INTERNATIONAL PEACEKEEPING

International Peacekeeping

The Yearbook of
International Peace Operations

edited by

MICHAEL BOTHE AND BORIS KONDOCH

Volume 7

2001

KLUWER LAW INTERNATIONAL
THE HAGUE / LONDON / NEW YORK

A C.I.P. Catalogue record for this book is available from the Library of Congress.

ISBN 90-411-1920-5
ISSN 1380-748-X

Published by Kluwer Law International,
P.O. Box 85889, 2508 CN The Hague, The Netherlands.

Sold and distributed in North, Central and South America
by Kluwer Law International,
101 Philip Drive, Norwell, MA 02061, U.S.A.
kluwerlaw@wkap.com

In all other countries, sold and distributed
by Kluwer Law International, Distribution Centre,
P.O. Box 322, 3300 AH Dordrecht, The Netherlands.

Printed on acid-free paper

International Peacekeeping:
The Yearbook of International Peace Operations

Table of Contents

Documents on CD-ROM

UN Security Council Resolutions, 1 January - 31 December 2001 – Overview

The Terrorist Attacks of 11 September 2001

UN Security Council Resolution 1368 (2001)
UN Security Council Resolution 1373 (2001)
UN Security Council Resolution 1377 (2001)
UN Security Council Resolution 1378 (2001)
Press Statement on Terrorism by the President of Security Council (SC/7152 of 21 September 2001)
UN Security Council Condemns, 'In Strongest Terms', Terrorist Attacks on United States, SC/7143, 4370th Meeting (PM) of 12 September 2001
UN Press Statement by the Security Council President on Terrorist Attacks in United States (SC/7141 of 11 September 2001)
US: Letter Dated 7 October 2001 from the Permanent Representative of the United States of America to the United Nations Security Council Addressed to the President of the Security Council (S/2001/946 of 7 October 2001)
NATO: Statement by the North Atlantic Council in Response to the Terrorist Attacks Against the United States (Press Release (2001) 124 of 12 September 2001)
NATO: Statement by NATO Secretary General, Lord Robertson of 2 October 2001
US: Public Law 107-40 (Joint Resolution to Authorize the Use of United States Armed Forces Against Those Responsible for the Recent Attacks Launched Against the United States), S.J.RES 23 of 18 September 2001)
US: Presidential Military Order – Detention, Treatment, and Trial of Certain Non-Citizens in the War Against Terrorism of 13 November 2001

Lakhdar Brahimi's Briefing to the Security Council, UN Verbatim
Transcript of 13 November 2001
The Bonn Agreement: Agreement On Provisional Arrangements in
Afghanistan Pending The Re-establishment of Permanent Government
Institutions of 5 December 2001
UN Security Council Resolution 1386 (2001)

Basic Documents on Peace Operations
Annual Report of the Secretary-General on the Work of the Organization
2001 (A/56/1 of 6 September 2001)
Report of the Secretary-General: No Exit Without Strategy: Security
Council Decision Making and the Closure or Transition of United Nations
Peacekeeping Operation (S/2001/394 of April 2001)

Documents on Sanctions Adopted under Chapter VII UNC
The Bossuyt Report: The Adverse Consequences of Economic Sanctions
on the Enjoyment of Human Rights, Review of Further Developments in
Fields with Which the Subcommission Has Been or May Be Concerned,
Economic and Social Council (E/CN.4/Sub.2/2000/33 of 21 June 2000),
working paper prepared by Mr. Marc Bossuyt
UN Office of the Spokesman for the Secretary-General (OSSG) Use of
Sanctions under Chapter VII of the UN Charter

International Society for Military Law and the Law of War
Recommendations of the International Society for Military Law and the
Law of War, XVth International Congress, Lillehammer, 6-10 June 2000

List of Ongoing UN Peacekeeping Missions

Map
Ongoing Peacekeeping Missions

Preface

In the editorial to the last issue of the journal 'International Peacekeeping', we announced that the publication would be continued in the form of a Yearbook. Both the publisher and the editors are still convinced that this form present definite advantages as compared with the previous form of a publication covering only two or four months in each issue. This new form of publication is now presented to the public. As it is new, it may not be perfect. Thus, comments and suggestions by our readers would be greatly appreciated.

Technically, this volume deals with the period following the one covered by last issue of the Journal, i.e. the year 2001. For the question of peace operations, this was a relatively calm period between major events. The last reporting period was dominated by a new development in the area of peace operations, namely the fully fledged taking over of governmental responsibility by the United Nations in the Kosovo and in East Timor. During the reporting period, the events of September 11 shocked the world. Its aftermath will require extensive political and legal evaluation but this has to be left to future volumes. It was necessary, however, to include these events in the documentation section.

We have tried to implement the concept announced in the said editorial: the emphasis is on principled comment and evaluation of current events. Thus, the Yearbook opens with three articles on the recently created UN administrations in East Timor and Kosovo. André de Hoogh from the University of Groningen discusses the legal basis and limitations of the legislative powers of the Security Council as illustrated by the case of the United Nations Transitional Administration in East Timor (UNTAET). In the same context Rachel Opie's article surveys the relationship between peace operations and human rights. John Cerone, a former legal advisor within the Human Rights Policy Bureau of the United Nations Interim Administration Mission in Kosovo (UNMIK/OSCE) and a member of the working group that drafted UNMIK Regulation 2001/4, analyses the human rights framework applicable to trafficking in persons and its incorporation into UNMIK Regulation 2001/4.

The following three articles address different issues of international peacekeeping in a more long term perspective. The last decade and the future of peace operations in Africa are evaluated by Peter Viggo Jakobsen. The article by Andrzej Sitkowski draws the readers' attention to the doctrinal implications of the Srebrenica, Rwanda and Brahimi Report. Andrew Solomon provides a careful analysis of the role of the United Nations Observer Mission in Georgia (UNOMIG).

The next two articles focus on certain aspects of two conflicts in the Middle East. Boris Kondoch analyses the lawfulness of sanctions imposed on Iraq. The Bossuyt Report and an overview of the use of sanctions by the Security Council are documents related to the topic of his article and can be found in the documentary part. Avishai Ehrlich's and Margaret Johannsen's article on Israel's interrogation of Palestinians from the Occupied Territories shows the dilemma of a democratic state to combat terrorism, and to respect democratic values and the rule of law at the same time.

International adjudication is a major element of peace processes. Two contributions are devoted to this problem area. Delia Chatoor's article on CARICOM's experience in the negotiations of the Rome Statute of the International Criminal Court is a good example of how a small group of states can have a positive impact on the development of international law. Erwin Müller and Patricia Schneider from the Institute of Peace Research and Security Policy at the University of Hamburg analyse the functioning conditions of international jurisdiction from an empirical perspective.

The events which dominated the last previous reporting period have triggered an intensive international discourse in the form of international conferences which are reported in this volume. A conference on 'Civil and Military Administrations in International Peacekeeping Operations' was held at the US-German George C. Marshall European Centre for Security Studies in Garmisch-Partenkirchen between 12-16 March 2001. The issues discussed and papers delivered are summarised by Dieter Fleck from the German Ministry of Defence. Two of the papers presented are reprinted in the yearbook, one by Vladimir Shustov on transitional civil administration within the framework of UN peacekeeping operations and the other by James Burger on legal issues in peacekeeping and humanitarian assistance.

Another conference report edited by Kathleen Dowley contains various papers discussing the Kosovo's Final Report of the Independent Commission which was asked to investigate and evaluate western actions in Kosovo. The conference report contains papers by well-known scholars, such as Richard Falk and Ivo Daalder. Graça Almeida Rodrigues, Professor of the New University in Lisbon, contributes a brief conference paper on 'Nation Building in East Timor.'

For technical reasons, it has been decided to put the rich, perhaps exceedingly rich documentation in the form of a CD-ROM. This form of distribution presents advantages as to the physical volume as well as the cost of the publication. But readers are invited to comment on this choice.

As indicated above, an important part of the documentation relates to the terrorist attacks which took place on 11 September 2001 in New York, Washington D.C. and Pennsylvania. In Resolution 1368 the Security Council condemned these acts as threat to international peace and security and recognized the inherent right of individual or collective self-defence in accordance with the UN Charter. On the same day, the North Atlantic Council released a statement which claimed that the terrorist attacks should be regarded as an action covered by Art. 5 of the Washington Treaty according to which "an armed attack against one or more of the Allies in Europe or North America shall be considered an attack against them all". On 2 October 2001, NATO Secretary General, Lord Robertson stated that the evidence against Al-Qaida headed by Osama Bin Laden and protected by the Taliban was "clear and compelling". On 18 September 2001, the US Public Law 107-40 authorized the US President to use all "necessary and appropriate force" against those responsible for the attacks against the United States and invoked the right of self defence. On 7 October 2001, the US Permanent Representative informed the UN Security Council that the US had initiated "the exercise of its inherent right of individual and collective self-defence" and that the "US may find that (its) self-defence requires further actions with respect to other organizations and other states." In Security Council Resolution 1373 of 28 September 2001, the Security Council, acting under Chapter VII of the UN Charter, decided that all States should, *inter alia*, prevent and suppress the financing of terrorism; refrain from providing any form of support to entities or persons involved in terrorist acts; take necessary steps to prevent commission of terrorist acts; deny safe haven to those who finance, plan, support or commit terrorist acts; and prevent the movement of terrorist or terrorist groups by effective border controls. The Security Council also called upon all States to take appropriate measures in conformity with the relevant provisions of national and international law before granting refugee status, for the purpose of ensuring that the asylum-seeker has not planned, facilitated or participated in the commission of terrorist acts. Furthermore, the Security Council established a committee to monitor implementation of resolution 1373. A highly controversial document is President Bush's military order which establishes the competence of US military tribunals to try certain individuals who are not US citizens for violations of the laws of war and other applicable laws. The order contains a provision which prohibits that any person tried by a military tribunal can seek any remedy or maintain any proceeding in a federal or state court in the US, a foreign court or international tribunal. Two documents related to the future of Afghanistan after the Taliban regime are Lakhdar Brahimi's Briefing to the Security Council and the so-called Bonn Agreement. The latter document has been endorsed by Security Council Resolution 1386.

Like in previous volumes of "International Peacekeeping" the yearbook contains the "Annual Report of the Secretary-General on the Work of the Organization". An important document in the field of peace operations is the Report of the Secretary-General "No Exit Without Strategy: Security Council Decision Making and the Closure or Transition of United Nations Peacekeeping Operation," containing guidelines and questions which the Security Council may take into account when it decides to launch, close or significantly alter the mandate of a peace operation. The last document contains the recommendations of the XVth International Congress of the International Society for Military Law and the Law of War on "Military Support to Civil Authorities", held in Norway between 6-10 June 2000.

Michael Bothe/Boris Kondoch

Attribution or Delegation of (Legislative) Power by the Security Council?
The Case of the United Nations Transitional Administration in East Timor (UNTAET)

*André J.J. de Hoogh**

Introduction

After the result of the popular consultation in East Timor was announced on 4 September 1999,[1] with 78.5 % of practically all registered voters voting against autonomy within Indonesia and for independence,[2] the country was thrown into a period of organised chaos and destruction. Militias, organised and supported by the Indonesian army and authorities,[3] killed,

---

*   Dr. André J.J. de Hoogh is lecturer in international law, University of Groningen. I would like to thank the members of the working group The Law of International Institutions of the Netherlands Society of International Law, and especially Dr. Niels Blokker, for their comments on a draft of this contribution. Special thanks goes to my colleagues Erik Koppe (Department of International Law) and Solke Munneke (Department of Constitutional Law) for their detailed observations regarding said draft.

[1]   The consultation was conducted by the United Nations Mission in East Timor (UNAMET), created by Security Council Resolution 1246, adopted 11 June 1999, (all Security Council resolutions may be found through http://www.un.org/documents/scres.htm; all websites visited September 2001). The consultation was based on Agreement between the Republic of Indonesia and the Portuguese Republic on the Question of East Timor, Agreement regarding the Modalities for the Popular Consultation, and East Timor Popular Consultation, all concluded 5 May 1999, through http://www.un.org/peace/etimor99/etimor.htm.

[2]   Letter Secretary-General to the president of the Security Council, S/1999/944, 3 September 1999, at http://www.un.org/peace/etimor/docs/N9925500.pdf.

[3]   See Report of the International Commission of Inquiry on East Timor to the Secretary-General, A/54/726, S/2000/59, 31 January 2000, at http://www.unhchr.ch/huridocda/huridoca.nsf/(Symbol)/A.54.726, +S.2000.59.En; National Commission on Human Rights, Indonesia, Executive Summary Report on the investigation of human rights violations in East Timor, 31 January 2000, reproduced at http://www.etan.org/news/2000a/3exec.htm; and also D. Kingsbury, 'The TNI and the militias' in D. Kingsbury (ed.), *Guns and ballot boxes, East Timor's vote for independence* (Monash Asia Institute, Clayton, 2000), pp. 69-80.

1

M. Bothe and B. Kondoch (eds.),
International Peacekeeping. The Yearbook of International Peace Operations, Volume 7, 2001, 1–41.

damaged and plundered both public and private buildings on a large scale.[4] Already before the referendum, with militia activity on the increase and tensions growing, Indonesians had started to leave the country. As the result of the consultation meant that East Timor would become independent, Indonesians and East Timorese in the armed forces, police and the civil administration fled also. As the Australian led International Force East Timor (INTERFET) entered the territory and secured control over it,[5] it was confronted by a total lack of civil authorities (including judges, prosecutors, lawyers and police), and a heavily damaged infrastructure.[6]

It is no wonder then that already in the resolution authorising INTER-FET (para. 11), the Security Council asked the Secretary-General to plan and prepare for a transitional administration. The Secretary-General did so in a report,[7] and on that basis the Security Council created the United Nations Transitional Administration in East Timor (UNTAET) in resolution 1272.[8] The Security Council once again determined the situation in East Timor to constitute a threat to peace and security, and laid down that UN-TAET (para. 1; emphasis added):

> (...) will be endowed with overall responsibility for the administration of East Timor and *will be empowered to exercise all legislative and executive authority, including the administration of justice*;

It further authorised UNTAET to take all necessary measures to fulfil its mandate (para. 4).

Through the Transitional Administrator (the Special Representative of the Secretary-General, Vieira de Mello), UNTAET has taken this power of legislation seriously, and has to date promulgated 68 regulations (4 in 1999; 36 in 2000; 28 in 2001).[9] In its very first regulation it determined the

---

[4] Generally Report of the Security Council Mission to Jakarta and Dili, 14 September 1999, S/1999/976, at http://www.un.org/peace/etimor/docs/9926220E.htm; Report of the Secretary-General on the situation in East Timor, 4 October 1999, S/1999/1024, 16 pp.

[5] INTERFET was authorised by Security Council Resolution 1264, adopted 15 September 1999.

[6] Report Secretary-General on East Timor, 4 October 1999, pp. 3-4 and 8.

[7] Report Secretary-General on East Timor, 4 October 1999, pp. 6-14.

[8] Security Council Resolution 1272, adopted 25 October 1999.

[9] All to be found through http://www.un.org/peace/etimor/UntaetN.htm. Besides regulations there are also directives, whose texts have not, unfortunately, been put on the UNTAET website (but on the intranet instead).

law applicable in East Timor, basically Indonesian law (minus some security and defence laws) insofar as this complies with internationally recognised standards of human rights.[10] Its later regulations have covered topics, such as the national consultative council, the transitional government, election of the constituent assembly, and Council of Ministers (1999/2, amended through 2000/24 and 2000/33; 2000/23; 2001/1 and 2001/11; and 2001/28);[11] a transitional judicial service commission (1999/3, amended and supplemented by 2000/11, 2000/14, 2000/16, 2000/25, 2000/30 on the organisation of courts and public prosecution, and 2000/15 on jurisdiction over crimes such as genocide, war crimes, crimes against humanity, torture); the police and prison system, and legal aid (2001/22, 2001/23, and 2001/24); a central fiscal authority (2000/1); the use of currencies (2000/2) and the determination of the US Dollar as official currency (2000/7 and 2001/14); a tax and customs regime (2000/12); a prohibition on land transactions by Indonesians (2000/27); a defence force and military code (2001/1, 2001/9, and 2001/12); a central civil registry (2001/3); firearms, ammunition, and explosives (2001/5); registration of motor vehicles (2001/6) and regulation of road traffic (2001/8); and the Commission for Reception, Truth and Reconciliation (2001/10).

The broad range of legislative measures described in the previous paragraph illustrates a shift from peacekeeping to peace-building. This development had already been noticed by former Secretary-General Boutros-Ghali,[12] and has taken on its clearest form recently in Kosovo and East Timor. In its report,[13] the Panel on United Nations Peace Operations dis-

---

[10] Sections 2 and 3, Regulation 1, UNTAET/REG/1999/1, 27 November 1999 (with retroactive force as of 25 October; section 8).

[11] Website of the transitional administration at http://www.gov.east-timor.org/old/.

[12] Secretary-General, An Agenda for Peace, Preventive diplomacy, peacemaking and peacekeeping, A/47/277 and S/24111, 17 June 1992, paras. 20, 46-59, at http://www.un.org/Docs/SG/agpeace.html. See also Secretary-General, Supplement to An Agenda for Peace, A/50/60 and S/1995/1, 3 January 1995, paras. 33-56, at http://www.un.org/Docs/SG/agsupp.html.

[13] Report of the Panel on United Nations Peace Operations, 21 August 2000, A/55/305-S/2000/809, xv and 58 pp., to be found through http://www.un.org/peace/reports/peace_operations/ (hereinafter Brahimi Report). Further C. de Coning, 'The UN Transitional Administration in East Timor (UNTAET): Lessons Learned from the First 100 Days' (2000) 6 *International Peacekeeping* (Kluwer Law International, The Hague) 83-90; H. Strohmeyer, 'Collapse and Reconstruction of a Judicial System: The United Nations Missions in Kosovo and East Timor' (2001) 95 *American Journal of International Law* 46-63; and M. Matheson, 'United Nations Governance of Postconflict Societies', *ibid.* 76-85.

cusses the phenomenon of transitional civil administration in relation to United Nations Mission in Kosovo (UNMIK) and UNTAET, and poses the question (perhaps rhetorically):[14] "(...) whether the United Nations should be in this business at all, (...)." Pursuing this further, the Panel goes on to address a pressing issue, namely that of 'applicable law'. It observes that both missions were confronted by situations where local judicial and legal capacity was non-existent, and that the law and legal system applicable before the relevant conflict were questioned or rejected by key groups considered as victims.[15] Its recommendation in this respect is to have international legal experts, including individuals that have experience with transitional administration mandates, study the feasibility and utility of drawing up an interim criminal code to be used until the reestablishment of local rule of law and law enforcement capacity.[16] Applying such an interim criminal code would certainly be far more practicable than relying on pre-existing applicable law. Peacekeeping personnel, sent out in a flurry, will generally be unfamiliar with the laws and legal system of any specific State (except perhaps of their State of nationality).

A fundamental question is what its legal basis would be. Why should one consider the United Nations, and more particularly the Security Council, to be competent to impose a criminal code, if only temporarily, upon the inhabitants of a certain territory? Indeed, the grant of full legislative power to peacekeeping or peace-enforcement operations, and the exercise of such powers by for instance UNTAET, raises many legal questions. Does the Security Council possess legislative powers? If so, what constitutes the legal basis for an affirmative answer? In Section 1 the enforcement powers of the Council, the legal basis of peacekeeping, and their application in the case of East Timor will be examined. Next, in Section 2, will be discussed the attribution or delegation of powers by the Security Council in the fields of enforcement, adjudication and legislation. Finally, Section 3 will investigate certain (inherent) limits to these powers, by reference especially to the experience of UNTAET.

---

[14] Brahimi Report, at 13, para. 78 (more broadly 13-14, paras. 76-83).

[15] Brahimi Report, at 14, para. 79.

[16] Brahimi Report, at 14, para. 83. Also recommended by Strohmeyer, *supra* note 13, 62-63.

Section 1: Enforcement and peacekeeping

1.1 Chapter VII and Chapter VI ½ Charter

The United Nations was created after the Second World War, and a collective security system was established in its constituent instrument, the Charter.[17] Its basic elements concerned the obligation of members of the United Nations to settle their disputes peacefully (article 2, para. 3),[18] the prohibition to use force (article 2, para. 4),[19] and the powers of the Security Council to maintain or restore international peace and security (articles 39, 41 and 42 in conjunction with 24 and 25). These latter powers were especially laid down in Chapter VII of the Charter, of which the opening provision (article 39) states:

> The Security Council shall determine the existence of any threat to the peace, breach of the peace or act of aggression and shall make recommendations, or decide what measures shall be taken in accordance with articles 41 and 42, to maintain or restore international peace and security.

Measures under article 41 do not involve the use of armed force, are to be applied by Members, and may include interruption of economic, transport, communication and diplomatic relations. Under article 42 the Council may take action by air, sea or land forces to maintain or restore international peace and security. Decisions of the Security Council, adopted in accordance with the Charter, are to be accepted and carried out by Members (article 25). Finally, article 103 stipulates that in case of conflict between obligations under the Charter and those under other international agreements, the obligations under the Charter shall prevail.

---

[17] The 1945 Charter of the United Nations (1945) 39 *American Journal of International Law* (Supplement) 190-215.

[18] Article 2, para. 3, Charter: "All Members shall settle their international disputes by peaceful means in such a manner that international peace and security, and justice, are not endangered."

[19] Article 2, para. 4, Charter: "All Members shall refrain in their international relations from the threat or use of force against the territorial integrity or political independence of any state, or in any manner inconsistent with the Purposes of the United Nations."

As the Second World War ended and times quietly slipped into the Cold War, the Security Council's envisaged activist role became stillborn. Although the Charter of the United Nations was intended to remedy some of the defects of the Covenant, which had become all too obvious during the League of Nations period,[20] the built in check on Security Council power and balance between the great powers, the veto, inhibited the adoption of any measures of the Security Council under Chapter VII of the Charter (article 27, para., Charter). Thus for the first 20 years of its existence, the power of decision granted in article 39 to adopt enforcement measures under articles 41 and 42 was not applied.[21] Only with the Rhodesian crisis of 1965 onwards, when a white minority regime assumed power and unilaterally declared independence, did the Security Council adopt comprehensive measures under article 41.[22] This was to be followed by an arms embargo against South Africa in 1977.[23] When Gorbachov became leader of the Soviet Union and initiated his programme of *glasnost* and *perestrojka*, this contributed to the fall of the Berlin wall in 1989 and the reunification of Germany. After a *coup d'état* the Soviet Union dissolved in 1991, with the Russian Federation taking over its permanent seat in the Security Council. All this brought about a renaissance of the Security Council, and already in 1990 it determined a breach of the peace in relation to Iraq's invasion of Kuwait, adopted comprehensive trade measures against Iraq (applied also to Kuwait's occupied territory), and authorised members co-operating with Kuwait to intervene militarily (*infra* subsection 2.1).[24] Since then the Council has acted in relation to an unprece-

---

[20]   With the experiences of the Italian invasion of Abyssinia and the Japanese take-over of Manchuria. Cf. J. Frowein, 'Article 39' in B. Simma, (Ed.), *Charter of the United Nations, A Commentary* (Oxford University Press, Oxford, 1994), pp. 605-616, at 606-607 (see also Frowein's commentaries on Articles 40 to 43, in *ibid.*, respectively pp. 617-621, 621-628, 628-636, 636-639); and P. Malanczuk, *Akehurst's Modern Introduction to International Law* (7th revised edition, Routledge, London, 1997), pp. 23-26. The 1919 Covenant on the League of Nations (1919) 13 *American Journal of International Law* (Supplement) 128-140.

[21]   In a non-binding fashion the Council recommended that members furnish assistance to South Korea to counter the armed attack by North Korea. See Security Council Resolution 83, adopted 27 June 1950.

[22]   Security Council Resolution 232, adopted 16 December 1966.

[23]   Security Council Resolution 418, adopted 4 November 1977.

[24]   Respectively Security Council Resolutions 660 (adopted 2 August 1990), 661 (adopted 6 August 1990), and 678 (adopted 29 November 1990). Earlier breaches of the peace had been determined in relation to the Koreas (Security Council Resolution 82, adopted 25 June 1950), the Falklands/Malvinas conflict (Security Council

dented number of crises, both by adopting measures of article 41 and by authorising military action.[25]

Security Council inaction was only to be expected with regard to military action under article 42, since the agreements envisaged in article 43 between the Council and members have never been concluded. Consequently, the Security Council has never had forces at its disposal ready to take action under article 42 *on its call.* Two developments occurred intended to remedy this: the adoption of the Uniting for Peace resolution by the General Assembly;[26] and the establishment of peacekeeping operations, at first by the General Assembly.[27]

Leaving aside the former development, controversy erupted over the establishment of peacekeeping operations by the Assembly rather than the Council, the organ specifically endowed with primary responsibility for the maintenance of international peace and security (article 24). France and the Soviet Union saw this as an attempt to sidetrack the Security Council, within which they held the power of veto (article 27, para. 3). Arguing that the setting up of peacekeeping was outside (*ultra vires*) the competence of the General Assembly, they refused to pay their allotted contributions. The Assembly decided to request an advisory opinion of the International Court of Justice on the matter.

In its opinion the Court held that the Security Council possesses *primary* but not *exclusive* responsibility for the maintenance of international peace and security.[28] The competence of the General Assembly to deal with international peace and security *generally* or even in relation to *specific situations* was not particularly controversial. However, arguments against Assembly competence for setting up peacekeeping operations focused on the last sentence of article 11, para. 2, which provides:

> Any such question on which action is necessary shall be referred to the Security Council by the General Assembly either before or after discussion.

Resolution 502, adopted 3 April 1982) and the Iraq-Iran war (Security Council Resolution 598, adopted 20 July 1987), but no enforcement measures were adopted.

[25] Generally Malanczuk, *supra* note 20, pp. 395-415.

[26] General Assembly Resolution 377 (V), Uniting for Peace, adopted 3 November 1950, at http://www.un.org/Depts/dhl/landmark/pdf/ares377e.pdf.

[27] Generally S. Ratner, *The New UN Peacekeeping, Building Peace in Lands of Conflict after the Cold War* (Macmillan, London, 1997).

[28] International Court of Justice, *Certain Expenses of the United Nations (Article 17, paragraph 2, of the Charter)*, Advisory Opinion, ICJ Reports 1962, p. 151, at 163.

The Court held that the word 'action' must be read to mean "coercive or enforcement action", and it indicated that:[29]

> The 'action' which is solely within the province of the Security Council is that which is indicated by the title of Chapter VII of the Charter, namely 'Action with respect to threats to the peace, breaches of the peace, and acts of aggression'.

Thus the Court is of the opinion that article 11, para. 2:[30]

> (...) *empowers the General Assembly*, by means of recommendations to States or to the Security Council, or to both, *to organize peace-keeping operations, at the request, or with the consent, of the States concerned.*

And it is precisely because of this aspect of peacekeeping, the request or consent of the States concerned, that the Court expounds that the operations United Nations Emergency Force (UNEF) and Opérations des Nations Unies au Congo (ONUC) did not constitute *enforcement* action in the sense of Chapter VII Charter.[31] In this regard the Court apparently considered that enforcement action might entail the use of armed force against any State, and particularly against any State determined by the Security Council, under article 39, to have committed an act of aggression or to be responsible for a breach of the peace.[32] The claim of the Court that the activities of ONUC did not include a use of armed of force against any member may be disputed in that the Secretary-General (who held exclusive command over ONUC) was authorised, among other things to use requisite force to apprehend and detain (pending legal action or deportation) foreign military and paramilitary personnel in the Congo.[33] As is well

---

[29] *Expenses Opinion*, quotation at 165, reference to coercive or enforcement action at 164 (and also 163).

[30] *Expenses Opinion*, 164. Emphasis added.

[31] *Expenses Opinion*, 166 (further 170-172 for UNEF, and 175-177 for ONUC).

[32] *Expenses Opinion*, 177.

[33] Security Council Resolution 169, adopted 24 November 1961, para. 4. See also Security Council Resolutions 143, adopted 14 July 1960, para. 2, and 145, adopted 9 August 1960, para. 1. Cf. M. Bothe, *Peacekeeping,* in Simma, *supra* note 20, pp. 565-603, at 591; and Malanczuk, *supra* note 20, pp. 418-420.

known the foreign military present in the Congo was Belgian.[34] Furthermore, ONUC in the end also took action against those Congolese opposition forces fighting for the secession of Katanga.[35] As such, it cannot be said that it adhered to a feature that later became the determinant condition, namely the consent *of all parties concerned*.[36]

As to the legal basis of establishing peacekeeping operations the Court apparently was of the view that this constitutes an express power of the General Assembly under article 11, para. 2, Charter, which enables the Assembly to make recommendations to the State(s) concerned. The Court did not identify any express power of the Council to organise peacekeeping operations, as it had not been asked to do so, although it appears that it did not view the Congo operation as an exercise of enforcement power under Chapter VII.[37] As the provisions of Chapter VI also do not provide such a basis, being concerned with the pacific settlement of disputes, authors have been wont to regard the organisation of peacekeeping operations by the Security Council as an implied power situated somewhere in between Chapters VI and VII and the late Secretary-General Hammarskjold coined the phrase 'Chapter VI ½'.[38] Certainly it is odd to think that the Assembly would be in possession of an express power in this respect, whereas the Council could invoke no more than an implied or assumed power.[39]

---

[34]   Security Council Resolution 143, adopted 14 July 1960, para. 1.

[35]   See Dissenting Opinion Koretsky, *Expenses Opinion*, pp. 267-272. Note I. Seidl-Hohenveldern/G. Loibl, *Das Recht der Internationalen Organisationen einschliesslich der Supranationalen Gemeinschaften* (7. überarbeitete Auflage, Carl Heymanns Verlag, Köln, 2000), at 305, para. 2027.

[36]   Cf. Bothe, *supra* note 33, p. 590; Ratner, *supra* note 27, pp. 26-31; and E. Suy, 'Peace-Keeping Operations' in R.-J. Dupuy, (Ed.), *A Handbook on International Organizations* (2nd edition, Martinus Nijhoff Publishers, Dordrecht, 1998), pp. 539-562, at 549-550.

[37]   *Expenses Opinion*, 177.

[38]   Secretary-General Hammarskjold, quoted in Ratner, *supra* note 27, p. 57 and endnote 6, at 268 (more broadly pp. 56-61).

[39]   D. Ciobanu, 'The power of the Security Council to organize peace-keeping operations' in A. Cassese (Ed.), *United Nations peace-keeping, Legal essays* (Sijthoff & Noordhoff, Alphen aan den Rijn, 1978), pp. 15-53, who concludes that peacekeeping by the Security cannot be based on express or implied powers, but is based on an assumed power constituted by practice and acceptance of the members (40-41); and Bothe, *supra* note 33, pp. 590-591. Frowein, *supra* note 20 (on Article 40 and 42), respectively at 619 and 632, answers in the negative as to article 40 as legal basis for peacekeeping, but this grafted upon his view that provisional measures under this provision are binding (620-621), and denies this also in relation to article 42. Suy,

1.2 Enforcement and consent regarding INTERFET and UNTAET

As to the authorisation of INTERFET and the establishment of UNTAET by the Security Council different issues arise (*infra* sections 2 and 3), though their legal bases are the same in both cases, namely consent and the exercise of powers by the Security Council.

As the situation spun out of control in East Timor, especially after the announcement of the result of the referendum, there was incessant pressure upon Indonesia to allow a peacekeeping force into the territory.[40] However, the representative of Indonesia remarked:[41]

> Furthermore, a peacekeeping mission under the present circumstances could hardly be effective when there is no peace to keep; rather, it would evolve into a peace-enforcing mission.

As it happens this scenario did not occur. Perhaps such would have been the case if Indonesia had kept up its support of the pro-autonomy militias even when INTERFET entered the territory and secured control over it. As it was, and however reluctantly, Indonesia by voice of president Habibie did give its consent to an international security presence on 12 September 1999, and this was duly noted by the Security Council in its resolution authorising INTERFET.[42] Indeed, INTERFET and its successor have not been forced to engage in enforcement action to any significant degree.[43] However, the Security Council did not only provide it with a mandate proper for a peacekeeping operation, namely armed action only in self-defence, but also with the authorisation to take all necessary measures to fulfil its mandate (to restore peace and security in East Timor, to protect and support UNAMET, and within capabilities to facilitate humanitarian assistance).[44] In assigning these tasks and powers the Security Council

---

supra note 36, p. 544, claims that article 40 is most frequently mentioned as the most suitable legal basis.

[40] Security Council, S/PV.4043, 11 September 1999, at http://www.un.org/peace/etimor/docs/9985750E.htm and at http://www.un.org/peace/etimor/docs/9985756E.htm.

[41] Representative for Indonesia, Wibisono, *ibid.*, at the second website mentioned in the previous footnote.

[42] Security Council Resolution 1264, preamble, para. 10.

[43] E.g. incident on 19 January 2000, reported at http://www.un.org/peace/etimor/news/N19100.htm.

[44] Note report of 10 February 2001, at http://www.un.org/peace/etimor/news/News10.html.

based itself on Chapter VII of the Charter, and determined that the situation in East Timor constituted a threat to peace and security. Consistent practice of the Security Council evidences that this constitutes an exercise of enforcement power,[45] and not merely the use of recommendations under article 39 or the application of provisional measures under article 40.

It may be noted here that the consent required of the Indonesian authorities could not have been replaced by that of the Portuguese authorities. Although Portugal continued to be the administrative power for East Timor,[46] and therefore is *de jure* entitled to act for East Timor, it could not authorise the stationing of troops on territory not under its control. Even if one were to claim that Portugal could agree to a peacekeeping operation (with self-defence options only), the consent of Indonesia would be lacking. Thus the requirement of consent *by all the parties concerned* would not have been fulfilled. As has been noted by others,[47] Indonesia's consent was hardly given voluntarily. However, if a situation is such that the Security Council would be competent to authorise the use of military force against a State, political pressure may be applied to obtain consent and thus prevent the necessity of armed action against that State.[48]

Insofar as UNTAET is concerned the situation is more complicated and is in fact reversed. As already noted UNTAET has been endowed with all legislative and executive power within East Timor (resolution 1272, para. 1), and this, *inter alia*, in order to provide security, to establish an effective administration, to support capacity-building for self-government (para. 2 and also para. 3). Ordinarily this would have required the consent of Indonesia as the State with effective control over the territory. However, by the time UNTAET was established on 25 October 1999, Indonesia had already severed its ties with East Timor (preamble, para. 4). This was indeed as it should be, since Indonesia's action in this amounted to performance of its obligation under Article 6 of the 5 May Agreement.[49]

---

[45] E.g. Malanczuk, *supra* note 20, pp. 389-390.

[46] International Court of Justice, *East Timor (Portugal v. Australia),* Judgment, ICJ Reports 1995, p. 90, at 103-104, paras. 30-33.

[47] M. Ruffert, 'The administration of Kosovo and East-Timor by the international community' (2001) 50 *International and Comparative Law Quarterly* 613-631, at 616.

[48] Practically all delegations present called upon Indonesia to accept a military presence (see *supra* note 40).

[49] As Indonesia failed to provide security and refused to agree to an international security presence in a situation of extreme chaos and destruction, one could argue that it

This provided for the obligation of Indonesia to take the constitutional steps necessary to restore to East Timor the status it held prior to its incorporation in 1976, if the Secretary-General determined on the basis of the result of the consultation that the proposed constitutional framework for autonomy was not acceptable to the people of East Timor. This indeed occurred and since Indonesia severed its links, it could no longer claim any power to represent the people of East Timor based on its factual control over the territory.

Consequently consent to the transfer of authority would not lie with Indonesia (though such consent was given beforehand in article 6), but with Portugal as the *de jure* administering authority. This consent was also already given before the fact, as the already mentioned article 6 also stipulated the obligation of Portugal (and of Indonesia) to agree on arrangements for a peaceful and orderly transfer of authority to the United Nations. Such arrangements seem to have been made on 28 September 1999 in a tripartite meeting of the Secretary-General and the ministers of foreign affairs of Portugal and Indonesia.[50]

However, although the required consent had thus been assured, the Security Council based its creation of UNTAET not merely upon such consent, but on Chapter VII of the Charter. It determined that the continuing situation in East Timor constituted a threat to peace and security, decided to establish UNTAET with overall responsibility for the administration of East Timor, empowered to exercise all legislative and executive power, and authorised to take all necessary measures to fulfil its mandate (resolution 1272, paras. 1 and 4). As is clear from the resolution (para. 3), the military functions performed by INTERFET would as soon as possible be taken over by the military component of UNTAET (designed to be of similar strength). Obviously then the legal basis for the powers exercised by UNTAET lies not only with the consent of Portugal, but also with the exercise of powers by the Security Council under Chapter VII of the Charter.[51] This then raises the question, to be discussed in subsection 2.3, whether the Security Council under that chapter possesses the power to

---

failed to perform another obligation under article 6, namely to agree on arrangements for a peaceful and orderly transfer of authority to the United Nations.

[50] Report Secretary-General, 4 October 1999, at 5 and 6. At 6 the Secretary-General observes (emphasis added): "The effectiveness of UNTAET will rest on its ability to perform its duties in close consultation and cooperation with the people of East Timor, *as it will have to exercise its authority on their behalf.*"

[51] This has been called, by Ruffert, *supra* note 47, at 618, robust peacekeeping.

grant legislative powers, whether by way of attribution or delegation, to peacekeeping operations.

Section 2: Attribution or delegation of powers by the Security Council

Before going into this, it is necessary to discuss the meaning to be attached to attribution of power and delegation of power, but also to examine the legal bases under which the Security Council has to date authorised others to engage in enforcement action (subsection 2.1) and under which it created Tribunals to prosecute and try individuals suspected of having committed serious violations of international (humanitarian) law (subsection 2.2).

Attribution or delegation of powers, in the context of international organisations, entails a grant of powers by States to an international organisation or by an organ of an organisation to another entity. A noticeable characteristic of the attribution of a power is that the attributing entity does not possess the *specific* attributed power itself,[52] and therefore the attributing entity cannot itself exercise the specific power.[53] This characteristic constitutes in essence the distinguishing feature of an attribution of power as set against a delegation of power. The delegation of a power means that a transfer of a specific power possessed by a certain entity (delegator), or at least of the right to exercise a power, is effected to some other entity (delegate).[54]

This transfer of power is not necessarily permanent. The delegating entity may reverse the transfer of power, and in a like manner may impose further restrictions on the exercise of that power.[55] It has even been held that an organ delegating a power may exercise its power concurrently with the delegate while the delegation lasts, and that in case of conflict deci-

---

[52] Note D. Sarooshi, *The United Nations and the Development of Collective Security, The Delegation by the UN Security Council of its Chapter VII Powers* (Oxford University Press, Oxford, 1999) p. 20 and p. 105.

[53] Especially Sarooshi, *ibid.*, pp. 101-105, who in the context of the establishment of tribunals by the Security Council characterises this as a delegation of powers. This appears to conflict with his claim, at 20, that one cannot delegate what one does not possess (invoking the Latin maxim *nemo dat quod non habet*).

[54] Sarooshi, *ibid.*, at 5, defines delegation in terms of the conveying of the exercise of a power to some other entity, although later on, at 7, he states that: "A delegation of power does not involve the transfer of a power *in toto*."

[55] H. Schermers/N. Blokker, *International Institutional Law, Unity within Diversity*, (3rd revised edition, Martinus Nijhoff Publishers, The Hague, 1995), p. 156, para. 230; Sarooshi, *supra* note 52, p. 7.

sions of the delegator prevail over those taken by the delegate.[56] Whether the same is true in case of the attribution of a power may very much be doubted. An attribution of power to take binding decisions, without any possibility of appeal or review, implies that the decisions thus taken could not be annulled or reversed (even if the specific power of decision-making could perhaps be taken away).[57] Whether the Security Council can attribute or delegate powers, and on what legal basis, will be examined next.

2.1 Delegation of enforcement powers

In regard to the powers held by international organisations, or organs thereof, it is generally held that these have to be either express (attribution or delegation of powers) or implicit (implied powers).[58] The latter kind of powers were recognised to exist by the International Court of Justice, which held in relation to the question whether the United Nations could press a claim against a non-member of the United Nations:[59]

> Under international law, the Organization must be deemed to have those powers which, though not expressly provided in the Charter, are conferred upon it by necessary implication as being essential to the performance of its duties.

---

[56] Sarooshi, *supra* note 52, p. 7. It may be suggested that the proper way to see this would not be that the delegator may take decisions in opposition to those of the delegate, but that the delegator may change the rules of the game, i.e. reverse the transfer of power and then exercise it itself or to impose restrictions on the exercise of power by the delegate. Thus Sarooshi's later observation (at 8), that the organ delegating could later exercise its power in a manner contrary to the way it was exercised by the delegate earlier, is the preferred way to go.

[57] International Court of Justice, *Effect of awards of compensation made by the U.N. Administrative Tribunal*, Advisory Opinion, ICJ Reports 1954, p. 47, at 58-59 and 60-62; Schermers/Blokker, *supra* note 55, pp. 156-157, para. 231; and Sarooshi, *supra* note 52, pp. 101-105.

[58] Schermers/Blokker, *supra* note 55, pp. 139-142, paras. 205-210, 147-152, paras. 217-223, and 158-163, paras. 232-236.

[59] International Court of Justice, *Reparation for injuries suffered in the service of the United Nations*, Advisory Opinion, ICJ Reports 1949, p. 174, at 182 (also 180 and 184). Cf. Khan, *Implied Powers of the United Nations* (Vikas Publications, Delhi, 1970), pp. 19-23; K. Skubiszewski, 'Implied Powers of International Organizations' in Y. Dinstein, (Ed.), *International Law at a Time of Perplexity, Essays in Honour of Shabtai Rosenne* (Martinus Nijhoff Publishers, Dordrecht, 1989), pp. 855-868, at 856-859 and 863-867; and N.D. White, *The Law of International Organisations* (Manchester University Press, Manchester, 1996), at 128-131.

The precise formulation of this doctrine of implied powers seems to have been regarded by some as overly broad, and judge Hackworth observed:[60]

> Powers not expressed cannot freely be implied. Implied powers flow from a grant of expressed powers, and are limited to those that are "necessary" to the exercise of powers expressly granted.

This difference of approach is relevant for the question whether or not the Security Council can be considered to possess the implied power to delegate its right to take armed action under article 42 to subsidiary organs, the Secretary-General, or to (member) States. The power would have to be implied, since no express power can be seen to exist in the Charter.[61] Only an express power to delegate enforcement action to regional arrangements or agencies is to be found in article 53 of the Charter.[62]

Sarooshi and Blokker do indeed argue that the Security Council possesses the implied power to delegate its power to take armed action under article 42 of the Charter.[63] Such a power to delegate would be necessary,[64] and therefore implied, because in the absence of the agreements envisaged in article 43 the Security Council lacks the means to accomplish its main

---

[60] Dissenting Opinion Hackworth, *Reparation Opinion*, 198.

[61] Contrary Frowein, *supra* note 20 (on Article 42), pp. 634-635, who sees authorisations as decisions under article 42 (suggesting application of the second sentence); T. Gill, 'Legal and some political limitations on the power of the UN Security Council to exercise its enforcement powers under Chapter VII of the Charter' (1995) 26 *Netherlands Yearbook of International Law* 33-138, at 57-58; N.D. White/Ö. Ülgen, 'The Security Council and the Decentralised Military Option: Constitutionality and Function' (1997) 44 *Netherlands International Law Review* 378-413, at 385-389; earlier White, *supra* note 59, pp. 191-198. Also Seidl-Hohenveldern/Loibl, *supra* note 35, pp. 301, para. 2019, and 305, para. 2029.

[62] Which in relevant part runs: "The Security Council shall, where appropriate, utilize such regional arrangements or agencies for enforcement action under its authority. But no enforcement action shall be taken under regional arrangements or by regional agencies without the authorization of the Security Council, (…)."

[63] Sarooshi, *supra* note 52, pp. 143-149; and N. Blokker, 'Is the Authorization Authorized?, Powers and Practice of the UN Security Council to Authorize the Use of Force by 'Coalitions of the Able and Willing'' (2000) 11 *European Journal of International Law* 541-568, at 547-549.

[64] Note Khan, *supra* note 59, pp. 133-134; Skubiszewsky, *supra* note 59, pp. 861-862, on the 'necessity' of implied powers; and contrary Seyersted, as quoted in White, *supra* note 59, p. 132, who argues for the notion of inherent powers that allow international organisations to perform any sovereign act, or act under international law, to the extent that their constitutions do not preclude this (more broadly pp. 131-133).

task of maintaining international peace and security. The counter-argument could be used that the Security Council cannot take action under article 42 (precisely because article 43 has not been implemented), and therefore should not be considered to possess an implied power to delegate something which it cannot undertake itself. Against this Sarooshi and Blokker argue the distinction between the power itself and the means necessary to exercise it.[65] They answer in the negative, sensibly enough, yet some doubts remain. In the end the choice for providing authorisations to members to engage in military enforcement action is *but one of the possible alternative means*.

In order to remain faithful to the set-up of the Charter it would be more appropriate to have members provide the Council with troops in relation to a particular crisis on an *ad hoc* basis,[66] than to authorise members to address the particular crisis themselves. The power of the Security Council to conclude agreements (treaties) with the member States to arrange troop contributions for addressing a particular crisis, not envisaged in the Charter, would constitute an implied power necessary to exercise its express power under article 42.

This is obviously unattainable from a political point of view, seeing the unwillingness of members to negotiate the agreements envisaged in article 43, and the unwillingness generally to put troops under UN command (especially when enforcement is at issue).[67] Politically, if not necessarily legally (though one might be tempted to exclaim: *ex injuria jus non oritur*, no right shall spring from a wrong), resort to authorisations is suspect because the need to utilise this alternative means arises only because of the failure of the members to negotiate in good faith the agreements of article 43.[68] The basic objection to be voiced as to the construct of authorisations

---

[65] Sarooshi, *supra* note 52, pp. 143-145; Blokker, *supra* note 63, p. 549.

[66] On this possibility, see Bothe, *supra* note 33, p. 590; and Frowein, *supra* note 20 (on Article 42), p. 633. Another possible means would be to change the mandate of a peacekeeping force operating already on the ground with consent of the parties concerned. Cf. Bothe, *supra* note 33, p. 590; earlier A. de Hoogh, *Obligations* Erga Omnes *and International Crimes, A Theoretical Inquiry into the Implementation and Enforcement of the International Responsibility of States* (Kluwer Law International, The Hague, 1996), at 316 and endnote 166 at 348. Sceptical about the advisability of doing this, Suy, *supra* note 36, pp. 558-559.

[67] Cf. The Clinton's Administration's Policy on Reforming Multilateral Peace Operations, (1994) 33 *International Legal Materials* 798-813. And also E. Warner, Coalition Defence and Reinforcing Forces, *ibid.*, 815-820; and C. Harper, 'Legal Authority for UN Peace Operations', *ibid.*, 822-829. Noted by Bothe, *supra* note 33, p. 575.

[68] Note Frowein, *supra* note 20 (on Article 43), p. 638.

is that article 42 envisages action *by the Security Council*, whereas the authorisations amount to action *by (member) States*. It is precisely this departure from the original scheme of the Charter, action *by the Security Council* (directed through the Military Staff Committee; article 47), that accounts for the increasing demand for express limits to the scope and timeframe of, and reporting regarding, authorisations.[69] Thus over the years authorisations have become less broad and more specific, have been given more limited timeframes (or with a mechanism allowing for termination), and have laid down specifics for reporting purposes.[70]

Considering the above, the conclusion must be that the power to delegate is not necessary for the exercise of the Council's express power. But can it be claimed that the Council's power to delegate is implied because it is necessary for the performance of its duties?[71] In this regard the Court noted in the Expenses Opinion in relation to the purposes of the UN:[72]

> These purposes are broad indeed, but neither they nor the powers conferred to effectuate them are unlimited. (...). But when the Organization takes action which warrants the assertion that it was appropriate for the fulfilment of one of the stated purposes of the United Nations, the presumption is that such action is not *ultra vires* the Organization.

The stated purpose of maintaining international peace and security (article 1, paragraph 1) is co-extensive with the primary responsibility of the Security Council to maintain international peace and security (article 24, paragraph 1). But a responsibility is not necessarily a duty. In performing its

---

69   White/Ülgen, *supra* note 61, 401-411; Sarooshi, *supra* note 52, pp. 155-163; and Blokker, *supra* note 63, 560-567.

70   *Ibid.* It is questionable whether one should see such developments as giving rise to legal limits to the power of the Security Council to delegate, or as political requirements necessary to ensure sufficient support for adoption of the resolution providing the authorisation.

71   A. Campbell, 'The Limits of the Powers of International Organisations' (1983) 32 *International and Comparative Law Quarterly* 523-533, at 532-533, discusses whether the word 'duties' would constitute a restriction to find implied powers possible only in case of mandatory measures.

72   *Expenses Opinion*, 168. The Court earlier rejected an argument that action for the maintenance of international peace and security must be financed through the agreements of Article 43, and it observed (*ibid.*, 167): "It cannot be said that the Charter has left the Security Council impotent in the face of an emergency situation when agreements under article 43 have not been concluded."

duty the Security Council is bound to the Organisation's purposes (and principles; article 24, paragraph 2), and the maintenance of international peace and security is to be effected through 'collective measures' (article 1, paragraph 1).[73] The most important specific powers granted for this purpose have been conferred in articles 39, 41 and 42 of the Charter. Thus it is the duty of the Security Council to determine the existence of any threat to the peace, breach of the peace or act of aggression, and to take action *itself* by air, sea or land forces under article 42 if it considers that the measures of article 41 would be inadequate or have proved to be inadequate.[74]

Now Blokker has observed that the question is whether the model of authorisations is generally acceptable to member States,[75] and Sarooshi has indicated that the source of the Council's competence to delegate to member States is subsequent practice.[76] In both cases there appears to be some entanglement between the concept of implied powers and that of internal customary law. Either the implied power to delegate exists (because it is necessary for the exercise of express powers or the performance of its duties), or it does not. If it does exist, the lack of acceptance by member States cannot distract from the existence of that power (though this might lead to a constitutional crisis similar to that engendered by the establishment of peacekeeping operations by the General Assembly).[77] If the implied power cannot be said to exist, the crucial question is whether the power to delegate could be based on the practice of the Security Council as generally accepted by the member States. The answer should be in the affirmative, and Blokker's very comprehensive analysis of Security Council practice and the views of member States shows such general acceptance.[78]

---

[73]   Schermers has indicated that the general purposes of international organisations are generally insufficient bases for extensive powers, that the major powers must be included in the constitution, and that only secondary, derived powers can be drawn from them as implied. H. Schermers, 'The Legal Bases of International Organization Action' in Dupuy, *supra* note 36, pp. 401-411, at 406-408.

[74]   Cf. Bothe, *supra* note 33, pp. 574-575.

[75]   Blokker, *supra* note 63, 567.

[76]   Sarooshi, *supra* note 52, pp. 146-149 (supported by interpretations of articles 42 and 53).

[77]   Cf. Skubiszewsky, *supra* note 59, pp. 859-860.

[78]   Blokker, *supra* note 63, 555-560, though criticism voiced about the lack of supervision and control by the Security Council has led to more restrictive mandates (*ibid.*, 560-567).

But this raises another interesting question: can the Security Council be considered to possess powers that are neither express nor implied? Again the answer should be in the affirmative. In the Namibia Opinion the ICJ rejected an argument by South Africa to the effect that a resolution had not been adopted because two permanent members had abstained. Article 27, paragraph 3, of the Charter requires that the nine affirmative votes necessary for the adoption of a decision include the concurring votes of the permanent members.[79] The ordinary meaning of this is that permanent members should vote in favour and not against or abstain. The Court noted:[80]

> (...) the proceedings of the Security Council extending over a long period supply abundant evidence that presidential rulings and the positions taken by members of the Council, in particular its permanent members, have consistently and uniformly interpreted the practice of voluntary abstention as not constituting a bar to the adoption of resolutions. (...) This procedure followed by the Security Council, (...), has been generally accepted by Members of the United Nations and evidences a general practice of that Organization.

It would seem then that a general practice of the Council generally accepted by member States may validate a practice of the Council in violation of a provision of the Charter.[81] By now then the power of the Security Council to authorise the use of force, as an assumed power,[82] is supported by a rule of internal customary law of the United Nations.[83]

---

[79] The French text makes more clear that the votes of permanent members must be among the nine affirmative votes: "Les décisions du Conseil de sécurité sur toutes autres questions sont prises par un vote affirmatif de neuf de ses membres dans lequel sont comprises les voix des tous les membres permanents, (...)."

[80] International Court of Justice, *Legal Consequences for States of the Continued Presence of South Africa in Namibia (South West Africa) notwithstanding Security Council Resolution 276 (1970)*, Advisory Opinion, ICJ Reports 1971, p. 16, at 22.

[81] Article 2, paragraph 1 (j), of the 1986 Vienna Convention on the Law of Treaties between States and International Organizations and between International Organizations, reprinted in (1986) 25 *International Legal Materials* 543-589, confirms this proposition (though it may be noted that general acceptance by the members of the organisation does not seem to feature as a separate requirement; but it does in relation to interpretation, see article 31, paragraph 2 (b)). Also Skubiszewski, *supra* note 59, p. 857.

[82] Note Ciobanu, *supra* note 39, pp. 40-41; and in a different context R. Wessel, 'The legality of the new functions of the Western European Union, The attribution of

André J.J. de Hoogh

2.2 Attribution or delegation of adjudicatory powers

The question of attribution or delegation of adjudicatory power has come up in recent years in relation to the establishment by the Security Council of the International Criminal Tribunal for the Former Yugoslavia (Yugoslav Tribunal),[84] and later of the International Criminal Tribunal for Rwanda.[85] Defence counsel for the first accused before the Yugoslav Tribunal, Dusko Tadić, argued that the establishment of a tribunal was outside the competence of the Council, and that the Council, not possessing any judicial powers, could not create a subsidiary organ endowed with such powers. In response the Appeals Chamber held:[86]

> Plainly, the Security Council is not a judicial organ and is not provided with judicial powers (though it may incidentally perform certain quasi-judicial activities such as effecting determinations or findings).

And it continued:[87]

> The establishment of the International Tribunal by the Security Council does not signify, however, that the Security Council has delegated to it some of its own functions or the exercise of some of

---

powers reconsidered on the occasion of the 50th anniversary of the Brussels Treaty' (1998) 51 *Studia Diplomatica* 15-28, at 22-25.

[83] Cf. B. Conforti, *The Law and Practice of the United Nations* (2nd Revised Edition, Kluwer Law International, The Hague, 2000), at 203-204. Earlier in this sense de Hoogh, *supra* note 66, pp. 305-309. In the Namibia Opinion, 46-50, paras. 91-105, the ICJ considered the exercise of the right to terminate the Mandate agreement to be validated under customary international law. Note also the extra-Charter competence conferred under article 11 of the 1958 Convention on Fishing and Conservation of the Living Resources of the High Seas, reprinted in (1958) 52 *American Journal of International Law,* 851-858, in which article 94, paragraph 2, of the Charter is declared applicable to decisions of a special commission.

[84] Security Council Resolution 827, adopted 25 May 1993 (the ICTY Statute may be found at http://www.un.org/icty/basic/statut/stat2000_con.htm).

[85] Security Council Resolution 955, adopted 8 November 1994 (Statute annexed to the Resolution).

[86] ICTY, Appeals Chamber, *Prosecutor v. Dusko Tadić a/k/a "Dule", Decision on the Defence Motion for Interlocutory Appeal on Jurisdiction,* 2 October 1995, para. 34, through http://www.un.org/icty/ind-e.htm.

[87] *Tadić Case, Jurisdiction,* para. 38. Also Gill, *supra* note 61, 85-86.

its own powers. Nor does it mean, in reverse, that the Security Council was usurping for itself part of a judicial function which does not belong to it but to other organs of the United Nations according to the Charter. The Security Council has resorted to the establishment of a judicial organ in the form of an international criminal tribunal as an instrument for the exercise of its own principal function of maintenance of peace and security, i.e., as a measure contributing to the restoration and maintenance of peace in the former Yugoslavia.

Obviously then the powers possessed by the Tribunal have not been delegated but attributed. The Tribunal's creation is apparently based on the consideration that there cannot be peace without justice. It may be speculated that international peace in the Balkan region could be jeopardised or endangered by the continuing liberty of individuals suspected to have committed crimes under international law, especially when such crimes had been planned, instigated, or tolerated by high level military and political leaders.[88] This has been the angle at the time of conclusion of the Dayton/Paris Peace Agreement, as it was laid down in the Constitution of Bosnia and Herzegovina, in article IX, that:[89]

> No person who is serving a sentence imposed by the International Tribunal for the Former Yugoslavia, and no person who is under indictment by the Tribunal and who has failed to comply with an order to appear before the Tribunal, may stand as a candidate or hold any appointive, elective, or other public office in the territory of Bosnia and Herzegovina.

However this may be, when the Security Council established the Tribunal in resolution 827, it merely stated that it was convinced that the establishment of the Tribunal and prosecution of responsible individuals would contribute to halting and redressing violations of international humanitarian law (preamble, para. 7) and would contribute to the restoration and maintenance of peace (preamble, para. 6).

---

[88] Note article 7 of the Statute on command responsibility.

[89] General Framework Agreement for Peace in Bosnia and Herzegovina, Annex 4: Constitution of Bosnia and Herzegovina, 14 December 1995 (Bosnia and Herzegovina; Croatia; Federal Republic of Yugoslavia), Paris, reprinted in (1996) 35 *International Legal Materials* 117-128.

However, as to the legal basis of the power of the Security Council to establish the Yugoslav Tribunal the Appeals Chamber held:[90] "(...) the International Tribunal matches perfectly the description of 'measures not involving the use of force'." Clearly the creation of the Yugoslav Tribunal could be considered to constitute a measure *not* involving the use of armed force.[91] However, this is beside the point. While there may be borderline cases as to what constitutes a use of armed force (one may refer to calls upon members to enforce, by use of force if necessary, trade embargoes),[92] this is obviously not in question here. Similarly the argument that the list of measures mentioned in article 41 is illustrative, and not limitative, does not hold sway.[93] The Chamber seems to interpret article 39 in the sense that the Security Council can only decide upon the kind of measures expressed in articles 41 and 42.[94] Since such would be the case, the Chamber then has no option but to base the establishment of the Tribunal either on article 41 or on article 42. As no issue of armed force is at stake,[95] the choice for article 41 then is clear-cut.

What the Appeals Chamber fails to take into account is that the establishment of the Tribunal and the powers that the Tribunal wields do not amount to coercive or enforcement action. The Appeals Chamber noted in relation to the powers under articles 41 and 42 that:[96] "These powers are coercive vis-à-vis the culprit State or entity." However, in making the choice for article 41 as legal basis, the Chamber does not explain in what way the establishment of the Tribunal would have *coercive* or *enforcement* character.[97] The distinction between powers of legislation, of adjudication,

---

[90] *Tadić Case, Jurisdiction*, para. 37. In agreement with the Appeals Chamber, Frowein, *supra* note 20 (on Article 41), p. 626. Dupuy generally supports the competence of the Security Council to establish the tribunals. P.-M. Dupuy, 'Le maintien de la paix' in Dupuy, *supra* note 36, pp. 563-604, at 588-590.

[91] *Tadić Case, Jurisdiction*, para. 33.

[92] E.g. Security Council Resolution 665, adopted 25 August 1990.

[93] *Tadić Case, Jurisdiction*, para. 35. Also Frowein, *supra* note 20 (on Article 41), p. 625.

[94] *Tadić Case, Jurisdiction*, para. 32.

[95] Contrary Conforti, *supra* note 83, pp. 207-208, who considers the creation of the tribunals to constitute a 'belligerent' measure under article 42 Charter.

[96] *Tadić Case, Jurisdiction*, para. 31. See also *Expenses Opinion*, 163 (and 164).

[97] Sarooshi, *supra* note 52, p. 5, notes (apparently in relation to action under article 42 and not so much in relation to measures under article 41): "The nature of the power being transferred is in essence coercive, and when this is combined with the capability of Member States to exercise this coercive element it can truly be said that there is a delegation of power and not just authority or competence." Before this he had

and of enforcement,[98] is not wholly absent from the Charter, as may be seen by reference to the power of the General Assembly to regulate the relations between staff and the United Nations (article 101, para. 1, Charter). In this regard the International Court of Justice held regarding the question whether the General Assembly could create a Tribunal competent to decide disputes with binding effect for the Assembly itself:[99]

> By establishing the Administrative Tribunal, the General Assembly was delegating the performance of its own functions: it was exercising a power which it had under the Charter to regulate staff relations. In regard to the Secretariat, the General Assembly is given by the Charter a power to make regulations, *but not a power to adjudicate upon, or otherwise deal with, particular instances.*

Furthermore, in a number of provisions the Charter mentions 'preventive or enforcement action', 'enforcement measures', 'enforcement action', or 'preventive or enforcement measures' (articles 2, para. 5; 2, para. 7, with reference to Chapter VII; 5; 50; and 53, para. 1). Such references are consistently viewed as referring to the measures of articles 41 and 42 and seen to possess coercive or enforcement character.[100] Coercion and enforcement are concepts that relate to action or measures being taken against a State or

---

observed (*ibid.*): "In many cases this will involve a delegation of competence which enables the delegate to carry out acts which would otherwise be unlawful. However, a characteristic of power, the implicit coercive or forceful element that demands compliance with a decision, cannot always be delegated."

[98] Schermers/Blokker, *supra* note 55, pp. 150-152, paras. 221-223.

[99] International Court of Justice, *Effect of Awards Opinion*, at 61. See also Dissenting Opinion Hackworth, *ibid.*, 77-81. The text quoted appears to some extent to indicate the exercise of an express power. Earlier the Court had concluded to the existence of an implied power enabling it to establish the Administrative Tribunal. *Ibid.*, 56-58. See Campbell, *supra* note 71, 525-527.

[100] Implicitly L. Goodrich/E. Hambro, *Charter of the United Nations, Commentary and Documents* (2nd, revised edition, Stevens & Sons, London, 1949), at 316; Kodjo, Article 53 in J.-P.Cot/A. Pellet, (Eds), *La Charte des Nations Unies, Commentaire article par article* (2e édition, revue et augmentée, Economica, Paris), pp. 816-831, at 819 and 824; Frowein, *supra* note 20 (on Article 42), p. 632; Schermers/Blokker, *supra* note 55, pp. 904-905, paras. 1451-452 (coercion), 924-942, paras. 1482-1512 (enforcement measures under Chapter VII); Gill, *supra* note 61, 48 and 52. The French text of the Charter translates 'enforcement' by 'coercition'.

a specific entity.[101] Their purpose is to put pressure on such a State or entity to agree to or adopt specific measures.

While it may be granted that the Tribunal exercises powers of decision-making, it does not coerce (member) States or entities. Its power is to adjudicate upon the alleged criminal responsibility of individuals. In a general sense then this may function as deterrence against unlawful behaviour of the 'targeted' States, entities, or individuals. Yet this constitutes a different kind of pressure than coercive or enforcement measures, which affect the targeted State or entity directly. In fact, in a later decision the Appeals Chamber observes:[102]

> (…) the International Tribunal does not possess any power to take enforcement measures against States. Had the drafters of the Statute intended to vest the International Tribunal with such a power, they would have expressly provided for it. In the case of an international judicial body, this is not a power that can be regarded as inherent in its functions.

Although an obligation has been placed upon members of the United Nations to co-operate with the Tribunal (Security Council resolution 827, para. 4; article 29 Statute), the exercise of judicial powers does not amount to coercion or enforcement. The obligation to co-operate could perhaps be seen as coercive or enforcement vis-à-vis the former Yugoslav republics (though it is not clear why such republics as Slovenia and Macedonia would be targeted for enforcement).

In the Tadić Case the Appeals Chamber did contemplate the existence of more general powers, other than those of articles 41 and 42, as a possible basis for the establishment of the Tribunal, but chose to base itself upon the express powers of article 41.[103] Yet this would have been the way forward. Article 41 measures are intended to have members apply meas-

---

[101] Frowein, *supra* note 20 (on Article 39), p. 616 notes that parties fighting in a civil war seem to come under the jurisdiction of the Security Council.

[102] ICTY, Appeals Chamber, *Prosecutor v. Tihomir Blaskic, Judgment on the Request of the Republic of Croatia for Review of the Decision of the Trial Chamber of 18 July 1997*, 29 October 1997, para. 25 (relevant footnote omitted), through http://www.un.org/icty/ind-e.htm.

[103] *Tadić Case, Jurisdiction*, para. 31. At another place, para. 37, it observed that the Security Council possesses both decision-making and executive powers regarding the maintenance of international peace and security.

ures against a State or entity to force it 'to give effect to its decisions'.[104] Such measures are 'to give effect to its decisions', though what these decisions are or may amount to is not clear.[105] These decisions are not the determination of article 39 or the decision to resort to enforcement measures under articles 41 or 42, nor a combination of the two.[106] The determination of one of the situations of article 39, standing alone, does not entail any consequences.[107] Thus it would not make sense to see the decisions referred to in article 41 as the determination of article 39. Similarly it would be absurd to consider giving effect to its decisions as the decision to impose enforcement measures. The Court in the Expenses Opinion mentioned that:[108]

> (...) it is the Security Council which is given a power to impose an explicit obligation of compliance if for example it issues an order or command to an aggressor under Chapter VII. It is only the Security Council which can require enforcement by coercive action against an aggressor.

The power to impose an obligation of compliance by way of order or command is not expressed in so many words in the Charter. At most one can see the decisions referred to in article 41 as a witness to such a power. As Schermers and Blokker note, some explicit powers presume the existence of implied powers, and they provide the following example:[109] "The right of sanction implies a right to recognize violations." Indeed it does, but one may add another implied power: the right to sanction and the right

---

[104] Armed action under article 42 is not only intended to force a State or entity to comply with Security Council demands, but could involve the implementation of those demands by use of armed force. Nevertheless, this does constitute coercive or enforcement action as may be seen from the authorisations in Resolutions 678 (paras. 1 and 2) and 940 (adopted 31 July 1994, para. 4), since a period of grace is provided during which voluntary compliance with the specific demands of the Council would forestall use of the authorisation.

[105] Note D. Schweigman, *The Authority of the Security Council under Chapter VII of the UN Charter, Legal Limits and the Role of the International Court of Justice,* (Proefschrift Erasmus Universiteit Rotterdam, 2001), at 37.

[106] Contrary Frowein, *supra* note 20 (on Article 41), p. 624.

[107] Cf. White, *supra* note 59, p. 102.

[108] *Expenses Opinion*, 163.

[109] Schermers/Blokker, *supra* note 55, p. 159, para. 233 (further pp. 897-901, paras. 1439-1443).

to recognise a violation imply a determination as to the measures necessary to redress or remedy the violation.[110]

In effect, the establishment of the Tribunal should rather be seen to concretise the object to be achieved, that is, the *maintenance or restoration* of international peace and security. The mere determination of a threat to the peace, breach of the peace, or act of aggression, does not tell us anything as to what should happen to forestall the threat to the peace (maintenance) or to remedy the breach of the peace or act of aggression (restoration). Of course the Council may decide upon the measures of articles 41 or 42, but these must have some purpose, some goal, or how would one know if and when these enforcement measures could, or even should, be terminated. For this reason the Security Council cannot only decide upon the measures of articles 41 and 42 in a binding manner, but may also formulate decisions which are binding upon the aggressor State, the State responsible for a breach of the peace, or the State contributing to a threat to the peace. This constitutes an implied power of the Council under articles 39, 41 and 42.[111] The practice of the Security Council is replete with demands of the Security Council to adopt specific measures that are addressed to specific parties.[112] Should such demands be heeded by the parties concerned, good faith implementation of those demands would take away the basis for resorting to coercive or enforcement action. Any system of law, and also a collective security system, must favour voluntary compliance by its subjects or members over enforced compliance.[113] Whether the basis for granting legislative powers to peacekeeping operations is the same as for the grant of adjudicatory powers to the tribunals will be discussed next.

2.3 Attribution of legislative powers

First to be answered is the question posed in the introduction, that is, whether the Security Council possesses legislative power? In this regard, Sands and Klein have observed that:[114]

---

[110] Schermers/Blokker, *supra* note 55, pp. 900-901, para. 1443.

[111] Cf. Sarooshi, *supra* note 52, pp. 95-98.

[112] Earlier de Hoogh, *supra* note 66, pp. 170-171, 172-173, 178-179, 181-184.

[113] Cf. de Hoogh, *supra* note 66, pp. 236-237 and 239-240.

[114] P. Sands/P. Klein, *Bowett's Law of International Institutions*, 5th edition, (Sweet & Maxwell, London, 2001) pp. 280.

It is largely agreed in that respect that the powers to adopt normative acts binding on members in the "external sphere" must be expressly stated in the organisation's constituent instruments and may not be implied.

However, the reference to 'normative acts', in their chapter on the legislative or normative function of international organisations, should somewhat surprisingly not be read in the context of any separation of powers. Rather they relate legislative or normative acts to the power to take decisions binding on members.[115] This is the more obvious as they continue to discuss the mandatory effect of Security Council decisions (article 25 Charter).[116] Further on they point to the grant of legislative power to UNTAET and indicate that their use of the phrase 'legislative functions' to describe norm-making activities of international organisations is not entirely inappropriate.[117]

A word on terminology is indispensable in this context and this concerns the meaning to be attached to 'legislative power' or the 'power to legislate'. Oxman has hypothesised that three characteristics must be present to constitute international legislation: written articulation of rules; that have legally binding effect as such; and have been promulgated by a process to which express authority has been delegated *a priori* to make binding rules without affirmative *a posteriori* assent to those rules by those bound.[118] It would certainly be prudent to add to this that such rules imply future application to an indeterminate number of cases or situations. Thus Stein has remarked that the result of legislation will be a norm applicable in more than one case and he questions whether one could call Security Council resolutions legislation.[119]

---

[115] Sands/Klein, *ibid.*, p. 261; in the same sense K. Dicke, 'National Interest vs. the Interest of the International Community – A Critical Review of Recent UN Security Council Practice' in J. Delbrück, (Ed.), *New Trends in International Lawmaking – International Legislation in the Public Interest*, (Duncker & Humblot, Berlin, 1996), pp. 145-169, at 164-165 (but see also p. 225).

[116] Sands/Klein, *ibid.*, pp. 281-282.

[117] Sands/Klein, *ibid.*, p. 285. See also Schermers/Blokker, *supra* note 55, p. 142, para. 210, in relation to the European Union and the European Communities.

[118] B. Oxman, 'The International Commons, the International Public Interest and New Modes of International Lawmaking' in Delbrück, *supra* note 115, pp. 21-60, at 28-30.

[119] T. Stein, 'Comment' in Delbrück, *supra* note 115, pp. 212-213, at 212. Contrary C. Schreuer, 'Comment', in *ibid.*, pp. 213-215, at 214, who feels that the creation of a

This goes to the heart of the matter. The Security Council does not determine or elaborate rules that would be applicable to any future situation. It determines the existence of *a* threat to the peace, *a* breach of the peace, or *an* act of aggression, and then decides what to do about it. Naturally, the measures of articles 41 and 42 may be wide in scope and target: the more members involved, the more activity may be expected. But all these measures will be taken to redress a *particular* situation and usually a *particular* member will be targeted.[120] This is no different in relation to the measures of article 41, which the Security Council may decide upon in a binding fashion and must be applied by all members. Although all members are bound to apply them, they all relate to a particular situation and will not be extended to future cases or situations unless the Council so decides. Clearly then, the Security Council does not possess the power to legislate.[121]

As noted in the introduction, the Security Council has decided that UNTAET is empowered to exercise all legislative and executive authority (resolution 1272, para. 1). In view of the general deterrence against the commission of violations by States, entities or individuals, the establishment and functioning of the *ad hoc* tribunals might be considered to constitute coercive or enforcement action against a State or some other entity. However, as argued above, this view is unpersuasive. In relation to the question of attribution of legislative power by the Security Council, this is even more questionable. Of course one might again entertain the thought that the mere adoption of legislation, that is adoption of rules binding upon certain subjects of law, would amount to general deterrence and therefore to coercive or enforcement action against States or entities. But this view is even less persuasive. The tribunals' exercise of adjudicatory power is related to certain specific situations. The exercise of legislative power by UNTAET, although granted in view of the specific situation of East Timor, is unrelated to any specific case or situation. The grant of legislative power to a peacekeeping operation is for internal purposes only (though one may speculate that the peacekeeping operation could conclude binding agreements, for instance on border controls, with neighbour-

---

war crimes tribunal and the adoption of its statute amount to legislation by the Security Council.

[120] Note Sarooshi, *supra* note 52, p. 98, note 51.

[121] In a different context the ICJ denied it possessed any legislative power. International Court of Justice, *Legality of the Threat or Use of Nuclear Weapons*, Advisory Opinion, ICJ Reports 1996, p. 226, at 237, para. 18. Also Declaration Vereshchetin, *ibid.*, 279-280; and Dissenting Opinion Oda, *ibid.*, 372.

ing States), that is, it is to be exercised in relation to the general population and objects and property within a certain territory. Nationals of other States may be affected by such legislation if they come within the territory concerned, but the legislative measures adopted are not generally directed against any State or entity (but *infra* section 3.1).

Nevertheless, it has been argued by Matheson that the governance functions exercised by UNTAET (and UNMIK) come within the scope of measures under article 41 of the Charter, arguing that the measures listed in article 41 are exemplary and not exclusive.[122] This has also been the position of the Appeals Chamber in the Tadić Case,[123] in which it also rejected an argument that article 41 envisages implementation of the measures decided upon by members rather than by (organs of) the United Nations.[124] In this regard it noted:[125]

> Logically, if the Organization can undertake measures which have to be implemented through the intermediary of its Members, it can *a fortiori* undertake measures which it can implement directly via its organs, if it happens to have the resources to do so. It is only for want of such resources that the United Nations has to act through its Members. (...). Action by Member States on behalf of the Organization is but a poor substitute *faute de mieux*, or a "second best" for want of the first.

Yet this is wide of the mark. Either the Security Council possesses the power to take action itself, or it does not. To suggest that because the Council has the power to bind the Members to take measures it possesses the power to take those measures itself, is to negate the express language of the Charter in envisaging implementation of measures by Members (article 41) and/or the taking of action by the Council itself (article 42). Even if one would consider measures by Members to constitute a substitute *faute de mieux* or second best, then this is because States in negotiating the Charter have opted for this. It is no good trying to remedy a less than ideal situation, if that is what it is, by postulating powers not expressed in the text.

---

[122] Matheson, *supra* note 13, 83-84.

[123] *Tadić* Case, *Jurisdiction*, paras. 33-36.

[124] *Tadić* Case, *Jurisdiction*, para. 32.

[125] *Tadić* Case, *Jurisdiction*, para. 36.

Thus, in the same vein as the establishment of the *ad hoc* tribunals, the grant of legislative power is based on the implied power of the Security Council to determine the specific measures necessary to maintain or restore international peace and security.[126] As can be seen from the quotation at the beginning of this section, Sands and Klein found that a power to adopt normative acts must be express. But since they claim this to be based on the Council's power to take binding decisions, one may safely assume that they would consider UNTAET's legislative power to be based upon the Council's delegation of its express power.[127]

Be that as it may, the implied power of the Security Council to attribute legislative powers to peacekeeping operations raises questions regarding the limits to the Council's implied power and to the exercise of legislative powers. In relation to East Timor and UNTAET these will be discussed first as to the legal bases of the power to attribute, and secondly as to the bounds of international law and domestic jurisdiction.

Section 3: The bases and bounds of legislative power in East Timor

3.1 The maintenance of international peace and security and consent

As indicated in section 1.2, the legal bases for the establishment of UNTAET have been the consent of Portugal and the exercise of enforcement powers by the Security Council under Chapter VII. Turning first to the latter basis, the Council determined the existence of a threat to peace and security, delegated its enforcement power under article 42 (first to INTERFET, then to UNTAET), and attributed legislative power to UNTAET under its implied power to determine the specific, concretised measures necessary to maintain or restore international peace and security. A common feature of the Council's exercise of powers under Chapter VII of the Charter is that such exercise must be necessary for, or stand in an arguable relation to, the maintenance or restoration of international peace and security.[128] This follows from the text of article 39 in that the purpose of the

---

[126] Cf. Dicke, *supra* note 115, p. 164; and J. Verhoeven, 'Les activités normatives et quasi normatives' in Dupuy, *supra* note 36, pp. 413-484, at 419, though he observed: "Nul n'a cependant sérieusement soutenu qu'il permettrait au Conseil de sécurité d'exercer par voie de décision des activités proprement normatives, (…)."

[127] Sands/Klein, *supra* note 114, pp. 261, 280, 281-282, and 285; in the same sense Dicke, *supra* note 115, pp. 164-165.

[128] Cf. Dicke, *supra* note 115, pp. 164 and 167; Schweigman, *supra* note 105, pp. 189-191.

measures to be taken is the maintenance or restoration of international peace and security.

However, the Appeals Chamber rejected an argument against the discretionary power of the Council in evaluating the appropriateness of the measure taken, the establishment of the Tribunal, and its effectiveness in achieving the objective of restoration of international peace and security.[129] The Appeals Chamber indicated in a cursory manner that the choice of means and their evaluation are left to the wide discretionary powers of the Security Council (as this entails a political evaluation of complex and dynamic situations). However, though it had earlier held that such discretion was not unlimited, it did not actually review the exercise of this power as to the choice of means.[130]

Regarding the attribution of *all legislative power* to UNTAET by the Security Council, it is necessary to take into account the source of the Council's powers, namely the maintenance or restoration of international peace and security under Chapter VII. The powers of the Security Council under Chapter VII may have broad discretionary character, but in the end they are not unlimited. To bestow upon a peacekeeping or peace enforcing operation *all legislative power* cannot be justified solely by reference to the Council's powers under Chapter VII. *Mutatis mutandis*, the exercise of legislative power by the relevant peacekeeping operation would also have to stand in an arguable relation to the maintenance or restoration of international peace and security. Yet some of the regulations adopted by UNTAET do not bear witness to this. It may be hard to divine such an arguable relation to international peace and security as to regulations on a central fiscal authority (2000/1), the determination of the US dollar as official currency (2000/7), a tax and customs regime (2000/12), a central civil registry (2001/3), the registration of motor vehicles (2001/6), and the regulation of road traffic (2001/8).

On the other hand, other regulations are more directly related to the maintenance of international peace and security, such as those on the prohibition of land transactions by Indonesians (2000/27), the defence force (2001/1 and 2001/9), and on firearms, ammunition and explosives (2001/5). Others can be considered to be necessary to promote the stability of East Timor in anticipation of its independence, such as those on the na-

---

[129] *Tadić Case, Jurisdiction*, para. 39.

[130] *Tadić Case, Jurisdiction*, paras. 32 and 39. In this latter paragraph it held that the legality and validity in law of a chosen measure could not be determined *ex post facto* by reference to its success or failure in achieving the restoration of international peace and security.

tional consultative council (1999/2, 2000/24 and 2000/33), the transitional government (2000/23), and the election of a constituent assembly (2001/2 and 2001/11); the applicable law (1999/1), the transitional judicial service commission and the organisation of the court system (1993/3, 2000/11, 2000/14, 2000/16, 2000/25, 2000/30); jurisdiction over crimes against humanity, genocide, war crimes and torture (2000/15), and the Commission for Reception, Truth and Reconciliation (2001/10).

Assuming then that not all legislative activity undertaken by UNTAET can be said to relate to the maintenance of international peace and security, an alternative legal basis must be found. This one can see in Portugal's consent to UN administration, given already in article 6 of the 5 May agreement, and which was confirmed in the tripartite meeting of 28 September 1999 on the arrangements for the peaceful and orderly transfer of authority to the UN. As Portugal was, and still is, the administering authority, its consent sufficed to provide the United Nations with *de jure* authority regarding all activities unrelated to the maintenance of international peace and security. However, although such authority is in principle all embracing, one may wonder whether substantive limitations do not apply by reason of rules of international law or because of East Timor's future domestic jurisdiction.

3.2 Domestic jurisdiction and some bounds of international law

At the outset it should be noted that international organisations are subjects of international law, and therefore bound by obligations under customary international law, their constitutions and treaties to which they are parties.[131] Thus the United Nations as an organisation is bound by (international) law,[132] and this will be the case also for specific organs such as the Security Council.[133] Naturally the Security Council possesses wide discre-

---

[131] International Court of Justice, *Interpretation of the Agreement of 25 March 1951 between the WHO and Egypt*, Advisory Opinion, ICJ Reports 1980, p. 73, 89-90.

[132] Generally J. Delbrück, 'Peacekeeping by the United Nations and the Rule of Law' *in* J. Akkerman/P. van Krieken/C. Pannenborg, (Eds.), *Declarations On Principles, A Quest For Universal Peace*, (A.W. Sijthoff, Leyden, 1977), pp. 73-99, who discusses this from the viewpoint of rule of law and the principle of legality.

[133] *Tadić Case, Jurisdiction*, para. 28, in which the Appeals Chamber held that: "(...) neither the text nor the spirit of the Charter conceives of the Security Council as *legibus solutus* (unbound by law)." Contrary Schweigman, *supra* note 105, pp. 195-196, as to customary international law (but more restrictive, 196-201, in relation to *jus cogens* and the quasi-judicial role of the Council).

tionary powers under articles 39, 41 and 42 of the Charter, though this should not be taken to mean that its actions are not subject to legal considerations or to review.[134] In this regard questions were raised by Matheson whether the Security Council could change the final political status of a territory (by recognising its independence, transferring it from one State to another, determining its boundaries, or giving it permanent autonomy) and whether the Council could make permanent changes in the legal system of a territory (by determining the political structure or promulgating a permanent constitution)?[135] He answers affirmatively, but this is difficult to accept.[136]

Article 24, paragraph 2, stipulates that the Security Council in exercising its responsibility for the maintenance of international peace and security shall abide by the purposes and principles of the United Nations. The purposes and principles of the UN are laid down in articles 1 and 2 of the Charter. Pride of place among these is article 2, paragraph 7, which provides that nothing in the Charter shall authorise the United Nations to intervene in matters which are essentially within the domestic jurisdiction of members. Among these matters of domestic jurisdiction are a State's choice of political, economical, social and cultural system and the formulation of foreign policy.[137] It may be granted that the last sentence provides that this shall not prejudice the application of enforcement measures under Chapter VII.[138]

Yet it would be too easy simply to deny article 2, paragraph 7, application if other purposes or principles suggest limits to the Council's power.[139] Article 1, paragraph 2, proclaims as purpose of the United Na-

---

[134] Contrary Gill, *supra* note 61, pp. 61-68 and 116-121 (though arguing for limitations based on the purposes and principles of the United Nations (72-90)).

[135] Matheson, *supra* note 13, 84-85.

[136] Though this author has in the past argued that far-reaching guarantees against repetition may be demanded, and imposed, as against States that have committed international crimes. De Hoogh, *supra* note 66, pp. 167-184. These could entail under certain circumstances the removal of a government directly responsible for the commission of such crimes (174-179). Contrary Schweigman, *supra* note 105, pp. 169-171.

[137] International Court of Justice, *Case concerning military and paramilitary activities in and around Nicaragua, Merits*, ICJ Reports 1986, p. 14, at 107-108, para. 205.

[138] Schweigman, *supra* note 105, pp. 178-179 (and note 785, at 177-178).

[139] See especially Gill, *supra* note 61, pp. 72-90, who argues extensively and correctly that the right of self-determination precludes the imposition of any form of government on the population of a State or other entity, and that the provisions of the Char-

tions respect for the principle of self-determination. As elaborated in common article 1, paragraph 1, of the Covenant on Civil and Political Rights and the Covenant on Economic, Social and Cultural Rights,[140] this entails the right of a people to freely choose its political system. Article 2, paragraph 4, prohibits members using force against the territorial integrity or political independence of a State (or in any manner inconsistent with UN purposes). Furthermore, article 1, paragraph 1, indicates the UN must promote the settlement of disputes in accordance with international law and justice, and this is strengthened by article 2, paragraph 3, imposing an obligation in similar terms upon members.

Though the attribution of legislative power to UNTAET entitles it to adopt far-reaching regulations, in exercising its power UNTAET should take into account that some matters are within the domestic jurisdiction and to be decided, or not, by the people of East Timor once it becomes independent. This is so even taking into consideration the *de jure* authority of Portugal and its transfer thereof to the United Nations. In the words of the Friendly Relations Declaration, a non-self-governing territory has a status separate and distinct from that of the administering State.[141] So as not to prejudice East Timor's future independence and domestic jurisdiction, UNTAET should duly respect its internal and external affairs.

There can be little doubt that the ratio of respect for internal affairs has led UNTAET to establish the national consultative council in regulation 1999/2, and all subsequent regulations up to and including those establishing the provisional government (2000/23) and organising the elections of 30 August 2001 for the constitutional assembly (2001/1 and 2001/11). By now the elections for the constitutional assembly have taken place, and they were largely won by FRETELIN which gained 55 out of 88 seats.[142]

---

ter have as their main purpose maintaining the independence, security and territorial integrity of its member States. Also Schweigman, *supra* note 105, pp. 162-183.

[140] The 1966 Covenant on Civil and Political Rights, and the 1966 Covenant on Economic, Social and Cultural Rights, both through http://www.unhchr.ch/html/intlinst.htm.

[141] General Assembly Resolution 2625 (XXV), 24 October 1970, Annex: Declaration on Principles of International Law concerning Friendly Relations and Co-operation among States in accordance with the Charter of the United Nations, reprinted in (1970) 9 *International Legal Materials* 1292-1297, para. 6 under the principle 'equal rights and self-determination of peoples'.

[142] Report, 6 September 2001, at http://www.un.org/News/dh/20010906.htm#3.

On this basis, the Transitional Administrator has established the Second Transitional Government of East Timor.[143]

Besides taking care not to interfere with the internal affairs of East Timor (though all regulations are adopted by the Transitional Administrator under the authority conferred by the Security Council), UNTAET has similarly respected the external affairs of East Timor. The successful negotiations on a new agreement on the mineral resources in the sea between East Timor and Australia bear witness to this. The Memorandum of Understanding between Australia and East Timor carefully indicates that the agreed text *is suitable for adoption as an agreement upon East Timor's independence*.[144] Most likely this agreement will be the first treaty to be ratified by the government in accordance with the constitutional requirements of an independent East Timor.

So far the discussion has been about applicable limits protecting the internal and external affairs of East Timor. As the United Nations, and the Security Council, is generally bound by international law, so also UNTAET must be considered bound. Regulation 1999/1 already requires that all persons undertaking public duties or holding public office shall, when exercising their functions, observe internationally recognised human rights standards as reflected in specified documents and treaties (section 2; and section 3 on applicable law). Yet international law may require more than this.

UNTAET must abide, for instance, by those rules of customary international law determining the prescriptive criminal jurisdiction of States.[145] In general, there will not be any problem regarding the application of territorial or any of the established principles of extra-territorial jurisdiction.[146] Other States or entities will be involved only insofar as the legislation concerned amounts to extra-territorial jurisdiction. Such would be the case, for instance, if legislation would be adopted making it a criminal offence for nationals to kill somebody when abroad (active nationality principle). However, UNTAET is entitled to exercise its power if it remains within the bounds of customary international law.

---

[143] Regulation No. 2001/28, 19 September 2001.

[144] Memorandum of Understanding of Timor Sea Arrangement, initialled 5 July 2001, at http://beta.austlii.edu.au/au/other/dfat/special/MOUTSA.html. Emphasis added.

[145] Cf. Malanczuk, *supra* note 20, pp. 109-117.

[146] UNTAET has determined that jurisdiction over crimes exists in accordance with the applicable (Indonesian) law. See section 5 of regulation 2000/11, adopted 6 March 2000.

Importantly it has exercised its power to provide for universal jurisdiction over the following crimes: genocide; war crimes; crimes against humanity; and torture.[147] Noticeable in this respect is that this jurisdiction applies generally to crimes committed before 25 October 1999 (section 2.4), provided it is consistent with section 3.1 of regulation 1999/1 or any other UNTAET regulation. This opens up the way not merely to prosecuting those committing crimes in 1999, but also to prosecuting those responsible for committing crimes under international law all the way back to Indonesia's invasion in December 1975.[148] Provided that the intertemporal dimensions of such jurisdiction are kept in mind, this may yet lead to justice for some of the individuals responsible for killing over 200,000 East Timorese.

Final observations

In consequence of the wave of death and destruction following the announcement of the result of the referendum and in view of the desertion of East Timor by Indonesian authorities, the Security Council in resolution 1272 established the United Nations Transitional Administration for East Timor. The Security Council empowered UNTAET to exercise all legislative and executive authority, including the administration of justice. By voice of the Transitional Administrator, Vieira de Mello, UNTAET has made extensive use of its power to legislate. This contribution has been devoted to uncovering the legal bases for UNTAET's extensive powers.

In a general sense these legal bases are the consent of Portugal (and of Indonesia) and the exercise of powers by the Security Council under Chapter VII of the Charter. Consent by Portugal and Indonesia was expressed in article 6 of the 5 May Agreement, which established that a peaceful and orderly transfer of authority to the United Nations would be effected if the people of East Timor rejected autonomy within Indonesia. In its resolution establishing UNTAET the Security Council determined

---

[147] Regulation 2000/15, adopted 6 June 2000.

[148] Generally D. Machover, 'International humanitarian law and the Indonesian occupation of East Timor' in Catholic Institute for International Relations/International Platform of Jurists for East Timor (IPJET), *International Law and the Question of East Timor*, 1995, pp. 205-222; J. Dunn, 'Genocide in East Timor: the Attempt to Destroy a Society and its Culture' in IPJET, *The East Timor Problem and the Role of Europe*, 1998, pp. 83-94; and R. Clark, 'East Timor and an International Criminal Court' in *ibid.*, pp. 95-106.

that the situation in East Timor constituted a threat to peace and security, empowered UNTAET to exercise all legislative and executive authority, and authorised UNTAET to take all necessary measures to fulfil its mandate. Clearly the Security Council acted pursuant to its powers under Chapter VII of the Charter.

However, it is not immediately clear which powers under that chapter could form the basis for the grant of legislative powers to a peacekeeping operation. In order to investigate this issue properly, the practice of the Security Council in delegating its enforcement powers to States and in establishing *ad hoc* international criminal tribunals was discussed. It was concluded that the delegation of enforcement powers could be based on an assumed power validated by a rule of internal customary law of the United Nations.

The legal basis of the establishment of the Yugoslav Tribunal is not based, as the Appeals Chamber has held, on article 41, but on the implied power to determine what specific measures have to be taken to maintain or restore international peace and security. Article 41 as legal basis must be discarded, because the establishment of the Tribunal and the powers it wields over individuals do not amount to coercive or enforcement measures against a State or entity. As the Security Council itself does not possess any adjudicatory powers, the grant of adjudicatory power to the Tribunal is not a case of delegation but of attribution of powers.

In the same vein the Security Council does not possess the power to legislate, since it always exercises its powers under Chapter VII in relation to a particular case or situation. The measures it decides upon under article 41 must be applied by all member States, but are always connected to a particular case or situation and will only be extended to cover future occurrences by express decision of the Council. Since the Council does not possess the power to legislate, the grant of such power to peacekeeping operations cannot be considered delegation but constitutes attribution.

Members have conferred on the Security Council the (primary) responsibility to maintain international peace and security, and its powers must be exercised so as to maintain or restore international peace and security. In consequence, the exercise of those powers should be necessary for, or stand in an arguable relation to, the maintenance or restoration of international peace and security. Thus it can be doubted whether the grant of *all* legislative authority to a peacekeeping operation can be validated by reference to the Council's powers under Chapter VII. Such doubts would be exacerbated where the Council would not even purport to act under Chapter VII.

The legislative powers of UNTAET are exercised in relation to the population of East Timor, and extensive use has been made of such powers. Some of UNTAET's regulations touch directly on issues of international peace and security (the defence force; firearms, ammunition and explosives), while others relate to the building of institutions (transitional government; elections for a constitutional assembly). However, if the exercise of Security Council powers should stand in an arguable relation to the maintenance of international peace and security, the same should be the case for the exercise of legislative powers by a peacekeeping operation. From this perspective some UNTAET regulations would not stand the test of scrutiny (the registration of motor vehicles; the regulation of road traffic). For such regulations an additional legal basis would be required, which can be found in Portugal's consent, as *de jure* administering power, to the transfer of authority to the United Nations.

Furthermore, as East Timor is bound for independence due consideration should be given to matters within its domestic jurisdiction. As to internal affairs, UNTAET has tried to respect these by establishing Timorese institutions such as the consultative council, the provisional governments and the constitutional assembly. In the negotiations with Australia on the status and exploitation of their shared sea, a matter of external affairs, UNTAET has concluded an agreement that will be subject to ratification by an independent East Timor. As international organisations are bound by customary international law, so also UN peacekeeping operations are bound. UNTAET has shown itself sensitive to this especially in its proclamation of the principles of extra-territorial criminal jurisdiction, which will form the basis of criminal proceedings before Timorese courts.

Many of the issues discussed in this contribution will be relevant also for an assessment of the way in which the United Nations Mission in Kosovo has exercised its powers. There, however, the situation is more complicated. The resolution by which the Security Council established UNMIK did not make any reference to a power to legislate.[149] In paragraph 11 it stated the responsibilities of the international civil presence to include: "Promoting the establishment, pending a final settlement, of substantial autonomy and self-government in Kosovo (...);" and also: "Organizing and overseeing the development of provisional institutions for democratic and autonomous self-government pending a political settlement, including the holding of elections;"

---

[149]   Security Council Resolution 1244, adopted 10 June 1999.

Apparently this has been interpreted to include or imply a power to legislate, because in its first regulation UNMIK posited this power.[150] However, the arrangements of substantial autonomy and self-government in Kosovo must respect the sovereignty and territorial integrity of the Federal Republic of Yugoslavia (FRY).[151] From this perspective some of the regulations adopted may be criticised. Why should one consider substantial autonomy and self-government to include a complete divorce of Kosovo's legal system from that of the FRY's? Whereas in its first regulation (section 3) UNMIK had determined the applicable law to be that of the FRY on 24 March 1999 (when NATO's bombardments started), in regulation 24 (section 1) it determined the applicable law to be the law in force in Kosovo on 22 March 1989 (when measures restricting Kosovo's autonomy were taken).

But this means that the applicable law is now that of a State that no longer exists, the Socialist Federal Republic of Yugoslavia. Would it not have been better to stick to measuring up FRY laws against UNMIK regulations and internationally recognised standards of human rights? The applicable law in Kosovo set by UNMIK will make it harder to reintegrate Kosovo in the FRY. As such it comes awfully close to creating facts on the ground, and as simply one of the stepping stones on the way to Kosovar independence.[152]

Postscript

The waves caused by the terrorist attacks against the United States on 11 September 2001 continue to grow in amplitude also within the United Nations. The day after the attacks the Security Council adopted resolution 1368, in which it regarded the attacks as a threat to international peace and security, and recognised the right to individual and collective self-defence in accordance with the Charter.[153] The Council further called upon States to work together to bring to justice the perpetrators (para. 3), and on the

---

[150] Section 1, paragraph 1, UNMIK/REG/1999/1, adopted 25 July 1999. All UNMIK regulations through http://www.un.org/peace/kosovo/pages/regulations/regs.html.

[151] Resolution 1244, preamble, para. 10, and para. 1 in conjunction to Annex 2 (paper agreed to by the Federal Republic of Yugoslavia), point 8.

[152] Note the recommendation of the self-appointed Independent International Commission on Kosovo that Kosovo ought to become conditionally independent. See information and report at http://www.kosovocommission.org/.

[153] Security Council Resolution 1368, adopted 12 September 2001, respectively para. 1 and preamble.

international community to redouble efforts to prevent and suppress terror-ist acts (para. 4).

One day after submission of this contribution the Security Council adopted resolution 1373.[154] The Security Council acted under Chapter VII of the Charter, and decided that all States shall (para. 1) prevent and sup-press the financing of terrorist acts; criminalise the wilful provision or col-lection of funds, by their nationals or within their territories, intentionally used, or in the knowledge that they are to be used, for carrying out terrorist acts; freeze funds, financial assets, or economic resources of persons who commit, participate in, or facilitate terrorist acts (and of entities owned or controlled by, or entities and persons acting on behalf of or directed by, such persons); prohibit making funds (etc.) available to such persons or entities. The Security Council further decided (para. 2) on a number of measures to be taken or complied with by States (refrain from supporting terrorist acts, prevent terrorist acts, provide early warning to other States, deny safe havens, etc.).

Many of the measures decided upon by the Security Council in the wake of the 11 September attacks had already been set out in resolution 1269.[155] But the Council has taken the opportunity to make these measures binding on (member) States. Leaving aside the fact that the Security Council cannot take decisions binding on non-member States, there is cause for concern here. Many of the measures adopted could fall under the implied power of the Council to determine the *specific* measures necessary to maintain or restore international peace and security. What is noticeable, however, is that the Council purports to be acting under Chapter VII with-out determining the existence of a threat to the peace, breach of the peace or act of aggression. This is all the more curious as the circumstances ob-viously warrant such a determination (arguably resolution 1368 contains an implied determination).

But perhaps this omission is deliberate. Contrary to what one would expect, the measures imposed by resolution 1373 are not geared towards redressing the threat(s) to international peace and security generated by the 11 September attacks. The measures that must be implemented by (mem-ber) States will be relevant for addressing the present crisis, but will also involve application well beyond the immediate future to include any (at-tempted) act of international terrorism wherever committed, by whoever committed, and against whomever committed. Thus, as a matter of fact,

---

[154] Security Council Resolution 1373, adopted 28 September 2001.

[155] Security Council Resolution 1269, adopted 19 October 1999, paras. 2 and 4.

resolution 1373 amounts to international legislation by the Security Council.[156] This contribution argued that the Security Council does not possess the power to legislate. If that is the correct view, the measures decided upon by the Council in resolution 1373 are *ultra vires*.

---

[156] It may be noted that the measures set out in paragraph 1 of Resolution 1373 correspond to some of those required under the International Convention for the Suppression of the Financing of Terrorism, adopted by the General Assembly, 9 December 1999, at http://untreaty.un.org/English/Terrorism/Conv12.pdf.

The Human Rights Framework Applicable To Trafficking in Persons And Its Incorporation into UNMIK Regulation 2001/4

John Cerone*

With the General Assembly's adoption of the text of the Protocol to Prevent, Suppress and Punish Trafficking in Persons in November 2000, the international community achieved a degree of consensus on an issue that has been the subject of politically-charged and morally-loaded debate since it undertook to elaborate the draft in December 1998 – whether and how to incorporate a human rights approach into this new international legal instrument which would supplement the United Nations Convention Against Transnational Organized Crime.[1]

Trafficking in persons is a complex phenomenon, encompassing such issues as gender discrimination, economic exploitation, and globalisation. As that complexity has been revealed, so has the international discourse on the issue become more sophisticated,[2] acknowledging the great variety of

---

*   As a Legal Advisor within the Human Rights Policy Bureau of the United Nations Interim Administration Mission in Kosovo (UNMIK/OSCE), the author was a member of the Working Group that drafted UNMIK Regulation 2001/4. He is presently serving as Executive Director of the War Crimes Research Office at the Washington College of Law (American University). The views expressed in this article are solely those of the author.

[1]   Protocol to Prevent, Suppress and Punish Trafficking in Persons, Especially Women and Children (the "Trafficking Protocol"), supplementing the United Nations Convention against Transnational Organized Crime, adopted 15 November 2000, UN Doc. A/RES/55/25 (2000).

[2]   A quick glance at the differences in approach between the 1949 Convention for the Suppression of the Traffic in Persons and the text of the Protocol illustrates the extent of this evolution. From a human rights perspective, the Protocol is a significant advance over the 1949 Convention. While the latter required states to punish offenders and to implement specific enforcement measures, it failed to employ a rights-based approach, focusing almost exclusively on the criminalization of trafficking and providing minimal protections to victims. Convention for the Suppression of the Traffic in Persons and of the Exploitation of the Prostitution of Others ("1949 Convention"), Dec. 2, 1949, opened for signature Mar. 21, 1950, 96 U.N.T.S. 272, 282 (entered into force July 25, 1951). Further, the 1949 Convention provides a definition that makes the consent of the 'victim' irrelevant and that accounts for only one form of trafficking – the case of trafficking for the purpose of prostitution. As stated by the Special Rapporteur on violence against women: "Due to its ill-defined and

M. Bothe and B. Kondoch (eds.),
International Peacekeeping. The Yearbook of International Peace Operations, Volume 7, 2001, 43–98.
© 2002 *Kluwer Law International. Printed in the Netherlands.*

configurations in which, and purposes for which, it occurs, as well as, in the words of the Special Rapporteur on Violence Against Women, "the continuum of women's movement and migrations" within which trafficking exists.[3]

Another aspect of this complexity is the range of actors typically involved – from the 'travel agents' and 'employment recruiters' in countries of origin, to the corrupt law enforcement officials in transit countries, to the 'bosses' who control the entire process. It is now well established that governments are not absolved of responsibility simply because acts violating human rights are committed by persons other than state officials. Further, such responsibility is not limited to cases where non-state actors are acting on behalf of the state. Human rights law imposes a duty on states to prevent and respond to violations committed by non-state actors, even when there is no connection between such actors and the state.[4]

The complexity of trafficking is also reflected in the finally agreed upon definition of trafficking in persons,[5] which is broad enough to cover all actors and intermediaries and to respond to the realities faced by victims of trafficking. This definition has found immediate application in Kosovo, where the absence of law enforcement following the withdrawal of Serbian and Yugoslav forces in June 1999, coupled with the slow build-up of effective interim police services, enabled organized crime to flourish – and with it, the trade in human beings.

This article sets forth an analysis of the legal responsibilities of states under human rights law for violations committed in a trafficking context, and demonstrates how Regulation 2001/4 of the United Nations Interim Administration Mission in Kosovo (UNMIK) establishes the legislative foundation for fulfilling those responsibilities in Kosovo. Section I describes the situation in Kosovo, highlighting the particular features of trafficking in persons in a post-conflict territory under United Nations admini-

---

broad terminology, a weak enforcement mechanism and its uniquely abolitionist perspective, the 1949 Convention has failed to attract widespread support." Report of the Special Rapporteur on violence against women, its causes and consequences, Ms. Radhika Coomaraswamy, E/CN.4/1997/47.

[3] Report of the Special Rapporteur on violence against women, its causes and consequences, Ms. Radhika Coomaraswamy, on trafficking in women, women's migration and violence against women, E/CN.4/2000/68, 29 February 2000.

[4] *Velásquez-Rodríguez* case, Judgment of July 29, 1988, Inter-Am.Ct.H.R. (Ser. C) No. 4 (1988).

[5] Much of the debate over the text of the Protocol concerned the definition of trafficking in persons.

stration. Section II examines the modes of state accountability that apply in a trafficking context, outlining the spectrum from pure state action to pure non-state action, with particular emphasis on the latter. Section III presents a legal analysis of human rights violations typically occurring in a trafficking context, and the obligations of states to prevent and respond to those violations. Section IV provides a commentary on UNMIK Regulation 2001/4, illustrating the incorporation of these obligations into the applicable law of Kosovo. Finally, Section V concludes the analysis and commentary by emphasizing the need for implementation of the Regulation, as well as other measures designed to address the underlying causes of trafficking in persons.

I. The Situation in Kosovo in 2000

While remaining part of the Federal Republic of Yugoslavia (FRY), Kosovo has been under United Nations administration since June 1999. The United Nations Interim Administration Mission in Kosovo (UNMIK), together with the NATO-led Kosovo Force (KFOR), exercises full public authority in Kosovo.[6] Among the responsibilities expressly set forth in the Security Council Resolution establishing UNMIK is the protection and promotion of human rights.[7]

A. Trafficking in Kosovo

Although the state of inter-ethnic relations in Kosovo has been and continues to be so appalling that the Special Representative of the UN Secretary-General (SRSG) had to abandon for the foreseeable future the goal of multi-ethnic integration in favour of a plan of 'peaceful co-existence', there is one sector in which inter-ethnic cooperation has fostered a thriving economy. While communication among ordinary citizens across the Ibar River in the divided town of Mitrovica has been at a standstill since the summer of 1999, organized criminal elements have had no difficulty overcoming their cultural and historical differences in order to enrich each other through the exploitation of trafficked women.[8]

---

[6] See J. Cerone, 'Minding the Gap: Outlining KFOR Accountability in Post-Conflict Kosovo' (2001) *EJIL* 469, 471.

[7] Security Council Resolution 1244 (1999) ("Resolution 1244"), para. 11(j).

[8] 'UN Swoops on Kosovo Sex Trade', BBC News, 17 November 2000 (http://news.bbc.co.uk/hi/english/world/europe/newsid_1028000/1028249.stm)

The International Organization for Migration (IOM) conducted comprehensive interviews with 130 trafficking victims between February 2000 and February 2001.[9] All of the victims were women, and the vast majority had been forced into prostitution.[10] According to IOM, most of these women had been sold three to six times while en route to Kosovo. During their travel to Kosovo, they were completely deprived of freedom of movement,[11] beaten and raped by the traffickers, and already forced into prostitution while still in the transit countries. Upon arrival in Kosovo, most of the victims continued to be subjected to physical, mental, and sexual abuse; were denied freedom of movement, including access to health care;[12] made to live in unsanitary conditions; and forced to have unprotected sex.

("[T]he operation has highlighted the co-operation between Serbs and Albanians involved in the sex trade").

[9] Situation Report, Counter-Trafficking Unit, Pristina Office, International Organization for Migration (February 2001) ("IOM Report"). The IOM Pristina office based its report on 130 documented cases arising between February 2000 and February 2001. The report is largely based on victim testimonies and UNMIK Police reports. While the number of cases may seem low, the actual number of trafficked persons in Kosovo is believed to be much higher. *Id.* There are several reasons for this. First, IOM documents only those cases where it assists the victim with repatriation. Thus, it only documents the cases of victims who: are identified as victims of trafficking according to IOM criteria; have not been ordered expelled by a court (see below); and choose to be repatriated. Second, Kosovo has been very slow in developing significant law enforcement capacity. Coupled with the impenetrability of the local communities rooted in a historical distrust of public officials and the undeniable grip of organized crime in Kosovo (see "NATO soldiers raid Kosovo brothels", CNN. com, November 17, 2000, 5:48 AM EST), the capacity of UNMIK Police to carry out trafficking investigations is seriously limited. Third, there is a serious lack of appropriate police personnel to conduct trafficking operations in terms of both the specialized training required and gender balance. (Even as of the time of writing, out of over 4,000 UNMIK Police officers, there are only 138 women). Fourth, in an area of utter lawlessness, trafficking cases have not been made a priority by UNMIK law enforcement. Fifth, victims, facing at best the prospect of prosecution and expulsion and at worst retaliation against themselves and their families, are reluctant to contact the police for assistance. This is compounded by the fact that few of the victims speak English or Albanian.

[10] Others types of exploitation included forced domestic work and dancing. *Ibid.*

[11] The travel documents of victims are commonly seized by the traffickers, and then turned over to subsequent purchasers. *Ibid.*

[12] According to the IOM Report, medical care was given to victims in emergency situations, particularly when the symptoms could affect their 'performance'. *Ibid.*

The primary perpetrators of trafficking in Kosovo tend to be non-state actors. However, there is growing evidence of participation of public actors. In recent months, the involvement of UNMIK personnel, including international police officers, in trafficking networks has come to light.[13]

The lack of adequate training, sensitivity, and awareness of legal professionals in Kosovo[14] exacerbates the violations already suffered by victims. When trafficking victims have appeared before the Kosovo courts, they have been afforded neither legal counsel nor a professional interpreter, and have been met with hostility from the bench.[15] In most cases, they have been convicted of prostitution and/or illegal entry into Kosovo,

---

[13] See "Kosovo: two UN police officers repatriated due to 'professional misconduct'" UNMIK Press Briefing, 13 August 2001 ("The United Nations Interim Administration Mission in Kosovo (UNMIK) today said two of its police officers had been repatriated to their home countries because of professional misconduct. The repatriation occurred following an UNMIK investigation into charges that four of its police officers were involved in the movement of women for the purposes of prostitution... While the four policemen committed professional misconduct 'to varying degrees,' evidence was not found to support criminal charges, the spokesman said"); "UNMIK expels two police for prostitution links," Kosovo Live News Report, 13 August 2001 ("One US policeman was alleged to have used an UNMIK vehicle to transport prostitutes from the Serbian border in exchange for money and sex. Another US officer and a Romanian were said to have warned a brothel owner that police were planning a raid on his premises"). See also "Kosovo: A Review of the Criminal Justice System, 1 September 2000 – 28 February 2001," Report of the OSCE Mission in Kosovo (March 2001) (trafficking victims stating that "they were brought by [the defendant] from Mitrovica/Mitrovice to Kosovo Polje/Fushe Kosova in a white UN vehicle driven by a Russian UN staff member...").

[14] "Kosovo: A Review of the Criminal Justice System, 1 September 2000-28 February 2001", Report of the OSCE Mission in Kosovo (March 2001) ("As trafficking-related offences usually involve forced prostitution, there are concerns that judicial personnel may harbour some prejudice. The large number of prosecutions of foreign women in Kosovo for prostitution appears to support these concerns ... During the investigation hearings, despite the degrading and brutal circumstances of the victim's experiences, which involved descriptions of multiple beatings, rape and forced prostitution, the investigating judge ordered that the two victims separately confront the defendant, Nikqi with their testimony. The confrontation between Nikqi and one of the victims dissolved into a shouting match which the investigating judge did not intervene to stop and he appeared to find the interaction entertaining"). The majority of judges in Kosovo today are Kosovo Albanians, most of whom had not practiced law in the ten years since Kosovo's autonomy was revoked by the Belgrade authorities in 1989. In addition, several layers of discrimination (discrimination against women, foreign women, and foreign women perceived to have engaged in prostitution) seem to underlie the court's hostility toward victims. *Ibid*

[15] Few of the victims speak Albanian, the language in which Kosovo court proceedings are usually conducted.

sentenced to a fine and/or imprisonment for 30 days, and ordered expelled from Kosovo for a period of three years.[16]

B. Victim Profile

Among the IOM cases, almost all of the victims are Eastern European women trafficked into Kosovo through Serbia-proper and the Former Yugoslav Republic of Macedonia (FYROM). Over sixty percent of the victims are from Moldova, the poorest country in Europe. IOM has also documented two cases of internal trafficking (i.e., trafficking of persons entirely within Kosovo).

The majority of victims are adult women between 18 and 24 years of age. Just fewer than ten percent of the victims are between the ages of 14 and 17.

More than half of those who were employed in their countries of origin made less than 40 DM ($20 USD) per month. Indeed, most of the victims who initially decided to go abroad[17] did so pursuant to a false promise of employment elsewhere in Europe.[18]

While personnel of international organizations are disproportionately represented among individuals procuring 'services' of trafficked women in Kosovo, the clientele consists mainly of Kosovan people.

C. The Legal Environment

As noted above, UNMIK serves as the governing body of Kosovo, with the SRSG retaining final executive and legislative authority.[19] Although Kosovo is not a state and UNMIK not a sovereign, UNMIK is bound by

---

[16] The victims in such cases are not assisted by IOM irrespective of the wish of the victim to return to her country of origin. IOM's policy is to deny assistance to anyone who has been ordered expelled by a court as the organization does not want to become a mechanism for deportation. To date, UNMIK has not enforced any of the expulsion orders.

[17] While some victims had been abducted from their countries of origin, the majority had been trafficked by deception.

[18] IOM Report.

[19] Resolution 1244, *supra* note 7, at para. 10. See also Report of the Secretary-General on the United Nations Interim Administration Mission in Kosovo ("Report of the Secretary-General"), para. 35, S/1999/779, 12 July 1999 ("35. The Security Council, in its resolution 1244 (1999), has vested in the interim civil administration authority over the territory and people of Kosovo. All legislative and executive powers, including the administration of the judiciary, will, therefore, be vested in UNMIK.")

international human rights law by virtue of its mandate[20] and as part of the law applicable in Kosovo.

The basis of the applicable law is set forth in UNMIK Regulation 1999/24, as amended. It states that the applicable law consists of the regulations promulgated by the SRSG as well as the law in force in Kosovo on 22 March 1989.[21] The regulations prevail if a conflict arises between these two sources of law. Regulation 1999/24 further stipulates, "[i]n exercising their functions, all persons undertaking public duties or holding public office in Kosovo shall observe internationally recognized human rights standards".[22] It then provides an extensive list of major international human rights instruments from which these standards are to be drawn.[23]

---

[20] See *supra* note 7. See also "Statement on the Right of KFOR to Apprehend and Detain", Office of the Acting SRSG, UNMIK, 4 July 1999 (noting that KFOR would be bound by international human rights standards in the performance of its duties in Kosovo).

[21] UNMIK Regulation 1999/24, § 1.1. The regulation continues: "If a court of competent jurisdiction or a body or person required to implement a provision of the law, determines that a subject matter or situation is not covered by the laws set out in section 1 of the present regulation but is covered by another law in force in Kosovo after 22 March 1989 which is not discriminatory and which complies with section 3 of the present regulation, the court, body or person shall, as an exception, apply that law". *Ibid* at § 1.2.

[22] *Ibid* at § 1.3. The SRSG has confirmed that members of the Kosovo judiciary are bound by this provision. See "Six Month Review", Legal System Monitoring Section, OSCE Mission in Kosovo (August 2000). ("In a letter to the President of the Belgrade Bar Association, dated 14 June 2000, the SRSG confirmed that Section 3 of *Regulation 1999/24* applies to judges and that this means they must not apply any provisions of the domestic law that are inconsistent with international human rights standards").

[23] This list includes: Universal Declaration on Human Rights of 10 December 1948 ("UDHR"); European Convention for the Protection of Human Rights and Fundamental Freedoms of 4 November 1950 and the Protocols thereto; International Covenant on Civil and Political Rights of 16 December 1966 and the Protocols thereto; International Covenant on Economic, Social and Cultural Rights of 16 December 1966 ("ICESCR"); International Convention on the Elimination of All Forms of Racial Discrimination of 21 December 1965 ("CERD"); Convention on the Elimination of All Forms of Discrimination Against Women of 17 December 1979 ("CEDAW"); Convention Against Torture and Other Cruel, Inhumane or Degrading Treatment or Punishment of 17 December 1984 ("CAT"); and International Convention on the Rights of the Child of 20 December 1989 ("CRC").

John Cerone

While several provisions of the law in force on 22 March 1989 are relevant to the crime of trafficking,[24] they are clearly inadequate for confronting the crime, as it exists today or for responding to the needs of victims. First, there is no express criminalization of trafficking. Second, penalties for some trafficking-related crimes are not proportional to the gravity of the crime.[25] Finally, and of particularly serious concern in an environment where the rule of law has not been consolidated, there is no provision for victim assistance.

II. Modes of state accountability under human rights law

This section sketches, in summary fashion, the normative framework for analysing state responsibility under human rights law[26] for acts committed by state actors, acts attributable to the state, and conduct of non-state actors acting independently of any state affiliation or connection. This discussion examines practice under both international and regional human

---

[24] Article 18, Law on Public Peace and Order ("By an imprisonment of up to two months shall be punished for minor offence ... [t]he one who forces another into prostitution, hires premises for this purpose or in some other way mediates in prostitution"). Article 251, Criminal Code of the Socialist Federal Republic of Yugoslavia (1977) ("SFRY Code") ("Whoever recruits, induces, incites or lures female persons into prostitution, or whoever takes part in any way in turning a female over to another for the exercise of prostitution, shall be punished by imprisonment for a term exceeding three months but not exceeding five years. If the offence described ... has been committed against a female under age or by force, threat or ruse, the offender shall be punished by imprisonment for a term exceeding one year, but not exceeding 10 years"). Note that the most relevant provision, article 251 of the SFRY Code, is gender-specific, thereby excluding the possibility of a male victim.

[25] The maximum sentence for a conviction under article 18 of the Law on Public Peace and Order is two months' imprisonment.

[26] While many of the cases cited in this section do not arise directly under human rights law, they all address the general law of state responsibility for internationally wrongful acts. This section deals essentially with the so-called "secondary rules" of state responsibility. See First Report on State Responsibility, Special Rapporteur of the International Law Commission on State Responsibility, 24 April 1998, A/CN.4/ 490, at para. 12. The link between these rules and substantive human rights law can be seen in the context of the accelerating convergence between the law of state responsibility for injury to aliens and human rights law. See Restatement (Third) of the Foreign Relations Law of the United States ("Restatement"), Introductory Note to Part VII, vol. 2, at 1058 (1987); D. Shelton, 'Private Violence, Public Wrongs and the Responsibilities of States' (1989) 13 *Fordham Intl. L. J. 1*, 23.

rights regimes and includes references to reports of UN Working Groups and Special Rapporteurs.[27]

A. Introduction

A few preliminary considerations should be kept in mind. First, it is universally recognized that all states are under a duty to carry out their international obligations in good faith.[28] It is also well established that breaches of international obligations can arise through acts or omissions.[29] Finally, the International Court of Justice ("ICJ") has held that with respect to treaty interpretation, a contextual approach, rather than a literal approach, should be employed.[30] That being said, it is important to recall that "[t]he objective of international human rights law is not to punish those individuals who are guilty of violations, but rather to protect the victims and to provide for the reparation of damages resulting from the acts of the States responsible".[31] It is therefore crucial that the interpretation of human rights treaties reflects this focus on protecting and providing reparations to victims.

---

[27]   Given the increasing role played by *opinio juris* in the formation of international law, such reports may provide evidence of the existence of rules of customary law, especially when endorsed by the Human Rights Commission or another intergovernmental body. For the proposition that *opinio juris* now dominates the formation of customary law, see *North Sea Continental Shelf Cases (F.R.G. v. Denmark; F. R. G. v. Netherlands)* 1969 I.C.J. 4; *Case Concerning Military and Paramilitary Activities In and Against Nicaragua* 1986 I.C.J. 14 (holding that if states explain their behaviour by invoking exceptions to rules, then this shows that they adhere to those rules).

[28]   See the Vienna Convention on the Law of Treaties, art. 26, April 24, 1970, 8 *I.L.M.* 679, Jul 69.

[29]   *Corfu Channel (U.K. v. Albania)*, 1949 I.C.J. 4,23 (Judgment of Apr. 9). See also Restatement, *supra* note 26 at § 207; *United States Diplomatic and Consular Staff in Tehran (U.S. v. Iran)*, 1980 I.C.J. 3 (Judgment of May 24) (court found that in addition to its direct responsibility for approving the acts, Iran's failure "to take appropriate steps ... by itself constituted a clear and serious violation" of international law); *Velásquez-Rodriguez* case, *supra* note 4, at para. 170 ("[U]nder international law a State is responsible for the acts of its agents undertaken in their official capacity and for their omissions").

[30]   *The Legal Consequences for State of the Continued Presence of South Africa in Namibia (South West Africa) Notwithstanding Security Council 271* (1970) [1971] ICJ rep. P. 31, para. 53. See also Vienna Convention, *supra* note 28, at art. 31(1).

[31]   *Velásquez-Rodriguez* case, *supra* note 4, at para. 134.

Article 2(1) of the International Covenant on Civil and Political Rights ("ICCPR") states, "Each State Party to the present Covenant undertakes to respect and to ensure to all individuals within its territory and subject to its jurisdiction the rights recognized in the present Covenant..."[32] In its General Comments, the Human Rights Committee[33] has construed this provision to oblige states to protect the rights contained in the Covenant against non-state interference.[34] Article 2 of the Convention on the Elimination of All Forms of Discriminations Against Women[35] ("CEDAW" or "Women's Convention") and Article 7 of the International Convention on the Protection of the Rights of All Migrant Workers and Their Families[36] ("Migrant Workers Convention") use similar language. The regional human rights institutions have similarly interpreted comparable provisions[37] in their respective treaties.[38]

---

[32] International Covenant on Civil and Political Rights, G.A. res. 2200A (XXI), 21 U.N. GAOR Supp. (No. 16) at 52, U.N. Doc. A/6316 (1966), 999 U.N.T.S. 171, entered into force Mar. 23, 1976. Note that a state is responsible not just for those in its territory, but also for those subject to its jurisdiction.

[33] The Human Rights Committee is the body charged with monitoring the implementation of the ICCPR. Its General Comments are authoritative interpretations of states' obligations under the Covenant (U.N. doc. CCPR/C/SR 371, para. 1; F. Newman/D. Weissbrodt, *International Human Rights: Law, Policy, and Process* (2nd Ed. 1996) 94).

[34] The practice of the Human Rights Committee demonstrates the existence of a legal duty on the part of states to protect rights against non-state interference. See, e.g., its General Comments 6, 10, 16, 17, 18, 20, 21, 27, and 28. In General Comment 27, the Human Rights Committee stated, "The State party must ensure that the rights guaranteed in article 12 are protected not only from public, but also from private interference". General Comment 27, at para. 6 (1999).

[35] Convention on the Elimination of All Forms of Discrimination against Women, art. 2, G.A. res. 34/180, 34 U.N. GAOR Supp. (No. 46) at 193, U.N. Doc. A/34/46, entered into force Sept. 3, 1981.

[36] International Convention on the Protection of the Rights of All Migrant Workers and Their Families, art. 7, U.N.GAOR 3rd Comm., 45th Sess., Annex, Agenda Item 12, at 1519, U.N. Doc. A/RES/45/ 158 (1991). The Migrant Workers Convention has not entered into force.

[37] See American Convention on Human Rights ("American Convention"), art. 1(1), O.A.S. Treaty Series No. 36, 1144 U.N.T.S. 123 entered into force July 18, 1978, reprinted in Basic Documents Pertaining to Human Rights in the Inter-American System, OEA/Ser.L.V/II.82 doc.6 rev.1 at 25 (1992); [European] Convention for the Protection of Human Rights and Fundamental Freedoms ("European Convention"), art. 1, 213 U.N.T.S. 222, entered into force Sept. 3, 1953.

[38] In addition to the *Velásquez-Rodriguez* case, *supra* note 4, see Applic. 15599/94, *A v. U.K.*, report of 18 Sep. 1997 (European Commission on Human Rights stating,

In the *Velásquez-Rodriguez* case, the Inter-American Court of Human Rights found that agents who acted under cover of public authority carried out the disappearance of Manfredo Velásquez. The court stated, however, that "even had that fact not been proven, the failure of the State apparatus to act, which is clearly proven, is a failure on the part of Honduras to fulfil the duties it assumed under Article 1(1) of the Convention, which obligated it to ensure Manfredo Velásquez the free and full exercise of his human rights."[39]

Earlier in its opinion, the court had surmised, "what is decisive is whether a violation of the rights recognized by the Convention has occurred with the support or the acquiescence of the government, or whether the State has allowed the act to take place without taking measures to prevent it or to punish those responsible".[40] This statement reflects the twin obligations to respect and ensure human rights.[41]

In either case the government would be held responsible. In the former case, where the violation has occurred with the support or the acquiescence of the government, the state would be directly responsible for the violation act itself. In the latter case, the state would be responsible for failing to ensure the right through the exercise of due diligence.[42]

"[E]ven in the absence of any direct responsibility for the acts of a private individual under Article 3 of the Convention, State responsibility may nevertheless be engaged through the obligation imposed by Article 1 of the Convention 'to secure ... the rights and freedoms defined in Section 1 of this Convention'").

[39] *Velásquez-Rodriguez* case, *supra* note 4, at para. 182.

[40] *Ibid* at para. 173.

[41] The court also speaks of the government's "duty to respect and guarantee [the Convention] rights". *Velásquez-Rodriguez* case, *supra* note 4, at para. 173. As states are not strictly liable for the acts of non-state actors, the word 'guarantee' may be strong. As the *Velásquez-Rodriguez* court itself noted, "of course, while the State is obligated to prevent human rights abuses, the existence of a particular violation does not, in itself, prove the failure to take preventive measures". *Ibid* at para. 175.

[42] As stated in the Report of the Representative of the Secretary-General on Mass Exoduses And Displaced Persons, "Abuses committed by non-State actors generally do not entail the responsibility of the States under human rights treaties, unless they are instigated, encouraged or at least acquiesced to by the Government concerned; otherwise they are typically labelled as infractions of a country's domestic laws. In such cases, the State is expected to take measures, to the best of its ability, to prevent further displacement, to alleviate the plight of the displaced and to bring those responsible to justice". Mass Exoduses And Displaced Persons, Report of the Representative of the Secretary-General, Mr. Francis Deng, Addendum, E/CN.4/1998/53/Add.

The obligations to respect and to ensure rights apply to those states that are parties to the relevant treaties. They also bind all states to the extent that these obligations have become part of customary international law.[43] As noted above, these obligations apply in Kosovo by Security Council mandate as well as by UNMIK Regulation.

B. State interference with human rights – the failure to respect rights

State interference with human rights can occur through conduct of the state or through conduct attributable to the state.

1. State actors

Where the actor is an official part of the machinery of the state, the state is responsible for his or her acts. This is true even where the actor is acting *ultra vires*, or beyond the scope of his official capacity.

In the *Velásquez-Rodriguez* case, the Inter-American Court stated:

> Whenever a State organ, official or public entity violates one of [the rights recognized in the Convention], this constitutes a failure of the duty to respect the rights and freedoms set forth in the Convention. This conclusion is independent of whether the organ or official has contravened provisions of internal law or overstepped the limits of his authority: under international law a State is responsible for the acts of its agents undertaken in their official capacity and for their omissions, even when those agents act outside the sphere of their authority or violate internal law.[44]

---

[43] While a state may not be bound by a particular obligation under customary law if it has been a persistent objector to that obligation, a state may not be a persistent objector to rules of *jus cogens*. Judge Weeramantry of the International Court of Justice, in his dissenting opinion in the *Legality of the Threat or Use of Nuclear Weapons* case, provided a catalog of rules of *jus cogens*: "the rules of *jus cogens* include: 'the fundamental rules concerning the safeguarding of peace, and notably those which forbid recourse to force or threat of force; fundamental rules of a humanitarian nature (prohibition of genocide, slavery and racial discrimination, protection of essential rights of the human person in time of peace and war)...'" *Legality of the Threat or Use of Nuclear Weapons* (dissenting opinion of Judge Weeramantry) 1996 I.C.J. 226 (citing Recueil des cours de l'Académie de droit international de La Haye, Vol. 134 (1971), p. 324, footnote 37). See also Restatement, *supra* note 26 at § 702.

[44] *Velásquez-Rodriguez*, *supra* note 4, at paras. 169-170.

This rule is also given form in the International Law Commission's Draft Articles on State Responsibility,[45] and is confirmed by international practice.[46]

2. Conduct of non-state actors attributable to the state

The state is responsible for the acts of non-state actors where such acts are attributable to the state.[47] Conduct of a non-state actor is imputed to the

---

[45] The Draft Articles on State Responsibility were finally adopted by the Commission in August 2001 and have been referred to the General Assembly. While the Draft Articles are not binding law, they are largely in accord with decisions of the International Court of Justice and are highly persuasive evidence of the state of customary law. Article 7 provides: "The conduct of an organ of a State or of a person or entity empowered to exercise elements of the governmental authority shall be considered an act of the State under international law if the organ, person or entity acts in that capacity, even if it exceeds its authority or contravenes instructions". Draft Articles on Responsibility of States for Internationally Wrongful Acts ("Draft Articles"), art. 7, A/CN.4/L.602/Rev.1, 26 July 2001.

[46] See *Youman's* claim 4 UNRIAA 110, 3 ILR 223 (1926) (unlawful acts by militia imputed to the state of Mexico); see also the *Mossé* case, 13 UNRIAA 516, 5 ILR 146 (1929). An example of a state actor acting *ultra vires* is provided by the Special Rapporteur on Torture. In a 1999 report the rapporteur wrote: "By letter dated 23 September 1998, the Special Rapporteur advised the Government that he had received information indicating that the detention of women in so-called 'safe-custody' is a practice employed by the Bangladesh law enforcement system even though there is no basis in Bangladesh law for this form of detention. Women are reportedly placed in 'safe-custody' on a judge's approval of a police application. A judge can grant an application for 'safe-custody' solely on his own discretion. Frequently, this form of custody is used for women victims of rape, sexual assault, trafficking in women, and kidnapping. This practice is cause for concern as it allegedly denies women their liberty, facilitates ill-treatment and serves more as a form of punishment than as a safety provision. Women in 'safe-custody' are said to be held with and treated like convicted criminals. Since there is no budget allocation to provide for women in 'safe-custody', they usually have to do other prisoners' laundry in order to obtain a share of their rations". Civil and Political Rights, Including Questions Of Torture And Detention, Report of the Special Rapporteur, Sir Nigel S, Rodley, E/CN.4/1999/61, para. 79. The fact that there these actions on the part of law enforcement personnel are not authorized by Bangladesh law does not preclude direct state responsibility for the acts.

[47] See *U.S. v. Iran, supra* note 29. See also 1992 Declaration on the Protection of All Persons from Enforced Disappearance, G.A. res. 47/133, 18 December 1992 (holding states responsible where private individuals act "on behalf of" the government); Convention against Torture and Other Cruel, Inhuman or Degrading Treatment or Punishment, G.A. res. 39/46, [annex, 39 U.N. GAOR Supp. (No. 51) at 197, U.N. Doc. A/39/51 (1984)], entered into force June 26, 1987, Article 1(1) (holding states

John Cerone

state when: that actor is in fact acting on the instructions of, or under the direction or control of, that state in carrying out the conduct; the conduct is subsequently adopted by the state; or the actor is exercising elements of governmental authority either pursuant to state authorization or in the absence or default of the official authorities.

a. Acting on the instructions of, or under the direction or control of, the state

Article 8 of the Draft Articles states: "The conduct of a person or group of persons shall be considered an act of a State under international law if the person or group of persons is in fact acting on the instructions of, or under the direction or control of, that State in carrying out the conduct".[48]

An example of its application is provided in a 1996 report of the Special Rapporteur on violence against women, its causes and consequences. In her Report on the mission to the Democratic People's Republic of Korea, the Republic of Korea and Japan on the issue of military sexual slavery in wartime, she describes the operation and use of "comfort stations" by the Japanese military. Comfort stations were facilities that housed

---

responsible for torture where it is inflicted "at the instigation of … a public official or other person acting in an official capacity").

[48] Draft Articles, art. 8, *supra* note 44. In the absence of specific instructions, a fairly high degree of control has been required to attribute the conduct to the state. According to the Commentary on the Draft Articles, "Such conduct will be attributable to the State only if it directed or controlled the specific operation and the conduct complained of was an integral part of that operation. The principle does not extend to conduct which was only incidentally or peripherally associated with an operation and which escaped from the State's direction or control". Commentary to Draft Articles, Report of the International Law Commission, 53rd Session, A/56/10. It should also be noted that different strands of jurisprudence have emerged as to the level of control required over organized, hierarchical groups. While the International Court of Justice has held that the proper standard for attribution is "effective control" over the group (*Military and Paramilitary Activities in and against Nicaragua (Nicaragua v. United States of America)*, Merits, I.C.J. Reports 1986, p. 14), including direction and participation in the particular act, the International Criminal Tribunal for the former Yugoslavia has found "overall control" to be sufficient and has not required direction or participation by the state in the specific conduct (Case IT-94-1, *Prosecutor v. Tadić*, (1999) *I.L.M.*, vol. 38, p. 1518). In finding further that the state could be held responsible even for acts contrary to specific instructions, the ICTY Appeals Chamber noted that, generally speaking, "the whole body of international law on State responsibility is based on a realistic concept of accountability, which disregards legal formalities and aims at ensuring that States entrusting some functions to individuals or groups of individuals must answer for their actions, even when they act contrary to their directives". *Ibid* at para. 121.

women who rendered sexual services in wartime for the use of armed forces. According to the special rapporteur, most of the women kept at the comfort stations were taken against their will.[49]

While "[l]ater in the war, the military relinquished, for the most part, its involvement in the running and operation of comfort stations to private operators who were either approached by army agents or who applied for permits on their own initiative",[50] the rapporteur maintains that the government of Japan remained responsible because, among other reasons, it continued to exercise control over the stations, as evidenced by the regulations it promulgated for them. She writes:

> These regulations are some of the most incriminating of the documents to have survived the war. Not only do they reveal beyond doubt the extent to which the Japanese forces took direct responsibility for the comfort stations and were intimately connected with all aspects of their organization, but they also clearly indicate how legitimised and established an institution the stations had become. The Special Rapporteur is absolutely convinced that most of the women kept at the comfort stations were taken against their will, that the Japanese Imperial Army initiated, regulated and controlled the vast network of comfort stations, and that the Government of Japan is responsible for the comfort stations. In addition, the Government of Japan should be prepared to assume responsibility for what this implies under international law.[51]

b.   Subsequent adoption

Acts of non-state actors that may not be initially imputable to the state will become so if the state adopts them. In *U.S. v. Iran*, the International Court of Justice held that although the initial attack on the U.S. Embassy was undertaken by actors who were neither agents nor organs of the state, Iran was responsible for their actions because of its subsequent approval and its decision to maintain the occupation of the embassy.[52]

---

[49]   Report on the mission to the Democratic People's Republic of Korea, the Republic of Korea and Japan on the issue of military sexual slavery in wartime, E/CN.4/1996/53/Add.1, Addendum. The special rapporteur considers the case of women forced to render sexual services in wartime by and/or for the use of armed forces a practice of military sexual slavery. *Ibid* at para. 6.

[50]   *Ibid* at para. 26.

[51]   *Ibid* at para. 20, 95.

[52]   See *U.S. v. Iran*, *supra* note 29, at paras. 56, 61, 63, 67, 73, 74, 76, 79.

This rule is expressed in Article 11 of the Draft Articles. It states, "Conduct which is not attributable to a State under the preceding articles shall nevertheless be considered an act of that State under international law if and to the extent that the State acknowledges and adopts the conduct in question as its own".[53]

c.   Exercising elements of governmental authority

The Draft Articles also provide for attribution where the non-state actor is exercising elements of governmental authority either pursuant to state authorization or in the absence or default of the official authorities. Examples of the exercise of elements of governmental authority by non-state actors would include a government hiring a private company to provide security services for a prison or delegating judicial functions to a customary court.

Article 5 reads:

> The conduct of a person or entity which is not an organ of the State ... but which is empowered by the law of that State to exercise elements of the governmental authority shall be considered an act of the State under international law, provided the person or entity is acting in that capacity in the particular instance.[54]

In its 1996 report, the ILC demonstrates that the international community broadly accepts this rule. It states:

> [This article] dealt with entities that were not part of the State but nonetheless exercised governmental authority, a situation that was of increasing practical importance given the recent trend towards the delegation of governmental authority to private-sector entities. That provision had not been subject to any criticism by Governments; if anything, the concern was that the provision should be sufficiently broad to encompass the proliferation of those diverse entities.[55]

---

[53]   Draft Articles, *supra* note 44, at art. 11.

[54]   Draft Articles, *supra* note 44, at art. 5.

[55]   Report of the International Law Commission on the work of its forty-eighth session, 6 May-26 July 1996, GAOR – Fifty-first Session, Supplement No. 10 (A/51/10), at para. 375.

Article 9 concerns conduct carried out in the absence or default of the official authorities. It provides that state responsibility will arise from the mere *de facto* exercise of governmental authority in the absence or default of the official authorities and in circumstances such as to call for the exercise of those elements of authority.[56]

3. Complicity

Human rights institutions have increasingly found degrees of state involvement not rising to the level established for attribution under the Draft Articles to be sufficient to render the state responsible for the acts of non-state actors.

It is a general principle of domestic law that where one is complicit in another person's act, both are held responsible for committing the act. Black's Law Dictionary states, "One is liable as an accomplice to the crime of another if he gave assistance or encouragement or failed to perform a legal duty to prevent it with the intent thereby to promote or facilitate commission of the crime".[57] While this rule is reflected to some extent in international law in the situation of two states acting in complicity,[58] general international law has not provided for state responsibility where state actors are complicit in the conduct of non-state actors but where such complicity does not rise to the level set forth in Article 8 of the Draft Articles. Notwithstanding this lacuna, a growing corpus of international jurisprudence and practice has developed the principle of state responsibility for complicity in the acts of non-state actors, at least in the context of human rights law.

Varying degrees of state knowledge and involvement, ranging from acquiescence to active support, can constitute complicity. As such, a variety of factual situations can give rise to complicity. Black's Law Dictionary defines acquiescence as "Conduct recognizing the existence of a transaction, and intended, in some extent at least, to carry the transaction, or permit it to be carried, into effect ...[It] implies active assent".[59] A clear example of acquiescence would be where law enforcement officials intentionally vacated an area in order to permit a violation to be perpetrated by non-state actors. Thus, where police intentionally cleared out of an area,

---

[56]   Draft Articles, *supra* note 44, at art. 9.

[57]   *Black's Law Dictionary* 17 (6th ed. 1990).

[58]   See Draft Articles, *supra* note 44, at art. 16.

[59]   *Black's Law Dictionary* 24 (6th ed. 1990).

knowing that a privately organized death squad was going to murder people there, the state could be held liable for violating the right to life.

A number of international instruments provide for state responsibility where the state supports, consents to, or acquiesces in the act.[60] While these provisions may be said to constitute a *lex specialis* applicable solely within the framework of those instruments, they can be said to contribute to the development of state responsibility under human rights law generally.

An example of the application of this principle in human rights jurisprudence can be found in the *Massacre at Riofrío Case* of the Inter-American Commission on Human Rights. In that case, petitioners alleged that members of the Colombian army collaborated with a group of paramilitaries in the execution of a number of individuals in the municipality of Riofrío, Colombia. Before analysing the alleged violations of the standards of the American Convention on Human Rights,[61] the Commission addressed the question of whether the acts of the paramilitaries, otherwise regarded as non-state actors[62], could be attributed to the state of Colombia, thus "call[ing] into question its responsibility in accordance with international law."

The Commission recalled that the Inter-American Court of Human Rights has noted, "It is sufficient to show that the infringement of the rights recognized in the Convention has been *supported or tolerated* by

---

[60] See, e.g., 1992 Declaration on the Protection of All Persons from Enforced Disappearance, G.A. res. 47/133, 18 December 1992 (holding states responsible where private individuals act "with the support, direct or indirect, consent or acquiescence of the Government"); Torture Convention, *supra* note 46, at art. 1(1) (holding states responsible for torture where it is inflicted "with the consent or acquiescence of a public official or other person acting in an official capacity"). See also Mass Exoduses And Displaced Persons, Report of the Representative of the Secretary-General, Mr. Francis Deng, Addendum, E/CN.4/1998/53/Add. ("Abuses committed by non-State actors generally do not entail the responsibility of the States under human rights treaties, unless they are instigated, encouraged or at least *acquiesced to* by the Government concerned") (emphasis added); Restatement, *supra* note 26, at § 702 ("A state violates international law if, as a matter of state policy, it practices, *encourages or condones*" human rights violations, including genocide and others capable of being committed by non-state actors).

[61] American Convention, *supra* note 36.

[62] Although Colombia has been found responsible for creating and supporting such paramilitary groups as part of its counterinsurgency efforts, the subsequent withdrawal of lawful support from and even criminalisation of such groups rendered untenable the argument that they were *de jure* state agents or otherwise authorized to exercise elements of governmental authority.

the government".[63] Having found evidence that "agents of the State helped to coordinate the massacre, to carry it out, and, as discovered by domestic courts, to cover it up", the Commission concluded that the "State is liable for the violations of the American Convention resulting from the acts of commission or omission by its own agents and by private individuals involved in the execution of the victims".[64]

In analysing whether the conduct at issue amounted to a violation of the right to life under the American Convention, the Commission found Colombia to be "responsible for the acts of its agents *as well as for those perpetrated by individuals who acted with their complicity* to make it possible to carry out and cover up the execution of the victims in violation of their right not to be arbitrarily deprived of their lives, as established in Article 4..."[65] It therefore found that the arbitrary deprivation of life perpetrated by paramilitaries acting in complicity with agents of the state constituted a breach of the American Convention by Colombia.

Finally, the reports of the special rapporteurs are replete with examples of government complicity. In his Report on the mission of the Special Rapporteur to the Islamic Republic of Iran, the Special Rapporteur on the promotion and protection of the right to freedom of opinion and expression writes that threats and use of violence by irregular groups of private persons against professionals in the field of information "are at times publicly defended by prominent members of the government bureaucracy, in the full knowledge that such actions have taken place outside the confines of the law."

Examples of clear complicity are also found in reports of the Special Rapporteur on violence against women. In a preliminary report she writes:

> In Thailand, the sexual intercourse experienced by girls 15 years or younger always constitutes statutory rape. Instead of punishing the rapist, i.e. the client or the brothel owner as an accomplice to the rape, in Thailand the girls who do complain are often arrested and sent back to the brothel upon payment of a fine. Women who are trafficked are usually smuggled across borders with the bribed com-

---

[63]   *Riofrio Massacre*, Inter-American Commission on Human Rights, REPORT N° 62/ 01, CASE 11.654, COLOMBIA, April 6, 2001, para. 48 (citing Int. Amer. Ct. H.R. *Pan-iagua Morales et al Case, Sentence of March 8, 1998*, paragraph 91) (emphasis added).

[64]   *Ibid* at para. 52.

[65]   *Ibid* at para. 57.

plicity of the border guards. Victims of trafficking report extensive police usage of brothels for free.[66]

By way of conclusion to the section on state interference with human rights, it may be instructive to note a statement of the Special Rapporteur on Torture that reflects different modes of state responsibility. Reporting on the subject of torture and other cruel, inhuman or degrading treatment or punishment in Pakistan, the rapporteur writes:

> [T]he Special Rapporteur advised the Government that he had received reports, according to which private landlords or waderas, particularly in Sindh province, were running private jails wherein bonded rural labourers were kept captive and were subjected to severe ill-treatment. Detention and torture in such private jails was said to occur *often with the knowledge, connivance or direct involvement of the police and other organs of the State*. Several private jails in Sindh were said to be maintained by elected members of the National Assembly.[67]

Mere *knowledge* of violations perpetrated by non-state actors is insufficient to engage a state's responsibility under the obligation to respect rights. (However, knowledge coupled with a failure to take action may engage a state's responsibility for failure to ensure rights, as explained below.) *Connivance* is a form of complicity, making the state responsible for the violation. Finally, the state is fully responsible due to the *direct involvement* of state actors.

C. Non-state interference with human rights – the failure to ensure rights

Acts of non-state actors that would constitute human rights violations if committed by the state may give rise to state responsibility even when there is no connection between the perpetrators and the state.

In the *Velásquez-Rodriguez* case, the Inter-American Court stated:

---

[66] Preliminary report submitted by the Special Rapporteur on violence against women, its causes and consequences, Ms. Radhika Coomaraswamy, E/CN.4/1995/42, para. 213.

[67] Report of the Special Rapporteur, Mr. Nigel S. Rodley, E/CN.4/1995/34, para. 550 (emphasis added).

An illegal act which violates human rights and which is initially not directly imputable to a State (for example, because it is the act of a private person or because the person responsible has not been identified) can lead to international responsibility of the State, not because of the act itself, but because of the lack of due diligence to prevent the violation or to respond to it as required by the Convention.[68]

The court reasoned that the Article 1(1) obligation to "ensure" the free and full exercise of the rights recognized by the Convention implied the duty of the states parties to "organize the governmental apparatus and, in general, all the structures through which public power is exercised, so that they are capable of juridically ensuring the free and full enjoyment of human rights".[69] The court elaborated on the states' duties to "prevent the violation or respond to it," stating, "the States must prevent, investigate and punish any violation of the rights recognized by the Convention and, moreover, if possible attempt to restore the right violated and provide compensation as warranted for damages resulting from the violation".[70]

"The 'due diligence' standard has been generally accepted as a measure of evaluating a State's responsibility for violation of human rights by private actors".[71] There is ample evidence to support this assertion. Applica-

---

[68] *Velásquez-Rodriguez* case, *supra* note 4, at para. 172. See also *Kiliç v. Turkey*, European Court of Human Rights, Application N° 22492/93, 28 March 2000.

[69] *Ibid* at para. 166. See also Final report on the situation of human rights in Afghanistan submitted by the Special Rapporteur, Mr. Felix Ermacora, in accordance with Commission on Human Rights resolution 1994/84, E/CN.4/1995/64, para. 20 ("[Article 2 of the Covenant] means that the State must not only refrain from committing human rights violations but that it should also prevent the violation of human rights and provide remedies for alleged human rights violations. Therefore, the structure and organization of the State must correspond to the cited requirements").

[70] *Ibid* at para. 167.

[71] Preliminary report submitted by the Special Rapporteur on violence against women, its causes and consequences, Ms. Radhika Coomaraswamy, E/CN.4/1995/42, para. 103 (citing Moore, Int. Arb. 495 (1872)). Note also a parallel development in refugee law. A well-founded fear of persecution is now deemed to include the failure of a state to protect individuals from conduct of non-state actors. *See Islam v. Secretary Of State For The Home Department; Regina v. Immigration Appeal Tribunal And Another; Ex Parte Shah (Conjoined Appeals)*, 25 March 1999, House of Lords, Lord Steyn ("Notwithstanding a constitutional guarantee against discrimination on the grounds of sex a woman's place in society in Pakistan is low. Domestic abuse of women and violence towards women is prevalent in Pakistan. That is also true of many other countries and by itself it does not give rise to a claim to refugee status.

tion of the 'due diligence' standard can be seen in the reports of UN special rapporteurs,[72] UN special representatives,[73] and the Secretary-General;[74] comments,[75] views,[76] and concluding observations[77] of human rights treaty bodies; reports on expert group meetings;[78] resolutions of the

---

The distinctive feature of this case is that in Pakistan women are unprotected by the state: discrimination against women in Pakistan is partly tolerated by the state and partly sanctioned by the state").

[72] *Ibid* Report on the question of the use of mercenaries as a means of violating human rights and impeding the exercise of the right of peoples to self-determination, submitted by Mr. Enrique Bernales Ballesteros, Special Rapporteur, E/CN.4/1995/29 (noting obligation of states to prevent, prosecute, and punish mercenary activities, whether "organized by public bodies or private persons"); Joint report of the Special Rapporteur on the question of torture, Mr. Nigel S. Rodley, and the Special Rapporteur on extra judicial, summary or arbitrary executions, Mr. Bacre Waly Ndiaye, Visit by the Special Rapporteurs to the Republic of Colombia from 17 to 26 October 1994, E/CN.4/1995/111, para. 115.

[73] Mass Exoduses And Displaced Persons, Report of the Representative of the Secretary-General, Mr. Francis Deng, Addendum, E/CN.4/1998/53/Add. ("[In the event of abuses committed by non-State actors], the State is expected to take measures, to the best of its ability, to prevent further displacement, to alleviate the plight of the displaced and to bring those responsible to justice").

[74] Report of the Secretary-General on Violence against women migrant workers, A/51/325, para. 53 ("States should be held accountable, in accordance with the 'due diligence principle', for their inaction on issues of violence against women migrant workers").

[75] CEDAW, General Recommendation 19, A/47/38, para. 9 (1992) ("Under general international law and specific human rights covenants, States may also be responsible for private acts if they fail to act with due diligence to prevent violations of rights or to investigate and punish acts of violence, and for providing compensation").

[76] CERD, Communication No. 4/1991, *L.K. v. The Netherlands* (finding that state violated Article 4(a) of CERD in failing "to investigate with due diligence and expedition" in response to racist remarks and threats made to complainant by private persons).

[77] Concluding observations of the Committee on the Elimination of All Forms of Racial Discrimination: United Arab Emirates, A/50/18 ("The Committee recommends that the State party show the utmost diligence in preventing acts of ill-treatment being committed against foreign workers, especially foreign women domestic servants, and take all appropriate measures to ensure that they are not subjected to any racial discrimination").

[78] Expert group meeting on children and juveniles in detention: application of human rights standards (Vienna, 30 October - 4 November 1994), Report of the Secretary-General, E/CN.4/1995/100, para. 44 ("[We] urge States to apply due diligence to prevent and investigate such acts of exploitation against children and to ensure that appropriate sanctions are applied against the adults who exploit the children, rather than against the children who are victims of such crimes").

Commission on Human Rights[79] and the Economic and Social Council;[80] Declarations by the General Assembly,[81] and the writings of publicists.[82]

Due diligence to prevent violations clearly requires legislative prohibition of the violation behaviour and enforcement. Legislative prohibition and enforcement alone, however, are not generally successful in preventing violations and are thus insufficient to meet a state's obligation.[83] States must take *effective* measures to meet their obligations in this context. This follows from the principle of good faith and has been echoed by various human rights bodies.[84] It is for this reason that the Inter-American Court

---

[79] The elimination of violence against women, Commission on Human Rights resolution 1996/49, para. 4 (emphasizing "the duty of Governments to refrain from engaging in violence against women and to exercise due diligence to prevent, investigate and, in accordance with national legislation, to punish acts of violence against women and to take appropriate and effective action concerning acts of violence against women, whether those acts are perpetrated by the State or by private persons and to provide access to just and effective remedies and specialized assistance to victims").

[80] ESC, Res. 1996/12, Elimination of violence against women (endorsing the UN Declaration on the Elimination of Violence against Women and Commission on Human Rights resolutions 1995/85 and 1996/49).

[81] Declaration on the Elimination of Violence against Women, G.A. res. 48/104, 48 U.N. GAOR Supp. (No. 49) at 217, U.N. Doc. A/48/49 (1993), art. 4(c) (declaring that states are under a duty to exercise due diligence to prevent, investigate, and, in accordance with national legislation, punish acts of violence against women, whether those acts are perpetrated by the state or by private persons).

[82] D. Sullivan, *The Public/Private Distinction in International Human Rights Law* 130; S. Farrior, 'The International Law on Trafficking in Women and Children for Prostitution: Making it Live Up to its Potential' (1997) 10 *Harv. Hum. Rts. J.* 213, 225 ("By virtue of Article 2 of the Covenant, states violate their obligations under the Covenant if they fail to exercise due diligence to end slavery and the slave trade by private actors within their jurisdiction"); R.J. Cook, 'State Responsibility For Violations of Women's Human Rights' (1994) 7 *Harv. Hum. Rts. J.* 125; D. Shelton, 'Private Violence, Public Wrongs and the Responsibilities of States' (1989) 13 *Fordham Intl. L. J.* 1, 23.

[83] Over-reliance on criminal justice responses raises additional concerns. See Sullivan, *supra* note 82, at 133 ("[A]ny analysis of the use of criminal penalties as a response to domestic violence must consider whether effective restraints on the exercise of police power are in place").

[84] *Velásquez-Rodriguez* case, *supra* note 4, at para. 167; Human Rights Committee, General Comment 16; ESCR Committee, General Comment 5, para. 11 (1994); *Artico v. Italy*, series A, 37 ECtHR 16 ("The [European] Convention is intended to guarantee not rights that are theoretical or illusory but rights that are practical and effective"); *A v. U.K.*, *supra* note 37, at para. 48 (European Commission stating that "[i]n order that a State may be held responsible it must in the view of the Commis-

emphasized that states are under a duty to employ "all those means of a legal, political, administrative and cultural nature that promote the protection of human rights and ensure that any violations are considered and treated as illegal acts, which, as such, may lead to the punishment of those responsible and the obligation to indemnify the victims for damages".[85] The court recognized that "[i]t is not possible to make a detailed list of all such measures, since they vary with the law and the conditions of each State Party".[86] In addition, they will vary with the nature of the right violated. However, a list of general measures can be extracted from international practice, bearing in mind the principles of effectiveness and reasonableness.[87]

Recent practice has included measures such as education and awareness-raising,[88] government condemnation of violations,[89] rehabilitation and

---

sion be shown that the domestic legal system ... fails to provide practical and effective protection of the rights guaranteed...").

[85] *Velásquez-Rodriguez* case, *supra* note 4, at para. 175. See also Human Rights Committee, General Comment 17, (each state has a duty to take "*every possible economic and social measure* ... to reduce infant mortality and to eradicate malnutrition among children and to prevent them from being subjected to acts of violence and cruel and inhuman treatment or from being exploited by means of forced labour or prostitution, or by their use in the illicit trafficking of narcotic drugs, or by any other means") (emphasis added).

[86] *Ibid.*

[87] D. Shelton, 'Private Violence, Public Wrongs and the Responsibilities of States' (1989) 13 *Fordham Intl. L. J.* 1, 23 (asserting that due diligence requires "reasonable measures of prevention that a well administered government could be expected to exercise under similar circumstances").

[88] Report of the Special Rapporteur on violence against women, its causes and consequences, Ms. Radhika Coomaraswamy, E/CN.4/1999/68, para. 25(vii); Report by Mr. M. Glélé-Ahanhanzo, Special Rapporteur on contemporary forms of racism, racial discrimination, xenophobia and related intolerance, E/CN.4/1996/72/Add.1; Report on the situation of human rights in Rwanda submitted by Mr. R. Degni-Ségui, Special Rapporteur of the Commission on Human Rights, E/CN.4/1995/, para. 140; ESCR Committee, General Comment 5 (1994); Concluding observations of the Committee on the Rights of the Child: Sudan, CRC/C/15/Add.10, para. 22.

[89] Follow-up to the Fourth World Conference on Women: Implementation of Strategic Objectives and Action in the Critical Areas of Concern, Thematic issues before the Commission on the Status of Women, Report of the Secretary-General, E/CN.6/1998/5, para. 12; Principles on the Effective Prevention and Investigation of Extra-legal, Arbitrary and Summary Executions, Principle 8, endorsed in ESC Resolution 1989/65.

From journal to yearbook

International Peacekeeping is a yearbook devoted to reporting upon and analysing all aspects of international peacekeeping but with an emphasis upon legal and policy issues. International Peacekeeping provides the interested public - diplomats, civil servants, politicians, the military, academics, journalists, and serious citizens - with an up-to-date source of information on peacekeeping, enabling them to keep abreast of the most important developments in the field. This is achieved not only by the provision of "basic documents", such as Security Council Resolutions or Reports from the UN Secretary-General, but also by expert commentatories on world events connected with peacekeeping operations. Thus, *International Peacekeeping* not only has a recording and documentary function, for those who wish to be kept well-informed, but also plays a role in forming opinions on the further development of peacekeeping as an instrument. Peacekeeping is treated in a pragmatic light, seen as a form of international military cooperation for the preservation or restoration of international peace and security, attention being focused primarily on UN peacekeeping operations.

In addition, the *Yearbook* will focus more academically on of the use of sanctions, aspects of international criminal law and military operations from the perspective of jus ad bellum and the *jus ad bello*. The *Yearbook* is the continuation of the journal *International Peacekeeping*.

Call for papers

As of volume 8, Harvey Langholtz (The College of William & Mary) will be the Editor-in-Chief of the Yearbook, which will contain the following sections:

* Articles
* The Chronicle
* Documents
* Book reviews
* Notes

The *Yearbook* is interested in receiving articles to be considered for publication. Manuscripts should be written in standard English and may be delivered in attachment by e-mail to Harvey Langholtz at hjlang@wm.edu o̶ ̶b̶ Harvey Langholtz, 127 Jameswood, Williamsburg. A. Articles should not be longer than ̶ ̶0̶0̶0̶ ̶ words). Further instructions for authors can Chief.

support services for victims,[90] training for law enforcement personnel,[91] ratification and implementation of other international human rights instruments,[92] improving access to legal remedies on both the domestic and international planes,[93] implementation of the recommendations of international human rights bodies and mechanisms,[94] protection of complainants and witnesses to violations,[95] promoting research and compiling statistics on violations,[96] publishing reports on the state's responses to violations,[97]

---

[90] Joint report of the Special Rapporteur on the question of torture, Mr. N. S. Rodley, and the Special Rapporteur on extra judicial, summary or arbitrary executions, Mr. Bacre Waly Ndiaye, Visit by the Special Rapporteurs to the Republic of Colombia from 17 to 26 October 1994, E/CN.4/1995/111, para. 121 (recommending effective reparation to the victims or their dependants, including adequate compensation and measures for their rehabilitation); Report of the Special Rapporteur on violence against women, its causes and consequences, Ms. Radhika Coomaraswamy, E/CN.4/1999/68, para. 25(vi).

[91] Situation of human rights in Cambodia, Report of the Special Representative of the Secretary-General for Human Rights in Cambodia, Mr. M. Kirby, E/CN.4/1996/93, para. 61; Declaration on the Elimination of Violence against Women, *supra* note 80, at art. 4(i).

[92] Report of the Special Rapporteur on violence against women, its causes and consequences, Ms. Radhika Coomaraswamy, E/CN.4/1999/68, para. 25(i); Report by Mr. M. Glélé-Ahanhanzo, Special Rapporteur on contemporary forms of racism, racial discrimination, xenophobia and related intolerance, E/CN.4/1996/72/Add.1.

[93] Principles on the Effective Prevention and Investigation of Extra-legal, Arbitrary and Summary Executions, Principle 8, endorsed in ESC Resolution 1989/65; Expert group meeting on children and juveniles in detention: application of human rights standards, Report of the Secretary-General, E/CN.4/1995/100; Situation of human rights in Cambodia, Report of the Special Representative of the Secretary-General for Human Rights in Cambodia, Mr. M. Kirby, E/CN.4/1996/93, para. 61.

[94] General Assembly resolution 53/116, Traffic in Women and Girls, A/RES/53/116, para. 3 (1999).

[95] Principles on the Effective Prevention and Investigation of Extra-legal, Arbitrary and Summary Executions, Principle 15, endorsed in ESC Resolution 1989/65.

[96] Declaration on the Elimination of Violence against Women, *supra* note 80, at art. 4(k).

[97] Declaration on the Elimination of Violence against Women, *supra* note 80, at art. 4(g); Principles on the Effective Prevention and Investigation of Extra-legal, Arbitrary and Summary Executions, Principle 17, endorsed in ESC Resolution 1989/65.

providing financial support to organizations that combat discrimination,[98] and changing patterns of socialization that perpetuate discrimination.[99]

Such measures are particularly important in countries where the rule of law is not entirely stable. In such cases, the government may be unable to effectively punish perpetrators,[100] and, consequently, must more diligently act to prevent violations by addressing the underlying conditions that lead to them.

As the special rapporteur on violence against women has noted:

> [T]he test is whether the State undertakes its duties seriously ... If statistics illustrate that existing laws are ineffective in protecting women from violence, States must find other complementary mechanisms to prevent domestic violence. Thus, if education, dismantling of institutional violence, demystifying domestic violence, training of State personnel, the funding of shelters and other direct services for victim-survivors and the systematic documentation of all incidents of domestic violence are found to be effective tools in

---

[98] Report by Mr. M. Glélé-Ahanhanzo, Special Rapporteur on contemporary forms of racism, racial discrimination, xenophobia and related intolerance, E/CN.4/1995/78/Add.1.

[99] Expert group meeting on children and juveniles in detention: application of human rights standards, Report of the Secretary-General, E/CN.4/1995/100; Report of the Special Rapporteur on violence against women, its causes and consequences, Ms. Radhika Coomaraswamy, E/CN.4/1997/47, para. 15.

[100] A report of the Special Representative on Cambodia states: "The lack of integrity of some of the courts also undermines justice. In November 1998, the Special Representative sent a letter to the General Prosecutor about the beating to death of a young woman by a brothel owner in Banteay Meanchey. A charge of voluntary manslaughter against the brothel owner had been dismissed by the investigating judge of the Banteay Meanchey Provincial Court, who cited 'lack of evidence' as grounds for dismissal despite the testimonies of 11 eyewitnesses to the beating. Also in November, the General Prosecutor sent a letter to the Banteay Meanchey prosecutor, noting the existence of procedural errors and recommending that charges of involuntary manslaughter, battery with injury, and violation of the law against trafficking in women be filed against the brothel owner. In December 1998, a representative of the Ministry of Justice went to Poipet to investigate the case. His investigation was hindered by veiled threats and intimidation by the local authorities. That same month, the President of the Banteay Meanchey Court stated that the evidence in the case (the 11 testimonies) had been lost; he seemed reluctant to file additional cases against the brothel owner, stating that the latter was being supported by powerful people in the military". Situation of human rights in Cambodia, Report of the Special Representative of the Secretary-General for Human Rights in Cambodia, Mr. T. Hammarberg, E/CN.4/1999/101, para. 58.

preventing domestic violence and protecting women's human rights, all become obligations in which the State must exercise due diligence in carrying out.[101]

D. Caveat

The line between complicity and failure to exercise due diligence is highly fact-sensitive.[102] Another way in which state responsibility is engaged in the context of violations by non-state actors is by the state's failure to provide an effective remedy in accordance with its treaty obligations.[103] It is important to remember that although the same acts may implicate all three types of responsibility, these are separate modes of state responsibility and breaches of independent legal obligations. They offer separate bases for holding states accountable.

The application of various, related modes of state responsibility is illustrated in the *Riofrio* case described above. In that case, the Inter-American Commission found Colombia responsible for: violations of the rights to life and to humane treatment perpetrated by paramilitaries acting in com-

---

[101] Report of the Special Rapporteur on violence against women, its causes and consequences, Ms. Radhika Coomaraswamy, E/CN.4/1996/53, paras. 37, 141.

[102] See *Velásquez-Rodriguez* case, *supra* note 4, at para. 177 ("Where the acts of private parties that violate the Convention are not seriously investigated, those parties are aided in a sense by the government, thereby making the State responsible on the international plane").

[103] Under Article 2(3)(a) of the ICCPR, each state party undertakes "[t]o ensure that any person whose rights or freedoms as herein recognized are violated shall have an effective remedy, notwithstanding that the violation has been committed by persons acting in an official capacity". ICCPR, *supra* note 32, at art. 2(3)(a). Similarly, Article 13 of the European Convention provides, "Everyone whose rights and freedoms as set forth in this Convention are violated shall have an effective remedy before a national authority notwithstanding that the violation has been committed by persons acting in an official capacity". European Convention, *supra* note 36, at art. 13. In a case where a physical injury was inflicted by a private school headmaster, the European Commission found that the U.K. had breached its obligation under Article13 because the "English legal system ... provided no effective redress". Applic. 14229/88, *Y v. U.K.*, report of 8 Oct. 1991, Res. DH (92)63, para. 45. Note that this case was settled before reaching the European Court. Although in a similar case that did reach the court it found that there was no violation of Article 13, the court did not base its decision on the fact that the injury was inflicted by a non-state actor. But the efficacy of this provision has been limited by statements of the court to the effect that Article 13 "does not go so far as to guarantee a remedy allowing a Contracting State's laws as such to be challenged before a national authority on the ground of being contrary to the Convention or to equivalent domestic legal norms". *Costello-Roberts v. U.K.*, Series A no. 247-C, p. 62, para. 40.

plicity with state agents, violation of the right to judicial protection, and failure to ensure the rights protected under the Convention.[104]

The due diligence standard is particularly useful for victims as a means of avoiding the substantial hurdles involved in proving complicity or state control. Regardless of whether state responsibility is engaged through state involvement or by a failure to prevent or respond, the state is fully accountable.

III. Human Rights Norms Typically Violated in the Context of Trafficking in Persons

It is universally recognized that trafficking in women constitutes a grave human rights violation.[105] The UN General Assembly has recently reaffirmed that "sexual violence and trafficking in women and girls for purposes of economic exploitation, sexual exploitation through prostitution and other forms of sexual exploitation and contemporary forms of slavery are serious violations of human rights".[106]

The scope of this analysis is limited to the civil and political rights of adult women, representing the overwhelming majority of known trafficking victims in Kosovo. Further, while trafficking victimizes persons of all ages and genders and is carried out for a variety of exploitative purposes, this analysis focuses on the case of adult women trafficked for the purpose of exploitation in the sex industry.

A whole other body of international law is applicable to the rights of children, and is thus beyond the scope of this analysis.[107] It should also be

---

[104] *Riofrio case, supra* note 62.

[105] See e.g., Vienna Declaration and Programme of Action A/CONF 157/23, World Conference on Human Rights, Vienna, 14-16 June 1993, Part I, §18 ("Gender-based violence and all forms of exploitation, including those resulting from cultural prejudice and international trafficking, are incompatible with the dignity and worth of the human person and must be eliminated"); Beijing Declaration and Platform for Action of the Fourth World Conference on Women, China, 4-15 September 1995 (Strategic objective D3. Eliminate trafficking in women and assist victims of violence due to prostitution and trafficking).

[106] A/RES/55/67, 31 January 2001.

[107] This body of law is highly developed and should be employed for the protection of females under the age of majority, with full regard for the key principle of non-discrimination, the evolving capacities of the child, and the child's right to healthy survival and participation. See, e.g., Optional Protocol to the Convention on the Rights of the Child on the sale of children, child prostitution and child pornography, adopted and opened for signature, ratification and accession by General Assembly

noted that there is a growing and dynamic jurisprudence on economic, social, and cultural rights being developed by UN experts, scholars, and NGOs. Both international and domestic institutions are paying increasing attention to the issue of violations by non-state actors in the context of economic, social, and cultural rights analysis. Women who have been trafficked and women in the sex industry frequently experience violations of their economic, social, and cultural rights.[108] In addition, denials of these rights are among the causes of trafficking.

The human rights violations discussed below may occur while the victim is in the country of origin, in transit, in the destination country, or throughout all three phases of the trafficking process.

A. Rights Implicated

Trafficking in women involves the violation of several human rights.[109] Trafficking entails violations of freedom from torture or cruel, inhuman, or degrading treatment or punishment;[110] the protection against arbitrary or unlawful interference with privacy, family, home, or correspondence;[111] the right to information (a constituent part of the right to expression); free-

---

resolution A/RES/54/263 of 25 May 2000. See also, ILO Convention 182 on the Worst Forms of Child Labour, 1999.

[108] Such as the right to health, the right to an adequate standard of living, and the right to adequate housing.

[109] See, e.g., Concluding observations of the Human Rights Committee: Nepal, 10/11/94, CCPR/C/79/ Add.42., para. 7 ("The persistence of practices of debt bondage, trafficking in women, child labour, and imprisonment on the ground of inability to fulfil a contractual liability constitute clear violations of several provisions of the Covenant"). The above enumeration of rights implicated is not intended to be exhaustive.

[110] Council of Europe, Parliamentary Assembly, Recommendation 1325, para. 3 (1997) ("Considering traffic in women and forced prostitution thus defined to be *a form of inhuman and degrading treatment* and a flagrant violation of human rights, the Assembly feels the need for urgent and concerted action on the part of the Council of Europe, its individual member states and other international organisations" (emphasis added)).

[111] Note the application of this right to violations of physical and moral integrity. See, e.g., *Airey v. Ireland*, 32 Eur. Ct. H.R. (ser. A) (1979) (finding that Ireland failed to ensure applicant's right to respect for private and family life because it had not provided an accessible legal procedure for her to obtain a legal separation from a husband who had been threatening her with violence).

dom from discrimination on the basis of race,[112] gender, or other status;[113] and freedom from slavery and servitude.

Further, the conditions to which trafficked women are ultimately subjected in the destination country can be extreme and deplorable and potentially implicate all human rights. Violations that may be particularly common include: violations of the right to life; torture or cruel, inhuman, or degrading treatment or punishment; violations of the right to liberty and security of the person; arbitrary or unlawful interference with privacy, family, home, or correspondence; discrimination on the basis of race and gender; and slavery and servitude.

1. Right to Information

Article 19(2) of the ICCPR states: "Everyone shall have the right to freedom of expression; this right shall include freedom to seek, receive and impart information and ideas of all kinds, regardless of frontiers..."[114]

The deceit and misinformation commonly used by traffickers to lure victims into accompanying them[115] violate this right.[116]

---

[112] See J. Chuang, 'Redirecting the Debate over Trafficking in Women: Definitions, Paradigms, and Contexts' (1998) 11 *Harv. Hum. Rts. J.* 65, 69 ("[R]acial factors can drive international trafficking across borders for the purpose of recruiting foreign women to meet the racial preferences of certain brothel clientele" (citing Human Rights Watch, Global Report on Women's Human Rights 232-33 (1995)); Communication From the European Commission to the Council and the European Parliament on Trafficking in Women for the Purpose of Sexual Exploitation 5 ("It also appears that demand for 'exotic' prostitutes is growing..."); Report of the Special Rapporteur on violence against women, its causes and consequences, Ms. Radhika Coomaraswamy, E/CN.4/1997/47 ("Today, women are primarily trafficked from the South to the North ... [T]rafficking in women is fuelled by poverty, racism and sexism").

[113] "Other status" in this context includes discrimination on the basis of social and economic status.

[114] ICCPR, art. 19(2). See also UDHR, art. 19; CEDAW, art. 10(h).

[115] Report on the mission of the Special Rapporteur to Poland on the issue of trafficking and forced prostitution of women (24 May to 1 June 1996), E/CN.4/1997/47/Add.1., para. 60, 62 ("Methods of recruitment are varied, but all of them intend to deceive the victim about the true nature of her employment abroad, lure her into a confidence relationship with the trafficker and eventually create an inescapable dependency on the eventual 'employer' ... These women are sometimes aware of what is expected of them abroad and often agree to leave their country in expectation of a substantial increase in income. What they are not aware of, however, are the conditions of virtual slavery and debt bondage they might find themselves in abroad").

[116] In addition, states must be careful to avoid direct violation of this right in the formulation of protective measures. For example, many of the proposals to 'end traffick-

2. *Freedom from Discrimination on the Basis of Gender*

Among the causes of trafficking of women are systemic discrimination against women in public and private life and the subordination of women generally. The special rapporteur on violence against women reports, "[T]he lack of rights afforded to women serves as the primary causative factor at the root of both women's migrations and trafficking in women. The failure of existing economic, political and social structures to provide equal and just opportunities for women to work has contributed to the feminisation of poverty, which in turn has led to the feminisation of migration, as women leave their homes in search of viable economic options".[117]

CEDAW expressly obliges states to "take *all appropriate measures*, including legislation, to suppress *all forms of traffic* in women and exploitation of prostitution of women".[118] In addition, as trafficking is driven largely by women's economic vulnerability and macroeconomic/ globalisation factors, several other provisions of CEDAW are implicated, includ-

---

ing' include shutting down mail order bride businesses as facilitating trafficking, and a whole host of Internet regulations, all of which impinge upon the freedom of expression.

[117] Report of the Special Rapporteur on violence against women, February 2000, *supra* note 3. See also Volume I: Annual General Assembly Report of the Human Rights Committee, 21/09/94, A/49/40, para. 252 ("The Committee regrets that [Togo] has not yet embarked on all the necessary reforms to cope with the factors and difficulties impeding equality of men and women in order to fully implement article 3 of the Covenant. The reported cases of traffic of women, the effect of certain customs and traditions, as well as the lack of effective government measures aiming at promoting equality of the sexes constitute matters of grave concern"); Communication From the European Commission to the Council and the European Parliament on Trafficking in Women for the Purpose of Sexual Exploitation 5 ("IOM studies indicate that the causes of migration related to trafficking in women can be found, *inter alia*, in the ... marginalisation of women in the source countries. Poor or non-existent education is also of critical importance, and in areas where unemployment is high, women tend to be more severely affected than men"); Rights of the Child: Sale of Children, Child Prostitution and Child Pornography, Report submitted by Mr. Vitit Muntarbhorn, Special Rapporteur, UN ESCOR, Commission for Human Rights, 50th Sess., Agenda Item 22, at 3, UN Doc. E/CN.4/1994/84/Add.1 (1994).

[118] CEDAW, art. 6 (emphasis added). Note that the Optional Protocol to the Women's Convention could prove a powerful vehicle for addressing trafficking violations. The Protocol allows complaints to be brought by women alleging violations of their rights under the Convention. In addition, the Committee could conduct an inquiry where it receives reliable information regarding grave or systematic violations of the Convention. Trafficking could be addressed under either mechanism.

ing the Article 10 right to equality in the field of education and the Article 11 right to equality in the field of employment.

Another right implicated by trafficking is the freedom from discrimination in realizing the right to health.[119] As stated in the Beijing Declaration and Platform for Action of the Fourth World Conference on Women, "Women and girls who are victims of this international trade are at an increased risk of further violence, as well as unwanted pregnancy and sexually transmitted infection, including infection with HIV/AIDS".[120]

The physical and mental abuse that trafficking victims suffer[121] violates the right to be free from gender-based violence. The UNGA has recognized that:

> Violence against women is a manifestation of historically unequal power relations between men and women, which have led to domination over and discrimination against women by men and to the prevention of the full advancement of women, and that violence against women is one of the crucial social mechanisms by which women are forced into a subordinate position compared with men.[122]

The special rapporteur provides an account of a typical arrival in a destination country:

> Once in Berlin, the women were sold mainly to Turks, who confiscated their passports and informed them of their future as prostitutes.

---

[119] CEDAW, art. 11(1)(f) ("The right to protection of health and to safety in working conditions, including the safeguarding of the function of reproduction") and art. 12(1) ("States Parties shall take all appropriate measures to eliminate discrimination against women in the field of health care"). See also UDHR, art. 25(1) ("Everyone has the right to a standard of living adequate for the health and well-being of himself and of his family, including food, clothing, housing and medical care and necessary social services"); ICESCR, art. 12(1) ("The States Parties to the present Covenant recognize the right of everyone to the enjoyment of the highest attainable standard of physical and mental health").

[120] Beijing Declaration and Platform for Action of the Fourth World Conference on Women, China, 4-15 September 1995, Objective D, §122. The increased risk of contracting a fatal illness, such as AIDS, would also constitute a threat to the right to life.

[121] See Preliminary report submitted by the Special Rapporteur on violence against women, its causes and consequences, Ms. Radhika Coomaraswamy, E/CN.4/1995/42, paras. 205-213.

[122] Declaration on the Elimination of Violence Against Women, *supra* note 80, preamble.

Those who resisted were confined, starved, threatened, battered and raped, until they agreed to provide sexual services to clients, mostly on a call-in basis and always escorted by a driver/bodyguard for DM 120 to 150 per client.[123]

Finally, discrimination on the grounds of race, gender, and socio-economic status frequently leads to the denial of a legal remedy, and thus impairs access to justice.

3.Freedom from Slavery and Servitude
States are obliged under customary law and a number of treaties to abolish slavery and forced labour, including debt bondage,[124] regardless of whether the condition is being imposed by public or private actors.[125]

Article1(1) of the Slavery Convention defines slavery as "the status or condition of a person over whom any or all of the powers attaching to the

---

[123] Report on the mission of the Special Rapporteur to Poland on the issue of trafficking and forced prostitution of women (24 May to 1 June 1996), E/CN.4/1997/47/Add.1., para. 23.

[124] Slavery Convention, 60 L.N.T.S. 253, entered into force March 9, 1927; Protocol amending the Slavery Convention, 182 U.N.T.S. 51, entered into force December 7, 1953; Supplementary Convention on the Abolition of Slavery, the Slave Trade, and Institutions and Practices Similar to Slavery, 226 U.N.T.S. 3, entered into force April 30, 1957; Convention for the Suppression of the Traffic in Persons and of the Exploitation of the Prostitution of Others, 96 U.N.T.S. 271, entered into force July 25, 1951. Note that the 1957 Supplementary Slavery Convention also prohibits institutions and practices similar to slavery, including debt bondage, serfdom, the sale or inheritance of a woman, and child exploitation. Supplementary Slavery Convention at art. 1.

[125] Note that subjecting women to slavery-like conditions would also constitute a violation of the right to work under Article 23 of the UDHR ("Everyone has the right to work, to free choice of employment, to just and favourable conditions of work"; "Everyone who works has the right to just and favourable remuneration ensuring for himself and his family an existence worthy of human dignity"); Article 6(1) of the ICESCR ("The States Parties to the present Covenant recognize the right to work, which includes the right of everyone to the opportunity to gain his living by work which he freely chooses or accepts, and will take appropriate steps to safeguard this right"); and Article 11 of CEDAW ("States Parties shall take all appropriate measures to eliminate discrimination against women in the field of employment in order to ensure, on a basis of equality of men and women ... [t]he right to work ...; [t]he right to the same employment opportunities ...; [t]he right to free choice of profession and employment ...; [t]he right to protection of health and to safety in working conditions, including the safeguarding of the function of reproduction").

right of ownership are exercised".[126] From reports detailing the mechanics of trafficking,[127] it is clear that trafficking for the purposes of forced labour "constitutes a modern form of slavery".[128]

Several reports of the special rapporteur on violence against women and other human rights mechanisms indicate that trafficking victims frequently find themselves in slavery-like conditions in the destination country.

According to the special rapporteur, "many of these women are held in debt-bondage as they are expected to repay the amount forwarded to their parents by the recruiting agents".[129] Some women are locked in their rooms, or even chained to their beds.[130] She concludes that "[c]onditions under which many trafficked women are forced to work ... must be considered, without a doubt, to be within the realm of slavery and slavery-like practices", and notes that "[t]he Working Group on Contemporary Forms of Slavery of the Sub-Commission on Prevention of Discrimination and

---

[126] Slavery Convention, 60 L.N.T.S. 253, entered into force March 9, 1927. In addition, debt bondage, a practice specifically prohibited by the 1957 Supplementary Slavery Convention, is often used by traffickers in order to control trafficked women. See *supra* note 123. Article 3 of the Supplementary Convention requires states to take steps to suppress the slave trade.

[127] See, e.g., Report on the mission of the Special Rapporteur to Poland on the issue of trafficking and forced prostitution of women (24 May to 1 June 1996), E/CN.4/ 1997/47/Add.1, para. 66 ("Once the woman reaches her destination, her passport is usually taken away and given to the brothel owner, who thereby acquires control over her. She is beaten into submission and forced to consent to her new life as a prostitute").

[128] Council of Europe, Opinion of the Steering Committee for Equality between Women and Men (CDEG) on Parliamentary Assembly Recommendation 1325 (1997), CM/Del/ Dec(97) 592/3.1, para. 8; see also Report of the Human Rights Committee: 15/09/98. A/53/40, (1998) ("333. It is noted with appreciation that the [Italian] judiciary has begun to treat offences concerning trafficking of women and others for the purpose of prostitution as acts which can be assimilated to slavery and contrary to international and national law").

[129] Preliminary report submitted by the Special Rapporteur on violence against women, its causes and consequences, Ms. Radhika Coomaraswamy, E/CN.4/1995/42, para. 212 ("[Many of these women] may also be illegally confined to the brothels, through the practice of withholding passports or through more physically abusive means. In one known incident, five girl prostitutes in Thailand were burned to death in a brothel because they had been chained to their beds and could not get away").

[130] *Ibid*

Protection of Minorities has identified trafficking, defined as a contemporary form of slavery, as one of its priorities".[131]

In its General Comment 28, the Human Rights Committee placed the obligation to address trafficking squarely within the Article 8 prohibition on slavery.[132]

4. The Right to Life

In addition to the more immediate threat to the right to life posed by beatings and confinement,[133] trafficked women's lives are threatened by their exposure to potentially lethal diseases. The special rapporteur writes:

> In many cases, brothels restrict the use of condoms, as clients are willing to pay higher rates for unprotected sex. Sexual intercourse with multiple clients can lead to painful vaginal bruises and abrasions, which increases the women's exposure to STDs. ... Apart from the risk of infection through sexual intercourse with numerous clients, the increasing use of contraceptive injections in brothels puts these women at further risk of disease, as brothel owners often use the same, possibly contaminated, needle multiple times. The contraction of AIDS could lead to death, and other STDs contracted by these women may ultimately leave them infertile.[134]

---

[131] Report of the Special Rapporteur on violence against women, its causes and consequences, Ms. Radhika Coomaraswamy, E/CN.4/1997/47.

[132] The Committee stated, "Having regard to their obligations under article 8, States parties should inform the Committee of measures taken to eliminate trafficking of women and children, within the country or across borders, and forced prostitution. They must also provide information on measures taken to protect women and children, including foreign women and children, from slavery, disguised inter alia as domestic or other kinds of personal service. States parties where women and children are recruited, and from which they are taken, and States parties where they are received should provide information on measures, national or international, which have been taken in order to prevent the violation of women's and children's rights". General Comment 28, at para. 12.

[133] See Preliminary Report, *supra* note 128.

[134] Report of the Special Rapporteur on violence against women, its causes and consequences, E/CN.4/1999/68/Add.4, paras. 26 & 27.

5. Freedom from Torture or Cruel, Inhuman, or Degrading Treatment or Punishment

The beatings, multiple rapes, and other forms of violence to which trafficking victims are subjected amount to physical and psychological torture.[135] As explained by the special rapporteur:

> For whatever reason women are trafficked, they are frequently raped, beaten and psychologically tormented. Similar strategies have been documented as methods of torturers who target the individual victim and seek to disable the community to which the victim belongs, in the same way as traffickers utilize violence to terrorize victims of trafficking into submission.[136]

6. The Right to Liberty and Security of the Person

Trafficked women are typically deprived of their personal liberty and freedom of movement.[137] An example provided by the special rapporteur demonstrates how violation of this right can also lead to a violation of the right to life:

> [Many of these women] may also be illegally confined to the brothels, through the practice of withholding passports or through more physically abusive means. In one known incident, five girl prostitutes in Thailand were burned to death in a brothel because they had been chained to their beds and could not get away.[138]

B. The failure to respect rights

This Subsection provides examples of situations in which a state would be held responsible for breaching its obligation to respect rights.

---

[135] Report of the Special Rapporteur on violence against women, its causes and consequences, E/CN.4/1999/68/Add.4, para. 26 ("Moreover, subjected, in effect, to multiple rapes, these women suffer serious psychological consequences from their repeated victimization").

[136] Report of the Special Rapporteur on violence against women, its causes and consequences, Ms. Radhika Coomaraswamy, E/CN.4/1997/47.

[137] Report of the Special Rapporteur on violence against women, its causes and consequences, E/CN.4/1999/68/Add.4, para. 25 ("Using a combination of threats, physical force, illegal confinement and debt bondage, brothel owners prevent escape or negotiation by these women").

[138] Preliminary report submitted by the Special Rapporteur on violence against women, its causes and consequences, Ms. Radhika Coomaraswamy, E/CN.4/1995/42, para. 212.

A state is internationally responsible when its acts or omissions directly violate rights. For example, laws pertaining to property, inheritance, marriage, divorce, and residence may deny women independence, mobility, and legal autonomy, and can thus foster trafficking.[139] The enactment or maintenance of such laws constitutes an act of the state in breach of its obligation to take all appropriate measures to suppress trafficking in women. A state is similarly responsible when state actors themselves carry out the trafficking[140] or when state actors are directly involved in imposing the violative conditions under which the trafficking victim is kept. An example of the latter would be the practice of "safe custody"[141] by law enforcement officials in Bangladesh or the regulation of comfort houses by the Japanese military.[142]

When a non-state actor engages in trafficking on behalf of the state, the state's responsibility for failing to respect rights is again engaged. For example, in her report on military sexual slavery, the special rapporteur on violence against women states that private operators would traffic women for comfort stations on behalf of the Japanese military.[143]

According to the recent developments in human rights jurisprudence noted above, a state is also responsible when it is complicit in the trafficking. A variety of fact patterns can show complicity. For example, where

---

[139] See J. Chuang, 'Redirecting the Debate over Trafficking in Women: Definitions, Paradigms, and Contexts' (1998) 11 *Harv. Hum. Rts. J.* 65, 81.

[140] See Report of the Special Rapporteur on violence against women, its causes and consequences, Ms. Radhika Coomaraswamy, E/CN.4/1997/47 ("Reportedly, officials of both Myanmar and Thailand are involved in trafficking women from Myanmar to Thailand. 'In many instances, the girls could document instances of being transported into Thailand with policemen in uniform, armed and often in police vehicles").

[141] Civil and Political Rights, Including Questions Of Torture And Detention, Report of the Special Rapporteur, Sir N.S. Rodley, E/CN.4/1999/61, para. 79.

[142] Report on the mission to the Democratic People's Republic of Korea, the Republic of Korea and Japan on the issue of military sexual slavery in wartime, E/CN.4/1996/53/Add.1, Addendum.

[143] *Ibid*: ("In the quest for more women, private operators working for the military, as well as members of the Korean police force who worked in collaboration with the Japanese, would come to the villages and deceive girls with the promise of well-paid work. Alternatively, in the years preceding 1942, Korean police would arrive in a village recruiting for the 'Women's Voluntary Service Corps'. This made the process official, sanctioned by the Japanese authorities, and it also implied a certain level of compulsion"). These actions would also constitute violations of international humanitarian law. See *Ibid*.

border guards or police officers have been bribed[144] or where they are pa-
trons of brothels known to house trafficking victims,[145] they are complicit
in the trafficking operation.

However, as noted above, complicity can also arise out of acquiescence. If a border guard watches a large number of women cross the border each carrying only a handbag and following an established trafficking
pattern, his failure to act could be deemed complicity if there was any intent on the part of the government to allow the trafficking to continue.[146]

In some instances, different modes of a state's responsibility will be
simultaneously engaged. For example, the special rapporteur reports:

> According to a 30-year-old Bangladeshi woman who was trafficked
> to Pakistan at the age of 27, '... we were taken to a secluded place in
> the jungle before crossing the border to Pakistan under police cus-

---

[144] Report of the Special Rapporteur on violence against women, its causes and consequences, Ms. Radhika Coomaraswamy, E/CN.4/1997/47 ("Additionally, bribes are
often required to facilitate border crossing. ... Police officers are also notorious for
corruption and for abuse of power over trafficked women. According to a Nepalese
non-governmental organization, the only way to see a case of trafficking prosecuted
is to bribe the local police. Local government officials in Nepal undermined a village awareness program when they accused women who were teaching villagers
about migration and trafficking of lying, arguing that trafficking did not exist").

[145] Report of the Special Rapporteur on violence against women, its causes and consequences, Ms. Radhika Coomaraswamy, E/CN.4/1997/47 ("Yai's customers included
high-ranking Taiwanese policemen who received free sexual services in return for
protection"); Report of the Special Rapporteur on violence against women, its
causes and consequences, Ms. Radhika Coomaraswamy, E/CN.4/1997/47 ("Once in
Thailand the brothels are under protection and had the patronage of the police. One
of the girls tells that she saw the police in all the brothels where she worked. They
seemed to know the owner very well and were often around with their uniforms,
guns and walkie-talkies. They also often took the girls to the rooms or out for the
whole night. In Klong Yai the police had special arrangements with the owner and
could take the girls for free").

[146] The special rapporteur has noted some reasons why countries may be inclined to allow trafficking to continue unabated. Report of the Special Rapporteur on violence
against women, its causes and consequences, Ms. Radhika Coomaraswamy, E/CN.4/
1997/47 ("Countries of origin, many with a vested economic interest in and some
with an official policy of promoting international migration, have little incentive to
curb activities that may increase the generation of external revenue. It is estimated
that the Government of the Philippines earns US$ 2 billion from remittances by
overseas contract workers. Conversely, countries of destination associate high costs
with the retention within their borders of individuals residing illegally in their territory and have no incentive to do more than deport trafficked women back to their
home countries").

tody. The border officials kept the girls who were pretty and sexually abused them until the other lots of girls came, then the previous ones were released'.[147]

In this case, the state would be responsible for the abuse the officials inflicted, as well as for its complicity in the trafficking.

C. The failure to ensure rights

The state is also responsible where it fails to exercise due diligence to prevent and respond to violations. In this context, it is crucial to examine the underlying factors that contribute to human rights violations. As noted above, sexism, racism, and women's economic vulnerability all contribute to the trafficking of women.[148]

1. Due diligence measures

The international community has identified a number of measures that states should take in order to prevent and respond to human rights violations in this context.[149]

---

[147] Report of the Special Rapporteur on violence against women, its causes and consequences, Ms. Radhika Coomaraswamy, E/CN.4/1997/47.

[148] Concluding observations of the Committee on the Elimination of Discrimination against Women: Bulgaria ("Bulgaria Report"), 14/05/98, A/53/38, para. 256 ("The Committee suggests that in order to tackle the problem of trafficking in women, it is essential to address women's economic vulnerability, which is the root cause of the problem"). See also Concluding observations of the Committee on the Elimination of Discrimination against Women: Dominican Republic, 14/05/98, A/53/38, para. 33 ("The Committee expresses deep concern about the economic consequences of women's poverty. Women's migration to urban areas and to foreign countries render them susceptible to sexual exploitation, including trafficking and sex tourism, and prostitution. ... The Committee is concerned that notwithstanding the high level of poverty among women, and especially of women-headed households, no affirmative action measures are being taken to support women's efforts to break the cycle of poverty").

[149] These measures have been drawn from: General Assembly resolution 55/67, Traffic in Women and Girls, A/RES/55/67 (2001); General Assembly resolution 53/116, Traffic in Women and Girls, A/RES/53/116 (1999); Commission on Human Rights resolution 2001/48, 1997/44, and 1995/85; Follow-up to the Fourth World Conference on Women: Implementation of Strategic Objectives and Action in the Critical Areas of Concern, Report of the Secretary-General, E/CN.6/1998/5, para. 12; Concluding observations of the Committee on the Elimination of Discrimination against Women: Bulgaria ("Bulgaria Report"), 14/05/98, A/53/38, para. 256; Joint Action of 24 February 1997 adopted by the European Council on the basis of Article K.3 of the Treaty on European Union concerning action to combat trafficking in human be-

General steps that states should take include: unequivocal condemnation of trafficking and all other forms of violence against women; improving national, regional, and international communication, coordination, and cooperation; ratifying and implementing other international human rights instruments, especially CEDAW; implementing the recommendations of international human rights bodies and mechanisms; encouraging Internet service providers to adopt or strengthen self-regulatory measures to promote the responsible use of the Internet with a view to eliminating trafficking in women and girls; and promoting research and compiling statistics on violations, and continuously updating information on trafficking in women and girls, including the analysis of the modus operandi of trafficking syndicates; and publishing reports on the state's responses to violations.

States should also adopt measures addressing the underlying causes of trafficking. Such measures include: public education and awareness-raising (through, for example, information provided by the staff of consulates and embassies dealing with requests for visas and work permits); introducing an active and visible policy of mainstreaming a gender perspective in all policies and programs related to violence against women; ensuring wide dissemination of resource manuals for use in training and education programs; encouraging media sensitisation; developing policies and disseminating materials to promote women's safety in society, including specific crime prevention strategies that reflect the realities of women's lives and address their distinct needs in areas such as social development,

<hr/>

ings and sexual exploitation of children, 97/154/JHA, Doc. No. 497X0154, Official Journal L 063, 04/03/1997 p. 0002-0006, at I.B.(a); Council of Europe, Parliamentary Assembly, Recommendation 1325 (1997) on traffic in women and forced prostitution in Council of Europe member states; Report of the Special Rapporteur on violence against women, its causes and consequences, Ms. Radhika Coomaraswamy, E/CN.4/1999/68, para. 25(i); Declaration on the Elimination of Violence against Wo- men, *supra* note 80; CEDAW, General Recommendation 19, A/47/38 (1992); Concluding observations of the Human Rights Committee: Nepal,10/11/94, CCPR/C/79/ Add.42., paras. 13-14; Global Programme against Trafficking in Human Beings, An outline for action, Centre for International Crime Prevention 7 (1999); Concluding Observations of the Committee on the Elimination of Discrimination Against Women: Kyrgyzstan ("Kyrgyzstan Report"), 27/01/99, CEDAW/C/1999/I/L.1/ Add.3., para. 37; Report of the Special Rapporteur on violence against women, its causes and consequences, Ms. Radhika Coomaraswamy, E/CN.4/1997/47, para. 15; Report of the Human Rights Committee: 15/09/98, A/53/40, para. 312; Vienna Declaration and Programme of Action, 12/07/93, A/CONF.157/23; Report of the Secretary- General, E/CN.4/1995/100.

environmental design and educational programs in crime prevention; taking appropriate measures to address the root factors, including external factors, that encourage trafficking in women and girls for prostitution and other forms of commercialised sex, forced marriages and forced labour; providing support to organizations which combat discrimination; providing job opportunities and training to vulnerable women; providing support to organizations which combat discrimination; and changing patterns of socialization which perpetuate discrimination.

In the area of law enforcement, states should undertake the following: introducing training of immigration staff, in particular in consulates delivering visas and at border points, in order to ensure that such staff are fully aware of the problem, are provided with up-to-date information on trafficking methods and trends, and are trained to recognize potential victims; training for law enforcement personnel; penalizing all offenders involved, including intermediaries and persons in authority; making provisions to seize and confiscate profits from trafficking in women, and to close establishments in which trafficking victims are sexually exploited; for states which do not extradite their nationals for offences committed abroad, making it possible to prosecute nationals in their home country for acts of trafficking committed abroad, whether or not there has been a complaint from the country in which the crime was committed; ensuring that adequate investigation powers and techniques are available to enable the offences listed to be investigated and prosecuted effectively; adopting measures to ensure that acts of violence against women, whether in public or private, are recognized as criminal matters that are, as appropriate, open to public scrutiny and intervention; and enacting and/or enforcing legislation, and amending penal codes where necessary, to ensure effective protection against rape, sexual harassment and all other forms of sexual violence against women.

At an absolute minimum, states must ensure that trafficking victims are not penalized. Further, victim assistance should be afforded through: providing temporary residence visas during the pendency of any criminal, civil or other legal actions; providing refuges and support services for victims and their families, including medical and psychological assistance; improving access to legal remedies on both the domestic and international planes, including the provision of legal assistance; protecting complainants and witnesses to violations; creating the enabling conditions for women who are victims of trafficking to fully participate in the society of their country of origin upon their return; granting the various NGOs and associations for victims of trafficking access to courts in order to increase the effectiveness of action against trafficking and enforced prostitution; making free telephone help-lines for women victims widely available; assisting in child care and maintenance; and providing training for law enforcement, medical, judicial, immigration and other personnel who handle cases of trafficked women and girls, taking into account current research and materials on traumatic stress and gender-sensitive counselling techniques, with a view to sensitising them to the special needs of victims.

2. Evidence of a failure to exercise due diligence

This Subsection provides examples of evidence that could reveal a failure to exercise due diligence.

The failure to attempt to prosecute or punish offenders[150] or to provide some remedy for a violation would clearly implicate state responsibility. This would be the case, for example, if a state deported a trafficking victim without taking a statement for use in a criminal investigation or without providing reparations for the violation of her human rights.[151]

Note that the state may be under an independent obligation not to deport a trafficking victim depending on the situation she would face upon returning to her country of origin.[152] The Human Rights Committee has

---

[150] See, e.g., Report on the mission of the Special Rapporteur to Poland on the issue of trafficking and forced prostitution of women (24 May to 1 June 1996), E/CN.4/ 1997/47/Add.1., para. 99 ("The Special Rapporteur was able to observe that, as already mentioned, judges give very light, suspended sentences to perpetrators of trafficking, even though the law stipulates a minimum of three years' imprisonment").

[151] See Report of the Human Rights Committee: 15/09/98, A/53/40, para. 312 ("The Com- mittee regrets that women brought to Israel for purposes of prostitution, many under false pretences or through coercion, are not protected as victims of trafficking but are likely to be penalized for their illegal presence in Israel by deportation. Such an approach to this problem effectively prevents these women from pursuing a remedy for the violation of their rights under article 8 of the Covenant. The Committee recommends that serious efforts be made to seek out and punish the traffickers, to institute rehabilitation programs for the victims and to ensure that they are able to pursue legal remedies against the perpetrators").

[152] See Report on the mission of the Special Rapporteur to Poland on the issue of trafficking and forced prostitution of women (24 May to 1 June 1996), E/CN.4/1997/ 47/Add.1, paras. 101, 104 ("[In Western European countries other than] the Netherlands and Belgium, a woman from a Central or Eastern European country caught without a valid visa, involved in trafficking, will be immediately deported. ... Deported women return to their countries of origin, including Poland, with very little support. In some host countries, non-governmental organizations provide assistance, including vocational training, to women victims until their deportation, but once in their home countries they are completely on their own. Women who have returned are afraid that they will not be accepted by their families or local communities, they

held that "[i]f a State party deports a person within its territory and subject to its jurisdiction in such circumstances that as a result, there is a real risk that his or her rights under the Covenant will be violated in another jurisdiction, that State party itself may be in violation of the Covenant".[153]

One case provided by the special rapporteur demonstrates the variety of ways in which a state's responsibility can be engaged, depending upon its degree of involvement.

> The case of Hamida, 12, who had been trafficked from Bangladesh to India but escaped after she had been raped repeatedly by police officers at the brothel where she was forcibly prostituted, depicts the situation in which many trafficked women and girls end up. Hamida has been detained at Tihar jail in Delhi in 'safe custody' for two years. She would like to leave but cannot find a way out. The five policemen who raped her have been released on bail. So far they have not been prosecuted. The trial against two of the three traffickers is repeatedly obstructed due, amongst other things, to the repeated absence of the public prosecutor. Meanwhile Hamida's interpreter and sole support was removed from the case because he was 'developing a sympathetic corner for the victim' and is not allowed contact with Hamida, following a court order. Arrangements to send her back to her parents can only be made on instructions from the Home Ministry. Two years ago, the Bangladesh High Commission refused to admit her as a citizen, whereas it is now recognized that she is Bangladeshi.[154]

---

fear revenge and blackmail from their traffickers - all of which the women have to face mostly alone. In Poland, the Special Rapporteur found that there exist no programmes whatsoever for returning women: no police programmes, no shelters and only very few non-governmental organizations dealing with this problem, except for the recently established organization La Strada. The women victims receive no assistance in re-socialisation and in rebuilding their lives").

[153] Communication No 692/1996: *A. R. J. v. Australia*, 11/08/97, CCPR/C/60/D/692/1996, para. 6.9. Another option would be to argue that the entitlement under Article 5 of the Trafficking Convention to take part in the proceedings against the trafficker on the same terms as nationals requires at least postponing deportation from states where nationals do have the right to participate in such proceedings. However, any use of the 1949 Convention may be seen as endorsing it and should therefore be avoided.

[154] Report of the Special Rapporteur on violence against women, its causes and consequences, Ms. Radhika Coomaraswamy, E/CN.4/1997/47.

The state is responsible for the human rights violations resulting from the rape committed by the police officers and in subjecting her to "safe-custody". The failure to prosecute effectively may be either complicity or failure to exercise due diligence, and thus may give rise to the state's responsibility to respect or to ensure the victim's rights. If the failure to prosecute is accompanied by any intention to permit impunity, then the state is liable for complicity. If the failure is accompanied by no such intention, it amounts to a lack of due diligence, making the state responsible for failing to respond to the violation of her rights by the traffickers.

D. Application in Kosovo

The situation in Kosovo described in Section I has placed UNMIK in breach of international human rights law. Rights violated in the course of trafficking in Kosovo have included all of the rights enumerated in Section II *supra*.

The failure of UNMIK to take steps to prevent and respond to these violations, evidenced clearly by the treatment of victims in the criminal justice system, the impunity of perpetrators, and the absence of any sort of victim assistance, amounts to a violation of UNMIK's obligation to ensure these rights. Further, the participation of UNMIK Police and other UN personnel in trafficking may render UNMIK directly responsible for those human rights violations, constituting a further breach of international human rights law.

As a first step in correcting this state of affairs, UNMIK has promulgated a comprehensive regulation on trafficking in persons.

IV. Commentary on UNMIK Regulation 2001/4

On 12 January 2001, the Special Representative of the Secretary General for UNMIK promulgated Regulation 2001/4 on the prohibition of trafficking in persons in Kosovo.[155] A special inter-agency Legislative Working Group on Trafficking in Persons initially drafted the Regulation.[156] The

---

[155] UNMIK Regulation No. 2001/4 ON THE PROHIBITION OF TRAFFICKING IN PERSONS IN KOSOVO ("Regulation No. 4" or "the Regulation"), UNMIK/REG/ 2001/4, 12 January 2001. The Regulation is not intended to deal with the crime of prostitution, which is prohibited under the applicable law of Kosovo.

[156] The draft Regulation was subject to further modification by the Office of the UNMIK Legal Advisor and by UN Headquarters. As with all legislation, some provisions resulted from a process of political negotiation and compromise.

purpose of the Working Group in elaborating this regulation was to combine a criminal justice response with a human rights approach to this very complex manifestation of transnational organized crime. In particular, the working group intended to make the public authorities in Kosovo responsible for providing assistance to victims of trafficking in conformity with international law. In addition, while the Working Group knew that further legislation or statutory instruments would be required to implement some provisions of the Regulation, the working group intended to provide the legal basis for such further legislation in this Regulation.

The Regulation establishes the crime of trafficking in persons as part of the law applicable in Kosovo. Incorporating a human rights approach to trafficking, the Regulation also provides specific protection and reparations for victims including a defence to prosecution for prostitution, the right to apply for compensation, and access to legal, medical, and other services.

The Regulation is divided into three chapters, respectively providing for Criminal Acts and Penalties; Investigation, Confiscation, and Court Procedures; and Victim Protection and Assistance.

A. CHAPTER I: Criminal Acts and Penalties

Section 1 sets forth definitions for the terms and phrases used in the regulation. The Regulation employs a very broad definition of trafficking in persons. The breadth of the definition recognizes the complexity of trafficking. In particular, the purpose of employing a broad definition is to sweep within its scope all intermediaries in the trafficking process. It thus encompasses a wide range of means, purposes, and actors. The definition was taken, almost verbatim, from the recently adopted Protocol on Trafficking in Persons to the Convention on Transnational Organised Crime.[157]

Trafficking in persons is defined in Section 1.1(a) as:

> The recruitment, transportation, transfer, harbouring or receipt of persons, by means of the threat or use of force or other forms of co-ercion, of abduction, of fraud, of deception, of the abuse of power or

---

[157] Indeed, the breadth of the definition was a cause of concern for some Working Group members who considered that the definition as a whole may not be sufficiently precise to put potential offenders on notice of the contours of the proscribed conduct. They noted that the definition was taken from a treaty and that it is not uncommon for governments to make modifications to criminal definitions set forth in international legal instruments in order to tailor those definitions to the circumstances prevailing within their territories.

of a position of vulnerability or of the giving or receiving of payments or benefits to achieve the consent of a person having control over another person, for the purpose of exploitation.

The definition sets out three elements: the act ("recruitment, transportation, transfer, harbouring or receipt of persons"), the means ("by means of the threat or use of force or other forms of coercion, of abduction, of fraud, of deception, of the abuse of power or of a position of vulnerability or of the giving or receiving of payments or benefits to achieve the consent of a person having control over another person"), and the purpose ("for the purpose of exploitation"). These three elements must be met for the crime of trafficking to arise.[158] It is significant to note that international movement is not required.[159] Thus, trafficking may occur within a single state's borders.

Under Section 1.1(b), "exploitation" is deemed to "include, but not be limited to, the exploitation of the prostitution of others or other forms of sexual exploitation, forced labour or services, slavery or practices similar to slavery, servitude or the removal of organs". The language employed makes clear that this list is not exhaustive.

This definition of trafficking marks a significant advance over the conception of trafficking codified in the 1949 Trafficking Convention.[160] One

---

[158] Note, however, that in the case of minors, the 'means' element is not required. See *infra*.

[159] While the Trafficking Protocol is limited by the parameters of the parent convention, the Regulation is not so limited. Thus, international movement is not required for an act to qualify as trafficking under the Regulation.

[160] Under Article 1 of the 1949 Convention, states parties "agree to punish any person who, to gratify the passions of another: (1) Procures, entices or leads away, for purposes of prostitution, another person, even with the consent of that person; (2) Exploits the prostitution of another person, even with the consent of that person". Convention for the Suppression of the Traffic in Persons and of the Exploitation of the Prostitution of Others, Dec. 2, 1949, opened for signature Mar. 21, 1950, 96 U.N. T.S. 272, 282 (entered into force July 25, 1951). This definition is flawed for its under- and over-inclusiveness. It is under-inclusive in that it defines trafficking as applicable only to movement for the purposes of prostitution. It therefore excludes trafficking for non-sexual economic exploitation, such as forced factory or domestic work. It is over-inclusive in that it makes the consent of the victim irrelevant. The fact that consent is deemed irrelevant makes the convention itself rights violative by denying women's agency and demonstrates the criminal nature of the instrument. The convention's focus on criminalization is also seen in the fact that the definition turns on the intent of the trafficker, rather than on the circumstances of the person being moved.

of the main drawbacks of that definition was that it took no account of the possibility of consent by the person alleged to have been trafficked. As early as 1994, the UN General Assembly adopted a definition of trafficking that implicitly makes consent relevant.[161] The European Union[162] and the Council of Europe[163] have both elaborated definitions of trafficking in which the absence of consent is a necessary criterion. NGOs have also advocated making consent relevant in the definition of trafficking.[164]

Section 1.2 of the Regulation underscores the relevance of consent to the definition of trafficking. It states, "The consent of a victim of trafficking in persons to the intended exploitation set forth in section 1.1 shall be irrelevant where any of the means set forth in section 1.1(a) have been used against a victim of trafficking".

This provision implicitly preserves the agency of those who voluntarily choose to engage in a practice that may be considered exploitation by a judge. For example, where someone chooses of their free will to travel to work as a prostitute in the destination area, and where they have fully con-

---

[161] General Assembly Resolution 49/166 of 23 December 1994.

[162] See Joint Action of 24 February 1997 adopted by the Council on the basis of Article K.3 of the Treaty on European Union concerning action to combat trafficking in human beings and sexual exploitation of children, 97/154/JHA, Doc. No. 497X0154, Official Journal L 063 , 04/03/1997 p. 0002-0006, at I.B.(a) (employing a definition of trafficking that requires that "use is made of coercion, in particular violence or threats, or deceit is used, or there is abuse of authority or other pressure, which is such that the person has no real and acceptable choice but to submit to the pressure or abuse involved").

[163] See Council of Europe, Parliamentary Assembly, Recommendation 1325 (1997) on traffic in women and forced prostitution in Council of Europe member states ("The Assembly defines traffic in women and forced prostitution as any legal or illegal transporting of women and/or trade in them, with or without their initial consent, for economic gain, *with the purpose of subsequent forced prostitution, forced marriage, or other forms of forced sexual exploitation.* The use of force may be physical, sexual and/or psychological, and includes intimidation, rape, abuse of authority or a situation of dependence") (emphasis added).

[164] See also Global Alliance Against Traffic in Women ("GAATW"), Human Rights Standards for the Treatment of Trafficked Persons, January 1999, which defines trafficking as "All acts and attempted acts involved in the recruitment, transportation within or across borders, purchase, sale, transfer, receipt or harbouring of a person *involving the use of deception, coercion (including the use or threat of force or the abuse of authority) or debt bondage* for the purpose of placing or holding such person, whether for pay or not, in involuntary servitude (domestic, sexual or reproductive), in forced or bonded labour, or in slavery-like conditions, in a community other than the one in which such person lived at the time of the original deception, coercion or debt bondage" (emphasis added).

sented to all conditions of that travel and work, including consent to the location of work, then such a person would not have been trafficked. However, such consent must be informed,[165] and use of any of the means listed in Section 1.1(a) would vitiate any form of consent expressed by the victim. Further, this provision prevents the conviction for trafficking of facilitators of illegal migration who operate with the full consent of the migrant and who do not use any illicit means against her or him.

While Section 1.2 is also taken largely from the Protocol, it contains a slight modification. The Protocol does not expressly require that such means have been used against the 'victim'. That being the case, the attempt to make consent relevant where such means are not employed would not include cases in which the victim fully consented, but illicit means were used vis-à-vis someone else (e.g. fraud perpetrated against a border guard).[166] The phrase "against a victim of trafficking" was added in order to clarify that the improper means have to have been employed vis-à-vis the victim.

Section 1.3 eliminates the 'means' element in the case of child victims. It is sufficient to recruit, transport, etc. the child for the purpose of exploitation. The principle underlying this provision is that a child is incapable of consenting to exploitation.

Section 2 criminalizes the act of trafficking in persons, as well as organization and negligent facilitation of trafficking. The existing applicable law already provided for accomplice liability[167] as well as universal juris-

---

[165] Thus, such consent is relevant only where the victim has consented: to be moved; to the conditions of movement (transit conditions); to the purpose of the movement (e.g. type of job in destination country, invitation, simply to travel, etc.); to the end conditions (including location). Having all of this in mind, it is clear that someone can have consented to working as a prostitute, but still have been trafficked.

[166] Accompanied by a broad interpretation of 'the exploitation of the prostitution of others or other forms of sexual exploitation', a likely occurrence in the present jurisprudential environment, this would mean that someone who consents to facilitation of their illegal migration, such facilitation involving fraud or coercion or deception perpetrated against anyone in the process (e.g. visa issuer), and where such person intends to work as a sex worker in the destination country, irrespective of whether such sex work is legal in the destination country, it is entirely possible that the facilitator could be found guilty of trafficking in persons (an international crime) and that the illegal migrant would be considered a 'victim' of trafficking.

[167] See FRY Code, art. 22 ("If several persons jointly commit a criminal act by participating in the act of commission or in some other way, each of them shall be punished as prescribed for the act") and art. 24 ("Anybody who intentionally aids another in the commission of a criminal act shall be punished as if he himself had committed it, but his punishment may also be reduced").

diction. Thus, these were not included in the Regulation. The Working Group did not expressly provide for universal jurisdiction as it was generally agreed within the group that the FRY Criminal Procedure Code already provides for universal jurisdiction.[168]

For the crime of trafficking or attempted trafficking, Section 2.1 prescribes a punishment of two to twelve years' imprisonment. To establish the punishment, the Working Group looked to penalties for comparable crimes under the domestic law. The broad range was intended to correspond to the broad spectrum of modalities in which persons can participate in trafficking. Section 2.2 permits a higher penalty where the victim is under the age of 18 years. In such cases the maximum penalty is 15 years' imprisonment.

Section 2.3 prohibits organizing a group of persons for the purpose of committing trafficking in persons. Upon conviction, perpetrators are liable to a penalty of five to twenty years. This section was intended to be used to prosecute the 'bosses' who construct or coordinate the trafficking networks.

In order to overcome the difficulty of establishing the intent of intermediaries, Section 2.4 criminalizes the negligent facilitation of trafficking. The Working Group intended use of the word "facilitate" that the person in some way affirmatively assisted the traffickers. This would not include, for example, a border guard who simply failed to thoroughly inspect a victim's documents.[169]

Trafficking is almost always accompanied by the seizure of the victim's passport or other identification documents, as a means of coercing the victim and limiting her freedom of movement. Thus, Section 3 prohibits the withholding of identification papers. It states that "[a]ny person who, acting or purporting to act as another person's employer, manager, contractor or employment agent, intentionally withholds that other person's personal identification documents and/or passport commits a criminal act and shall be liable upon conviction to a penalty of six (6) months to five (5) years' imprisonment". As with section 2.4, this provision will enable prosecution where it is impossible to prove the intent to traffic. The

---

[168] FRY Code.

[169] This is without prejudice to any questions of state responsibility. UNMIK, for example, is required to conduct training for its border police, sensitising them to the issue and establishing special procedures for suspected traffickers and trafficking victims.

phrase "purporting to act" was inserted in order to avoid limiting the relationships described to a more restrictive meaning under the applicable law.

Section 4 prohibits using or procuring the sexual services of a person in a situation of sexual exploitation. According to Section 4.1, "Any person who uses or procures the sexual services of a person with the knowledge that that person is a victim of trafficking in persons commits a criminal act and shall be liable upon conviction to a penalty of three (3) months to five (5) years' imprisonment". The provision incorporates a fairly high *mens rea* requirement. Perpetrators must know that the person whose services they are using is a victim of trafficking. While actual knowledge can be difficult to prove, the Working Group was of the opinion that knowledge could be inferred from the circumstances surrounding the use of such services. Section 4.2 increases the maximum penalty to ten years' imprisonment where the "person providing the sexual services ... is under the age of 18 years".

B. CHAPTER II: Investigation, Confiscation and Court Procedures

In light of the precarious security situation prevailing in Kosovo, special steps must be taken in the course of investigations in order to protect trafficking victims from the traffickers and their criminal networks. Section 5.1 provides that "[t]he taking of a statement by a law enforcement officer or investigating judge shall in no way inhibit or delay the voluntary repatriation of an alleged victim of trafficking". This provision recognizes that the longer victims remain in Kosovo, the longer their lives are in jeopardy, and, consequently, requires the police and judges to act expediently.

Section 5.2 requires that "[a]ppropriate measures be taken for witness protection during any investigation and/or court proceedings". As of the time of promulgation, no comprehensive witness protection program was in place in Kosovo.[170] In light of this gap, guidelines would have to be drafted setting forth the steps that police and judicial personnel must take in the course of trafficking investigations.

---

[170] As stated by the Legal System Monitoring Section of the OSCE Mission in Kosovo, "In particularly sensitive cases and those involving organised criminal activity, more substantial mechanisms for the protection of victims and witnesses are essential, such as the provision of immunity and longer-term protection of key witnesses (including, for example, a relocation programme). At this time, UNMIK has not yet formulated any guidelines for the protection of victims and witnesses in the courtrooms, nor established any mechanisms or programs for substantial witness protection. Working-groups led by UNMIK police have been established to address these issues". Report of the OSCE Mission in Kosovo, *Kosovo: A Review of the Criminal Justice System*, 1 September 2000-28 February 2001 (March 2001).

Section 6 provides for the confiscation of property and the closure of establishments. Section 6.1 permits the confiscation of assets that are used in connection with trafficking, including proceeds.[171] The personal property of victims is exempted from this provision. Section 6.2 empowers an investigative judge to close establishments associated with trafficking.

As part of the obligation to provide reparations to victims of human rights violations, Section 6.3 authorizes the establishment of a Reparations Fund for victims of trafficking. The Fund "shall be authorised to receive funds from, *inter alia,* the confiscation of property pursuant to section 6.1".

All of the provisions in Section 6 will require elaboration in the form of administrative directions or other statutory instruments before they can be implemented. For example, procedures for confiscation and closure, including the right to hearings and appeals, will have to be spelled out in an administrative direction.

Section 7 permits certain modifications to court proceedings in order to protect the victim. Sections 7.1 to 7.3 bar the use of evidence concerning the character or personal history of the alleged victim, including, for example, sexual or employment history. Such evidence can only be used if the defendant receives the express authorization of the president of the panel of judges. Such authorization may only be granted if "the evidence is of such relevance, and its omission would be so prejudicial to the defendant, as to result in a miscarriage of justice for the defendant if not allowed to be introduced".[172] This standard is intended to embody a balance

---

[171] While the FRY Code provides for confiscation of property, it may be "imposed only for the criminal acts for which it is expressly prescribed, and when a punishment of imprisonment for a term of at least three years has been imposed on the offender". FRY Code, art. 40.

[172] The Special Rapporteur had recommended an absolute bar on the introduction of character or personal history evidence. See Report of the Special Rapporteur on violence against women, February 2000, *supra* note 3, at para. 117 ("The personal history, the alleged 'character' or the current or previous occupation of the victim must not be used against the victim, nor serve as a reason to disqualify the victim's complaint or to decide not to prosecute the offenders. For example, the offenders must be prohibited from using as a defence the fact that the person is, or was at any time, a sex worker or a domestic worker"). Presumably, the absolute prohibition recommended by the Special Rapporteur is aimed at eliminating the evil of drawing unwarranted (and morally loaded) inferences rooted in sex discrimination. Initially, the draft Regulation prohibited introduction of character and personal history evidence, but many members of the group thought this was so broad as to impinge upon the defendant's right to a fair trial. The Working Group determined that evidence of employment history may in some cases be relevant as it may tend to negate one of

between the right of the accused to a defence and the victim's right to privacy.[173]

Section 7.4 permits the judge to exclude the public or to permit witnesses to testify through, for example, closed circuit television. This is particularly important when trafficking victims may be further traumatized by the close presence of the alleged trafficker or the general public.

In response to the continuing punishment of trafficking victims by the Kosovo courts, Section 8 excludes the criminal responsibility of trafficking victims for certain acts that they may have committed as a result of their having been trafficked. Section 8 states, "A person is not criminally responsible for prostitution or illegal entry, presence or work in Kosovo if that person provides evidence that supports a reasonable belief that he or she was the victim of trafficking". It reflects the general principle of law that a person cannot be held criminally responsible where his or her act was not committed voluntarily.

C. CHAPTER III: Victim Protection and Assistance

The purpose of Chapter III is to spell out the responsibilities of the public authorities toward victims of trafficking.

Section 9 authorizes the appointment of a Victim Assistance Coordinator who will be responsible for organizing the provision of services to victims. In carrying out that responsibility, Section 9.1 stipulates that the Coordinator "shall liase with the relevant law enforcement authorities, international and non-governmental or other organisations, and administrative departments as necessary".

Section 9.2 imposes a financial limitation on the ability of the Coordinator to perform his or her function. It provides that "[e]xpenses arising from the implementation of the provisions under Chapter III of the present regulation shall be funded, to the extent resources are available, and from donor contributions made specifically for this purpose and recorded as designated donor grants in the Kosovo Consolidated Budget". Section 10

---

the elements of the crime (i.e., the means requirement). An alternative proposal prohibited the introduction of character evidence, and allowed evidence of personal history (e.g. employment history) only in exceptional cases with the approval of the court after in camera review, this latter provision being modelled after rape shield laws. The final text provides for the possible use of either type of evidence, but subjects both to the same review process.

[173] The European Court of Human Rights has recognized that in certain cases it is necessary for the authorities to take steps to protect victims and witnesses, even where such steps may infringe on the right of the defendant to confront witnesses. See *Dorson v. Netherlands* (1996) 22 ECHR 330.

confirms that victim assistance will be provided only to the extent funds are available to do so.

Section 10 elaborates on the types of assistance to be afforded to trafficking victims. Section 10.1 states:

> Upon the request of a person who provides to the Victim Assistance Coordinator reasonable grounds for belief that she or he is a victim of trafficking, the following services shall be provided to that person, subject to availability of resources provided in accordance with section 9.2:
> (a) Free interpreting services in the language of their choice;
> (b) Free legal counsel in relation to trafficking issues (criminal or civil);
> (c) Temporary safe housing, psychological, medical and social welfare assistance as may be necessary to provide for their needs; and
> (d) Such other services as shall be specified in an administrative direction.

As noted above, the provision of these services is "subject to availability of resources," and is thus not guaranteed. The provision of other services to be detailed in an administrative direction would include repatriation and reintegration assistance, which was deleted from an earlier draft of the Regulation.

Section 10.2 ensures that these services and facilities will be made available to victims "regardless of any charges of prostitution or of illegal entry, presence or work in Kosovo that may be pending against them". In this regard, it is important to note that the Coordinator, according to Section 10.1, makes an independent determination of whether or not the person requesting services is a victim of trafficking.[174] Thus, even if courts continue to charge and convict trafficking victims for prostitution, the Coordinator will still be empowered to provide assistance to them.

Section 10.3 requires police officers to inform trafficking victims of their right to the services listed. It also requires police officers to liase with the service providers, which is especially important pending the appointment of a Coordinator.

---

[174] An administrative direction should expressly provide for the right to appeal from an adverse determination by the Coordinator.

Section 11 concerns deportation proceedings against trafficking victims. This section was designed to prevent Kosovo courts from handing down expulsion orders against trafficking victims. It states:

> A conviction for prostitution or a conviction for illegal entry, presence or work in Kosovo shall not be the basis for deportation if the person who is to be deported is a victim of trafficking.

As part of the applicable law, this section also provides a legal basis for UNMIK to refrain from expelling trafficking victims who have been ordered expelled by a court notwithstanding the existence of this provision.

In the event that a trafficking victim will face persecution if returned to his or her country of origin, Section 12 permits the possibility that the victim may be granted temporary residence in Kosovo or other assistance. Section 12.1 states:

> If a victim of trafficking expresses a wish to not be returned to her or his country of citizenship or previous habitual residence based on a claim of persecution, such a claim shall be evaluated by the appropriate authority, pursuant to the applicable law, who may determine that the victim may be granted residence in Kosovo or such other assistance as deemed appropriate.

This section was drafted in open terms in recognition of certain unresolved antecedent questions (e.g., who the appropriate authority in Kosovo would be, etc.). In addition, use of the term "persecution" without spelling out the bases of persecution was intended to permit broader protection than that provided under the Refugee Convention.[175] Section 12.2 preserves any other rights the victim may have under international refugee or human rights law.[176]

---

[175] 1951 Convention Relating to the Status of Refugees, entry into force 22 April 1954.

[176] There are several cases in which trafficking victims may also be refugees. First, given the vulnerability of their situation, refugees are more likely to become victims of trafficking to a further destination. Second, the mechanism of flight of a refugee may constitute trafficking. Finally, in cases of trafficking for the purpose of forced prostitution, a victim may become a refugee *sur place* if she or he would face persecution if returned home due to having worked as prostitute (whether voluntarily or not).

D. Final Provisions

The final provisions of the Regulation are standard provisions. Section 13 authorizes the Special Representative of the Secretary-General to issue administrative directions for the implementation of the Regulation. Section 14 confirms that the Regulation supersedes any provision in the applicable law that is inconsistent with it. Finally, 12 January 2001 is established as the entry into force date in Section 15.

E. Immunity

While Regulation No. 4 is silent on the issue of immunity, a prior regulation provides far-reaching immunity for UNMIK, KFOR, and the personnel of both. Under UNMIK Regulation 2000/47, immunity is extended to UNMIK and KFOR as entities, including the property of both.[177] While high-ranking UNMIK officials are afforded blanket immunity, other UNMIK personnel have only functional immunity.[178]

All KFOR personnel are provided blanket immunity. KFOR personnel are "immune from jurisdiction before courts in Kosovo in respect of any administrative, civil or criminal act committed by them in the territory of Kosovo". Regulation 47 also states that they are "subject to the exclusive jurisdiction of their respective sending States" and are "immune from any form of arrest or detention other than by persons acting on behalf of their respective sending States".[179]

Regulation 2000/47 also provides for the waiver of immunity.[180] In light of the growing evidence of perpetration of or complicity in trafficking by UNMIK and KFOR personnel, the waiver provisions must be invoked in order to avoid falling afoul of human rights law.[181]

---

[177] UNMIK Regulation 2000/47 on the Status, Privileges and Immunities of KFOR and UNMIK and Their Personnel in Kosovo ("Regulation 2000/47"), Sections 2.1 and 3.1,UNMIK/REG/2000/47, 18 August 2000.

[178] "UNMIK personnel, including locally recruited personnel, shall be immune from legal process in respect of words spoken and all acts performed by them in their official capacity. ... UNMIK personnel shall be immune from any form of arrest or detention." Regulation 2000/47, Sections 3.3 and 3.4.

[179] Regulation 2000/47, Section 2.4.

[180] While the immunity of UNMIK personnel may be waived by the UN Secretary General, "[r]equests to waive jurisdiction over KFOR personnel shall be referred to the respective commander of the national element of such personnel for consideration". Regulation 2000/47, Section 6.

[181] Alternatively, states may themselves prosecute their nationals. However, as states are unlikely to prosecute in these cases and may not even have legislation providing

V. Conclusion

While the promulgation of UNMIK Regulation 2001/4 is to be welcomed for its progressive approach to the phenomenon of trafficking in persons, providing the legislative foundation can only be the beginning of UNMIK's work in this field. UNMIK must act diligently to prosecute offenders and to make sure that the remedies envisioned in the Regulation are effective.

As a whole, Regulation 2001/4 reflects the complexity of the trafficking problem, encompassing such issues as gender discrimination, economic exploitation, globalisation, and the movement of people. In order to move forward and effectively address the problem, UNMIK must implement preventive and remedial measures that recognize these broader dimensions.

In addition, UNMIK cannot by itself adequately address all aspects of trafficking. It must cooperate with the Yugoslav authorities, as well as countries throughout the region and beyond, to jointly confront the issue of transnational organized crime, and to address the global inequalities that cause trafficking to flourish.

---

a jurisdictional basis to do so, the best course of action would be to waive the immunity of the perpetrators.

International Human Rights Promotion
and Protection Through Peace Operations:
A Strong Mechanism?

*Rachel Opie**

Introduction

The latest form of peace operations, as deployed in Kosovo and East
Timor, do already constitute a mechanism for the promotion and protection of international human rights. The peace operation, particularly
through the processes of peace building, constitutes a mechanism which is
attempting to rebuild and reconstruct societal institutions, and is doing so
with the explicit objective to promote and protect international human
rights standards. In respect of existing human rights mechanisms, the
peace operation is another step in their development as it directly involves
the wide implementation of the standards into a wide national context.
What remains to be seen is whether the inherent strength of this mechanism will be realised. Currently, as the United Nations Interim
Administration Mission in Kosovo (UNMIK) and United Nations
Transitional Authority in East Timor (UNTAET) demonstrate,
international human rights are part of the fabric of the operations. They
also play a very considerable role in the tasks of the operations. What is
shown to be one of the determinative factors for the realisation of the
strength of this mechanism is the capacity of the United Nations (UN) to
cope with the enormous and inherent difficulties of post-conflict
situations. However, as this article will indicate, some of these difficulties
are proving insurmountable for the UN. Consequently, the political
management of the structures that the operations are putting in place is not
enhancing the realisation of structural capacity for the promotion and
protection of human rights as provided, but is rather undermining it.

---

*   LLB/BA graduate from Victoria University of Wellington, New Zealand. In writing
     of this article, I would like to warmly acknowledge the time, suggestions and en-
     couragement given by Professore Andrea de Guttry, Dr. André de Hoogh, Professor
     Ian Macduff and Dr. Anne Opie. This research was made possible by a grant from
     the Scuola Superiore Sant'Anna, Pisa, Italy.

M. Bothe and B. Kondoch (eds.),
International Peacekeeping. The Yearbook of International Peace Operations, Volume 7, 2001, 99–151.
© 2002 *Kluwer Law International. Printed in the Netherlands.*

Section One

This section will provide a brief overview of the current form of peace operations, and the relationship of peace operations with international human rights in the current global order. The development of these institutions demonstrate the attempts of the UN to adjust to and remain relevant in the light of changing geopolitical circumstances and the needs arising from these circumstances. One effect of the adaptation by the UN is that international human rights are becoming recognised as vital to the conceptions of successful conflict resolution. Therefore, human rights impact significantly on the activities of peace operations, and following the trend of greater understanding about the role of human rights for conflict resolution, they will continue to play a part. On the basis of this presumption, the peace operation has become an important mechanism in the system for the promotion and protection of human rights.[1] This is because the human rights component utilises existing human rights mechanisms such as investigating, reporting and monitoring of past human rights violations and the current human rights situation, but it also goes further by actively implementing human rights norms and standards through other activities undertaken in the peace operation. This has the potential to be particularly effective as the process of implementation is occurring at the same time as overall societal re-building and re-establishment, allowing human rights to inform the underlying structural and relational aspects of the post-settlement society.

---

[1] I understand the 'promotion of human rights' to be a continual process consisting of the implementation and development of activities and instruments that function to increase people's and the broader society's understanding and knowledge of international human rights norms and standards. More specifically, what it means to have rights, what the rights are, and increasing the awareness of ways to protect those rights. Therefore, promotion of human rights is largely about education and increasing the visibility of the existence and the substance of rights. The 'protection of human rights' I understand as the creation, strengthening and deepening of structures and institutions that ensure ongoing promotion, existence, and realisation of human rights, and which serves to create a culture of human rights and institutions to guard against possible future human rights violations and ultimately the resurgence of violent conflict. Ideally, it should also include structures to ensure the realisation of and to guarantee rights. other than civil and political rights which are presently the primary focus of peace operations to the exclusion of, in particular, social and economic rights.

1.1 Setting the Scene: Peace Operations and Human Rights

The end of the Cold War has affected the geopolitical order in numerous ways. In the area of peace and security, the previously existing world order, based on the division of the world into two political zones, either suppressed or intensified conflict depending on the geographical region[2]. Now, although globally we are not necessarily experiencing 'new forms of conflict'[3] or an overall increase in conflict[4], conflict is being defined and explained in new ways. What previously would have been explained by East-West rivalry, is now being seen as the result of a collapsed society, social unrest due to a lack of democracy, "or the ravages caused by a dictatorship"[5]. Concurrently, conflict is not only occurring on the peripheries, as the conflict in the Balkans indicates, media coverage of conflict is increasingly making it part of the 'global consciousness', and conflict is having more impact on the lives of people previously not affected through the global repercussions of all conflict, including intra-state conflict. Further, the ways of managing of this new 'disorder' are yet to be discovered and implemented successfully. As Rausmann has argued, it has now become imperative that a strong global system with new actors, roles and rules comes into being[6].

Arguably, the beginnings of the development of this new global system are visible. The end of the Cold War, and thus superpower constraint, saw the UN playing a greater, more active role in global affairs. In the area of peace and security, and further in the area of peace operations, this trend was clear.[7] Increasing publicly expressed awareness of the role the UN had the potential to play was coupled with developments in the conceptualisa-

---

2   J.P. Lederach, *Building Peace: Sustainable Reconciliation in Divided Societies* (United States Institute of Peace Washington, DC, 1997), at 6.

3   L.J. Rasmussen, 'Peacemaking in the 21st Century: New Rules, New Roles, New Actors' in Zartman, William I., and J. Lewis Rasmussen (eds), *Peacemaking in International Conflict: Methods and Techniques* (United States Institute of Peace Press: Washington, D.C., 1997), pp. 23-50, at 37.

4   There has been an increase in 'minor armed conflicts' in which fewer than 25 people have died in a given year. See Lederach, *supra* note 2, at 6.

5   Y. Daudet et al, 'Conflict Resolution: New Approaches and Methods', in *Peace and Conflict Issues* (Paris: UNESCO Publishing, 2000), at 25.

6   Rasmussen, *supra* note 3, at 38.

7   The overall term which will be used here is 'peace operations' to make a distinction with traditional peacekeeping. The former aims to implement peace, rather than with the later which just 'freezes' it. See Rasmussen, *supra* note 3, at 39.

tion of the role peace operations as part of a broader involvement in global conflict resolution. This process has seen what Griffin has termed "retrenchment, reform and regionalization"[8] to describe the very real tempering of enthusiasm and initiatives, as the realities of undertaking peace operations became more apparent after the activism of the UN in the latter 1990s. However, peace operations form a substantial, and an ever-evolving aspect of the strategy of the UN in conflict resolution and management and in its broader role in global peace and security.[9]

I will not retrace the evolution of peace operations from traditional peacekeeping operations here because of the already extensive existing literature and discussions in this area.[10] Suffice it to say that the evolution has been one of increasing multi-functionality, multidimensionality, and complexity of operations, as traditional forms of peacekeeping were found to be inadequate to respond to the changing demands of conflicts. This is particularly so because the UN has become increasing involved in intra-state conflict, until relatively recently 'off limits' on grounds of state sovereignty and non-intervention, which is generally speaking, more complex, more violent, and more difficult to resolve.[11]

A major feature of the evolution in peace operations has been the inclusion of peace building as a primary and substantial task. With the operations in Kosovo (United Nations Interim Administration in Kosovo (UN-

---

[8] See M. Griffin, 'Retrenchment, Reform and Regionalization: Trends in UN Peace Support Operations' in (1/1999) 6 *International Peacekeeping* (Frank Cass/London) 1-31.

[9] Griffin, *supra* note 8, at 4.

[10] See, for example, A. Parsons, *From Cold War to Hot Peace: UN Interventions 1947-1995* (Penguin Books: London, 1995); W.J. Durch, 'Keeping the Peace: Politics and Lessons of the 1990s' in W.J. Durch, (ed) *UN Peacekeeping, American Policy and the Uncivil Wars of the 1990s* (St. Martin's Press: New York, 1996), pp. 1-34; N.D. White, *Keeping the Peace: The United Nations and the Maintenance of International Peace and Security* (Manchester University Press: Manchester, 1993); J. Mackinlay, (ed), *A Guide to Peace Support Operations* (The Thomas J. Watson Jr. Institute for International Studies, Brown University, 1996) at http://www.brown.edu/Departments/Watson_Institute/Publications/index.html; O. Ramsbotham/ T. Woodhouse, *Encyclopedia of International Peacekeeping Operations* (ABC-CLIO: California, Inc, 1999). See also, Th.G. Wiess/D.P. Forsythe/R.A. Coates, *The United Nations and Changing World Politics* (2nd ed, Westview Press, Boulder, 1997) for a more general discussion.

[11] N. Græger, 'Human Rights and Multi-functional Peace Operations' in R.G. Patman (ed), *Universal Human Rights?* (Great Britain: Macmillan Press, 2000), pp. 175-190, at 179.

MIK))[12] and East Timor (United Nations Transitional Authority in East Timor (UNTAET)), peace operations have reached a new level of complexity. The international community, in its various forms and with its various tasks, is directly involved and overtly embedded in the political processes of the 'hosting' country.

There has been a corresponding evolution in the area of international human rights, largely in the continual development in the definition of human rights standards and norms, their incorporation into documents of varying legal status, and the attainment, by a number, of the status of customary international law.[13] Alongside this, has been the development of the machinery within the UN to protect these human rights norms and standards, primarily through monitoring, reporting and complaints procedures. Concurrently, a crucial aspect in this evolution is the increasing acceptability of human rights discourse, and the growing explicit recognition of the importance of human rights-based solutions in areas of peace and security in order to achieve a long-lasting solution to the conflict.[14]

With the inclusion of human rights as a component of peace operations, the evolutions in peace operations and in the system of international human rights are increasingly inter-twined. David P. Forsythe argues that now "human rights and international security [are]difficult to deconstruct and fully separate."[15] This trend reflects both change in the nature and aims of peace operations, and the overall growth and visibility of human rights discourse through the formal recognition that human rights are vital

---

[12]   Establishment and authorisation of UNMIK is Security Council resolution U.N. Doc S/RES/1244 (10 June 1999). The authorising resolution for UNTAET is Security Council resolution U.N. Doc S/RES/1272 (25 October 1999). All official documents, including reports, resolutions and regulations, pertaining to UNMIK can be found at http://www.un.org/peace/kosovo/pages/kosovo1.shtml. All official documents, including reports, resolutions and regulations pertaining to UNTAET can be found at http://www.un.org/peace/etimor/docs/UntaetD.htm.

[13]   Human rights which have attained the status of customary international law are the rights against torture, genocide, slavery, and the principle of non-discrimination. See M.N. Shaw, *International Law* (4th ed, Cambridge University Press: Cambridge, 1997).

[14]   In some cases this was recognised by the parties to the conflict. For example, in El Salvador and Guatemala human rights occupied a primary position in the respective peace agreements, and thus the subsequent international presence.

[15]   D. Forsythe, 'Human Rights and International Security: United Nations Field Operations Redux' in M. Castermans-Holleman/F. Van Hoof/J. Smith (eds), *The Role of the Nation-State in the 21st Century: Human Rights, International Organisations and Foreign Policy – Essays in honour of Peter Baehr* (Kluwer Law International/The Hague, 1998), pp. 265-76, at 267.

Rachel Opie

for the achievement of the aims of the new form of peace operations.[16] As dominated by the 'human rights component', it is now a framework through which international human rights standards can be implemented in a post-settlement territory.

1.2 The Human Rights Component as a Mechanism for Human Rights Promotion and Protection

There has been a recent policy shift within the UN, supported by a large amount of rhetoric about the importance of human rights, which aims to 'mainstream' human rights into all the activities of the Organisation. In the report of the Secretary-General on *Renewing the United Nations: A Programme for Reform*, the intention is explicitly expressed to extend human rights activities through the reorganisation and restructuring of the human rights secretariat and *"the integration of human rights into all principal United Nations activities and programmes."* [17]

The result of the policy change for the promotion and protection of human rights should not be underestimated. However, it should also be seen as a long awaited fulfilment of a legal requirement to have the promotion and protection of human rights a primary objective of the UN. The mandate of the Charter of the United Nations 1945 ("the Charter"), to integrate the promotion and protection of human rights into all the activities of the UN can, for the UN and its specialised agencies, as Karen Kenny argues, "be understood as a constitutional requirement."[18]

Article 1 of the Charter establishes the purposes of the UN which includes achieving international co-operation "in promoting and encouraging respect for human rights".[19] Further, the UN is mandated to integrate human rights into all its activities. Article 55 provides that "with the view to the creation of conditions of stability and well-being which are necessary for peace and friendly relations among nations...the United Nations

---

[16] D. García-Sayán, 'Human Rights and Peace-Keeping Operations' in (3/1995) 29 *University of Richmond Law Review* 41-65, at 49.

[17] Report of the Secretary-General *Renewing the United Nations: A Programme for Reform*, U.N. Doc., A/51/950 (14 July 1997), at http://www.un.org/reform/track2/ hilights.htm. See also para. 196 at http://www.un.org/reform/track2/focus.htm#HR. Emphasis added.

[18] K. Kenny, 'Fulfilling the Promise of the UN Charter: Transformative Integration of Human Rights' (1999) 10 *Irish Studies in International Affairs* 43-52, at 44.

[19] The Charter of the United Nations, ("the Charter") 26 June 1945, Article 1 (3). The text can be found at the University of Minnesota Human Rights Library at http://www1.umn.edu/humanrts/instree/ ainstls1.htm

shall promote a universal respect for, and observance of, human rights and fundamental freedoms for all without distinction as to race, sex, language, or religion."[20] That this is also a direct obligation of the Member States is established in Article 56.[21] Kenny argues that human rights are at the forefront of the other aims of the Organisation, including the maintenance of peace and security and, consequently, the integration of human rights in to UN work "should not be seen as a mere policy decision of the secretary-general; rather it is a legal imperative flowing from the UN Charter and the nature of the international human rights law - as well as an operational imperative flowing from the practical observance that the denial of human rights is a source of international instability."[22]

Therefore, while the shift in policy headed by the Secretary-General is a welcome development, it should be seen in the context of a previously existing legal requirement significantly under-prioritised by the UN and member states. The inclusion, as discussed below, of a human rights component in peace operations also needs to be seen in this light.

Previous to the efforts to mainstream human rights into all UN activities, the development of mechanisms concentrated on both monitoring of international human right standards as expressed in the UN treaties and conventions, and dealing with the complaints of human rights violations. In brief, the conventional charter-based mechanisms are treaty monitoring bodies monitoring the implementation of the particular applicable treaty. They include activities of state reporting, state complaints and individual complaints under a particular treaty[23]. The extra-conventional mechanisms

---

[20]   The Charter, *supra* note 19, Article 55 (c).

[21]   The Charter, *supra* note 19, Article 56 reads "all Members pledge themselves to take joint and separate action in co-operation with the Organisation for the achievement of the purposes set forth in Article 55."

[22]   Kenny, *supra* note 18, at 44.

[23]   These mechanisms include the International Covenant on Economic, Social and Cultural Rights 1966 (ICESCR), Articles 16 - 18 set out procedure for state reporting; the International Covenant on Civil and Political Rights 1966 (ICCPR), Articles 41 - 42 establish state reporting and complaints procedures; The First Optional Protocol to the ICCPR 1966 establishes individual complaints mechanisms; International Convention on the Elimination of All Forms of Racial Discrimination 1969 (CERD), Article 9 provides for state reporting; the Covenant Against Torture and Other Cruel, Inhumane or Degrading Treatment or Punishment 1984 (CAT), Articles 19-22 set out procedures for state reporting and state and individual complaints; Convention on the Elimination of All Forms of Discrimination Against Women 1981 (CEDAW), Article 18 provides for state reporting; Convention on the Rights of the Child 1989 (CRC), Article 44 provides for state reporting. All the texts of these con-

incorporate Special Rapporteurs, Special Representatives, Special Envoys and Independent Experts, Working Groups and the Complaints Procedure 1503, all of which are now coordinated by the Office of the High Commissioner of Human Rights (OHCHR), the Commission of Human Rights (CHR) and its Sub-Commission. They include mechanisms for standard-setting, thematic investigations, and country-specific activities.

Similarly, other UN bodies were involved in human rights monitoring. The General Assembly has authority to make recommendations for actions regarding human rights and situations of human rights violations, and can pass resolutions condemning a state for human rights violations.[24] The Security Council acts as a mechanism through the developing practice of the establishment of peace enforcement operations under Chapter VII of the United Nations Charter on the grounds that the human rights violations contributed to the existence of a threat to international peace and security,[25] and by being the competent body for peace operations, so establishing the broad framework of promotion and protection of human rights in peace operations that is the subject of this article. Finally, the International Court of Justice (ICJ) and the International Tribunals established in the Former Yugoslavia, Rwanda and Sierra Leone are clearly intended to function to protect and promote human rights through their work in prose-

---

ventions, their status and ratification information at University of Minnesota Human Rights Library at http://www1.umn.edu/humanrts/instree/ainstls1.htm

[24] Practice has shown that the General Assembly can also be a mechanism for the promotion and protection of human rights in relation to establishing peacekeeping operations when the Security Council is prevented from acting, for example, through the exercise of the veto power. An example of this was the establishment and deployment of United Nations Emergency Force (UNEF I) in 1956. General Assembly resolution 997 (2 November 1956) established a force "to secure and supervise the cessation of hostilities" in Egypt and Israel. The legality of authorisation and subsequent deployment was tested by in the International Court of Justice in the *Expenses Case* (ICJ Rep. 1962, at 177) but was held to be legal. See S. Morphet, 'United Nations Peacekeeping and Election-Monitoring' in A. Roberts, and B. Kingsbury (eds) *United Nations, Divided World: The UN's Roles in International Relations* (2nd ed, Clarendon Press: Oxford, 1998), pp. 183-239, at 185, and P. Malanczuk, *Akehurst's Modern Introduction to International Law* (7th ed, Routledge: New York, 1997) at 417.

[25] H. Boekle, 'The United Nations and the International Protection of Human Rights: An Appraisal' (6/1997) 5 *International Peacekeeping* (Kluwer Law International/ The Hague) 182-193, at 191.

cution of persons responsible for violations of international humanitarian law.[26]

The culmination of the invigoration of activity in the area of human rights in the early 1990s was the creation of OHCHR in 1993. It was intended to facilitate the "continued adaptation of the United Nations human rights machinery to the current and future needs in the promotion and protection of human rights ..."[27] The High Commissioner was mandated with the task of [promoting] the universal respect for and observance of all human rights,"[28] and was given the "principal responsibility for United Nations human rights activities under the direction and authority of the Secretary-General ..." Following that, the High Commissioner was given a number of responsibilities, which can be broadly defined as providing, enhancing and coordinating activities which will serve to protect and promote all human rights.[29]

It can be argued that there is a lack of ongoing support for the OHCHR, demonstrated by the minimal funding allocated, and little actual institutional support.[30] However, its creation was a principal structural innovation for human rights in the UN, and it gave a firm institutional basis for the further development of human rights and incorporation of human rights-based activities into the UN system. It also served, significantly, to indicate the growing realisation of the importance of human rights as a major concern of the UN.

It is the OHCHR which has been responsible for the creation and rapid institutionalisation of the mechanisms of technical cooperation and field presences through which the OHCHR assists countries in the promotion

[26] Kenny, *supra* note 18, at 43. Articles 92-96 of the Charter establish the International Court of Justice (ICJ). Security Council resolution 827, U.N. Doc. S/RES/827, (25 May 1993), created the International Criminal Tribunal for the Former Yugoslavia (ICTY). Security Council resolution 955, UN Doc. S/RES/955 (8 November 1994), created the International Criminal Tribunal for Rwanda (ICTR). Security Council resolution 1315, U.N. Doc. S/RES/1315 (14 August 2000) authorised the establishment of a "Special Court" in Sierra Leone. The Report of the Secretary-General on the Establishment of a Special Court for Sierra Leone, UN Doc. S/2000/915 (4 October 2000), provides the details for the Court, at http://www.un.org/documents

[27] General Assembly Resolution, U.N. Doc. A/RES/48/141, (7 January 1994).

[28] A/RES/48/141, *supra* note 27, at para. 3 (a).

[29] A/RES/48/141, *supra* note 27, at para. 4.

[30] See, for example, 'Robinson quits UN human rights post' in *The Guardian Weekly* March 22-March 28 (Vol.164, No.13), at 1, where she cites frustrations at the lack of support for the OHCHR as a major reason for her resignation. She withdrew her resignation later.

and protection of human rights in particular areas. The movement of human rights to the field can be considered the major innovation in international promotion and protection of human rights since the end of the Cold War.[31] Karen Kenny describes it as "a watershed move into the implementation of human rights."[32] To state the obvious, while standard-setting, and investigative, monitoring and reporting mechanisms remain essential, human rights remain abstracted without their concrete realisation. Likewise, the previously established mechanisms have clearly been insufficient in dealing with human rights violations, and a new strategy was required. The development of technical cooperation and field presence activities were the beginnings of an approach that is moving towards the actual implementation of the norms and standards. Further, it represents an important shift whereby the UN is no longer confined to operating in the international sphere, but is able to directly contribute to the process of the promotion and protection of human rights at national level.[33]

'Human rights components' in peace operations take this form of activity one step further through their direct intention to introduce and incorporate international human rights in post-settlement states.[34] The human rights component has two vital roles. It is an important aspect in moving a society beyond a situation of conflict and the surrounding related culture of conflict,[35] and is a critical mechanism for the spreading and implementation of human rights norms and standards. It has the potential to be par-

---

[31]   M. Nowak, 'The New Trend Towards Re-Politicising Human Rights' in Castermans-Holleman/Van Hoof/Smith (eds), *supra* note 14, pp. 151-61, at 157.

[32]   Kenny, *supra* note 18, at 45.

[33]   H. Hey, 'Peace Operations: New Opportunities for the United Nations to Promote and Protect Human Rights in the 21st Century' in Castermans-Holleman/Van Hoof/Smith (eds), *supra* note 15, pp. 307-26, at 326.

[34]   The ability of human rights to play a role in peace operations was enhanced by formation of the Memorandum of Understanding (MOU) between OHCHR and the UN Department of Peacekeeping (DPKO) on 5 November, 1999. It aimed to increase the effectiveness of UN peacekeeping and human rights activities through enhanced cooperation between the two agencies.

[35]   There is a ongoing debate as to whether human rights can be a determining factor in attaining peace, and human rights could also lead to unrest and conflict through the greater awareness by people of previously unknown human rights norms. See B.V.A. Röling, 'Peace Research and Peace-keeping' in A. Cassese (ed),*United Nations Peace-keeping: Legal Essays* (Sijthoff and Noordhoff International Publishers: Alphen aan den Rijn, 1978), pp. 245-252, at 249. However, this article is dealing with human rights as an important factor in the process of leading a society beyond conflict once a form of settlement has been reached.

ticularly effective because the overall goal, and thus 'ideal' outcome, of a 'human rights component' is the embodiment of international human rights into the fabric of the society, structurally and culturally. Depending on the success of the operation and of the component, human rights standards will then inform the structure of the post-settlement society, and will continue to remain in play, impacting on (to an unknown degree) the nature of societal relations from that point on. (This also, of course, depends on the continuance of supporting factors, such as a democratic government and the respect of the state for human rights, functioning human rights machinery, for example, human rights commissions or Ombudsperson institutions, and human rights education).

The peace operation represents another mechanism for the effective distribution, incorporation, and the ongoing future presence of human rights in post-conflict societies. It provides the framework for their potentially extensive influence on all aspects of an operation. In addition, while it is not possible to be definitive, it is likely that the trend of including human rights components in peace operations will continue, and will remain a significant aspect of the work of the UN. Therefore, this mechanism for the promotion and protection of human rights is vital to the general international system of human rights and requires greater visibility as such in its various dimensions.

Section Two: Human Rights in Peace Building

This section will discuss the concept of peace building, and how the human rights component is inextricably linked to its aims and objectives. The evolution of peace building as a fundamental strategy for the resolution of conflict has meant that it has become a primary task in peace operations. Human rights have a strong and important relationship with peace building and are essential for its aims and purposes. The desired outcomes of peace building are dependent on the development of human rights-based institutions and culture. It is this centrality of the human rights component to peace building which gives peace operations the potential strength as a mechanism for the promotion and protection of human rights. On the assumption that peace building will continue to be a feature of the work of the UN, the dominant presence of human rights through human rights-based activities in peace operations works to increase and re-inforce the realisation of international human rights.[36]

2.1 The Characteristics of Peace Building in UN Peace Operations

The concept of peace building was first formalised in the *Agenda for Peace* where "post-conflict peace-building" was identified as a phase of the international community's intervention in conflict situations.[37] There is no accepted definition for peace building but it does broadly encompasses three elements:[38]

- external (international) intervention to help create the conditions con-ducive to peace.
- rehabilitation, reconstruction and reconciliation of societies which have experienced (and may be continuing to experience) armed con-flict; and
- creation of the security-related, political and/or socio-economic mechanisms to facilitate the building of working relationships and/or trust between the parties to the conflict, so to prevent a resumption of conflict;

Although not implemented to the same degree as the aspects above, ad-dressing the root causes of the conflict as sources of enmity and potential destabilisation for a peace process is key to peace building. Together, these elements are intended to achieve the ultimate goal: a just, stable and sustainable peace, or perhaps less ambitiously, reducing the risk of re-sumption of violent conflict, and contributing to the creation of conditions "most conducive to reconciliation, reconstruction and recovery."[39]

---

[36] Human rights based activities are those which are inspired by international human rights standards and norms. One example is the exercise of institution-building or structural (re)creation and development done in accordance with internationally rec-ognised standards of human rights.

[37] Report of the Secretary-General *The Agenda for Peace: Preventive Diplomacy, Peacemaking and Peacekeeping* pursuant to the statement adopted by the Summit Meeting of the Security Council on 31 January 1992, U.N. Doc., A/47/277-S/24/111 (17 June 1992) at http://www.un.org/Docs/SG/agpeace.html

[38] C.-P. David, 'Does Peace Building Build Peace?' (1/1999) 30 *Security Dialogue* 25-45, at 27.

[39] O. Ramsbotham, 'Reflections on UN Post-Settlement Peacebuilding' (1/2000) 7 *InternationalPeacekeeping* (Frank Cass/London) 169-189, at 172.

Operationally, peace building by the UN includes, but not exclusively, the creation or strengthening of national institutions, monitoring elections, promoting human rights, providing for reintegration and rehabilitation programs, and creating conditions for resumed development.[40] The form of this intervention has been primarily one of "structural negotiation."[41] It is based on the premise that establishing the structures of a Western liberal democracy and market economy, which includes the dominant focus on civil and political rights, will serve to address the causes of conflict and continue to exist as means of peaceful resolution of future disputes after the international presence has departed.

However, the predominant focus on societal structures is increasingly being recognised as insufficient for resolving violent, protracted conflict and attaining sustainable peace. An alternative view of peace building encompasses, at a minimum, another level of engagement with the society. Related, it requires that peace is not simply viewed as a 'stage', but as "a dynamic social construct".[42] This wider view incorporates different approaches, for example, 'peace building-from-below', to work with the emotional and psychological aftermath of conflict, or the "cognitive" structures, which play a defining role in the nature of relationships,[43] and to provide options to embedded cultures of violence. It is premised on the belief that for most people who have been affected by violent conflict, it has been a process of loss, pain and suffering, and therefore there exist deep grievances, which, if there is to be a move towards peace, must be properly engaged with and reconciled. Peace building in this sense "has as its primary goal the *healing of human relations* within the target community..."[44] It is an overtly political process which ideally should create a situation whereby there is a "reciprocated sense among actors of moral obligation to refrain from violence, coupled with a commitment to seek and abide by peaceful means of resolution of political disputes."[45] It is at this level that reconciliation can occur.

---

[40]   Report of the Secretary-General to the Security Council *Causes of Conflict and Promotion of Durable Peace and Sustainable Development in Africa*, UN Doc. S/1998/318, 16 April 1998, para. 63, at http://www.un.org/ecosocdev/geninfo/afrec/sgreport/index.html

[41]   F. Wilmer, 'Social Construction of Conflict and Reconciliation in the Former Yugoslavia' in (4/1998) 25 *Social Justice* 90-113, at 93.

[42]   Lederach, *supra* note 2, at 20.

[43]   Wilmer, *supra* note 41, at 93.

[44]   Griffin, *supra* note 8, at 9. Emphasis added.

[45]   Wilmer, *supra* note 41, at 93.

Peace building is a relatively new aspect of the overall international peace and security strategy of the UN and it is undergoing constant re-conceptualisation. The UN is still following a particular operational model, one that is largely based on the belief, albeit not borne out in practice, in the ability of liberal democratic structures to work as sufficient transformative means to move a society from violent conflict to peace.[46] However, increasingly there is an awareness that structural development without deeper societal reconciliation is not leading to lasting peace.

Equally importantly, human rights have a vital role to play in working with the 'cognitive structures' of a post-settlement society. The close and mutually reinforcing relationship of peace and human rights is recognised in Articles 1 and 55 of the Charter, and has been discussed previously with reference to Karen Kenny.[47] Increasingly it is understood that violations of human rights are not only a consequence of conflict, but are a factor of instability and insecurity which may spark conflict.[48] The recognition of this has been formalised by the inclusion of human rights in peace operations, in particular through peace building, notwithstanding that conceptually and in practice there is significant room for improvement.

Human rights influence the structural and institutional framework which supports all other initiatives taken and without which the work done within the operations has a greater chance of collapse after, or even before, the departure of the international community. They facilitate structural development grounded in principles of participation, equality, and non-discrimination, and highlight how other structures contrary to human rights standards and norms have previously existed. As such, the process creates the foundations and the basic societal capacity for a culture of on-going future realisation of human rights, and the greater potential for sustainable peace.

Furthermore, human rights-based activities foster the introduction and assimilation of ideas and values which have the potential to alter the bases of relationships between previously polarised groups in post-settlement societies. It is an area through which, as peace building evolves beyond its focus on structural development, the present role of human rights could be significantly increased and deepened. In this context, human rights constitute an important framework within which to address the underlying and

---

[46] See the discussion by Wilmer, *supra* note 41.

[47] Above, at p. 4. See Kenny, *supra* note 18.

[48] Græger, *supra* note 11, at 182.

not so readily expressed 'roots' of conflict, and provide an adaptable base from which to begin to transform them, ideally culminating in the resolution of the conflict. Owen Fiss argues that human rights can be seen as primarily social ideals and therefore "operate as ideals do – as aspiration. They are not a projection of an idle utopia, but inform and infuse expectations and demands of the here and now. They constitute a culture ... and as such serve as a basis for discussion, criticism, and even more, concrete action."[49] Human rights viewed in this sense provide an alternative conception of societal organisation than one immersed in a paradigm of violent conflict. In this respect, human rights are fundamental to the processes of reconciliation, and re-definition and restoration of relationships on all levels of society, from intra-familial to state-citizen relations.

2.2 Defining the Human Rights Component

What constitutes the human rights component is naturally a matter of definition. Generally, it has been viewed restrictively, limited to human rights operations falling directly within the ambit of the formal 'Human Rights Component'. This Component is considered to represent the sole contribution of human rights to the peace operation. However, this definition fails to give a true picture of the role of human rights. Instead, the human rights component is constitutive of all human rights-based activities. It is not limited to the formal human rights structure provided directly by the mandates, but influences the undertakings of all other components.

There are two primary forms of human rights operations (HROs): those that together form a human rights component of a peace operation, and those that exist independently of other forms of international intervention or in the absence of any other international presence. It is the former that will be the focus of this article but the basic features of both are largely synonymous. While, HROs are difficult to define because of the diversity of functions and goals they incorporate, Karen Kenny, drawing on Stephen Golub, nonetheless identifies HROs as having the following features:

Organized by an intergovernmental body such as the UN; based in a country for at least several months, as opposed to visiting it for shorter periods; central functions at the very least include observing, or more typically include investigating, documenting and/or reporting on, human rights violations and situations likely to give rise to such violations, and often

---

[49]   O.M. Fiss, 'Human Rights as Social Ideals' in C. Hesse/R. Post (eds) *Human Rights in Political Transitions: Gettysburg to Bosnia* (Zone Books: New York, 1999) pp. 263-76, at 266.

additional tasks such as human rights education and technical assistance; and staffed by at least a dozen monitors, and typically several dozen or more.[50]

However, HROs that contribute to a peace operation have to be considered in the light of the context of the peace operation itself. As such, they are part of peace building in the attempt to negotiate and oversee political transitions, and in terms of the approaches to peace building to date involve "the design and supervision of constitutional, judicial and electoral reforms, the observation, supervision, organization and conduct of elections, creation of national institutions, including civilian police forces."[51]

Finally, and in addition, human rights are more generally intended to inform the entire peace operation and form the basis of a significant proportion of the activities undertaken. Therefore, while most recent peace operations have had a defined 'human rights component', the actual human rights-based activities that take place in a peace operation are significantly more extensive and exist outside those defined boundaries. This is demonstrated in the following discussion of the peace operations of UN-MIK and UNTAET.

Section Three: The UNMIK and UNTAET Experiences

The operations in Kosovo and East Timor represent the two last stages in the evolution of peace operations by the UN. Here, the UN has undertaken previously unprecedented involvement in the political processes and societal rebuilding of two territories so as to transform the societies from a situation of violent conflict to peace. Despite the aim to establish structure in Kosovo which would lead to 'substantial self-government', it remains a

---

[50]   K. Kenny, 'Introducing the Sustainability Principle to Human Rights Operations' in (4/1997) 4 *International Peacekeeping* (Frank Cass/London) 61-78, at 61-62. On the basis of this list, she identifies the following as having been HROs: the Human Rights Division of the United Nations Observer Mission in El Salvador (ONUSAL); the International Civilian Mission in Haiti (MICIVIH); the human rights component of the United Nations Transitional Authority in Cambodia (UNTAC); the United Nations Human Rights Field Operation in Rwanda (HRFOR); the United Nations Mission for the Verification of Human Rights in Guatemala (MINUGUA); and the OSCE mission in Bosnia and Herzegovina after the Dayton Agreement on 21 November 1995.

[51]   R. Müllerson, 'Fifty Years of the United Nations' in R. Blackburn and J.J. Busuttil, *Human Rights for the 21st Century* (Pinter: London, 1997), pp. 140-161, at 151.

province of the Former Republic of Yugoslavia (FRY) and the sovereignty and territorial integrity is reaffirmed in resolution 1244. In contrast, the issue of sovereignty was avoided when planning for UNTAET.[52] Instead, for the first time, albeit not explicitly, the Security Council bestowed full sovereign powers to the UN over East Timor, to be exercised through UNTAET.[53] In East Timor, the UN is in a new position whereby it has complete control and responsibility for the reconstruction of a post-settlement society. Through the comparison of the peace operations in Kosovo and East Timor, this section will centre the arguments made above in the context of the two continuing operations.

A general analysis of the mandates will indicate the similarities in the approach of the peace operations deployed in Kosovo and East Timor despite the differences in region, history, culture, politics and form of conflict. This includes the approach to human rights, with one modification. The treatment of human rights in UNMIK and UNTAET differs in their respective mandates, but going beyond the primary authorising documents it can be seen that human rights are intended to be part of the fabric of the operation. The extent of their intended presence is the key to the potential strength of the human rights component as a mechanism. I will demonstrate that peace operations incorporate a very substantial human rights-basis through the activities, carried out in the framework of peace building, that can broadly be said to form the human rights component of the operation.

---

[52] J. Chopra, 'The UN's Kingdom in East Timor' in (3/2000) 42 *Survival*, 27-39, at 29. Note, however, that in the initial stages of planning, before the deployment of UNAMET to organise and hold the popular consultation, the issue of sovereignty was at the forefront of discussions between the Governments of Portugal and Indonesia and the UN. In the "5th of May" Agreement between the Republic of Indonesia and the Portuguese Republic on the Question of East Timor (5 May 1999), the position of the Government of Indonesia was clearly stated: "the proposed special autonomy should be implemented only as an end solution to the question of East Timor with full recognition of Indonesian sovereignty over East Timor." See Preamble, at http://www.un.org/peace/etimor99/agreement/agreeframe_Eng01.html

[53] Security Council Resolution, U.N. Doc. S/RES/1272 (25 October 1999), para. 1. It states that UNTAET "will be endowed with overall responsibility for the administration of East Timor and will be empowered to exercise all legislative and executive authority, including the administration of justice." This power is exercised through the Special Representative of the Secretary-General.

3.1 The Mandates and Structures of UNMIK and UNTAET

UNMIK and UNTAET are defined as an 'integrated, multidimensional' operations. They are operations that are intended to be a form of temporary governance in territories undergoing processes of political transition. They are under the authority of the Security Council of the UN, vested in the Secretary-General, and exercised by the Special Representative of the Secretary-General (SRSG) who forms the apex of the 'on the ground' organisational structure. All the legislative and executive powers, including those of the administration of the judiciary, are vested in the interim administration or transitional authority.[54] The SRSG has full executive power, and in the field of legislative power is able to change, repeal or suspend any laws "to the extent necessary for carrying out his functions, or where existing laws are incompatible with the mandate, aims and purposes of the civil administration."[55] In both operations, the SRSGs hold an enormous degree of power, which is relatively unchecked. However, the inclusion of human rights in the operations provide a clearly important restraint on the exercise of the power of the SRSG.

The overall structure of UNMIK and UNTAET represents the primary difference between the two operations. UNMIK is unique in the respect that no operation before has been designed in which other intergovernmental organisations have worked alongside the UN in such an 'equally cooperative' relationship. A different intergovernmental organisation is responsible for a different component. The mandate states that "the four components of UNMIK will act in an 'integrated manner' to attain the objectives set out in paragraph 11" of resolution 1244 (1999).[56] This is particularly important in the light of the admission that the tasks that are intended to be carried out would go beyond the competence and capabilities of one organisation, and thus while there are specific tasks assigned to

---

[54] Report of the Secretary-General on the Interim Administration Mission in Kosovo, U.N. Doc. S/1999/779 (12 July 1999) para. 35; Security Council Resolution 1272, U.N. Doc. S/RES/1272 (25 October 1999), para. 1; Report of the Secretary-General of the Situation in East Timor, U.N. Doc. S/1999/1024, (4 October 1999), para. 26.

[55] Report of the Secretary-General, S/1999/779, *supra* note 54, para. 39; Report of the Secretary-General, S/1999/1024, *supra* note 54, para. 32. By contrast, the mandate for UNTAET goes further, excluding the provision that the Special Representative must act to the extent necessary, or where the laws are incompatible with the mandate. Rather, Paragraph 32 provides, "The Special Representative will have the power to enact new laws and regulations, and to amend, suspend or repeal existing ones."

[56] Report of the Secretary-General, S/1999/779, *supra* note 54, para. 53.

each component, cooperation between them is considered essential.[57] The relevance to human rights can be seen; the structure calls for a degree of fluidity between organisations and components, thereby allowing for human rights activities and considerations to inform all components of the operation.

The four components are as follows: the UN is responsible for the Civil Administration component in which public administration/civil affairs, police, and judicial affairs are incorporated. The Institution-Building component is lead by the Organisation for Security and Cooperation in Europe (OSCE). This component is responsible for democratisation and institution-building, elections, and human rights. UNHCR is responsible for the Humanitarian component, which incorporates humanitarian assistance, and mine action, and the EU is the overseeing agency for the Reconstruction component. The military component, KFOR, composed primarily by NATO personnel, was authorised by the Security Council, and remains separate from the interim administration.[58] However, close coordination is required with UNMIK.

While it was stated by the Secretary-General in his report of 12 July 1999 that the "cooperation of the lead agencies and those other organizations which will contribute to the four components will set a precedent for the future",[59] this model of organisation for peace operations was not followed in respect of East Timor. Rather, the UN is responsible for overseeing all the components of the operation and their tasks. It can be argued, however, that the UN does not possess the experience or expertise to undertake a mission like this on its own, and in fact multi-organisational input is required. This is overcome by UNTAET being mandated to work with other agencies where necessary. The report of the Secretary-General provided for the conclusion of "such international agreements with States and international organizations as may necessary for carrying out of the functions of UNTAET in East Timor."[60] This is further stressed in the authorising resolution which states that the Security Council "recognizes that, in developing and performing its functions under its mandate, UNTAET will need to draw on the expertise and capacity of Member States,

---

[57] See Report of the Secretary-General, S/1999/779, *supra* note 54, para. 118.

[58] Security Council Resolution 1244, *supra* note 12, at Annex Two.

[59] Report of the Secretary-General, S/1999/779, *supra* note 54, para. 118.

[60] Report of the Secretary-General, S/1999/779, *supra* note 54, para. 35.

Rachel Opie

United Nations agencies and other international organizations, including the international financial institutions."[61]

The main components of UNTAET were determined as being a:

- Governance and Public Administration component which includes five divisions: judicial affairs, civilian police, economic, financial and development affairs, public services, and electoral affairs, and provides for district administrations;
- Humanitarian Assistance and Emergency Rehabilitation component; and
- Military component.[62]

Broadly, the objectives of both the missions are the same. They focus on:

- institutional development and capacity-building in areas of democracy and good governance, the judiciary, civil society, including the media,
- correctional facilities and the police, hoping thus to create the conditions for effective administration;
- development of the institutional capacity for supporting and holding of elections;
- undertaking confidence-building measures;
- both short-term and long-term humanitarian assistance, rehabilitation and reconstruction;
- the emergency provision of, and reconstruction of public services; and,
- the promotion of economic and social recovery and development through economic reconstruction.

As will be discussed below, UNMIK was also specifically mandated to promote and protect human rights. This was not an explicit objective of UNTAET.

Therefore, while the operational structure differs in the sense of UNMIK being jointly run by regional organisations and the UN, and UNTAET being a 'UN operation', the overall framework is very similar. The division of tasks between components is roughly the same, and the objectives concentrate on the same areas of institutional and capacity-building. In broad terms, this indicates a basic structural approach to peace building

---

[61] Security Council Resolution 1272, S/RES/1272, *supra* note 12, para. 5.

[62] See Report of the Secretary-General, S/1999/1024, *supra* note 54.

as undertaken by the UN, and implies a model which is now, or may become, institutionalised within the UN.

3.2 The Human Rights Components of UNMIK and UNTAET

This uniformity of approach is carried through to the treatment of human rights, and how human rights are incorporated into the peace operations through the human rights components. By looking at the peace operations of UNMIK and UNTAET it can be seen that the provision for human rights is significant. This is both in terms of the power of influence on the operations in their entirety, and in terms of the types of activities intended to be undertaken by the operations. Here, these activities are conceived as also contributing to the human rights component along with the HROs that have previously been seen to be constitutive of the human rights component. Together, they allow for a considerably broader conception of what constitutes a human rights component and thus a more accurate picture of the role of human rights in a peace operation.

At an initial glance, the mandates authorising UNMIK and UNTAET provide for differing degrees of inclusion of human rights in each operation. However, the common use of the regulation-making powers by SRSGs which effectively put human rights at the core of both the peace operations, and the similar provisions for the human rights supporting structures, means the intended role of human rights in the peace operations of UNMIK and UNTAET is very strong indeed. [63]

3.2.1 Human Rights as the Foundation for UNMIK and UNTAET and the Standards Applied

In UNMIK and UNTAET, human rights considerations are legally required to form the basis of the operations. This builds on the structural provisions for human rights discussed briefly below but goes further because it effectively makes human rights a consideration for all who are working within the operations. Therefore, human rights should impact on all the work done by the operation. In this sense, human rights exist outside of the previously defined human rights component, and as a key to the whole operation.

---

[63] See below for the discussion of how this was done through UNMIK Regulation No.1999/1. On the Authority of the Interim Administration in Kosovo, U.N. Doc. UNMIK/REG/1999/1 (23 July 1999), and UNTAET Regulation No. 1 On the Authority of the Transitional Administration in East Timor U.N. Doc UN-TAET/REG/1999/1 (27 November 1999).

Rachel Opie

The mandate for UNMIK provides for the promotion and protection of human rights as a primary objective.[64] The Secretary-General defines what he considers this to mean and thus what is needed to fulfil the objective:

In its resolution 1244 (1999), the Security Council requests UNMIK to protect and promote human rights in Kosovo. In assuming its responsibilities, UNMIK will be guided by internationally recognized standards of human rights *as the basis for the exercise of its authority* in Kosovo. UNMIK *will embed a culture of human rights in all areas of activity,* and *will adopt human rights policies in respect of its administrative functions.*[65]

This paragraph is further strengthened by Regulation No. 1/1999 promulgated by the SRSG in establishing the applicable law.[66] Section Two of this regulation is the most relevant for this discussion. It provides:

Observance of internationally recognised standards:
In exercising their functions, all persons undertaking public duties or holding public office in Kosovo shall observe internationally recognized human rights standards and shall not discriminate against any person on any ground such as sex, race, colour, language, political or other opinion, national, ethnic or social origin, association with a national community, property, birth or other status.

A later regulation, section 1, paragraph 3 of UNMIK Regulation No. 1999/24 gave greater clarity as to what, in the context of Kosovo, constituted internationally recognised standards of human rights. The wording of the provision does not exclude other possible documents incorporating human rights standards, but explicitly includes:

- The Universal Declaration of Human Rights of 10 December 1948;
- The European Convention for the Protection of Human Rights and Fundamental Freedoms of 4 November 1950 and the Protocols thereto;
- The International Covenant on Civil and Political Rights of 16 December 1966 and the Protocols thereto;

---

[64] Security Council Resolution 1272, *supra* note 12, para. 11(j).

[65] Report of the Secretary-General, S/1999/779, *supra* note 54, para 42. Emphasis added.

[66] UNMIK/REG/1999/1 *supra* note 63.

- The International Covenant on Economic, Social and Cultural Rights of 16 December 1966;
- The Convention on the Elimination of All Forms of Racial Discrimination of 21 December 1965;
- The Convention on the Elimination of All Forms of Discrimination Against Women of 17 December 1979;
- The Convention Against Torture and Other Cruel, Inhumane or Degrading Treatment or Punishment of 17 December 1984;
- The International Convention on the Rights of the Child of 20 December 1989.[67]

Therefore, not only is the promotion and protection of human rights a primary objective for the operation in Kosovo but it is explicitly provided that the 'internationally recognised standards of human rights' are legally required to constitute the foundation of the operation. The applicable law binds all authorities, including the SRSG, of the Transitional Administration. Therefore, human rights will be a primary consideration in all decision-making and formulation of initiatives by the operation. As such, the potential for human rights to have the key influencing role in UNMIK is significant.

In contrast, in its objectives UNTAET is mandated to facilitate the promotion and protection of human rights through the tasks of institution-building[68] and through compliance of the indigenous security structures with international human rights norms and standards.[69] However, the promotion and protection of human rights is not an objective in and of itself. It appears, therefore, that the protection and promotion of human rights for the operation in East Timor is only intended to be a consequence of the objective of creating "non-discriminatory and impartial institutions",[70] and not a determinative factor in the undertaking of the operation as a whole.

However, in the first exercise of his regulation-making power, the SRSG for East Timor allows a different conclusion to be drawn. Section 2 of UNTAET Regulation No. 1999/1 reads:

---

[67] UNMIK Regulation No. 1999/24 U.N. Doc. UNMIK/REG/1999/24 On the Law Applicable in Kosovo (12 December 1999), s. 1(3).

[68] Report of the Secretary-General, S/1999/1024, *supra* note 54, para. 29(h) provides, "to create non-discriminatory and impartial institutions, particularly those of judiciary and police, to ensure the establishment and maintenance of the rule of law and to promote and protect human rights."

[69] Report of the Secretary-General, S/1999/1024, *supra* note 54, para. 29(m).

[70] Report of the Secretary-General, S/1999/1024, *supra* note 54, para. 29(h).

Rachel Opie

Section Two
Observance of internationally recognized standards
In exercising their functions, all persons undertaking public duties or holding public office in East Timor shall observe internationally recognized human rights standards, as reflected, in particular, in:

- The Universal Declaration on Human Rights of 10 December 1948;
- The International Covenant on Civil and Political Rights of 16 December 1966 and its Protocols;
- The International Covenant on Economic, Social and Cultural Rights of 16 December 1966;
- The Convention on the Elimination of All Forms of Racial Discrimination of 21 December 1965;
- The Convention on the Elimination of All Forms of Discrimination Against Women of 17 December 1979;
- The Convention Against Torture and other Cruel, Inhumane or Degrading Treatment or Punishment of 17 December 1984;
- The International Convention on the Rights of the Child of 20 November 1989.

They shall not discriminate against any person on any ground such as sex, race, colour, language, religion, political or other opinion, national, ethnic or social origin, association with a national community, property, birth or all other status.[71]

Obviously, this is essentially the same as Section 2 of UNMIK Regulation No. 1999/1. The differences are that paragraph 3 of UNMIK Regulation No. 1999/24 has been incorporated into section 2 of UNTAET Regulation No. 1999/1, and for clear geographical and therefore applicability reasons, the European Convention for the Protection of Human Rights and Fundamental Freedoms 1950, and its Protocols, have not been included.

As has been seen in the description of the objectives of UNTAET, the primary, if not sole focus, is various forms of public service. Although not specifically using the words 'protection and promotion', by legally requiring all those working in the transitional administration to 'observe' internationally recognised standards of human rights, this regulation requires that human rights are a primary consideration for all activities in the op-

---

[71]   UNTAET/REG/1999/1 *supra* note 63.

eration. If read alongside paragraph 42 of Security Council resolution 1024 which defined what was to be considered promotion and protection of human rights in UNMIK, the effect is very similar. By legally requiring that internationally recognised standards of human rights are 'observed' by all those in the public arena or undertaking public duties, the regulation is effectively making those standards the 'basis for the exercise of authority in East Timor, allowing a resulting 'culture of human rights', and ensuring that human rights policies will be adopted by the interim administration in the exercise of its functions.

Furthermore, the purpose of these provisions is to provide a foundation on which the applicable law of Kosovo and East Timor must be made and reviewed. They also provide a tool for guiding the day-to-day application of the law. The applicable law in Kosovo was eventually determined to be that before 22 March 1989, the regulations promulgated by the SRSG, and their subsidiary instruments. Where there is a gap in this law, the law in existence after 22 March 1989 can be applied. However, that application is subject to the accordance of that law with internationally recognised standards of human rights.[72] In East Timor the applicable law is that in existence prior to 25 October 1999 provided that it does not conflict with the internationally recognised standards included in section two above. In accordance with this, UNTAET Regulation No. 1999/1 provided that a number of Indonesian laws which were directly in conflict with internationally recognised standards of human rights were no longer considered law in East Timor.[73]

Consequentially, while the mandates provide the legal authority and guidance for the implementation of the peace operations, UNMIK and UNTAET Regulations No. 1999/1, and UNMIK Regulation No.1999/24 directly and legally bind all those the working in the civil administration to the observance of international human rights standards. They also subject the application of the national laws to international human rights standards. What then becomes determinative of the actual role of human rights

---

[72]   UNMIK/REG/1999/24 *supra* note 67, ss. 1 and 2. This regulation amended UN-MIK/REG/1999/1 as a result of the refusal of Kosovo Albania judges and prosecutors to apply the law after 22 March 1989 because it constituted the law applied in Kosovo after its loss of autonomy to Serbia.

[73]   UNTAET/REG/1999/1 *supra* note 63, s. 3. Section 3.2 lists the inapplicable Indonesian laws as: Law on Anti-Subversion, Law on Social Organizations, Law on National Security, Law on National Protection and Defence, Law on Mobilization and Demobilization, Law on Defence and Security. 25 October 1999 is the date on which UNTAET was authorised to be deployed in East Timor.

in peace operations, is what to "be guided", to "observe", and to "embed a culture of human rights", means in light of the current practice.

3.2.2 Supportive Structures for Human Rights in UNMIK and UNTAET

In addition to forming the basis of UNMIK and UNTAET, the mandates for each operation provide for a clear human rights structure which aids in the 'direct' promotion and protection of human rights and acts as a focal point for the overall integration of human rights considerations throughout the operations. Firstly, the SRSGs are to be directly advised by a human rights 'unit'. In UNMIK, this is a Senior Human Rights Adviser who is mandated to directly advise the SRSG on human rights issues and to "ensure a pro-active approach on human rights in *all* UNMIK activities..."[74] In UNTAET, an Office for Human Rights Affairs is intended to advise the SRSG in the exercise of "his/her duties",[75] which by implication covers all the activities of the operation.

Secondly, in UNMIK, human rights are granted further structural support within the 'formal' human rights component overseen by OCSE as an aspect of the Institution-Building component. Within this, a "core of human rights monitors and advisors"[76], a gender advisory unit, and very importantly, the establishment of an Ombudsperson Institution[77] are provided for. Here, the mandate indicates the extent of overlap human rights will have with other tasks, and particularly with those defined as 'civil administration', for example judicial affairs, and with institution-building generally. Although these activities are allocated to other components, they have an obvious human rights-basis because they are informed by, and are implementing, relevant norms and standards of human rights throughout the processes of their establishment.

The mandate for UNTAET does not provide for a 'formal' human rights component. But, the mandate does provide for a predominance of human rights-based activities within the framework of the operation, and a supporting human rights structure. The mandate makes provisions for a human rights structure similar to UNMIK. Paragraph 42 of the report of the Secretary-General establishes an East Timorese Human Rights Institution which will function as a focal point for all human rights activities, and

---

[74] Report of the Secretary-General, S/1999/779, *supra* note 54, para. 49. Emphasis added.

[75] Report of the Secretary-General, S/1999/1024, *supra* note 54, para. 41.

[76] Report of the Secretary-General, S/1999/779, *supra* note 54, para. 87.

[77] Report of the Secretary-General, S/1999/779, *supra* note 54, para. 89-90.

will provide human rights input into *all* other activities of the operation.[78] It is also directly mandated to provide assistance and guidance to the SRSG. As with the human rights aspect of the Institution-Building component in UNMIK, this Institution is staffed with human rights monitors, investigators and advisors, and is also tasked with developing the East Timorese capacity in human rights. Further, a Public Information Office is provided for whose role is to develop democratic media, and to promote understanding and respect for human rights standards and institutions.[79]

These provisions for human rights in UNMIK and UNTAET result in a structure which is sufficient to ensure that human rights impact on the operations taken in their entirety. The provision of a central institution ensures human rights-based activities can be undertaken and coordinated. Through the lines of communication that are opened to the SRSG and other components and agencies working both within and in coordination with the administrations, the influence of human rights on all activities is facilitated. However, the extent that this structure is able to be fully utilised to ensure widespread and significant influence is also dependent on other critical factors, such as resources and the overall management approaches.

This analysis indicates the depth of inclusion that is provided for international human rights. It demonstrates that human rights have the potential to pervade all aspects of the peace operations in Kosovo and East Timor, including where a specific human rights component has not been mandated. Therefore, it is not sufficient to limit the conception of the 'human rights component' to that which is currently 'formally' ascribed as such. Rather, it is important to view the human rights component as that which encompasses all the activities and tasks of a peace operation which are human rights based, and takes account of the extent to which human rights can impact on all decision-making and policy implementation of an operation through their legally required observation and consideration.

The importance of taking a broader view, for the purposes of this article, is to properly understand the degree with which human rights can potentially be promoted and protected within the context of a peace operation. It indicates the substantial presence of human rights in peace operations, and therefore highlights the potential strength of the human rights component as a mechanism in the international system of protection and promotion of human rights. In consideration of the fact that the promotion

---

[78] Report of the Secretary-General, S/1999/1024, *supra* note 54.
[79] Report of the Secretary-General, S/1999/1024, *supra* note 54, para. 43.

Rachel Opie

and protection of human rights is a legal requirement for the UN and its agencies, peace operations provide an important opportunity for the UN to fulfil this obligation. Understanding the actual position of human rights, could in the light of the rhetoric surrounding, and the actual practice of, inclusion of human rights in peace operations, assist the UN in this process.

Section Four: Human Rights in UNMIK and UNTAET:

4.1. Case Study of the Establishment of the Judiciary as a Human Rights-Based Initiative

The following section discusses UNMIK's and UNTAET's implementation of human rights standards in Kosovo and East Timor through the development and establishment of their judicial systems. In addressing this issue, I intend to base my inquiry on the following two questions: How is the establishment of the national judicial systems being carried out in accordance with international human rights standards in the post-conflict societies? What is the gap between the institutional capacity of the legal bodies to promote and protect human rights and the reality in respect of the current capacity? My focus is therefore on how the processes of change from a conflict situation to a situation of peace are being managed by the UN in peace operations, and how they affect the potential of peace operations to promote and protect human rights.

I have chosen to focus on the development of the judicial institutions consistently with international human rights standards for a number of reasons. A primary objective of a peace operation is the development of the judicial system.[80] Such a development is vital to the processes of rebuilding a more secure and functioning society based on the rule of law and respect for law, order and respect for human rights. Similarly, creating

---

[80] See, for example, H. Strohmeyer, 'Collapse and Reconstruction of a Judicial System: The United Nations Missions in Kosovo and East Timor' (2001) 95 *The American Journal of International Law* 46-63, who concludes that a major lesson learnt from UNMIK and UNTAET is that the administration of justice should be a high priority, at p. 47, and the Report of the Secretary-General S/1999/1024 *supra* note 54, in which the Secretary-General identifies the establishment of a working justice system to be one of the primary "urgent needs" facing the Transitional Administration, para 23, and Report of OSCE: Mission to Kosovo *Strategy for Justice* (June 2001) at http://www.osce.org/kosovo/documents/reports/justice where it is stated that there is continuing recognition that the implementation of a fair and effective justice system is the key to the success of UNMIK, p. 1.

a functioning judicial system that meets the basic requirements of independence and impartiality is a benchmark from which the progress of the peace operation and the current potential for human rights protection and promotion can be assessed.[81] The value of establishing such a benchmark for human rights is based on two presumptions. Firstly, the judicial system is founded on the principles of the rule of law and is a primary instrument through which international human rights standards are applied in the national context. As such, it can provide an indication of the achievements or failures in the human rights aspects of the operations. Secondly, defining the establishment of the judiciary as a key goal may mean that this initiative would receive more resources and political support than others deemed not so essential in the first stages of peace building.

Finally, the establishment of a judicial system has previously not been generally conceived of as part of the human rights component. In UNMIK, the task was given to the civil administration component,[82] and in UNTAET it was the responsibility of the governance and public administration component.[83] However, the following discussion will demonstrate the significant role that human rights has played in the processes of establishment of the judiciaries, and therefore supports the assertion that the human rights component should be formally seen as wider than it currently is.

4.2. The Establishment of the Judicial Systems Consistent with International Human Rights

There are many ways in which the justice systems are being established in Kosovo and East Timor consistent with international human rights. Two primary ways are, on the one hand, the establishment of the judicial systems on the fundamental principles necessary in order to ensure a judicial system in which it is possible to realise human rights to justice.[84] On the

---

[81] In Report of the Secretary-General on the United Nations Transitional Administration in East Timor (for period 27 January-26 July 2000) U.N. Doc S/2000/738 (26 July 2000), where he states that one of the key areas which was identified by the SRSG in East Timor, Sergio Vieira de Mello, to act as a benchmark that would guide the activities of the Mission towards minimum goals was "a credible system of justice in which fundamental human rights are respected", at para 68.

[82] See Report of the Secretary-General, S/1999/779, *supra* note 54.

[83] See Report of the Secretary-General, S/1999/1024, *supra* note 54.

[84] For the purposes of this article, 'rights to justice' incorporate the rights to equality before the law, equal protection of the law without discrimination, effective remedies by a competent, fair, independent and impartial tribunal, public hearing, protection from arbitrary arrest, the presumption of innocence. For reference, these rights

second, the utilisation of the justice system is the critical mechanism through which it is possible to investigate and prosecute past, present, (and inevitably future) human rights violations. Such a process enables the exercise the right of justice, and the direct promotion and protection of international human rights standards in the national setting. I have chosen to look at these particular aspects for three primary reasons.

(1) An independent and impartial judiciary and the investigation into, and prosecution of, human rights violations are two pressing tasks of the peace operations.
(2) Both are crucial to the establishment of judiciaries founded on international standards of human rights which will have the capacities to uphold human rights standards, both in terms of day to day operations and through their ability to deal with the specific consequences of conflict and past, current and future human rights violations.
(3) They serve to illustrate how the peace operations are directly involved in the active implementation of international human rights norms and standards during the process of peace building, and the importance of such operations in human rights promotion and protection.

My initial brief discussion is on how the peace operations are incorporating human rights into the justice systems of Kosovo and East Timor through the promulgation of regulations. I then discuss how the ideal situation as presented by the regulations establishing the justice system is not the reality in Kosovo and East Timor. The post-conflict environments in which the UN is attempting to establish these judicial systems are complex. One of the consequences of this is that the UN's management of these processes has, in some cases, not appeared to be fully adequate. Therefore, while the creation of the judicial system is a crucial step for the incorporation of international human rights standards into these national institutions, the shortcomings of the approaches by the UN to the task of peace building are undermining the potential for a full realisation of human rights in Kosovo and East Timor.

---

are, for example, documented in the ICCPR, Articles 9, 10, 14, 15, 16 and 26, *supra* note 23.

4.2.1 How the Judicial Systems are Consistent with International Human Rights

The conflicts in Kosovo and East Timor destroyed a significant percentage of the countries' infrastructure, resulted in the deaths or dispersal of large proportions of the populations, and created a highly politicised environment. Apart from the other numerous and tragic consequences, this was to have an enormous impact on the ability of the peace operations to put in place working judicial systems.

In Kosovo, law and order had completely collapsed. Due to the systematic discrimination that was imposed on the Kosovo Albanians since 1989, there were virtually no Kosovo Albanians working within Kosovo's civil service. This was particularly so in the judiciary where the overwhelming percentage of judges and prosecutors were Kosovo Serbs. Following the NATO intervention, those few Kosovo Albanians who did work in the public service were soon targets of threats, intimidation and violence as perceived traitors and representatives of the previous regime.

East Timor's minimal judicial infrastructure was completely destroyed in the post-consultation violence, and all legal resources including furniture, books, court equipment, court records, had been burned or were rendered not usable.[85] Those East Timorese who had been part of the civil administration under the Indonesian occupation, including judges, prosecutors and lawyers were seen as sympathetic to Indonesia and as perpetrators of the occupation. They largely left East Timor after the results of the popular consultation were announced.

It is in light of this reality, and the other pressing areas calling for rapid attention that the efforts to re-build or, in the case of East Timor, to actually construct for the first time,[86] the judicial systems by UNMIK and UNTAET have to be contextualised. There were and continue to be substantial practical difficulties facing the UN. Further, there are inherent tensions in the processes of peace and state-building in post-conflict societies. Placing this work within context recognises that the substantial and ongoing challenges facing the operations were accentuated by the circumstances in which the transitional administrations were put in place.[87] This

---

[85] Strohmeyer *supra* note 80, at. 50.

[86] See, H. Strohmeyer, 'Building a New Judiciary for East Timor: Challenges of a Fledgling Nation' (2000) 11 *Criminal Law Forum* 259.

[87] This statement should also be qualified somewhat in relation to the situation in East Timor. In Chopra, *supra* note 52 , at p. 28, Jarat Chopra makes the following comment after a description of the devastation that was wrought on East Timor: "Nevertheless, by the time UNTAET began to deploy in November, there were conditions

Rachel Opie

article, therefore, is not attempting to "lay the blame" for the ongoing problems experienced in achieving the aims and goals of the peace operations solely at the feet of the UN. However, it will identify areas where approaches by the UN have not assisted the process.

4.2.2 How the Judicial Systems are Consistent with International Human Rights: Established in Accordance with Basic Principles

The development of the judicial systems in Kosovo and East Timor were a direct response to the need to establish the rule of law, law and order, and to respond to past, present and future human rights needs. In resolution 1244, UNMIK was mandated to "maintain civil law and order."[88] A primary component of this was identified as the "immediate re-establishment of an independent, impartial and multi-ethnic judiciary."[89] In resolution 1024, the Secretary-General provided that UNTAET would establish "non-discriminatory and impartial institutions, including a judiciary and a civilian police force, to ensure the establishment and maintenance of the rule of law and to promote and protect human rights."[90]

Establishing these systems in law has been done by the promulgation of regulations by the Special Representatives of the Secretary-General in Kosovo and East Timor.[91] The approach taken has been to focus on the

---

for success that are rarely available to peace missions. The belligerent power had completely withdrawn, and an effective multinational force could credibly guarantee internal and external security...the local population openly welcomed the UN..." While I am in accordance with Chopra, that these conditions called for East Timor to become a success story for the UN, this does not detract from the fact that what was being undertaken in East Timor had not been undertaken before, and that the conditions were not conducive to a simple implementation of mandate.

[88] S/1999/1244, *supra* note 12, para. 11(i)

[89] Report of the Secretary-General S/1999/779, *supra* note 54, para. 66.

[90] Report of Secretary-General S/1999/1024, *supra* note 54, para 29 (h).

[91] The authority to promulgate regulations in Kosovo was assumed by the SRSG in an announcement that he would perform executive functions until new legitimate authorities were established (See, Report of the Secretary-General S/1999/799, *supra* note 54, para. 18.) Further, UNMIK/REG/1999/1, *supra* note 67, s. 1 reads: "All legislative and executive authority with respect to Kosovo, including the administration of the judiciary, is vested in UNMIK and is exercised by the Special Representative of the Secretary-General." In East Timor the executive authority was vested in the SRSG by Security Council resolution S/RES/1999/1272, *supra* note 12, para. 6, by which the Special Representative "as the Transitional Administrator, will be responsible for all aspects of United Nations work in East Timor and will have the power to enact new laws and regulations, and suspend or repeal existing ones." And likewise in UNTAET Regulation 1999/1 which reads, with the necessary alterations to

creation of the primary institutions of Western-type judicial systems founded on the principles of independence and impartiality. The regulations that established the judicial advisory bodies for the appointment and removal of judges and prosecutors, the offices of judges and prosecutors, and the organisation of the court system, together constitute a systematic structure which puts in place the formal procedural safeguards for an independent and impartial judiciary.[92] While it was not until the Constitutional Framework for Provisional Self-Government in Kosovo that the basic principles of independence and impartiality were pointedly given legal force, this regulation does establish the separation of powers,[93] the rights to an independent and impartial court,[94] and the independence and impartiality of judges.[95] Earlier in the development of the East Timorese judicial system, UNTAET Regulation No. 2000/11 establishes the independence of the judiciary, and the independence and impartiality of judges.[96]

From the point of view of the consistency of national institutions with international human rights standards, this approach is one important step in providing the necessary safeguards through which human rights to justice can be realised. The principles of independence and impartiality are fundamental to the rule of law and therefore to the form of justice system being (re)created in Kosovo and East Timor. If realised, these principles would be the basic building blocks on which other rights to justice could also subsequently be guaranteed. Without them, the entire process of justice would be cast in doubt and could likely result in judicial systems without credibility or legitimacy in the eyes of those who are subject to them.

---

make it applicable to East Timor, the same as UNMIK Regulation 1999/1, *supra* note 63.

[92] The relevant regulations are as follows: UNMIK/REG/1999/6 On the Recommendations for the Structures and Administration of the Judiciary and the Prosecution Service (7 September 1999); UNMIK/REG//1999/7 On Appointment and Removal From Office of Judges and Prosecutors (7 September 1999); UNTAET/REG/1999/3 On the Establishment of a Transitional Judicial Service Commission (3 December 1999), UNTAET/REG/2000/11 On the Organization of the Courts in East Timor (6 March 2000).

[93] UNMIK Regulation No. 2001/9, U.N. Doc UNMIK/REG/2001/9 On A Constitutional Framework for Provisional Self-Government in Kosovo (5 May 2001), Chapter 2.a.c

[94] UNMIK/REG/2001/9, *supra* note 93, s. 4, 9.4.3.

[95] UNMIK/REG/2001/9, *supra* note 93, s. 4, 9.4.8.

[96] UNTAET/REG/2000/11, *supra* note 92, Part I. General Provisions

Rachel Opie

However, putting in place the structural foundations does just represent one step. In any context, let alone post-conflict environments, declaring the need for and establishing bodies and procedures in order to protect and uphold basic principles does not equate with the existence in reality of systems which effectively function to observe and guarantee these principles. The introduction of the basic principles of independence and impartiality through founding regulations has not resulted in independent or impartial judicial systems in Kosovo and East Timor.

4.2.3 How the Judicial Systems are Consistent with International Human Rights: Mechanism for investigation and prosecution of human rights violations

The conflicts in Kosovo and East Timor resulted in widespread and systematic violations of the human rights of the civilian populations. The task of bringing the perpetrators to justice, crucial for the process of peace building, has essentially been given to the newly established judicial systems. It therefore represents a critical test as to whether the ability of judicial systems are able to demonstrate their ability and capability to fulfil the needs and expectations for justice that exist.

In directly being responsible for the investigation of past and present human rights violations and the process of prosecution, the judicial systems in Kosovo and East Timor are fundamentally responsible for the promotion and protection of international human rights standards. These systems represent a primary instrument with which the international standards can be directly implemented and guaranteed in a national context. Similarly, on the premise that they do possess a deterrent value, the judicial systems are a mechanism for the future promotion and protection of human rights.

While in Kosovo all cases concerning human rights violations are heard through the 'regular' court system, the initiative of establishing the Serious Crimes Panel in East Timor has provided the East Timorese with a feasible avenue for the investigation and prosecution of human rights violations that occurred during the occupation by Indonesia and post-consultation violence.[97] This is the first time that such an institution has been developed in the context of the national court system in a post-conflict country. Regulation 2000/15, directly recalling the recommenda-

---

[97] The Serious Crimes Unit is the body that undertakes investigations into the allegations of serious crimes.

tions of the International Commission of Inquiry of East Timor,[98] establishes panels of judges in the District Court of Dili with exclusive jurisdiction to hear cases dealing with serious criminal offences concerning events
that happened in East Timor prior to 25 October 1999.[99] "Serious crimes"
for the purposes of the Panel are the following, their definitions based on
of the Rome Statute of the International Criminal Court:[100]

- Genocide
- War crimes
- Crimes against humanity
- Murder
- Sexual Offences

---

[98] Report of the International Commission of Inquiry on East Timor to the Secretary-
General, U.N. Doc. A/54/726 - S/2000/59 (31 January 2000). Para 146: "The East
Timorese]must not be forgotten in the rush of events to redefine relations in the region, and their basic human rights to justice, compensation and the truth must be
fully respected. This is a responsibility which the United Nations must shoulder both
in the short and long terms, in particular in its trusteeship relation with the people of
East Timor as it administers the territory towards independence; Para 152: The
United Nations should establish an independent and international body charged
with:·conducting further systematic investigations of the human rights violations and
violations of international humanitarian law in East Timor during the period from
January 1999; identifying the persons responsible for those violations, including
those with command responsibilities; ensuring reparations for the violations from
those responsible; prosecuting those guilty of serious human rights violations within
the framework of its function to ensure justice; and considering the issues of truth
and reconciliation; Para 153: The United Nations should establish an international
human rights tribunal consisting of judges appointed by the United Nations, preferably with the participation of members from East Timor and Indonesia. The tribunal
would sit in Indonesia, East Timor and any other relevant territory to receive the
complaints and to try and sentence those accused by the independent investigation
body of serious violations of fundamental human rights and international humanitarian law which took place in East Timor since January 1999 regardless of the nationality of the individual or where that person was when the violations were committed."

[99] UNTAET Regulation No. 2000/15, U.N. Doc UNTAET/REG/2000/15 On the Establishment of Panels With Exclusive Jurisdiction Over Serious Criminal Offences
(6 June 2000), s. 2.4.

[100] The Rome Statute of the International Criminal Court. Opened for signature on 17
July 1998. U.N. Doc. A/CONF.183/9. Adopted by the United Nations Diplomatic
Conference of Plenipotentiaries on the Establishment of an International Criminal
Court on 17 July 1998.

- Torture[101]

In effect, this regulation imports "a regime created for a radically different setting, the International Criminal Court (ICC), into a district court of one of the world's poorest nations."[102] It provides a model of the type of institution that can be created in the context of a peace operation that directly aims to protect humanitarian and human rights law standards. It further represents an initiative developed with the intention of ensuring the actual enforcement of human rights standards, and their future protection on the basis that these instruments do possess some deterrent value. However, it remains to be seen whether the Panel will fulfil the expectations for justice that have been created. It represents another key test, within the broader test of the judicial system as a whole, of the ability of the UN to manage the institutions it creates.

4.2.4 How the Judicial Systems are Coherent with International Human Rights: Establishment of extra-judicial mechanisms

Extra-juridical initiatives have also been taken in Kosovo and East Timor which aim at furthering the ability of the systems to both investigate and provide certain avenues of recourse for other types of human rights violations. In Kosovo, an Ombudsperson Institution was established by UN-MIK Regulation No. 2000/38 and has since been included in the Constitutional Framework as a provisional institution for self-government.[103] It provides the "accessible and timely mechanisms for the review and redress of actions constituting an abuse of authority by the interim civil administration or any emerging central or local institution."[104]

The Ombudsperson Institution has jurisdiction to hear complaints of human rights violations and actions that constitute an abuse of authority.[105] More generally, the office has wide powers to monitor the human rights

---

[101] UNTAET/REG/2000/15, *supra* note 99, s. 1.3. For a detailed analysis of the law to be applied by the Special Panels see S. Linton, 'Rising from the Ashes: The creation of a viable criminal justice system in East Timor' (2001) 5 *Melbourne Law Review* at http://www.austlii.edu.au/au/journals/MULR/2001/5.html.

[102] Linton, *supra* note 101, Part E.

[103] UNMIK/REG/2001/9, *supra* note 93, s. 4, chapter 10.

[104] UNMIK Regulation No. 2000/38, U.N. Doc UNMIK/REG/2000/38, On the Establishment of the Ombudsperson Institution in Kosovo (30 June 2000), s. 1.2.

[105] UNMIK/REG/2000/38, *supra* note 104 , s. 3. The jurisdiction of the Ombudsperson is confined to allegations of violations of human rights due to an abuse of authority that have occurred after the establishment of the Institution.

situation, undertake investigations and make recommendations.[106] It is a very important step for the protection and promotion human rights and freedoms through the provision of an avenue for recourse against abuse of power or institutionalised practices which lead to violations of human rights.[107] In addition, it provides a vital mechanism for complaints regarding the judiciary, and as such can assist in ensuring its independence and the impartiality. Despite the fact it cannot directly prevent human rights violations occurring, it does represent an important safeguard against impunity and against future repetitions of violations.

In East Timor, a form of truth and reconciliation commission has been established in order to deal with the process of overcoming the consequences of the conflict and the related process of community reconciliation. The Commission for Reception, Truth and Reconciliation (CRTR) can undertake investigations into allegations of human rights violations that occurred during the "political conflict"[108] to determine the "truth" in

---

[106] UNMIK/REG/2000/38, *supra* note 104. Functions of the Ombudsperson are set out in s. 4.

[107] UNMIK/REG/2000/38, *supra* note 104, s. 1.2. The section reads: "The Ombudsperson shall promote and protect the rights and freedoms of individuals and legal entities and ensure that all persons in Kosovo are able to exercise effectively the human rights and fundamental freedoms safeguarded by international human rights standards, in particular the European Convention on Human Rights and its Protocols and the International Covenant on Civil and Political Rights."

[108] 'Political conflicts' were defined in s.1.j to be "armed and non-armed struggles and discord related to the sovereignty and political status of East Timor, the organisation or governance of East Timor, the illegal Indonesian invasion and occupation of East Timor, or any combination of the foregoing." 'Human rights violations' are defined as violations of international human rights standards, violations of international humanitarian law, and criminal acts "committed within the context of the political conflicts in East Timor between April 25 1974 and 25 October 1999." Section 1.c defines international humanitarian law as including Geneva Conventions of 12 August 1949; the Protocols Additional to the Geneva Conventions of 12 August 1949, and relating to the Protection of Victims of International and non-International Armed Conflict of June 8 1977; and the Convention on the Prohibition or Restrictions on the Use of Certain Conventional Weapons Which May be Deemed to be Excessively Injurious or to have Indiscriminate Effects of 10 October 1980; and the laws and customs of war, see UNMIK/REG/2000/38, *supra* note 104. April 25 1974 was the date on which the Portuguese Armed Forces Movement (AFM) overthrew the Caetano Regime and 25 October 1999 was the date on which the Security Council passed resolution 1272 (1999), and UNTAET was authorised to be deployed to East Timor.

Rachel Opie

respect of these violations. [109] It has a specific function to identify practices and polices of both State and non-State actors which require reform to prevent future human rights violations.[110] Other related tasks are assisting in and promoting reconciliation and the reintegration of people who have been deemed to have harmed their communities, and promoting human rights.

This mechanism is not intended to 'challenge' the mainstream justice system and provide an avenue to dealing with violations of human rights without the necessary safeguards. On the contrary, the regulation includes safeguards to ensure it is appropriate mechanism used in relation to the crime committed[111] and it incorporates human rights protections such as the rights to representation and legal aid.[112] The recommendatory reports for reform are a very important aspect for preventing recurrences of human rights violations, and is thus an important tool for future human rights protection and promotion.

4.2.5 How the Judicial Systems are Consistent with International Human Rights: Conclusion

The above discussion has shown that human rights are an important influence in the conception of the judicial systems in Kosovo and East Timor, and it is possible to see the intended role of international human rights in these systems. The regulations governing the establishment of independent and impartial national judicial systems provide the direct mandate and le-

---

[109]   UNTAET Regulation No. 2001/10, U.N. Doc UNTAET/REG/2001/10 On the Establishment of a Commission for Reception, Truth and Reconciliation in East Timor (13 July 2001). Section 3: Objectives and Functions of the Commission: 3.1 The objectives of the Commission shall include: (a) inquiring into human rights violations that have taken place in the context of the political conflicts in East Timor; (b) establishing the truth regarding past human rights violations; (c) reporting the nature of the human rights violations that have occurred and identifying the factors that may have lead to such violations; (d) identifying the practices and policies, whether of State or non-State actors which need to be addressed to prevent future recurrences of human rights violations; (e) the referral of human rights violations to the Office of the General Prosecutor with recommendations for the prosecution of offences where appropriate; (f) assisting in restoring the human dignity of victims; (g) promoting reconciliation; (h) supporting the reception and reintegration of individuals who have caused harm to their communities through the commission of minor criminal offences and other harmful acts through the facilitation of community based mechanisms for reconciliation; and (i) the promotion of human rights.

[110]   UNTAET/REG/2001/10, *supra* note 109, s. 13.1.

[111]   UNTAET/REG/2001/10, *supra* note 109, ss. 22.2, 27.5, 27.6 and 32.

[112]   UNTAET/REG/2001/10, *supra* note 109, s. 18.

gal capacity to investigate and make findings or prosecute for international human rights violations within a framework that is consistent with international human rights standards and provide the mechanisms for their promotion and protection. In this sense, the peace operations have managed a considerable achievement – that of a workable, comprehensive system of the primary structures of the judicial systems, based on international standards of human rights.

Establishing such a system through regulation is also an indication of how the UN is attempting to tackle the challenges posed by being the authority responsible for managing the change from conflict to peace. These regulations show that the approach the UN is taking is one of structural establishment, firmly rooted in the fundamental principles of Western justice and human rights. It is this approach, therefore, that has been deemed essential for enabling the process from conflict to peace and for enabling that process to move forward and be sustainable.

4.3 Political Management and its Impact on the Judicial Systems

Appearances have the tendency to be deceptive, or at a minimum, not to tell the whole story and what has been presented above in the context of the regulatory framework for the judicial systems in Kosovo and East Timor represents the ideal picture. However, the structural establishment of a judicial system is not equivalent to the existence of a establishment of a working legal system with the capacities and abilities to guarantee international standards of human rights.

In any situation, let alone a post-conflict situation, it would be a challenging task to implement such a working reality within the space of two years. In addition, the peace operations in Kosovo and East Timor have faced and continue to face immense difficulties coming to grips with the tasks that are required of them to fulfil their mandates. This is clearly demonstrated in the management approaches that have limited the potential of the structural frameworks that were put in place. The Secretary-General summarised the effects of the mismanagement, and subsequent systematic breakdown on human rights, in his report to the Security Council where he states in relation to the situation in Kosovo that:

> "violations of the human rights of all communities in Kosovo continue to be a major concern of UNMIK. Systemic problems in the criminal justice system have sustained a climate of impunity. There are persistent complaints from ethnic minorities that criminal incidents against them are not fully investigated or prosecuted in com-

parison with crimes against the majority community. Pre-trial detention is of major concern, both with regard to its length and access by
detainees to attorneys and the outside world. This was illustrated by
the recent hunger strike in Mitrovica by Kosovo Serb and Roma detainees complaining both about the length of their detention before
trial and alleged bias in the treatment they had received, in contrast
to the treatment of the majority community. With the number of
criminal trials now increasing, the right to a fair trial is also of concern, including access by defendants to legal advice of sufficient
quality to ensure that they are adequately defended".[113]

The following analysis of UNMIK and UNTAET's approaches to the
management of the judicial systems they established through regulation is
based on the premise that for a system to function there are two key aspects that have to be present: the creation of the framework of a viable
system, and the 'successful' management of that system. Here, the notion
of the management incorporates two primary aspects: the decisions relating to the approach taken to any given situation in process of establishing
the judiciary, that is, the "political management" of the situation; and the
provision and allocation of resources, for example, material or personnel.

I am not intending to discuss the issue of resources despite the fact that
this is a major issue affecting peace operations, because the lack of resources is very widely acknowledged. Moreover, even with the resources
necessary the peace operations will not fulfil their aims and objectives for
the judicial systems, let alone the overall peace operations, in Kosovo,
East Timor, or in future operations without a modification of their 'political management' approach. As is discussed below, instances of political
management have had direct repercussions for the ability of the judicial
systems to work as intended and have undercut the potential for human
rights standards to be realised, protected and promoted through a system
that is crucial for doing just that. The lack of adequate engagement with
the situation on the ground and a lack of political support and instances of
political interference mean that the achievements the UN can claim in respect of establishing human rights-based structures are undermined. In this
sense, the provision of more resources would not overcome the shortcomings of the operations. Finally, it is understood that the entire responsibility for the transitional process does not lie with the peace operations. They

---

[113] Report of the Secretary-General on the Interim Administration Mission in Kosovo,
UN Doc. S/2000/538, (6 June 2000), para. 47.

cannot control the minds and actions of autonomous individuals. Neither are they free and independent bodies but do face the political and economic constraints faced by the UN as a whole. It is not realistic to hold the UN, or individual peace operations, entirely culpable for the inability to move the transitory process from violent conflict to peace. There is an extent to which the societies themselves are also responsible.

4.3.1 The impact of the inability to deal with the situation on the ground on the independence and impartiality of the judicial systems

The discussion of instances of the 'political management' approaches of UNMIK and UNTAET which have impacted negatively on the ability to realise the potential of the judicial systems are not intended to be seen as individual instances of mismanagement by the peace operations. Instead, they should be understood as indicative of the larger issues confronting the peace operations. Broadly speaking, the instances discussed below raise the problems associated with the inability of the peace operations to engage with the post-conflict political situations. They demonstrate that problematic and reactionary measures have been taken. They also highlight the politicisation of peace operations, no doubt due to their connection with the political organisation of the UN, and the consequent existence of political interference and lack of political will. Both these factors are resulting in a situation where while one stage of the process of building the structures is underway, the process of the management of those structures is significantly reducing their potential effectiveness.

4.3.2 Lack of security leading to reactionary regulatory measures

The inability of UNMIK and UNTAET to deal with the broad issue of security in Kosovo and East Timor has resulted in reactionary initiatives, some of which are directly undermining the aims and purposes of the peace operations. While in Kosovo, the lack of security continues to pose a considerably greater pervasive problem, [114] in both countries it impedes the progress of the operations.

It is not feasible or realistic to expect that only the actions and initiatives taken by the peace operations will create a secure environment and

---

[114] F.M. Lorenzo, 'The Rule of Law in Kosovo: Problems and Prospects' (2000) 11 *Criminal Law Forum* 127-142, at 135. The security issue has other consequences for the judicial systems such as the lack of necessary security and protection of witnesses which will not be discussed in this article. See also, Report of the International Crisis Group, *Kosovo Report Card: ICG Balkans Report No. 100* (Pristina/Brussels, 28 August 2000), at http://www.intl-crisis-group.org/, at 30.

create law and order. The Secretary-General states this succinctly when he reports that "continuing violence in the province[of Kosovo] remains the single most important threat to the attainment of the international community's goals. It is also the most serious threat to the right of ordinary men and women of Kosovo to enjoy a peaceful and secure life. Most residents abhor the violence that troubles the province, yet they remain unwilling to cooperate fully with UNMIK in tackling the causes and perpetrators of such violence. UNMIK cannot act alone in this regard."[115] However, the achievement of law and order is a goal of both operations, and is necessary for the achievement of other goals. The fact that its ongoing lack is impacting negatively on the other aspects of the operations is well illustrated by the impact on the judiciary.

Two following examples indicate how the peace operations are attempting to counter the effects of the lack of security on the judiciary through ad hoc measures. Further, they demonstrate clearly the futility and the inadequacy of focusing on structural reconstruction, and establishing institutions which are consistent with international human rights principles, when there are not the enabling conditions for peace. In this sense, there is a strong case made for the extension of the currently held notions of what constitutes peace building to a focus on addressing the root causes of the violent conflict.

In the contexts of Kosovo and East Timor, where there is a historical lack of confidence in the judicial system, the actual manifestation of these principles in the working reality of the judicial systems is crucial for re-establishing the systems credibility and legitimacy. However, the lack of security is impacting significantly on the ability of the judicial systems to guarantee the basic principles of independence and impartiality. In attempts to overcome this, the SRSGs promulgated various regulations to counter the actual and probable existence of bias on the part of judges and prosecutors facing intimidation, threats and violence. UNMIK Regulations 2000/6[116], 2000/34[117] and 2000/64,[118] provide for international judges and

---

[115]   Report of the Secretary-General on the United Nations Interim Administration Mission in Kosovo, U.N. Doc. S/2001/218 (13 March 2001), para. 65.

[116]   UNMIK Regulation No. 2000/6, U.N. Doc. UNMIK/REG/2000/6 On the Appointment and Removal of Judges From Office of International Judges and Prosecutors (15 February 2000).

[117]   UNMIK Regulation No. 2000/34, U.N. Doc. UNMIK/REG/2000/34 On Amending UNMIK Regulation No. 2000/6 (27 May 2000).

prosecutors in the courts throughout Kosovo, and for the assignment of international judges and prosecutors and/or a change of venue during proceedings if "considered necessary to ensure the independence and impartiality of the judiciary or the proper administration of justice."[119] Following the initiative in Kosovo, UNTAET Regulation No. 2000/25 was promulgated which enabled international judges and prosecutors to be appointed to the Serious Crimes Panel. [120]

In neither instance have the regulations resulted in independent judicial systems which can guarantee the administration of justice with impartiality. The inability to guarantee overall security has meant that security issues continue to plague the system.[121] One Kosovar judge was quoted as saying, in respect of threats and intimidation of judges and prosecutors, that "they have to live with it."[122] Similarly, Amnesty International, in its latest report on East Timor states that continuing threats and intimidation directed towards members of the judiciary in order to influence proceedings means that with the result that the judiciary does not appear to be free, independent or impartial.[123]

Another reactionary, ad hoc response to the lack of security and the urgent need to establish law and order, was the promulgation of regulations extending the periods of pre-trial detention beyond the maximum six month period established by the International Covenant on Civil and Political Rights 1966 (ICCPR) and the European Convention for the Protection of Human Rights and Fundamental Freedoms 1950 (ECHR).[124] This

---

[118] UNMIK Regulation No. 2000/64, U.N. Doc. UNMIK/REG/2000/64 On Assignment of International Judges/Prosecutors And/Or Change of Venue (15 December 2000). The preamble states: "recognizing that the presence of security threats may undermine the independence and impartiality of the judiciary and impede the ability of the judiciary to properly prosecute crimes which gravely undermine the peace process and the full establishment of the rule of law in Kosovo..."

[119] UNMIK REG/2000/64, *supra* note 118, s. 1.1.

[120] UNTAET Regulation No. 2000/25, U.N. Doc. UNTAET/REG/2000/25 On Amending Regulation No. 1999/3 (3 August 2000).

[121] Report of the Secretary-General S/2001/218, *supra* note 115, para 6.

[122] OSCE Report, *Kosovo – A Review of the Criminal Justice System 1 September 2000-28 February 2001*, at http://www.osce.org/kosovo/documents/reports, at 49.

[123] Report of Amnesty International, *East Timor: Justice Past, Present and Future* (27 July 2001) at http://www.amnesty.org, at 9.

[124] ICCPR, Art 9: "(1) Everyone has the right to liberty and security of person. No one shall be subjected to arbitrary arrest or detention. No one shall be deprived of his liberty except on such grounds and in accordance with such procedure as are established by law. (2) Anyone who is arrested shall be informed, at the time of the arrest,

Rachel Opie

was done in order to attempt to deal with the inability of the court system to cope with the demand being placed on it, particularly in the earlier stage of its establishment.

The effects of these regulations are two-fold. Firstly, they threaten the protection of basic human rights to justice. UNMIK Regulation No. 1999/26[125] contains no standards or criteria for determining when a person can be held for the longer period, nor at what point this extension can be terminated and by whom.[126] The decision-making process is not subject to provisions for periodic review of the extension, or a mechanism through which the suspect can exercise the right of review of an order for detention.[127] UNTAET Regulation No. 2000/14 permits an indefinite extension of pre-trial detention, but it does contain safeguards.[128]

---

of the reasons for his arrest... (3) Anyone arrested shall be brought promptly before a judge or other officer authorized by law to exercise judicial power and shall be entitled to trial within a reasonable time or to release. It shall not be the general rule that persons awaiting trial shall be detained in custody, but release may be subject to guarantees to appear for trial, at any stage of the judicial proceedings, and, should the occasion arise, for the execution of judgement. (4) Anyone who is deprived of his liberty by arrest or detention shall be entitled to take proceedings before a court, in order that court may decide without delay on the lawfulness of his detention and order his release if the detention is not lawful. (5) Anyone who has been the victim of unlawful arrest or detention shall have an enforceable right to compensation." Article 9(3) and (4) of the ICCPR correspond to Articles 5(3) and (4) of the ECHR.

Art 14: "(1) All persons shall be equal before the courts and tribunals. In the determination of any criminal charge against him, or of his rights and obligations in a suit at law, everyone shall be entitled to a fair and public hearing by a competent, independent and impartial tribunal established by law...(3) In the determination of any criminal charge against him, everyone shall be entitled to the following minimum guarantees, in full equality: includes informed promptly of charge, time and facilities for defence, tried without undue delay..."

[125] UNMIK Regulation No. 1999/26, U.N. Doc UNMIK/REG/1999/26 On the Extension of Periods of Pre-trial Detention (22 December 1999).

[126] Report of Amnesty International, *Amnesty International's Recommendations to UNMIK on the Judicial System* (ai-index EUR 70/006/2000, 4 February 2000), Recommendation 2, at http://www.amnesty.org.

[127] Report of OSCE Department of Human Rights and Rule of Law, *Observations and Recommendations of the OSCE Legal Monitoring Section: Report No. 6, Extension of Custody Time Limits and the Rights of Detainees: The Unlawfulness of Regulation 1999/6* (Pristina, 29 April 2000), at http://www.osce.org/kosovo/documents/ reports, at 3.

[128] These include mechanisms for periodic review of detention, and enables the suspect to request a review, or an appeal, of the orders for detention at either stage of further detention. See UNTAET Regulation No. 2000/14, U.N. Doc UNTAET/REG/

Secondly, the process of making these regulations was in contravention of international human rights standards. According to the ICCPR, the "prevailing circumstances" that must exist in order to justify derogation from the rights against deprivation of liberty and for fair trial must constitute a public emergency. [129] However, in neither Kosovo nor East Timor was this state of affairs held to exist. As required by Article 4 of the ICCPR, there were no declarations of public emergencies, and the Secretary-General was not informed of the derogations or the reasons for them.

In the context of the security situation and the difficulties faced in administering justice efficiently, legally validating a practice which has arisen may have been the only conceivable alternative. However, it is suggested that the mode in which this option was executed is at fault. In effect, these regulations are reactions to systematic weaknesses of the peace operations, in this instance manifested in the inability to cope with the security situation. The promulgation of the regulations was contrary to the objective to promote and protect human rights of the peace operations. The regulations were made in direct contravention of the procedures for derogating from basic human rights as established in the ICCPR and ECHR, and they serve to threaten the protection of the rights to fair trial, in particular the rights to fair trial in a reasonable time or to release.[130]

2000/14 On Amending Regulation No. 2000/11 (10 May 2000), articles 12a.3, 12a.6 and 12a.12 respectively.

[129] Art 4: "(1) In time of public emergency which threatens the life of a nation and the existence of which is officially proclaimed, the States Parties to the present Covenant may take measures derogating from their obligations under the present Covenant to the extent strictly required by the exigencies of the situation, provided that such measures are not inconsistent with their other obligations under international law and do not involve discrimination solely on the ground of race, colour, sex, language, religion, or social orientation. (2) No derogation from articles 6, 7, 8 (paragraphs 1 and 2), 11, 15, 16, and 18, may be made under this provision. (3) Any state party to the present Covenant availing itself of the right of derogation shall immediately inform other States Parties to the present Covenant, through the intermediary of the Secretary-General of the United Nations, of the provisions from which it has derogated and of the reasons by which it was actuated. A further communication shall be made, through the same intermediary, on the date on which it terminates such derogation."

[130] Report of Amnesty International, *East Timor: Building a New Country Based on Human Rights* (ai-index ASA 57/005/2000, 28 August 2000), at http://www.amnesty.org, s. 4.12

Rachel Opie

4.3.2.1 Political Interference Undermining Independence and Impartiality
Managing the relationships inextricably linked with the deployment of
peace operations in the context of very politically charged and difficult-to-
navigate situations is an important aspect of the 'political management' of
the peace operations. It is obvious that peace operations cannot be politically neutral mechanisms. The concern is rather that in the nature of international politics, the political considerations of affected states, contributing, hosting, or otherwise, are impacting, often very detrimentally, on the
capacity and ability of the operations to fulfil their mandates. In Kosovo
and East Timor, political considerations culminating in political interference or lack of political support for operation initiatives are affecting the
judicial systems to realise their capacities as promulgated by regulation.
These two outcomes of choices of political management in Kosovo and
East Timor are undermining and limiting the capacities of the judicial systems to provide independent and fair trials for human rights violations, and
in the case of East Timor, have effectively assisted in the closing down of
the option for justice through an Indonesian system.

4.3.2.1.a KFOR and the judicial system
Instances where KFOR officials have refused to follow court orders by
Kosovo Albanian judges to release Kosovo Albanian suspects raise a fundamental tension inherent in peace operations – what ever the course of
action decided to be taken risks impacting negatively on the operational
goals. The refusals to follow the court orders were made in the context of
a very and unusually high rate of release of people in detention which was
undermining the efforts to restore order and security.[131] The rate of release
was also undermining the credibility of the judicial system, contributing to
the appearance of impunity for some in Kosovo. [132] Notwithstanding this,
this does constitute interference by the security forces in Kosovo in the
administration of justice. It undermines the basic tenant of the separation
of powers, and the actual independence of the judiciary which then has direct repercussions for the appearance of the independence of the judiciary
and its legitimacy.

More recently, reports of KFOR officials deliberately withholding information because they want to protect intelligence sources, and of pre-

---

[131] Report of Lawyer's Committee on Human Rights, *A Fragile Peace: Laying the
Foundations for Justice in Kosovo* (October 1999), at http://www.lchr.org/feature/
kosovo/kosovofeature.htm.

[132] Lorenzo, *supra* note 114, at 132.

venting civilian police carrying out initial investigations and then not disclosing the information they obtained,[133] illustrate political interference in the processes of criminal investigation. Christer Karphammar, a Swedish jurist who worked as a public prosecutor and as the first international judge in Kosovo, was quoted as saying that he knows of several cases in which UN and senior KFOR officials blocked the prosecution of former KLA members on the grounds that prosecution could endanger personnel from NATO member states. In the framework of the role, and duties of KFOR, this does not seem an appropriate reason for such interference. It undermines the objective of the operation to provide justice for victims of human rights violations, and to provide an effective, independent and impartial judicial system. The result is obvious; as Karphammar said, the effect was that during his 18-month tenure in Kosovo, "the judiciary was not allowed to work independently."[134]

4.3.2.1.b Ministry of Justice and the Prosecution Service
In East Timor, political interference by the Ministry of Justice in the Public Prosecution Service is threatening the ability of the judiciary to guarantee independence.[135] Linton writes euphemistically, "UNTAET's Ministry of Justice...which used to be responsible for the prosecution service when it was composed of purely East Timorese prosecutors, continues to play a particularly active and influential role vis-à-vis the new Public Prosecution Service."[136]

This was recently elaborated on by the former acting General Prosecutor and acting Deputy General Prosecutor for Serious Crimes in East Timor between June to September 2000, Carlos Vasconcelos. At the Annual Conference of the International Association of Prosecutors (Sydney, Australia, 2-7 September 2001), he expressed outrage at the level of interference by the Ministry of Justice in the Prosecution Service:

As acting General Prosecutor responsible for the prosecution service in East Timor, I faced UNTAET's Minister of Justice who seemed never to

---

[133]   J.R. Smith, 'Rule of Law is Elusive in Kosovo; UN, NATO Criticized For Inaction on Violence' *The Washington Post* (Sunday, July 29 2000), at A1.

[134]   Smith, *supra* note 133, at A1.

[135]   UNTAET Regulation 2000/16, U.N. Doc. UNTAET/REG/2000/16 On the Organisation of the Public Prosecution Service in East Timor (6 June 2000) provides that "public prosecutors shall act...without improper influence, direct and indirect, from any source, whether within or outside the civil administration of East Timor." Section 4.2.

[136]   Linton, *supra* note 101, Part III.f.

Rachel Opie

have heard of the fundamental principles of the separation of powers and of prosecutorial independence... I was privy to a series of very serious, but elementary, professional errors that could have exposed, and still can expose, UNTAET and its leadership to international ridicule. I never dreamt that I would encounter such a degree of political interference, incompetence and mismanagement in the United Nations... I have experienced [it] on a scale that is literally condemning the East Timorese to a dysfunctional and morally bankrupt criminal justice system.[137]

There have not been any publicised responses to this charge of interference in the Prosecution Service. While the effects of such interference are not immediately obvious, this does threaten compliance with the basic principles on which the justice system has been based, thus subsequently undermining its credibility.

4.3.2.2 Lack of Political Will Undermining capacity for Investigation and Prosecution of Human Rights Violations

4.3.2.2.a Managing the relationship with the Government of Indonesia

A key factor in the administration of justice for human rights violations in East Timor is the co-operation of the Government of Indonesia. The approach followed by UNTAET to facilitate this co-operation represents a clear illustration of the influence of the political considerations of member states of the UN on the peace operations. In the context where past strong diplomatic pressure has resulted in the Government of Indonesia conceding to the requests of the international community, the approach used, now having been followed for almost two years, could be defined as a lack of political will to push Indonesia to bring to justice those involved in the human rights violations in East Timor. The statement of the Secretary-General in his May 2001 report provides some indication of the approach that has been consistently followed:

The Indonesian Parliament's decision to establish an ad hoc tribunal to deal with gross violations of human rights in East Timor was seen as a positive step. However, the relevant decree signed by President Wahid on 24 April limits the jurisdiction of a tribunal to acts committed after the ballot on 30 August 1999 ... This is *deeply disappointing*, especially since UNTAET had provided evidence and access to witnesses to the Indonesian authorities in the course of their investigations. UNTAET has not yet received access to evidence and witnesses provided for in the memoran-

---

[137]   On East Timor Alert Network (ETAN) website at http://etan.org7et2001c/august/26-31/25cv.htm.

dum of understanding with Indonesia on cooperation in legal, judicial and human rights-related fields, concluded on 6 April 2000. UNTAET is pursuing this matter with the Government of Indonesia and is *urgently seeking clarification* concerning the jurisdiction of the ad hoc tribunals.[138]

There has been a virtual lack of initiatives on the part of the Indonesian Government for dealing with human rights violations. The Indonesian Government has successfully deterred any prospect of an international tribunal to hear allegations of human rights violations, and has largely put off the creation of its own mechanisms to deal with the allegations of human rights violations committed by its army, police and militias. Even in light of the most recent widening of the scope of the jurisdiction of the Ad Hoc Human Rights Commission,[139] referred to above in the Secretary-General's statement, by Indonesian President Megawati Sukarnoputri after loud domestic and international protest, the Commission is still to be established.[140] The trying of the first suspects was further postponed until September 2001, and as of yet no proceedings have begun. This demonstrates that "urgently seeking clarification" is not translating into action on the part of the Indonesian Government. In addition, political support and resources in Indonesia are by no means guaranteed. With the lack of international and UNTAET pressure, it is very debatable whether the East Timorese will ever get justice by this mechanism.

4.3.2.2.b Lack of Support for Domestic Mechanisms

Further to the lack of political will to push for mechanisms for dealing with allegations of human rights violations in Indonesia, there is a similar lack of will, as manifested in a lack of political support, to ensure that the East Timorese system can successfully undertake the process of investigation and prosecution. Much of the necessary evidence, and the perpetrators

---

[138] Interim Report of the Secretary-General on the United Nations Transitional Administration East Timor, U.N. Doc. S/2001/436 (2 May 2001), para 18. Emphasis added.

[139] This Presidential Decree (23 April 2001) limited the jurisdiction to the violations that occurred in East Timor, after 30 August 1999, the date of the popular consultation which would have prevented the hearing cases that concerning violations that occurred from the occupation in 1975. See "Summary" of the East Timor NGO Forum Briefing Paper to International Donors Conference, (Canberra, June 2001), at http://www.smp.minihub.org/Resources.htm, s. .2.

[140] Megawati Sukarnoputri widened the jurisdiction to include crimes committed between April and September 1999.

of the crimes, are in Indonesia.[141] However, in Indonesia, there is considerable opposition to compliance with the co-operative memorandum of understanding (MOU)[142] the Government made with UNTAET for the purpose of facilitating investigation into human rights violations.[143] The results for the ability of the judicial systems in East Timor to deal effectively
with past human rights violations seem clear. In June 2001, the East Timor
NGO Forum said that "unless the MOU is adhered to the judges of the
Special Panel may have no further cases to hear in a few months time."[144]

Despite the problems of access to evidence, the continuing limited action by the Government of Indonesia makes it vital that UNTAET ensure
that the mechanisms it has created for the investigation and prosecution of
human rights violations have the capability to administer justice sufficiently. While there has been progress, it has been very slow, and multiple
problems facing and being experienced by the Serious Crimes Unit are seriously obstructing its ability to deliver justice. Instead, there is increasing
anger and a lack of faith in the system on the part of the East Timorese
who have seen few outcomes and East Timorese NGOs, important partners in human rights violations investigations, are unwilling or refusing to
work with the Unit.[145]

In Kosovo, the lack of political support for an initiative similar to the
Serious Crimes Panel is contributing to potentially serious infringements
of the rights to justice of both the victims and the alleged perpetrators.
Starting in April 2000, the framework of a Kosovo War and Ethnic Crimes
Court (KWECC) was established, to find a, albeit partial, solution to the
recognised problem of fair trials for serious crimes. The inability to actually implement the KWECC has meant that cases involving allegations of

---

[141]   Memorandum to the UN Commission on Human Rights (10 March 2001) on recommendations for the UN Commission on Human Rights, the East Timor Action
Network (ETAN), at http://etan.org/news/20001a/03hrmemo.htm.

[142]   Memorandum of Understanding between the Republic of Indonesia and the United
Nations Transitional Administration in East Timor regarding Cooperation in Legal,
Judicial and Human Rights Related Matters, 6 April 2000.

[143]   Report of the Secretary-General on the Transitional Administration in East Timor
(for period 27 July 2000 to 16 January 2001), UN Doc. S/2001/42, para 25.

[144]   See East Timor NGO Forum Briefing Paper *supra* note 139, s. 2.

[145]   Amnesty International Report, *supra* note 123, at 35. The overall situation is leading
for stronger and more widespread calls for the international tribunal that was recommended by the International Commission of Inquiry, *supra* note 98. Concurrently
however, the political will and international attention on the issue is rapidly declining. It seems unlikely that the Security Council will take the authoritative action.

human rights violations which are not taken by the ICTY, are being proc-
essed through the 'regular' justice system.

The case of *Miroslav Vuckovic* highlights the serious threat this can
pose to the rights to justice of individuals and in general. The trial against
Vuckovic, a Kosovo Serbian, for genocide was held in the District Court
of Mitrovica/Mitrovice before a panel of five judges – one international
and the rest, including the presiding judge, Kosovo Albanians. The Prosecutor was a Kosovo Albanian. OSCE found that the evidence was "insufficient to prove the required genocidal intent to destroy the Kosovo Albanian group as such in whole or part."[146] Vuckovic was convicted of genocide and sentenced to 14 years imprisonment. As of yet, no written verdict
has been provided. On the basis of past experience, and particularly in
highly charged cases like this one, this does not bode well for the system
of restitution of justice following the war in Kosovo, or for the rights of
defendants.

Reactionary and ad hoc measures to try and overcome the pervasive issue of security in the post-conflict environments, and the clear infiltration
of the Realpolitik that restricts the general ability of the UN into the workings of the peace operations are impacting negatively on the aims and purposes of the peace operations of UNMIK and UNTAET. In the context of
establishing the judicial systems in Kosovo and East Timor, it has been
shown that the peace operations are achieving considerable success in establishing societal structures based on the international human rights standards, thus with the capacity to guarantee their realisation. However, the
potential that this holds for the actual guarantee and realisation of international human rights standards is currently significantly restricted through
the nature of the political management that is dominating the peace operations. The predominance of a structural approach to peace building is also
having a clear limiting effect.

The basic principles on which the judicial systems were established,
and the ability of the initiatives created to fulfil their tasks of investigating
and prosecuting human rights violations, are being undermined by the
very peace operations which have as their direct objective the promotion
and protection of human rights. It is resulting in the appearance of the
place of human rights in the operations, and their tasks, not being translated into reality.

---

[146] OSCE Report, *supra* note 122, at 97. For more detail on this case, see pages 9597,
and for more on the treatment of genocide charges in Kosovo Courts see Section 9.

Rachel Opie

Conclusion

The UN's involvement in managing a transition from violent conflict to peace has impacted on the role of human rights in the latest form of peace operation. International standards of human rights have become a critical factor in the UN approach to its role in maintaining international peace and security. This is especially clear when what constitutes 'the human rights component' of an operation is understood as including all the human rights-based activities undertaken. Through peace building, international human rights standards are being "nationalised" by the development of the primary structures of a post-conflict society in accordance with such standards.

However, in determining whether the peace operation constitutes a strong mechanism for human rights promotion and protection, two factors have emerged. First, the focus on the structural development approach being taken in response to the demands on peace building has consequences for the fulfilment of the objectives and aims of the operation. It fails to engage completely with the political and social situations of the post-conflict society. This has the danger of undermining the achievements gained and rendering them unworkable. In respect of the judicial systems in Kosovo and East Timor, it has been shown that this is jeopardising the much needed processes of building confidence in the judicial systems, and of getting justice for victims of human rights violations, further contributing directly to the difficulties in assisting the societies to move from violent conflict to peace.

Second, this calls for the conclusion that what is required is a more holistic approach. To quote the words of Griffin, the "healing of human relations" needs to become a fundamental aspect of the peace building strategy. Following a human rights-based approach holds significant promise in this regard, particularly as it intends to deal with the social, economic and political consequences of the conflict. The human rights-based approach would also contribute significantly to the strength of the peace operation as a mechanism for human rights. The point has been made above that as it is currently conceptualised, the peace operation is not a strong mechanism. Its strength depends on being able to transform the structures which have been developed 'on paper' and as constructed physically, and the ideals and standards they uphold, into the actual fabric of the post-conflict society. More specifically, a human rights-based approach would satisfy the UN obligations to promote and encourage respect for human rights, and further to ensure the achievement of the objective of the peace operations themselves to protect and promote human rights, through the development of a culture of human rights.

Therefore, the latest forms of peace operations, as in Kosovo and East Timor, constitute another stage in the development of international capacity to promote and protect human rights. Through their ability to fundamentally determine the type of societal structures that will be put in place in post-conflict societies, and through the objective of the operations as mandated by the Security Council to promote and protect international human rights standards, peace operations take the implementation of international human rights standards another step further. However, this is not the equivalent to constituting a strong mechanism. While human rights-based initiatives already play a considerable role in peace operations, this is not equivalent to a human rights-based approach. It is proposed that transforming the approach of the peace operations to that of a human rights-based one would better serve the needs of the peace operations, further fulfil the obligations of the UN, and result in a strong mechanism for the promotion and protection of human rights.

UN Peace Operations in Africa Today and Tomorrow[1]

*Peter Viggo Jakobsen**

For better or worse, the African continent has played a crucial role in the development of the United Nations' (UN) peace operations during the last 40 years. The first UN operation in Africa, ONUC in the Congo (1960-64),[2] also represented the first UN attempt to carry out a peace enforcement operation in an internal conflict. ONUC started out with a Chapter VI mandate as a peacekeeping operation based on the principles of consent, impartiality and non-use of force except for self-defence, but it gradually evolved into a full-scale peace enforcement operation in which the UN contingents were authorized to take offensive actions against the rebels in the Katanga province.[3] ONUC succeeded militarily as the Katanga rebels were defeated, but the patient died because the operational difficulties and the divisions among the five permanent members of the Security Council deterred the UN from going beyond peacekeeping again for the remainder of the Cold War era.

The importance of Africa grew after 1988 where the improved climate in the Security Council paved the way for a dramatic increase in the number of UN peace operations. The 13 operations conducted prior to 1988 are dwarfed by the 41 conducted between January 1989 and January 2001. 18 of the post-Cold War operations have taken place on the African continent and several of them were as innovative and proved as influential on subsequent UN practice as ONUC. The UNTAG operation in Namibia (1989-90) is thus regarded as the first of the so-called multi-functional

---

*   Associate Professor, Institute of Political Science, University of Copenhagen.

[1]   An earlier version of this article was published in Danish as 'FN's fredsoperationer i Afrika i dag og i morgen' (2/2001) 130 *Militært Tidsskrift* 75-97.

[2]   For the complete list of UN peace operations in Africa see Appendix 1.

[3]   The classic peacekeeping operations are often referred to as Chapter VI½ operations, an expression first used by Dag Hammarskjöld, UN Secretary General between 1953-61. The reason is that peacekeeping operations are not mentioned in the Chapter and they are situated in a grey area between Chapter VI focussing on peaceful conflict resolution and Chapter VII containing the coercive instruments the UN can employ to maintain international peace and security. ONUC was a de facto but not de jure enforcement operation since no explicit reference to Chapter VII was ever made. See B. Huldt, 'Working Multilaterally: The Old Peacekeepers' Viewpoint' in D.C.F. Daniel/B.C. Hayes (eds.), *Beyond Traditional Peacekeeping* (St. Martin's Press, New York, 1995), pp. 103-104.

M. Bothe and B. Kondoch (eds.),
International Peacekeeping. The Yearbook of International Peace Operations, Volume 7, 2001, 153–180.

peace operations, e.g. operations with a combination of both civilian and military tasks; UNOSOM II in Somalia (1993-95) was the first UN attempt to conduct a peace enforcement on its own since the Congo operation; UNOMIL in Liberia (1993-97) was the first UN operation to be conducted jointly with a regional organization, the Economic Community of West African States (ECOWAS); UNAMSIL in Sierra Leone

(1999-) represents the first UN try at what UN Secretary-General Kofi Annan defines as 'robust peacekeeping', that is, finding a middle way between traditional peacekeeping with consent from the parties and peace enforcement without consent; lastly UNMEE in Eritrea/Ethiopia (2000-) is the first operation where the UN Standby High Readiness Brigade (SHIR-BRIG) has been deployed.

In addition to being path-breaking and challenging, the UN operations in Africa have generally been characterized by minimal Western support and a dramatic lack of resources. An analysis of the African operations will therefore provide the best basis for judging what the UN is (in)capable of today and tomorrow. This is so for two reasons. The level of commitment and resources are unlikely to become much lower and the challenges unlikely to become much higher. Secondly, Africa will become the central area of operations for the UN in the decade ahead because the demand for peace operations will be higher here than anywhere else, and because no other organizations or states are capable or willing to take on this thankless task. The UN operations have had more than their fair share of problems in the 1990s, and commentators have been queuing to make their call on the UN to terminate its involvement in peace operations and give way to more capable actors,[4] be they states, regional organizations or private military companies. The argument made here is the opposite, namely that there is no alternative to the UN in Africa and that the UN will continue to play a pivotal role in peace operations in the new century.[5] Commentators have written obituaries of UN peace operations each and every time they have run into trouble, and they always have been proven wrong. As a consequence, this article will analyse the most important peace operations conducted in Africa after the end of the Cold War in order to establish a basis for making a judgement about what we can expect of the UN in Africa today and tomorrow.

---

[4]   See for instance M. Ignatieff, 'A Bungling U.N. Undermines Itself,' *The New York Times*, 15 May 2000, p. A19; and C. Krauthammer, 'Let Peacekeeping Rest in Peace' *The Washington Post*, 2 June 2000, p. A33.

[5]   For an elaboration of this point see P.V. Jakobsen, 'Overload, not marginalization, threatens UN peacekeeping' (2/2000) 30 *Security Dialogue* 167-178.

The first part of the article undertakes a chronological analysis of the eight most important peace operations that the UN has conducted in Africa since 1989. UNTAG, UNAVEM II, ONUMOZ, UNOSOM II, UNAMIR, UNAVEM III, UNAMSIL and UNMEE are analysed briefly by means of four questions: (1) What type of operation was conducted? (2) What tasks were the UN force asked to do? (3) To what extent was the UN force capable of solving these tasks? and (4) What consequences did the outcome have for subsequent UN operations? These analyses form the basis for the assessment of the UN's capacity for conducting peace operations today which is made in the second part of the article. The third part analyses the three alternatives to the UN that have been most popular in the debate: 'give war a chance,' subcontracting to private military companies and 'African solutions for African problems.' The fourth and final part of the article discusses the prospects for UN peace operations in Africa tomorrow in the decade ahead.

1.UNTAG (1989-90) in Namibia

UNTAG was deployed in order to implement a peace agreement between South Africa and the rebel movement South West African People's Organization (SWAPO) that would pave the way for Namibia's independence. The 8,000-strong UNTAG was the first major operation the UN initiated after the end of the Cold War and its multi-functionality subsequently became the defining feature of the major peace operations conducted in the 1990s. A multi-functional peace operation distinguishes itself from a classic peacekeeping operation or observer mission by having both civilian and military contingents, a combination of civilian and military tasks and a civilian head of mission: a special representative of the Secretary-General (SRSG).

The UNTAG force consisted of 4,500 soldiers, 2,000 civilians and 1,500 police observers. Numbers were boosted by the presence of 1,000 electoral observers during the elections. UNTAG was tasked to monitor the withdrawal of the South African forces from Namibia; the disarmament of SWAPO forces and their return from Angola; human rights; the local police; and the conduct of free and fair elections. UNTAG should also enable the safe return of refugees and the main responsibility for this task was given to the United Nations High Commissioner for Refugees (UNHCR).

UNTAG was successful in the sense that South Africa got out, SWAPO got in and Namibia gained her independence. Nevertheless, the operation suffered from so many operational shortcomings resulting from deployment delays, lack of vehicles, poor logistics etc., that it is open to question to what extent the success can be attributed to UNTAG. The delayed arrival meant that the force was not in place when SWAPO units broke the cease-fire and began to enter Namibia. The SRSG therefore had to ask the South African Army to stop the incursion and the result was 350 dead SWAPO insurgents. That the peace process survived this incident can only be explained by factors that the UN force did not control. Firstly, the conflict was relatively easy to solve. It only involved two parties and the UN merely had to oversee the withdrawal of the South African forces and the conduct of elections. Compared to some of the subsequent operations such as UNAVEM and ONUMOZ where the UN was tasked to persuade former enemies to share power and coexist peacefully within the same country, this was quite a simple task. Secondly, South Africa was under heavy pressure from the United States to honour the peace agreement. Thirdly, none of the parties had strategic or economic interests in the continuation of the conflict, and fourthly, none of the neighbouring states tried to derail the peace process.[6]

Paradoxically, the success in Namibia had a negative impact on the UN's next multi-functional peace operation in Africa, because it helped to persuade the Security Council that UNAVEM II in Angola could be implemented successfully on the cheap with a very small UN force.

2. UNAVEM II (1991-92) in Angola

UNAVEM II was a discount version of the Namibia operation. The objective was similar, namely to monitor the implementation of a peace agreement between the government of Angola and the rebel movement União Nacional para a Independência Total de Angola (UNITA), which like the one in Namibia was supposed to result in the conduct of free and fair elections. The UN force consisted of 350 military observers, 126 civilian police observers, 242 civilians and 400 electoral observers and was headed by a SRSG. The operation was based on a chapter VI mandate and can with its many different observer tasks best be described as a multi-functional observer mission. It was tasked to observe the cease-fire; the

---

[6]   The analysis of UNTAG builds on V.P. Fortna, 'United Nations Transition Assistance Group' in W.J. Durch (ed.), *The Evolution of UN Peacekeeping: Case Studies and Comparative Analysis* (St. Martin's Press, New York, 1993), pp. 353-375; D. Pankhurst, 'Namibia' in O. Furley and R. May (eds.), *Peacekeeping in Africa* (Ashgate, Aldershot, 1998), pp. 207-222. The factual data for this and all the operations analysed have been found on the UN website: http://www.un.org/Depts/dpko/dpko/ops.htm.

local police; the disarmament and demobilisation of the armed forces; the establishment of new national army; and the presidential and legislative elections.

Prior to the establishment of UNAVEM II, 70 UN military observers (UNAVEM I) had successfully monitored the withdrawal of foreign forces from Angola and even been able to end the operation a month ahead of schedule. This success and the positive result in Namibia convinced the Security Council that the success of UNAVEM II was virtually assured and that only a small observer force would be required to see it through. Warnings from several African countries that a much larger force would be required were ignored.[7] Unfortunately, the assumption on which UN-AVEM II was based, that the parties would honour the agreement they had signed, turned out to be erroneous as electoral defeat induced UNITA to resume the war.

It is much debated whether UNAVEM II would have been successful if the Security Council had chosen to deploy a larger force. The operation was hopelessly understaffed and the budget much too small. The 400 electoral observers were thus supposed to cover 6,000 polling stations in a country two-thirds the size of Western Europe. They were consequently only capable of spending an average of 20 minutes at each station making it impossible to credibly refute the allegations of fraud that UNITA used to reject the result of the election.[8] Three other problems are also regarded as important for the failure, namely that the peace agreement did not contain provisions for power-sharing (none of the parties were interested in this), that demobilization of the two armies was not completed at the time of the election, and that the UN did not have any say in the design of the peace agreement or a mandate allowing it to influence its implementation.[9]

The SRSG, Margaret Anstee, has subsequently made the case that UNAVEM II 'very nearly did bring it off,' and that it would have succeeded if UNAVEM II had been given a larger force and more influence

---

[7]   W. Kühne, 'Lessons from peacekeeping operations in Angola, Mozambique, Somalia, Rwanda and Liberia' *Chaillot Papers*, No. 22 (December 1995), p. 18; N. MacQueen, 'Peacekeeping by attrition: The United Nations in Angola' (3/1998) 36 *The Journal of Modern African Studies* 401.

[8]   M.R. Berdal, 'Whither UN Peacekeeping?' *Adelphi Paper*, No. 281 (1993), p. 37.

[9]   M.J. Anstee, 'Angola: the forgotten tragedy. A test case for UN peacekeeping,' (6/1993) 11 *International Relations* 495-511; Kühne, *supra* note 7, pp. 18-21; A. Malaquias, 'The UN in Mozambique and Angola: Lessons Learnt' (2/1996) 3 *International Peacekeeping* (Frank Cass/London) 87-103.

on the implementation of the peace agreement.[10] Other commentators disagree arguing that the UNITA's leader Jonas Savimbi would have rejected the election result in any event because he remained convinced that he could win a military victory, and because he did not want to give up the lucrative diamond mines under UNITA control.[11] That a 8,000-strong UN force (UNAVEM III), as we shall see below, was unable to end the civil war in 1995-97, supports the latter position.

Fortunately, the failure in Angola and the criticism that followed in its wake induced the UN to change tack and adopt a different strategy in its next multi-functional peace operation in Mozambique.

3. ONUMOZ (1992-94) in Mozambique

As was the case with UNTAG and UNAVEM II, ONUMOZ was also mandated to monitor the implementation of a peace agreement, here between the government and the rebel movement Resistencia Nacional Mozambicana (RENAMO), that was supposed to lead to elections. ONUMOZ was deployed on a Chapter VI mandate and asked to verify the cease-fire, monitor the withdrawal of foreign forces, integrate former government troops and rebels into a new national army, disarm, demobilize and reintegrate former soldiers into society, coordinate and monitor humanitarian assistance, provide technical assistance and monitor the electoral process. Monitoring of the local police was later added to the mandate when the parties had accepted a UN role here also. At full strength the UN force numbered 7,437, of which 861 were civilians, and 1,087 police observers. In addition 2,500 electoral observers were present during the elections. To enhance coordination the UN for the first time established a separate office for coordinating the humanitarian aspects of the operation (UNO-HAC).

ONUMOZ was a success. The majority of the armed forces were demobilized, the election was held and the civil war brought to an end. The success can in part be attributed to the fact that UN learned from the failure in Angola and deployed a much larger force with a more realistic budget and a mandate that gave it a say in the implementation of the peace agreement. To deny the loser of the election the possibility of going back

---

[10] Anstee, *ibid.*, p. 497.

[11] D.C. Jett, *Why Peacekeeping Fails* (Macmillan Press Ltd, Houndsmills, 2000), pp. 117-119; S.J. Stedman, 'Spoiler Problems in Peace Processes' (2/1997) 22 *International Security* 39-40.

to war, the UN tried hard to complete demobilization before the election.[12] This effort was not entirely successful as RENAMO held back 2-15,000 soldiers because it did not trust the government to honour its promises if it won the election.[13] Still RENAMO did not go back to war and this can in part be explained by heavy pressure from the international community and the financial inducements that the SRSR, Aldo Ajello, was able to employ because his national government Italy had provided him with a USD35 million fund to assist RENAMO's transition to a democratic party.[14] For a period of 13 months (Sept 1993-Oct 1994) Ajello paid REMANO's leader USD 300.000 a month to reward his cooperation with the UN.[15]

Although the UN did not repeat the mistakes from Angola, it remains an open question how much credit one should give to ONUMOZ for the success. The operation suffered from most of the weaknesses that normally characterize UN peace operations. Delays meant that ONUMOZ only became operational eight months after the peace agreement had been signed, the new office for humanitarian coordination did not work, many police observers lacked the basic skills required to fulfil their work, the mine clearing programme turned into a white elephant and the demobilization and reintegration programme was marred by delays. The reason that these problems did not derail the peace process, most observers agree, is that it was supported by a number of factors outside of ONUMOZ control: the parties no longer regarded military victory as possible; international support for the peace process was strong; the neighbouring states and the donors put heavy pressure on RENAMO's leader to accept his defeat at the polls; the parties depended heavily on external economic support as Mozambique lacks the natural resources that have enabled parties in other

---

[12]   The strong influence that the UNAVEM II experience had on ONUMOZ is evident from E. Berman, *Managing Arms in Peace Processes: Mozambique* (UNIDIR, Geneva, 1996), pp. 34-39.

[13]   C. Alden, 'United Nations Peacekeeping in Africa: Lessons for the OAU and SADC' *Accord Occasional Paper*, No. 1 (Accord, Durban, 1997), p. 9; B.F. Walter, 'Designing Transitions for Violent Civil War' in B.F. Walter and J. Snyder (eds.), *Civil Wars, Insecurity and Intervention* (Columbia University Press, New York, 1999), p. 57. Moreover, the disarmament that did occur was very uneven. See A. Vines, 'Disarmament in Mozambique' (1/1998) 24 *Journal of Southern African Studies* 191-205.

[14]   'Key Actors in the War and Peace Process' in *The Mozambican Peace Process in Perspective* (Accord, London), http://www.c-r.org/acc_moz/keyactors.htm downloaded 29 May 2002.

[15]   R. Synge, *Mozambique. UN Peacekeeping in Action 1992-94* (United States Institute of Peace Press, Washington, D.C., 1997), p. 60.

conflicts to sustain their war effort; and the soldiers were so exhausted from war that they rioted because they felt that the demobilization process proceeded too slowly.[16]

Unfortunately, the success of ONUMOZ did not have much impact on subsequent operations because it was overshadowed by the failure in Somalia.

4. UNOSOM II (1993-95) in Somalia

In December 1992, following the collapse of UNOSOM I, the Security Council gave a 38,000-strong US-led intervention force UNITAF a Chapter VII mandate to establish a secure environment for the delivery of humanitarian assistance. UNOSOM II took over from UNITAF in May 1993 and although it was considerably smaller, 30,800, it was still mandated to disarm the Somalia militias and take control of all of Somalia; tasks that UNITAF had deemed beyond its capacity. In addition UNOSOM II was also tasked to provide humanitarian assistance; clear mines; repatriate refugees and internally displaced; assist in the rebuilding of political institutions; the civilian administration and the police. UNOSOM II was the first UN-controlled operation ever to be given a peace enforcement mandate from the start.

As you are probably aware, the operation failed. The unilateral US decision to withdraw after 18 US Rangers were killed in an unsuccessful attempt to capture clan leader Aideed effectively ended the operation. The reasons for the failure is a topic of heated debate. Some believe that UNOSOM II was doomed from the start because the UN had taken on an impossible task. Others point to the many mistakes and problems that marred the operation. UNOSOM II not only suffered from the 'usual' problems such as inadequate planning, poor logistics, shortages of materiel, budgetary constraints, poorly qualified staff, bureaucratic and slow decision-making procedures, inadequate intelligence and lack of coordination among the UN organizations involved. On top of all this came specific problems stemming from a poorly managed handover from UNITAF to UNOSOM II, mistakes made by the Americans before the UN took

---

[16] For ONUMOZ see S. Barnes, 'Peacekeeping in Mozambique' in O. Furley and R. May (eds.), *Peacekeeping in Africa* (Ashgate, Aldershot, 1998), pp. 159-177; Berman, *supra* note 12; H. Broer and M. Emery, 'Civilian Police in U.N. Peacekeeping Operations' in R.B. Oakley, M.J. Dziedzic and E.M. Goldberg (eds.), *Policing the New World Disorder Peace Operations and Public Security* (NDU Press, Washington, DC., 1998), http://www.ndu.edu/ndu/inss/books/policing/chapter10.html; Jett, *supra* note 11; and Malaquias, *supra* note 9.

over, contingents who refused to carry out risky assignments (the Italians even rejected that the force was mandated to use force beyond self-defence), and American operations conducted outside the UN chain of command, including the one that cost the lives of the 18 Rangers.[17]

This is not the place to enter into this debate; for our purposes the important thing to note is that the UN drew the lesson from Somalia that it lacked the capacity to carry out peace enforcement operations in ongoing conflicts in order to coerce the parties to cease fire, and that the world organization should refrain from undertaking such operations in the future.[18] In addition, UNOSOM II made the Western powers, and in particularly the US, allergic to participation in new operations in Africa. The failure in Somalia thus contributed heavily to the tragedy in Rwanda.

5. UNAMIR (1993-94) in Rwanda

The fact that UNAMIR has a greater resemblance with UNAVEM II than ONUMOZ suggests that the Security Council ignored the lessons learned in these two operations. UNAMIR was given a Chapter VI mandate to monitor the implementation of a peace agreement that Rwanda's Hutu-dominated government and the Tutsi-dominated rebel movement the Rwandan Patriotic Front (RPF) had signed in August 1993. More specifically, the UNAMIR force was tasked to assist in ensuring the security of the capital city of Kigali; monitor the cease-fire agreement, including establishment of an expanded demilitarized zone and demobilization procedures; monitor the security situation during the final period of the transitional government's mandate leading up to elections; assist with mine-

---

[17] For UNOSOM II see W. Clarke and J. Herbst, *Somalia and the Future of Humanitarian Intervention* (Princeton University, Center for International Studies Monograph Series, No. 9, New Jersey, 1995); D.C.F. Daniel and C.H. Bradd with C.J. Oudraat, *Coercive Inducement and the Containment of International Crises* (United States Institute for Peace Press, Washington, DC, 1998); J.L. Hirsch and R.B. Oakley, *Somalia and Operation Restore Hope* (United States Institute for Peace Press, Washington, DC, 1995); R.G. Patman, 'The UN Operation in Somalia' in R. Thakur/C. Thayer (eds.), *UN Peacekeeping in the 1990s* (Westview, Col: Boulder, 1995), pp. 95-114; and *The Comprehensive Report on Lessons Learned from United Nations Operation in Somalia (UNOSOM), April 1992 - March 1995* (The Lessons Learned Unit of the Department of Peacekeeping Operations, New York, 1995).

[18] K. Annan, 'Renewing the United Nations: A Programme for Reform' UN doc. A/51/950, 16 July, 1997, para. 107; B. Boutros-Ghali, 'Supplement to An Agenda for Peace. Position paper of the Secretary-General on the occasion of the Fiftieth Anniversary of the UN' A/50/60-S/1995/1, 3 January 1995, para 77.

clearance; and assist in the coordination of humanitarian assistance activities in conjunction with relief operations.

Just like UNAVEM II, the operation was based on the assumption that the parties would honour the peace agreement they had signed, and the small UNAMIR force (2,548 soldiers and 200 civilians) was very limited in its ability to influence the parties. As it turned out, the hawks within the Rwandan government had no intention of honouring the agreement which would deprive them of all their power and privileges, and the result was the genocide of the Tutsies with cost 800,000 people their lives.

When the genocide started in the beginning of April 1994, the RPF launched an intervention in Rwanda to stop it. The Security Council did not take any effective action. Instead it reacted by withdrawing UNAMIR, leaving behind only a symbolic contingent of 270. Attempts to assemble an African intervention force stranded on Western and primarily US unwillingness to provide the required support, and the Security Council ended up giving France a Chapter VII mandate to establish a safe zone for refugees. Operation Turquoise carried out by 2,500 French soldiers began on 23 June and the civil war ended with a RPF victory three weeks later.

UNAMIR's effectiveness was limited by a long list of factors: delays in deployments which meant that the force just had reached full strength when the genocide began; the SRSG arrived three months into the operation, a factor which hampered cooperation with the force commander; inadequate funds; materiel shortages; severe logistical problems (because no member state would provide a well-equipped logistics battalion, this task was left to Bangladesh, who could neither equip nor support its own contingent); an inadequate intelligence capacity; and poorly trained and equipped contingents.

However, the principal factor leading to the disaster was the Somalia syndrome that the Western countries, and especially the US, suffered from. Reluctance on the part of the Western members of the Security Council to become involved in another operation in Africa meant that the strength of UNAMIR was reduced from the 8,000 recommended by the UN assessment team to 2,500, and the Security Council also rejected a proposal from the UN Secretary-General that UNAMIR should take part in the disarmament of the armed forces. Requests from UNAMIR's force commander, Romeo A. Dallaire, for ammunition, reinforcements and armored personnel carriers and permission to confiscate weapons depots were rejected by the UN Secretariat in New York, and the Security Council also ignored a proposal from Belgium calling for a reinforcement of UNAMIR.[19]

Dallaire has subsequently claimed that a well-trained 5,000-strong force could have prevented the genocide, and this seems likely provided that the force had been deployed before the genocide began.[20] The only positive thing about UNAMIR is that it induced the Western powers to re-think their approach to Africa and peace operations in general. Operation Turquoise helped to put peace enforcement delegated by the Security Council to states and regional organizations back on the agenda, and the Western powers also embarked on a number of initiatives aimed at en-hancing the African capacity for peacekeeping.

6. UNAVEM III (1995-97) in Angola

When setting up UNAVEM III to assist in the implementation of a new peace agreement signed in November 1994, the UN tried to draw on its experience from UNAVEM II, UNOMOZ and UNAMIR. The Security Council authorized the establishment of a large multi-functional peace op-eration consisting of 7,000 soldiers, 350 military observers, 260 police observers and a civilian staff of 420. UNAVEM III was mandated to assist the Angolan parties in restoring peace and achieving national reconcilia-tion; to supervise, control and verify the disengagement of forces and to monitor the cease-fire; to supervise control and verify the demobilization of the armed forces and the formation of a joint national army; to verify and monitor the police; to provide humanitarian assistance; and to partici-pate in mine-clearance activities. This mandate put UNAVEM III in a bet-ter position than its predecessor to influence the implementation of the

---

[19]   For UNAMIR see R. Connaughton, 'Wider Peacekeeping – How Wide of the Mark?' *British Army Review*, No. 111 (December 1995) 55-64; I. Carlsson/H. Sung-Joo/R. M. Kupolati, *Report of the Independent Inquiry into the Actions of the United Nations during the 1994 Genocide in Rwanda* (New York, 15 December 1999), http://www.un.org/News/ossg/rwanda_report.htm; Kühne, *supra* note 7, pp. 31-36; B.D. Jones, 'Military Intervention in Rwanda's 'Two Wars': Partisanship and Indif-ference' in B.F. Walter/J. Snyder (eds.) *Civil Wars, Insecurity and Intervention* (Co-lumbia University Press, New York, 1999), pp. 136-138; *The Comprehensive Report on Lessons Learned from United Nations Assistance Mission for Rwanda (UNAMIR), October 1993-April 1996* (The Lessons Learned Unit of the Department of Peacekeeping Operations, New York, 1997); and C. Winther, 'The International Response to the Conflict and Genocide in Rwanda' in K.E. Jørgensen (ed.), *Euro-pean Approaches to Crisis Management* (Kluwer Law International, 1997), pp. 83-105.

[20]   A.J. Kuperman, 'Rwanda in Retrospect' (1/2000) 79 *Foreign Affairs,* 94-118.

peace agreement and the new agreement also contained provisions for power-sharing and improved military guarantees aimed at making it more acceptable to UNITA.[21]

When UNAVEM III withdrew in 1997 some progress had been made: a government of national unity and a joint army had been formed, and some of UNITA's forces had been disarmed and demobilized. However, UNITA's leader Savimbi held back his elite units and remained unwilling to surrender control of 'his' diamond mines. Fighting resumed in December 1998 and resulted in the withdrawal of UNAVEM IIIs successor, a smaller observer mission (MONUA), from Angola in 1999.

Not even with a larger force, more resources, a stronger mandate and - on paper at least - a better peace agreement did the UN succeed in bringing peace to Angola. Force commander Philip Sibanda subsequently complained that UNAVEM III was hampered by inadequate resources, and that it might have succeeded if he had been given the 15,000 soldiers that the UN assessment team had recommended prior to the start of the mission, more vehicles and adequate air transport.[22] However, it seems highly unlikely that an additional 8,000 troops would have made a decisive difference, given that UNAVEM III to succeed would have had to force Savimbi to comply with the peace agreement, i.e. be in a position to defeat UNITA militarily if necessary.

7. UNAMSIL (1999-) in Sierra Leone

An authorized force of 17,500 makes UNAMSIL the largest UN peace operation since UNOSOM II. The operation is multi-functional and deployed to support the implementation of a peace agreement between the government of Sierra Leone and the rebel movement Revolutionary United Front (RUF). UNAMSIL is mandated to assist the government in the implementation of the disarmament, demobilization and reintegration plan; to provide security at key locations and Government buildings, in particular in Freetown, important intersections and major airports; to coordinate with and assist, the Sierra Leone law enforcement authorities in the discharge of their responsibilities; to facilitate the free flow of people, goods and humanitarian assistance; and to provide electoral support.

---

[21] For UNAVEM III see Kühne, *supra* note 7, pp. 20-21; and MacQueen, *supra* note 7.

[22] P. Sibanda, 'United Nations Operations in Southern Africa: Mandate, Means and Doctrine in UNAVEM III' in M. Malan (ed.), *Boundaries of Peace Operations: The African Dimension* (Institute for Security Studies, ISS Monograph Series, No. 44, Pretoria, 2000), http://www.iss.co.za/Pubs/Monographs/No44/UnitedNations.html.

UNAMSIL is a chapter VII operation with a mandate to use 'all neces-sary' means in order to fulfil its mandate, maintain freedom of movement and protect UN personnel and civilians against attacks 'within its capabili-ties and areas of deployment.' UN Secretary-General Kofi Annan charac-terizes UNAMSIL as a: 'robust peacekeeping force – impartial in terms of its political position vis-à-vis the parties, but strong in its ability to deter attacks and to defend itself and its mandate should this become neces-sary.'[23] Western and NATO doctrines would classify the operation as peace enforcement,[24] but Annan is politically prevented from doing so, be-cause a majority of UN member states, including the Western ones, since the failure in Somalia has been strongly opposed to UN involvement in peace enforcement.[25]

This opposition is also clear from the low level of support that UNAM-SIL has received from UN member states. It has been a struggle to find troops and UNAMSIL has suffered from deployment delays; inadequate logistical support; lack of modern equipment; poorly trained personnel; premature withdrawals of contingents; internal bickering; reluctance among troop contributions to allow their continents to take part in combat operations; allegations of corruption; and an inadequate intelligence capacity.[26]

---

[23] K. Annan, 'Secretary-General Stresses Need to Address Issues Related to UNAM-SIL's Command and Control Structure, Equipment Shortfalls and Mandate' *UN Press Release*, SG/SM/7514 PKO/95, 23 August 2000.

[24] For an analysis of Western doctrines see P.V. Jakobsen, 'The Emerging Consensus on Grey Area Peace Operations Doctrine: The Emerging Consensus on Grey Area Peace Operations Doctrine: Will It Last and Enhance Operational Effectiveness?' (3/2000) 7 *International Peacekeeping* (Frank Cass/London) 36-56.

[25] The FN is also characterizing its ongoing operation in East Timor (UNTAET) as a peacekeeping operation although it with its Chapter VII mandate and authority to use 'all necessary means' to accomplish its tasks in reality is a peace enforcement operation. The 'all necessary means' is a standard UN term usually reserved for peace enforcement operations. It was thus employed in connection with the Gulf War and in most of the other enforcement operations that the UN has authorized in the 1990s (UNITAF, Operation Turquoise, the American intervention in Haiti in 1994 and the NATO operations in Bosnia and Kosovo).

[26] T. Deen/I. Kemp, 'Shoestring peacekeeping' (17 May 2000) 33 *Jane's Defence Weekly*; D. Farah, 'Old Problems Hamper U.N. In Sierra Leone' *The Washington Post*, 11 June 2000, p. A25; S. Gordon/J. Higgs, 'Briefing UN Mission in Sierra Leone: Peace at what price?' (27 September 2000) 34 *Jane's Defence Weekly* 27-34; E. MacAskill, 'UN gets warning shot on peacekeeping' *The Guardian*, 9 September 2000.

UNAMSIL's weaknesses were put on display in May 2000 when RUF captured a large amount of materiel from the UN force and took over 500 UN soldiers hostage. The crisis induced Great Britain to a hasty deployment of 700 paratroopers to evacuate Western citizens and stabilize the situation.[27] UNAMSIL salvaged some of its tainted honour by rescuing 233 UN soldiers in a daring rescue operation in July 2000,[28] but the situation remains uncertain. Although Annan has succeeded in increasing the size of UNAMSIL to 17,500 (his target is 20,500),[29] the prospects for ending the civil war in the near future do not look bright because it has proven difficult to prevent RUF from sustaining its military capacity through the sale of diamonds.[30]

Since the final outcome of UNAMSIL remains unclear at the time of writing, it is obviously too early to tell what implications it will have for future UN operations. It is equally unclear what lessons the UN will draw from the debacle in May 2000. The Brahimi Report which was released in August 2000 effectively represents an attempt by Annan to use the humiliation of UNAMSIL as an argument for giving the UN a capacity for 'robust peacekeeping,' so that repetitions can be avoided.[31] His attempt will almost certainly fail, however, as many governments and commentators view the fate of UNAMSIL as additional proof that the UN should stick to Chapter VI activities and leave Chapter VII operations to regional organizations and coalitions of states with the willingness and capability to conduct them effectively.[32]

---

[27] E. MacAskill/R. Norton-Taylor, 'Flawed evidence led to mission creep' *The Guardian*, 16 May 2000.

[28] D. Farah, 'U.N. Rescues Hostages in Sierra Leone' *The Washington Post*, 16 July 2000, p. A20.

[29] UN Doc. S/2001/228, 14 March 2001, para. 10.

[30] D. Farah, 'Liberian President Pledges to Cut Sierra Leone Rebel Ties' *The Washington Post*, 20 January 2000, p. 21; E. MacAskill/D. Pallister, 'Crackdown on 'blood' diamonds' *The Guardian*, 20 December 2000; N. Onishi, 'Africa Diamond Hub Defies Smuggling Rules' *The New York Times*, 2 January 2001.

[31] Annan made no attempt to hide what he thought the conclusion the report should reach. Compare K. Annan, 'Secretary-General Delivers Commencement Address at Paul Nitze School of Advanced International Studies, John Hopkins University' *UN Press Release*, SG/SM/7421, 25 May 2000; and L. Brahimi et al., *Report of the Panel on the United Nations Peace Operations* (UN Doc. A/55/305-S/2000/809, 21 August 2000).

[32] See for instance M. Hirsh, 'Calling All Regio-cops. Peacekeeping's Hybrid Future' (8/2000) 79 *Foreign Affairs* 2-8; and R. Thakur, 'The U.N.'s impossible task' *Japan Times*, 28 May 2000.

8. UNMEE (2000-) in Ethiopia and Eritrea

UNMEE is a rare example of a classic peacekeeping operation. It is deployed to monitor a peace agreement between the governments of Ethiopia and Eritrea and has been tasked to monitor and verify the withdrawal of the armed forces and the establishment of a security zone. It is also involved in humanitarian mine-action activities, the coordination of humanitarian assistance and human rights activities. The operation is led by a SRSG, has a Chapter VI mandate and has an authorized strength of 4,200 soldiers including 220 military observers and 127 civilians. Although it has a civilian head of mission (SRSG) and some civilian tasks, it would be misleading to view it as a multi-functional operation.

All signs are that the operation is a success story in the making and according to the UN Secretary-General its effectiveness is not hampered by the usual operational difficulties. On the contrary, Annan has praised the SHIRBRIG countries (Canada, Denmark and the Netherlands, who provided 1,964 soldiers) and the other contributors for 'their prompt and generous contributions, which allowed a quick and efficient deployment of the force.'[33]

Unlike the other African peace operations, it has not been difficult to find well-trained troops from the Western countries (Denmark actually fought a long and hard battle to be allowed to participate), and the explanation is of course that this operation compared to the alternatives, the Democratic Republic of Congo and Sierra Leone, is relatively safe and much more likely to succeed. That the war ended with a decisive defeat for Eritrea significantly reduces the risk of renewed fighting; the level of cooperation from the parties is quite high; both parties are state governments with relatively disciplined armies, not unpredictable warlords; the measure of success is simple: establish a new border; none of the neighbouring countries are trying to derail the peace process; and the operation enjoys the backing of a united Security Council. As a member of the Danish contingent put it: 'This is a holiday not a mission.'[34] These favourable conditions were also reflected in the welcome the commander of the Danish contingent gave his troops when they arrived:

---

[33] UN Doc. S/2001/202, 7 March 2001, para. 25.

[34] W. Shawcross, 'UN Peacekeeping Lessons in Africa' *International Herald Tribune*, 16 December 2000.

'The situation is very peaceful. In a short while we will take in your weapons for storage. Only guards will be allowed to carry weapons. The rest of you won't need them.'[35]

Considering that interstate wars today are placed on the list of endangered species and that very few operations are conducted in a best case scenario, it seems unlikely that UNMEE will have much impact on future UN peace operations in Africa or elsewhere. It may, however, be used as yet another argument in favour of restricting the UN to Chapter VI activities.

9. Assessing the UN capacity for peace operations today

A comparison of the eight operations suggests that the UN at a minimum will need to acquire the coercive capacity that Annan wants in order to significantly improve its success rate. In the three operations where UN efforts proved successful (ONUMOZ, UNMEE and UNTAG), the parties could be persuaded to cooperate and the peace process enjoyed the support of neighbouring states and the international community in general. Conversely, in the operations that failed the UN was faced with one or more parties who actively sought to derail the peace process (UNAMIR, UN-AVEM II + III, UNAMSIL and UNOSOM II), because peace would result in a loss of power, status and income. In the three successful cases, mediation, diplomatic pressure, economic sticks and carrots and the presence of UN forces proved sufficient to keep the peace process on track, in the five failures these instruments failed to do the trick, and the two UN attempts to coerce the recalcitrant parties to accept a peace agreement or process have (thus far) failed (UNAMSIL and UNOSOM II). The conclusion which is supported by other UN operations is in other words that the UN does not have the capacity to coerce parties to cease fire and solve their differences peacefully against their will. As a consequence, it will in most cases be a combination of external factors that the UN force cannot control (exhaustion, lack of funds to finance continued fighting, support from neighbouring countries, transnational companies and the great powers for the peace process) that ultimately decide whether an operation succeeds or fails.

That a capacity for peace enforcement is key to success is also suggested by the fact that the operational shortcomings, which characterized all the operations except UNMEE, did not prove decisive for their out-

---

[35] C. Brøndum, 'God start for danskerne i Eritrea' *Berlingske Tidende*, 10 December 2000, p. 8.

come. The presence of an effective peacekeeping force cannot be regarded as a necessary condition for success since both the UNTAG and ONU-MOZ operations succeeded in spite of severe operational problems. Such problems cannot explain the failures of the two UNAVEM operations, UNAMSIL and UNOSOM II either. Only in the case of UNAMIR can one make a credible case that a well-equipped force with the same mandate could have made a difference and limited the loss of life significantly, while the RPF defeated the government forces. Had UNAMSIL had better personnel and better equipment the humiliation in May 2000 could have been avoided – after all 700 British troops proved enough to stabilize the situation, but in order to succeed in persuading/coercing RUF to lay down its arms and surrender control of its diamond fields, it is likely to need more than the 17,500 personnel it presently has. Similarly well-equipped and well-trained UNAVEM II+III and UNOSOM II forces could not have coerced their opponents effectively without major reinforcements.

In short, the principal reason why five of the eight operations failed, was not that the UN forces were badly trained, equipped and supported, but that the concept was wrong, i. e. that the Security Council deployed peacekeeping forces in situations where there was a need for peace enforcement contingents like the ones NATO has deployed in the Balkans. Both UNAMSIL and UNOSOM II functioned effectively as peacekeeping forces even though they had Chapter VII mandates because they lacked the capacity to coerce the parties to accept peace agreements against their will.

Although a well-equipped and well-trained force is always to be preferred and although operational effectiveness on occasion can make the difference between failure and success, the conclusion nevertheless remains that improvements in operational effectiveness in themselves will have a limited effect on the UN's rate of success. As long as the UN lacks a peace enforcement capacity, it will only succeed in peace operations when the parties want peace or can be enticed/pressured with diplomatic and economic instruments to enter and implement cease-fires and peace agreements. Effective peacekeeping forces can hold hands but they cannot twist arms and coerce recalcitrant parties to respect peace agreements or UN resolutions.

UN peace operations are therefore unlikely to prove more successful in the coming decade than they have in the past because UN forces more often than not will be deployed in conflicts where cooperation from at least one of the parties will be limited. All the major peace operations in the

1990s have been characterized by limited or a lack of consent from (one of) the parties, and there is nothing to suggest that this is about to change.

The logical solution to this problem is of course to give the UN the capacity to conduct robust peacekeeping (read: peace enforcement) as the Brahimi Report and Annan recommend. This is not possible, however, because the large majority of member states resist giving the UN military teeth. The widespread resistance in the Third World stems partly from fear that the establishment of such a capability would be financed by development funds, partly from fear that the great powers on the Security Council would use such a capacity selectively to advance their own interests. Needless to say, a handful of Third World governments also have reason to fear that it might be used against them.[36] The permanent members are also unenthusiastic about the proposal because they are unwilling to foot the bill and, more importantly, see an interest in preserving their monopoly on deciding where and when effective military interventions should be launched. A third factor blocking the establishment of a UN peace enforcement capacity is the strong aversion to casualties that the Western states currently suffer from. This aversion makes them very reluctant to contribute troops to peace enforcement operations under UN command. That no Western country has been willing to contribute with contingents to UNAMSIL and the British refusal to put their troops in Sierra Leone under UN command illustrate the problem in a nutshell. Since it seems safe to conclude that the UN will not be given a peace enforcement capacity in the foreseeable future, the next part of the article will take a closer look at the three alternatives to the UN that have been most popular among commentators and Western policy makers in recent years.

10. Alternatives to the UN?
The debate in recent years have focussed on three alternatives to the UN when it comes to peace enforcement activities: 'give war a chance,' sub-contracting to private military companies and the African do-it-yourself solution. The name of the first alternative is the title of a provocative *Foreign Affairs* article by Luttwak from 1999 which makes the case that the UN should refrain from launching peacekeeping operations until the parties have tired of fighting or one of them has won a decisive military victory. The only thing the UN, according to Luttwak, accomplishes by inter-

---

[36] For Third World reactions to the Brahimi Report see L. Brahimi, 'Peacekeeping and Conflict Resolution,' The 2001 Alastair Buchan Memorial Lecture delivered on 22 March 2001 at Arundel House, IISS; and B. Crossette, 'U.N. Plan for a New Crisis Unit Opposed by Wary Poor Nations,' *The New York Times*, 26 November 2000.

vening earlier is to prolong the conflicts and force UN troops to become passive spectators to outrages and massacres. So as long as the UN is unprepared to help the strongest party win faster and more decisively and lacks the capacity to coerce the parties to cease fire, the best course of action is to stay away.[37]

Luttwak's argument should not be dismissed out of hand for it reflects the conclusion drawn above, that it is very limited what a UN force without a peace enforcement capacity can do in situations where (one of) the parties have signed a peace agreement in bad faith. His solution is already being practiced. War has been given plenty of chances in Burundi, the Democratic Republic of Congo and Sudan to give just a few examples, and war was also given a chance in the conflict between Eritrea and Ethiopia. UNMEE was only deployed after Ethiopia had defeated Eritrea decisively and it was clear that both parties were ready for peace.

The problem with Luttwak's solution is that it is infeasible in many cases. The armed conflicts that dominate the international system today have a number of features that make them hard to ignore. They do not burn themselves out, as Luttwak assumes, but tend to go on and on because none of the parties are strong enough to win a decisive victory. Civilian casualties are much higher than before and this attracts the attention of the media. Media coverage of massacres on civilians and the fact that the conflicts drag on will often make it very difficult for Western governments to resist calls for military intervention until the parties have tired of fighting, unless it is clear to everyone that an intervention is likely to fail (until the death of Laurent Kabila the Democratic Republic of Congo was an obvious case in point). Non-intervention was eventually not a live option for Western decision makers in Northern Iraq, Bosnia, Somalia, Rwanda or Kosovo and there will be more conflicts in the future where nasty television footage (or fear that it might appear) will pressure Western government to 'do something' in Africa. However, since the Western powers on the Security Council more often than not are unwilling to run the risks of intervening themselves, the deployment of a UN peacekeeping operation represents a convenient way of signalling a commitment to world peace as they can usually count on other countries to supply the troops. This dilemma is not about to disappear which is why the Security Council will continue to authorize peacekeeping operations with slim prospects of success.

---

[37] E.N. Luttwak, 'Give War a Chance' (4/1999) 78 *Foreign Affairs* 36-44.

Finally, it also creates difficulties for Luttwak's solution that it tends to be hard to determine in advance whether the parties sign a peace agreement because they want peace or because they want time to regroup and prepare the next offensive. Once troops have been put on the ground, it will usually be too costly (morally and politically) to follow Luttwak's advice and withdraw if the parties renege on their commitments. The withdrawals of United Nations Emergency Force (UNEF I) from the Sinai in 1967 and UNAMIR from Rwanda in 1994 illustrate the problem. The UN was given much of the blame for the Six-Day War and the genocide that followed in the wake of these withdrawals. The genocide in Rwanda has made it very hard for the UN to withdraw, once troops have been committed, and it was actually this difficulty which led to the humiliation of UNAMSIL in the Spring of 2000. UNAMSIL was originally deployed to cooperate with the 15,000-strong Economic Community of West African States Cease-fire Monitoring Group (ECOMOG) force already operating in Sierra Leone. The basis for this operation quickly collapsed, however, following a decision by Nigeria to withdraw the majority of its 12,000 soldiers in ECOMOG. The shadow of Rwanda made it impossible for the UN to withdraw and the unwillingness of member states to contribute the troops and funds required to fill the vacuum created by the Nigerian withdrawal set the stage for the disaster.

To sum up, even though Luttwak's alternative is and will continue to be used, especially in Africa where it is easier for Western leaders to ignore massive human rights violations than in most other places, conflicts generating unbearable pressure on Western leaders 'to something' will continue to occur in Africa.

The second alternative to UN peacekeeping is as controversial as the first: sub-contracting to private military companies who offer a great variety of military services ranging from military training to the planning and conduct of military campaigns.[38] Interest in this alternative was primarily generated by the results Executive Outcomes (EO), a private military company consisting of former soldiers from the South African Defence Force, achieved in Angola and Sierra Leone in the mid-1990s. Hired by the Angolan government, EO provided different forms of technical assistance, trained 5,000 troops and 30 pilots and took part in the planning and

---

[38] For such proposals see K. O'Brien, 'Military-Advisory Groups and African Security: Privatized Peacekeeping?' (3/2000) 5 *International Peacekeeping* (Frank Cass/London) 78-105; J. Schulhofer-Wohl, 'Should We Privatize The Peacekeeping?' *The Washington Post*, 12 May 2000, p. A 47; and D. Shearer, 'Private Armies and Military Intervention' *Adelphi Paper*, No. 316 (1998).

conduct of offensive operations against UNITA. The EO-led operations resulted in the recapture of important diamond areas and oil installations from UNITA and induced the rebels to sign the peace agreement that paved the way for the deployment of UNAVEM III. One of UNITA's conditions for signing was that EO left the country. EO achieved this result with a force of 570 and the loss of 20 men.

EO was equally successful in Sierra Leone where it on a government contract trained and equipped a large pro-government militia, provided logistical support, planned and participated in offensive operations with planes, helicopter gunships and soldiers. In less than a year, the EO-led forces succeeded in driving RUF out of the capital Freetown, reopening the main roads into Freetown, regaining control with important mining districts and destroying the RUF headquarters. As had been the case in Angola, the EO campaign forced the rebels to the negotiating table and RUF also demanded the departure of EO just like UNITA had done. EO employed 300-400 personnel when the operation in Sierra Leone was at its highest and lost only two men.[39]

It should be pointed out immediately that the successes were short-lived in both places and that the EO involvement failed to put an end to either of the civil wars. This said, the results achieved by EO do demonstrate that private military companies in some conflicts would be capable of providing the peace enforcement capacity that is necessary for success. They are unlikely to be allowed to do so, however. Private military companies like EO, who provide combat services to their clients have been getting a bad press in recent years, and the combination of bad publicity and the adoption of a new law in South Africa regulating the activities of private security firms caused EO to terminate its activities in 1998. Although the termination probably should been seen as a public relations exercise (former EO staff still ply their trade in Africa and elsewhere), it still suggests that the UN Security Council is unlikely to start hiring private military companies to conduct peace enforcement activities on its behalf in the near future.[40]

---

[39] D.J. Francis, 'Mercenary intervention in Sierra Leone: Providing national security or international exploitation?' (2/1999) 20 *Third World Quarterly* 326-327, 329-330; H.M. Howe, 'Private security firms and African stability: the case of Executive Outcomes' (2/1998) 36 *The Journal of Modern African Studies* 311-317; D. Shearer, 'Dial an army' (8-9/1997) 53 *The World Today* 204.

[40] K.R. Nossal, 'Bulls to Bears: The Privatization of War in the 1990s' in G. Carbonnier/S. Fleming (eds.), *War, Money and Survival* (International Committee of the

On the other hand, the future looks bright for the private military companies that refuse to offer combat services and restrict themselves to training and equipping government forces or offer protection services. The UN Secretariat has begun to hire private firms to protect their staff and has also considered using them for other types of security tasks that none of its member states are willing to take on.[41] Most recently, the UN has begun to hire private intelligence firms to enhance the enforcement of UN sanctions.[42] The great powers are also increasingly employing private military companies. The American government used personnel from a private military company for the OSCE observer mission in Kosovo in 1998-99 instead of its own officers, and American, British and French companies are increasingly helped by their national governments to obtain contracts abroad.[43] Private military companies can also be expected to become more involved in the training of African government forces because this form of military assistance play a key role in the strategy Western governments have adopted to realize the third alternative to the UN: the African do-it-yourself solution.

'African solutions to African problems' has been the slogan for the Western Africa policy since the genocide in Rwanda, and it must understood in the context of the Security Council practice of authorizing regional organizations or coalitions of the willing to conduct Chapter VII operations in their own regions. The Western states would like to see this model employed more often in Africa to avoid having to send their own troops to the region.

The main problem with this alternative is of course that the African countries presently lack the capacity to conduct peace enforcement operations effectively. Bajusz and O'Prey concluded in 1996 that only eight African countries, Botswana, Ethiopia, Ghana, Kenya, Nigeria, Senegal, South Africa and Zimbabwe, could field contingents meeting the minimum training and equipment standards,[44] and since then the situation is

---

Red Cross, Geneva, 2000), pp. 36-39; K.A. O'Brien, 'PMCs, myths and mercenaries: The debate on private military companies' (1/2000) 145 *RUSI Journal* 59-64.

[41] Jakobsen, *supra* note 5, p. 168; O'Brien, *supra* note 36, pp. 91-92.

[42] C. Lynch, 'Private Firms Aid U.N. on Sanctions,' *The Washington Post*, 21 April 2001, p. A15.

[43] O'Brien, *supra* note 40.

[44] W.D. Bajusz/K.P. O'Prey, 'An All-African Peace Force: An immediate Option or Long-Term Goal for the Region?' *Strategic Forum*, No. 86 (Institute for National Strategic Studies, Washington, D.C., 1996), http://www.ndu.edu/inss/strforum/forum86.html.

likely to have worsened rather than improved. This lack of capacity was also demonstrated by the two largest peace enforcement operations that have been conducted to date by African nations: the ECOMOG operations in Liberia and Sierra Leone. In Liberia the operational problems were as bad as the ones we have described in the UN operations analysed above and on top comes problems with corruption, serious human rights violations and looting.[45] In Sierra Leone the 15,000 strong ECOMOG force fared just as badly as UNAMSIL almost losing Freetown to a much smaller and badly equipped rebel force. The principal reason for the defeat, according to press reports, was poor leadership and low morale among the troops who had not been paid for months.[46]

A quick survey of the three African organizations with the highest capacity for crisis management does not give much basis for optimism either. The Organization of African Unity (OAU) is the least capable of the three. Even though OAU since 1993 has been trying to establish a capacity to prevent, manage and solve conflict, it has thus far only succeeded in setting up a modest organizational capacity and fielding a couple of small observer missions. Further improvements are hindered by disagreements among its member states and economic difficulties, and the OAU Chiefs of Staff have explicitly ruled out OAU involvement in peace enforcement operations.[47]

The capacity of the Southern African Development Community (SADC) is a little greater.[48] The members have agreed to establish a peacekeeping capacity and this has resulted in the establishment of a regional training centre and a number of regional training exercises. SADC has yet to conduct its first joint operation and although the capacity exists, it seems unlikely that the members will be able to agree on launching one

---

[45]   H. Howe, 'Lessons of Liberia' (3/1997) 21 *International Security* 145-176; M.M. Khobe, 'The Evolution and Conduct of ECOMOG Operations in West Africa' in M. Malan, (ed.) *Boundaries of Peace Operations: The African Dimension* (Institute for Security Studies, ISS Monograph Series, No. 44, Pretoria, 2000), http://www.iss.co. za/Pubs/Monographs/No44/ECOMOG.html; F. Olonisakin, 'African 'Homemade' Peacekeeping Initiatives' (3/1997) 23 *Armed Forces and Society* 349-372.

[46]   B. Ankoma, 'Sierra Leone: Why Gen Shelpidi was fired' *New African*, No. 374 (May 1999) 16-18.

[47]   D. O'Brien, 'The Search for Subsidiarity: 'The UN, African Regional Organisations and Humanitarian Action' (3/2000) 7 *International Peacekeeping* (Frank Cass/London) 65.

[48]   SADC has 14 members: Angola, Botswana, the Democratic Republic Congo, Lesotho, Malawi, Mauritius, Mozambique, Namibia, Seychelles, South Africa, Swaziland, Tanzania, Zambia and Zimbabwe.

in the near future. Thus far, they have resorted to unilateral interventions and only asked for SADC approval after the fact. The current instability in Zimbabwe is also reducing the prospects of joint SADC operations.

ECOWAS is the only African organization with peace enforcement experience.[49] Its ECOMOG forces have conducted such operations in Liberia, Sierra Leone and Guinea-Bissau, and steps are now being taken to strengthen its capacity further. An institutional capacity for conflict resolution is being set up and ECOWAS also plans to create a rapid reaction force consisting of stand-by units from its member states.[50] While this is all good news, the severity of the problems that has characterized ECOMOG operations suggests that Western assistance on a major scale will be required in order to enhance the effectiveness of future operations. Moreover, the inherent limitations of the organization should also be borne in mind. Nigeria has been the single most important contributor in terms of manpower, materiel and funds to the ECOMOG operations. Without Nigerian participation the enforcement capacity of ECOWAS is virtually non-existent.

The lack of indigenous peace enforcement capacity in Africa means that massive assistance from the West will be required to create it, and such assistance is not forthcoming at the moment. Western assistance to date has primarily focussed on peacekeeping training and institutional development and done relatively little to enhance the African capacity for peace enforcement.[51] This may now be changing as the Americans and the British have initiated training programmes that go beyond peacekeeping to prepare African contingents for service in Sierra Leone.[52] Moreover, the British are also supporting efforts to develop a common African doctrine for the conduct of peace operations that go beyond traditional peacekeep-

---

[49] ECOWAS has 15 members: Benin, Burkina Faso, Cape Verde, Côte d'Ivoire, Gambia, Ghana, Guinea, Guinea-Bissau, Liberia, Mali, Niger, Nigeria, Senegal, Sierra Leone and Togo.

[50] G. Ikeh, 'ECOWAS Conflict Prevention and Resolution Mechanism' *Panafrican News Agency*, 21 June 1999.

[51] For an overview and analysis of the various training programmes see E. Berman/K. Sams, *Constructive Disengagement: Western Efforts to Develop African Peacekeeping* (Institute for Security Studies, ISS Monograph Series, No 33, Pretoria, 1998), http://www.iss.co.za/Pubs/Monographs/No33/Contents.html; M. Malan (ed.) *Resolute Partners: Building Peacekeeping Capacity in Southern Africa* (Institute for Security Studies, ISS Monograph Series, No. 21, Pretoria, 1998), http://www.iss.co.za/Pubs/Monographs/No21/Contents.html

[52] J. Perlez, 'G.I.'s to Be Sent To Train Africans for Sierra Leone' *The New York Times*, 9 August 2000.

ing.[53] However, these initiatives do not alter the overall conclusion that it will take a very long time to establish the African capacity for peace enforcement that is required in order to enable the Africans to manage their own conflicts.

Since none of the three popular alternatives to the UN can stand up to closer scrutiny, the question remains what tomorrow will bring for UN peace operations in Africa?

11. UN peace operations in Africa tomorrow

The lack of any viable alternative means that the UN will remain the key player involved in peace operations in Africa in the decade ahead. The UN will continue to deploy observer missions and multi-functional Chapter VI peace operations on its own or jointly with African organizations. In a few exceptional cases, we can also expect to see the UN become involved in 'robust peacekeeping' with Chapter VII mandates. This is likely to happen when the Security Council comes under pressure to do something in a specific crisis and no other volunteers can be found. Peace enforcement operations authorized by the UN and led by Western great powers cannot be ruled out since both the British and the French may continue to find themselves in situations where they perceive an interest or obligation to take action in an emergency occurring in one of their former colonies.

That the UN will continue to play a key role will not prevent the three 'alternatives' from having an impact. Western governments are likely to continue to follow Luttwak's advice and give war a chance whenever they can get away with it. This will not always be possible because the media, non-governmental organizations, the UN Secretary General and the African countries on occasion will succeed in pressuring Western governments to intervene, as was the case with the British intervention in Sierra Leone in May 2000.[54]

Private military companies will increasingly be hired to provide security for UN staff and train government armies. It is highly unlikely that

---

[53] P.R. Wilkinson, 'Peace Support Under Fire: Lessons From Sierra Leone,' *ISIS Briefing on Humanitarian Intervention*, No. 2 (London: International Security Information Service, 2000), http:/www.isisuk.demon.co.uk/0811/isis/uk/hiproject/no2.html. The doctrine is available at http://www.iss.co.za/Pubs/Other/PeaceSupportManualMM/Contents.html.

[54] Ironically the British government ended up being criticized in this case anyway. Critics complained that the governments had deployed the troops too hastily without any clear idea about that they were supposed to do. See MacAskill/Norton-Taylor, *supra* note 27.

they will hired by the UN to conduct enforcement operations, however. While the use of mercenaries and private military companies for combat services will continue, it will be marginal compared to the roles played by the UN and the African organizations.

The efforts undertaken to enhance the African peacekeeping capacity will intensify and gradually begin to bear fruit in the form of more effective African contributions to peace operations conducted by the UN and their own regional organizations. The African countries are likely to continue to favour participation in UN operations to operations conducted by other actors because the UN reimbursement system reduces the cost of such participation.

The Western ambition to enable the Africans to manage their own conflicts remains a long-term project and its prospects for success will depend more on Western efforts in the fields of development and democratisation than on their peacekeeping programmes. Training the African armies will not make much difference unless the African states are strengthened also.

The joker in the African game in the next decade is the European Union (EU). The 60,000-strong rapid reaction force that the EU members will have established (on paper) in 2003 is bound to end up in Africa. Most European troops will be tied down in the Balkans but the remainder will go to Africa. This is so for three reasons. Firstly, the EU will come under a lot of pressure to demonstrate the usefulness of its new force the moment it is declared operational. Secondly, Africa is the region where the demand will be highest and the geopolitical space greatest. There will not be any need for new peace operations in Europe in the coming decade, and the Americans are unlikely to allow anything but symbolic EU operations in strategically important regions like the Caucasus or the Middle East. Thirdly, EU members are likely to have interests or feel compelled to initiate peace operations in their former colonies in Africa from time to time, and they will do their utmost to use the rapid reaction force to this end. Thus, it is not a question of if, but when, the EU will become involved in peace operations in Africa in the next decade. The hard question is to predict the level of the EU's commitment? Large EU operations are unlikely for the simple reason that the capacity does not exist, but small operations involving 5-10,000 personnel are likely. The EU is hence not in a position to threaten the dominant role of the UN in the decade ahead either.

Appendix I

Chronological list of UN peace operations in Africa (29 May 2002)

Mission Acronym	Mission Name	Duration	Max. Force *
ONUC	United Nations Operation in the Congo	July 60-June 64	19,828
UNAVEM I	United Nations Angola Verification Mission I	Jan 89-June 91	70
UNTAG	United Nations Transition Assistance Group in Namibia	Apr 89-Mar 90	8,000
MINURSO	United Nations Mission for the Referendum in Western Sahara	Apr 91-	261
UNAVEM II	United Nations Angola Verification Mission II	June 91-Feb 95	718
UNOSOM I	United Nations Operation in Somalia I	Apr 92-Mar 93	4,469
ONUMOZ	United Nations Operation in Mozambique	Apr 92-Dec 94	8,524
UNOSOM II	United Nations Operation in Somalia II	May 93-Mar 95	30,800
UNOMUR	United Nations Observer Mission Uganda-Rwanda	June 93-Sept 94	81
UNOMIL	United Nations Observer Mission in Liberia	Sept 93-Sept 97	748
UNAMIR	United Nations Assistance Mission for Rwanda	Oct 93-Mar 96	5,540 **
UNASOG	United Nations Aouzou Strip Observer Group	May 94-June 94	15
UNAVEM III	United Nations Angola Verification Mission III	Feb 95-July 97	8,030
MONUA	United Nations Observer Mission in Angola	July 97-Feb 99	934
MINURCA	United Nations Mission in the Central African Republic	Apr 98-Feb 00	1,350
UNOMSIL	United Nations Observer Mission in Sierra Leone	July 98-Oct 99	70

Peter Viggo Jakobsen

UNAMSIL	United Nations Mission in Sierra Leone	Oct 99-	17,50 0
MONUC	United Nations Organization Mission in the Democratic Republic of Congo	Dec 99-	90
UNMEE	United Nations Mission in Ethiopia and Eritrea	Sept 00-	4,517

* Electoral observers are not included.
** UNAMIR was doubled in size after the genocide.

Reflections on The Peacekeeping Doctrine

Andrzej Sitkowski*

The ultimate purpose of the first peacekeeping operation, the United Nations Emergency Force in Egypt (UNEF), was to provide political cover for the withdrawal of the Anglo-French-Israeli invaders from the territories occupied during the Suez Crisis. It was thus conceived of as a face-saving operation of a unique kind.[1] At that time and later during the Cold War, the presence of the UN troops did help to avoid the direct military involvement and a confrontation by the superpowers.

Peacekeeping was never defined by any UN organ or by its Secretariat. This lack of an official definition would have allowed for adjustments to be made to UN missions in keeping with the nature of conflicts. The UN chose instead to petrify the UNEF's guidelines into a doctrine, which it has applied indiscriminately thereafter. For decades, the UN has been deploying international military contingents equipped with the same face-saving guidelines as those introduced for UNEF, even when one of the faces to be saved is a genocidal killer's. Non-violent use of international armed forces was the unimpeachable basis of the doctrine until the publication of Kofi Annan's groundbreaking report on Srebrenica and Ingvar Carlsson's report on Rwanda in 1999. The following article discusses the doctrinal implications of these reports and the relevant findings of a recent comprehensive review of peacekeeping.

1. A Doctrine for a Neutral United Nations

The peacekeeping doctrine and its inflexibility in the changing world is a fitting expression of the United Nations' profound, if undeclared, shift in role. From a world body intended by its Charter to restrain aggressors and prevent wars it became a good offices organization for mediating, monitoring and reporting from areas of conflict.

---

*   Former United Nations consultant, staff member and peacekeeper. Writes a book "Flag against Guns, UN Peacekeeping: Myth and Reality".

[1]   B. Urquhart, *Hammarskjold* (Harper Colophon Books, New York, 1984), p. 194.

M. Bothe and B. Kondoch (eds.),
International Peacekeeping. The Yearbook of International Peace Operations, Volume 7, 2001, 181–196.
© 2002 *Kluwer Law International. Printed in the Netherlands.*

Andrzej Sitkowski

The United Nations took on its new role with remarkable ease, beginning in Palestine in 1947-48. Trygve Lie proposed the creation of a 5,000 to 10,000 man international force to implement the UN plan for partition only after the assassination of the UN Mediator Count Folke Bernadotte but quickly abandoned the proposal in the face of opposition from member states.[2] No Secretary-General until Boutros Boutros-Ghali's misconceived military adventure in Somalia challenged the neutral role, and some embraced it eagerly.[3] Dag Hammarskjold considered the idea of a stand-by UN military intervention force quite unsound.[4] His successor, U Thant, went further and maintained, in relation to the conflict in Cyprus, that it would be 'a little insane for the UN Force to set about killing Cypriots, whether Greek or Turkish, to prevent them from killing each other'.[5] For Kurt Waldheim even a British offer to add aircraft to strengthen the UN Force's deterrence capacity on Cyprus during the Turkish invasion in 1974 was unacceptable.[6] Javier Perez de Cuellar maintained that the use of force by peacekeepers amounted to a breach of impartiality and had devastating results for the missions.[7] Boutros-Ghali managed, rather awkwardly, to argue publicly both for and against peace enforcement. In 1993, referring to the UN combating General Aidid in Somalia, the Secretary-General said: 'We have to be in position to apply military force for peace'.[8] Two years later, he baldly declared that he was always against peace enforcement, admitting indirectly his opposition to the Charter of the organization that he headed.[9] In confirmation of this stance Boutros-Ghali later pronounced

---

[2] T. Lie, *In the Cause of Peace* (The Macmillan Company, New York, 1954), p. 192-193.

[3] UN Document A/50/60-S/1995. In the 'Agenda for Peace' Boutros-Ghali advanced proposals for more effective peacekeeping and also recognized the organisation's role in peace enforcement. In absence of any substantial support from the Member States Boutros-Ghali watered down his proposals in the 'Supplement to An Agenda for Peace' reproduced in the same document.

[4] Urquhart, *supra* note 1, 230. Although the UN troops resorted to the use of force in their operation in the Congo's secessionist province of Katanga in the early 1960s, Hammarskjold did everything possible to avoid it.

[5] United Nations Department of Public Information (ed), *The Blue Helmets* (New York, 1996), p. 156.

[6] K. Waldheim, *In the Eye of Storm* (Weidenfels & Nicholson, London, 1986), p. 86.

[7] J. Perez de Cuellar, *Pilgrimage for Peace* (St. Martins Press, New York 1997), p. 43 and p. 495.

[8] B. Boutros-Ghali, Interview in *Der Spiegel*, No.29/1993.

[9] B. Boutros-Ghali, Interview in *Die Zeit*, No.40/1995.

the UN 'a neutral intervening force and honest broker'.[10] The member states either did not mind, did not notice or just wanted this shift in role. There was no support for a different United Nations.

Three guiding principles comprise the peacekeeping doctrine: consent of the parties to the conflict, impartiality and use of force only in self-defence. All are difficult if not impossible to observe in the turmoil of the non-interstate conflicts now prevailing. Moreover, it is arguable whether any UN peacekeeping action can be deemed impartial, short of mediating, monitoring and reporting, none of which requires the deployment of armed forces. (For example, the escort by UN troops of a humanitarian convoy to a besieged town is not, contrary to appearances, impartial. Bringing about the town's surrender by cutting off all supplies is a military goal, which the UN action counters.) Non-use of force except in self-defence is the most ambiguous principle. It is nevertheless supposed to mark the distinction between peacekeeping and peace enforcement. This distinction, in turn, constitutes the core of the UN politics of military intervention as conceived by Boutros-Ghali: 'The logic of peacekeeping flows from premises that are quite distinct from these of enforcement and the dynamics of the latter are incompatible with the political process that peacekeeping is intended to facilitate. To blur the distinction between the two can undermine the viability of a peacekeeping operation and endanger its personnel'.[11] The distinction is, however, blurred from the start by the UN definition of self-defence. The guidelines for UNEF II proposed by Waldheim in 1973 and approved by the Security Council in Resolution 341 provide in paragraph (e) that the UN contingents' will not use force except in self-defence. Self-defence would include resistance to attempts by forceful means to prevent it from discharging its duties under the Security Council's mandate ...'.[12] This understanding of self-defence became, in theory at least, standard for all peacekeeping operations.

Members of UN Forces from the Commander to the privates face hard choices. For example, is forcibly removing an illegal roadblock obstructing the progress of a UN convoy an act of self-defence or an offensive action? The UN mission to Cambodia illustrates how mutually exclusive but seemingly correct interpretations within the command of an operation can arise. The Force's Commander, General John M. Sanderson (Australia),

---

[10]   *The Blue Helmets, supra* note 5, 5.

[11]   UN Document A/50/60-S/1995, *ibid*, para.35.

[12]   *The Blue Helmets, supra* note 5, 60.

Andrzej Sitkowski

and his Deputy, General Michel Loridon (France), differed on the appropriate strategy to take with the Khmer Rouge who, contrary to previous agreements, were preventing UN peacekeepers from entering their zone. The Deputy insisted that it was within the mission's mandate to use force, if need be, to compel rebels to honour the UN troops' freedom of movement. The Commander believed that such an action would amount to an offensive, which was outside the mission's mandate. Both Generals might have been correct in their interpretation, but the Deputy was sent packing.[13]

Not surprisingly, the option of negotiations, and when they had failed, of retreat, was chosen more often than not over the use of force to defend the mandates. This choice was made at all levels of the peacekeeping operations, except when UN personnel and property were directly attacked. But even that exception was not always observed, as numerous instances of hostage taking and confiscation of UN equipment demonstrated. The disciplining of military personnel for not standing their ground in defence of UN mandates is unheard of, even when whole troop units surrendered.

Despite the prevailing tactics of appeasement, most UN peacekeeping missions were sucked into the violence by the dynamics of the conflict. The use of force crept, however, into most missions unwittingly and erratically, leaving the results more to chance than to professional military performance. Moreover, the non-use of force doctrine did not prevent the necessity for body bags: over 1,500 UN personnel have lost their lives in the course of all operations.

2. Bosnia: The Peacekeeping Fundamentalism at Work

Annan's report on the fall of Srebrenica is a case study on the application in Bosnia and Herzegovina of the UN peacekeeping doctrine of impartiality and non-violence at its most extreme.[14] The UN Secretariat in New York and its civil representatives in the field resisted until the bitter end the use of force in discharging the Security Council mandates.

On 30 May 1995, 40 days before the fall of Srebrenica, Boutros-Ghali submitted to the Security Council a major report addressing the mandate, the attitudes of the parties and the safety of the (misnamed) United Nations Protection Force (UNPROFOR).[15] Arguing for a revision '...of the

---

[13]   S.M. Hill/S.P. Malik, *Peacekeeping and the United Nations* (Aldershot Dartmouth, 1996), p. 175.

[14]   UN Document A/54/549 (1999).

[15]   *The Blue Helmets, supra* note 5, 557.

UNPROFOR mandate so that it would include only those tasks that a peacekeeping operation could be reasonably expected to perform in the circumstances prevailing in Bosnia and Herzegovina', the Secretary General wanted UNPROFOR to abandon 'any actual or implied commitment to use force to deter attacks' against the safe areas, and wanted force, including air power, to be used only in self-defence. From the context of the report it is clear that Boutros-Ghali was referring to self-defence in its narrow understanding, as it concerns direct actions against UN personnel alone and not the defence of the UN mandates. Endeavouring to put UN-PROFOR back on the safe track of traditional peacekeeping, Boutros-Ghali entered into a rather unconventional argument with the Security Council, which presented its own interpretation of Resolution 836 of 4 June 1993. In paragraph 9 the Security Council Resolution had authorized UNPROFOR '... in carrying out the mandate...acting in self-defence, to take the necessary measures, including the use of force, in reply to bombardments against safe areas by any of the parties or to armed incursion into them or in the event of any deliberate obstruction in or around those areas to the freedom of movement of UNPROFOR or of protected humanitarian convoys.' The Secretary General maintained that the reference to 'self-defence' was confirmation that UNPROFOR's mandate 'did not include any provision for enforcement.' The confusion about what should be considered peacekeeping, peace enforcement and self-defence reached its peak. Boutros-Ghali's plea against the use of force concluded with a declaration of the UN's objectives, namely 'the quest for peace, the protection of human life and the rejection of a culture of death. These objectives will take time to attain and they will be attained only through the successful use of non-military methods. Amid a cacophony of sordid facts the new declaration sounded hollow. What the Rwandan and Bosnian missions expressed was not the rejection of a culture of death but the appeasement of that culture's true believers and practitioners. Preachers of non-violence are not in the habit of dispatching armed men to areas of burning conflict, as the Secretary-General did.

Annan acknowledges the UN's fundamental error of judgement in insisting on the application of peacekeeping rules in a situation where there was no peace to keep. He states specifically that the Secretariat was 'wrong to declare repeatedly and publicly that we did not want to use air power against the Serbs except as a last resort, and to accept shelling of the safe areas as a daily occurrence.' He also recognizes that the success of the Bosnian Serb war aims was ultimately determined on the battlefield and not at the negotiating table. Lastly, Annan admits that '[w]hen, in June

1995 the international community provided UNPROFOR with a heavily armed rapid reaction force, we argued against using it robustly to implement our mandate'.[16] This admission squarely contradicts the standard UN justification for the failure of peacekeeping operations as an inevitable outcome of the lack of clear mandates and the means to discharge them properly. What is made less clear in Annan's report is that UNPROFOR lacked credibility from the outset due to its policy of appeasing the belligerents and taking no risks in confronting them. UNPROFOR thereby surrendered its freedom of movement, the basic privilege of UN personnel, and was subject to forceful obstructions and humiliating searches. It is far from certain that a more assertive UN stance in this respect would have led to violent confrontations, as the advocates of appeasement claimed.

Despite the UN Secretariat's resistance, force had been used by UNPOFOR troops and NATO aircraft in actions of close air support and in air strikes. The attitudes of the UN military leaders in Bosnia about discharging their mandate and using force differed considerably. Although restricted by the policies and orders of the civilian authority of the Special Representatives of the Secretary General in the Former Yugoslavia, the UNPROFOR Commanders in Bosnia did have some margin of freedom. The four men who occupied the post between September 1992 and December 1995 proved that the individual attitudes and qualities of the military leaders can influence the conduct and outcome of a mission to a greater degree than is commonly recognized.

For General Philippe Morillon (France, nicknamed 'the Hero of Srebrenica' for personally entering the besieged town and promising in the name of the UN safety to its inhabitants), the principle of the non-use of force was paramount, even when the Security Council wanted the use of force to be considered. Acting under Chapter VII of the UN Charter, the Security Council in Resolution 770 of 13 August 1992 invited the Secretary General to consider further measures necessary to ensure unimpeded delivery of humanitarian supplies. The reaction came indirectly from the UNPROFOR Commander. In September 1993, Morillon declared in Sarajevo that his command, which was to be enlarged to 6,000 troops from 1,400, had no intention of using force to lift sieges. He then announced, however, that '[o]ur first priority here will be to try to deblock not only Sarajevo but all towns and cities that are besieged ...' Lastly, Morillon stated that the existing rules would continue to apply, meaning that the UN troops could return fire to protect themselves or those under their protec-

---

[16]   UN Document A/54/549, *ibid*, para. 480, 488 and 497.

tion against a clearly identifiable target responsible for an act of aggression.[17]

Morillon thereby made a public departure from the standard UN peacekeeping rule that troops had the right to use force in self-defence when faced with forceful obstructions in discharging mandates. He even restricted the troops' right to return fire directed at themselves: clear identification of the target responsible for an attack is a tall order in the chaos of war. Under Morillon's command the UNPROFOR troops acquiesced in illegal roadblocks and searches of on-duty UN vehicles by warring parties.

An incident resulting in the death of Hakija Turajlic, Deputy Prime Minister of Bosnia and Herzegovina, demonstrated the dangers inherent in these practices. On 8 January 1993, Orthodox Christmas Day, a small convoy of UN armoured personal carriers (APC) returning from the Sarajevo airport was blocked by the Serbs, who had been alarmed by the arrival of a Turkish airplane and who, due to the holidays, were more than usually intoxicated. One of the APCs was carrying an unidentified passenger at the request of the Bosnian Presidency to UNPROFOR. The APC's crew complied with the Serbs' demand that they present their identification papers, but the passenger refused. To enable his identification the crew opened the rear doors for the first time. They were opened again upon the arrival of a Serbian Liaison Officer, who spent about five minutes in the APC talking to Turajlic. After the Officer left the vehicle, the doors could not be reclosed because of the pressure of the crowd, which had become larger and more excited. As a result of the negotiations led by the Commanding Officer of the French Battalion, Colonel Sartre, the other APCs in the convey were allowed to depart. Finally, the UN officer obtained Serbian clearance over the radio for the release of the APC with Turajlic, but before it was confirmed at the check-point, a highly agitated Serb fired a burst from his semi automatic pistol over Sartre's shoulder at the Bosnian Deputy Prime Minister. The Serbs immediately cleared the road, and Turajlic was driven to the UNPROFOR Sector headquarters hospital, where he was pronounced dead on arrival.

The accounts of the events are more or less identical in the Report of the Special Commission of Inquiry set up by the Secretary General,[18] the

---

[17] 'UN Intends To Open All Bosnian Roads Without A Fight', *International Herald Tribune*, 23 September 1992.

[18] UN Document S25130 (1993). The Commission was jointly headed by Sahabzada Yaqub-Khan (Special Representative of the UN Secretary-General for Western Sa-

statements of Colonel Sartre and the APC's crew members and the memoirs of Morillon.[19] The conclusions drawn by the Commission and the General differ. Morillon and his men claimed that the tragedy was due to their ignorance of Turajlic's identity and their resultant failure to make special security arrangements. The General did not see that his troops bore any responsibility and was satisfied that the Inquiry 'made justice to all rumours, accusations and calumnies circulated all over the world'.[20] In fact, the Inquiry found that UNPROFOR had failed to establish effective security corridors between the airport and the city. Instead of controlling the belligerents it had allowed to be itself controlled. The Inquiry also noted that the UNPROFOR's standing operating procedure provided that 'under no circumstances will the doors of APCs be opened'. Turajlic was killed through an opened door. There were no publicly known consequences of these and other inquiry findings.

General Francis Briquemont (Belgium) replaced Morillon in July 1993. Testifying before a commission of the French National Assembly, Briquemont gave a negative appraisal of the mission in virtually all its aspects: the strictly neutral initial mandate had become gradually militarised, resources were inadequate, the rules for a recourse to legitimate self-defence were ambiguous, the mission's civilian leadership was in disarray, the governments contributing troops were meddling in their deployment and the cooperation with NATO and the European Union was unsatisfactory. Briquemont made it clear that instead of his predecessor's minimized mandate he would favour robust action from the outset. He found himself, however, entrusted with an ambivalent role – semi-military, semi-diplomatic – and left out without clear directives.[21] The General gave up the UNPROFOR Command after half a year.

His successor, General Sir Michael Rose (United Kingdom), was no less aware of the military weaknesses of his contingents. Rose considered the lack of an airmobile reserve the most serious and bemoaned the lack of necessary military hardware and effective command structures.[22] The General was nevertheless prepared to act within these limitations. Nothing

---

hara) and by General Lars-Eric Wahlgren (Commander of the UN Interim Force in Lebanon).

[19]   P. Morillon, *Croire et Oser* (Bernard Grasset, Paris, 1993), pp. 141-149.

[20]   P. Morillon *ibid*, p. 144.

[21]   Assemblée Nationale, Commission des affaires étrangères, Rapport d'information No 1950. Sur la politique d'intervention dans les conflits, par M. Jean-Bernard Raimond, Député (Paris, 1994), 112-118.

[22]   Sir M. Rose, *Fighting For Peace* (Warner Books, London, 1999), p. 366.

can better illustrate the different attitude than Rose's own reminiscence: 'as I drove for the first time from the airport to Sarajevo, we swept through the main Serb roadblock, Sierra Four, without stopping. A year before, a Bosnian Government minister had been killed there, sitting in the back of a French armoured personnel carrier'.[23] Rose did not hesitate to take matters into his own hands. (For example, he commandeered a platoon of Danish Leopard tanks that was waiting in vain in Split for clearances from New York and Zagreb to proceed to Tuzla to help Rose protect humanitarian convoys, he ordered after due warning illegal roadblocks to be forcibly dealt with, and he was determined to engineer a situation in which he could legitimately call in NATO strikes in order to demonstrate an assertive UN approach to peacekeeping.[24] His more robust approach was opposed not only by the operation's civilian leaders but also by Rose's immediate superior, the UN Force Commander in Zagreb, General Bertrand de la Presle (France). While recognizing the Danish tanks' effectiveness in actions of self-defence, he firmly opposed equipping UNPRO-FOR with additional heavy armour for fear of provoking an escalation in violence.[25] Under the circumstances, Rose was satisfied with UNPRO-FOR's performance in Bosnia and thought, rather optimistically, that it had succeeded 'in breaking the traditional moulds of peacekeeping' A new way of responding multilaterally to civil wars and international disorder that lay somewhere between traditional peacekeeping and combat had been developed.[26]

General Rupert Smith (United Kingdom), who replaced Rose in January 1995 as the head of UNPROFOR, adopted a similarly assertive stance. It did not endear him to one of the staunchest guardians of UN impartiality in Bosnia at the time, the UN Chief Political Officer in Sarajevo. Here is Corwin's telling assessment of Smith's role in Bosnia: 'There was no longer any question in my mind that Smith was fighting a war with Mladic and that Smith would win, but I was also convinced that the UN had never given Smith any clear authorization to fight that war. I am not in any way suggesting that Smith was taking powers not authorized to him. The operative word here is 'clear'. Smith was working in a grey area and when the language of the Security Council resolutions was in any way dubious,

---

[23] *Ibid*, p.25.

[24] *Ibid*, p. 52, 53 and 361.

[25] B. de la Presle, *Opérations des Nations Unies, Leçons de terrain* (Foundation Pour les Etudes de Défense, Paris, 1995), p. 295-296.

[26] Rose, *supra* note 22, 363-364.

he would ask for interpretation from the UN and from the U.K. government. Once he was assured that he could legally pursue his aggressive
stance against Mladic, he would proceed. Mladic may have deserved no
better, but what irritated me was that Smith was operating under a UN
flag'.[27] The former UN Chief Political Officer in Sarajevo goes on to state
that Smith was wrong even when he obtained a UN clearance for his actions. Corwin protested, for example, the General's decision to turn over
to the Bosnian government fifty thousand sandbags to be used to protect
the traffic, including humanitarian convoys, on the Igman road to Sarajevo
from Serbian shelling.[28]

Smith's assertiveness was still no match for the general UN policy of
appeasement. He had to endure massive hostage takings of his men by the
Bosnian Serbs and the fall of the safe areas. His last task was to wind UN-
PROFOR up. By the end of 1995, a NATO-led multinational Implementation Force (IFOR) took over the peacekeeping. Many of Smith's soldiers
simply stayed put, exchanging their Blue Helmets for green ones and
hoisting the NATO flag in place of the lowered UN flag. The war was
over, and the bruised Bosnian Serbs now left in peace the same men whom
they had so often harassed as members of UNPROFOR. NATO proved to
have better credentials. Who would ever think of taking the Alliance's
soldiers hostage?

3. Rwanda: The Peacekeeping Paralysis[29]

In comparison with the multiethnic complications, international confusion
and the gradual militarization of the UNPROFOR's mandate in ex-
Yugoslavia, the story of the United Nations Assistance Mission for
Rwanda (UNAMIR) is straightforward and for that reason perhaps the
more sinister.

The Independent Inquiry chaired by Carlsson described the UNAMIR's
overwhelming failure as follows: 'A force numbering 2,500 should have
been able to stop or at least limit massacres which began in Rwanda....
However the fundamental capacity problems... led to the terrible and humiliating situation... of a force almost paralysed in the face of a wave of

---

[27] P. Corwin, *Dubious Mandate* (Duke University Press, Durham 1999), p. 206.

[28] *Ibid*, p. 194-195.

[29] Unless otherwise stated, all information and quotations reproduced in this section
originate from the 'Report of the Independent Inquiry into the Actions of the United
Nations During the 1994 Genocide in Rwanda' of 25 December 1999 released by
the UN in digital form (http://www.un.org/news/ossg/rwanda).

some of the worst brutality humankind has seen in this century.' The Inquiry's report provides ample evidence that the commitment of the UN leaders both in New York and Rwanda to a minimalist interpretation of the peacekeeping doctrine was among the leading causes of that paralysis.

UNAMIR was established by Security Council Resolution 872 of 5 October 1993 with a mandate that included 'contributing to the establishment and maintenance of a climate conducive to the secure installation and subsequent operation of the transitional Government'. Boutros-Ghali recommended that '...the Mission would establish, supervise and monitor a new demilitarised zone and continue to provide security in Kigali'.[30] For the benefit of the military the mandate's diplomatic language had to be translated into rules of engagement (ROE). UNAMIR's Force Commander, the much-decorated Canadian General Romeo A. Dallaire, undertook this task. His draft explicitly allowed the mission to respond, even with force, to crimes against humanity and other abuses. (Paragraph 17 stated: "There may also be ethnically or politically motivated criminal acts committed during this mandate which will morally and legally require UNAMIR to use all available means to halt them. Examples are executions, attacks on displaced persons or refugees.") Headquarters never replied formally to Dallaire's request for the draft ROE's approval, but General Maurice Baril, then Military Adviser to the Secretary-General, told the Inquiry that he considered Dallaire's draft a good one. He also said that the Headquarters did not have a procedure for the requested approval. The Force Commander, not having received a formal reply, must have considered the draft ROE approved and in effect. The Inquiry judged such a conclusion reasonable. Moreover, the ROE were accepted by all UNAMIR's contingents (with some minor amendments made by the Belgians), as Daillaire later testified at the trial of Jean-Paul Akayesu, the former mayor of Taba, before the UN International Criminal Tribunal for Rwanda.[31] The same draft of the ROE was resent to New York after the genocide began and, the Inquiry stated, 'Headquarters did not object to para.17 concerning the crimes against humanity.'

Akayesu's defence attorney, Nicholas Tiangaye, suggested that if the United Nations was unable to end the massacres, government authorities could not have been expected to do so. 'Why did UNAMIR not apply Ar-

---

30   *The Blue Helmets, supra* note 5, 343.

31   Transcript of proceedings of 25 February 1998 of the International Criminal Tribunal for Rwanda, Case No: ITCR-96-4-T. Arusha. Typescript, 105. Unpublished.

ticle 17?', he asked.[32] Dallaire's response: 'I did not order offensive operations ... because I was not, fundamentally, neither equipped nor provided
with enough supplies, neither was I fundamentally mandated and this was
confirmed to me by my superiors.' The General simply disowned his own
ROE. Although admitting that morally speaking he had the right to give
the order to attack those perpetrating the massacres, the General added: 'if
you look at my mandate of 5 October you would not see any reference ...
to write what I wrote under paragraph 17 ....' Finally, after this self-
critical performance, Dallaire pointed out to the Tribunal that '... on the
evening of 7th April, technically speaking, [because of the breakdown of
the cease-fire] I no longer had a mandate. ... I could simply have ordered
that people should pack up and leave'.[33] UNAMIR's inaction was fully in
line with the underlying UN Headquarters policy, which had been summarized in a cable from New York in January 1994: '... the overriding consideration is the need to avoid entering into a course of action that may
lead to the use of force and unanticipated repercussions'. Nothing was going to change this directive.

On 11 January 1994, Dallaire sent Baril a telegram entitled 'Request
for Protection of Informant'. The informant in question was a senior
trainer in the Interahamwe militia, who had been put into contact with
UNAMIR by the Prime Minister Designate, Faustin Twaguramungu. Identified later as Jean-Pierre, the informant offered three pieces of information: first, that there were plans to force the withdrawal of Belgium's UN
contingent through the murder of Belgian soldiers, second, that arrangements were being made for the extermination of all Tutsis at a rate of
1,000 people every 20 minutes, third, that there was a major weapons
cache in Kigali ready for distribution. The information made it evident that
the henchmen in Rwanda had learnt the lessons from Somalia where, after
suffering 18 American casualties, the UN operation quickly collapsed.
Dallaire told Headquarters in the same cable that he intended to act within
the next 36 hours. He requested guidance as to how to protect the informant but not as to his other actions. There are conflicting accounts about
who in New York read the cable and when, but it is not disputed that it
was never disclosed to the Security Council. The Secretariat's reaction
was quick and clear. On the same day, UNAMIR was told that Headquarters could not approve the lifting of the weapons cache, as such an action

---

32 S. Buckley, 'General Accuses UN of Failure to Stem Rwanda Genocide', *International Herald Tribune*, 4 Feb 1998, 27.
33 ITCR Transcript, *ibid*, 171-173.

went beyond the mission's mandate. Booh Booh, the civilian head of UNAMIR, and Dallaire were instructed to inform President Habyarimana, to demand corrective action and to refrain from any action that might involve the use of force. Meetings were held with the President and the leaders of an extremist political party. Nothing came of the meetings, except that those preparing the genocide had been forewarned. The sinister scenario of events predicted by Jean-Pierre thereafter acquired the inevitability of a Greek tragedy. Ten Belgian soldiers were murdered, the Belgian contingent was withdrawn, 800,000 people including moderate Hutus were killed across the country and the UNAMIR's strength was reduced to few hundred men.

The curtain went up for the well-rehearsed drama on 6 April 1994. The plane carrying Habyarimana and the President of Burundi, Cyprien Ntayramira, was shot down approaching Kigali. A group of extremists dismissed Prime Minister Agathe Uwilingiyimana and the bloodbath began. Dallaire and Booh Booh sought for the moderate politician to address the nation on the radio, but she was murdered instead, as were ten UNAMIR Belgian paratroopers sent to protect her, after they had surrendered to Rwandan government soldiers. No attempt was made to rescue them. Dallaire stated before the Belgian Senate Inquiry that he saw a couple of soldiers in Belgian uniforms on the ground at the Kigali Camp, but that he did not know if they were injured or dead. The General ordered the driver to stop, but he refused. The driver happened to be a major in the Rwandan Government Forces, members of which had killed the soldiers that Dallaire saw. (The UN Inquiry is silent as to why the General could not have afforded his own driver). Dallaire did not learn of his soldiers' deaths until about 15 hours after they had been taken hostage. On the same day, several other prominent Rwandan officials were killed or kidnapped while the UNAMIR troops assigned to protect them fled or looked the other way. Thousands of civilians seeking UN protection at the compound of the École Technique Officielle were massacred upon being abandoned by the UNAMIR troops stationed there.

The success of the plotters of the genocide would have been complete if not for the progress of the Tutsi-dominated Rwandese Patriotic Front Army (RPF). The RPF defeated the Government Forces, established new authorities in Kigali and triggered the flight of two million Hutus, who feared revenge. UNAMIR kept trying to reactivate the cease-fire, which amounted to stalling the progress of the only party willing and able to stop the massacres. Only after most of the fighting and killing was over did the UN Secretariat and the Security Council admit the genocide in Rwanda.

They decided in June 1994 to deploy UNAMIR II, this time with 5,500 men but again with the traditional peacekeeping mandate.

UN troops' presence implied protection and made the potential victims highly visible to their persecutors. The pretence of protection reduces to complicity in murder, notwithstanding the fact that on the margin of the killing orgies UNAMIR saved or evacuated a few thousand people. 'The rivers were full of corpses when I arrived', stated Dallaire.[34] There were many more when he left. Among the dead were none of the machete-wielding, amok-running killers who could have been eliminated by the UN soldiers.

4. Brahimi's Report: The Distinction between Peacekeeping and Peace Enforcement Confirmed

The report of the High-Level Panel appointed by the Secretary General under the chairmanship of Lakhdar Brahimi (Algeria) to undertake a comprehensive review of peacekeeping makes for substantial and refreshing reading.[35] Concerning the peacekeeping doctrine and strategy, however, the Panel fully commits itself to the old principles and reinforces the ambiguity of the peacekeeping-peace enforcement distinction. So: 'The Panel concurs that the consent of the local parties, impartiality and use of force only in self-defence should remain the bedrock principles of peacekeeping' and further 'The Panel recognizes that the United Nations does not wage war. Where enforcement action is required, it has consistently been entrusted to coalitions of willing States, with the authorization of the Security Council, acting under Chapter VII of the Charter'.[36]

It is not helpful that the interpretation of the 'bedrock' principles comes close to denying what has to date been understood as self-defence. 'Once deployed', the Panel concludes, 'United Nations peacekeepers must be able to carry out their mandates professionally and successfully and be capable of defending themselves, other mission components and the mission's mandate, with robust rules of engagement, against those who renege on their commitments to a peace accord or otherwise seek to undermine it by violence'.[37] There is no way of knowing in advance, however, what obstacles will be raised by the 'spoilers' of the mission's mandate. If peace-

---

[34]   *Ibid*, 204.

[35]   UN Document A/55/305-S/2000/809 (2000).

[36]   *Ibid*, para. 48 and 53.

[37]   *Ibid*, para.55.

keepers are expected to defend the mandate, they must be ready to take any appropriate coercive action, be it manhandling a drunken militiaman standing in the middle of the road, shelling the 'spoilers'' artillery positions or even calling in close air support. The most common challenge to mandates is the restriction of the UN forces' freedom of movement. Here, it may be worthwhile to refer to the experience in Cambodia again. Loridon seeks to force his way into the Khmer Rouge zone in defence of the mandate. Sanderson, who recognizes that '...the United Nations does not wage war...', has him dismissed. Both find support for their interpretations in the Panel's advice.

5. Conclusion

The Brahimi Panel's commitment to the strict distinction between peacekeeping and peace enforcement actions conforms to the conclusions of Annan's report on Srebrenica, as it calls for the same approach.[38] The pervasive ambivalence within the UN about the role of force in the pursuit of peace continues and is not merely a theoretical concern. Those who believed that UN peacekeeping reached its nadir in Srebrenica and Rwanda were proven wrong in Sierra Leone. When confronted by gangs of deranged rebels, whose trademark was chopping off the limbs of civilians, including women and children's, the peacekeepers surrendered en masse with their arms and equipment.[39] Released later due to a mix of negotiations and pressure, they were joined by more and more international troops. The UN force, equipped with a traditional peacekeeping mandate, grew to 12,500 men by the end of the year 2000. The rebels maintain their hold on the diamond-rich northern territories and their harassment of the local population.

After all his recent efforts to restore the organization's military credibility, Annan was reduced to seeing UN peacekeepers again operating in a situation where there was no peace to keep. He recently announced in Freetown that 'the United Nations are not waging a war for restoring peace in Sierra Leone.' One of his lieutenants explained why: 'those who have the military capacity for fighting the rebels do not want to come. Those who agree to come do not want to make the war'.[40] Many Sierra

---

[38]   UN Document A/54/549, *ibid*, para. 498.

[39]   C. Lynch, 'In Sierra Leone UN Forces Robbed of Guns', *International Herald Tribune*, 8 February 2000.

[40]   A.B. Pour, 'Les Nations Unies tentent de sauver leur mission en Sierre Leone', *Le Monde*, 4 décembre 2000.

Leonians now yearn for the mid-'90s when a small mercenary force, Executive Outcomes, drove the rebels out of much of the country.[41]

The doctrine based on a distinction between peacekeeping and peace enforcement is divorced from the reality of most contemporary armed conflicts, is wasteful and has crippling effects at all levels of UN peacekeeping missions. The symbolic presence of international troops waving the Blue Flag provides, however, a smokescreen, a substitute for an effective intervention. There is a constant demand for such a commodity on the international political market.

Those tempted to peer deeper into the abyss of peacekeeping versus peace enforcement may be well advised to heed Rose: '... it is impossible to draw a clear line between the permissible use of force in a peacekeeping operation and an act of war. The limit that I termed the "Mogadishu Line" is defined by the goals pursued, the levels of force, the strategic imperatives facing the combatants and the political circumstances existing at that time'.[42]

---

[41] W. Shawcross, 'UN Peacekeeping Lessons in Africa', *International Herald Tribune*, 16-17 December 2000. As Shawcross often accompanies Kofi Annan on his trips, his indiscretion on mercenaries might carry some weight. According to Broder, 'In 1995, Executive Outcomes, a private South African military firm hired by the embattled Freetown government, used no more than 300 men to restore order in the country over 21 months for a total cost of $35 million. By contrast, the UN maintains 11,500 UN peacekeepers in Sierra Leone, costing an estimated $260 every six months. Meanwhile, the rebellion ... is still raging with no sign of let-up.' J. Broder, 'Mercenaries: The Future of UN Peacekeeping?, (2000) FoxNewsCom, updated 26 June. http://www.foxnews.com/world/ 062300/un_broder.sml).

[42] Sir M. Rose, *supra* note 22, 354.

United Nations Observer Mission in Georgia: Keeping the Peace and Observing the Peacekeepers

Andrew Solomon*

"The tensions and conflict situations that exist in the newly independent States of the Former Soviet Union carry much significance for regional stability and international peace and security."[1]

"It is definitely not in Russia's interest to see outside mediation and peacekeeping operations on the territory of the former Soviet Union."[2]

"The UN's experience in the territories of the ex Soviet Union probably reflects the minimum level possible UN involvement as a global authority."[3]

I. Introduction

In the decade following the disintegration of the Soviet Union, no less than six of the fifteen former Soviet republics have experienced some form of armed conflict pitting government forces against either ethnic separatists

---

*   Andrew Solomon is presently a Legal Analyst and Co-Director of Research at the Central and East European Law Initiative (CEELI) in Washington DC. He has extensive experience working with international organizations, most recently having served as a Legal Analyst for the OSCE. He has also worked for the Legal Department of the OHR (Office of the High Representative) in Bosnia and the UNHCR. He also spent five years at the Brookings Institution as an analyst of US foreign policy and international affairs. Andrew Solomon holds a *juris doctor* from Catholic University of America; a masters of arts in international affairs from American University; and a bachelors of arts in political science from Temple University.

[1]   Report of the Secretary General Concerning the Situation in Abkhazia, Georgia, 3 March 1994, UN Doc. S/1994.

[2]   "Is the Union Being Reborn. Theses of the Council on Foreign and Defence Policy", Nezavisimaya gazeta (Moscow), May 23, 1996 cited in L. Johnson, *Keeping the Peace in the CIS: The Evolution of Russian Policy* (1999) at 32.

[3]   L. Johnson/C. Archer, *Peacekeeping and the Role of Russia in Eurasia* (Westview Press, 1996) at 207.

M. Bothe and B. Kondoch (eds.),
International Peacekeeping. The Yearbook of International Peace Operations, Volume 7, 2001, 197–235.
© 2002 Kluwer Law International. Printed in the Netherlands.

or religious insurgents.[4] Not only have these conflicts threatened the political independence and territorial integrity of these newly independent states, they have challenged the international community's overall capacity for managing armed conflicts in the post-cold war world. Moreover, these conflicts have exposed the limitations of international peacekeeping operations in areas where the Russian Federation remains the principal regional power. Although international organizations including the United Nations (UN) and the Organization for Security and Cooperation in Europe (OSCE) are involved in mediating disputes in the former Soviet Union and observing ceasefire agreements, the heavy lifting of maintaining security and peacekeeping in this region remains a Russian orchestrated affair.

The Russian Federation has been quite determined to gain not only tacit acceptance, but explicit international recognition of its lead role in guaranteeing peace and stability throughout the former Soviet Union. In addressing the UN General Assembly on 26 September 1994, then President Boris Yeltsin not only stated that the territories comprising the former USSR were vital to Russian security interests, but also proclaimed the Russian Federation's authority to intervene as a "peacemaker".[5] While the international community has, for the most part, conceded that Russia's historical interests in the region and proximity to the conflicts therein necessitates that it play an important part in any peacekeeping operation on the territory of the former Soviet Union, the international community is cautious of acknowledging that these newly independent states fall within Russia's sphere of security interests.[6] It has therefore made it clear that any peacekeeping operations Russia seeks to undertake should remain accountable to the United Nations. On the one hand, the international community has come to appreciate and rely on the deployment of Russian and Commonwealth of Independent States (CIS) peacekeepers, while on the other hand, there is general concern that Russia may utilize peacekeeping as a means to re-establish its traditional hegemony in the wake of the Soviet Union's

---

[4] These include the following countries and conflicts: Armenia (Nagorno-Karabakh), Azerbaijan (Nagorno-Karabakh), Georgia (Abkhazia and South Ossetia), Russian Federation (Chechnya, North Ossetia, Ingushetia), Kyrgyzstan, (Islamic insurgency), Tajikistan (Islamic insurgency), and Uzbekistan (Islamic insurgency).

[5] V. Socor, *Yeltsin At UN on CIS Affairs*, RFE/RF Daily Report, September 27, 1994.

[6] W.H. Lewis, *Russia as Peacekeeper* in Problems of Post-Communism, (January/February 1995).

demise, and create a region of satellite states in what Russia refers to as the "near abroad."[7]

Efforts to resolve the Georgia-Abkhaz conflict illustrate how the United Nations and the Russian Federation have creatively addressed and reconciled what could be viewed as their seemingly incompatible interests in order to put an end to armed conflict on the territory of the former Soviet Union. First, the Russian Federation and the United Nations developed a flexible division of labour or "dual mediator" model in which a clearly interested party (the Russian Federation) and a neutral international body (the United Nations) cooperated to resolve a complex dispute. In this case, Russia was able facilitate the end of hostilities and negotiate a ceasefire agreement by relying on its historical role in the region as well as its commensurate political leverage. At the same time, the United Nations added legitimacy and the power of international norms to the process.[8] Secondly, through parallel deployments of an armed Russian-led Commonwealth of Independent States Peacekeeping Force (CISPKF) along with the unarmed United Nations Observer Mission in Georgia (UNOMIG), Russia achieved its long sought after goal of legitimacy while the UN was assured of some supervisory control by the international community.

UNOMIG represents something of a breakthrough by internationalizing peacekeeping in the former Soviet Union. The deployment of UN military observers to oversee a ceasefire agreement in an internal conflict as well as the operations of an independent peacekeeping operation raises several important legal issues associated with peacekeeping. This paper will explore these legal issues and assess how efforts to deploy a peacekeeping mission in Georgia and Abkhazia have complied with the basic principles of international peacekeeping, namely a clear and practicable mandate, cooperation of the parties with peacekeeping forces, and the minimum use of force.[9] It will do so by examining UNOMIG's evolving mandate, the challenges of negotiating a Status of Forces Agreement in an internal conflict, and how unarmed military observers which operate without rules of engagement are equipped to provide for their security and accomplish their

---

7   L. Johnson/C. Archer, *supra* note 3, at 14.

8   Melanie C. Greenberg et al. (eds), *Words Over War: Mediation and Arbitration to Prevent Deadly Conflict* (2000) at 15.

9   Boutros Boutros-Ghali, 'Empowering the United Nations' (1993) 71 *Foreign Aff.* 89, 91.

mission. Where appropriate and possible given the limited amount of resources, this discussion will also assess how mandates, SOFAs, and rules
of engagement serve as a basis for Russian peacekeeping operations.

II. The Parties to the Conflict

The Georgian-Abkhaz conflict involves a region of the world that was
relatively unknown to the international community at the time armed conflict erupted between the Government of Georgia and Abkhaz separatist
forces in 1992. Due to its geographical location within the former Soviet
Union and Moscow's traditional sphere-of-influence, the international
community had little contact with the Caucasus region or experience dealing with issues unique to the peoples that live there at the time Georgia descended into chaos.[10] The Caucasus's complex set of heretofore unfamiliar
players and history challenged the ability of observers to decipher events,
make appropriate conclusions, and develop an adequate response to the
outbreak of hostilities. For the sake of clarity, this section will therefore
provide some background on the key players in the conflict, i.e. the Republic of Georgia and the separatist Abkhaz region.

A. The Georgians
Georgia is one of several independent and sovereign states that comprise
the Caucasus region. It is a mountainous country that spans 69,000 square
kilometres. It borders on Armenia and Azerbaijan in the southeast, Turkey
in the southwest, Russia to the north, and the Black Sea to the west. [11]
Along with its neighbours, the country is situated at a crossroads of civili-
zations and cultures. Throughout most of its 2,500 year history, control
over Georgia territory passed from Mongol, Arab, Persian, and then Ottoman empires. At the end of the eighteenth century, the Georgian nation
sought the protection of Tsarist Russia from the Ottoman Turks.[12]

Georgia eventually became a protectorate of Moscow in 1783, and was
fully incorporated into the Russian empire shortly afterwards.[13] After a

---

[10] Georgia was a constituent part of the Soviet Union for most of the twentieth century.

[11] See Map of Region.

[12] P. Aven, 'Post Soviet Transcaucasia' in R. Allison (ed), *Challenges for the Former Soviet South*. (Royal Institute for International Affairs, 1996), at 162.

[13] A. Brown et al. (eds), *The Cambridge Encyclopaedia of Russia and the Soviet Union* (Cambridge University Press, 1982) at 459-60.

brief period of independence between 1918 and 1921, Georgia then joined with its Caucasus neighbours of Armenia and Azerbaijan in establishing the Federal Union of the Soviet Socialist Republics, which formed part of the nascent Soviet Union.[14] It was not until 1936 that Georgia became a separate and distinct part of the Soviet Union – the Georgian Soviet Socialist Republic. Georgia officially remained one of the Soviet Union's fifteen republics until it declared independence on April 9, 1991.[15] However, it would not be until December 1991 that the Soviet Union would cease to exist, and Georgia would be truly sovereign and independent.

The country is perhaps best known for two Georgian figures that shaped the course of history in the 20th century. The first, Joseph Stalin, ruled the Soviet Union and its satellite states in eastern Europe with an iron fist from 1924 until his death in 1953. Not only was he responsible for expanding Moscow's sphere of influence deep into the heart of Europe, it was under Stalin that millions of Soviets and others were sentenced to forced labour and death in the *Gulag* (state labour camps). In contrast, Georgia's current president and former Soviet Foreign Minister, Eduard Shevardnadze, is largely credited with bringing the cold war to an end under the direction of Mikhail Gorbachev, and liberalizing the communist political system through the policies of *glasnost* (openness) and *perestroika* (restructuring). After the collapse of the Soviet Union and several years of instability in Georgia that culminated in the ouster of the country's first democratically elected but authoritarian President Zviad Gamsuhhurdia in 1992, Shevardnadze was called upon to return to his native Georgia and take up the presidency, a post similar to one he held during the 1970s. Since his return Georgia has made considerable progress on the path to democracy and a market oriented economy.[16]

The presence of large petroleum reserves in the nearby Caspian Basin has made Georgia an important player in the high stakes game of constructing pipelines to transport this lucrative commodity from the region to

---

[14] *Id.*

[15] On April 9, 1991, the Georgian parliament "endorsed", but did not vote on, "a statement by Gamsakhurdia declaring Georgia independent of the USSR." See E. Fuller, *Eduard Shevardnadze's Via Dolorosa* 2 RFE/RL RESEARCH REPORT (October 29, 1993) at 17.

[16] D. Zurabishvili, *Shevardnadze's One Man Democracy*, Institute for War & Peace Reporting (September 1996), available at http://www.ipwr.net.

western markets.[17] With the support of the United States, Georgian territory is poised to host two internationally financed pipelines that would by-
pass Russian territory and thereby deprive Moscow of important revenues
as well as strategic control over oil from the Caspian. [18] Georgia's success
in securing backing for these as well as its increasingly western orientation, such as its active membership in NATO's Partnership for Peace program, has exacerbated relations with Moscow.

Georgia faces other challenges of independence in an often volatile region, one replete with ancient and recent episodes of ethnic intolerance
and strife. Although Georgia enjoys relatively peaceful and stable relations
with its neighbours, the same can not be said about other countries in the
region. To Georgia's south, Azerbaijan and Armenia have been locked in a
twelve-year political and military stalemate over the status of the Arme-
nian populated enclave inside Azerbaijan – Nagorno-Karabakh.[19] In addition, several of the Russian Federation's restive Caucasian republics, including Chechnya, border Georgia to the north.[20] Since 1995, Moscow has
fought two destructive wars with Chechen separatists that have left the territory in ruins and resulted in the displacement, injury, and death of several hundred thousand non-combatants and combatants alike. Despite
these military confrontations on its borders, Georgia has managed to steer
clear of being drawn into any external conflicts.

In contrast to its success in preventing these external conflicts from
spilling over onto its territory, Georgia has experienced three major internal conflicts since achieving independence. The first involved a civil war
between forces loyal to the country's first post-independence President,
Zviad Gamsakhurdia, and opposition forces which deposed him in January
1992 and now constitute aspects of the Georgian government.[21] The second and third conflicts deal with the country's inability to manage an ethnically diverse society. Although its roughly five million inhabitants are

---

[17] H. Guliev, *Oil in Troubled Waters*, Institute for War & Peace Reporting (April 1997),
available at http://www.ipwr.net.

[18] See W. Constantinos Papadonopoulos, Pipeline Geopolitics in the Caspian Sea (1997)
36 *SUM Tex.J Bus. L.* 1, 12.

[19] See the discussion of Nagorno Karabakh in L. Drobizheva et al., (eds), *Ethnic Conflict in the Post Soviet World: Case Studies and Analysis* (M.E. Sharpe, 1996) at
227-254.

[20] See Map of the region.

[21] U.S. Department of State, *Fact Sheet: Georgia* (9 May 1994).

mainly of ethnic Georgian origin (70.1 per cent), Armenians (8.1 per cent), Russians (6.3 per cent), Azerbaijnis (5.7 per cent), Ossetians (3 percent) and Abkhaz (1.8 per cent) have also resided in Georgia for centuries.[22] Similarly, while Orthodox Christianity is the predominant religion, approximately 11 per cent of the population is Muslim.[23] Managing this ethnic mosaic has complicated Georgia's independence and territorial integrity.

Although the Ossetians and Abkhaz live for the most part in regions that have been granted special autonomous status by the central government, they have both attempted to secede from Georgia. For instance, in 1990, South Ossetia declared its independence in an attempt to unite with North Ossetia, a region of Russia. After a two year low-intensity conflict between the central government and Ossetian separatist forces, the parties negotiated an end to the conflict with the help of the Russian Federation.[24] Shortly afterwards, however, Georgia found itself embroiled in an even more serious ethnic conflict and open warfare that threatened to tear the republic apart, this time with the Abkhaz minority population.

B. The Abkhaz

The Abkhaz trace their history back several thousand of years to ancient tribes that occupied present day Abkhazia, a 3,000 square mile strip of land situated along the Black Sea coast. [25] Some three-quarters of Abkhazia is mountainous but its long coastline is subtropical – a natural resource that gave rise to an extensive tourist industry during the Soviet period.[26] Abkhazia shares a border with the Russian Federation in the north and the Georgian region of Mingrelia to the south. While they recognize the Georgians as their historical neighbours, the Abkhaz vigorously assert that their language and culture are distinctly different. Instead, they argue that the Abkhaz language and culture are more akin to those of the Caucasian peoples inhabiting Russia rather than those of their historical Geor-

---

[22] U.S. Department of State, *Background Notes: Georgia* (November 1998).

[23] *Id.*

[24] *Id.*

[25] See the facts and figures of Abkhazia on the region's unofficial website located at http://www.abkhazia.org and Brown, *supra* note 12 at 63-4.

[26] A. Minisharvo, 'Abkhazia: God's Country' (11-17-2000) 58 *IWPR Caucasus Reporting Service.*

gian neighbours.[27] Moreover, unlike the Georgians which are Orthodox Christians, the Abkhaz have largely practiced Islam since the 16th century.[28]

Like the Georgians' struggle for independence amidst powerful empires, the Abkhaz have also sought self-determination and independence, even though they were often a minority in their own land throughout much of their history. They sought this independence primarily by shifting alliances between competing regional powers and ethnic rivals, including a short-lived alliance with the Georgians. Although a Kingdom of Abkhaz and Georgians achieved independence in the 8th and 10th centuries, it was subsequently defeated by the Ottoman Turks. As a result, the Abkhaz were forced to live under foreign rule once again.

With the subsequent collapse of eight centuries of Ottoman rule in the region, Tsarist Russia sought to extend its empire in the Caucasus, beginning with Abkhazia. Abkhazia became a Russian protectorate in 1810 and was then forcibly annexed by Moscow in 1864. Although the Abkhaz did resist Russian rule, they also viewed Russia, and the Soviet Union thereafter, as a protector of their interests against the Georgians who have come to outnumber them in the territory of Abkhazia over time.

In March 1921, four years after the Russian Revolution, Abkhazia was designated as one of the Soviet Union's various Union Republics. As such, Abkhazia exercised considerable autonomy in governing itself *vis-à-vis* the Georgian population. This period only lasted for three months after which time the administration of Abkhazia was transferred to what eventually became the Georgian Soviet Socialist Republic.[29] In February 1931, Abkhazia was officially made an autonomous republic within Georgia. In the Abkhazian Autonomous Republic of Georgia, the Abkhaz population continued to fear that the Georgians would eliminate their political autonomy and destroy the Abkhaz cultural entity.

A history of tension between the Abkhaz and the Georgians was complicated by the minority status of the Abkhaz within the autonomous republic and by periodic campaigns known as Georgianisation, first by the Soviet and later by the Georgian government from about 1930 through the

---

[27]   S. K. Batalden et al., *The Newly Independent States of Eurasia. Handbook of Former Soviet Republics* (1993); at 111.

[28]   *Id.*

[29]   C. Dale, 'The Case of Abkhazia' in Johnson, *supra* note 3, at 112.

late 1950s.[30] During this period, the authorities banned instruction in the Abkhaz language and persecuted Abkhaz intellectuals and literary figures. These campaigns also resulted in a significant increase in the number of Georgians living in Abkhazia. What was only a population of 10 per cent in the 1930s rose to 46 per cent by 1952.[31] According to the 1989 Soviet census, the Georgians constituted 45.7 per cent of the total population in Abkhazia while ethnic Armenians and Russians comprised 14.6 percent and 14.3 per cent respectively.[32] In contrast, the 93,000 Abkhaz living on the territory of Abkhazia declined to only 17.8 percent of the total population by the end of the 1980s.[33]

In an attempt to address Abkhaz grievances associated with the relative decrease in the overall population, and their representation in political institutions, the Georgian government eventually reserved the majority of party and government positions for ethnic Abkhaz. This measure, however, only exacerbated an already tense situation. A huge rift resulted between the Georgian and Abkhaz political elites. Because the Georgians still controlled the top spots, the Abkhaz continued to feel disenfranchised. For their part, the Georgian majority in Abkhazia resented the disproportionate distribution of political and administrative positions to the Abkhaz. For the Abkhaz, they continued to view themselves as a minority in their own land throughout the Soviet period and at the outset of Georgian independence in 1991. It was at this point, the Abkhaz resumed their efforts for self-determination. As the Soviet Union disintegrated, the Abkhaz and the Georgians found themselves heading for war.

III. Ethnic Tensions Give Rise to Armed Conflict

The ensuing Georgian-Abkhaz conflict involved peoples who had for decades lived in close proximity, often mixed together in the same communities. The ethnic Abkhaz fought for expanded autonomy or full independ-

---

[30]   Batalden et al., *supra* note 26, at 112.

[31]   A. Minisharvo, 'Abkhazia: God's Country' *IWPR Caucasus Reporting Service*, No. 58, November 17, 2000.

[32]   *Natsionalnyi sostav naseleniya SSR po dannym vsesoyuznoi perepisi naseleniya 1989* (National census of the population of the Soviet Socialist Republics, 1989), USSR State Committed for Statistics, Moscow (1991).

[33]   *Id.*

ence while the Georgian government in Tbilisi and ethnic Georgians in Abkhazia sought to preserve the territorial integrity of their newly independent state. In short, the Georgian-Abkhaz conflict is a secessionist ethnic conflict between a parent state and a minority ethnic group taking place on the backdrop of a disintegrating empire and weakened regional hegemony.

What initially began as a disagreement over political representation and Abkhazia's territorial status quickly turned into a violent armed conflict in August 1992 that lasted as open warfare for more than one year. By the time it was over, the intense fighting left 10,000 to 15,000 dead and at least 8,000 wounded.[34] In addition, approximately 250,000 persons, mostly ethnic Georgians living in Abkhazia, were displaced from their homes and forced to flee the region.[35] The conflict resulted in the expulsion of Georgian authorities and *de facto* independence for Abkhazia, but the dispute between remains formally unresolved to this day. The Georgians and the Abkhaz currently remain frozen somewhere between war and peace.

A. Abkhaz Separatism and the War of Laws

In the years immediately preceding the break-up of the Soviet Union, many of the USSR's 170 ethnic minorities began pressing for greater autonomy, while others began to demand outright independence. During this period, friction between Georgian and Abkhaz authorities – tense for decades – intensified over the legal status of Abkhazia *vis-à-vis* Georgia. The first real salvo in the attempt to separate Abkhazia from Georgia was fired on 25 August 1990 when the Abkhaz parliament declared the sovereignty of the Abkhaz people.[36] Shortly thereafter, the Georgian Supreme Soviet or legislature annulled this act and declared that Abkhazia remains a constituent part of a federative Georgian republic pursuant to the 1921 Treaty of Union between Georgia and Abkhazia.[37]

In March 1991, Moscow organized a referendum on the preservation of the USSR as an attempt to undermine calls for independence emanating

---

[34] Human Rights Watch, *Georgia and Abkhazia: Violations of the Laws of War and Russia's Role in the Conflict* (March 1995) at 5.

[35] C. Dale, *The Dynamics and Challenges of Ethnic Cleansing: The Georgia Abkahzia Case.* UNHCR Country Paper, August 1997.

[36] Greenberg, *supra* note 8, at 21.

[37] Aven, *supra* note 11, at 174.

from specific republics including Georgia. While Georgia's independence minded leadership boycotted the vote, the Abkhaz population, however, participated and overwhelmingly demonstrated its allegiance to Moscow by voting in favour preserving the Soviet Union with a reported 98 per cent of the vote.[38] Abkhaz representatives then acceded to an agreement of confederation between "thirteen peoples of the North Caucasus and Abkhazia", an act the Georgian leadership promptly condemned.[39] By voting overwhelmingly in support of continuing the Soviet Union and then agreeing to form a confederation with their perceived ethnic kin, the Abkhaz demonstrated to the Georgians their unwillingness to remain under Georgian control and desire to secede if Georgia pressed forward with its intention to declare its independence from the Soviet Union.

At the end of 1991, Georgia did emerge as one of fifteen successor states of the Soviet Union, but its *de facto* and *de jure* control over Abkhazia remained tenuous. It subsequently embarked upon a process to consolidate the Georgian state, a process which ultimately fuelled further separatist sentiment in Abkhazia. In February 1992, the Georgian leadership rejected its Soviet-era Constitution and voted to return to the pre-Soviet Georgian Constitution of 1921 which had the effect of reducing Abkhazia's legal autonomy within Georgia. In response, the Abkhaz parliament voted on June 1992 to return to an obscure Soviet Constitution drafted in 1925 under which Abkhazia enjoyed autonomy within Georgia. The Abkhaz claimed that since Abkhazia was an autonomous republic within Georgia under the old Soviet Constitution, by seceding from the Soviet Union and denouncing its constitution on its territory, Georgia thereby invalidated Abkhazia's status as part of Georgia.[40] In response, the Georgian parliament demanded the dissolution of the Abkhaz parliament, the resignation of its government, and new elections.[41] It also cut electricity and telephone service to the Abkhaz capital, Sukhumi, for several hours in an attempt to intimidate the Abkhaz.[42] Undeterred, the Abkhaz

---

[38] Greenberg, *supra* note 8, at 17.

[39] *Confederation of Peoples Proclaimed*, Radio Liberty Daily Report, August 26, 1992, at 1. Also, see discussion of the run up to armed conflict in Human Rights Watch, *supra* note 33, at 14.

[40] Aven, *supra* note 11, at175.

[41] *Abkhazia Heats Up*, Tbilisi Radio, July 1, 1992, cited in *FBIS-SOV-92-127*, July 1, 1992 at 67.

[42] *Id.*

again declared their sovereignty roughly one month later on July 23, 1992. In the ensuing weeks, tensions between the two sides simmered.

B. Escalation and Armed Conflict

Interestingly enough, the initial outbreak of violence in Abkhazia was not directly related to the political standoff between the Abkhaz leadership in Sukhumi and the Georgian government in Tbilisi, but was rather an outgrowth of an entirely different political struggle involving opponents to the Georgian government. This opposition group, loyal to former President Gamsukhurdia, had taken representatives of the Tbilisi government hostage in the Gali region of Abkhazia.[43] In response, a mechanized battalion of the Georgian National Guard, a quasi-official militia group commanded by Defence Minister Tengiz Kitovani, and comprised of 1,000 men, five tanks, a helicopter and ten cannons, entered Abkhazia on 13 August 1992.[44] Their mission was reportedly to free the hostages.

Although this operation and show of force resulted in the eventual release of the hostages, the Georgian National Guard did not withdraw from Abkhazia. Instead, the Kitovani-led forces marched on Sukhumi where they took control of the airport, stormed government buildings including the Abkhaz parliament, and drove the Abkhaz leadership along with interior ministry troops and para-military forces from the city. Hundreds of individuals were reportedly killed and significant numbers of refugees fled across the border into Russia or into other parts of Georgia.[45] By 19 August 1992, the Georgian flag had been raised above the Abkhaz Council of Ministers building and the entire territory of Abkhazia, except for the town of Guadata where Abkhaz forces had fled, was declared to be under Georgian control.[46]

Following the fall of Sukhumi and the Abkhaz retreat to the city of Guadata, the Abkhaz called upon Russia to intervene, a plea that resulted in the arrival of an unknown number of Russian military personnel and volunteers from Chechnya, Ingushetia, as well as other Russian regions.[47]

---

[43]   *Georgian Officials Taken Hostage*, Radio Liberty Daily Report, August 13, 1992.

[44]   Human Rights Watch, *supra* note 33, at 14.

[45]   *Id*.

[46]   Interfax, August 19, 1992, cited in *FBIS-SOV-92-161* August 19, 1992, at 70.

[47]   M. Glenny, 'The Bear in the Caucasus' (March 1994) *Harper's Magazine*, at 52. See also, Human Rights Watch, *supra* note 33, at 14.

Also, on 3 September 1992, a Russian brokered agreement put a temporary end to hostilities but this agreement was soon violated by both sides.
Subsequent ceasefire agreements were negotiated in December 1992, May
1993, and July 1993, but efforts to permanently end the hostilities failed
following several attempts by the Abkhaz to retake Sukhumi.[48] For a year
following their expulsion from Sukhumi and the south-eastern territory of
Abkhazia, Abkhaz forces continued to regroup and mount offensive operations which some observers allege were funded, supplied, and directed by
elements of the Russian military and security apparatus.[49] On 16 September 1993, Abkhaz forces launched a major offensive in which they besieged Sukhumi and ultimately forced the Georgian military to abandon
the capital on 27 September 1993.[50] The Abkhaz continued to press their
military gains and by December 1993 had forced the Georgian military to
regroup on the eastern side of the Inguri River, effectively securing the *de
facto* independence of the Abkhaz republic.

IV. Negotiating An End to the Conflict and Consent to Peacekeepers.

A. Moscow Accord of 3 September 1992

Following the Abkhaz appeal for Russian intervention, Moscow brokered
a ceasefire agreement between the Abkhaz leadership and the Government
of Georgia on 3 September 1992. Although this agreement collapsed following the resumption of hostilities on 1 October 1992, it did lay the
framework for later negotiations based on respect for the territorial integrity of the Republic of Georgia.[51] Moreover, the accord provided for the
disarming of militias and illegal armed formations, the partial withdrawal
of Georgian armed forces from Abkhazia, an exchange of prisoners, the re-

---

[48] E. Fuller, *Russia's Diplomatic Offensive in the Transcaucasus*, RFE/RL Research Report, October 1, 1993, at 30; see also T.W. Murphy, The Commonwealth of
Independent States: Mechanism for Stability or Domination? 5 *USAFA J. Leg. Stud.*
57, 66.

[49] J. Feinberg, *The Armed Forces in Georgia*, Centre for Defence Information (March
1999), at 12.

[50] *Abkhaz Retake Sukhumi*, Reuters, September 29, 1993.

[51] United Nations Department of Peacekeeping Operations, *Georgia-UNOMIG Background*,   available   at
http://www.un.org/Depts/DPKO/Missions/unomig/unomigB.htm

turn of displaced persons to their homes, and the resumption of state functions by the Abkhaz leadership.[52]

Perhaps more importantly, this accord served as a precedent for the resolution of the conflict by identifying the importance of an international peacekeeping mission in overseeing compliance with the ceasefire agreement.[53] Specifically, the agreement created a tripartite observation mechanism which included participation by, not only representatives of Georgian and Abkhaz forces, but the Russian military as well. Furthermore, at the time the parties signed the agreement, they issued an appeal to the United Nations to assist in its implementation. On 27 September 1992, Georgia appealed to the Conference for Security and Cooperation in Europe (CSCE) for a "fact-finding mission" after reports of Russian assistance to Abkhaz separatists. At about this time the UN authorized the deployment of a preliminary observation team to the region in September and a follow-up team in late October 1992.[54]

While Russia had taken the lead in negotiating this initial agreement, following the appeals by the parties for international negotiators, talks proceeded under the aegis of the UN with active mediation on the part of Russia. After the 3 September 1992 agreement collapsed, the UN Secretary General appointed a Special Envoy to Georgia who took part along with Russian diplomats pressuring each side to return to the negotiating table.[55] Efforts by the Special Envoy to achieve a peaceful settlement of the conflict continue until now.

B. Guadata Agreement of 27 July 1993

The second phase of efforts to negotiate a settlement to the conflict provided for the introduction of some type of peacekeeping operation. It culminated with the ceasefire agreement of 27 July 1993, brokered by the Russian government. Meeting in the Abkhaz city of Guadata, the parties to the conflict agreed on several important points regarding the introduction of peacekeepers. First, the parties agreed to activate the tripartite Russian-Abkhaz-Georgian monitoring groups originally provided for in the 3 September 1992 agreement in order to "supervise the observance of the cease-

---

[52] Excerpts of the agreement are available at http://www.abkhazia-georgia.parliament.ge in the Protocols & Agreements Section.

[53] Greenberg, *supra* note 8, at 18.

[54] U.S. Department of State, *supra* note 20, and *Id.*, at 19.

[55] See United Nations Department of Peacekeeping Operations, *supra* note 50.

fire regime."[56] According to the terms of the agreement, these monitoring groups enjoyed complete freedom of movement throughout the area of conflict, but only after notifying the competent authorities as to their arrival. Also, the parties stipulated to adopt immediate and effective measures to curtail any behaviour or conduct deemed by the monitoring groups to violated the ceasefire agreement in some way. Similarly, the parties agreed to respond efficiently to the recommendations of the monitoring groups.[57]

Attention soon turned toward the possibility of introducing some form of international presence, in addition Russian monitors. In the Guadata agreement, the parties stipulated that "it is essential to [immediately] invite international observers and peacekeepers to be deployed in the conflict zone" the size and composition of which would be determined in consultation with the Secretary General of the United Nations.[58] Moreover, both the Abkhaz and Georgians agreed that "a multinational police force shall be established in the conflict zone for the purposes of maintaining order."[59]

In response, the Security Council authorized the deployment of a small team of military observers to monitor compliance with the agreement and serve as the foundation for an expanded UN observer mission once it was clear that a withdrawal of Georgian forces from Abkhazia was underway.[60] This advance team of observers arrived on 8 August 1993, and established headquarters in Sukhumi. Shortly thereafter, observer teams began regular road patrols to monitor compliance with the ceasefire agreement.[61] On 24 August 1993, roughly three weeks after the advance team's deployment, the Security Council adopted Resolution 858, establishing the United Nations Observer Mission in Georgia (UNOMIG) for a period of six months subject to extension if recommended by the Secretary General.[62] The Security Council also recognized the deployment of monitoring groups composed of Georgian, Abkhaz, and Russian military units which, according

---

[56] See Section 2, *Agreement on a Ceasefire in Abkhazia and Arrangements to Monitor its Observance*, UN Doc. S/26250.

[57] *Id.*, Section 4

[58] *Id.*, Section 5.

[59] *Id.*, Section 6.

[60] Security Council Resolution 854 (1993), U.N. Doc. S/RES/854, 6 August 1993.

[61] See United Nations Department of Peacekeeping Operations, *supra* note 50.

[62] Security Council Resolution 937 (1994), U.N. Doc. S/RES/937, 21 July 1994.

to the language of the Resolution, were apparently operating under an independent mandate – mostly likely the 27 July 1993 agreement itself.

The resumption of hostilities from 16 November until 27 November undermined the UNOMIG's ability to fulfil its original mandate, and forestalled the deployment of a larger mission into the area of conflict. After recognizing there was no peace to keep or a viable agreement to oversee, the Security Council adopted what may be deemed to be a wait and see approach. As Georgian and Abkhaz forces engaged each other, the advance team of observers stayed in place. It was authorized under Security Council Resolution 881 of 4 November 1993 to maintain contacts with parties to the conflict and monitor the situation. This interim mandate was first extended on 22 December 1993, and was then followed by additional extensions on 31 January and 4 March 1994.[63]

C. Moscow Agreement of 14 May 1994

In February 1994, the United Nations and Russia convened additional negotiations, first in New York and then in Moscow. At about this time, the Georgian government, and the Commonwealth of Independent States formally requested that the United Nations authorize the deployment of peacekeeping troops along the Georgian-Abkhaz border.[64] In response, the Secretary-General specifically advised the UN Security Council that peacekeepers were inappropriate in the existing climate existing.[65] As a result of United Nations inaction, Georgia formally requested that Russian troops take part in a CIS peacekeeping operation in June 1994.[66] After about a month of intensive negotiations, the parties agreed to yet another ceasefire on 4 April 1994, followed shortly thereafter by a landmark agreement – the Agreement on a Ceasefire and Separation of Forces – that formalized the deployment of international observers and also provided formal consent to the introduction of Russian peacekeepers operating under the auspices of the Commonwealth of Independent States.[67]

---

[63]   Security Council Resolution 892 (1993), U.N. Doc. S/RES/892, 22 December 1993; Security Council Resolution 896 (1994), U.N. Doc. S/RES/896, 31 January 1994; and Security Council Resolution 901 (1994), U.N. Doc. S/RES/901, 4 March 1994.

64   *Georgia Appeals to UN, Russia for Help in Ending Renewed Conflict*, United Press International, February 9, 1994.

[65]   *UN Still Rules Out Georgia Peacekeeping Force*, Reuters, March 21,1994.

[66]   Murphy, *supra* note 47.

[67]   *Agreement on a Ceasefire and Separation of Forces Signed in Moscow on 14 May 1994*, UN Doc. S/1994/583.

This agreement satisfied both the parties to the conflict as well as the negotiators.[68] The Georgians received the international presence they were originally pressing for and an armed peacekeeping force, albeit a Russian one. Meanwhile, the Abkhaz believed the presence of Russian peacekeepers would freeze the situation and allow them to secure *de facto* independence. For its part, Moscow viewed this agreement as providing formal UN recognition to CIS peacekeeping. The United Nations was prepared to delegate to Russia this peacekeeping responsibility partly because the UN lacked capacity to deploy a peacekeeping force itself and partly because it had come to recognize Georgia and Abkhazia as falling within Russia's sphere of influence.[69] These interests were ultimately reflected in the terms of the agreement.

Although the Moscow agreement failed to provide a formula for a negotiated settlement, it did provide a formula for implementing the ceasefire and its verification by international peacekeepers. First, it established a completely demilitarized "security zone" of twelve kilometres on each side of the Inguri River that divides Georgian and Abkhaz territory. The agreement then created a restricted weapons zone extending a further twelve kilometres from the eastern and western borders of the security zone. Heavy weapons and military equipment were to be withdrawn from the area and stored in designated areas subject to UN verification. Finally, it guaranteed freedom of movement of international observers within these zones and the surrounding areas.[70]

Furthermore, in a Protocol to the 14 May 1994 agreement, the parties authorized and formally consented to the deployment and of the CIS peacekeeping force (CISPKF). The Protocol identified the following functions of the CISPKF: maintaining the ceasefire; promoting the safe return of refugees and displaced persons; and supervising the security and restricted weapons zone. In this sense, the Protocol acted as a mandate for the CISPKF.[71] In addition, the Protocol contained provisions that resembled elements of a status of forces agreement. For example, it states that

---

[68]   P. Baev, *Russia's Policies in the Caucasus* (1997).

[69]   D. Danilov, *Russia's Role in Abkhazia*, Accord (1999).

[70]   See *Agreement on a Ceasefire and Separation of Forces Signed in Moscow on 14 May 1994, supra* note 66.

[71]   See Protocol in *Id.*

"the force shall comply with local laws and regulations" of Abkhazia and Georgia.[72]

V. Deployment of Peacekeepers

One week after representatives of the Abkhaz leadership and the Georgian government signed the 14 May 1994 agreement, the Security Council adopted Resolution 937 in which it decided to increase the strength of UNOMIG and provide it with an expanded mandate.[73] The separate CISPKF was concurrently deployed in accordance with the terms of the cease-fire agreement.[74]

A. United Nations Observer Mission in Georgia

The United Nations Observer Mission in Georgia was first established after the Abkhaz and Georgians signed what appeared to be a viable cease-fire agreement brokered by the Russian Federation on 27 July 1993. Roughly two weeks later, the UN Security Council authorized the deployment of a small team of military observers to monitor compliance with the agreement.[75] The UN intended that these military observers serve as an advance team for an expanded observer mission that deploy once it was clear to the Security Council that the parties were respecting the ceasefire. After the Secretary General concluded the ceasefire was indeed holding, he informed the Security Council that the conditions were conducive to an expanded peacekeeping mission.[76] Acting in response to the Secretary General's recommendation, the Security Council adopted Resolution 858 on 24 August 1993 thereby establishing the observer mission in Georgia. [77]

Since 1993, UNOMIG has deployed several hundred military observers on a rotating basis to monitor compliance with the ceasefire agreement and report on the conduct of the CIS's peacekeeping operations. Although the

---

[72]   *Id.*

[73]   Security Council Resolution 937, *supra* note 66.

[74]   Security Council Resolution 854, *supra* note 59.

[75]   *Id.*

[76]   See *Report of the Secretary General Concerning the Situation in Abkhazia, Georgia,* U.N. Doc. S/1994/818, 12 July 1994.

[77]   Security Council Resolution 858 (1993), U.N. Doc. S/RES/858, 24 August 1993.

Security Council initially authorized only a small contingent of 38 military observers, the peacekeeping operation has grown considerably and is now comprised of 103 military observers from 22 countries.[78] Moreover, these military observers are supported by 90 international civilian personnel, and roughly 150 national staff.[79] Although mission headquarters were originally based in both Pitsunda, as well as Sukhumi itself, the two head-quarters were consolidated in Sukhumi in July 1998 because of security concerns. The UN also operates a liaison office in Tbilisi, and an office for the protection and promotion of human rights in Sukhumi.

In the security and restricted weapons zones, there are sector headquar-ters in the towns of Gali (on Abkhaz side of the Inguri River) and Zugdidi (on the Georgian side of the Inguri River). Prior to 1999, UNOMIG also operated out of local team bases in the villages of Zemo-Bargevi and Okumi (Abkhazia) as well as in Kahati and Jvari (Georgia), but these bases were closed due to staffing and security concerns.[80] From its mission and sector headquarters, UNOMIG observers patrol their areas of respon-sibility using two person teams of mobile ground patrols as well as weekly helicopter patrols.[81]

The decision to deploy a UN military observer force rather than a more robust or full fledged peacekeeping force demonstrated the unwillingness of Security Council members to challenge the Russian's sphere of influ-ence, and clearly articulated desire to resolve the conflict there with mini-mal participation on the part of the international community. To a lesser but nevertheless still important extent, it also reflected a general concern that the UN peacekeeping apparatus was overburdened, and the realization that UN member states would not provide the requisite military personnel or hardware for a robust peacekeeping force.[82] The only way Russia would accept an international presence on the ground, the argument goes, is if it was a weak and inconsequential force. Under these circumstances, the

---

[78] U.S. Department of State, *Fact Sheet: Peacekeeping in Georgia. UNOMIG* (30 March 2000).

[79] United Nations Department of Peacekeeping Operations, *Georgia – UNOMIG Facts and Figures*, available at http://www.un.org/Depts/DPKO/Missions/unomig/ uno-migF.htm

[80] See Map of the region.

[81] United Nations Department of Peacekeeping Operations, *supra* note 50.

[82] S.N. MacFarlane, *Arms Control, Conflict, and Peace Settlements: The Caucasus*, Centre for Security Policy (Geneva), Occasional Paper, No. 8 (August 2000).

UN's only option was to deploy a token force of unarmed observers. As a result, UNOMIG's ability to bring peace has been compromised somewhat because it plays a secondary role in peacekeeping to that of Russia.[83] By other accounts, the presence of UNOMIG has stabilized the security situation in the conflict zones, reduced the loss of life, and also facilitated the efforts of humanitarian agencies to operation in the field.[84]

B. Commonwealth of Independent States Peacekeeping Force

The Commonwealth of Independent States Peacekeeping Force (CISPKF) numbered roughly 3,000 at the outset of its June 1994 deployment. It maintained this force level for about two years but subsequently reduced its numbers significantly. Presently, the number of CIS peacekeepers in Abkhazia stands at roughly 1,600.[85] Although the hardware at its disposal also fluctuates, the operation has recently deployed 1 helicopter wing (6 helicopters in total), 1 artillery battery, and 150 armoured personnel carriers.[86] Since their introduction, these forces have deployed principally along the Inguri River, thus separating Georgian and Abkhaz military formations. While it is standard Russian peacekeeping practice to deploy checkpoints along the ceasefire line and engage in "linear peacekeeping", the CISPKF also engages in limited military patrols through the security zone.[87]

Even though the 14 May 1994 agreement provides specifically for the deployment CIS peacekeepers, no CIS country other than Russia has contributed men or financial resources to the operation. One of the first CISPKF commanders admitted as much in 1996 when he described the composition of the force and the nature of the operation. According to Vasily Yakushev, "Our forces are called collective ... I want everyone to hear

---

[83] S.N. MacFarlane, *The UN Role in Abkhazia*, available at http://www.abkhazia-gorgia.parliament.ge.

[84] Greenberg, *supra* note 8, at 29.

[85] For an analysis of Russia's military resources and force strength in Georgia, see L. Johnson, *Keeping the Peace in the CIS: The Evolution of Russian Policy* (1999) at 45.

[86] See *Peacekeeping Operations in the Conflict Regions of the CIS*, Centre for Political and International Studies (Moscow) available at http://www.isn.rsuh.ru/cpis/english/projects.pkeep.htm.

[87] R. Allison, *Peacekeeping in the Soviet Successor States*, Institute for Security Studies of the Western European Union, Chaillot Paper 18 (November 1994).

me when I say that the collective is Russia."[88] Some sources report, however, that a token force of Tajik soldiers have deployed along with the Russians.[89] For their part, the Ukrainians have offered peacekeepers but only under an expanded international force with United Nations command.

These peacekeepers operate officially under the CIS rubric, but they are not in fact a multilateral force. Rather, the CISPKF is a Russian operation under the general command of the Russian Deputy Minister of Defence.[90] Most of the peacekeepers were originally Russian soldiers and officers that had previously served in the former USSR armed forces stationed in Abkhazia. As such, they were viewed by many of the Georgians as biased in favour of the Abkhaz.[91] Additional peacekeeping contingents were dispatched from Russia to complement the force on the ground but these peacekeepers were mostly Russian airborne troops that lacked any peacekeeping training at all. Some were, reportedly, conscripts with little military training let alone peacekeeping training.[92] Like their predecessors, many of these peacekeepers were also accused of rough behaviour toward civilians and a complete lack of impartiality in the conflict as well.[93] Since 1997, however, at least two battalions of Russian troops have received peacekeeping training at the Totskoye Peacekeeping Training Centre in the Volga Military District.[94] As part of their training, Russian peacekeepers develop skills in establishing contacts and developing dialogue with parties on opposing sides to a conflict, monitoring of ceasefire agreements through checkpoint operations and patrolling, as well as security and communications. [95]

---

[88] *Interview with Commander of Peacekeepers*, Moscow NTV, cited in FBIS-SOV-96 103, May 29, 1996.

[89] E. Marks, Dynamics of Peacekeeping in Georgia (September 1995) 45 *Strategic Forum*.

[90] R. A. Touzmohammad, *Domestic Conflict Resolution and the UN: Russia, the CIS, and Problems of International Law*, Institute for State and Law, Russian Academy of Sciences, Monograph, (date unknown).

[91] See D. Darchiashvili, The Russian Military Presence in Georgia: The Parties' Attitudes and Prospects (1997) 2 *Caucasian Regional Studies* 1.

[92] See Dale, in Johnson, *supra* note 3, at 115.

[93] Feinberg, *supra* note 48, at 42.

[94] *Id.*

[95] Johnson, *supra* note 3.

Andrew Solomon

VI. Peacekeeping Mandates

The United Nations Charter clearly provides that the main purpose of the UN is "to maintain international peace and security."[96] In situations where an armed belligerency between two sovereign states or between a state and a rebel force threatens international peace and security, the Charter empowers the UN Security Council to act. It may do so by taking peaceful measures, such as political and economic sanctions, as well as coercive measures including the use of force.[97] The UN has also relied on peacekeeping as a pragmatic response to international disputes and conflicts despite the fact that the Charter does not explicitly provide it with the legal basis to deploy peacekeeping operations. Instead, the power to establish a peacekeeping operation is considered derivative of the Security Council's general powers to respond to actual or potential situations that threaten peace by establishing subsidiary organs or by entrusting the Secretary General with certain functions.[98] Since its inception, the UN has increasingly relied on these general powers to deploy peacekeeping operations, especially in the wake of decolonization in Africa and the end of the cold war.

Before the Security Council may exercise its power to deploy a peacekeeping mission, it must adopt a Resolution establishing the operation and provides it with a mandate. The management of any peacekeeping operation depends on the basic document which functions as the mission's mandate. Without this document, the peacekeeping mission suffers from a lack of legal and political legitimacy. At the same time, the mandate must be clear, credible, and achievable. According to a former UN Secretary General, one of the basic conditions for any successful peacekeeping operation is "a clear and practicable mandate."[99] Although the diplomatic and political processes surrounding the establishment of a peacekeeping operation will invariably involve compromise for the sake of consensus build-

---

[96]   UN Charter art. 1.

[97]   See UN Charter arts. 33, 40, 41, and 42.

[98]   See M. Bothe/Th. Dörschel, *UN Peacekeeping: A Documentary Introduction* (1999) at xv.

[99]   See paragraph 51 of *Agenda For Peace: Preventative Diplomacy, Peacemaking, and Peacekeeping, Report of the Secretary General*, UN Doc. A/47/277 - S/2411, 17 June 1992.

ing, the mandate should avoid ambiguity. Ambiguity may give rise to legal and political difficulties in the field that can undermine the mission's credibility and eventually destroy its ability to function.[100]

In addition to reflecting these political and legal concerns, mandates also have the practical effect of outlining the structure of the mission and determining whether the force shall be comprised of unarmed military observers or lightly armed peacekeepers. It will also define the mission's principal objectives and responsibilities and provide it with the resources and authority to protect itself and carry out its mission.[101] Normally, the content of the mandate will vary according to the nature of the conflict but it should always seek to identify realistic objectives and responsibilities. Depending on the nature of the conflict, a mandate may authorize the peacekeepers to engage in wide variety of responsibilities. Peacekeepers, for example, may supervise troop withdrawals and ceasefire agreements, implement peace accords, as well as monitor governmental transitions. In addition, peacekeeping operations may observe elections and verify implementation of human rights agreements.[102] One of the more flexible aspects of peacekeeping is that an operation's mandate may change or evolve in accordance with the situation on the ground.

A. UNOMIG's Evolving Mandate

Before UNOMIG was officially established, the UN Security Council approved the deployment of roughly ten military observers on 6 August 1993 in a three paragraph document that authorized them to "help verify compliance" with the July 1993 ceasefire agreement.[103] Since that time, the Security Council created UNOMIG and issued upwards of twenty resolutions concerning the Georgian-Abkhaz conflict, most of which serve as an extension of the mission's original mandate. These mandates, including the most recent extension issued on 31 January 2002, are much more detailed and typically run fifteen to twenty paragraphs in length. The large number of mandates may be explained by the fact that each mandate is subject to

---

[100] P.R. Wilkison/R.J. Rinaldo (eds.), *Principles for the Conduct of Peace Support Operations*, United Nations Institute for Training and Research (New York, 1996) at 71.

[101] S.M. Hill/S.P. Malik, *Peacekeeping and the United Nations* (1996).

[102] For a list of various mandates see S.R. Ratner, *The New UN Peacekeeping: Building Peace in Lands of Conflict After the Cold War* (1996) at 18-19.

[103] Security Council Resolution 854, *supra* note 59.

Security Council renewal after six months. While this may have the tendency of bureaucratizing the mission and forcing those involved in the deployment to be constantly engaged in drafting status reports and memorandum for the UN Secretariat, it also ensures that the conflict remains on the Security Council's agenda. In addition, it has allowed the Security Council the flexibility it needs to revise and expand the mission's mandate in response to changes on the ground as well as within UN political and diplomatic circles.

1. Resolution 858

In issuing UNOMIG's original mandate on 24 August 1993, the Security Council provided a very general outline of its objectives and responsibilities. Specifically, Resolution 858 authorized the deployment of up to eighty-eight military observers to verify compliance with the ceasefire agreement, investigate reported ceasefire violations, and resolve any such violations to the satisfaction of the parties to the agreement.[104] Surprisingly, the mandate did not provide much guidance or create any specific mechanism by which UNOMIG could resolve the violations it uncovered. Instead, it simply "call[ed] upon" all parties to "cooperate fully" with UNOMIG. Apparently, this initial mandate was left as vague as possible in order to create the necessary consensus among Security Council members, including Russia, and facilitate consent by the parties to the conflict. Although it was extended on several occasions during the ensuring 11 months, this initial mandate remained virtually unchanged until the Russian brokered ceasefire agreement of 14 May 1994.

Perhaps the most interesting aspect of the initial mandate was the inclusion of a paragraph in which the Security Council officially "welcomed" the deployment of the tripartite monitoring groups that included Russian peacekeepers. While this provision is not considered an authorization for Russian peacekeeping, it was considered important acknowledgment of Russia's role in resolving the conflict. After several years of seeking UN legitimization of its peacekeeping efforts in the territories of the former Soviet Union, this document undoubtedly pleased the Russian delegation. It also reflects the Security Council's position that Russia would play a central role in any settlement of the conflict. This position was made clearer and reaffirmed by ensuing mandates.

---

[104]   Security Council Resolution 858, *supra* note 76.

2. Resolution 937

In Resolution 937, the Security Council provided UNOMIG with an expanded mandate in response to significant changes on the ground, most notably the 14 May 1994 ceasefire agreement in which the parties to the conflict agreed to withdraw their forces from a security zone to be monitored by both international observers and the CISPKF.[105] In this Resolution, the Security Council not only outlined UNOMIG's fundamental mission but also provided the basis for all subsequent mandates. Under the terms of this expanded mandate, UNOMIG was authorized to monitor implementation of the ceasefire agreement including compliance with prohibitions on activities within the security and heavy weapons zones; investigate and resolve any reported or alleged violations; oversee storage areas for heavy weapons equipment withdrawn from the two zones, and to monitor the withdrawal of troops. In addition to these tasks, which are primarily military in nature, UNOMIG was also asked to "contribute to conditions for the safe and orderly return of refugees and displaced persons."[106]

This expanded mandate is also notable for its treatment of Russia and the deployment of CIS peacekeepers. First, the mandate recognizes Russia as the "facilitator" of negotiations between the Georgian and the Abkhaz sides, a designation that is repeated in each and every subsequent mandate.[107] In yet another nod to Russia's role in the region, the mandate also welcomes the Russian contribution to the CIS peacekeeping force. At the same time, however, the mandate provides that UNOMIG will "observe the operation of the CIS peacekeeping force within the framework of the implementation of the Agreement."[108] The effect of this Resolution was to give rise to a system of peacekeeping that several observers have described as "subcontract peacekeeping."[109] In this situation, an international organization such as the United Nations authorizes specific states to carry out peacekeeping on its behalf while reserving for itself the authority to supervise the operation. Because the United Nations was pre-occupied with peacekeeping missions in the Balkans and Africa, the argument goes, it was willing to contract out peacekeeping to the Russians in Georgia and

---

[105] Security Council Resolution 937, *supra* note 61.

[106] *Id.*, at para. 6(I).

[107] *Id.*, at para. 2.

[108] *Id.*, at para. 6(A).

[109] Greenberg, *supra* note 3, at 20-21.

Abkhazia. Others have opined that the arrangement whereby the United Nations would take a backseat to the Russians was nothing more than a *quid pro quo* for Russian acquiescence to UN approval of military intervention in Haiti by the United States.[110]

3. Subsequent Resolutions

The structure of the peacekeeping operation originally provided for in Resolution 937, as well as its relationship to the Russian-led CISPKF, have remained largely unchanged since 1994. Subsequent UN Resolutions that extended the mandate have largely focused on demonstrating the Security Council's political resolve in finding a peaceful solution to the conflict and reminding both the Abkhaz and Georgians that they are expected to cooperate with UNOMIG and implement the terms of the ceasefire agreement. In Resolution 971, the Security Council first expressed deep concern over the lack of progress in refugee returns, and then asked the Secretary General to examine how "additional steps" may be taken within UNOMIG's existing mandate to increase refugee returns.[111] Most extensions also call upon the parties to ensure that UNOMIG enjoys complete freedom of movement as well as reminding them of their commitments regarding the mission's security. For example, in Resolution 1065, the Security Council was sufficiently concerned over the danger to UNOMIG personnel from recently laid mines that it condemned the act and called upon the parties to prevent any future mine laying.[112]

VII. Status of Forces Agreements and Peacekeeping Operations

The deployment of a peacekeeping operation, consented to by the host government, is customarily accompanied by a Status of Forces Agreement (SOFA). Whereas the mandate authorizes and provides the legal basis for the deployment of peacekeepers, it is the SOFA which guarantees the legality of the peacekeepers conduct on the territory of a sovereign country and outlines the conditions under which the force shall operate. The SOFA normally does so by identifying the responsibilities, rights, immunities, and privileges of the peacekeeping operation and its individual members

---

[110]   *Behind the Scenes at the UN*, Associated Press, August 2, 1994.
[111]   Security Council Resolution 971 (1995), U.N. Doc. S/RES/971, 12 January 1995.
[112]   Security Council Resolution 1065 (1996), U.N. Doc. S/RES/1065, 12 July 1996.

vis-à-vis the domestic laws and regulations of the consenting host government.[113]

Invariably, these agreements begin with the recognition that the host government exercises complete jurisdiction within its territory, subject to any explicit exceptions to that jurisdiction.[114] A SOFA will therefore seek agreement over specific behaviour and acts for which peacekeeping force is exempted from local law and regulation.[115] It involves balancing the "sovereign prerogative" and the interests of the host government with the operational needs and interests of the peacekeepers.[116] A well drafted SOFA that clearly provides the basic rules and procedures governing the relationship of the peacekeeping force with the host government serves as the foundation for cooperative relations between the parties and enhances the effectiveness of the peacekeeping force in carrying out its mandate. [117]

As previously mentioned, SOFAs are intended as agreements to exempt peacekeepers from local law and regulations by providing them with specific privileges and immunities. In this sense, SOFAs should be viewed in conjunction with protections afforded to UN peacekeepers under international law. For instance, peacekeepers operating under the auspices of the UN enjoy certain general protections from domestic law and regulations in the exercise of their official functions pursuant to Article 105 of the UN Charter.[118] These protections are more specifically enumerated in the Convention on the Privileges and Immunities of the United Nations.[119] Moreover, peacekeepers and their staff may enjoy protections under the Vienna

---

[113] W.G. Sharp, Sen. (ed), *UN Peace Operations: A Collection of Primary Documents and Readings governing the Conduct of Multilateral Peace Operations* (American Heritage Custom Publishing Group, 1995), at 224-45.

[114] U.S. Department of State, *Backgrounder: Status of Forces Agreements,* (http://usinfo.state.gov/regional/ea/easec/newsofa.htm).

[115] In situations involving the deployment of peacekeepers under the coercive authority of the United Nations Security Council (i.e. no consent of the receiving country), peacekeepers enjoy absolute immunity from local jurisdiction. No agreement with the receiving country is required. See Sharp, *supra* note 112.

[116] Richard J. Erickson, Status of Forces Agreements: Sharing of Sovereign Prerogative (1994) *Air Force Law Review*, at 137-1555.

[117] Miguel de Brito, *The Relationship Between Peacekeepers, Host Governments and the Local Population*, Monograph No. 10, Conflict Management, Peacekeeping and Peace Building (April 1997).

[118] See UN Charter, Article 105.

[119] *Convention on the Privileges and Immunities of the United Nations*, 33. U.N.T.S. 261.

Convention on Diplomatic Relations.[120] While UN member states are obligated to provide these basic protections to personnel associated with UN peacekeeping operations operating on their territory, SOFAs will normally incorporate reference to these protections and then include other detailed provisions governing issues such as freedom of movement, capacity to contract, and criminal jurisdiction.

A. Negotiating the Elements of a SOFA
1. General Considerations
SOFAs and the provisions contained therein may be negotiated by the simplest of means such as an exchange of diplomatic notes. Alternatively, they may be the product of intensive bilateral or multilateral negotiations between parties. Similarly, a SOFA may be narrow or broad in scope. How SOFAs are negotiated as well as what they contain ultimately depend on a combination of at least three factors: the nature and duration of the military activity of the peacekeeper in the host nation; the relationship between the contributing states and the host government; and the political environment within the host government.[121] For example, a diplomatic note may be sufficient when peacekeepers or military personnel are deployed for a brief period or are engaged in a limited humanitarian mission. For situations involving the basing of thousands of troops, an extensive negotiation culminating in a detailed document will most likely be required in order to address the rules and procedures governing the support and conduct of those troops. For more limited deployments, the parties may elect to narrow the scope of the SOFA to what may be considered as the core elements of SOFAs.

Regardless of the form a SOFA takes, all SOFAs generally contain provisions addressing criminal jurisdiction as well as entry/exit requirements, customs and taxes, claims for damages, authority to contract, vehicle registration, and communication support.[122] These provisions usually involve the host nation waiving specific legal and regulatory requirements or extending benefits to the peacekeeping operation deemed necessary for the peacekeepers' day to day activity. It is probably the issue of criminal

---

[120] *Convention on Diplomatic Relations and Optional Protocols*, U.N.T.S. 7310-7312

[121] For a thorough discussion of types of SOFAs and how they may be concluded see G. Bowens, *Legal Guide to Peacekeeping Operations* (1998) and Erickson, *supra* note 115.

[122] For a basic checklist and discussion of typical SOFA provisions, see *id*.

jurisdiction, however, which is the most important aspect of concluding a SOFA and may be potentially the most controversial because it involves notions of state sovereignty. In keeping with the general rule of international law that a government of a sovereign country exercises jurisdiction over all persons within its territory, a SOFA will normally recognize the host government's primary or exclusive jurisdiction in cases involving a peacekeepers violation of domestic law.[123] At the same time, the SOFA will establish a system of concurrent jurisdiction. Under the formula of concurrent jurisdiction, the host government may exercise its primary jurisdiction in cases involving criminal offences exclusive to domestic law. The peacekeeping force exercises jurisdiction over offences committed within the peacekeeping mission (*inter se* cases) as well as offences committed by peacekeepers during the course of their official duty.[124] In this way, the host government retains a residual amount of jurisdiction while the peacekeepers enjoy substantial protections from criminal liability and sanction. Resolving these issues is an important aspect in defining the relationship between the host government and the peacekeeping operation.

2. UN Model SOFA for Peacekeeping Operations

In October 1990, pursuant to a request of the General Assembly, the Secretary General prepared a model SOFA intended to serve as a basis for future agreements between the UN and governments hosting UN peacekeeping operations.[125] The UN model SOFA addresses general issues of the operation's status, status of individual members of the peacekeeping force, administrative facilities for the mission, and the settlement of disputes.[126] In addition to recognizing basic privileges of the peacekeepers in areas such as entry, residence and departure; the use of permits and licenses; and immunity from local laws and regulations, the UN model SOFA explicitly invokes the Convention on the Privileges and Immunities of the United Nations in an effort to provide the maximum protection to UN peacekeepers.

---

[123] U.S. Department of State, *supra* note 113.

[124] Erickson, *supra* note 115.

[125] Model Status-of-Forces Agreement For Peacekeeping Operations, UN Doc. A/45/594, 9 October 1990.

[126] *Id.*

B. General UNOMIG SOFA Issues

1. Timing

The timing of an agreement governing the status of peacekeeping forces is important for a variety of reasons. Because a SOFA is aimed at enhancing cooperation between the peacekeeping operation and the host government, it is advantageous to negotiate the agreement prior to the deployment of the force. In this way, all major issues may be identified and resolved before disputes arise. Failure to do so could undermine the working relationship between the parties and threaten the ability of the peacekeeping operation to meet the goals provided for in the mandate.[127] It also places the peacekeepers in a vulnerable position, leaving them without the ability to defend themselves as well as exposing them to criminal prosecution.

While the United Nations followed this approach at the outset of its involvement in negotiating the introduction of a peacekeeping operation in Georgia, it ultimately deployed a force without first negotiating a agreement on the status of peacekeeping forces. In authorizing preparations for the first deployment of international observers to monitor the 27 July 1993 ceasefire agreement between Abkhaz and Georgian forces, the Security Council called upon the Georgian authorities to negotiate a status for forces agreement in order to facilitate this deployment.[128] There is no indication from UN documents or other sources that such an agreement was reached prior to the 8 August 1993 deployment of observers. Moreover, the fact that the Security Council again called for a status of forces agreement in Resolution 858, the initial mandate of the UNOMIG peacekeeping operation, suggests no prior agreement had been reached over the status of military observers in Abkhazia.[129]

While it remains unclear whether a SOFA or similar agreement governing the status of the advance team of observers was ever reached, it is clear that UNOMIG personnel deployed in the absence of a SOFA. This fact is revealed in the Secretary General Report of 14 October 1994 in which he stated, "I have initiated an exchange of letters with the Government of Georgia with a view to concluding an agreement on the status of UNOMIG. I expect that such an agreement will be concluded in the near

---

[127] *Id.*

[128] Security Council Resolution 849 (1993), UN Doc. S/RES/849, 9 July 1993.

[129] Security Council Resolution 858, *supra* note 76.

future."[130] It was not until the Report of 6 January 1995, roughly two weeks before the expiration of the operation's mandate, that the Secretary General confirmed an exchange of letters with the Georgian government resulted in a status of forces agreement governing UNOMIG.[131] Despite the risks to the peacekeeping personnel and the possibilities for disputes with parties to the conflict and the CISPKF, UNOMIG was nonetheless deployed and forced to operate without a SOFA for at least six months. Fortunately, no reported controversies arose during this period that impeded the ability of the mission to deploy and begin operations.

2. Parties to the SOFA and Internal Conflicts

In traditional peacekeeping operations involving interstate conflict, the parties to a SOFA agreement would normally include the government of the hosting state as well as the United Nations. This is, however, not the case for internal conflicts where multiple parties may exert *de facto* jurisdiction in areas where peacekeepers are deployed. The increasing number of peacekeeping operations deployed in the wake of internal conflicts required some form of agreement be considered with separatist governments or guerrilla authorities. In apparent recognition of this need, the UN model SOFA did not distinguish between *de facto* or *de jure* authorities for the purpose of concluding the agreement. In Section II of the model SOFA (Application of the Convention), the term "government" is construed to incorporate those authorities exercising *de facto* control over the area of peacekeeping operations.[132] While concluding an agreement with separatist authorities may enhance the security and effectiveness of the peacekeeping operation, this may be opposed by a host government claiming *de jure* control over a separatist region. Therefore, the process of drafting a SOFA in the context of an internal conflict may require additional diplomatic efforts to address the issue of sovereignty and territorial integrity of the host country.

In the context of the UNOMIG deployment, the UN took the initial approach of recognizing the Government of Georgia as the sole authority competent to enter into a SOFA or similar agreement. In this sense, the

---

[130] *Report of the Secretary-General Concerning the Situation in Abkhazia, Georgia*, UN Doc. S/1994/1160, 14 October 1994.

[131] *Report of the Secretary-General Concerning the Situation in Abkhazia, Georgia*, UN Doc. S/1995/10, 6 January 1995.

[132] See UN Model SOFA provided in M. Bothe/Th. Dörschel, *supra* note 97, at 59.

UN appeared to resist the approach suggested by the UN model SOFA. Resolutions 849 and 858 (the initial authorization and first UNOMIG mandate) explicitly call upon the authorities in Tbilisi to conclude a status for forces agreement.[133] There is no mention of the Abkhaz authorities in this regard. This omission may reflect the United Nations determined support for the territorial integrity of the Georgian state. Similarly, it is perhaps an example of hesitancy on the part of the UN to recognize the *de facto* authority exercised over Abkhazia by the separatist forces.

While these are legitimate concerns given the propensity of international law to recognize states rather than non-state actors, the fact remains that the deployment of international military observers involved patrols in areas controlled by Abkhaz forces rather than the Georgian government. A SOFA or similar agreement with the Abkhaz authorities would seem to have been a prudent option to ensure the safety of the observers as well as increasing their effectiveness. Instead, the UN preferred to negotiate the status of the ceasefire observers with the recognized government in Tbilisi. It may have been seeking to fill the security vacuum by repeatedly calling on all parties to take steps to ensure the security of UNOMIG personnel and cooperate with the mission. [134]

The United Nations, however, pursued a different approach following the resumption of hostilities in August 1993 and the taking of additional territory by the Abkhaz. It was then that the United Nations recognized that *de facto* control over territory by the Abkhaz necessitated some detailed agreement with them over the deployment of the peacekeeping operation. In Resolution 937, providing UNOMIG with an expanded mandate, the Security Council explicitly requested that "necessary arrangements with the Abkhaz authorities be concluded without delay."[135]

VIII. Rules of Engagement in Peacekeeping Operations

The use of force is a controversial aspect of peacekeeping, one that may negatively impact on the effectiveness of UN peacekeeping operations as a

---

[133] Security Council Resolution 849, *supra* note 127 at para. 6; and Security Council Resolution 858, *supra* note 76, at para. 8.

[134] Security Council Resolution 892, *supra* note 62, at para. 6; and Security Council Resolution 896, *supra* note 62, at para.14.

[135] Security Council Resolution 892, supra note 62, at para. 8.

mechanism for the resolution of international and internal conflicts. Because UN peacekeeping involves the intervention of military personnel into the affairs of a sovereign state or states, peacekeeping has been traditionally based on securing the consent of the parties to the conflict as well as exhibiting and maintaining the impartiality of the operation.[136] Similarly, peacekeepers have traditionally been guided by the principle of non-use of force. According to Brian Urquhart, "[peacekeepers] will in no circumstances have military objectives or take sides."[137] Consent, impartiality, and the non-use of force make peacekeeping more palatable to states concerned with protecting their sovereignty.

The extent to which a peacekeeping operation employs armed force in its duties collides with the principles of consent and impartiality, and may ultimately undermine the effectiveness of the mission and the accomplishment of the mandate because it infringes on the sovereignty of the host state. While peacekeepers may, on occasion, be forced to use armed force to defend themselves from hostile acts or in order to carry out their mandate, they do so at the risk of jeopardizing the overall mission. For example, when a peacekeeping operation engages in the use of force, it may be viewed as taking the side of one party to the conflict. The party against whom force was employed may then either cease cooperating with the mission, threaten to revoke its consent, or even take hostile action against the peacekeepers. It is therefore necessary that the deployment of a peacekeeping operation be accompanied by clear rules of engagement.

International peacekeeping may involve the deployment of either armed military forces or unarmed military observers. Normally, rules of engagement would only be relevant to discussions of armed military forces because it is this type of force that possess the capacity to employ force when they or their mission are threatened. In contrast, unarmed military observers, like those deployed as part of the United Nations Observer Mission in Georgia, must rely on the protections afforded them under the SOFA or the UN Convention on the Privileges and Immunities of the United Nations. Military observers may also rely on diplomatic engagement and political persuasion in order to protect themselves and carry out their mission, but this often leaves them exposed. Although rules of engagement

---

[136] P.R. Wilkinson/R.J. Rinaldo, *supra* note 99, at 71.

[137] See B. Urquhart and F. Heisbourg, 'Prospects for a Rapid Response Capability: A Dialogue' in O.A. Otunnu /M.W. Doyle (eds), *Peacemaking and Peacekeeping for the New Century* (1998) at 193-94.

(ROEs) typically do not apply to unarmed military observers, these types of peacekeepers must develop some standards for assessing and responding to the general security situation.

A. The Purposes and Functions of Rules of Engagement

Rules of engagement have been identified as the primary tool for regulating the use of force and may be considered a cornerstone of military operations during times of peace or conflict.[138] They govern the use of force by identifying the circumstances in which armed force may be used as well as its permissible extent and degree. They are designed with three purposes in mind: providing for the security of military personnel; ensuring successful accomplishment of the military mission; and ensuring that the force conform its conduct to the obligations set forth by international humanitarian law.[139] Rules of engagement are normally issued by military authorities and then communicated down the chain of military command to force commanders and military personnel in the field.

1. Ensuring Compliance with International Humanitarian Law

Rules of engagement are considered matters of operation and as such do not create legal obligations. At the same time, they are based on legal principles codified in domestic and international law. Alleged violations of the rules of engagement will be reviewed and investigated by the military command with both domestic and international law in mind. Where the excessive use of force is identified as a violation of the rules of engagement, the offender may be prosecuted under military law and subjected to a court martial.[140]

Contemporary international humanitarian law may be characterized as the intersection of the laws of war, human rights law, as well as arms control law and refugee law. International humanitarian law is not concerned with the cause of war; instead it simply identifies what rules apply to the conduct of parties once an armed conflict is objectively said to exist.[141] As such, its chief purpose has been to place constraints on the use of force in an armed conflict in order to make it more orderly and less traumatic. This

---

[138]   Bowens, *supra* note 120, at 185.

[139]   R.J. Grunwalt, 'The JCS Standing Rules of Engagement: A Judge Advocate's Primer' 42 *A.F.L.REV.* 245 at 256.

[140]   J.T. Dworken, 'Rules of Engagement: Lessons from Restore Hope' (September 1994) *Military Review*, at 28.

[141]   L. Malone, *International Law* (1998), at 143.

is accomplished by requiring the use of force conform to principles of distinction and proportionality. Rules of engagement will normally reflect these principles in proscribing what is a valid target, under what conditions may these targets be fired upon, and what weapons may be employed in this effort.[142]

2. Providing Self-defence

Rules of engagement increase the physical security of the force and the ability of the force to protect itself. While the use of force in self-defence is generally regarded as an inherit right in customary international law, it must be proportional to the real or perceived threat.[143] Proportionality is extremely relevant to the discussion of the amount of force that is authorized by the rules of engagement. Normally, the rules of engagement will authorize a military force to take appropriate action in self-defence but stress that when force is used in this regard, it must be reasonable in terms of its intensity, duration, and magnitude.[144]

The main issue surrounding the use of force in self-defence is whether the peacekeepers need to first absorb the harm resulting from a hostile act before responding, or whether the peacekeeper may act in anticipation of a hostile act. Rules of engagement are much clearer in situations involving hostile acts. In situations where hostile acts are present, rules of engagement would clearly authorize the use of force. They would most likely describe the hostile act and then proscribe the type of weapon that may be used in that situation and proportionality of the response.[145] Situations involving hostile intent are much more difficult for rules of engagement to address.

3. Facilitating Accomplishment of Mandate

Rules of engagement also function as a guide to commanders in utilizing their forces by helping to characterize the nature of the mission and identi-

---

[142] G. R. Phillips, 'Rules of Engagement: A Primer' (1993) 4 *Army Law*, at 14.

[143] The UN Charter recognizes the right of both collective and individual self-defence in Article 51. Similarly, the Security Council and General Assembly have authorized peacekeeping operations to use force. For a discussion of the use of force under international law see K.E. Cox, 'Beyond Self-Defence: United Nations Peacekeeping Operations & the Use of Force' 7 *Denv. J. Int'L. & Pol'y* 239, 250

[144] See Grunawalt, *supra* note 138, at 251.

[145] Phillips, *supra* note 141 at 18.

Andrew Solomon

fying how force may be used to accomplish the peacekeeping mandate. Although rules of engagement do not provide a mission statement, they may help the military commander and the soldier in the field better understand their mission and therefore enhance the likelihood that the mission succeeds. Rules of engagement set parameters on the use of force and allow the peacekeepers to rely on force in those circumstances that are authorized under the ROEs. Although ROEs should rightly be thought of in terms of restricting the use of force and thereby preventing an overreaction, in this context they actually work to prevent an under-reaction.[146] When rules of engagement are clear, a peacekeeper may employ force without hesitation.

B. ROE's and the Use of Force In UN Peacekeeping: Expanding the Definition of Self-defence

As UN peacekeeping operations have evolved, so too have the rules governing the use of force. The end of the cold war has witnessed the emergence of a "second generation" of peacekeeping operations that have been characterized by expanded and more complex missions. For example, in addition to performing traditional functions like observing ceasefire agreements, troop re-deployments, and disarmament, UNPKO personnel are now engaged in delivering humanitarian aid, providing support to refugee populations, and protecting safe areas for vulnerable populations. In addition, many peacekeepers are responsible for maintaining law and order.[147] More often than not, these new tasks are being performed following volatile internal conflicts or in the wake of a collapsed state, situations that pose a real threat to the physical safety of the peacekeepers. In response to these complexities and the dangers of contemporary peacekeeping, the rules governing the use of force by United Nations peacekeeping operations have undergone significant expansion.

1. The Use of Force Only in Self Defence or Defence of Others
The traditional approach to the use of force by UN peacekeepers is quite clear: peacekeepers may use force only in defence of the peacekeeping operation itself and strictly in response to an armed attack.[148] In other words,

---

[146]   *Id.*

[147]   Ratner, *supra* note 101, at 9-24.

[148]   See the report of Dag Hammarskjold in *United Nations Emergency Force, Summary Study of the Experience Derived From the Establishment and Operation of the*

the use of force is authorized in situations where the peacekeeper fears for his or her personal security or the security of another peacekeeper. Moreover, peacekeepers may use force in self-defence but they may not take the initiative in doing so. According to a study on early UN peacekeeping operations, this narrow definition of self-defence was appropriate when the force's mandate was limited to maintaining cease-fire agreements between well trained and disciplined armed forces located on two sides of a demilitarised zone.[149] In these types of situations, a limited amount of force was often all a peacekeeper required to protect itself in carrying out its mission. If the mandate is expanded to include other tasks or if the peacekeepers are required to operate in areas populated by many civilians, they may require more flexibility in using force to defend itself. It wasn't until the UN's experience in Congo in 1960 that the limitations of a narrow view of the use of force became clear. In this situation, the peacekeepers were unable to prevent the deterioration of the situation by using only that amount of force sufficient for self-defence. After this mission, it became clear to many that there existed the need to broaden the definition of self-defence in order to allow the operation to carry out its mandate.[150]

2. *Using Force to Defend the Mandate*

Under the broader definition of self-defence, the circumstances in which force may be used have been expanded from only those involving the personal safety of the peacekeepers. Instead, peacekeepers may now use force in response to attempts by force from carrying out their mandate. According to a former UN Secretary General, the current rules of engagement allow UN peacekeepers to use force "if armed persons attempt by force to prevent them from carrying out their orders."[151]

In recent years, the Security Council has explicitly authorized the use of force in situations that go well beyond the narrow view of personal self-defence. For example, in Somalia, Bosnia, Croatia, and Rwanda, UN peacekeepers were authorized to use force to deliver humanitarian assistance. In Bosnia and Croatia, UN peacekeepers were authorized to use force to protect safe areas and also secure the mission's freedom of

---

Force: Report of the Secretary General, UN GAOR, 13th Session, Agenda Item 65© P 179, U.N. Doc. A/3943 (1958)

[149] Cox, *supra* note 142, at 250.

[150] *Id.*

[151] Boutros Boutros-Ghali, *supra* note 9, at 89, 91.

movement. These missions illustrate the contemporary trend toward robust rules of engagement and empowering peacekeepers with the authority to not only defend themselves but to defend their ability to achieve their mandates.

C. UNOMIG and General Issues of Security

Although a ceasefire has been in place since 1994, the issue of UNOMIG's security is an important one. On various occasions since deploying, UNOMIG personnel have found themselves in the middle of growing tensions and an often deteriorating security system. Unfortunately, military observers have been injured, killed, and taken hostage in the process. For example, on 8 June 1998, three military observers where severely injured while on patrol when their vehicle hit a land mine.[152] On 21 September 1998, UNOMIG personnel were ambushed in the centre of Sukhumi by unknown forces, resulting the injuries to four observers.[153]

As previously indicated, the United Nations peacekeeping operation in Georgia is currently comprised of unarmed military observers, supported by international civilian personnel. They patrol a demilitarized zone and oversee a ceasefire in clearly marked vehicles but enjoy no other tangible means of protecting themselves or accomplishing their mission. As unarmed observers, UNOMIG personnel do not operate under rules of engagement that assist them in identifying potential threats or respond to hostile acts with the use of force. According to one UNOMIG observer, "we are the dog that barks but has no bite."[154] Instead of relying on the use of force, UNOMIG personnel have had to rely on other instruments. These include: language of the mandate calling on the parties to cooperate with UNOMIG; diplomatic engagement and political persuasion on the ground; and cooperation with the CISPKF which has formally agreed to "cooperate with the United Nations mission and help create conditions favourable for the efforts of the United Nations."[155] In response, the Georgian government

---

[152] *Truce Means Nothing in Western Georgia*, Interfax Moscow, cited in FBIS-SOV-UNMO-98-160, June 10, 1998.

[153] See *Report of the Secretary-General Concerning the Situation in Abkhazia, Georgia*, UN Doc. S/1998/1012, 29 October 1998.

[154] Unfortunately, this cite remains incomplete. See Chapter 4, "Peacekeeping", in an otherwise un-attributable publication.

[155] *Letter Dated 21 June 1994 From the Permanent Representative of the Russian Federation to the United Nations Addressed to the Secretary-General*, UN Doc. S/1994/732, 21 June 1994.

has dispatched interior ministry troops to patrol in the vicinity of UNOMIG facilities in areas under its control while the Abkhaz leadership detailed a contingent of "Presidential Guards" to provide security for UNOMIG in Sukhumi.[156] While these alternatives may have provided some security to the mission, UNOMIG has continued to endure threats to its security and been prevented from freely moving through its area of operations and working to fulfil its mandate.

IX Conclusion

Despite the fact that the United Nations has failed to deliver a peace to the peoples of Georgia and Abkhazia, UNOMIG represents the first occasion in which an international peacekeeping operation has deployed to territories of the former Soviet Union. In addition to monitoring compliance with a ceasefire agreement between the parties to the conflict and supporting efforts to negotiate a peaceful settlement to the conflict, UNOMIG has proven its worthiness in supervising the operations of the Russian-led peacekeeping force. Not only has it given transparency to Russian conduct in the region but it may also go quite far in improving the quality of Russian peacekeeping in future conflicts. In the event another armed conflict on the territory of the former Soviet Union threatens international peace and security and warrants the introduction of peacekeepers, the international community will be better prepared to deploy such a mission and co-operate with Russian or CIS peacekeeping contingents.

---

[156] Feinberg, *supra* note 48, at 41.

Torture to Serve Security?

*Avishai Ehrlich/Margret Johannsen**

1. Terrorism and human rights: The case of Israel's interrogation of Palestinians from the Occupied Territories

1. Terrorism: The Challenge for Democracy and the Rule of Law
Terrorist violence poses a particular political challenge for democratic states. As recent history shows, there is a tendency among state institutions to go beyond the limits set by the rule of law, and undermine the due process of law and human rights guarantees – in the name of necessity.

Thus, according to the European Court of Human Rights, in 1971 the Northern Irish police were in breach of the ban against inhuman and degrading treatment while questioning prisoners, imputed members of the Irish Republican Army (IRA).[1] In the Federal Republic of Germany in 1977, while the President of the Employers' Association, Hanns Martin Schleyer, was taken hostage in a blackmail attempt, imprisoned members of the Red Army Faction (RAF) were denied the right to communicate freely with their defence lawyers through a law banning contacts.[2] In

---

* Dr. Avishai Ehrlich, senior lecturer, works at Tel Aviv University and the Academic College of Tel Aviv-Jaffa. He was previously a researcher at the Hebrew University of Jerusalem and at the London School of Economics. He has also lectured at Middlesex University, London and at York University, Toronto. a.ehrlich@mta.ac. il.

Dr. Margret Johannsen, senior researcher, works at the Institute for Peace Research and Security Policy at the University of Hamburg (www.ifsh.de). Her fields of research include the Middle East, Arms Control, and Terrorism. Johannsen@rrz.uni-hamburg.de.

[1] In their report published on 2 September 1976, the European Commission for Human Rights labelled these interrogation methods 'torture'. The European Court of Human Rights on the other hand dismissed the term 'torture' and labelled the methods applied as being inhumane and degrading. Cf. the verdict of the European Court of Human Rights: *Case of Ireland v. The United Kingdom*, Ref. No. 5310/71 of 18 January 1978.

[2] Cf. Presse- und Informationsamt der Bundesregierung, *Dokumentation zu den Ereignissen und Entscheidungen im Zusammenhang mit der Entführung von Hanns Martin Schleyer und der Lufthansa-Maschine 'Landshut'*, Bonn 1977, Anlage 6, pp. 9-14. For an evaluation according to constitutional law, cf. M. Schröder, Staatsrecht

M. Bothe and B. Kondoch (eds.),
International Peacekeeping. The Yearbook of International Peace Operations, Volume 7, 2001, 237–265.
© 2002 *Kluwer Law International. Printed in the Netherlands.*

Spain during the 1980s, it appears the Minister of the Interior set up and financed an organisation that made assassination attempts on members or sympathisers of the secret Basque Homeland and Freedom (ETA) organisation in order to crush the militant Basque separatist movement.[3]

This demonstrates a fundamental dilemma in democratic states. In the fight against terrorism there is a tendency among state institutions responsible for security to place security above the benchmarks established in international agreements, thus protecting their own members from recrimination. It cannot be taken for granted that, whilst ensuring their security, democratic states are also upholding democratic legal procedures and values. The debate about what is permissible in the fight against terrorism is an area wherein competing societal forces from authoritarianism to liberalism forge the relationship between citizen and state. When the state feels challenged by terrorist organisations, generally authoritarian forces are strengthened and liberal forces weakened.

Thus, democratic states confront a twofold challenge from terrorism: they must demonstrate their ability to protect the lives and property of their citizens from illegitimate violence and, at the same time, maintain the democratic rights and values of society. The fact that one goal may be easier to reach if it is subordinated to the other constitutes the fundamental dilemma of the democratic state founded according to the rule of law. However, its legitimacy is dependent on striving to achieve both goals simultaneously, and developing measures to fight terrorism, which are compatible with democracy.

This article deals with the eroding effect that terrorism has on the norms of the democratic state. The analysis is based on years of interrogations by the Israeli General Security Services (GSS; in Hebrew, *Shin Bet* or *Shabak*)[4] who, with the permission of the state exerted 'moderate physical pressure' on Palestinian prisoners in order to obtain information that, according to the GSS, would help prevent terrorist attacks. In September 1999, lawyers for the victims of these 'semi-legal torture operations' and Palestinian, Israeli and international human rights organisations reaped the fruits of their petitions and campaigns when the Israeli Supreme Court de-

---

an den Grenzen des Rechtsstaates', in: *Archiv des öffentlichen Rechts (AöR)* 103 (1978), pp. 121-148 (137-138).

[3] Cf. W.L. Bernecker, 'Das Baskenland zwischen Terrorismus und Friedenssehnsucht', in: R. Wandler, ed., *Euskadi. Ein Lesebuch zu Politik, Geschichte und Kultur des Baskenlandes*, Berlin 1999, pp. 9-41 (31); W.L. Bernecker et al., *Spanien-Lexikon. Wirtschaft, Politik, Kultur, Gesellschaft*, München 1990, p. 415.

[4] In the following, the terms 'secret service' or 'GSS are used.

clared these interrogation procedures illegal. The public debate preceding this verdict highlighted the fact that a democratic state may not only institute torture, but also approve and confer legitimacy upon such procedures. This is a striking contradiction which leads to the above-mentioned tendency towards an erosion of democratic legal procedures and values when dealing with terror.

2. The Ban on Torture in International Law and its Validity in Israel
International law prohibits torture. The implementation of this interdict is based upon the UN Convention against torture and other cruel, inhuman or degrading treatment or punishment of 10 December 1984.[5] In its preamble, the Anti-Torture Convention reinforces the prohibition of torture in the following documents: The United Nations Charter (1945),[6] in particular Article 55 of the Universal Declaration of Human Rights of 10 December 1948,[7] Article 5 and the International Covenant on Civil and Political Rights of 19 December 1966 (ICCPR),[8] Article 7. In addition, the Anti-Torture Convention makes reference to the UN Declaration to the General Assembly on the protection of all persons against torture and other cruel, inhuman or degrading treatment or punishment (1975).[9] In Israel the Anti-Torture Convention has been in force since 2 November 1991, the Civil Covenant since 3 January 1992.[10] Moreover, torture is also prohibited ac-

---

[5] In the following denoted as the 'Anti-Torture Convention'. Cf. United Nations Office of Public Information, *Yearbook of the United Nations 1984*, Vol. 38, New York 1988, pp. 813-819. The Anti-Torture Convention came into force in 1987.

[6] Cf. United Nations Office of Public Information, *Yearbook of the United Nations 1946-47*, p. 831-843. Further: BGBl 1973 II, pp. 430, 505.

[7] UN Doc. A/RES/217 (III), in: *Yearbook of the United Nations 1948-49*, p. 535-537.

[8] In the following shortened to the 'Civil Covenant'. Cf. United Nations Office of Public Information, *Yearbook of the United Nations 1966*, pp. 423-431. The Civil Covenant came into effect in 1976.

[9] Resolution 3452 (XXX) of 9. December 1975, adopted without vote by Assembly. Cf. United Nations Office of Public Information, *Yearbook of the United Nations 1975*, pp. 624-625.

[10] Israel did not accede to the Protocol of the Civil Covenant. Individual petitions to the Human Rights Commission against the state cannot be filed in Israeli cases. The Anti-Torture Convention was ratified with reservations according to Article 28: Israel neither recognized the jurisdiction of the Committee against Torture, nor the necessity to examine accusations of systematic torture, nor the requirement of requesting that the accused participating state co-operate in these examinations. However, Israel has fulfilled the reporting requirements of Article 19 of the Anti-Torture Convention.

cording to international customary law. According to Israeli law, international customary law is a component of the Israeli legal system, but not international treaty law, i.e. the Anti-Torture Convention. The latter could only be applied in legal procedures if they were explicitly adopted into Israeli law through legislative action. However, as cited numerous times by the Committee Against Torture established according to Article 17 of the Anti-Torture Convention, this has not occurred.

Furthermore, torture is punishable under Israeli law. Israeli Basic Law[11] on Human Dignity and Liberty (1992) guarantees the preservation of life, body and dignity of any person, and thus prohibits maltreatment which, according to Article 16 of the Anti-Torture Convention, is illegal.[12] Moreover, according to the Convention on the Law of Treaties signed in Vienna 23 May 1969,[13] Israel is required to comply with international law regardless of the domestic legal situation. Thus there can be no doubt – and this was never questioned by any of the sides – that Israel is bound by the requirements of the convention, even though they have not been explicitly incorporated into Israeli Law through legislation.

However, there was controversy over whether the requirements of the Anti-Torture Convention could be applied to the Israeli interrogation practices for so-called security prisoners. Israel denied the accusations of torture made in documents of numerous Committees during 1994,[14] 1997[15] and 1998,[16] as well as those made in a public hearing in 1988.[17] Israel re-

---

[11] This term is not equivalent to German Basic Law. Israel does not have a constitution, but a series of 'Basic Laws' (in the meantime numbering 11) in which the fundamental norms of the State of Israel are articulated.

[12] Cf. http://www.israel-mfa.gov.il/mfa/go.asp?MFAH00hi0. The Israeli 1994 countries report explicitly cites this fundamental guarantee to explain the validity of the prohibition of maltreatment set out in Article 16 of the Anti-Torture Convention.

[13] Cf. BGBl, 1985 II, p. 926.

[14] Cf. Committee against Torture, 4 February 1994, 'Initial reports of States Parties due in 1992: Israel.04/02/94.CAT/C/16/Add.4', http://www.unhchr.ch/tbs/doc.nsf/MasterFrameView/c7f20ebdd71b91ccc12563610039133f?Opendocument, 16 April 2001.

[15] Cf. Committee against Torture, 18 February 1997, 'Second periodic reports of States parties due in 1996: Israel. 18/02/97.CAT/C/33/Add.2/Rev.1.(State Party Report)' http://www.unhchr.ch/tbs/doc.nsf/MasterFrameView/653f6da51dc104d6802564640 056 8ed6?Opendocument, 16 April 2001.

[16] Cf. Committee against Torture, 6 March 1998, 'Second periodic reports of States parties due in 1996: Israel. 06/03/98. CAT/C/33/Add.3 (State Party Report)' http://www.unhchr.ch/tbs/doc.nsf/MasterFrameView/5736c7280ccfe131802565e80 0519b3b?Opendocument, 16 April 2001.

fused to accept that the methods used in these interrogations contravened the prohibitions of the Anti-Torture Convention. The prisoners' lawyers and the Israeli and international human rights organisations fighting against these interrogation practices had no doubt that these methods constituted torture and were therefore a breach of Israeli as well as international law.

Like the Universal Declaration of Human Rights and the Declaration to the General Assembly, the Anti-Torture Convention differentiates between torture and other forms of treatment and punishment considered cruel, inhuman or degrading. Thus it conforms to the widespread understanding that torture is narrowly interpreted to include only those methods in which the victim is subjected to extreme pain. On the other hand, in contrast to this narrow definition, torture also includes psychological suffering. Article 1 defines torture as

> 'any act by which severe pain or suffering, whether physical or mental, is intentionally inflicted on a person for such purposes as obtaining from him or a third person information or a confession, punishing him for an act he or a third person has committed or is suspected of having committed, or intimidating or coercing him or a third person, or for any reason based on discrimination of any kind, when such pain or suffering is inflicted by or at the instigation of or with the consent or acquiescence of a public official or other person acting in an official capacity. It does not include pain or suffering arising only from, inherent in or incidental to lawful sanctions'.[18]

The ban on torture is universal. This is because the right to life and freedom from bodily harm are elementary human rights which even in a state of emergency cannot be forsworn. They are a part of the 'humanitarian minimum standard', *jus cogens* and thus of a peremptory nature.[19] Article 2 of the Anti-Torture Convention explicitly states that torture is not even justified under exceptional circumstances, e.g. war. This is the prevailing

---

[17]   Cf. Committee against Torture, 4 September 1997, 'Summary record of the first part (public) of the 295th meeting: Israel. 04/09/97. CAT/C/SR.295. (Summary Record)' http://www.unhchr.ch/tbs/doc.nsf/MasterFrameView/87b2a1733266b4ca802565150 05915a3?Opendocument, 16 April 2001.

[18]   Convention Against Torture and Other Cruel, Inhuman or Degrading Treatment or Punishment, 33. Set., No. 1 (February 1985), pp. 31-35 (31).

[19]   Cf. K. Radke, *Der Staatsnotstand im modernen Friedensvölkerrecht*, Baden-Baden 1988, p. 186; further: pp. 196-205.

opinion among international law jurists,[20] thus the state of emergency established during the War of Independence following the Declaration of the State of Israel cannot be used to justify torture.[21] However, the prohibition to invoke, as justification for torture, exceptional circumstances is not repeated with regard to other forms of maltreatment mentioned in Article 16. Could Israel have used this circumstance to legitimise its interrogation procedures?

In extreme cases of the threat of terrorist violence, Israel took advantage of the right to exert 'moderate physical pressure' on prisoners to gain intelligence information they required to fend off danger. According to the Israelis, these interrogation methods were not violations of international law.[22] In the report on efforts to implement the convention, and the public hearings on the reports – filed by Israel for the first time in 1994 and again in 1997 – the Israeli representative called the methods 'unpleasant', but denied that they were torture in terms of Article 1, or cruel, inhuman or degrading treatment or punishment according to Article 16 of the Anti-Torture Convention.[23] In the reports and hearings, Israel cited the unusual security threat that terrorism poses. As the Anti-Torture Convention explicitly excludes justification of torture under any exceptional circumstances, one might assume that 'moderate physical pressure' would be justified to effectively combat terrorism, particularly when the application of physical violence is below the level prohibited by Article 16. However, the Committee against Torture, to whom these reports were submitted, reached another conclusion. It asserted that in the interrogation of Palestinian prisoners, methods were applied that both contravened the ban on

---

[20] In contrast, Brugger maintains that if there were a hypothetical 'bomb ticking' in the Federal Republic of Germany then there would be exceptions to the rule which would allow lifting the ban on torture if the state could not protect its citizens. However, in such a case, the state would have to take legal precautions including certain rules of investigation. Cf. W. Brugger, „Darf der Staat ausnahmsweise foltern?', in: *Der Staat*, 1996, pp. 67-97. Raess warns that this could lead to an insidious erosion of the ban on torture. Cf. M. Raess, *Der Schutz vor Folter im Völkerrecht*, Dissertation 1988, Zürich 1989, p. 112.

[21] Cf. I. Zamir, 'Human Rights and National Security', in: *Israel Law Review*, Vol. 23, No. 2-3, 1989, pp. 376-406 (383); further: 'The state of emergency', in: *The Jerusalem Post*, Internet Edition, 22. November 1999 http://www.jpost.com, 22 November 1999.

[22] Cf. CAT/C/16/Add.4. (FN 14), § 35: "It should be noted that the use of such moderate pressure is in accordance with international law." Further: CAT/C/33/Add.2/Rev.1. (FN 15), § 7.

[23] Cf. CAT/C/SR.295 (note 17), § 18.

torture and violated the prohibition of cruel, inhuman or degrading treatment or punishment.[24]

3. The Situation in Israel: Torture of Palestinian Prisoners

Contrary to Israeli protestations, torture and maltreatment of Palestinian prisoners from the occupied territories *was* common practice. These practices have to be seen within the context of the occupation of Palestinian territories and Palestinian resistance, which have lasted for decades.

3.1 The Political Situation: Occupation and Resistance

In 1967 during the Six-Day War, Israel occupied the area west of Jordan (including East Jerusalem and the Gaza Strip), which was inhabited by Palestinians. A military government was established in these occupied territories – except in East Jerusalem, which was annexed by Israel; the new administration operated partly according to Jordanian law, partly Israeli law and partly by means of special ordinances. Palestinians accused of hostile activities were generally brought before a military court, though they could file an appeal to the Supreme Court of Israel. Soon after seizing power, Israel began confiscating public and private Arab land; the founding of numerous Jewish settlements on this confiscated land served to incorporate the occupied territories into Israel in the long-term.

Palestinian resistance began almost immediately after the occupation. The Palestine Liberation Organisation (PLO) led this movement. Several PLO groups[25] resorted to terrorist strategies and conducted attacks in Israel as well as internationally. In December 1987, an insurrection (known as the *Intifada*) against the occupation began in the occupied territories. In the 1988 Palestinian Declaration of Independence, the PLO expressed its willingness to recognise the existence of an Israeli state for the first time. This smoothed the path for the peace process – the 1991 Madrid Conference and the 1993 'Oslo' Declaration of Principles. The *Intifada* ended with the 'Oslo' agreement. In 1994, the Palestinian Authority was established in Jericho and the Gaza Strip. Despite a series of agreements, Israel continued to implement its settlement policy in the occupied territories al-

---

[24] Cf. 'Concluding observations of the Committee against Torture: Israel. 18/05/98. A/53/44, paras. 232-242. (Concluding Observations/Comments)' http://www.unhchr.ch/tbs/doc.nsf/MasteFrameView/daf82ddcda36946e80256609004b7df9?Opendocument, 16 April 2001.

[25] The PLO is an umbrella organisation in which the broad spectrum of Palestinian resistance groups is assembled.

though this was in violation of international law and the Palestinians repeatedly committed terrorist attacks on Israeli civilians.

3.2 The Legal Situation: The State under the Rule of Law and Emergency Law

Israel regards itself as a nation in a permanent state of war. This is demonstrated *inter alia* in the power of the government which, in its role as a 'secondary legislative body', is empowered to impose emergency regulations which supersede existing laws. Despite the temporary nature of these emergency regulations, they have been enforced and renewed repeatedly by the Knesset since 1948. Thus a dual reality has been created in which, on the one hand democratic laws and human rights norms exist, and on the other, they have been selectively abrogated by the government.[26] For example, these regulations allow the government to detain people without prosecution and trial for long periods. Most often during these periods of so-called administrative arrest, interrogations occur in which 'physical pressure' is applied. The prisoner is denied access to lawyers and family members and held in solitary confinement. Another ordinance, which is used to justify the imprisonment and interrogation of Palestinians, is the 1948 Prevention of Terrorism Ordinance. It broadly defines a terrorist organisation, gives the authorities the power to determine whether an organisation is terrorist and establishes under what circumstances people should be considered members of a terrorist organisation. It does not contain the right of appeal.[27]

The Israeli Penal Code prohibits civil servants from using force or violence. According to regulations for taking evidence, forced confessions are not permissible.[28]

3.3 GSS, the Counter-Espionage and Internal Security Service

GSS is responsible for internal security and secret service intelligence in Israel and the occupied territories. It reports to the Prime Minister, draws its authority in the occupied territories from military regulations and is supported by border police, army and the police. Its agents conduct inter-

---

[26] For more on defence and emergency laws, cf. A. Rubinstein, *The Basic Law of the State of Israel* (in Hebrew) Tel Aviv 1980, pp. 218-224; 380-389.

[27] Cf. The State of Israel, 'The Law' http://www.Israel.mfa.gov.il/mfa/go.asp? MFAH07tu0, 16 April 2001.

[28] Cf. S. Cohen/D. Golan, 'The Interrogation of Palestinians During the Intifada: Ill-treatment, "Moderate Physical Pressure" or Torture?' *B'tselem*, (Jerusalem, March 1991), pp. 17-18.

rogations in prisons, detention centres or police stations; during questioning the prisoners are legally in the hands of prison staff or the army. After interrogation, they are handed over to the police who record their confessions. Interrogating officers of the GSS seldom appear in court.

The public is excluded from scrutiny of the GSS. If a prisoner maintains that a confession was extorted through violent means, the court can try to ascertain whether this indeed was the case; the judge must make a decision based on the credibility of the interrogating officer or that of the prisoner – except in cases where proof of torture or mistreatment is available.

3.4 A Short History of Torture in Israel

The first accusations of ill-treatment and torture were made during the early 1970s, though they were not documented in detail. In 1977 the London *Sunday Times* published a series on the torture of Palestinians in Israeli prisons. It was based on dozens of cases in which beatings, electric shocks, immersion in freezing water, etc, were described. Between 1978 and 1983, during Menachim Begin's government, the number of cases decreased considerably. However, since 1984 Amnesty International, Al-Haq and Palestinian and Israeli lawyers have ascertained that there has been an increase in the cases of cruel treatment of prisoners. During the first months of the *Intifada*, the number of cases of administrative detention increased dramatically and so too the number of interrogations. During the *Intifada* the intelligence network of the GSS collapsed and new methods for obtaining intelligence information were required. The result was a marked increase in the systematic application of 'physical pressure' in interrogations. According to official estimates, the GSS interrogated around 30 000 Palestinians during the *Intifada*.[29]

In 1986 Israel signed the Civil Covenant and the Anti-Torture Convention thus establishing commitments to international agreements that were at variance with the GSS's intelligence requirements. Against this background the Landau Commission was created in 1987.

---

[29] Cf. Public Committee Against Torture in Israel (PCATI) http://stoptorture.org.il/
english/pcati.html, 16 April 2001.

3.5 The Landau Commission Report[30]

The Landau Commission Report, drawn up under the leadership of Judge Moshe Landau, President of the Supreme Court, is an extensive and complex document. The first section of this report describes the threats of terrorism, the false testimony by the GSS interrogation officers on violently coerced confessions and the application of 'physical pressure' in interrogations. The second part, relating to the specific instructions given to the GSS on the use of 'physical pressure', remains classified to this day.

Since 1971, increasing numbers of Palestinian prisoners testified in court that they were violently coerced into making confessions. Interrogation officers denied these accusations to prevent the prisoners' acquittal, following internal directives from the GSS. This practice lasted from 1971 to 1986; the courts tended to trust GSS blindly. According to the Landau Report, after the scandal became public, these incriminating practices were ceased. Landau has recently admitted that this assessment proved false.[31] The Report unambiguously denounced GSS's lies, though the Commission did not recommend criminal proceedings against GSS officers on the grounds that this would not serve society and would undermine the efforts of the security service. The Commission saw its main task in rehabilitating the General Security Service; according to the Report, bringing GSS members to court for criminal offences would not facilitate this process. It was deemed more important to prescribe investigating methods which would not permit interrogation officers to give false testimony. The Commission did not disapprove of the methods in themselves, only the fact that GSS officers lied to the court. They were in agreement with GSS that in the context of terrorist violence investigations could only be effective if specific forms of violent force were used. However, they were convinced that these methods had to be justified legally and morally; efficiency criteria per se were not sufficient and therefore an effort was made in the Report to validate the application of 'physical pressure' legally and morally.

---

[30] Cf. State of Israel, *Report of the Commission of Inquiry into the Methods of Investigation of the General Security Service Regarding Hostile Terrorist Activity*, Part One, Jerusalem, October 1987.

[31] Judge Landau: 'Apparently, there were double messages once again. There was the written code – the Landau Commission – and another oral code in the field.' Avi Shavit, 'Judgement Day', in: *Ha'aretz*, Magazine, 6 October 2000 (English Internet Edition) http://www3.haaretz.co.il/eng, 6 October 2000.

3.5.1 The Argument of Necessity as Justification

Israeli Penal Law exonerates a person from criminal prosecution for crimes which, in other cases, would be punishable if committed in self-defence or in the defence of another for whom one is responsible. This legal principle of exoneration is only valid when the act committed is the lesser evil, i.e. when danger is certain and immediate, and the response proportionate to the danger, and no alternative is available. In penal law, justification of necessity is only applicable to individuals; however, the Commission declared it relevant to the State and its representatives – in this case GSS – thereby determining that defence of the State, and the State's responsibility to defend its citizens, constitutes justification of such harmful acts. The most obvious, frequently-cited example is the 'ticking bomb': an arrested terrorist suspected of knowing the whereabouts of a bomb could be forced to divulge life-saving information if 'physical pressure' is applied. According to the Report, force is indeed necessary and morally valid under such circumstances.

The Landau Commission decreed that the legal use of necessity as justification was morally valid. In the case of a clash between values enshrined in criminal law and the moral commitment to save lives, defence of the state becomes a moral imperative – the lesser evil. If interrogating terrorists without applying force does not yield tangible results, use of force is justified *a priori* to break resistance. According to the Commission, this interpretation of the 'necessity justification' does not require additional legislation to permit physical pressure since the norms of international law are sufficient for implementation of these precautions. 'Necessity as justification' allows forceful coercion to extort information, thus information obtained this way can be used in court.

What is 'permitted pressure'? The Commission recommended non-violent, psychological pressure, intensive questioning, manipulation and subterfuge as a primary means of exerting pressure. If these methods are ineffective, the use of 'physical force' is inevitable. Nonetheless, the Commission did set limits, which were known only to the GSS and which specified that GSS interrogators be instructed in the clear-cut parameters so as to avoid excessive physical pressure being applied at an individual officer's discretion. The Report warned against slipping into the use of into methods employed by regimes 'we despise'. A democratic society confronted with terrorism must deal with the conflict between security, on the one hand, and the maintenance of the rule of law and morality, on the other. There are three ways to resolve this conflict:

1. Give GSS a free hand to act beyond the confines of the law. The Commission rejected this option outright, as it does not allow any control whatsoever and might lead to despotism.
2. Overtly insist on the commitment to legal methods and turn a blind eye to what actually takes place. This option was rejected in the report as hypocritical.
3. Adopt the rule of law. According to the Commission, the law must establish the appropriate framework for the practices of the Security Service. Stringent regulatory directives should be instituted; limits and compulsory instructions implemented, and rigorous supervision exercised. Interrogating officers who violate directives and exceed the limits must be brought to account.

3.5.2 Permissible Interrogation Methods

The interrogation methods permitted and the procedures prescribed by the Commission were contained in the secret section of the report. It became the task of various human rights organisations to obtain information on the basis of thousands of testimonies from interrogation victims. It emerged that the GSS was controlled by an internal investigative committee. Only in 1991 was this deemed unsatisfactory and supervision of GSS turned over to the Attorney General.[32] Criminal charges have never been brought against interrogating officers for the use of unauthorized methods, although there was a series of cases in which detainees died during or after the interrogations. The Report was heavily criticized by jurists and philosophers in Israel and abroad.[33]

---

[32] Cf. *Subjudice* – Monthly for lawyers (Hebrew), No. 6 (July/August 1992).

[33] The legal journal, the Israel Law Review, dedicated a complete issue to this critique. See: 'Symposium on the Report of the Commission of Inquiry into the Methods of Investigation of the General Security Service Regarding Hostile Terrorist Activity', Israel Law Review Association, Faculty of Law, Hebrew University of Jerusalem, Set. 23, No. 2-3 (Spring/Summer 1989) http://mishpatim.mscc.huji.ac.il/ilr/ilr23_2.htm, 16 April 2001. The Minerva Centre for Human Rights held a symposium on torture in 1995 http://humrts.huji.ac.il, 16 April 2001. Cf. also: L. Shelef, 'The Lesser Evil and the Most Good – On the Report of the Landau Commission on Terrorism and Torture', in: *Plilim* (Hebrew), 1990, pp. 185-219; D. Statman, 'The Question of the Moral Imperative and the Ban on Torture', in: *Mishpat Umimshal* (Hebrew), July 1997, pp. 161-196; A. Gilad, 'An Absolute Moral Imperative. Thou Shall not Torture', in: *Mishpat Umimshal* (Hebrew), June 1998, pp. 425-431.

4. The Anti-Torture Campaign Conducted by Human Rights Organisations and the Ban on Torture in the Decisions of the Supreme Court in
1999

In Israel and around the world, it is the non-governmental organisations
(NGOs) which are most energetically committed to defending human
rights and who lead the battle against torture. Their activities can be summarised as follows:

- providing legal advice to prisoners;
- compiling information, *inter alia* through on-site investigations;
- forwarding information to authorities and the media;
- obtaining and giving advice to parliamentarians;
- petitioning the judiciary, ministries and subordinate departments;
- lobbying foreign governments and institutions;
- publishing reports;
- co-operating with organisations to monitor the implementation of human rights agreements and improve legislation that protects human
rights.

4.1 International Human Rights Organisations against Torture in the Israeli-Palestinian Conflict

4.1.1 Amnesty International

The first report by Amnesty International (AI) on the torture of Palestinians in Israeli prisons was made in 1970.[34] It is based on material collected
during three visits to Israel between December 1968 and January 1970. AI
decided to publish the report after the Israeli government showed no willingness to establish a committee to investigate the accusations.[35] In its annual reports as well as its mission and special reports, AI continued to
document cases of torture and ill-treatment of Palestinian security prisoners by the GSS. They gave information about contacts between AI and the
Israeli authorities – meetings, inquiries, requests, recommendations and
other activities undertaken by AI to further their endeavours.[36]

Following the outbreak of the *Intifada* in December 1987 there was a
dramatic increase in the number of Palestinians arrested and mistreated. In

---

[34] Cf. Amnesty International, *Report on Torture*, London 1973, 1975, p. 231. In this
report the victims are referred to as 'certain prisoners'. However, it is clear from the
context that they are Palestinian prisoners.

[35] *Ibid*, p. 233.

[36] Cf. Amnesty International, *Torture in the Eighties,* London 1984, pp. 233-236.

its 1988 Annual Report[37] AI stated: 'The number of reports on torture and ill-treatment of Palestinian prisoners with the aim of extorting information or confessions from them, harassing or intimidating them has increased'.[38] Subsequently, AI reports became increasingly severe: in 1990 AI reported the 'torture and systematic maltreatment of political prisoners'[39] for the first time; in 1993 AI stated that 'Palestinians were exposed to systematic torture and mistreatment during questioning'.[40] Systematic torture and/or ill-treatment was noted in subsequent reports to the year 2000. Moreover in the 1998 Report it is explicitly stated that torture and ill-treatment were 'officially sanctioned'.[41] An AI report dated August 1996, entitled *'Under constant medical supervision: Torture, ill-treatment and the health-professions in Israel and the Occupied Territories'* looked at the problem of collaboration by doctors. A critical evaluation of human rights five years after the signing of the Israeli-Palestinian Declaration of Principles is made in a report entitled *'Israel/Occupied Territories and the Palestinian Authority: Five Years after the 'Oslo' Agreement – human rights sacrificed for security'*.[42]

As an advisory body to the Economic and Social Council (ECOSOC) of the United Nations, AI was influential in consultations with the Human Rights Commission and committees against torture.[43] They raised the issues of torture and ill-treatment regularly in verbal declarations to the Human Rights Commission[44] and, in 1997 and 1998, conveyed information to the Committee against Torture (CAT) on the use of torture in Israel.[45]

---

37   The Annual Reports of Amnesty International cover the preceding year; the annual report of 1990 for example covers the period from 1 January to 31 December 1989.

38   Amnesty International, *Report 1988*, London 1988, p. 240.

39   Amnesty International, *Report 1990*, London 1990, p. 131.

40   Amnesty International, *Report 1993*, London 1993, p. 169.

41   Amnesty International, *Report 1998*, London 1998, p. 208. This wording is also used in the next two annual reports.

42   Cf. Amnesty International, *Report 1999*, London 1999, p. 209.

43   E. Klein, 'Die Internationalen und Supranationalen Organisationen als Völkerrechtssubjekte', in: W. Graf Vitzthum (ed.), *Völkerrecht*, (Berlin/New York), pp. 267-391 (343-344); H. Cook, 'The Role of Amnesty International in the Fight Against Torture', in: Antonio Cassese (ed.), *The International Fight Against Torture. La lutte internationale contre la torture*, Baden-Baden 1991, pp. 172-186 (183).

44   Cf. the Annual Reports of AI from 1989 to 1999, London 1989-1999.

45   Cf. Amnesty International, *Report 1998*, London 1998, p. 209; *Report 1999*, London. 1999, p. 209.

4.1.2   Human Rights Watch

Human Rights Watch (HRW) was created from the Fund for Free Expression, founded in 1975 to monitor participating States' fulfilment of human rights commitments made in the Helsinki Final Act of the CSCE. HRW published an extensive study of Israeli interrogation procedures in the Occupied Territories a year after the signing of the Israeli-Palestinian Declaration of Principles. This study documents torture and maltreatment from the beginning of the occupation[46] and makes political recommendations to the governments of Israel and the US and member states of the European Union. The US administration is urged to suspend aid of $1.8 billion if torture continues, or to publicly explain the extraordinary circumstances justifying its continuation, as required by US law. European Union nations are advised to make economic relations with Israel dependent upon improvement of human rights for Palestinians, especially the elimination of torture.

Like AI, HRW has a special advisory status to ECOSOC. In May 1998, HRW commented on Israel's second report to the Committee against Torture.[47] It criticised Israel's persistence with its interrogation methods and expressed concern that Israeli initiatives were directed towards legalisation of torture and ill-treatment. In July 1998,[48] commenting on the first Israeli report to the Human Rights Commission on the implementation of the Civil Covenant, HRW called Israel's portrayal of interrogation methods deceptive, and reproached the Supreme Court for routinely accepting GSS's claim that physical force was indispensable and for not deciding on the legitimacy of specific interrogation techniques. HRW asked the Human Rights Commission to recommend that Israel incorporate the Civil Covenant regulations in national law; this would stop the use of torture immediately and make Israel's guidelines on interrogation public.

---

[46]   Human Rights Watch/Middle East, *Torture and Ill-Treatment. Israel's Interrogation of Palestinians from the Occupied Territories*, New York 1994.

[47]   Human Rights Watch, 'HRW Memorandum to UN Committee Against Torture' http://hrw.org/hrw/press98/may/isra0515.htm, 16 April 2001.

[48]   Cf. Human Rights Watch, 'Human Rights Watch Submission to the Human Rights Committee', 13 July 1998 http://hrw.org/hrw/reports98/Israel/Isrl988-02.htm, 16 April 2001.

4.1.3 Israeli and Palestinian Human Rights Organisations against the Use of Torture in the Israeli-Palestinian Conflict

Most human rights organisations in Israel and the Occupied Territories[49] are financed by donations from abroad and work closely with similar organisations in Europe and the US. The Israeli and Palestinian organisations are independent, but their activities overlap and occasionally they work together. Several of these organisations are particularly active on the issue of torture: *El Haq, Law, Addameer, B'tselem* and *PCATI.*

The Palestinian human rights organisation *El-Haq* (Arabic for *Justice* or *Law*), founded in 1980, was the first to be established in the West Bank. In 1995, it conducted a study[50] of torture and other cruel and degrading forms of treatment of Palestinians in Israeli custody during the years of the *Intifada* (1987-1994); more than 700 were interviewed. It found, *inter alia,* that 94percent of those interrogated were tortured or ill-treated.[51] In May 2000, *El-Haq* obtained special consultative status at the ECOSOC of the United Nations.[52]

Law, a Palestinian human rights organisation established in 1990 by a group of Jerusalem-based lawyers, defends human rights both in the PNA and the Occupied Territories, and documents human rights abuses. On the issue of torture, *Law* represents prisoners whom it regularly visits in Palestinian and Israeli prisons and interrogation centres. *Law* also organizes workshops and conferences and publishes a journal to raise awareness of human rights[53].

Addameer (Arabic for *conscious*) is a Palestinian NGO established in 1992 by human rights activists. It provides support to, and advocates the rights of, political prisoners and works to end torture through monitoring legal procedures and solidarity campaigns.[54]

B'tselem (Hebrew for *In the image*) – the Israeli Center for Human Rights in the Occupied Territories – was established in 1989 to change Israeli policy in the Occupied Territories, to ensure that residents' human

---

49 Cf. http://www.alternativenews.org/aic/aic.htm, 16 April 2001.

50 M. Phillips, 'Torture for Security: the Systematic Torture and Ill-Treatment of Palestinians by Israel' al-Haq 1995 http://www.alhaq.org/summaries/summary_torture. html, 16 April 2001.

51 Cf. http://www.alhaq.org/issues/hr_torture.htm, 16 April 2001.

52 Cf. Press Release 30 May 2000 http://www.alhaq.org/releases/pr_000530.htm, 16 April 2001.

53 Cf. http://www.lawsociety.org/aboutL/index.html, 16 April 2001.

54 Cf. http://www.addameer.org, 16 April 2001.

rights were protected and that the Israeli government fulfilled its obligations under international law. *B'tselem's* main activity is research, documentation and education; it also publishes a quarterly journal. The largest organisation of its kind in Israel, it has hundreds of volunteers who set up information stands, distribute materials, participate in public lectures and protest in the Occupied Territories[55]. *B'tselem* published the first detailed documentation of interrogation practices used by the GSS (1991). Since then, *B'tselem* has been most actively engaged in the fight against state sanctioned torture of Palestinian detainees.[56]

PCATI (Public Committee Against Torture in Israel) was established in 1990 to work for the abolition of torture and the restoration of full human rights in Israel's law and practices. *PCATI* documents, monitors and responds to cases of illegal interrogation within Israel, the Occupied Territories, the Palestinian National Authority and the Israeli-controlled Security Zone in South Lebanon. It provides legal aid and advocacy to individual victims of torture by filing individual petitions to the Israeli Supreme Court and by submitting petitions on matters of principle. *PCATI* also runs educational programs for the public at large, acts as a legislative watchdog and pressure group and serves as an international resource and clearing-house for information on the subject of torture.[57]

ACRI (The Association for Civil Rights in Israel) was established in 1972 to bolster Israel's commitment to civil liberties and human rights through legal action, education and public outreach. *ACRI* pursues its goals through litigation, preparation of educational curricula, by bringing violations to the attention of the authorities responsible, pressing for investigations and ensuring that corrective action is taken. *ACRI* counsels victims and provides expert advice to draft human rights legislation. On torture, *ACRI's* lawyers represented detainees in court.[58]

Some of these human rights organisations assist *Amnesty* and *Human Rights Watch* during visits to Israel, comment on Israeli reports to Amnesty and the Committee Against Torture, and engage in protest activities and demonstrations. Others work with professional groups whose work relates to the issue of torture: e.g. doctors and psychologists employed by the GSS to monitor the physical and mental fitness of detainees so as to avoid fatalities, and lawyers advising the GSS on how to remain within the

---

[55]   Cf. http://www.btselem.org, 16 April 2001.

[56]   Cf. http://www.btselem.org, 16 April 2001.

[57]   Cf. http://www.stoptorture.org.il/english/pcati.html, 16 April 2001.

[58]   Cf. http://www.nif.org/acri., 16 April 2001

limits of impunity. These organisations were able to raise awareness of the corrupting influence of this issue upon members of the professions.

Some organisations took on the role of advising Knesset Members; some collaborate with academic organisations to hold conferences and invite internationally-renowned personalities to criticize the practices of the judiciary and its compliance with the Landau Commission interpretations of the 'necessity' defence.[59]

4.2 Discussion of Israel's Interrogation Methods at the United Nations

Soon after the Six Day War in 1967, the United Nations dealt with the human rights situation in the Occupied Territories; a Special Commission was established which reported on information it had received on torture and acknowledged the credibility of the informants. Thereafter, a special working group established by the UN-Human Rights Commission stated that Israel had contravened the Geneva Convention by using force to obtain information and confessions from detainees.[60]

In 1991, after Israel ratified the Convention against Torture (1984) and the International Covenant on Civil and Political Rights (1966), the Committee against Torture and the Human Rights Committee examined Israel's reports on the implementation of the treaties, and the interrogation methods of the Israeli GSS.[61] The Committee against Torture recommended (in 1994, 1997, and 1998) that Israel introduce organisational and legal reforms in order to put an end to the interrogation practices of the GSS.

In 1994, the Committee against Torture criticised Israeli interrogation methods and the Landau Commission Report[62] by stating its concern that the latter created 'conditions leading to the risk of torture or cruel, or in-

---

[59] Cf. Minerva Center for Human Rights at Hebrew University Jerusalem http://humrts.huji.ac.il/torture.htm, 16 April 2001.

[60] Cf. Amnesty International, Report on Torture, London 1973, 1975, p. 229.

[61] According to Article 40 of the Civil Covenant and Article 19 of the Convention against Torture, the States Parties are obliged to submit periodic reports on the measures they have adopted in order to implement the Covenant and the Convention respectively. Israel submitted its first report on the implementation of the Convention against Torture on 25 January 1994 and the second one on 26 February 1998. Moreover, on 17 February 1997 Israel submitted a further special report that had been requested by the Committee against Torture on 22 November 1996. After a delay of more than five years, Israel submitted its first report on the implementation of the Civil Covenant on 9 April 1998.

[62] Cf. Chapter 3.

human or degrading treatment or punishment...'.[63] In subsequent observations the Committee chose less restrained language, listing seven interrogation methods that breached Article 1 and Article 16 of the Convention against Torture.[64] In May 1998 the Committee repeated its assessment, further criticising the breach of Article 2, paragraph 2, of the Convention which holds that no exceptional circumstances may be invoked as justification for torture.[65] In July 1998 the UN Human Rights Committee[66] stated that the interrogation methods already denounced by the Committee Against Torture also violated Article 7 of the International Covenant on Civil and Political Rights.[67] The Committee emphasised the inviolable character of the prohibition of torture as laid down in article 7, and urged Israel to cease using the methods referred to; it further demanded that any legislation enacted for the purpose of authorizing interrogation techniques explicitly prohibit all forms of treatment banned by article 7.

The long and laborious efforts of domestic and international human rights organisations, together with the cessation of terrorist activity during the peace process, culminated in September 1999 in the Israeli High Court's revision of the policy which had enabled the GSS to use 'physical pressure'[68]

---

[63] Cf. Committee against Torture, 12 June 1994, 'Concluding observations of the Committee against Torture: Israel. 12/06/94. A/49/44 – paras. 159-171. (Concluding Observations/Comments), para. 168(a)' http://www.unhchr.ch/tbs/doc.nsf/MasterFrameView/a8dc0b9a636a7a36c12563e20 033f2e4?Opendocument, 16 April 2001.

[64] And also constituted torture as defined in article 1 of the Convention. Cf. Committee against Torture, 9 May 1997, 'Concluding observations of the Committee against Torture: Israel. 09/05/97. A/52/44, paras. 253-260. (Concluding Observations/ Comments), § 257' http://www.unhchr.ch/tbs/doc.nsf/MasterFrameView/69b6685c 93d9f25180256498005063da?Opendocument, 16 April 2001.

[65] Cf. A/53/44, paras. 232-242 (FN 24), paras. 240(a), 238(a).

[66] The Human Rights Committee reports on the implementation of the Civil Covenant by the States Parties.

[67] Cf. Human Rights Committee, 28 July 1998, 'Consideration of Reports Submitted by States Parties Under Article 40 of the Covenant. Concluding Observations of the Human Rights Committee' http://www.unhchr.ch/tbs/doc.nsf/MasterFrameView/ 7ea14efe56ecd5ea8025665600391d1b?Opendocument, 16 April 2001

[68] Cf. M. Reinfeld, 'Court outlaws use of 'physical pressure', in: *Ha'aretz*, 7 September 1999. Possibly the decrease in the number of terrorist attacks in Israel since 1998 also played a role here. It is the result of the successful Israeli-Palestinian security cooperation under the supervision of the US Central Intelligence Agency CIA which was agreed upon in Wye Plantation in October 1998. Cf. M. Johannsen, ,Wye Plan-

4.3   The High Court's Decision
Following applications from seven human rights organisations, an extended panel of nine judges of the Israeli Supreme Court of Justice ruled, on 6 September 1999, that some methods of interrogation used by the GSS involving 'physical pressure' were illegal. The specific methods mentioned by the court were:

1)   violent shaking;
2)   the 'shabach' position: standing or sitting, hands and legs cuffed, head covered by a sealed sack, with continuous loud music being played;
3)   'frog crouch' position: crouching on the tip of the toes for long periods of time;
4)   sleep deprivation beyond that inherently required by the interrogation.

The court refrained from defining these methods as 'torture', but ruled that they constituted an illegal infringement of the rights of detainees and of their dignity. In contrast with the Landau Report, the High Court held that GSS investigators were only endowed with the same interrogation powers given to police investigators. The investigator's authority to conduct a fair investigation does not permit him to torture or treat a person in a cruel, inhuman or degrading manner.

The Court held that the 'necessity' defence as it appears in the Penal Law (article 34(11)), which negates criminal liability in certain circumstances, is not a basis for using physical pressure. Investigators may, however, avail themselves of the 'necessity' defence if, after the event, they face criminal charges for having used prohibited methods of investigation. In other words, the 'necessity' defence – the argument that an act was necessary to prevent a greater peril – cannot be the basis on which authorisation is given *in advance* to investigators because it refers to exceptional, unforeseen circumstances. It can only be used after the fact when interrogators face prosecution.

The judges ruled according to what they regarded as the prevailing legal situation, but they also referred to Israel's security problems and to the demands of fighting terrorism. The court's decision stated: '[T]he court must rule according to the law... if the law, as it stands today, requires mending, this issue is for the Knesset (legislature) to decide according to democratic principles and jurisprudence...'.[69] The court thus stated that it is for the Knesset to decide whether special legislation is required with regard to the interrogation methods of the GSS, subject to the provisions of the Basic Law: Human Dignity and Liberty.[70]

4.4 Political Assessment of the High Court Decision

The tireless work of NGOs non-governmental organizations in collaboration with dedicated lawyers contributed decisively to the High Court's decision of 6 September 1999. Waging a legal battle, the NGOs gained a political victory. They made sure that national security, an argument invoked by GSS for years to end all arguments, was no longer above the rule of law. In a Supreme Court case deal with an application against the pardon granted by the President to members of the GSS, Justice *Aharon Barak* declared in 1986: 'There is no security without law; the rule of law is a component of national security'.[71] Thirteen years later *Barak*, serving as Chief Justice, was instrumental in making this insight once guide the political practice.

In Israel and abroad, lawyers and NGOs publicly denounced both the interrogation practices of the GSS and the failure of the Israeli juridical system, and their criticism could not be ignored permanently by the judiciary because this would have damaged the self-image of its members. It is true that, as loyal servants of the state of Israel, they could hardly close their ears to the argument that the special threat to Israel necessitated special measures of protection for its citizens. However, part of their professional identity is the conviction that in Israel, i.e. in a liberal democracy, they serve, as law professionals, the rule of law. If the alleged necessities of the political situation lead to the erosion of the rule of law the lawyers who participate in the process are confronted with a dilemma they prefer not to face. The detailed bureaucratic procedures that had to be followed when 'moderate physical pressure' was to be applied may, for a number of years, have contributed to suppressing this dilemma. In the end, however, this could not work indefinitely because criticism of the interrogation practices, and particularly of the *Landau* Commission Report, was not only articulated by the 'enemies of the State of Israel', i.e. from the 'out-

---

[69] Cf. The Supreme Court of Israel, sitting as the High Court of Justice. H.C. 5100/94; H.C.4054/95; H.C.6536/95; H.C.5188/96; H.C.7563/97; H.C.7628/97; H.C.1043/99.

[70] Cf. 'Supreme Court Judgment Concerning the Legality of the GSS Interrogation Methods" http://www.israel-mfa.gov.il/go.asp?MFAH0foa0, 16 April 2001.

[71] I. Zamir, 'Human Rights and National Security', in: *Israel Law Review*, Vol. 23, Nos 2-3, Spring-Summer 1989, pp. 375-406 (394).

side', but also from the 'inside'. Top Jewish legal people from Israel, Great Britain and the USA were among the most vehement critics.

In the light of their assessment it would have been hardly convincing to denounce the criticism of the UN Human Rights organizations as merely rooted in an attitude critical of or even hostile to Israel as the Israeli political class frequently chooses to do when commenting on the UN. Occasionally Israel is accused of displaying a 'siege-mentality' which can be explained by the genocide of the Jews by the German National-Socialism as well as by the experience that, after the Proclamation of Independence, the newly proclaimed Jewish state found itself surrounded by enemies whose minds were set on its elimination. Such a mentality can in principle immunize against criticism from the outside. However, as significant portions of the Jewish Diaspora joined in this criticism, the immunizing mechanism failed to function in this case. Therefore, the collaboration of domestic Israeli and Palestinian human rights organizations with their international counterparts had an effect which took even the activists by surprise.[72] In the light of such considerations the High Court decision of 6 September 1999 can also be seen as an act of 'self-purification'.

However, the High Court decision also followed from the logic of the transformation of the Israeli-Palestinian conflict that took place in the course of the nineties. The interrogation methods of the Israeli GSS were part of the weaponry employed by the Israeli occupation forces against the uprising Palestinians. Since 1993, however, the conflict has become profoundly transformed. Israel and the PLO have committed themselves in principle to the solution of the Palestine conflict by means of negotiations. Despite all the tensions and obstacles that characterized the negotiating marathon in the seven years that followed the signing of the Declaration of Principles ('Oslo') there developed within Israel the belief that the parties to the conflict would eventually sign an agreement which would put an end to the occupation. It followed that the Palestinian government would take over from the Israeli government the prevention of acts of terrorism in Israel. At the time of the Court ruling, it seemed that there was going to be a change in the mode of conflict or even an end of the conflict. In the light of the expectation that the occupation would soon come to an end, mass arrests and intimidation by threatening the employment of torture and ill-treatment under the responsibility of the Israeli security organs seemed to become increasingly obsolete.

---

[72] S. Knaul, 'Folter in Israel ab jetzt verboten', in: *die tageszeitung*, 7 September 1999.

Finally since the collapse of the Soviet Union, there is more ideological pressure from the United States and the European Union to guard human rights. The disregard of human rights has become an ideological rallying point on which to base international politics and massive violations of human rights can lead to international sanctions and even military intervention.[73] To be true, for reasons of the double standard that prevails in international politics Israel need not worry about such eventualities. However, it is well aware that it would be beneficial to be in line with the new trend. Because due to its open economy and globalisation of trade Israel is also vulnerable to criticism which may make investors hesitate to put their money in the Israeli economy.

5. The Situation in Israel since the High Court Decision

Since the Supreme Court decision of September 1999, the evidence so far is that the prohibited methods of 'physical pressure' have ceased.[74] The challenge posed by the court to the Knesset was that, if the use of physical pressure was deemed absolutely necessary for state security, it should enact a law authorising it and put the question of positive legislation back on the agenda for public debate.

The public discourse on the necessity of 'physical pressure' which ensued following the court's decision related to a long-standing divide among Israel's political class with regard to basic values: between those for whom state security is supreme (stateists) and those whose main concern is with the rule of law and civil rights (liberals). Although there has always been a correlation between advocation of 'physical pressure' and hawkishness, the split ran across the political divide and not entirely along party lines. For example, the late Prime Minister Begin was against

---

[73] D.P. Forsythe, 'US foreign policy and human rights: The price of principles after the Cold War', in: Ipse (ed.), *Human Rights and Comparative Foreign Policy*, Tokyo/New York/Paris 2000, pp. 21-48 (34, 40-41). See the legal-philosophical discussion of the conflict between the requirement to protect the human rights and the prohibition of military force: W. Kerstin, 'Bewaffnete Intervention als Menschenrechtsschutz?', in: R. Merkel (ed.), *Der Kosovo-Krieg und das Völkerrecht*, Frankfurt a.M. 2000, pp. 187-231. For a critical analysis of the so called 'change of paradigm' in international law claimed by the proponents of the concept of 'humanitarian intervention' see N. Paech, '"Humanitäre Intervention" und Völkerrecht' in: U. Albrecht/P. Schäfer (eds), *Der Kosovo-Krieg*, Köln 1999, pp. 82-103.

[74] G. Levy, 'A year without torture', in: *Ha'aretz*, 3 September 2000. However, see also M. Reinfeld, 'Report: GSS still tortures, but less', in: *Ha'aretz*, 6 September 2000.

'physical pressure' and so were some of his followers, while Rabin was for it. Three main positions can be detected in the debate:

1) Those who approved of the court's decision and were against any form of legalised torture, even under strictest control.
2) Those who objected to legislation as it would restrict the GSS, preferring the status quo – i.e. a judicial or ministerial committee giving the GSS interrogators immunity against prosecution on the issue of 'physical pressure".
3) Those who wished to legislate for 'physical pressure", and impose clear limits on the situations and methods to be used by the GSS.

There were two paths to legislation, one proposed by the opposition Likud party and one by the government. Firstly, that of the opposition: Several days after the court's decision, the Likud took the initiative and established a committee to draft a law to allow the GSS the use of 'special methods" including 'moderate physical pressure'. The draft was tabled a few weeks later and 46 Knesset Members (out of 120) signed it.[75] The law suggested that a ministerial committee for security matters would determine in detail and in writing the specific methods, means and circumstances under which 'special methods' would be permitted.[76] In addition, the draft aimed to enshrine in law those procedures already permitted by the Landau Commission (1987); until the High Court's decision, these procedures patently failed to control the GSS. Though the Likud tabled its proposed legislation in November, it agreed to postpone any debate and readings of the law following a request by Prime Minister Barak. Barak promised that the government would shortly submit its own draft legislation and that the two proposals should be discussed together.

After the court's decision in September 1999, Barak convened the Ministerial Committee for Security and the divisions again emerged. As expected, the Minister of Justice (Beilin) was strongly opposed to any legislation which gave dispensation for 'special methods' to the GSS.[77] The Legal Advisor to the Government was, however, in favour. To pressure the government to reach a decision he refused to instruct the GSS on the

---

[75] G. Alon, 'Likud drafts a bill to let GSS use "special methods"', in: *Ha'aretz*, 15 November 1999.

[76] R. Rivlin, 'And the bomb is ticking' (Hebrew), in: *Ha'aretz*, 3 November 1999.

[77] A. Harel/M. Reinfeld/G. Alon, 'Beilin, A-G clash over need for new law on interrogation', in: *Ha'aretz*, 7 September 1999.

terms of interrogation and the circumstances under which he was prepared to ask the courts for immunity for GSS interrogators. This created a crisis as the GSS could not continue their work as they no longer knew whether they could act with impunity.[78] The opposition to the law in the government was supported by the head of the Knesset Committee for Constitution and by the influential head of the Knesset Committee for Foreign Affairs and Security.[79] By February it was reported that Barak was inclined to legislation which would extend the 'necessity defence' to GSS interrogation in advance.[80] Shortly after, the Ministerial Committee for Legislation headed by the Minister of Justice resolved against the legislation submitted by the Likud opposition.[81] In a debate in the Knesset called by the Likud in March on this topic, Prime Minister Barak voiced his moral commitment to the GSS in their work against terrorism. In April another team, comprising members of the Ministry of Defence and the Ministry of Justice, tabled its recommendations for the extension of the 'necessity defence' to give immunity in advance to GSS interrogators.

Two years have passed since the court's decision and no legislation has been enacted. The debate continues.[82] After the outbreak of the second *Intifada* in late September 2000 and the resumption of Palestinian terrorist attacks in Israel, there is mounting pressure by the GSS on the government to find legal ways that would grant interrogators the authority to exert physical pressure on those they are questioning.[83] If the armed conflict with the Palestinians continues it is quite likely that with or without legislation Israel will grant its GSS impunity to conduct interrogations using what has been euphemistically called 'physical pressure'.

6. Conclusions: The Security Dilemma

At the end of the twentieth century, torture – although it still exists – has become a taboo. As a rule, authorities deny that in their area of responsibility humans are being tormented, because under international law torture

---

[78] G. Alon, 'The Legal Advisor to the Government: "I cannot direct the GSS..."' (Hebrew), in: *Ha'aretz*, 5 November 1999.

[79] G. Alon, '"With brains – not with force" – Interview with Dan Meridor' (Hebrew), in: *Ha'aretz*, 8 September 1999.

[80] A. Eldar, 'A ticking time bomb of a question', in: *Ha'aretz*, 16 February 2000.

[81] G. Alon, 'Government rejects Likuds draft law on the legalisation of torture' (Hebrew), in: *Ha'aretz*, 29 February 2000.

[82] G. Levy, 'A year without torture', in: *Ha'aretz*, 3 September 2000; Dan Margalit, 'As long as terrorism is kept at bay', in: *Ha'aretz*, 4 September 2000.

[83] A. Benn, 'Mounting pressure on the rule of law', in: *Ha'aretz*, 21 February 2001.

is prohibited and they fear the possible consequences of an evident breach of law. The euphemistic terminologies they prefer, such as 'moderate physical pressure', are part of their strategy of denial, while at the same time, these euphemisms serve as means of upholding the practice.

In order to counter this strategy lawyers and human rights organizations committed to the fight against torture usually refuse to get bogged down in endless semantic, casuistic debates with perpetrators or their legal functionaries about definitions, redefinitions and refinements of what constitutes torture and ill-treatment. Instead they prefer to collect evidence of ill-treatment and disseminate this information widely, thus allowing each informed person to make up their minds, independently, without hierarchical mediation as to whether these practices are torture and ill-treatment and should not be tolerated.[84] Beyond the immediate confrontation with empirical data, this strategy gives the power of judgement back to the people. People can now follow and be involved in critical examination of the arguments produced as justifications for and against use of physical pressure against suspects in the context of fighting terrorism.

6.1 The 'Realist" Argument for a Law Allowing Torture

'Realist' thinkers usually employ a standard argument against the prohibition of use of physical pressure on detainees suspected or convicted of terrorist connections. They start from the premise that the state must guarantee the security of its citizens under all circumstances, including the extreme conditions of a terrorist threat. The example they cite most often is the extreme case of the caught suspect who may know the whereabouts of a 'ticking bomb'. Defenders of the use of force in interrogations argue that if two values clash, in this case, the physical integrity of a possible informant and the lives of innocent citizens, and if one cannot be guaranteed without violation of the other, then one has to choose the lesser evil. This is the logic behind the argument known as the 'necessity defence' which has been used in the Israeli legal system. If saving life and human rights cannot be reconciled – human rights must come second if thereby loss of lives can be prevented. An absolute prohibition of torture and ill-treatment that does not allow for any exceptions fails, claim 'realists', to take into consideration the dilemma which a state faces when it is challenged by terrorism.

---

[84] Cf. S. Cohen, 'The Impact of Information on Human Rights': Denial and Acknowledgment:, Minerva Centre on Human Rights http://humrts.huji.ac.il/denial.htm, 16 April 2001.

A democratic state, argue further the 'realists', draws legitimacy from its ability to assure its citizens and the world that security and democracy are compatible – even under extreme conditions. For this purpose, if the state allows the use of 'physical force' in special circumstances, it must create systems of tight control over the usage of physical force. Control is meant to serve two functions:

First, it is to manufacture the citizens' consent to the (putatively) limited violation of human rights. The citizens must be assured that this violation will not 'spill over' to other fields of life and will not extend to wider categories of people other than those directly involved in terrorism. 'Law abiding' people, so goes the argument, need not fear for themselves. This argument appeals to people's trust in public institutions and the 'order' they represent.

Second, it is to ensure that the state keeps watch over the institutions and agents who are allowed to use physical force. This stipulation is meant to fit the employment of force into the norms of government, thus 'civilizing' it functionally. In this regard control is considered necessary because it is to assure the state as well as the citizens that accountability, responsibility, transparency, flow of information and the 'rule of regulations' govern each and every area of the state's activities so that there would not develop 'a state within the state'– with secret and deviant internal norms and culture that flourishes under the protection of secrecy.

6.2 Arguments for and against a Law which Permits Torture in Extreme Cases

A democratic state which attempts to combat terrorism with measures that are compatible with the norms of human rights must choose between two procedures:

1) To legislate categorically against torture and ill-treatment; or
2) to positively and legally allow extreme measures in extreme situations.

Assuming that the democratic state perceives torture and ill-treatment in principle as wrong and evil, the question can be put in a different way: How can they best be prevented? Those who defend legislation which permits the appliance of physical pressure in special circumstances cite the most extreme situation, i.e. the situation of the 'ticking bomb' (or, for that matter, the extreme of the extreme case: a weapon of mass destruction in the hands of a terrorist); they want legislation in order to restrict the usage of 'physical pressure' to those extreme cases only. Those who object to use of 'physical pressure', by means of legislation or other 'semi-legal' procedures, want a categorical prohibition. They claim that even in the extreme cases interrogators using 'physical pressure' should withstand trial. If they plead that these measures were taken to save life the court could accept these, if proven, as 'the lesser of evils' behaviour and could acquit them. Positive legislation, they argue, is therefore superfluous.

A law which permits use of physical force in the extreme cases of interrogation provides for ambiguity and creates a twilight-zone. That is so because, as the law is necessarily abstract, it must be decided whether or not it is applicable to a specific, particular case. There is, however, the danger of a 'slippery slope' towards ever widening practices, as most real situations will not be clear-cut cases such as the favourite example of the 'ticking bomb'. For this reason control is deemed necessary over the people in charge of implementing the use of 'physical force'. However, on the basis of the Israeli experience, it can be argued that it is impossible to prevent such creeping deterioration by means of control.

Control by the state's institutions will run into numerous difficulties. Legalizing 'physical pressure' in interrogations will, most likely, lead to more, not less, secretiveness. As 'physical pressure' is contrary to international law it will always be done away from the public eye. Secrecy necessitates further mechanisms of inspection in order to uncover illegal acts hidden by the veil of secrecy. If cases of 'physical pressure' occurred and the interrogators overstepped the law the state, whose agents these interrogators are, would be tempted to leave the public in the dark. For such violations of the law – particularly if they occur repeatedly – mean that the state is not in complete control. As a result, the matter would tend to be covered up because the state would want to avoid admitting that it is ineffective. The torture and ill-treatment as well as the cumulative loss of control would be hidden from the public.

A system of controls of 'physical pressure' in interrogations of persons suspected of terrorist affiliations corrupts society, for it requires the participation of professionals such as lawyers, medical doctors and others. Lawyers may be asked to make sure that the interrogators do not overstep the law. As long as their participation is limited to this function it remains within their professional code, that is, making sure that the law is observed. If, however, they will be asked to assist to cover up legally the breaking of the law – their participation would constitute a breach of their professional code, more so, they will be colluding in the crime. Participation of medical doctors would always be incompatible with their professional code which is to preserve the life and well-being of people entrusted to them. If they work with the perpetrators of 'physical pressure' either to assure that 'limits' are not overstepped or to prevent permanent signs, damage, or death – they are, thus, themselves part of the team of tormentors.

Corruption, however, will not be limited to these professions only. An ever widening circle of the population will become part of the system that was once established to exercise control but tends to develop its own rules of secrecy. Journalists will hear about breaches of the law and might not report. Spouses or friends will be asked or threatened to keep silent. The number of such silent collaborators will increase. This leads to the gradual erosion of democratic values. The assertion that, if there is control, democracy will not be hurt by legalising 'physical pressure' in interrogations cannot be, thus, upheld. In the course of gradual tacit collusion by society of ever increasing numbers of cases of torture and ill-treatment there would come a point when control is no longer considered to be necessary. The system of control may *de facto* disappear.

6.3. Human Rights as Elements of Security in a Wider Sense

A state that allows legal use of torture will act against what is now regarded as an international code of behaviour. It will therefore be suspect and criticized. If domestic control fails to keep 'moderate physical pressure' within the limits of the law then external actors (such as allies or international organisations) will eventually intervene. International pressure can come in various forms: investigations, public condemnation, sanctions. When the practice has become known and criticised, the reputation of the torturing state will suffer. To be true, the road to becoming a pariah-state may be long. However, a number of detrimental effects can be encountered even before the pariah stage is reached: less foreign capital influx, difficulties in the arms trade, or, in the worst case, economic or military sanctions.

'Inviting' international pressure has repercussions: it can damage the sovereignty of the state and, by implication, its security. Abrogating human rights for the sake of security may not even 'pay': the price to be paid, in terms of the overall power of the state, may be much higher than the additional security the state gains by means of torture. After the collapse of many totalitarian states, a 'human rights regime' is becoming more and more part of security in a wider sense. Sovereignty is no longer accepted as an overriding argument in international law, the balance of human rights and security can no longer be seen as a zero sum game.

The Limits of Economic Sanctions under International Law: The Case of Iraq

Boris Kondoch*

"Let me conclude by saying that the humanitarian situation in Iraq poses a serious moral dilemma for this Organization. The United Nations has always been on the side of the vulnerable and the weak, and has always sought to relieve suffering, yet here we are accused of causing suffering to an entire population. We are in danger of losing the argument, or the propaganda war - if we haven't already lost it - about who is responsible for this situation in Iraq – President Saddam Hussein or the United Nations." [1]
Kofi Annan

1. Introduction

For a long time, it was commonly believed that sanctions were a humane alternative to war. Former US President Woodrow Wilson stated in 1919: "A nation that is boycotted is a nation that is in sight of surrender. Apply this economic, peaceful, silent, deadly remedy and there will be no need for force. It is a terrible remedy. It does not cost life outside the nation boycotted, but it brings a pressure upon the nation which, in my judgement, no modern nation could resist." [2]

During the last decade, however, sanctions have come under harsh criticism. The experience of the economic sanctions imposed on Iraq by the UN Security Council in 1990, and still in place eleven years later show

---

* Research Fellow, Institute of Public Law, Johann Wolfgang Goethe University, Frankfurt am Main. The author is grateful to Rita Silek (Ministry of Foreign Affairs/ Hungary) and Glen Rangwala (Campaign against Sanctions on Iraq) for critical comments. Remaining errors are, of course, the author's sole responsibility.

[1] Quoted in V. Gowlland-Debbas (ed.), *United Nations Sanctions and International Law* (2001), p. 16.

[2] Quoted in G.C. Hufbauer/J.J. Schott/K.A. Elliott, *Economic Sanctions Reconsidered* (Vol. 1, 1990), p. 9.

M. Bothe and B. Kondoch (eds.),
International Peacekeeping. The Yearbook of International Peace Operations, Volume 7, 2001, 267–294.
© 2002 Kluwer Law International. Printed in the Netherlands.

Boris Kondoch

the ethical and legal ambiguity of sanctions. In September 1999, the UN Co-ordinator for Iraq, Hans von Sponeck, called for an end to many of the sanctions against Iraq in order to facilitate larger flows of food and medicine.[3] In the same month, several speakers in the UN General Assembly's debate emphasised the need to lift the sanctions in order to end human suffering in Iraq.[4]

This article focuses on the UN sanctions regime imposed on Iraq and its compatibility with international law. After briefly defining sanctions and summarizing the UN sanctions debate, it analyses the Iraqi case and examines the legality of the sanctions regime. The objective is to determine whether the sanctions violate international law, in particular international humanitarian law and human rights law.[5]

---

[3] D. Jehl, 'UN Official Calls for an End of Sanctions against Iraq', *International Herald Tribune (IHT)*, 21 September 1999, 10.

[4] UN Press Release GA/9618, 30 September 1999.

[5] Lack of space precludes a comprehensive analysis on all aspects of the Iraqi sanction regime and of sanctions generally. A considerable amount of literature on the topic has already been published. See, for example, M. Brzoska, 'Der Schatten Saddams. Die Vereinten Nationen auf der Suche nach zielgerichten Sanktionen', *Vereinte Nationen* (2001) 56; M. Brzoska (ed.), *Design and Implementation of Arms Embargo and Travel and Aviation Related Sanctions. 'Results of the Bonn-Berlin Process'* (2001); P. Conlon, 'Legal Problems at the Centre of the United Nations Sanctions' (1996) 65 *Nordic Journal of International Law* 73; P. Conlon, 'The Humanitarian Mitigation of UN Sanctions' (1996) 39 *GYIL* 249; D. Cortright/G. Lopez, *The Sanctions Decade. Assesing UN Strategies in the 1990s* (2000); D. Cortright/A. Millar/G.A. Lopez, *Smart Sanctions: Restructuring UN Policy in Iraq* (2001); C.-A. Fleischhauer, 'Wirtschaftliche Zwangsmassnahmen in Recht und Praxis der Weltorganisation. Die Anwendung von Sanktionen durch die Vereinten Nationen in der Golfkrise' (1991) *Vereinte Nationen* 41; W.J.M. van Genugten/G.A. de Groot (ed.), *United Nations Sanctions* (1999); V. Gowlland-Debbas (ed.), *United Nations Sanctions and International Law* (2001); R. Göbel/J. Guilliard/M. Schiffmann, *Der Irak – Ein belagertes Land* (2001); S. Graham-Brown, *Sanctioning Saddam: The Politics of Intervention in Iraq* (1999); R.E. Hull, *Imposing International Sanctions: Legal Aspects and Enforcement by the Military* (1997) http://www.ndu.edu/inss/books/sanctions/contents.html; C.C. Jonyer, 'Sanctions, Compliance and International Law: Reflections on the United Nations' Experience Against Iraq' (1991) 32 *Virginia Journal of International Law* 1; H. Köchler, *Ethical Aspects of Sanctions in International Law. The Practice of the Sanctions Policy and Human Rights*, http://i-p-o.org/sanctp.htm; M. Kulessa, 'Von Märchen und Mechanismen', *Vereinte Nationen* (1996) 89; W.M. Reisman/D.L. Stevick, 'The Applicability of International Law Standards to United Nations Economic Sanctions Programmes' (1998) 9 *EJIL* 86; G. Simons, *The Scourging of Iraq* (2nd ed., 1998); D. Starck, *Die Rechtmäßigkeit von UNO-Wirtschaftssanktionen in Anbetracht ihrer Auswirkungen auf die Zivilbevölkerung* (2000); K. Van Brabant, *Sanctions: The Current Debate* (1999);

2. Definition of Collective Sanctions Applied by the Security Council

Collective sanctions can be generally defined as "collective measures imposed by organs representing the international community, in response to perceived unlawful or unacceptable conduct by one of its members and meant to uphold standards of behaviour required by international law."[6] The UN Charter does not define the term "sanctions", but sanctions are cited in it as measures that the Security Council may take under Chapter VII against a state in order to restore or maintain international peace and security. Such measures may not include the use of armed force but may include the interruption of economic relations and communications as well as the severance of diplomatic relations.

Economic sanctions are the most contentious types. Economic sanctions may compromise a wide range of measures such as a selective or comprehensive ban on trade, a prohibition on some or all capital and service transactions with the government or nationals of the offending country, an interdiction of transport and communication, and a freezing of assets.

Economic sanctions based on Chapter VII are to be distinguished from economic countermeasures.[7] The latter are bilateral, imposed in peacetime, and generally considered to be lawful unless not prohibited by the national law. Economic sanctions based on Chapter VII are also distinct from economic sanctions recommended by the Security Council or the General Assembly that are not binding on the UN members states.

Unlike individual sanctions, measures taken under Art. 41 of the UN Charter by the Security Council are mandatory i.e. implementation is not left to members' discretion since member states have an obligation under Art. 25 of the UN Charter to implement the Security Council decisions.

N.D. White, 'Collective Sanctions: An Alternative to Military Coercion?' (1994) 12 *International Relations* 75.

[6] N. Schrijver, 'The Use of Economic Sanctions by the UN Security Council: An International Law Perspective' in H.G. Post (ed.), *International Economic Law and Armed Conflict* (1994), p. 125.

[7] L. Boisson De Chazornes, 'Economic Countermeasures in an Independent World', *ASIL Proceedings* (1995) 337; on countermeasures see Art. 30 of the International Law Commission (ILC) Draft on State Responsibility in (1979) *Yearbook of the International Law Commission*, Vol. II, 47. Shrijver concludes from the ILC's Draft on State Responsibility, that collective sanctions imposed by the UN Security Council are subsumed under the word countermeasure as in the heading of draft Art. 30 and in the word measure in the text, N. Shrijver, *supra* note 6, 126.

3. Criticism of Comprehensive Sanction Regimes Imposed by the United Nations

The Security Council has imposed sanctions a mere 14 times in 56 years. Prior to 1990, sanctions were only imposed on Southern Rhodesia and South Africa. Since the end of the Cold War, the Security Council has imposed sanctions increasingly often, in the cases of Afghanistan, Angola, Ethiopia and Eritrea, the former Yugoslavia, Federal Republic of Yugoslavia, Haiti, Iraq, Libya, Liberia, Rwanda, Sierra Leone, Somalia and Sudan.[8] In parallel, debate about sanctions has intensified. Sanctions have been criticised for the following main reasons.[9]

3.1. The Ethical Dilemma
Sanctions are widely considered to hurt innocent civilians while sparing the political leaders. In the 1995 Supplement to the Agenda for Peace,[10] UN Secretary-General Boutros Boutros-Ghali termed sanctions a "blunt instrument" and questioned whether inflicting suffering on vulnerable groups in the target country is a legitimate means of putting pressure on political leaders. He proposed the establishment of a mechanism to monitor the application of sanctions and to evaluate their impact on the target state.[11]

Similar concerns have been voiced by numerous UN agencies and NGOs.[12] Among them is the International Federation of the Red Cross and Red Crescent Societies, which expressed in its World Disaster Report

---

[8] Use of Sanctions under Chapter VII of the UN Charter by the Office of the Spokesman for the Secretary General, http://www.un.org/News/ossg/sanction.htm.

[9] For more detail, see M. Kulessa/D. Starck, 'Peace Through Sanctions? Recommendations for German UN Policy', 4 *International Peacekeeping* (Kluwer Law International, 1998), 144.

[10] Reprinted in 2 *International Peacekeeping* (Kluwer Law International, 1994/95) 21, 24.

[11] Similar concerns have been raised by the current UN Secretary General Kofi Annan, see for example, *Annual Report of the Secretary General Report on the Work of the Organization* UN Doc. A/53/1 (1998), 62; *The Causes of Conflict and the Promotion of Durable Peace and Sustainable Development in Africa* (1998), 25.

[12] See, for example, Campaign Against Sanctions on Iraq, http://www.cam.ac.uk/societies/casi/; The Fourth Freedom Forum, http://www.fourthfreedom.org; International Action Centre, http://www.iacenter.org/iraq.htm; Voices in the Wilderness, http://www.nonviolence.org/vitw/.

1995[13] a growing misgiving about the humanitarian impact of sanctions.[14] The President of the International Committee of the Red Cross (ICRC) voiced particular concern about the situation in Iraq to the General Assembly on 28 November 1998, noting that the high price paid by the most vulnerable groups of the county's population was apparent.[15]

Almost every sanctions regime contains provisions allowing humanitarian exemptions for essential needs such as food and medicine in order to mitigate the regime's otherwise comprehensive impact. Nonetheless, as a major study on the impact of armed conflict on children pointed out "humanitarian exemptions tend to be ambiguous and are interpreted arbitrarily and inconsistently. .... Delays, confusion and the denial of requests to import essential humanitarian goods cause resource shortages. While these effects might seem to be spread evenly across the target populations, they inevitably fall most heavily on the poor."[16] Recent statements from various UN committees have also reflected a desire to take the humanitarian impact of sanctions into account. The Subgroup on the Question of UN Imposed Sanctions stressed that unintended side effects on civilians should be minimized by making an appropriate humanitarian exception in the Security Council resolutions.[17]

Likewise, the UN Committee on Economic, Social and Cultural Rights stated in December 1997 that more attention needed to be paid to safeguarding the rights of the vulnerable in target countries and that sanctions might violate basic economic, social, and cultural rights.[18]

Critics of UN sanctions have accordingly suggested that more targeted or smart sanctions be developed which would reduce the unintended adverse consequences of sanctions regimes. Smart sanctions are conceptualised to hurt the political leaders or those responsible for the threat or

---

[13]   International Federation of Red Cross and Red Crescent Societies (ed.), *World Disasters Report* 1995 (1995) 19-27.

[14]   For further reading, see, 'The Humanitarian Consequences of Economic Sanctions' in *Principles and Response in International Humanitarian Assistance and Protection*; 26th International Conference of the Red Cross and Red Crescent.

[15]   See also ICRC, *Iraq: A Decade of Sanctions* (1999).

[16]   *Promotion and Protection of the Rights of Children/ Impact of Armed Conflict on Children*, UN Doc. A/51/306, para. 128.

[17]   UN Doc. A/52/242.

[18]   See UN Committee on Economic, Social and Cultural Rights, *The Relationship between Sanctions and Respect for Economic, Social and Cultural Rights*, UN Doc. E/C.12/1997/8.

breach of the peace, while sparing the civilian population.[19] The concept of smart sanctions was endorsed by the current UN Secretary General Kofi Annan in his Millennium Report.[20]

3.2. Lack of Transparency

Once sanctions are in place, they are supervised by a sanctions committee[21] of the Security Council, which operates secretly and cannot be monitored or held publicly accountable. The UN General Assembly demanded that the transparency of the sanctions committees be increased.[22] The Security Council expressed its intention to move in this direction, calling in a presidential statement for a formal mechanism to assess the potential impact of sanctions and to monitor their effect.[23]

3.3. Double Standards

Another criticism is that sanctions imposed by the Security Council are based on biased or unevenly applied standards. When sanctions were imposed on Iraq to induce it to withdraw from Kuwait, sceptics pointed out that many invasions and occupations by other countries such as Turkey, Israel, and Indonesia had not resulted in the imposition of sanctions. All existing sanctions regimes except on the former Yugoslavia are targeted at countries of the south.[24]

3.4. Missing Legal and Constitutional Concept

The lack of institutional arrangements to objectively address the humanitarian impact of sanctions has limited the United Nations's capacity to respond to the adverse humanitarian consequences of the sanctions regimes

---

[19] For further information, see *Smart Sanctions – Targeting UN Sanctions*, http://www. smartsanctions.ch/start.html.

[20] *Millenium Report*, http: //www.un.org/millennium/sg/report/, 49-50.

[21] H.P. Kaul, 'Die Sanktionsausschüsse des Sicherheitsrates. Ein Einblick in die Arbeitsweise und Verfahren' (1996) *Vereinte Nationen* 96. See in the case of Iraq, P. Conlon, *United Nations Sanctions Management: A Case Study of the Iraqi Sanctions Committee, 1990 – 1994* (2000).

[22] General Assembly Resolution 242, Annex II (1997), UN Doc. A/52/242.

[23] Notes by the President of the Security Council, Ambassador Celso Amorim, *Work of the Sanctions Committee*, UN Doc. S/1999/92. Another problem is the isolation of sanctions committees from information about the humanitarian situation of countries under sanctions, see Working Group of Sanctions, Draft Report of 14 February 2001, http://www.cam.ac.uk/societies/casi/info/scwgs140201.html.

[24] See C. Dias, 'Die Peitsche des Nordens' (2/1996) *Der Überblick* 18.

effectively. The UN Department of Humanitarian Affairs commissioned a study in 1998[25] that recommended that guiding legal principles for the imposition of sanctions be established and clear objectives be defined. A working paper submitted by the Russian Federation stressed that sanctions regimes must pursue well defined purposes, have a time frame, be subject to regular review and provide clearly stipulated conditions for their determination, and not be politically motivated.[26] For its part, the so-called "Bossuyt Report" which was prepared at the request of the Sub-Commission on the Promotion and Protection of Human Rights, recommended a six prong test in order to evaluate a sanctions regime.[27] According to this test, the first issue to be examined is whether the sanctions are being imposed for a valid reason, meaning there must be a threat of or an actual breach of international peace and security. Second, the sanctions must target the proper parties who are responsible for the threat or breach of the peace and not the innocent civilians. Third, only proper goods or objects - not humanitarian goods – may be targeted. Fourth and fifth, sanctions must be reasonably limited by time and effectiveness. Sixth, the protest of governments, NGOs, intergovernmental bodies, scholars, and the general public must be taken into account.

3.5. Lack of Effectiveness

Sanctions' record in bringing about fundamental changes in the policies of the target countries is poor. Any changes usually took years.[28] A 1991 study calculated that sanctions had proven effective in mere 34 per cent of 115 cases.[29] The cases studied, however, included only two comprehensive sanction regimes imposed by the UN Security Council, namely the ones against Southern Rhodesia and South Africa.

3.6. Effects on Third States

Sanctions often cause hardship to the neighbours and major trading partners of the targeted countries,[30] in the case of the sanctions imposed on

---

[25] C. Bruderlein, *Coping with the Humanitarian Impact of Sanctions*, http://www.relief web.int/ocha_ol/pub/sanctions.html.

[26] UN Doc. A/AC182/L100 (1998), para. 41-47.

[27] *The Adverse Consequences of Economic Sanctions on the Enjoyment of Human Rights (The Bossuyt Report)*, E/ CN. 4/ Sub. 2/ 2000/ 33 of 21 June 2000.

[28] For further reading, see R.A. Pape, 'Why Economic Sanctions Do Not Work' (1997) 22 *International Security* 90.

[29] G.C. Hufbauer/J.J. Schott/K.A. Elliott, *supra* note 5, 93-94.

[30] L.L. Martin/J. Laurenti, *The United Nations and Economic Sanctions* (1997), p. 21.

Iraq, 21 countries have claimed losses in their revenues as a result of damage to their economic links with Iraq.[31]

4. Sanctions against Iraq

On 2 August 1990, Iraq invaded Kuwait. Two days later, Iraq proclaimed that Kuwait was an integral part of Iraq. On 9 August 1990, the Security Council declared in Resolution 660[32] that a breach of the peace had occurred and called for Iraq to withdraw immediately from Kuwait. Sanctions were imposed on Iraq on 6 August 1990 by Resolution 661, which required all states to ban imports from and exports to Iraq and Kuwait. It also barred the transfer of funds to both countries and required a freeze on the bank accounts affected. Exceptions were provided for only in the case of "supplies intended strictly for medical purposes, and, in humanitarian circumstances, foodstuffs" as well as in the case of "payments exclusively for strictly medical or humanitarian purposes, and, in humanitarian circumstances, foodstuffs." On 9 August 1990, the Council adopted Resolution 662, declaring the annexation null and void and demanding that Iraq rescind the action. The main objectives of the sanctions, as indicated in particular in Security Council Resolutions 660 and 662, were:

a) to bring the invasion and occupation of Kuwait by Iraq to an end,
b) to restore the sovereignty, independence, and territorial integrity of Kuwait,
c) to restore the authority of the legitimate government of Kuwait, and
d) to protect the assets of the legitimate government of Kuwait.

Security Council Resolution 661 established a committee to examine reports on the progress of implementation of the resolutions.[33] The Sanctions Committee was not, however, given the task of determining whether Iraq

---

[31] These states invoked Article 50 of the UN Charter which provides that any state which is affected with special economic problems caused by preventive or enforcement measures imposed by the Security Council shall have a right to consult the Council regarding the solution of those problems, UN Docs. S/22021 (1990) and S/22193 (1991). See in detail, P. Conlon, 'Lessons From Iraq: The Functions of the Iraq Sanctions Committee as a Source of Sanctions Implementation Authority and Practice' (1999) 35 *Virginia Journal of International Law* 632.

[32] S/RES/660 (1990).

[33] See also S/RES/661 (1990).

complied with its obligations under the relevant Security Council resolutions to the degree necessary to ease or lift, partly or wholly, the various prohibitions. Subsequent Security Council resolutions assigned additional monitoring tasks to the Committee. The sanctions were later augmented by Resolution 670, which confirmed that Resolution 661 applied to all types of transport, including aircraft. Exceptions were made where the Council had given prior consent. Resolution 665 adopted on 25 August 1990 endorsed a naval interdiction to ensure the strict implementation of the sanctions imposed by Resolution 661. On 13 September 1990, the Council adopted Resolution 666, which established guidelines to govern international humanitarian assistance. Per Resolution 669 adopted on 24 September 1990, the Council was authorized to review requests for assistance from countries that faced economic difficulties due to the implementation of the sanctions. Convinced of the need to apply even greater pressure on Iraq, the Council adopted Resolution 678, giving Iraq "one final opportunity as a pause of good will to fully implement Resolution 660 and all subsequent relevant Resolutions." Should Iraq fail to do so, the member states co-operating with Kuwait were authorized "to use all necessary means to uphold and implement the resolutions" and "to restore peace and security in the area." The deadline of 15 January 1991 passed, and the US-led Gulf-Coalition attacked Iraq. Within 100 days, Kuwait was liberated. A provisional end to the hostilities was brought about by Iraq's acceptance of Resolution 686, which demanded that Iraq cease hostile actions towards the Gulf Coalition, release detainees and prisoners, accept liability for damages, and implement all twelve previous resolutions.[34] A formal cease-fire was set forth by Resolution 687 on 3 April 1991.[35] The sanctions regime was kept in place after the cease-fire for a different purpose. The regime was henceforth intended to compel Iraq to fulfil its obligations resulting from that resolution, namely:

a) the respect for the inviolability of the border between Iraq and Kuwait,
b) the demarcation of the boundary between Iraq and Kuwait,
c) the deployment of United Nations observer unit to monitor the Khor Abdullah and the demilitarised zone,
d) the destruction, removal or rendering harmless, under international supervision, of all weapons of mass destruction and ballistic missiles with a range greater than 150 kilometres,

---

34   S/RES/686 (1991).
35   S/RES/687 (1991).

e)   liability for any direct loss, including environmental damages due to the annexation,
f)   the repatriation of all Kuwaiti and third country nationals,
g)   the requirement not to commit or support international terrorism, and
h)   the return of all property seized by Iraq.[36]

These eight criteria had to be fulfilled by the Iraqi government in order for the sanctions to be lifted. No resolution imposing sanctions since then have had such specific and varied terms. Resolution 687 declared that the full trade embargo would remain in place, pending periodic reviews every 60 days (para. 21) and every 120 days (para. 289) of Iraqi compliance with the obligations of Resolution 687. The sanctions were only slightly modified to allow the import of food and material for certain civilian needs and humanitarian purposes. Resolution 687 formalized the so-called "no-objection" procedure according to which the proving of humanitarian need was no longer required in the Sanctions Committee. The export of food-stuff as well as materials and supplies was permitted as long as the Sanctions Committee was notified.

Resolutions 706 and 712 proposed a partial lifting of the sanctions, which would have enabled Iraq to sell US$ 1.6 billion of oil worth partly for the purchase of humanitarian supplies. Iraq would in return have been subject to strict UN monitoring of the contracts and distributions of humanitarian goods purchased with the proceeds from the oil sales. For over five years, the programme did not come into effect, at first due to Iraq's rejection of the terms on which the Council was prepared to authorize limited oil sales and later due to the difficulties of working out for implementation arrangements.

In reaction to the deteriorating humanitarian situation in Iraq, the Security Council passed Resolution 986. Resolution 986 of 4 April 1995 allowed Iraq to sell up to US$ 1 billion of oil every 90 days and use 66 % of

---

[36]   On the various aspects of Resolution 687, see for example, B. Graefrath, 'Iraqi Reparations and the Security Coucil'(1995) 55 *ZaöRV* 1; B. Graefrath/ M. Mohr, 'Legal Consequences of an Act of Aggression: the Case of Iraqi Invasion and Occupation of Kuwait' (1992) 43 *ÖZöRV* 109; R.B. Lillich, *The United Nations Compensation Commission* (1995); T. Marauhn, 'The Implementation of Disarmament and Arms Control Obligations Imposed upon Iraq by the Security Council' (1992) 52 ZaöRV 781; S. Sur, *Security Council Resolution 687 of 3 April 1991 in the Gulf Affair: Problems of Restoring and Safeguarding Peace* (1992); F. Tanner (ed.) *From Versailles to Baghdad Post War Armament of Defeated States* (1992); United Nations Department of Public Information, *The United Nations and the Iraq-Kuwait Conflict, 1990-1996* (The United Nations Blue Book Series, Vol. IX).

the proceeds for humanitarian supplies. On 20 May 1996, the UN and Iraq concluded a memorandum of understanding that codified the practical arrangements for the so-called "oil-for-food" agreement. Under the "oil-for-food" programme[37], Iraq may sell up to US$ 5.2 billion worth of oil in a six month period. A third of the proceeds is to go to compensate victims of the Iraqi invasion of Kuwait and a fixed amount is set to be aside for aid to the Kurdish regions.[38]

The next turning point came when UNSCOM ascertained in 1998 that Iraq had not fulfilled its obligations under Resolution 687 to disarm all its weapons of mass destruction.[39] In December 1998, UN inspectors were withdrawn prior to the punitive air strikes by the United Kingdom and the United States.[40] After the so-called Operation Desert Fox[41], the inspectors

---

[37] For further information, see United Nations Office of the Iraq Programme, http://www.un.org/Depts/oip/.

[38] Further Security Council Resolutions regarding the sanctions imposed on Iraq include S/RES/1051 (1996), S/RES/1111 (1997), S/RES/1115 (1997), S/RES/1129 (1997), S/RES/1134 (1997), S/RES/1137 (1997), S/RES/1143 (1997), S/RES/1153 (1998), S/RES/1158 (1998), S/RES/1175 (1998), S/RES/1194 (1998), S/RES/1210 (1998), S/RES/1242 (1999), S/RES/1266 (1999), S/RES/1281 (1999), S/RES/1284 (1999), S/RES/1302 (2000), S/RES/1330 (2000), S/RES/1352 (2001), S/RES/1360 (2001), and S/RES/1382 (2001).

[39] See the letter of 15 December 1998 from the Secretary-General transmitting reports of UNSCOM and IAEA to the Security Council, UN Doc. S/1998/1172.

[40] UNSCOM reported regularly to the Security Council. The reports are available at http://www.un.org/Depts/unscom/. For further information on UNSCOM, see the personal accounts of former UNSCOM inspectors R. Butler, *The Greatest Threat* (2000); C. Duelfer, 'Arms Reduction: The Role of International Organisations, the UNSCOM Experience' (2000) 5 *Conflict & Security Law* 105; S. Ritter, *Endgame* (1999) and T. Trevon, *Der unsichtbare Tod* (1999). An excellent military analysis of Iraq's efforts to rebuild its conventional forces, its attempts to proliferate and its struggle to block UN weapons inspections is offered in A.H. Cordesman, *Iraq and the War of Sanctions* (1999).

[41] See on the legality of the use of force N. Krisch, 'Unilateral Enforcement of the Collective Will: Kosovo, Iraq, and the Security Council' (1999) 3 *Max Planck Yearbook of United Nations Law* 59; D. Leurdijk/R. Siekman, 'The Legal Basis for Military Action against Iraq' (1998) 4 *International Peacekeeping* (Kluwer Law International) 71; J. Lobel/M. Ratner, 'Bypassing the Security Council: Ambiguous Authorization to Use Force, Ceasefires and the Iraqi Inspection Regime' (1999) 93 *AJIL* 124; M. Weller, 'The Threat or Use of Force in a Unipolar World: The Iraq Crisis of Winter 1997/98' (1998) 4 *International Peacekeeping* (Kluwer Law International) 63; N.D. White, 'The Legality of the Threat of Force against Iraq' (1999) 30 *Security Dialogue* 75; R. Zedalis, 'Dealing with the Weapon Inspections Crisis in Iraq' (1999) 59 *ZaöRV* 37; S.M. Condron, 'Justification for Unilateral Action in Re-

did not re-enter because the Security Council members could not agree on how to monitor Iraqi weapons and when – or if – to begin lifting the sanctions. Since the establishment of the cease-fire, the issue of lifting the sanctions has been debated at length among the five permanent members of the Security Council.[42] Russia, France, and China have been sympathetic to an immediate lifting of the sanctions. The UN Security Council has come up with several draft proposals on sanctions and inspections but has been unable to agree on new weapons inspections. The United States and United Kingdom have not been able to convince the other permanent members of the Council that strict sanctions should be kept even if Iraq agrees to new inspections. A proposal tabled by the United Kingdom and the Netherlands and supported by the United States provided for an UN-SCOM replacement agency to be called the United Nations Commission on Inspection and Monitoring (UNCIM).[43] On 17 December 1999, the Security Council adopted Resolution 1284 replacing UNSCOM with the United Nations Monitoring Verification and Inspection Commission (UNMOVIC).[44] Since then, however, UN weapon inspectors have not been allowed to re-enter Iraq.

New proposals for modifying the sanctions regime were launched by the United Kingdom, France, and Russia in summer 2001.[45] No agreement on them, however, has been reached. The "oil-for-food" programme remains in place as established under Security Council Resolution 1382 of 29 November 2001.[46] It will terminate after 150 days, and the Security Council will have to decide how to proceed with the unsatisfactory situation in Iraq.

---

sponse to the Iraqi Threat: ACritical Analysis.of Operation Desert Fox (September 1999) 161 *Military Law Review* 115.

[42] R. Zedalis, 'An Analysis of Some of the Principal Leading Questions Relating to UN Weapons Inspections in Iraq' (1998) 67 *Nordic Journal of International Law* 249.

[43] The draft is accessible at http://www.cam.ac.uk/societies/casi/info/uk-dutch.html.

[44] For updated information on UNMOVIC, see http://www.un.org/Depts/unmovic/index.htm.

[45] The drafts are accessible at: http://www.cam.ac.uk/societies/casi/info/scdeb0105 a06.html.

[46] S/RES/1382.

5. The Impact of Sanctions Imposed on Iraq

The humanitarian problems caused by economic sanctions are illustrated best by the example of Iraq,[47] as the regime imposed on Iraq is the most comprehensive in UN history. From 1991 on, an increasing number of reports documenting the adverse impact on the impact of sanctions began to circulate. Humanitarian agencies agree that conditions in Iraq have continued to deteriorate even after the initiation of the "oil-for-food" programme.

Several UN agencies and human rights organizations have produced reports on malnutrition due to the food blockade and on severe health problems due to the absence of medicines and water purification systems.[48] A 1996 study estimated a ten per cent drop in Iraq's GDP since the imposition of the UN sanctions. A joint UNICEF and Iraqi government survey [49] pointed to a deterioration since the Gulf War and the imposition of sanctions.[50] The mortality rate among children under the age of five doubled from 56 per 1,000 live births between 1984-89 to 131 between 1994-99. The survey's principal conclusion is that Iraq should be allowed to raise additional proceeds and to spend the proceeds more freely. Various UN agencies have estimated that the sanctions have contributed to hundreds of thousands of deaths. In late September 1998, the UN Humanitarian Co-ordinator for Iraq, Denis J. Halliday, resigned to protest against the continuation of economic sanctions, claiming that these were killing innocent people and children.[51] According to UNICEF, 5,000 to 6,000 children under the age of five die each month. According to UNFP and the ICRC, approximately 70 per cent of women are suffering from anaemia. Malnutrition is partly caused by a massive deterioration in the basic infrastructure, such as water supply and waste disposal systems. Lastly, when evaluating the impact of sanctions one must also take the social costs into

---

[47] S. Willett, *The Gulf Crisis: Economic Implications* (1990); P. Clawson, *How Has Saddam Survived?*, *Economic Sanctions: 1990-93* (1993).

[48] See Subgroup on the 'Question of United Nations Imposed Sanctions', General Assembly Resolution 242, Annex II (1997).

[49] UNICEF, *Iraq Child and Maternal Mortality Surveys*, http://www.unicef.org/reseval/ iraqr.html.

[50] See also on this aspect, M.M. Ali/I.H. Shah, "Sanctions and Childhood Mortality in Iraq" (2000) *The Lancet* (2000) 355; R. Garfield, *Morbidity and Mortality Among Iraqi Children from 1990 to 1998: Assessing the Impact of Economic Sanctions* (1999), http://www.fourthfreedom.org/sanctions/garfield.html.

[51] See Interview with D.J. Halliday, http://www.globalpolicy.org/security/sanction/ dhall2.htm.

account. The sanctions had deep consequences on Iraqi and Islamic family values, according to Denis J. Halliday, Child begging, for example, has become commonplace.[52]

The humanitarian panel, one of three panels set up by the Security Council after the US-UK strikes in December 1998 to find a new basis for Councils policies regarding Iraq, concluded that Iraq had experienced a shift from relative affluence to massive poverty.[53]

The United States blames the Iraqi government and not the sanctions regime for the severe living conditions. Samuel R. Berger, the national security advisor, pointed out in the latest UNICEF report that the child mortality rates were declining in the autonomous region, which is under the same sanctions regime as the rest of Iraq but where the food delivery is organized by the UN.[54] The implications, however, that the different rates are the result of the different implementation arrangements has been dismissed by UNICEF.[55]

Although the extent to which human hardship is attributable to the economic sanctions as opposed to Iraqi government policy is subject of considerable debate.[56] There is no doubt that the economic sanctions have had a severe impact on the country's population. On the one hand, much of the humanitarian suffering could have been mitigated had Iraq accepted the oil-for-food programme in 1991 and not delayed its implementation after the establishment of the oil-for-food programme by Resolution 986 in 1995. On the other hand, the Security Council cannot evade its own responsibility. It has imposed and maintained the current sanctions regime that has been used by the Iraqi government against the most vulnerable groups of its population to generate support for lifting the sanctions. The oil-for-food programme has been not effective enough to alleviate the suffering.

---

[52] D.J. Halliday, 'The Impact of The UN Sanctions on the People of Iraq' (2/1999) 28 *Journal of Palestine Studies* 32-33.

[53] UN Doc. Annex II S/1999/356.

[54] S.R. Berger, 'The Iraqis are Victims of Saddam, Not of the Outside World', *IHT*, 20 October 1999, http://www.iht.com/IHT/TODAY/WED/ED/edberger.html.

[55] S. Graham-Brown, UNICEF establishes Blame in Iraq, http://www.igc.apc.org/globalpolicy/security/sanction/iraq1/iraq11.htm.

[56] B. Crossette, 'Iraq Ignoring UN Call to Use Oil Wind Fall for Children', *IHT*, 11 August 1999, 5; B. Crossette, 'UN Chief Faults Iraq over Aid Programme for Mothers and Children', *IHT*, 25 August 1999, 7; D. Cortright/G.A. Lopez, 'Are Sanctions Just? The Problematic Case of Iraq' (1999) 52 *Journal of International Affairs* 743-45.

6. Legal Evaluation

The following paragraphs seek to clarify the legal rules applicable to collective sanctions in times of peace and armed conflict. The analysis then addresses the question whether the Security Council violated international law by imposing and upholding sanctions against Iraq.

6.1. The Power of the Security Council to Impose Sanctions

The power of the Security Council to impose sanctions rests upon Art. 41 of the UN Charter. Before adopting measures under Art. 41, the Security Council must have determined in accordance with Art. 39 of the UN Charter "the existence of any threat to the peace or breach of peace, or an act of aggression" and make recommendations or decide what measures are to be taken "to maintain or restore international peace and security."

The Council determined in Resolution 660 that there existed "a breach of international peace and security as regards the Iraqi invasion of Kuwait" before adopting sanctions by Resolution 661. Iraq's was the only case in which the illegal invasion of another country was given as the justification for imposing sanctions. One of the unsettled issues regarding the imposition of sanctions on Iraq is whether the Security Council acted in accordance with international law when it kept the sanctions in place after the main purpose of the Security Council policy, i.e., the liberation of Kuwait, had been fulfilled and whether Iraq could still be seen as a threat to the peace.

It may be argued based on the wording of Resolution 687, that the Council assumed a continuing threat to the peace from Iraq's possession of weapons of mass destruction (see in particular the preamble to Resolution 687). Although Art. 39 of the UN Charter provides the Council with a wide margin of appreciation, such an argument alone appears to be legally doubtful because international law does not generally prohibit the possession of weapons of mass destruction, except when agreed by sovereign states limiting the amount of armaments.

The wording of Resolution 687[57] also suggests that the Council decided that a continuing threat to the peace existed out of fear of Iraq's latent tendency to use weapons of mass destruction. The presumption of the Council appears to be reasonable given Iraq's past aggressive conduct: Iraq had committed an act of aggression against Kuwait and had used poison gas in the First Gulf war against Iran and against the Kurdish population in the 1980s.

---

[57] See, for example, paragraphs 4, 8, 14, 23 of the preamble of Resolution 687.

6.2. *Legal Limitations to the Security Council's Measures under Chapter VII*

It has been argued that the Security Council can act above international law and therefore no legal limitations exists on measures adopted by it under Chapter VII.[58] This interpretation is based on the wording of Arts. 103 and 25 of the UN Charter. Specifically, Art. 103 states that "in the event of a conflict between the obligation of the Members of the United Nations under the present Charter and their obligation under any other international agreement, their obligation under the present Charter shall prevail." According to Art. 25 of the UN Charter, the UN Members "agree to accept and carry out the decisions of the Security Council in accordance with the Charter." This interpretation cannot, however, be accepted for the following reasons:

a) According to Art. 24(1) read together with Arts. 1 and 2 of the UN Charter the Council's decisions must be in accord with the purposes and principles of the United Nations. Promoting and encouraging respect for human rights and fundamental freedoms are among these purposes, and therefore the Council always has to take them into account when acting under Chapter VII. Since, as argued by some legal commentators,[59] humanitarian law can be perceived as 'human rights in armed conflicts', the Council is also bound by rules of international humanitarian law.

b) Another limitation is imposed by legal norms regarded as *jus cogens*. The doctrine of *jus cogens* was developed in the late 1960s and can be found in Art. 53 of the Vienna Convention on the Law of Treaties, 1969. Norms regarded as *jus cogens* are non-derogable from them and it is generally accepted that these standards also apply to Security Council enforcement measures taken under Chapter VII of the UN Charter.[60] As the hard core of human rights and international humanitarian law constitute *jus cogens*, these norms apply to measures imposed by the Security Council under Chapter VII.

---

[58] See, for example, G. Oosthuizen, 'Playing the Devil' s Advocate: The United Nations Security Council is Unbound by Law' (1999) 12 *LJIL* 549.

[59] L. Doswald-Beck/S. Vite, 'International Humanitarian Law and Human Rights Law' (1993) No. 293 *ICRC Review* 94.

[60] T.D. Gill, 'Legal and Some Political Limitations on the Power of the UN Security Council to Exercise Its Enforcement Powers under Chapter VII of the Charter' (1995) 26 *NYIL* 33, 79.

This view is also supported by the statement of Justice Weeramantry of the International Court of Justice in the Lockerbie case that "the history of the United Nations ... corroborates the view that a limitation on the plenitude of the Security Council's power is that those powers must be exercised in accordance with the well-established principles of international law."[61]

c) The Security Council, as laid down in Arts. 24-26 of the UN Charter, is to bear responsibility for the maintenance of international peace and security. It would be contrary to its role if the Council disregarded the rule of law[62] since a peaceful world order can only be realized through respect for the rule of law.[63]

6.3. Legal Limits to Collective Sanctions Under Art. 41 of the UN Charter
No international treaty explicitly deals with the issue of the legal limits of economic sanctions. Art. 41 of the UN Charter, which empowers the Security Council to impose sanctions, is silent on the questions regarding the precise scope and duration of sanctions. Moreover, due to the infrequency of sanctions prior to the end of the Cold War, only few scholars commented on the issue. There is nonetheless a scholarly consensus that the non-derogable provisions of human rights law[64] and provisions of international humanitarian law demarcate the limits of the permissibility of economic sanctions.[65]

---

[61] *Order with regard to request for the Indication of Provisional Measures in the Case Concerning Questions of Interpretations and Application of the 1971 Montreal Convention Arising from the Aerial Incident at Lockerbie (Libya v United States)*, ICJ (1992); 31 *ILM* (1992) 694-696.

[62] Other authors have also suggested that the principle of good faith constitutes a limit to the enforcement powers of the Security Council. See V. Gowlland-Debbas, 'Security Council Enforcement Action and Issues of State Responsibility' (1994) 43 *ICLQ* 93-94.

[63] H.-P. Gasser, 'Collective Economic Sanctions and International Humanitarian Law - An Enforcement Measure under the United Nations Charter and the Right of Civilians to Immunity: An Unavoidable Clash of Policy Goals' (1996) 56 *ZaöRV* 880-881.

[64] As the non-derogable provisions of human rights apply in times of peace and of an armed conflict, the relevant rules are discussed in the section relating to legal limitations during times of peace.

[65] H.-P. Gasser, *supra* note 63, 871; R. Normand, *Iraqi Sanctions, Human Rights and Humanitarian Law*, http://www.merip.org/mer/mer200/normand.htm; A. Reinisch, 'Developing Human Rights and Humanitarian Accountability of the Security Council for the Imposition of Economic Sanctions' (2001) 95 *AJIL* 851-872; D. Starck,

6.3.1. Legal Limitations in Times of Armed Conflict

International humanitarian law can be defined as "those international
rules, established by treaty or custom, which are specifically intended to
solve humanitarian problems directly arising from international and non-
international armed conflicts and which for humanitarian reasons, limit the
right of the parties to a conflict to use methods and means of warfare of
their choice or protect persons and property that are or may be affected by
the conflict."[66]

Although international humanitarian law does not directly address the
legality of sanction regimes imposed by the Security Council in the course
of an armed conflict, it is widely agreed that specific rules can be found in
the four Geneva Conventions, the Protocols thereto, and relevant customary international law. The purpose of these instruments is to provide civilians with a minimum protection from the effects of armed conflict. They
define certain population groups as particularly vulnerable and specifically
mentions sectors exempt from blockades. The lack of addressing collective sanctions in the Geneva Conventions and the Additional Protocols can
be explained by the fact that the drafters at that time did not anticipate that
non-military measures such as collective sanctions could contribute to
thousands of deaths. This fact, however, does not preclude the application
of international humanitarian law, since this area of international law is
highly adaptive and widely interpreted in a dynamic way. It would otherwise be also impossible to apply international humanitarian law to new
types of weapons. As the former Senior Legal Advisor of the ICRC, H.-P.
Gasser convincingly argues, "while the safeguards of international humanitarian law have been established primarily to protect the civilian
population against the effects of military operations in an armed conflict
between the two belligerents, considerations of humanitarian policy
clearly suggest that they also apply to enforcement measures based on
Chapter VII of the UN Charter."[67] This holds true at least for sanctions
adopted in the course of an armed conflict.[68]

---

supra note 5, 227-370; P.C. Szasz, 'Das kleinste Übel' (2/1996) Der Überblick 27-
29.

[66] H.-P. Gasser, *International Humanitarian Law* (1993), p. 16.

[67] H.-P. Gasser, *supra* note 63, 885.

[68] The view that international humanitarian law is directly applicable to economic
sanctions has not been followed by D. Starck due to the non-military character of the
sanctions. The author does, however, apply international humanitarian law to economic sanctions by analogy. See in detail, D. Starck, *supra* note 5, 235.

6.3.1.1. Prohibition on Starvation as a Method of Warfare

As food is essential for the human survival, starvation has been used as a method of warfare for centuries. Starvation can be defined "as an effect, the condition or process of perishing from insufficient food intake, a state of extreme malnutrition, which may be caused by physical inability to eat or insufficient food supplies."[69] Under international humanitarian law, starvation as a method of warfare is prohibited. This rule is embodied in Art. 54 of the Additional Protocol I and Art. 14 of Additional Protocol II. It can be regarded as *jus cogens*.[70] No collective sanctions may be imposed in such a manner as to cause the civilian population to starve. If a significant segment of a civilian population falls below subsistence level economic sanctions violate the prohibition on starvation.

It may questioned whether a subjective element must be shown for the crime of starvation to be established. According to Art. 54 of the Additional Protocol I, starvation is prohibited "as a method of warfare." The word "method" suggests that the party whose actions cause starvation has the knowledge and the will to act in this manner. According to Art. 8 (2)(b)(xxv) of the ICC Statute starvation as a method of warfare is a war crime only if the perpetrator intended to starve a civilian population as a method of warfare. On the basis of these two regulations, it may be concluded that the prohibition on starvation requires a subjective element.

6.3.1.2. Right to Humanitarian Assistance

If starvation is strictly forbidden as a method of warfare, the provisions dealing with the regulation of relief actions must also be considered to be absolutely binding. Under international humanitarian law, civilians enjoy a right to humanitarian assistance, though different rules apply to international and non-international armed conflicts.

6.3.1.2.1. Right to Humanitarian Assistance in International Armed Conflicts

Art. 23 of the Fourth Geneva Convention obligates states during an international armed conflict to authorise and facilitate the free passage and distribution of the following relief goods:

---

[69] G.A. Mudge, 'Starvation as a Means of Warfare' *International Lawyer* 4 (1969/ 1970) 236.

[70] D. Starck, *supra* note 5, 282.

- medical supplies for the benefits for all civilians;
- religious objects for the benefits for all civilians; and
- essential foodstuffs, clothing and tonics intended for children under 15, expectant mothers, and maternity cases.

Art. 70 of Additional Protocol I has extended the right to receive relief goods to all members of the civilian population. It adds goods that constitute the minimum necessary for the survival of persons in war times with the consent of the state concerned.

According to Arts. 9/9/9/10 of the four respective 1949 Geneva Conventions, the ICRC and other impartial humanitarian organizations may be subject to the consent to the parties to the conflict to undertake humanitarian activities for the protection and relief of protected persons.

6.3.1.2.2. Right to Humanitarian Assistance in Non-international Armed Conflicts

According to Art. 3 common to the 1949 Geneva Conventions humanitarian and relief actions should be undertaken, subject to the consent of the parties concerned.

Pursuant to Art. 18(2) of Additional Protocol II, relief societies may offer their services and if necessary provide impartial humanitarian relief, again subject to the consent of the parties concerned.

6.3.1.2.3. Relief Assistance in Naval Blockades

Art. 23 of the Fourth Geneva Convention and Art. 70 of Additional Protocol I also apply to naval blockades. An exception to naval blockades must be granted if the civilians of the blockaded country are threatened by starvation or severe shortage of medical supplies.[71]

6.3.1.2.4. Relief Assistance to Occupied Territories

Arts. 55 and 59 of the Fourth Geneva Convention establish a regime to protect civilians in an occupied territory. Art. 55 sets out the principle that the occupying power assumes on the responsibility of insuring the supply of food and medicine to the occupied territory. Art. 69(1) of Additional Protocol I extends that responsibility to the provision of clothing, bedding, means of shelter, other essential supplies and religious objects.

In contrast to Art. 23 of the Fourth Geneva Convention, Art. 55 applies to the civilian population as a whole. Art. 59 requires that if the occupying

---

[71]   H.-P. Gasser, *supra* note 63, 886.

power cannot provide the necessary supplies, it must authorize third parties, like the Protecting Power or the ICRC, to carry out relief actions.[72]

6.3.1.3. Rule of Distinction

Under the rule of distinction, which is one of the fundamental principles of international humanitarian law, belligerents are required to distinguish between civilians and combatants at all times and to direct their attacks only against military targets.[73]

Collective sanctions cannot therefore be aimed at the entire population, in an attempt, to influence the regime without being a clear violation of the principle of distinction.

6.3.1.4. Proportionality

Collective sanctions are also limited by the principle of proportionality, which is an essential element of the law of armed conflict. Examples of its application can be found in Arts. 51 and 57 of Additional Protocol I. Art. 57 (b) of Protocol I prohibits any "attack which may be expected to cause incidental loss of civilian life, injury to civilians, damage to civilian objects ... which would be excessive in relation to the concrete and direct military advantage anticipated." For example, "a remote advantage to be gained at some unknown time in the future would not be a proper consideration to weigh against civilian losses."[74] This principle applied to a sanctions regime means that the goal intended to be achieved by the sanctions must justify the humanitarian hardship they cause.

6.3.2. Legal Limitations During Times of Peace

The application of the above-mentioned rules of international humanitarian law either directly or by analogy to economic sanctions has been proposed even outside the context of an armed conflict. Direct application is based on the idea that as long as the consequences of an armed conflict are felt in peacetime, the Security Council is bound by the rules of international humanitarian law. It remains unclear, however, when and on which basis the effects of an armed conflict can no longer be felt. Such a vague approach also finds no foundation in customary international law. Application by analogy of international humanitarian law to sanctions during

---

[72]   See also Art. 70 I of Additional Protocol I and, Art. 18(2) of Additional Protocol II.

[73]   See Art. 47 of Additional Protocol I.

[74]   W.A. Solf in M. Bothe/K.J. Partsch/W.A. Solf, *New Rules for Victims of Armed Conflict* (1982), p. 365.

peacetime is proposed on the grounds that the sanctions are always the same measures having the same effects regardless whether there is an armed conflict in the target state. Following *"a maiore ad minus"* reasoning this view argues that the rules of international humanitarian law restricting the lawfulness of sanctions during times of war should apply all the more in times of peace.[75]

Application of international humanitarian law by analogy during peacetime must, however, be rejected for two reasons. Firstly, international humanitarian law has been expressly developed to protect the vulnerable in armed conflicts and not to protect civilians during peacetime. Secondly, the application of norms by analogy requires that a given situation is not sufficiently regulated by the existing legal rules. However, civilians are sufficiently protected from the adverse effects of sanctions during peacetime by human rights law and the genocide convention, as elaborated in the following paragraphs.

6.3.2.1. The Right to Life

The right to life is incorporated in numerous international human rights instruments, such as Art. 6 of the International Covenant on Civil and Political Rights, 1966; Art. 2 of the European Convention for the Protection of Human Rights and Fundamental Freedoms, 1950; and Art. 4 of the African Charter of Human Rights, 1981.

It is disputed whether the right to life should be interpreted narrowly or broadly. According to a narrow interpretation, the right to life applies only to cases where life is arbitrarily taken through execution, torture and the like but not through starvation and hunger.[76] The UN Human Rights Committee rejects such a narrow interpretation and argues that the right to life requires that states adopt positive measures.

In order to resolve this legal dilemma, one must consider the right to life together with the human rights provisions guaranteeing the right to food and the right to be free from hunger. Most important among these provisions is Art. 11 of the International Covenant on Economic, Social and Cultural Rights, 1966, which states that:

---

[75] See, for example, M. Sassòli, 'Sanctions and International Humanitarian Law' in V. Gowlland-Debbas (ed.), *supra* note 5, 244; D. Starck, *supra* note 5, 241-245.

[76] Y. Dinstein, 'The Right to Life, Physical Integrity and Liberty' in L. Henkin (ed.), *The International Bill of Rights* (1981), p. 115.

"1. The State Parties ... recognize the right of everyone to an adequate standard of living ... including food ... . The State Parties will take appropriate steps to ensure the realization of this right ... .
2. The States Parties ..., recognize the fundamental right of everyone to be free from hunger."

It can be concluded from this article that states are obligated to provide essential goods to those in need. If this interpretation cannot be accepted, it is at least prohibited to deliberately acting as to deprive human beings of food and to cause hunger and starvation.[77]

6.3.2.2. The Rights of the Child

One of the groups most vulnerable to the adverse consequences of sanctions are children. The rights of children are laid down in the United Nations Convention on the Rights of the Child, 1989, which currently stands as the most widely ratified international agreement. Most relevant in the context of sanctions are Arts. 6 and 24 of the Convention, according to which every child has the inherent right to life and the right to the highest attainable standard of health and access to medical services.

6.3.2.3. The Prohibition on Genocide

Another limitation can be also drawn from the prohibition on genocide,[78] which may be viewed as a "collective right to life". According to Art. 1 of the Convention on the Prevention and Punishment of the Crime of Genocide, 1948, genocide is prohibited both in times of peace and war.

Pursuant to Art. 2 a), b), and c) of the Convention, genocide is, *inter alia*, "killing members of the group", "causing serious bodily, or mental harm to members of the group", or "deliberately inflicting on a group conditions of life calculated to bring about its physical destruction in whole or in part", committed with the intent to destroy, in whole or in part, a national, ethnic, racial, or religious group, as such. Collective sanctions can accordingly constitute genocide, if they amount to the deliberate starvation of a group, committed with the intent to destroy it.

---

[77] A. Segall, 'Economic Sanctions: Legal and Policy Constraints' (1999) No. 836 *ICRC Review* 763.

[78] Recent incorporation of the prohibition on genocide as an international crime are found in Art. 6 of the Statute of the International Criminal Court, Art. 4 of the Statute of the International Criminal Tribunal for the Former Yugoslavia, Art. 2 of the Statute of the International Criminal Tribunal for Rwanda.

6.3.2.4. The Principle of Proportionality
The principle of proportionality also represents as a criterion in determining the legality of collective sanctions imposed during peacetime. It is not only well established under international humanitarian law, but it can also be found in almost all branches of international and national law.

Proportionality in the context of collective sanctions requires that a careful balance be struck between the United Nations interest in attaining the goal of a sanctions regime and its interest in avoiding unacceptable harm to the civilian population.[79]

7. Legal Assessment of the Sanctions Imposed on Iraq

From a legal perspective, the Iraqi sanctions regime can be divided into two distinct phases: the first from the adoption of sanctions by Security Council Resolution 661 on 6 August 1990 until the end of Operation Desert Storm and the second from the establishment of the cease-fire by Security Council 687 on 3 April 1991 to the present. In the Second Gulf War, international humanitarian law became applicable on 2 August 1990 when Iraq invaded Kuwait.[80] Concerning the first phase it may be argued that the Security Council Resolution 661 was not in conformity with the prohibition on starvation (see 6.3.1.1.) since it allowed the payments for foodstuffs only in humanitarian circumstances. In practice, allowance was rarely given until the adoption of Security Council Resolution 666 on 13 September 1990.[81] Resolution 661 established therefore an almost complete food embargo. The mere existence of a food embargo does not, however, automatically violate the prohibition on starvation. It must be shown that the sanction regime had such an effect on a significant part of the Iraqi population that its standard of living fell below a subsistence level. The lack of objective reports prior to the end of the armed conflict regarding food availability makes it impossible to ascertain the extent to which the

---

[79]   J. Delbrück, 'Proportionality' in R. Bernhardt (ed.), *Encyclopedia of Public International Law*, Instalment 7 (1984), p. 396.

[80]   Kuwait is a party to the four Geneva Conventions 1949 and to both Additional Protocols. Although Iraq has only ratified the four Geneva Conventions, all the rules applicable here are rules of customary international law, which are binding on all belligerents, irrespective of which treaty they are party to, including the UN.

[81]   R. Provost, 'Starvation as a Weapon: Legal Implications of the United Nations Food Blockade Against Iraq and Kuwait' (1992) 30 *Columbia Journal of Transnational Law* 584.

food shortage can be attributed to the military campaign as opposed to the sanctions. Even if there were clear evidence that the Council's sanctions caused starvation among the Iraqi population, the specific intent on the part of the Security Council to starve the Iraqi people cannot be proven, since there is little information available regarding the motives and reasons behind the Security Council's and the Sanctions Committee's actions.[82] Furthermore, the Council's decision to exclude "supplies strictly intended for medical purposes" and "in humanitarian circumstances, foodstuffs" from sanctions as well as the Sanctions Committee's practice of allowing the food shipments after the adoption of Security Council Resolution 666 indicates that the Council did not intend to starve the Iraqi people.

Security Council Resolution 661 nonetheless violates the rules of international humanitarian law governing relief to the civilian population (see 6.3.1.2.). The civilian population of any territory has the right to receive relief goods such as essential foodstuffs and medical supplies in times of armed conflict. No exceptions to these rules are permissible under international law. Resolution 661 was in conformity with the above mentioned rules in respect of medical supplies as these items were exempted from the ban, but foodstuffs were only exempted from the embargo in humanitarian circumstances, which can be regarded as a clear violation of international humanitarian law. According to Art. 23 of the Fourth Geneva Convention, religious objects for the benefits for all civilians; and clothing and tonics intended for children under 15, expectant mothers, and maternity cases should have been exempted from the sanctions regime as well.

The Council acted in accordance with the principle of distinction (see 6.3.1.3.). There is no evidence that the sanctions were targeted at the entire Iraqi people. The sanctions were imposed only to change Iraqi government policy, i.e., their main aim was to end the occupation of Kuwait.

International humanitarian law in the Iraqi case generally ceased to have effect when the armed conflict was ended with the cease-fire established by Resolution 687. International humanitarian law still remained to the pending issues from the Second Gulf War, such as the repatriation of the prisoners of war.[83] Military operations have, however, been launched against Iraq on several occasions following the cease-fire[84], and one may argue that there is an armed conflict and international humanitarian law is

---

[82] R. Provost, *ibid.*, 584.

[83] H.-P. Gasser, *supra* note 66, 23.

[84] See, for example, C. Gray, 'After the Ceasefire: Iraq, the Security Council and the Use of Force' (1994) 65 *BYIL* 135.

still applicable. In 1991 and 1992, the coalition forces established the northern and southern no-fly zones in response to Iraqi efforts to suppress the Shiites and Kurds, respectively.[85] A year later, the United States launched air strikes against Iraq, suspecting that it was behind a conspiracy to assassinate former US President George Bush during a visit to Kuwait.[86] In the aftermath of Operation Desert Fox, the United States and the United Kingdom continued strikes in the no-fly zones.[87] In view of these military operations, it may be argued that there is still an armed conflict and international humanitarian law applies.[88]

Settlement of this issue hangs on the definition of armed conflict. The Geneva Conventions do not provide such a definition. According to the ICRC Commentary, an armed conflict is "any difference arising between two States leading to the intervention of members of the armed forces ..., even if one of the parties denies the existence of a state of war. It makes no difference how long the conflict lasts, or how much slaughter takes place."[89] For its part, the Appeals Chamber in the *Tadic* case [90] held that "an armed conflict exists whenever there is a resort to armed force between States or protracted armed violence between governmental authorities and organized armed groups or between such groups within a State. International humanitarian law applies from the initiation of such armed conflicts and extends beyond the cessation of hostilities until a general conclusion of peace is reached ... ." Both definitions are formulated very generally and lack clarity. It appears, however, to be clear that fighting must reach a certain degree of intensity as to amount to an armed conflict. Many isolated events, such as naval incidents or border clashes, do not constitute an armed conflict.[91] In the case at hand, it is arguable that the

---

[85] See in more detail, H. Cook, *The Safe Haven in Northern Iraq* (1995); P. Malanczuk, 'The Kurdish Crisis and Allied Intervention in the Aftermath of the Second Gulf War'(1991) 2 *EJIL* 114.

[86] W.M. Reisman, 'The Raid on Baghdad: Some Reflections on its Lawfulness and Implications' (1994) 5 *EJIL* 120.

[87] R.J. Zedalis, 'The Quiet, Continuing Air War Against Iraq: An Interpretative Analysis of the Controlling Security Council Resolutions' (2000) 55 *ZöR* 181; 'Breite Kritik am Angriff der USA im Irak', *Neue Züricher Zeitung*, 19 February 2001, 1.

[88] See, for example, *The Bossuyt Report*, *supra* note 27, para. 73.

[89] J. Pictet, *Commentary on the IV Geneva Convention Relative to the Protection of Civilian Persons in Time of War* (1958), p. 20.

[90] *The Prosecutor v Tadic*, Appeal Chamber Judgement, IT-94-1-AR72, at para 70.

[91] C. Greenwood, 'Scope of Application of Humanitarian Law' in D. Fleck (ed.), *The Handbook of Humanitarian Law in Armed Conflicts* (1995), p. 42.

US-UK military attacks after Operation Desert Storm have never reached such a degree of intensity as to amount to an armed conflict. If so, that the sanctions since the adoption of the cease-fire the sanctions would no longer have to conform to the standards of international humanitarian law but to the non-derogable provisions of human rights law (see 6.3.), which are also applicable during the times of an armed conflict, as well as the principle of proportionality (see 6.3.1.4. and 6.3.2.4.) and the prohibition on genocide (see 6.3.2.3).

As to possible human rights violations, in particular violations of the right to life (see 6.3.2.1.) and the rights of the child (6.3.2.2.), it has to be taken into account that the sanctions have clearly contributed to the human suffering in Iraq (see 5.). Some observers claim, that the Iraqi government bears sole responsibility for the situation and therefore for the human rights violations. This claim is based on the failure of the Iraqi government to comply with the provisions of Resolution 687, regarding the disarmament of Iraq and its partial use of the proceeds from the oil sale to purchase on dubious items instead on food and medicine. It is arguable, that, there would be no longer sanctions in place if Iraq had completely complied with all terms of the cease-fire resolution. Even so, Iraq's irresponsible behaviour would not entitle the Security Council to breach its independent obligation to promote and respect the human rights of the Iraqi people. The Council should have taken a far less drastic approach towards Iraq after it had become apparent that the Iraqi people were severely suffering under the sanctions and that the "oil-for-food" programme had not sufficiently alleviated their plight.[92] From that moment on, that Council has violated the human rights of the Iraqi people.

The next question to be answered regarding the collective sanctions on Iraq is whether they are proportional. The regime is now in place for over 11 years, and its success, as measured by Iraqi compliance with the cease-fire resolution, has been mixed.[93] However, the major problem that is the disarmament of Iraq remains unresolved. It is disputed whether Iraq's weapons of mass destruction have been eliminated. No UN inspections took place in Iraq since winter 1998 and therefore no objective data is

---

[92] R. Normand, *supra* note 64.

[93] Iraq fulfilled several obligations imposed by Resolution 687 for example in respect of the boundary demarcation, compensation payments and no further acts of aggression have been committed against Kuwait. But Iraq did not comply fully with its obligation to return missing Kuwaiti persons and property. See in more detail, K. Katzman, *Iraq: Compliance, Sanctions, and U.S. Policy*, CRS Issue Brief for Congress, updated 29 November 2001.

available whether Iraq still poses a threat to international peace and security. One may question whether this objective can be achieved at all as long as Saddam Hussein remains in power and as long as some of these weapons can be readily produced. Since too many Iraqi people have suffered and died as a result of the sanctions, and only insufficient progress has been made in disarming Iraq, the sanctions regime in its present form cannot be considered proportional.

It has been claimed that the sanctions on Iraq amount to genocide (see 6.3.2.3.).[94] None of the commentators accusing the Security Council of committing the crime of genocide can, however, prove a specific intent by the Council to destroy the people of Iraq in whole or in part. The Council's mere awareness that sanctions contribute to the human hardship cannot be equated with the intent required to qualify the sanctions as genocide. The Bossuyt Report concludes that the current sanctions regime raises questions under the genocide convention. In this context, Bossuyt quotes from an 1996 interview of the former United States Ambassador to the UN, Madeleine Albright. Asked whether the half-million deaths caused by the sanctions were worth it, she answered "I think it's a very hard choice, but the price, we think is worth it." Even if this were the official opinion of the US government[95] the intent to destroy the Iraqi people cannot be deduced from the policy of one Security Council member: the motives and intentions of all members of the Council would have to be taken into account. In addition, the calls of Russia and France to modify the current sanction regime in order to mitigate the suffering of the Iraqi people contradict an alleged intent of the Council to commit genocide.

---

[94]   See Ramsay Clark's Letter to the Security Council, http://www.transnational.org/features/sanctionsIraq.html; E. Davidsson, *The Economic Sanctions Against the People of Iraq: Consequences and Legal Findings*, http://www.aldeilis.net/jus/econsanc/sanctionsed.pdf, 34-35; D. Halliday/P. Bennis, 'Die Auswirkungen der Sanktionen und die US Politik' in R. Göbel/J. Guilliard/M. Schiffmann, *supra* note 5, 64; G. Simons, *supra* note 5, 242.

[95]   See also the US Reactions to the Bossuyt Report by Ambassador George Moose, US Representative to the UN and Other International Organizations in Geneva of 17 August 2000, http://www.us-mission.ch/press2000/0817moose.htm.

The Role of Small States in International Diplomacy: CARICOM's Experience in the Negotiations on the Rome Statute of the International Criminal Court

*Delia Chatoor**

1. Introduction

The Caribbean Community and Common Market (CARICOM) is geographically located in an arc enclosing the Caribbean Sea. It consists of thirteen (13) independent States[1] with a 2000/2001 population of approximately 5. 2 million inhabitants. All, except Suriname, are former colonies of the United Kingdom (UK) and achieved their Independence during the period from the 1960s to the 1980s. In addition to maintaining most of the political and education structures of the colonial power, the newly Independent States retained the Common Law system.

One of the first diplomatic acts of all the independent states was to seek membership in the United Nations (UN) and its Specialized Agencies. Some also sought solidarity in the Non-Aligned Movement and the Group of 77. The regional organization, the Organization of American States (OAS), also attracted the states and in 1967, Trinidad and Tobago applied and was accepted as the first CARICOM Member State of the OAS.

There was, however, a major obstacle to membership for all CARICOM States. According to the then Article 8 of the OAS Charter, Belize and Guyana were debarred from membership because both countries had unresolved border disputes with Guatemala and Venezuela respectively. Persistent campaigns by CARICOM, however, led to successful applications for Belize and Guyana and they ratified the OAS Charter on 8 January 1991.

As small states with even smaller military resources, CARICOM has traditionally supported the rule against intervention by other States. This concept was endorsed by them and reflected the provisions of the 1966

---

* ICRC Head of Office for the Caribbean Community States based in Port of Spain, Trinidad and Tobago. Attorney at Law, Foreign Service Officer with the Government of Trinidad and Tobago prior to appointment with the ICRC, that is, since 1983. Served at the UN from September 1988 to February 1996.

[1] The thirteen member states of CARICOM are: Antigua and Barbuda, Bahamas, Barbados, Belize, Dominica, Grenada, Guyana, Jamaica, St. Kitts and Nevis, St. Lucia, St. Vincent and the Grenadines, Suriname and Trinidad and Tobago.

M. Bothe and B. Kondoch (eds.),
International Peacekeeping. The Yearbook of International Peace Operations, Volume 7, 2001, 295–310.
© 2002 *Kluwer Law International. Printed in the Netherlands.*

United Nations General Assembly Resolution 2131 (xx) wherein it was declared:

> "No State has the right to intervene, directly or indirectly, for any reason whatever, in the internal or external affairs of any other State. Consequently, armed intervention and all other forms of interference or attempted threats against the personality of the State or against its political, economic or cultural elements are condemned".

This philosophy was complimented by the acceptance of the peaceful settlement of disputes, the rule of law and the right of self-determination and independence of peoples and nations.

It was partly because of the concerns of the proliferation of weapons of mass destruction and the fact that these weapons could be used by irresponsible and criminally inclined individuals that the Government of Trinidad and Tobago in 1988 sought to bring the matter before the United Nations. There was also the worrying threats to CARICOM's economies and their socio-political fabric by the illicit trafficking in narcotic drugs across national borders. These activities, it was argued, were more oppressive in small states with their peculiar vulnerabilities.

2. Reactivation of the Issue on the Establishment of an International Criminal Court

At the Third Special Session of the United Nations General Assembly on Disarmament held in 1988, President Arthur N. R. Robinson (then Prime Minister of the Republic of Trinidad and Tobago) proposed that "the United Nations should commence discussion on the criminal responsibility of individuals (including mercenaries) who act in breach of the relevant norms of international law with particular reference to the provision of treaties banning the use of certain types of weapons".

President Robinson also suggested "that there would be the need eventually to examine the existing international codes, the possibilities for using international commissions of inquiry, and of instituting in the long term an international criminal court".

At the forty-third Session of the United Nations General Assembly in 1988, the Government of Trinidad and Tobago, therefore, sought to concretise its reflections through the introduction of a new agenda item along the following terms:

"Liability for the illegal transfer and/or use of prohibited weapons and/or use of prohibited weapons and weapons or substances which cause unnecessary human suffering ...".

It was further explained that the proposal was made in the context of disarmament and international peace and security.

The item was allocated to the First Committee of the United Nations General Assembly (UNGA) but there was no discussion and Trinidad and Tobago requested its deferral to the next UNGA in 1989.

Throughout 1988 CARICOM governments also became increasingly concerned about another matter: the alleged attempts by a large developed country to extend its domestic authority to Caribbean countries without regard to the sovereignty and independent legal system of those countries. In a letter dated 8th July 1988 addressed to the then President of the United States of America, Mr. Ronald Reagan, the Honourable Vere C. Bird, Prime Minister of Antigua and Barbuda and Chairman of the Conference of Heads of Government of the Caribbean Community expressed regret at "any effort on the part of anyone to subvert the principles of natural justice" which he declared were at "the foundation of the democratic way of life of CARICOM Countries".

CARICOM Governments were troubled by allegations levelled against a standing Prime Minister on illegal activities involved in drug trafficking and other corrupt practices. It was thought that an independent mechanism would be more effective in investigating such allegations.

Led by the Government of Trinidad and Tobago, the decision was taken to reformulate the 1988 Agenda Item and introduce it at the forty-fourth UNGA Session in 1989. It was explained that certain forms of criminality had assumed a transnational character which severely limited the effectiveness of countries to combat these crimes when acting within the confines of their domestic jurisdictions. The crimes included acts of genocide, torture, crimes against diplomats and the illicit traffic in drugs across national frontiers.

It was argued that such crimes posed grave threats to the integrity of states and they had the potential to undermine their stability, security and development. International criminal jurisdiction could, therefore, make a significant contribution to the maintenance of international peace and security and ensure appropriate examination of alleged criminality.

Trinidad and Tobago was mindful of the various stillborn attempts advanced for the establishment of an international criminal court (ICC). Legal experts, advising the Government of Trinidad and Tobago, recommended that any new proposal at the United Nations would need to reflect an issue of international importance. It was, therefore, decided that the illicit traffic in narcotic drugs on an international scale could be the issue to catch the attention of States. There was, therefore, a careful analysis of the 1988 United Nations Convention against Illicit Traffic in Narcotic Drugs and Psychotropic Substances which was adopted on 19th December 1988. A number of preamble paragraphs to that Convention provided the rationale for requesting the General Committee of the UNGA to allocate Trinidad and Tobago's proposal to the Sixth Committee and for serious consideration to be given to an international criminal court (ICC) to deal with drug trafficking.

In this regard, therefore, special attention was paid to Preamble Paragraphs 3, 4, 5 and 14. Preamble Paragraph 14 which read:

> "*Recognizing also* the importance of strengthening and enhancing effective legal means for international co-operation in criminal matters for suppressing the international criminal activities of illicit traffic", was thought to provide some measure of support for an international judicial institution to deal with a spiralling international problem.

CARICOM States, which supported the efforts of Trinidad and Tobago, pointed out that there were links between illicit traffic and other forms of criminal activities which posed serious threats to the States stability, security and sovereignty. The States conceded that they lacked the resources to counteract such threats.

CARICOM support for a permanent court, which would assist in the investigation and prosecution of international crimes, such as, drug trafficking, was based on the following considerations:

(a) solidarity among the Member States for a regional problem.
(b) concerns and fears that the illicit traffic in narcotic drugs and associated activities were undermining the countries' socio-economic, political and national security interests.
(c) apprehension that larger and more powerful states may engage in extra-territoriality policies in their attempts to address the spread of the illegal activities of drug traffickers.
(d) inadequate and poorly equipped security forces.
(e) judicial systems may also be inadequate to put on trial powerful drug lords and trace the proceeds of illegal activities.

With these thoughts in mind, Trinidad and Tobago recommended that the new agenda item be allocated to the Sixth (Legal) Committee of the General Assembly. The reactions of United Nations Member States were, however, wide and ranged from total opposition (most Western European States, Canada, Latin American States and certain Asian States) to mild curiosity (African States). The objections were also varied and included the following arguments:

(a) an international court was inappropriate to address the problem.
(b) the newly adopted 1988 United Nations Convention against Illicit Traffic in Narcotic Drugs and Psychotropic Substances contained adequate mechanisms and the issue was more appropriately dealt with through existing and proposed bilateral and regional arrangements.
(c) the international community did not need another organization as there would be the financing issues to consider.
(d) the International Law Commission (ILC) had been examining the question of international criminal jurisdiction within the context of the draft Code of Crimes against the Peace and Security of Mankind and it was preferable to await the outcome of the discussions on the definitions of the crimes before addressing the issue of a penal/criminal tribunal.
(e) any punitive international body would more than likely be used against developing countries.

Trinidad and Tobago took note of the ILC's work and the United Nations General Assembly (UNGA) resolution of 1947[2] which had requested the Commission to:

(a) formulate the principles of international law recognized in the Charter of the Nuremberg Tribunal and in the Judgement of the Tribunal.
(b) prepare a draft code of offences against the peace and security of mankind, indicating clearly the place to be accorded to the principles mentioned in (a) above.

The draft Code of Crimes against the peace and security of mankind became a fixed item on the agenda of the Sixth Committee but it did not enjoy continuous years of discussion. In 1954, the General Assembly[3], not-

---

[2]   Resolution 177(II) of 21 November 1947.
[3]   Resolution 897 (IX) of 4 December 1954.

ing that the draft Code as formulated by the ILC raised issues related to the definition of aggression, and that the General Assembly had mandated a Special Committee to prepare a report on a draft definition of aggression, decided to postpone consideration of the draft Code until that Special Committee had submitted its report.

A definition of aggression was finally adopted by the UNGA in 1974[4] but it was not until 1981 that the ILC was invited to resume its work on the elaboration of a draft Code. There was however little or no discussion on an ICC.

Following the debate on Trinidad and Tobago's agenda item in 1989, the Sixth Committee, therefore, decided to recommend to the UNGA[5] that the ILC should "... when considering ... the item entitled" Draft Code of Crimes against the Peace and Security of Mankind", ... address the question of establishing an international criminal court or other international criminal trial mechanism with jurisdiction over persons alleged to have committed crimes which may be covered under such a code of crimes, including persons engaged in illicit trafficking in narcotic drugs across national frontiers..."

The Secretary-General was requested to transmit to the ILC any views expressed pursuant to paragraph 3 of resolution 44/32 of 4 December 1989, as well as the summary records of the agenda item. It was further decided that consideration of the question of establishing an international criminal court or other international criminal trial mechanism should be done when examining the report of the ILC.

The result of this decision led to the removal of Trinidad and Tobago's item as a separate agenda item in the Sixth Committee. The compromise was negotiated during informal consultations and had to be accepted by the main sponsor and all the co-sponsors. It is instructive to recall that the co-sponsors included all the CARICOM States, the Republic of Comoros, Costa Rica, Libya and Vanuatu.

Trinidad and Tobago was, however, fearful that the ILC would not devote much attention to the matter and like the draft Code, it could become buried in intellectual rhetoric. To stress the importance of a permanent court, the Government of Trinidad and Tobago launched a diplomatic blitz which involved bilateral discussions with members of the ILC and UN representatives and participation in various UN and regional conferences

---

4   Resolution 3314 (XXIX) of 14 December 1974.

5   Resolution 44/39 of 4 December 1989.

and meetings[6]. The issue was also placed on the agendas of the Conferences of Heads of State and Government of CARICOM and became a fixed item of Trinidad and Tobago's foreign policy.

The ILC did devote considerable time to the question of an international criminal jurisdiction. At its forty-fourth and forty-fifth sessions in 1992 and 1993, the Special Rapporteur, who had been appointed by the Commission to work on the draft Code, spent much of his time on the possible establishment of an ICC. This procedure eventually led, in 1994, to the adoption of a draft statute of an ICC. The Commission recommended that the General Assembly should convene an international conference of plenipotentiaries to study the 1994 text and to conclude a convention on the establishment of an ICC[7].

During the period 1990 to 1995, many regional and international situations developed which led to a reversal of the negative approaches to the establishment of an ICC and to a greater understanding of the need to address impunity.

3. The Role of CARICOM in the Period 1990 to 1998

The 1990s witnessed the collapse of the Berlin Wall, the end of the period of bipolarity, the unravelling of the former Yugoslavia, the butchery in Rwanda and the spread of non-international, ethnically-charged conflicts. For the Caribbean, there was an apparent loss of interest by some developed countries in the Region as a whole and this led one prime minister to state: "... as a result of the end of the Cold War, the Caribbean has declined in geo-political significance in the eyes of those countries to whom ideological rivalries mattered, and who saw the region as a potential location of international tension arising from the clash of conflicting ideologies"[8].

---

[6]   Eighth United Nations Congress on Crime Prevention and the Treatment of Offenders, Cuba. A draft statute of an international criminal court was prepared by an NGO committee of experts, chaired by Professor M. Cherif Bassiouni, in 1990 and submitted to the Congress. At that meeting, the Trinidad and Tobago delegation lobbied for a court and the Congress lent its support to the work of the ILC.

[7]   Officials Records of the General Assembly, forty-ninth Session, Supplement No.10 (A/49/10), chap. IIA

[8]   SOURCE: UWI-IIR – Distinguished Lecturer Series: "The New Realities of Caribbean International Economic Relations" – The Right Honourable Owen Arthur, Prime Minister of Barbados, 15th April 1996.

The Prime Minister further added that "the Caribbean region, with its long tradition of commitment to the practice of democracy, is wonderfully well positioned to accommodate many of the new political nuances that are now infusing its contemporary international economic relations arising from the end of the Cold War". One may, however, go further and add "...its contemporary international political relations".

The English-speaking Caribbean had no ethnic difficulties, all the States had democratically-elected Governments, elections were held every four to five years and there were no abhorrent abuses of human rights. At the United Nations and in other international fora, the CARICOM States gave unequivocal support to two important limbs of international relations as reflected in the Charter of the United Nations, namely:

- non-interference in the internal affairs of other States
- non-use of force in the conduct of international relations and in the settlement of disputes.

The Region as a whole, therefore, continued to support the United Nations' efforts on the establishment of an ICC even though the focus now devolved on war crimes, crimes against humanity and genocide. The so-called treaty-based crimes, such as illicit traffic in narcotic drugs and terrorism, were marginalized. There was also the understanding that the two ad hoc tribunals for the former Yugoslavia and Rwanda were of a very restricted competence and there had to be a more permanent system which would deal with those responsible for serious international crimes. Enforcement measures, for example, by the Security Council, were applicable to States so that the imposition of economic sanctions or even military action could not ensure that the individuals who incited the commission of serious international crimes were punished. CARICOM's concerns were, therefore, not highlighted even though Government representatives in their statements at the United Nations advocated for a broad-based approach to the ICC's jurisdiction. There were also repeated calls for transparency in the negotiating process and fair discussion on the proposals and concerns of developing countries.

While the negotiations on the ICC began to be more focussed on a very restricted list of crimes, namely, aggression, crimes against humanity, genocide and war crimes, support for the so-called "treaty-based crimes" of the illicit traffic in narcotic drugs and terrorism, was not forthcoming. In this regard, however, the Region has always supported the inclusion of all the so-called "core crimes" and shared the concerns of many on the role of the Security Council vis-à-vis the Court.

The threat of drug trafficking continued to be a daily reality to the Region and the vulnerability of the small sates was described in the following terms": the smallest states were stepping stones of a supply route that provides several options for methods of transportation, concealment and easy escape when detection appears imminent"[9]. Protective services were too small and inadequately equipped to address the growing situation.

At the Rome Conference on the ICC in 1998, CARICOM States made every attempt to bring international drug trafficking within the Court's jurisdiction. Discussions were held with various groups in the hope that there would be support. States requested a draft definition on the crime and a text was prepared and circulated to a number of delegations in the African, Asian and Latin American Groups.

CARICOM's proposal, contained in Conference document A/CONF. 183/C.1/L.48 dated 3 July 1998, reflected the main elements the Governments wished to have included. The chapeau, therefore, stated that the crimes involving the illicit traffic in narcotic drugs and psychotropic substances were "those crimes set out in article 3, paragraphs 1 and 2, of the 1988 United Nations Convention against the Illicit Traffic in Narcotic Drugs and Psychotropic Substances". The threshold for application and for triggering the jurisdiction of the Court would be when the offences were committed:

(a) On a large scale (and) (or) in a transboundary context; within the framework of an organized and hierarchical structure;
(b) with the use of violence and intimidation against private persons, juridical persons or other institutions, or members of the legislative, executive or judicial arms of government, (thereby) creating fear or insecurity within a State or disrupting its economic, social, political or security structures or with other consequences of a similar nature; or
(c) In a context in which corrupt influence is exerted over the public, the media and public institutions."

CARICOM no longer viewed large scale drug trafficking as a regional issue. It was seen as an international menace which posed a serious threat to the international peace and security of all states.

---

[9] Extract from "Current Capability and Future Requirements for Drug Interdiction in the New Century" – Commander Kayam Mohammed, Commander Officer, Trinidad and Tobago Coast Guard, CINSEC 97, March 18, 1997, Trinidad and Tobago.

In seeking to highlight this crime, CARICOM delegations at the Rome Conference reminded others that it was Trinidad and Tobago which braved and weathered the serious opposition against the establishment of an ICC during the early period of the debate. CARICOM delegates stressed during informal consultations with different interest groups that the illicit traffic in narcotic drugs had international dimensions; there were harmful consequences to the world's population; and national legislation on the subject varied thus making it difficult to establish a unified regime.

It is interesting to note that during a 1997 Caribbean Island Nations Security Conference (CANSEC), held in Trinidad and Tobago, a representative of the United States reported that "in 1996, trafficking organizations in the Eastern Caribbean were estimated to be responsible for over 100 metric tonnes of cocaine en route to the United States ... Together both the West Caribbean and the Eastern Pacific account for 75 per cent of the cocaine flow en route to the United States".[10]

The attraction of the Region was recognized and its vulnerability stressed. At the Rome Conference, however, the States in support of the inclusion of illicit drug trafficking and terrorism could not persuade the majority to include the crimes within the Court's jurisdiction. The compromises which eventually emerged contained the inclusion of a review mechanism (Article 123) of the Statute and Resolution E wherein it was recognized "that the international trafficking of narcotic drugs is a very serious crime, sometimes destabilizing the political and social and economic order in states". It was, therefore, recommended that "a Review Conference ... consider the crimes of terrorism and drug crimes with a view to arriving at an acceptable definition and their inclusion in the list of crimes within the jurisdiction of the Court".

Even though Trinidad and Tobago was one of the original members of the so-called "Like-Minded Group of States", there was very little support for all the major concerns of CARICOM. This negative response was further amplified when CARICOM States, at the Rome Conference, sought to include capital punishment as a punishment available to the ICC. This latter issue at one point threatened to unravel the negotiations but the Head of the Trinidad and Tobago delegation, Attorney General Ramesh Maharaj, articulating the position of CARICOM, stated that there was no inter-

---

[10] Quote from the address by Mr. Shane Hoffman, J2 Counter-Drug Division, USACOM – Deputy Counter-Drug Department, to the CINSEC 97. Author's Note: Some of geo-political threats to the Caribbean Region identified included: drug trafficking; militarization of drug policies; coups d'état; the threat of external intervention and money laundering.

national consensus on the abolition of capital punishment; that capital punishment was not a human right issue and that capital punishment was the penalty for murder domestically and given the nature of the offences within the Court's jurisdiction, the most serious penalty should be imposed. It was further argued that it would be difficult explaining the approach of the Government which, on the one hand advocated the death penalty domestically, but on the other supported a term of life imprisonment for crimes such as genocide.

A compromise had to be found and this was brokered by the Coordinator of the Working Group on Penalties, Rolf Fife of Norway with the support of the delegations of Trinidad and Tobago, Singapore, Saudi Arabia and Sudan. Article 80 reflects the hard fought compromise text which preserves the national application of penalties. This follows the principle of Complementarity.

Delegations, however, wanted the Diplomatic Conference itself to recognize that the provisions on penalties with the exclusion of capital punishment should not be viewed as a universal ban on that form of punishment. The President of the Conference, therefore, read in the final plenary session a statement which became part of the official records of the Conference.

Even with the inclusion of one safeguard for domestic procedures in the Statute and another in the Presidential statement, Trinidad and Tobago proceeded to abstain on the vote which adopted the Rome Statute. This reaction was, however, not a rejection of the Statute *in toto*. It was rather an attempt to express the Government's dissatisfaction with the exclusion of its key concerns. The final Act was, therefore, signed by the four CARICOM States present on the 19th July, 1998. These States were Barbados, Dominica, Jamaica and Trinidad and Tobago.

4. Post-Rome Developments and the Caribbean Community

Many States and certain non-governmental organizations were surprised at Trinidad and Tobago's abstention on the Rome Statute. The CARICOM Region nevertheless continued to demonstrate its unwavering support for the development of an international criminal justice system with an independent, impartial court at its helm. In order, therefore, to share its Rome experiences with those CARICOM States that could not participate, the Government of Trinidad and Tobago in March 1999 co-hosted with No Peace Without Justice (NPWJ) and other non-governmental organizations, an Inter-Governmental Regional Caribbean Conference on the ICC. The programme was intended for Attorneys General, Parliamentarians, experts in the field of international criminal law and other policy makers.

At the conclusion of the Conference, government representatives signed the Port of Spain Declaration on the International Criminal Court in which they, *inter alia*, declared "their commitment to pursue the process of ratification of the Rome Statute by their respective States within the shortest possible time" and "to encourage all States, members of the International Community to sign and ratify the Rome Statute".

In his perspective of the role which could be played by small states, Mr. Bill Pace, Convenor of the International NGO Coalition for the International Criminal Court stated at the Conference:

> "Many small island states have long understood that cooperation between governments and NGOs on issues which larger powers were hesitant to address was the beginning of a so-called New Diplomacy... Although largely ignored by the news media, this partnership has proven that positive results can be produced through mechanisms of international democracy, including results to which larger powers on occasion have to adapt. The ICC Statute is our most recent example of law-making through international democracy".

In order, therefore, to seek to preserve its infant democracy, Trinidad and Tobago sought to highlight the debilitating effects the illicit traffic in narcotic drugs was having on its fragile institutions and people. Such vulnerability has also made it possible for Trinidad and Tobago to support the work of the Preparatory Commission on the ICC even in the absence of this offence and to recommend that a workable compromise be found for the definition of the crime of aggression. This confidence in the potential of the ICC led Trinidad and Tobago to ratify the Rome Statute on 6th April 1999.

Other CARICOM States have signed and are examining their laws with a view to ratification and accession. Every regional and international event is used to reinforce the Region's support for a permanent court and for the inclusion of the illicit traffic and terrorism. In the General Debate of the fifty-fifth Session of the United Nations General Assembly, His Excellency Dr. Patrick Lewis, Permanent Representative of Antigua and Barbuda to the United Nations stated that his country would "like to remind [this body] that we remain disappointed that the International Criminal Court will not be dealing with illegal trafficking in narcotics, illegal trade in arms and terrorism". A similar sentiment was expressed by the Prime Minister of Trinidad and Tobago at the September 2000 Millennium Summit.

The Foreign Minister of Jamaica, His Excellency Paul Robertson at that same United Nations General Assembly Session remarked that Jamaica was looking "forward to the contribution that the Court will ultimately make to the strengthening of international jurisprudence, by addressing the serious crimes of global concern committed by individuals who hitherto escaped the reach of the law".

Most CARICOM Member States have, therefore, been participating in regional workshops under the auspices of international organizations (International Committee of the Red Cross), the Commonwealth, No Peace Without Justice, the NGO coalition and other institutions.

Limited resources have, however, hampered attendance at the sessions of the Preparatory Commission. Trinidad and Tobago continues to fly the CARICOM flag at the meeting and briefs delegations on a regular basis.

In addition to the limited ambit of the Court's jurisdiction, CARICOM States are concerned on what would be the financial cost to their treasuries. From the commencement of debate on the ICC, CARICOM States had advocated for a court which would be part of the United Nations system so that it would be able to benefit from its expertise in administrative and budgetary procedures and utilize the funds in the United Nations Regular Budget.

In its brief for the 1998 Rome Conference, Trinidad and Tobago sought to maintain its preference for a court which would be financed through the United Nations. This procedure was viewed as being stable and reliable; it would benefit from the United Nations oversight mechanisms and could attract a greater number of States. The system in the Rome Statute in Part 12 was reluctantly agreed to by the Region. It is, therefore, not unexpected for delegates, during workshops and meetings, to seek information on what could be their contribution to the Court.

In May 1998 prior to the Rome Conference, the President of Trinidad and Tobago, Arthur N.R. Robinson, stated:

> "As relatively small and relatively peaceful nations we must never allow ourselves to believe that the establishment of an ICC is irrelevant to our circumstances. On the contrary, we must work strenuously to ensure that such an impartial international body is formed

precisely in order to safeguard the interest and equality of nations and peoples such as our own".[11]

These sentiments continue to guide the Region in its consideration of the Rome Statute and its role in the administration of justice. Globalisation has brought with it many blessings but also many difficulties. Small States tend to be more susceptible to changes. Trinidad and Tobago could, therefore, identify with the following statement made by His Holiness Pope Pius XII when he said "... since in our times people easily change their place of residence and frequently pass from one state to another, it is desirable that at least the most serious crimes should have a sanction everywhere and, if possible, of an equal severity, so that the culprits may nowhere be able to escape or be shielded from the punishment of their crimes".[12]

5. Summary and Conclusion

The English-speaking Caribbean States generally work towards the maintenance of a unified foreign policy. They believe in the United Nations and rely on assistance from its many specialized agencies, bodies and funds. The rule of law and respect for democratic traditions and human rights are part of their outlook on foreign policy. These States are nevertheless acutely aware of their vulnerability and so they believe in strong, impartial and independent structures and systems to which they can turn to for assistance.

It was, therefore, not difficult for Trinidad and Tobago to gain the support of these States when it reintroduced the question of an international criminal jurisdiction. The concerns were the same, the challenges identical. Their historical antecedent also facilitated the common approach at the United Nations and in the Commonwealth.

The Region is alert to the fact that sixty ratifications are required for the Statute's entry into force. It has, therefore, been argued that the quicker this happens, greater would be the momentum. Out of the thirteen States,

---

[11] Quote from Message of His Excellency Arthur N R Robinson, President of the Republic of Trinidad and Tobago at the Opening Ceremony of a regional workshop on "Mechanisms for the Development of International Criminal Justice", 14 to 15 May 1998, Port of Spain.

[12] Quote from an address by His Holiness Pope Pius XII to the Sixth International Congress of Penal Law, 3rd October 1953.

three have ratified and one has acceded[13]. A number have also signed and they are considering ratification by 2002[14]. There is, however, the anxiety over implementing legislation and the ability of the States to cooperate with the Court as stipulated in Article 86.

Revision of domestic criminal justice systems would be very necessary in some countries and, in the absence of trained legislative draftsmen and with competing Governmental interests, some states could be forced to delay becoming states parties[15].

The Caribbean has enjoyed many years of peace and this could be an attraction to those seeking a haven from their violations of human rights and IHL. The states are aware of the untold misery brought on by internal armed conflicts. They see the Court, therefore, as one which would serve as a powerful deterrent against future crimes and violations of international law.

The ICC cannot stop these abuses. It will not have its own police or detention facilities. Great reliance will have to be placed on the States parties. The reality however is that an effective, impartial and independent court which is respected by all, could contribute to the maintenance of peace and security, could achieve justice for the victims of serious violations and could provide an alternative to use of domestic systems. As small developing countries, a viable alternative would not be unreasonable.

The Region, therefore, maintains its support for the Court and will no doubt continue to do so. However its main concerns – the illicit traffic in narcotic drugs, large scale money laundering, corruption of governmental and security officials, competing interests, capital punishment, illegal traffic in small arms, weak economies and threats of domestic instability – could determine whether all thirteen CARICOM States become party to the Rome Statute of the International Criminal Court.

All the States agree that justice demands that the offenders must be held accountable for the crimes they have committed. The International Criminal Court so long in coming should assist in this process and so contribute to international peace and also put an end to impunity.

---

[13] Belize and Trinidad and Tobago have ratified. Dominica has acceded.

[14] Antigua and Barbuda, Bahamas, Barbados, Jamaica and St. Lucia have signed.

[15] Trinidad and Tobago is working on implementing legislation which could become the model for the Region.

Delia Chatoor

Addendum

The seriousness of the illicit traffic in narcotic drugs in the Caribbean region continues to be articulated and highlighted by regional and international organizations. In its most recent report entitled *"Drugs in the Caribbean Region 1999-2000 Trends"*, the Barbados-based Caribbean Drug-Control Coordination Mechanism (CCM) stated:

> Cocaine trade represents 85 per cent of all income generated by the drugtrade in the Caribbean. Meanwhile, marijuana, the drug of choice in the region – and the only illegal narcotic substance produced within the Caribbean – remained stable during the last year, accounting for the remaining 15 per cent of Caribbean drug-related income".

The report also noted that there was a slight increase in the trafficking and consumption of heroin. Furthermore in 1999 more cocaine entered the US through the Caribbean corridor than through Mexico.

The CCM explained that there were external stimuli which exacerbated the drug problem. But a number of indigenous vulnerabilities contributed to the matter and encouraged international criminality, namely "weak economic and government structures, geographic location, poor living conditions (high levels of poverty), increased dependence on tourism and financial services which are vulnerable to money laundering".

It has, therefore, been argued that multilateral agreements, mutual legal assistance agreements, extradition treaties and increased marine patrols have not stemmed the flood. Domestic judicial and investigatory systems are inadequate to do the job of bringing the drug lords to justice. Only an impartial and effective international court could serve as a deterrent.

This rationale goes back to the case presented by Trinidad and Tobago, on behalf of CARICOM, in 1989 when it was decided that an international criminal court could facilitate the bringing to justice those who engage in the large-scale, transboundary illicit traffic in narcotic drugs and who indulge in money laundering and other criminal activities which undermine legitimate legal, political and socio-economic systems. The illegal trade in arms, notably small arms, has added another important dimension to the problem.

Therefore it does not seem likely the CARICOM Member States will reduce their concern and insistence on the inclusion of the illicit traffic in narcotic drugs unless there is a radical reverse of the situation.

Functioning Conditions of International Jurisdiction

*Erwin Müller/Patricia Schneider**

1. Introduction

If parties to a conflict make use of and accept decisions of international courts, these courts can contribute, as instruments of non-violent, peaceful conflict resolution, to a "civilisation of conflict resolution". The critical question therefore is under which conditions and circumstances these institutions can, according to the maxim "peace through law", develop positive effects. Since no effective global authority equipped with superior means of coercion that could guarantee compulsory jurisdiction exists, the creation of the conditions required for the establishment of a successful international jurisdiction is dependent on the willingness of disputing states to voluntarily recognize jurisdiction and sacrifice a substantial part of their sovereignty. The answer to our question lies in other words with the attitude towards international jurisdiction of sovereign states, acting in a macrocosm of like independent entities, eager to maintain their interests and to avoid foreign powers or third parties (like courts) disposing over them. Hence the question is not so much a legal one as a (power) political one, which must be answered by the application of social science theories and methods. A systematic empirical "inventory" of the system of international jurisdiction is required that explains in particular the system's deficits and thereby shows the starting point for its reorganization.

Without a doubt the International Court of Justice (ICJ), the United Nations' principal judicial organ, represents the most important jurisdictional institution for the peaceful settlement of international disputes globally. An empirical analysis of its performance is particularly suited to demon-

---

* Dr. E. Müller, senior researcher, and Dipl.-Pol. P. Schneider, researcher, work at the Institute for Peace Research and Security Policy at the University of Hamburg (www.ifsh.de). They co-edit the journal "Vierteljahresschrift für Sicherheit und Frieden (S+F)". This article is a result of studies conducted as part of the research project "Peace through Law" funded by the German Ministry for Education and Research. Patricia_Schneider@public.uni-hamburg.de.

M. Bothe and B. Kondoch (eds.),
International Peacekeeping. The Yearbook of International Peace Operations, Volume 7, 2001, 311–323.
© 2002 *Kluwer Law International. Printed in the Netherlands.*

strating the conditions under which international jurisdiction can function successfully.[1]

The following article begins with a discussion of the objective problems with an empirical analysis. These problems are primarily caused by the limited number of cases before the ICJ, and they stand in the way of highly desirable statistical conclusions being drawn. With these problems in mind, the article turns to the central issue of the conditions under which the ICJ is able to function successfully, which fundamentally depend on the parties to a conflict and the matter of the dispute. The most important variable is consistently the willingness of state parties to refer disputes to the Court, to take part in its proceedings and to comply with its judgments, a variable we call a "court-friendly attitude". Finally, a conclusion from the empirical findings depicted is drawn.

2. Methodological problems of a statistical analysis

An empirical review and analysis of the disputes referred to the International Court of Justice (approximately 100 at the moment) cannot be equated with a statistical review and analysis. Among other reasons the total number of cases is fairly small, making coincidence a factor of inappropriate weight. (Disputes referred by only one state, namely Yugoslavia's ten claims against NATO member states in 1999, which make up about a tenth of all cases before the Court, can influence the overall impression significantly.) Even if the total number of cases were large enough, it would make little sense to proceed solely on that basis. Follow-

---

[1] Materials from the ICJ cases and other relevant documents (the Statute etc.) as well as a register of ICJ-publications can be found at http://www.icj-cij.org/. See also: ICJ, *The International Court of Justice* (The Hague, 1996); International Court of Justice, *Reports of Judgments, Advisory Opinions and Orders* (The Hague, 1997) (and previous volumes); United Nations Department of Public Information (ed.), *Yearbook of the United Nations* (1998 and previous volumes); International Court of Justice, *Yearbook* (1997-98 and previous volumes). See also: R. Bernhardt (ed.), *Encyclopedia of Public International Law (EPIL)* (Amsterdam, 1992), for further references. About the conflicts see F.R. Pfetsch, *Konflikte seit 1945. Daten – Fakten – Hintergründe* (5 vols., Freiburg, 1991); F.R. Pfetsch, *Globales Konfliktpanorama 1990-1995* (Münster, 1995); K.J. Gantzel/T. Schwinghammer, *Die Kriege nach dem Zweiten Weltkrieg, 1945-1992: Daten und Tendenzen* (Münster, 1995); Arbeitsgemeinschaft Kriegsursachenforschung (AKUF), Das Kriegsgeschehen 2000: Daten und Tendenzen der Kriege und bewaffneten Konflikte (Opladen, 2001 and previous volumes).

ing set theory, subsets must be built that are by definition smaller than the total – often much smaller. To give an example, when assessing state parties' compliance with ICJ judgments, not to distinguish between marginal and highly relevant matters would be as sensible as not to distinguish in criminal statistics between petty offences and capital crimes. Since the number of highly relevant matters before the ICJ is much smaller than the number of marginal, the subset of cases of interest is of a statistically useless size.[2]

Nonetheless, certain empirical trends can be discerned. These trends shall be presented with all due caution regarding the claim of an exactness that cannot be guaranteed and with a warning that their extrapolation would be risky.

3. Conditions under which the ICJ is able to function successfully

The ICJ's prospects of success as an instrument of peaceful conflict resolution crucially depend on the behaviour of states as parties to a dispute, because the level of obligation and compulsion characterizing the international judicial system is highly insufficient. There is no ipso facto obligation for a state to take part in proceedings when one party files an application; in other words, the Court enjoys no compulsory jurisdiction independent from the will of the states or the parties to its Statute. Moreover, the means to execute a judgment is absolutely inadequate. If the losing party does not voluntarily comply with the judgment, the only recourse for the victorious party is to the UN Security Council, which then has complete discretion to decide whether or not it is necessary to take action (i.e. to make recommendations or to decide upon measures to give effect to the judgment). The corresponding Security Council resolution can be vetoed by its permanent members. (On the sole occasion that the Security Council considered such an application, the United States vetoed Nicaragua's demands for measures against it.[3])

---

[2] According to the mathematical-statistical level of knowledge, the random factor plays an extremely significant role in samples of this size. Even extraordinarily strong correlations are not immune to showing a significant interdependence that does not exist in reality. Considerable caution is therefore required.

[3] We refer to the case *Military and Paramilitary Activities in and against Nicaragua* (1984-91), in which Nicaragua filed an application seeking termination of the U.S. intervention in its civil war and obtained a favourable ICJ-Judgment on the merits. See J. Crawford, 'Military Activities Against Nicaragua Case Nicaragua v. United

For these and other reasons the ICJ-system depends on the "court-friendly attitude" of states. This attitude is determined partly by the willingness of the parties to the Statute to use the Court at all, but more by their willingness to participate in proceedings as respondent (ad hoc in a singular case, by accepting the "optional clause" of the ICJ Statute or by signing an agreement on peaceful conflict settlement or other treaties with a corresponding arbitration clause) and their willingness to comply even with unwelcome judgments.

The outstanding importance of the acceptance of the role of the respondent as an indicator of a "court-friendly attitude" and adherence to the law can be best understood by applying game theory to the following characteristic situation. The applicant state generally articulates a claim against the respondent state or claims a judgment favourable to it. The respondent can only (the possibility of a counter-claim being excluded) try to reject the claim. The applicant in this zero-sum game therefore has nothing to lose, even if the Court's judgment is not the one that it hoped for. The respondent – whatever the judgment – never has anything to gain. In other words, in their best case-scenarios, the applicant will secure a victory, whereas the respondent can only avoid a loss. In the worst case-scenario for each, the applicant does not gain anything, but the respondent suffers a loss. It should come as no surprise that a "rational actor" facing this (0/+ vs. 0/-) combination of risks and opportunities will be unlikely to play this "game" voluntarily when it has the slightest doubt about the outcome, let alone when a defeat seems inevitable. Accordingly, it is particularly interesting to examine which states are still willing to participate in this process and under which circumstances.[4] The question itself suggests the hypothe-

---

States, *EPIL*, Vol. III., pp. 371 et seq, and H. Mosler in B. Simma (ed.), *Charta der Vereinten Nationen. Kommentar* (Munich, 1991), p. 956.

[4] If actors are assumed to be guided by (egocentric) rationality, it is necessary to find an explanation for the "enigmatic" common situations where actors accept the disadvantageous role of the respondent. Game theory offers an explanation by drawing our attention to the phenomenon of "iterated" games, i.e. sequences of games containing repeated characteristic situations that provide the chance for actors to change roles. In the next phase of the game, the respondent may become the applicant and may expect that the original applicant will follow its example and accept the disadvantageous role of the respondent (expectation of reciprocity). Beyond game theory, other factors may encourage a state to accept international jurisdiction even in the aforementioned role. Such factors include the existence of imminent negative sanctions or the promise of positive sanctions (a "package deal") made by the other party to the conflict, a hegemonial power or an international organization that both parties are members of. This list of possible factors is not meant to be exhaustive.

sis that democracies and states under the rule of law are rather inclined to agree to this kind of peaceful conflict settlement due to the character of their social and political systems. They are generally regarded as those actors that show a strong "respect for the law".[5] In addition, one could hypothesize that a state's foreign relations are of particular importance, that is to say the degree to which it is the "enemy" or "friend" of the other party to a conflict.

As applicants, one could above all imagine smaller states. These states may tend to choose legal recourse to the ICJ, as they lack alternative means of protecting their rights.

The matter of the dispute can be identified as another important determinant of a "court-friendly attitude". The ICJ's rulings can work fundamentally different effects. It is one thing, for example, to be involved in a case concerning a small payment of compensation to a foreign national; it is another to put at risk a claim on a territory abundant in natural resources. That is why the degree of inclination towards international law and jurisdiction correlates significantly with the dimensions of the potential damage. This dynamic will likewise be examined in detail later.

As an interim finding, one might note that the essential parameters determining the prospects of an effective jurisdiction for the International Court of Justice have been identified, namely the jurisdictional system and its specific features, the actors and their characteristics relevant to our formulation of the question as well as the matters of dispute before the Court.

4. Friendliness of States to international jurisdiction

As a first indicator of their "court-friendly attitude" one can consider the willingness of states to accept the optional clause of the Statute of the ICJ (Art. 36 paragraph 2) recognizing the Court's jurisdiction as compulsory. The results are not very encouraging. For several decades, the ratio of parties to the Statute (almost exclusively UN member states, being such parties ipso facto) subjecting themselves to the optional clause (often with reservations) has remained approximately one third. The ICJ's functional

---

5   Political scientists have come to assume that democracies and states under the rule of law, being accustomed to settling internal conflicts by peaceful, e.g. judicial means, will be inclined to extend this habit to their foreign relations. See i. a. B. Russett/J.R. Oneal, *Triangulating Peace. Democracy, Interdependence, and International Organizations* (New York/London, 2001), pp. 53 et seq and pp. 64 and seq.

Erwin Müller/Patricia Schneider

precursor, the Permanent Court of International Justice (PCIJ) of the League of Nations era, enjoyed at times over 80 percent acceptance among potential parties. (See Table 1.)

Table 1: Percentage ratio of parties to the statutes of the Permanent Court of International Justice and the International Court of Justice accepting the optional clause concerning compulsory jurisdiction

Permanent Court of International Justice			
1925	64%	1935	85%
1930	69%	1940	64%
International Court of Justice			
1945	45%	1975	31%
1950	57%	1980	30%
1955	50%	1985	28%
1960	46%	1990	33%
1965	34%	1995	32%
1970	36%	2000	33%

Source: Own calculation on the basis of the data in ICJ, The International Court of Justice, Den Haag 1996, p. 42 and the sources in footnote 1.

At first sight, it may seem surprising that some non-democracies have also accepted the optional clause, whereas some democracies have refused to (e. g. Germany) and others have given notice of termination (e. g. USA, France). The number of democratic and non-democratic states accepting the optional clause is in fact roughly the same. Considering that democracies have been (and still are) a minority globally, however, the ratio of democracies accepting the optional clause is greater than that of non-democratic states. The conclusion may be drawn that democracies are comparatively more inclined to international jurisdiction, so far as one accepts this specific kind of obligation as an indicator.

The ICJ's practice shows a similar pattern: non-democratic states also appear before the Court as applicants and respondents. The quantitative difference between democratic and non-democratic states that have been involved in cases before the ICJ is not significant. (A more precise calculation would be problematic, since the current inclination of Yugoslavia and Congo to submit cases to the Court (14 actions) is skewing statistics considerably.) On this empirical basis, it can be stated that democracies as a whole are involved in ICJ-cases proportionally more often, both as applicants and respondents.[6] This observation does not say enough, however, about their friendliness towards international jurisdiction, as it does not say anything about their willingness to comply with a judgment. The same holds true for non-democracies. The question of compliance will be discussed below.

The question of whether major powers as well as smaller powers appear as applicants before the Court must be handled even more carefully. It is not surprising that smaller powers are involved more often, both as applicants and respondents, because their number is much higher. What is really interesting and possibly surprising is that even the biggest powers often make use of the ICJ, but only those that can be described as democratic. Neither the Soviet Union resp. Russia nor the People's Republic of China has ever been involved in cases as applicants; several claims were filed against the USSR, but it always refused to accept the Court's jurisdiction.[7] Among the smaller powers, Eastern European (after the beginning of the Cold War) and to a lesser extent East Asian states avoided the Court. Eastern European states' avoidance was a function of their social system and their dependence on the Soviet Union as a hegemonial power. "Third World" states, especially African, kept away from the Court, because they assumed – like the communist bloc – that the ICJ was an instrument of the West or the former colonial powers.[8] This attitude has by now shifted massively in the ICJ's favour. In no small part, the change is explicable by a change in the understanding of state sovereignty. State sovereignty as previously understood hindered states from applying to the ICJ or accepting its jurisdiction, because participation was associated with "subjection" to an alien jurisdiction.

As regards the most powerful democratic states, they stand atop the "ICJ-charts", measured by the frequency of their involvement into cases

---

[6] This observation also applies to the comparison between developed states and developing states, which is not surprising, since democracies are much more likely to be found in the developed world.

[7] Cf. J.A. Frowein, 'The International Court of Justice' in R.-J. Dupuy (ed.), *Manuel sur les organisations internationales/A Handbook on International Organizations* (Dordrecht/Boston/London, 1998), p. 165; H.-J. Schlochauer, 'International Court of Justice', *EPIL*, Vol. II, pp. 1093, and I. Seidl-Hohenveldern, *Völkerrecht* (Cologne et al. 1997), p. 337.

[8] For more on these and other causes, see H. Neuhold, 'Das System friedlicher Streitbeilegung der Vereinten Nationen' in F. Cede/L. Sucharipa-Behrmann (eds.), *Die Vereinten Nationen. Recht und Praxis* (Vienna/Munich, 1999), p. 62; K. Oellers-Frahm, 'International Court of Justice', *EPIL*, Vol. II, pp. 1104 et seq, and Seidl-Hohenveldern, op. cit., p. 337.

before the ICJ. (The fact that Yugoslavia managed on practically a single day to endanger the positions that they had achieved over decades shows the power of coincidence and illustrates the precarious character of such a ranking.) A plausible explanation for the fact that major powers are more often involved in ICJ-proceedings is that they are more often involved in international political conflicts than other states. (Put bluntly, you are more likely to be engaged in disputes if you are a global political player than if you are, say, Switzerland.)

In comparison thereto it is more meaningful to deal with the matters of dispute, especially their subjective meaning to those concerned ("amount in dispute") as an indicator of a "court-friendly attitude". There is a broad range of matters, from disputes of a fundamental importance to "small things". Quantitatively speaking, disputes about the delimitation of land or maritime frontiers or boundaries (continental shelf, exclusive economic zones and fishery zones) are highly represented among cases. Likewise, since the commencement of Yugoslavia's action against ten NATO States during the air-strikes of 1999, the number of cases that we would characterise as "last resort" increased (Nicaragua, Bosnia and Herzegovina, Yugoslavia, Congo). "Last resort" means that there is no other remedy for a state against an aggressor, e. g. because there is no protecting power or because no action is taken by the UN Security Council.[9]

The importance of the category "frontiers" should not require further explanation in light of the remarkable number of wars that have been waged over the course of border lines and territorial delimitations. The continental shelf possesses a remarkably high economic interest. (It is in this zone, for example, that more than 90 percent of the world's off-shore oil reserves are believed to be located.) Fishery cases do not in general lead to armed conflict, but they can provoke severe political strife, such as during the "cod war" between the United Kingdom and Iceland. (Iceland's GDP at the time was over 70 percent directly or indirectly dependent on its fishing industry.)

---

[9] See the cases listed in Table 2 (no. 12, 18, 22 and 23). Nicaragua sought aid and protection against an armed intervention by the United States in its civil war during the 1980s; Bosnia and Herzegovina was confronted with attacks directed by the Yugoslavian government during the war of secession, conducted by Bosnian Serbs; Yugoslavia in turn demanded the termination of NATO air strikes in 1999; and the Republic of Congo tried – or rather is trying - to stop African states from providing military support to opposition forces in its civil war. In all these cases, resort to the ICJ was the last and only chance to get an authoritative decision ordering the termination of the hostile acts of adversaries.

Of minor political significance are other issues and cases, e.g. regarding the protection of economic and other rights of citizens of applicant states. States' willingness to appear and to take part in the proceedings before the ICJ cannot, however, be presumed even in these minor cases. Even friendly countries and allies do not hesitate to file preliminary objections that aim at questioning especially the Court's jurisdiction. If a state of enmity exists between the parties, the prospects of participation are likely to tend to zero.

Cases that are really interesting are those with a high "amount in dispute". In contrast to the PCIJ, all of whose judgments were ultimately complied with, the ICJ has a long history of suffering setbacks, even though about 80 percent of its judgments have been obeyed. This ratio decreases to about 50 percent (on the part of the respondents) in contentious cases not submitted to the Court by agreement of the parties if the judgment on the merits favours the applicant. Raising preliminary objections against the Court's jurisdiction and an application's admissibility has become a habit. Disdain of provisional measures resp. interim measures of protection ordered by the court is a common principle. Non-compliance with judgments on the merit may sometimes have only been avoided because the judgments were not delivered for various reasons.

Table 2: "Court-hostile attitude": Indicators and Cases

	Preliminary objections**	Non-compliance with	
		Provisional measures	Judgment on the merits
1. United Kingdom / Albania ("Corfu Channel", 1947-49)	X	*	X
2. United Kingdom / Iran ("Anglo-Iranian Oil Co.", 1951-52)	X	X	*
3. Israel / Bulgaria ("Aerial Incident of 27 July 1955", 1957-59)	X	*	*
4. Cambodia/Thailand ("Temple of Preah Vihear", 1959-62)	X	*	X
5. United Kingdom / Iceland ("Fisheries Jurisdiction", 1972-74)	X	X	X
6. Germany / Iceland ("Fisheries Jurisdiction", 1972-74)	X	X	X

7. Australia / France ("Nuclear Tests", 1973-74)	X	X	*
8. New Zealand / France ("Nuclear Tests", 1973-74)	X	X	*
9. Greece / Turkey ("Aegean Sea Continental Shelf", 1976-78)	X	*	*
10. USA / Iran ("U.S. Diplomatic and Consular Staff in Tehran", 1979-81)	X	X	X
11. Burkina Faso / Mali ("Frontier Dispute", 1983-86)	X	X	-
12. Nicaragua / USA ("Military and Paramilitary Activities in and against Nicaragua", 1984-91)	X	X	X
13. Nicaragua / Honduras ("Border and Transborder Armed Actions", 1986-92)	X	*	*
14. Iran / USA ("Aerial Incident of 3 July 1988", 1989-96)	X	*	*
15. Libya / USA ("Questions of Interpretation and Application of the 1971 Montreal Convention ...", 1992-)	X	*	*
16. Libya / United Kingdom ("Questions of Interpretation and Application of the 1971 Montreal Convention ...", 1992-)	X	*	*
17. Iran / USA ("Oil Platforms", 1992-)	X	*	*
18. Bosnia and Herzegovina / Yugoslavia ("Application of the Convention on the Prevention and Punishment of the Crime of Genocide", 1993-)	X	X	*
19. Cameroon / Nigeria ("Land and Maritime Boundary between Cameroon and Nigeria", 1994-)	X	X	*
20. Paraguay / USA ("Vienna Convention on Consular Relations", 1998)	-	X	*
21. Germany / USA ("La Grand", 1999-2001)	-	X	-

22. Yugoslavia / NATO-States ("Legality of Use of Force", 1999-)	X	*	*
23. Congo/Burundi, Rwanda ("Armed Activities on the Territory of the Congo", 1999-2001), Uganda (1999-)	X	X	*

* = no provisional measures indicated or (so far) no judgment on the merits implying legal consequences passed on the respondent
** = raised in a formal or informal way
X = yes
- = no
Source: Analysis of the information contained in the sources cited in footnote 1.

Table 2 shows that the habit of raising preliminary objections is common to both non-democratic states and democracies as well as to both small and big powers. Furthermore, it is evident that democracies can be quite stubborn even with each other (e.g. Iceland and France vs. the United Kingdom and Germany or Australia and New Zealand, respectively), even if they are essentially friends or allies. This aversion to participating in judicial proceedings or complying with orders and judgments is even stronger when the respondent state is faced with a severe infringement of coercive statutes of international law in the sense of delicta juris gentium (e.g. an armed attack or genocide) that is liable in compensation.

In contrast to the legal device of preliminary objections, the disdain of provisional measures and judgments of the ICJ is a flagrant contempt of court resp. a grave breach of law. The picture drawn above does not, however, change in these categories. (See Table 2.) Even states proclaiming the rule of law do not differ from notorious "rogue states" in their conduct: self-interest comes before morality.[10] The ultimate conclusion to be drawn is that in cases concerning a really relevant matter, acceptance of international jurisdiction is avoided wherever possible. If objections fail and the proceedings continue, states will refuse to appear or participate and will ignore the Court's subsequent rulings and judgments, treating them as if they were an unreasonable demand.

---

[10] The information compiled in Table 2 demonstrates the validity of this statement very clearly. Among the states that did not comply with judgments on the merits are Iceland and the United States on one hand and Albania, Thailand and Iran on the other. The information also demonstrates that even pretty small countries will dare to disregard binding decisions of the UN's principal judicial organ.

Erwin Müller/Patricia Schneider

This gloomy picture is, however, incomplete. Several counter-examples of successful conflict settlement before the ICJ prove that parties to a conflict can develop a sense of settling their disputes on important matters peacefully. This is so even if the parties had been waging wars over the matter before or even during ICJ proceedings. In other cases, (renewed) armed conflicts have very likely been avoided by the appeal to the ICJ. This latter category includes among others the cases Honduras v. Nicaragua (1958-60), El Salvador / Honduras (1986-92), Burkina Faso / Mali (1983-86) and Chad / Libya (1990-94). All related to border or territorial disputes over areas of strategic or economic importance that were the focus of armed conflict, which was on the verge of recurring, continued briefly or seemed about to break out.[11] It is true that given the military weakness of the states involved there was no threat of a major war. Nonetheless, it cannot be denied that the ICJ has had an impact on preventing or terminating wars and thus has acted as a peacemaker loyal to the maxim "peace through law". The Court's success in helping to delimit the continental shelf between Libya on one hand and Tunisia or Malta on the other (1978-82 and 1982-85, respectively) should not be underestimated either. Moreover, it is an intriguing aspect of these cases that none of the parties involved could be described as a model democracy.

5. Conclusion

From the preceding empirical findings one can draw the following conclusion:
Both democratic states and non-democratic states make use of the International Court of Justice for authoritative dispute settlement or are involved in ICJ proceedings, albeit with different intensity.

-   With the qualifications listed above, this holds true for major and smaller powers.
-   The more important the matter of dispute the less inclined states are to settle it judicially, regardless of the characteristics of the parties: even states under the rule of law show contempt for the law, often fla-

---

[11] The territorial disputes terminated by this process had sometimes dragged on for decades, originating in the insufficient or incomplete delimitation of borders in colonial times, be it between colonies of different states or within a colony between administrative units, which later became the frontiers of independent states.

grantly. Nonetheless, the ICJ has enjoyed some success in settling significant matters of dispute.

The "brilliance and misery" of the ICJ are ultimately determined by the parties to the dispute, i.e. the states of the world, in the context of an outdated international system that lacks an effective global authority in respect of jurisdiction. Its main deficits in turn lie in the absence of compulsory jurisdiction on one hand and an insufficient means of enforcing judgments on the other.

Remedying these deficits is of the utmost importance and urgency. How to do so is not the subject of this article, which deals exclusively with empirical findings on these deficits. The most noteworthy finding here is that the democratic character of states or their democratisation does not vouch for a friendly attitude towards international jurisdiction. The maxim "peace through democracy or democratisation" cannot be used in the wider sense of "loyalty to international law through democracy".

Reconsidering
the Independent Commission on Kosovo's
Final Report

Original Papers Presented
at the Mohonk International Peace Conference
December 7-8, 2000
Mohonk Mountain House
New Paltz, NY

The scholars and practitioners included in this yearbook were invited to undertake a review of the *Final Report*[1] of the Independent International Commission on Kosovo, a Commission convened by Prime Minister Persson of Sweden to investigate and report on the legitimacy and adequacy of western actions in Kosovo. The goal was to learn from this experience and be better prepared to confront future crises. The Commission, co-chaired by Justice Richard Goldstone of South Africa and the Honourable Carl Tham of Sweden, concluded that NATO actions were "illegal but legitimate." They made additional recommendations for future reform of international law, UN decision-making and established new criteria for international action in the face of serious human rights abuses. With regards to Kosovo, they recommended "conditional independence."

Mohonk Mountain House, together with the State University of New York at New Paltz and the Carnegie Corporation of New York, agreed to host a seminar on the Final Report, to reconsider its conclusions in light of the regime change in the Federal Republic of Yugoslavia. Mohonk chose to host the event, given its special history as site of the International Arbitration Conferences held for years before the first world war, with the goal of achieving international peace. We invited guest speakers from the academic, policy, human rights and media worlds in order to ensure a diverse set of perspectives on the *Report* and its recommendations. The results exceeded our expectations, and the manuscripts included here represent

---

[1]   The Independent International Commission on Kosovo, *The Kosovo Report: Conflict, International Response and Lessons Learned* (Oxford University Press, 2000).

M. Bothe and B. Kondoch (eds.),
International Peacekeeping. The Yearbook of International Peace Operations, Volume 7, 2001, 325–402.
© 2002 *Kluwer Law International. Printed in the Netherlands.*

some of the very best thinking on the topic of humanitarian intervention today.

I am grateful for the support of many individuals in making the seminar possible: first, to Roger Bowen, former president of SUNY New Paltz, for his vision and leadership; the Carnegie Corporation of New York and Mohonk Consultations for their support; Gail Parisi-Morehouse and her staff for her help in co-coordinating the event; the Department of Political Science and my colleagues there for demonstrating patience with my preoccupation; and finally, the students in my Fall 2000 European Politics class for their energy and intellectual curiosity, especially Sally Santangelo, for her assistance in editing these papers.

I am confident that you will find the papers as stimulating as we did when we first heard them presented.

Professor Kathleen Dowley
Department of Political Science and International Relations
SUNY New Paltz
New Paltz, NY 12561

Table of Contents:

Mohonk International Peace Conference: Lessons from the Conflict in Kosovo

Introduction
President *Roger Bowen,* SUNY New Paltz

In May 1916, the Honorable James Brown Scott, who was then secretary of the Carnegie Endowment for International Peace, opened the 22nd, and, as it happened, the last Lake Mohonk Conference on International Arbitration in this very room at Mohonk Mountain House. The title of his address was "The Form of Agreement and Cooperation Necessary for the Creation of an International Court of Justice for the Decision of International Disputes." Speaking as the First World War was raging in Europe, Scott's speech was as much a lament as it was an entreaty. "Justice," he said, "is a very treacherous conception. To one man it may mean one thing, to another quite the reverse. Therefore, what we desire and what we must have for society is not merely the individual conception of justice, but what we may call the collective sense of justice."

Between 1895 and 1916, Mohonk conferences were convened annually to discuss such issues, right here, again, in this room, to ponder what is meant by a collective sense of justice. At the first annual conference, Benjamin Trueblood, who was then secretary of the American Peace Society, and later in 1899 author of a book entitled "The Federation of the World" waxed optimistically: "International arbitration springs out of that spirit of internationalism which has been growing more and more during this century. There has come to be in our century an international conscience." That, Trueblood believed, was the necessary and the sufficient condition for establishing an international court that would act upon a collective sense of justice and in this way put an end to the scourge of war.

Between the first and the last Mohonk Conferences, scores of North America's best known statesmen and judicial figures came here to Mohonk to endorse this grand, civilizing mission. Nicholas Murray Butler, Columbia University President from 1901 to 1945 and for 20 years secretary of the Carnegie Endowment, addressed the Mohonk Conference five times in as many years. Robert Lansing, who was Wilson's Secretary of State, spoke at Mohonk four times. William Taft, the former President of the United States, spoke annually in this room between 1910 and 1914. And the Canadian Minister of Labor and later Prime Minister Mackenzie King lectured here each year between 1910 and 1914. Andrew Carnegie himself was a member of the special committee on the national conference of arbitration and peace, and he advised the Mohonk Conference directly.

The Mohonk mission was spawned to put an end to war. It was, as the Smileys who created the Mohonk movement themselves were the first to admit, informed by Quaker idealism. Their idea and hope was to put an end to the scourge of war in the coming 20th Century. Optimism abounded, but it was also, we can see clearly in retrospect, unfounded.

President Emeritus of Harvard, Charles Elliot, summarized the proceedings of the 1915 Mohonk Conference in such a way as to capture, I believe, the mood of those who had worked so hard for over 20 years to find the means of peace in the early 20th Century, when he asserted that only by a process of education through suffering would human kind ever come to the conclusion that peaceful arbitration in settling disputes is preferable to war.

Well, the 20th Century, of course, was humankind's bloodiest century, and it provided necessary but lamentably insufficient education through suffering. And now with the Cold War a distant memory and international conflict more rare than ever before, the time has certainly arrived to take notice of this newest scourge threatening human life and rights on every continent, and that is intranational conflict or internal wars. As wars between nations happen less and less, and wars within nations occur more and more, I think it is important for all of us to take a close look at intranational conflict in Rwanda, Sri Lanka, certainly Chechnya in Russia, Israel and Palestine, Spain with the Basque separatists, Tibet, Assam in India, the Kurds in Turkey, the split in Angola between Unita and the government, Britain and Northern Ireland, and, of course, Kosovo itself. These are among the better known places where internal conflict or civil war or separatists' movements have fractured civil order and created a politics that brutalizes the wider population, a politics that reflects historical enmities and causes horrific loss of life.

Kosovo itself may in fact be a turning point. It was NATO's military intervention that was characterized by the Independent International Commission on Kosovo as illegal but legitimate. Illegal because it violated Yugoslavia's sovereignty: it violated sovereignty because it did not have permission from the UN Security Council to intervene. But legitimate, because NATO's purpose was thoroughly humanitarian, to preserve and to protect the lives of the Kosovar Albanians.

The Commission has argued that we need in this era of the early 21st century to close the gap between legality and legitimacy. But how do we close the gap? I think the Commission suggests that legalizing intervention for humanitarian purposes is the way to do it. But interestingly, by legalizing intervention, you must necessarily delegitimate national sovereignty, and therein lies the rub.

What would the Smiley Brothers, the originators of the Mohonk Conferences say about this recommendation coming from Mr. Goldstone's Commission? I think that they would quickly and without hesitation support the notion of placing human rights above national sovereignty, and that reflects, I think, their Quaker idealism. But I think that they would quickly say no to the notion of legalizing armed intervention. That's my guess.

Whatever response they may have had to this late 20th, early 21st Century phenomenon, I think they would nonetheless welcome the existence of this conference and the fact that we're holding it in this hallowed parlour as a positive sign. Whether Andrew Carnegie, or the Smileys, or Richard Goldstone, or Carl Tham, or the other members of the Kosovo Commission, all share in common the objective to understand the origins of conflict and its consequences and to look for ways to prevent future conflict, and certainly that is what motivated the Smileys to host the Mohonk conferences. Convening good people to study and discuss the bad things that people do is a worthy human enterprise.

The Independent International Commission on Kosovo
Justice *Richard Goldstone*, Commission Co-Chair

The Commission was the idea of the Swedish Prime Minister, Goran Persson, who became increasingly concerned after the 78 days of bombing and when the United Nations force went into Kosovo in the aftermath. The Swedish Prime Minister was concerned at the lack of objective analysis in the international community. Protagonists were arguing their side only and not seeing the other side. The supporters of NATO, and particularly in the NATO capitals, were exaggerating the causes which led NATO to go in. There were NATO supporting international lawyers who grossly, in my view, misinterpreted Security Council resolutions as giving international legal legitimacy to the intervention. The resolutions clearly did not authorize military intervention. Those resolutions, which had been unanimously agreed to by the Security Council, warned Milosevic to stop ethnic cleansing and threatened that if he didn't, other means would be considered by the Council. And some lawyers in NATO capitals, and particularly in the United States, argued that because there was reference to "other means", they indirectly sanctioned military intervention. It is dangerous to adopt that line. Such misinterpretation is calculated to cause Russia and China, certainly, and in reverse situations other of the leading members of the Security Council, to refuse even to be parties to more benign resolutions for fear of such misinterpretation. So it's a very double-edged sword.

Prime Minister Persson was concerned, also, on the other side that there were criticisms of the United Nations' intervention that were similarly not even handed. He conceived of the idea, which he discussed with his government, of setting up an independent international commission. It was really an experiment. It had not been done before. At about the same time, however, the United Nations Secretary-General, Kofi Annan, had set up, as you know, two commissions of inquiry looking into the events in Srebrenica and in Rwanda. And those were courageous efforts, I would suggest, on the part of the Secretary General. At relevant times, Kofi Annan had been the head of the Department of Peace-keeping at the United Nations and he obviously was well aware that he was likely to be criticized in the reports as indeed he was. So this was along the same continuum, if you will, of independent people looking at the performance in the one case of the United Nations itself, and in the case of this commission, into the bombing by NATO, what led up to it and its consequences.

Prime Minister Persson discussed the Commission with some of the heads of state of leading countries and received their support. Kofi Annan was approached, and he gave his warm support to the project. When Carl Tham and I saw him in July of last year, he volunteered to accept the report from the Commission in his official capacity as Secretary-General. This again was a characteristically courageous offer from him, but it was unusual. I have no doubt that none of his predecessors would remotely have considered agreeing ahead of time to accept a report from a commission which had not yet been fully constituted. We were yet to choose any of the other members of the Commission, and obviously he didn't know, nor did we, what was going to be in the report.

The Swedish government put up the initial funding, very generous funding, for the commission, but Prime Minister Persson did not want this to be seen as a Swedish Commission. That would have defeated his whole purpose. He decided that the chairman should be a non-European, non-North American, which is why he came to South Africa for somebody to head the commission. After I agreed to accept the invitation the Prime Minister inquired whether it would be acceptable to have as the co-chairman Carl Tham. I was delighted to agree.

Having done that, the Prime Minister made it clear that that was the end of his or the Swedish involvement. Carl Tham and I were free to invite anybody we wished to be members of the Commission. There was no restriction on the people to be invited or on the number, and the Commission was invited to draft its own terms of reference.

Carl Tham and I met for the first time in July of last year at Heathrow Airport. We both made a diversion to meet each other, and we immediately agreed that we wanted wide geographic distribution on the Commission, and we wanted appropriate gender balance. We the approached eleven other people from ten countries in Europe, North America, Africa and the Middle East to join the Commission.

The Commission has met five times. The first meeting was in Stockholm when we agreed on the terms of reference. We met again in New York as the guests of NYU Law School. We met in Budapest as guests of the Central European University with financial support from the Soros Foundation. We then met in Florence for the fourth meeting, again as guests of NYU Law School at their beautiful facility in Florence. The last meeting, at Carl Tham's suggestion, was in Johannesburg at the University of the Witwatersrand.

We held three very important seminars designed to inform the Commission. They were held in conjunction with three of the meetings of the Commission, the one in New York, the one in Budapest and the last in Johannesburg. Members of the Commission met with political leaders in Europe, in North America, and a wide spectrum of people from Kosovo. We also spoke to the principal participants who attended the Rambouillet and Paris meetings which failed to find a solution to the impasse and which led to the bombing. We received important background briefings which I think helped us get a broader picture and context of what happened in relation to Kosovo.

One of the early debates we had on the Commission concerned the point in time at which to begin looking at the events. One thing I've learned in my exposure to the former Yugoslavia is that its one part of the world, not the only one, but perhaps the most telling in respect of attaching importance to dates. You name a date in the former Yugoslavia as being important, and you are immediately labelled as being pro or anti something or other that happened on or about that date. Dates play a very important role. If you go to Belgrade, the starting date for any historical analysis is 1389 with the Battle of Kosovo. We decided on the Commission that we had a year to do our work, and there was no reason to go back to the 14th Century. We decided we would start in 1989 when autonomy was effectively withdrawn by Milosevic from the province of Kosovo.

We examined the evidence, and we really looked at a lot of material. In fact, one of the problems for our Commission was we had too much information, not too little information. Somebody said that one of the problems of the former Yugoslavia is that there's more history than can be consumed by the people of that area, and to an extent that's true. We had all of this material, but it became clear from looking at particularly objective analyses from various international organizations (UNHCR, the ICRC, the OSCE, the ICG, and many others) that after the withdrawal of autonomy in 1989 and the increased nationalism of the Milosevic regime, there was a huge increase in human rights abuses in Kosovo. At the same time, the LDK, the movement of Ibrahim Rugova was being built on a platform of independence for Kosovo, but wanting to achieve it by peaceful means. He became a popular leader of the ethnic Albanian population, which was the majority population of Kosovo. The Serb oppression continued, and the Albanian people of Kosovo began very efficiently and successfully to set up parallel organizations. They were being dismissed at a rapid rate from all official positions, such as police officers, teachers or even as judges. More Kosovar Albanians reached the conclusion that they had no option but to set up parallel organizations.

One of the findings of our Commission was at that point in the history of the early '90s in particular, the peaceful movement led by Rugova received virtually no support or recognition from Western powers. The neglect of that movement played a significant role in the establishment and popularizing of the KLA, of the Kosovo Liberation Army which decided that the only way to achieve independence and the only way to get attention from the international community was to resort to violence. Initially they attacked and murdered Serb police officers in Kosovo. They well knew that this would set in motion a cycle of violence.

The defining moment, of course, for the ethnic Albanians in Kosovo was the absence of Kosovo from the agenda at Dayton. That was the clearest possible signal from the major powers that Kosovo was to be ignored, and of course that was a huge success for the policy of violence of the KLA and a huge blow to the movement of Ibrahim Rugova. The KLA became more and more popular, and generally had wide popular support, which is not difficult to understand. The increase in violence, the cycle I referred to, came to the attention of the Security Council, and the two resolutions to which I referred earlier were passed making a determination that the violence in Kosovo was a threat to international peace and security. They were resolutions under Chapter 7 of the Charter and warned Milosevic of further action if the violence did not cease.

It did not cease. Milosevic ignored the Security Council in the sure knowledge that there would never be any question of a Western land invasion, and he regarded the Security Council and the threats as loud barking which wouldn't be followed by any hurtful biting. So the violence continued, and under the leadership of the United States, the NATO activation order was given, and was followed by the meeting at Rambouillet.

It must be recognized that the activation order itself was a contravention of the United Nations Charter. Article II outlaws not only the actual use of military intervention, but also the threat of it. The Rambouillet meeting was held, then, under the shadow of that activation order.

I need not dwell on the failure of Rambouillet and Paris which was followed by the 78 days of bombing. The time it took to bring Milosovic to his knees was the result of a gross miscalculation on the part of NATO. The evidence is abundantly clear, (notwithstanding subsequent denials) that the NATO leaders said and believed that it would take three or four days, or at most seven days of bombing to force Milosevic to capitulate. It was not anticipated at all that it would take anything near 78 days. With the use of hindsight, many of the NATO leaders said, well, of course, they realized it would take time; that they realized they were in for a long haul. That is not borne out by the statements that were made at the time.

We had a look at all of those things. We had a look at the eventual capitulation by Milosevic. Carl Tham and I had a very interesting hour and a half with President Martti Ahtisaari and in some ways an even more interesting meeting with Victor Chernomyrdin in Moscow. It was the two of them who went and negotiated the end of the bombing, and both of them had the same answer when Carl Tham and I asked them why Milosevic had changed his mind and did capitulate. The answer we got from both of them was that they didn't have the foggiest idea. They didn't quite know why Milosevic at that point capitulated.

The Commission sent two missions to Kosovo. We met with the important leaders, KLA leaders as well as Rugova and his people. We met with Bernard Kouchner on a number of occasions. We met with the UNHCR leaders there as well as with those from the European Union and the OSCE. We received interesting and relevant briefings from them.

So that was the sort of approach which the Commission took to its work. We considered the manner in which the war was fought, in the sense of whether or not NATO was guilty of war crimes. However, we decided that it would not be appropriate for us to be trespass on the jurisdiction of the Office of the Prosecutor of the International Criminal Tribunal which was at that time looking into this very question. When the Chief Prosecutor, Carla del Ponte, made public her internal report we decided to defer to her decision that there was insufficient evidence to justify an investigation into the culpability of any individual arising from the NATO intervention. However, we did comment negatively on the use of the cluster bombs that caused death and injury to innocent civilians and especially children.

Let me deal briefly with the major findings of the Commission. Firstly we found, as I've indicated already, that there were no real efforts at prevention. We found that there were steps the international community could have taken support the non-violent policy of the LDK. Observers could have been sent in. NGOs who were doing wonderful work there could have been supported more than they were. Generally, there could have been a greater civilian international presence which could possibly have made a difference.

We found that there were very mixed signals sent out by the international community, particularly by the Russian Federation which gave the impression of supporting Milosevic fully and certainly must have been giving him the green light or at least an amber light to go ahead with his completely unacceptable policies.

As far as the NATO campaign is concerned, as Roger Bowen has mentioned, we held that the NATO bombing was clearly a contravention of the United Nation's Charter, and therefore illegal under present international law. We used the word "legitimate." Perhaps it was an unfortunate choice of words. We've been criticized for really giving birth to an oxymoron. What we meant by legitimate was that it was morally and politically justifiable, and I think that that was clear from the statements we made, and it comes out very clearly from the report. As to the question of sovereignty, we came to the conclusion that where governments in the exercise of their sovereignty, ethnically cleanse their own citizens, abuse the fundamental human rights of their own citizens, this is a ground for intervention one way or another by the international community.

We recognized that there is thus this unfortunate gap between legality, black letter law on the one hand, and morality on the other. And that's an unhappy situation. I compare it to the position in Apartheid South Africa where oppressive and racist laws lacked all moral justification and all moral content. There was a gap between the law and morality. And, of course, the victim is justice. In South Africa, millions of black South Africans were put in prison for breaking immoral laws, and it became a badge of honour to be sent to prison. It was an embarrassment to political leaders if they hadn't been to prison. And the whole social fabric breaks down if there's no moral turpitude attached to violating the law.

And I suggest it's the same in the international community. Where there's this gap between the law and morality, the first victim is the United Nations, because it was bypassed by NATO the Commission has suggested that one way to narrow the gap would be for the General Assembly to consider a declaration setting out the conditions that should exist to justify military intervention for humanitarian purposes

We decided that we had to look at the final status of Kosovo. We felt that we had a moral obligation as a Commission not to ignore what for the Kosovar Albanians and for Kosovo generally was the most important issue concerning them. And we looked at all of the alternatives, which we've set out in the report. There was no good solution; there was no easy solution, and really what we had to choose was the least objectionable, the least unrealistic solution for Kosovo. We've called it Conditional Independence. We came to the conclusion that when over a million people are driven

from their homes, when some ten thousand of them had been murdered
and, when an unknown number of women have been raped, one cannot
expect those people to accept further rule from the government which was
responsible for their terrible victimization. I should remind you that when
the report was written, Milosevic was still in office. However, I don't believe that we would make any significant change to our report had we
written it a few weeks later after President Kostunica came to office. But
of course, the replacement of Milosevic by Kostunica has caused serious
problems for the Kosovar Albanians. While Milosevic was there, they
were getting support from the West in particular. Their plight was well
recognized.

And now that Kostunica has become the flavor of the month Kosovo is
again placed on the very furthest back burner. When our report came out,
according to the New York Times, a spokesperson for the State Department comment on the report was that it is premature to talk about the future status of Kosovo. If anything is calculated again to cause violence and
to cause a resurgence of the KLA in Kosovo, it is this approach. People
don't learn lessons. It's repeating this neglect of the early '90s and telling
the Albanian majority in Kosovo the only way you're going to regain the
attention of the international community is to revert to violence. It has already begun. The murder of Serb police officers across the border in Serbia now has occurred on a few occasions, and if the nettle isn't grasped,
then I think there's reason for tremendous pessimism for the immediate future in Kosovo.

Let me end by briefly talking about the reception of the report. It has been
out for only a few weeks, but it has met with a great deal of interest. It's
had a fair amount of media interest. It's had more than important reception
in the academic communities in major universities in a number of countries. It's been significant that the members of the Commission have been
invited to participate in a number of seminars in a number of countries, including Japan, in a number of European countries, this seminar, and another one in Boston next week. The Canadian government, which has been
very supportive of the Commission, invited us earlier this week to brief
government officials in Ottawa, and yesterday we had a meeting with non-
governmental organization representatives, also in Ottawa. We were told
by the deputy minister who was involved with Central Europe that our report was the only one that was referred to by the Canadian Parliamentary
report which recently came out on Kosovo.

We went to Kosovo to present our report there. We received a mixed reception, because the Kosovar Albanians want independence not tomorrow, but yesterday. In the early and middle '90s there were many solutions that were possible, including a form of autonomy within the Federal Republic of Yugoslavia. But in the aftermath of the ethnic cleansing Albanians have only one goal, and that's independence. I gave a lecture at the University in Prishtina which was attended mainly by faculty, not only law faculty, but right across the board. And they were very suspicious of this conditional independence. They don't like conditionality. Is it one year or three years or ten years or fifteen years? And of course, we can't tell them, because the condition we've laid down is a democratic government, not only on paper, but in substance, and adequate protection for Serb, Roma and other minorities and, vitally, economic viability. If Kosovo was given independence tomorrow without open borders, with antagonistic neighbours, in particular Serbia, from an economic point of view, Kosovo clearly cannot survive as an independent state.

Russia will not like our report. Moscow has become highly critical of the manner in which the United Nations is implementing Resolution 1244. We were presented during our visit to Moscow with a long list of their criticisms. They refer, inter alia, to the introduction of the Deutsche Mark as the currency of Kosovo as well as to the fact that we could visit Kosovo without visas from Belgrade (which would have been refused). All of this, they say is clearly inconsistent with 1244's clear words that Kosovo remains a province of the Federal Republic of Yugoslavia. Well, that's not the interpretation that Bernard Kouchner and the major European nations are giving to the UN mandate.

The State Department, as I've said, refuses to discuss the future status of Kosovo. We mention in the report they refused to meet with our Commission. We were told that by Ambassador Dobbins in July last year that the State Department took the gravest exception to a friendly government, Sweden, setting up a Commission to look into NATO. They would have nothing to do with us. And that, I would suggest was a remarkable reaction. I must say that it appeared to encourage non-governmental organizations in the United States, whether it was Carnegie or Ford or NYU Law School or SUNY, to give us a warmer reception. It also didn't do us any harm in two other respects. It insured the perception as well as the fact of our independence that we were refused any contact by the State Department in Washington and by the government in Belgrade. Also, the State Department's attitude, I think, meant that we received a warmer welcome in some of the European capitals. So good things sometimes come in strange packages.

The Canadian government, as I said, was very supportive and has generously supported our work. The best form of praise is emulation, and we are delighted that the Canadian government invited Garreth Evans, who I'm happy is with us, and Mohamed Sahnoun to lead a new independent international commission to look specifically at intervention and sovereignty.

That's where we are at the moment. There's been some criticism of the Commission's report, but that we welcome. The whole purpose of this sort of Commission is to stimulate debate, we hope more objective debate, and in that context we are really grateful indeed to President Bowen and to SUNY New Paltz and to the other people he mentioned for making possible this seminar.

Kosovo: The Missing Democratic Context

Benjamin Barber, Gershon and Carol Kekst Chair of Civil Society at the University of Maryland, Director, The Democracy Collaborative, New York

I should start by saying I am by no means a specialist or expert on the Balkans, on peace keeping, or on humanitarian intervention. With people like my friends Michael Ignatieff and Bob Keohane and Richard Falk and David Rieff, I would be foolish indeed to try to engage in any detailed discussion of the region, and I will not do that. Rather, I will try to provide a more general perspective for our discussion, as the Commission and others think about the future of Kosovo. Obviously what happened in Kosovo, the original tragedy as well as the subsequent intervention, were conditioned by larger European and global conditions that continue to press on us and to be relevant even after the confrontation is over.

As is implicit in the report itself, no real efforts were made at prevention. Intervention by arms, humanitarian or otherwise, always signals failure, and there were multiple failures already in place prior to the events that transpired starting in 1991 and 1992 in the Balkans. We can talk about the failure of Communism, which played a considerable role. In a larger sense, the failure of the Soviet Empire had a large impact on events. Then there was the failure of the Yugoslav statehood movement and the Tito experiment; the failure of later democratisation efforts (more about that in a moment). We can speak also about the failure of Europe as a model for and enforcer of national integrity, the failure of the United Nations, the failure of NATO and the failure, to some degree, of the United States as an enforcer of international justice. So this entire sequence of obvious tragedies is wrapped in and conditioned by prior failures that are not always so visible.

Moreover, these current failures have to be put into that larger context of a series of historical failures that created an almost impossible situation, something that I think is made very clear by the rich, textured character of the report. The report is judicious, careful, and extraordinarily thorough. It is also courageous, because it takes some controversial positions, some of which I think we'll have a chance to challenge and talk about today, some of which I myself want to at least raise questions about. But as Justice Goldstone notes, the purpose of a report like this is precisely to draw attention, provoke discussion, force us to assume a broader perspective, and perhaps for the first time help us to move in the direction of preventative action that will pre-empt another such situation from coming into being.

With that in mind, let me raise a number of contextual questions and put them in the setting of democratic and political theory more generally, leaving it to my better informed colleagues to comment directly about the Balkans situation. Let me start by making a paradoxical suggestion, as provocative and controversial as any that were made in the report. I would argue that with respect to the cultural wars, the ethnic and tribal fragmentation of the last 10 or 15 years, there is evidence for the proposition that imperialism actually worked in the 19th and early 20th Centuries and that the collapse of imperialism opened the way to the modern tragedy. With respect to the moderation (or suppression) of tribal passion, Soviet imperialism "worked"; the Austro-Hungarian empire worked. For imperialism as a device for tempering nationalism and sub nationalist fractiousness was rather efficacious, and the failure of empire unleashed disintegrative forces that were contrary to the emerging spirit of democracy. Imperialism collapsed for very good reasons to be sure, and I offer this argument not to legitimate empire or suggest that we return to it, but to remind us in the spirit of dialectic that empire nonetheless had its virtues – among them a capacity (however repressive) to deal with what was then called the nationalities question. The Balkans disaster is then, ironically, to some degree a feature of the collapse of empire. Certainly, the fall of the Soviet Empire and the collapse of Communist Yugoslavia (a product of the Austro-Hungarian Empire) unleashed a kind of anarchy that was a ripe setting for the kinds of ethnic nationalist and religious hatreds that flourished and led to what this report rightly calls the tragedy of Kosovo. As it also reminds us, Kosovo was only the last in a series of crises in Croatia, in Montenegro, and throughout the Balkans region.

The second contextual point I want to offer concerns the failures and insufficiencies of democratisation in the wake of the collapse of the Soviet Empire: for the crisis in democratisation has a great deal to do with the emergence of a Balkan crisis as well as with the inability of the United Nations system and the European system to deal effectively with it. Indeed, it was the absence of adequate democratisation that both helped to create the crisis and eventually obstructed an effective pre-emptive strategy on the part of the United Nations or the Europeans.

The failures of democratisation are evidenced in the two forms in which democracy appeared in the wake of the collapse of the Soviet Union (to the degree democracy appeared at all). In one form democracy appeared as a superficial, top-heavy importation of political institutions borrowed from the West. These borrowed institutions were set down in a vacuum in the relative absence of the kinds of robust civil society and civic institutions that had grounded democracy in Europe and America. Democracy lives only when it goes all the way down. In a book called *Strong Democracy*[2], I wrote about participatory or "strong" forms of democratic governance; strong democracy is another way of talking about deep democracy. Democracy cannot simply be about establishing a multi-party system, about elections, about parliaments, or about securing an independent judiciary and a free press. In the absence of an infrastructure of civic institutions, of social relationships, of political, social and religious attitudes, democracy becomes a kind of superficial skin graft that the body politic rejects. That has been what has happened in much of the ex-Soviet Empire, including the entities of Serbia, Slovenia, Croatia, Bosnia-Herzegovina. It may also prophesise the future (as the Report notes) with respect to Montenegro and Macedonia, which have their own problems with democratisation and which may be headed for violent civil strife.

If fractious internecine warfare can result from the insufficiencies of democratisation, confounding democracy with marketisation can be a serious impetus to civil unrest. For if democracy entails more than the importation of a political system or a foreign Bill of Rights, then it surely entails more than the import of market institutions and a willingness to engage in wholesale privatisation. In the world transitioning from communism or other undemocratic forms of government to democracy, the ideology of privatisation has become a powerful and insidious surrogate for democracy. The myth that prosperous consumers are the same thing as competent citizens and that a market society is a democratic society has acquired the power of myth. The myth of the market has been actively propagated by the well-to-do trading nations, in particular, by the government of the United States in its global presence. The lesson taught has been if you wish to democratise, privatise first! Establish a market economy, open your borders to a different kind of economic imperialism – the imperialism of speculative capital, of investments, of free labour markets – and you can achieve democracy, with or without a civic infrastructure or an

---

[2]   B. Barber, *Strong Democracy: Participatory Politics For a New Age* (Berkeley, University of California Press, 1984).

educated citizenry. We have seen where such lessons, all too well absorbed, have led in Russia, and we know where they have led in Eastern Europe. In the Balkans, where many people were persuaded that if they privatised their economy, if the old command economy of the Soviet system were dismantled, they would have democracy, they learned the hard way that the market is no defence against the incursions of religious and ethnic hatred. Only a robust and well grounded democracy can resist fractious breakdown, and the market hardly provided such a grounding. Tom Friedman likes to say no society with a McDonald's will make war on another society with a McDonald's, but this is to confuse the accurate claim that democracies rarely go to war with one another, with the far less certain claim that market societies rarely go to war with one another.

There were then in the Balkans two dangerous myths: the myth that democracy could be established top down via the import of free institutions, in the absence of a civic infrastructure; and the myth that a market society is the same thing as a democratic society and that citizens are no more than political consumers. Privatise your markets, read the myth, and you will be immunized against the kinds of problems that ultimately split the Balkans into warring factions and led to the tragedy to which this Report is a response. Together, these two myths bear a deep responsibility for the causal context within which the Balkan disaster emerged.

We can relate the issue of democratisation not just to the climate inside of Russia and inside of Serbia, inside of Kosovo or Croatia, but to the international climate as well. For Kosovo was but a single instance of the inability of the international community in any of its manifestations, whether the UN General Assembly or the Security Council or the International NGO community or NATO or even Europe, to pre-empt tribal and cultural and ethnic warfare. There is in fact a radical asymmetry in global society today, and this asymmetry has a great deal to do with the failures of the international system in the peace-keeping domain.

To put it rather baldly, we have managed over the last 30 years to globalise our markets in capital, in labour, in trade and in financial speculation – we have managed to globalise our corporations so that the multinational or transnational corporation has become the standard in business – without having in any way globalised our civic or political institutions. The economy is global while governance and civil society remain national and local. We have a Davos for corporate institutions but none for our Unions and foundations and NGOs. What has resulted is a radically asymmetrical global infrastructure in which economics is internationalised while democracy remains trapped inside the box of national sovereignty – unable to create an atmosphere within which genuine global cooperation around rule-making and peace-keeping might have been brought to bear on emerging situations of civil strife and ethnic warfare, not just in the Balkans, but in Africa, in Asia and where civil strife threatened.

In fact, and I won't belabour this though it goes to the heart of my analysis, this asymmetry has meant a globalisation of almost all of our vices but none of our virtues. Think about the character of globalisation today: we've globalised disease; globalised crime; globalised the drug trade. We've globalised the weapons trade, including the trade in nuclear weapons. We've also globalised terrorism, globalised prostitution, globalised pornography. And, most disastrously, (Nelson Mandela refers to it in the letter attached letter to the Report), we have globalised the exploitation and victimization of women and children. Women and children have been the primary victims not just of these tribal and fractious wars, (and they certainly have been that), but also of globalisation itself on the economic level. They are often the first to bear the burdens and the first to suffer the consequences, as was so evident in the painful documentation in this Report on the treatment of women and children during the period of civil strife – the use of rape as an instrument of war and repression, for example. Such depravities against women and children have become standard practice in our modern civil wars.

Not just in wartime, however. The analogy of the use rape as an instrument of war is the peacetime use of girls and boys – of virgins – as bait for the global pornographic trade that draws Western tourists to Thailand and other countries at peace. You can find sex tours advertised on the Internet. The global economy, in fact, is peacefully promoting many of the same kinds of horrors that were committed during the war in the Balkans and are justly condemned in the Report. As violence against children becomes integral to the new global market, it is increasingly difficult to assail violence against children during wartime without sounding hypocritical or self-serving. If the abuse of women is part of the infrastructure of the global market economy itself, how can it be singled out for criticism among civil warriors?

Pope John Paul said two years ago when he was on his mission to the Americas, "if globalisation is ruled merely by the laws of the market applied to suit the powerful, the consequences cannot be but negative." His prescience has been unhappily vindicated in the tragedy of Rwanda, the tragedy of Sierra Leone, the tragedy of the Balkans. And if you find my reference to Pope John Paul a little too easy, (after all, he is a professional moralist and it's his job to engage in moral exhortation), let me read you a passage from another pope, a more secular bishop who you might not expect to talk this who makes very much the same point. This secular Pope writes, "You hear talk about a new financial order, about an international bankruptcy law, about transparency and more. These issues are extremely important, but you don't hear a word about people. You don't hear about the underlying social structures that have to be developed. If we don't get the base right, we'll have great architecture, but the building will fall over." Which is what happened in the Balkans and many other parts of the world. "We live in a world that gradually is getting worse and worse and worse," he concludes; "It's not hopeless, but we must do something about it now." This moralizing Pope is James Wolfensohn, the president of the World Bank. And coming from him, such moralizing is a warning and a half.

I want to suggest, in other words, the context here for our discussion of what happened in Kosovo has to also include a understanding of this asymmetrical development of a global economy in which governance and NGO and civil society mechanisms of the sort that would have helped democracy root all the way down in Kosovo and indeed in Serbia itself is lacking globally as well and creates the condition here for these problems.

Let me offer a fifth contextual point and point briefly to the persistent of bigotry and racism and religious intolerance of our post-enlightenment and post-modernist world – alluded to in our discussions today but not fully elaborated. Kosovo's Albanian population, after all, is predominantly Muslim, and although theirs was certainly not by any means the only instance of repression born of bigotry, it was a significant factor not only in the original persecution, but I would argue, in securing the attention of Europe and the USA to the plight there. The fact that it was Muslims who were suffering and not Christians unfortunately bore some responsibility I fear for the lag in responsiveness from Europe and from the United States. We can also point to the larger question that Nelson Mandela raises in his powerful accompanying letter to this Report between the humanistic interventions in European theatres like the Balkans and the total absence of such intervention in Africa where we have seen an economic and political marginalisation, a pushing of the whole continent south of the Sahara and north of South Africa completely out of the sightlines of the concert of nations, the concert of markets. On almost every positive indicator you can deploy – trade, GNP, standard of living, Africa simply doesn't register; but on the negative indicators – violent death, AIDS, disease – it's off the charts the other way.

There has been a tendency then, in the underlying message, to suggest that African lives and European lives are not measured by the same standards; to suggest that Muslim suffering and Christian suffering somehow should not evoke the same immediate response. And that has been a contributing factor here, both to the development of the situation where Kosovar Albanians are concerned and the lack of rapid and effective response from Europe and America.

Let me make one more point about this – this one reflexive – because many people have used my work on *Jihad vs. McWorld*[3] to putatively show intractable these ancient racial and ethnic and religious hatreds are, and how really we can't do very much about them; for, they suggest, at the base of the human soul is a kind of dark place that even in this postmodern age re-emerges to capture and undo our more civilized side. What the Commission Report makes very clear and we need to remember here is that the role of bigotry, of race hatred, of tribal warfare is not simply a return to ancient prejudices or to a bottom-up recrudescence of nationalist bigotry. On the contrary, it's more often the top down conscious contrivance of manipulative elites who use new media to provoke dormant passions in order to instigate fear and suspicion where they were dormant or non-existent. One of the simplest and most shocking passages in the Report begins "Serbian intellectuals began openly to publish nationalist tracts and to discuss the "genocide" being practiced against Serbs," and so on. The fact is, leading intellectuals including (I'm ashamed to say) some of my own colleagues in democratic theory and practice, involved themselves in stirring up and provoking people at a local level. Their targets had in fact for years, even generations, lived together without any evidence of these supposedly deeply seated base passions. So that what we have witnessed in Kosovo is at least in part a conscious use and manipulation of forces they may be present in any community but are here being stirred up and deployed on behalf of the political ambitions of rapacious elites.

This same elite manipulation was in evidence in Rwanda where the State radio played upon mostly dormant passions, and indeed even directed Hutus how to respond to and resist Tutsi hegemony. There may

---

3   B. Barber, *Jihad vs. McWorld* (New York, Times Books, 1995).

have been passions already in place, but the leadership stirred them up and made them virulent and dangerous in ways that, had the elites gone in the other direction (as happened under the empires of the nineteenth century that put the lid on internecine passion), might have had a very different outcome.

Finally, let me say just a word about the more immediate context of the Report, the legitimacy and efficacy of humanitarian intervention by force of arms, in this case on the part of NATO and the United States. As the Report made clear, and as Justice Goldstone just said in his own remarks, it is of course quite silly to use the word "legitimate" in this context because the use of force across a sovereign nation's boundaries is always by definition illegitimate. So the question isn't whether intervention has some generic legitimacy – it never does. The question is whether it can be justified by the kind of necessarily compromised logic we use in the real world of political relations under the real and compromised conditions of actual peace and war.

What I want to say here is that this particular intervention in the Balkans – however flawed it was with respect to its generic legitimacy – was illegitimate in a variety of other ways, mostly avoidable, some of which have been made clear in the Report, some of which perhaps have not. The use of NATO, for example, which has pledged itself specifically in its charter to defensive deployments and then only in "humanitarian" interventions, created large political problems. We want to remember that shortly before the intervention, the Russians were told not to worry about the extension of NATO to their borders being contemplated by the West, because it would never be used for anything other than direct defence of the national sovereignty of its members. Yet shortly thereafter, it was put to use (perhaps very good reasons but they are not relevant to the logic here) to intervene in the Balkans. The situation was indeed tragic, but if you are viewing it from the Russian perspective you may find yourself saying: 'Yes, that's tragic, and maybe next they'll say Chechnya is a similarly tragic situation, or maybe there's a problem in St. Petersburg that requires humanitarian intervention. NATO was used in the Balkans in a manner contrary to its charter and in a fashion certain to raise fears in Russia.

I also think the failure to secure a UN blessing was a problem, although we know the UN is tainted in its own ways just as NATO is tainted and the United States is tainted. There are no pure players here. There is no one who can pretend to have a cleaner hand than anyone else. And even if there had been an agreement to work through the UN, the question was "which UN?" The Security Council (which surely would have been paralysed and incapable of action)? Or the General Assembly (which is tainted in another way)? The General Assembly has, to be sure, taken positions systematically over the years that represent a certain moral logic but is without the power of enforcement and which sometime appear as unrealistic or irresponsible (those who make the decisions do not necessarily put up the soldiers or expend the resources). So while it is a pity no UN blessing was sought, it would have been extremely difficult to obtain such a blessing, and obtaining it would have precipitated a whole new set of moral and legal issues.

Unhappily, the United States itself contributed to the illegitimacy of the project by the self-serving inefficiency of its air strategy. Not only did it refuse (again for good reasons rooted in American domestic politics) to commit the kinds of ground forces that might have guaranteed success, but it refused with less persuasive reasons to expose its pilots to any risk whatsoever. This zero-risk approach led it to the decision to fly missions above 15,000 feet where its pilots were perfectly safe (just as their targets were perfectly safe!) – so that, absent any meaningful interaction between pilots and their targets either way, everybody came out pretty well except the purposes of the original intervention. As things turned out, Milosevic's heavy weaponry and elite troops were almost untouched. Innocent civilians were inadvertently killed, and an embassy here and there was inadvertently bombed, but it was impossible to achieve real military success from a safe and secure 15,000 feet.

I would go further and argue the whole bombing strategy ultimately was a mistake. Every study ever that has been done from the World War II studies of the fire bombings in Nazi Germany to the studies of the impact on North Vietnam of American carpet bombing during the Vietnamese War suggest that bombing is an insufficient and often a counterproductive instrument whether the objective is to weaken a people's will or erode a nation's economic infrastructure. Nazi Germany's productivity went up all through the war, the fire bombings of its factory towns notwithstanding. Even had American pilots flown closer and more effective missions, it is not clear there would have been a significant impact. As it is, the bombings solidified support of Milosevic, even among those who otherwise might have been his adversaries.

The background for the weak American air strategy was of course the Powell doctrine – a consequence of the so-called Vietnam Syndrome that left the American military unwilling to fight a war in which victory is not certain and in which American casualties are not minimal. What the Powell Doctrine means is that America is unlikely to commit forces to ambiguous and uncertain situations (almost all civil war situations are both ambiguous and uncertain!), which is to say it will rarely commit at all and when it does it will commit in a way more attentive to its own casualties than effective outcomes with respect to vanquishing it enemies. A side issue, but one that may have influenced the Powell doctrine, concerns the privatisation of the American military, which means now military service is viewed by most people as just another job or a way to get credentialed for other jobs – certainly not a place where you risk your life and actually go out and die in the name of foreign causes. Finally, we can add, the historical isolationism of the United States played into the American ambivalence about intervention.

Our nation has always been an ambivalent hegemon. On the one hand, we're the last remaining super power – in the French view a clumsy "hyper-power." On the other hand, we're remarkably reluctant to act like one in the kind of brutal ways that might have made for a much more efficient intervention in Yugoslavia, once intervention had been decided upon. In this spirit, we are fanatic about our sovereignty, and about putting our own troops under NATO command (let alone anybody else's command) – even where we are intervening in and encroaching on the sovereignty of others. So ambivalence was another invisible condition for the tragedy that emerged in Kosovo.

Let me conclude by returning to my central theme, the role of democratisation and democratic institutions that go all the way down in deterring ethnic war – in deterring the kinds of nationalistic breakdown, the kind of tribalism and ethnic and religious bigotry that we've seen at work in the Balkans and on other continents around the world. A more democratic Europe defined by the Europeans and not the Euro might have had a better chance at pre-empting the conflict. A more responsible, decisive Europe could have nipped it in the bud. But a Europe defined primarily by economic interests, and lacking deep down moral and democratic integrity, was unable to act.

A more democratic Serbia, a more democratic Kosovo to begin with might have had institutions that would have prevented the worst from coming about. The Report notes in powerful ways how, early on, the League for Kosovo Democracy provided options that were not responded to by the European community and in time gave away then to the Kosovo Liberation Army where the possibilities of reconciliation and the avoidance of ethnic war had disappeared. And a more democratically constituted armed forces in the United States, one where ordinary citizens served and where Vietnam did not haunt the professional military's dreams, would have invited more discussion here about the meaning of casualties and the meaning of intervention (as it did in Vietnam when the draft was still in place). And finally, a more democratic global arena might have meant that there were institutions of governance and civil society around the world that would have facilitated intervention with a far greater legitimacy than NATO possessed.

In short, in a more democratic world, there will always be far less need for humanitarian intervention, and in a more democratic world – when intervention is necessary – it's likely to be both more legitimate and more efficacious. I don't want to suggest that democracy is a panacea, but it remains the human race's best hope in a perilous and often hopeless world.

The Hypocrisy of Humanitarian Intervention
David Rieff, Senior Fellow, World Policy Institute

I really think this report is an extremely dangerous and irresponsible document. I think it is a call for war. But before getting to the truly wrong-headed, let me pass by the merely idiotic. What astonishes me about the context of the report, by which I mean its sponsorship by the various left liberal foundations, though you have kept rather quiet about this, left liberal social democratic governments, the Nordics, Holland, the Canadian government, are the easy slaps at the U.S. in the report. Of course, anyone familiar with the rhetoric of the governments in question will be familiar with this approach. So let me be as clear as I can: I am not somebody who thinks that the issue of American military involvement is to be laughed at with cheap jibes about those cowards in the US Air Force who chose to fight the Kosovo campaign at 15,000 feet. First of all, I think anybody in this room who has not been under fire should be extremely careful about that thought, and when in doubt, put it out of his or her mind. Because it is not a joke to fire a rocket at any height, and it is not a joke to be fired upon. Let the authors of the report try it sometime. Frankly, I think the easy dismissal of the US military's concerns is an intellectual solecism and a moral disgrace.

It is also so hypocritical as to be beneath contempt. These same social democratic governments whose views dominate the report that talk about the necessity, indeed the moral obligation of humanitarian interventions, are the very governments that consistently cut their military forces. The Canadian government, for example, which has taken the lead in a number of these issues, is a government that has basically pared its forces to the point that those of us who lived in Bosnia during the war, as I did, remember how often we would pass Canadian battalions – and very nice fellows, all of them – and see them fixing their broken-down 1960s armoured personnel carriers by the side of the road. That is, when they were not cleaning their other antiquated weapons.

So before complaining endlessly about how the Americans don't sign this or that international treaty, and implying – and yes, politely as the wording is – that is the clear implication of this report, that the Americans are either cowards or have not understood that putting on a uniform implies risk. I hate to sound like that old Kipling poem, but when the shooting starts, it's the American Army that is expected to do the heavy lifting, and there is no evidence despite all the pious talk emanating from the

European capitals, from Ottawa, et cetera, of Europe, let alone poor Canada changing its fundamental military configuration on any of these issues. Which means that for the foreseeable future, the kind of humanitarian war this report champions, if it is to be engaged in at all, is going to be engaged in by the United States Army and Air Force. So have a care.

Now, for what is really wrong with the report. As I read it, the report is generally for humanitarian military intervention, though somewhat disguised as a critique of the Kosovo operation. I read its subtext as an effort to provide the legal, moral and historical rationale for a regime of international military intervention in last resort faced with substantial – or to put it in old fashioned terms, extraordinary – human rights or humanitarian violations. That is what is worth arguing about. But of course the report makes all kinds of historical and political claims about Kosovo and even Bosnia. Many of these are highly questionable; others represent the triumph of hope over experience taken to an absurd degree. And they need to be challenged if we are even to begin to think clearly about any of these matters. A call for humanitarian intervention as an international norm based on a misunderstanding of much of what has happened in the South Balkans is surely like building an amphitheatre on quicksand.

Let me get down to cases. The account in the report of the history of Kosovo is extremely – how should I phrase it – optimistic. Implicit in the entire account is that fundamentally things all went really wrong in 1989. Of course, I agree entirely with Judge Goldstone that the Balkans are a place where everyone wants to say, oh, yes, that date, but I have an earlier date to tell you about. In that decision, at least, the Commission was clearly entirely correct.

The problem is that by using 1989, there is an implicit assumption, and one that I think is actually borne out in some of the text of the report, that basically things were okay until 1989. And I simply don't think that was the case.

I also think that the report, rather like the policy of various international actors towards the Balkans, tends to rather misdescribe Kosovo as if it were Bosnia. The fundamental difference, at least to those of us who were in the Balkans during those wars, that we – and let me be blunt – unlike the authors of this report, experienced on the ground, is that whereas in Bosnia people basically got along, in Kosovo it was basically a zero-sum game. That was true from the beginning, no matter what date you give to that beginning. So already, the optimistic premise of the report is false.

Let me give an example: The account in the report of the various versions of Kosovar autonomy and relative independence in the Tito period is grossly inaccurate. And here, although I'm sort of a sworn enemy of greater Serbia and was made persona non grata by the Serbian government between 1993 and the fall of the Milosevic regime, not everything the Serbs said about Kosovo was false. Most importantly, when the Rankovic regime fell in Yugoslavia in 1966 – remember it? The authors of the report don't seem to – what happened subsequent to that was a kind of massive ethnic cleansing of Serbs.

Grim reality time, however unpleasant it may be for interventionist social-democrats: It has always been like that in Kosovo. Throughout its history, the dominant mode has been that of the zero sum game. Everyone played by those rules in the province, apart, that is, from a few liberal intellectuals in Prishtina to whose views I think this report attaches far too much weight.

If you actually look at the history of Kosovo in the Tito period, what you will see is actually Serbs on top, Albanians get the chop. Albanians on top, Serbs get the chop. And obviously since the federal government of Yugoslavia had a greater amount of force at its disposal, the force deployed against the Albanians was always going to be greater, and the force the Albanians were able to deploy against the Serbs was always going to be lesser, but that doesn't make it less of a zero-sum game. So already if we're talking about history, I think there are profound errors of interpretation in the report.

I also think this rather romantic reference to May '68, as if the LDK were the product if this period of revolutionary romanticism and modernization is very misleading. I don't think a historical analysis of the LDK would support that, let alone of other factions in Kosovo. The Kosovo story is not one of liberals versus conservatives but Albanians against Serbs. Sorry, but that's a fact, at least for the major political conflicts that unfolded between the fall of Rankovic and the present time (it has been in some ways even more marked since the victory of NATO).

Other errors: The report blames the international community far too much for its actions before 1999. I'll come back to the phrase "international community" I assure you. As far as blaming the international actors goes, the report attaches far too much importance to the supposed need to support Rugova and the LDK and far too little importance to the role of the diaspora in radicalising the Albanian side. I don't think it's simply a case of "we failed." Far from it.

Like all fundamentally sentimental understandings, there is a kind of fable of guilt in this report. We, the international actors, failed to support the LDK and civil society and the NGOs and all the nice people, and then the bad people, the thugs and the ethnic groups came and started provoking the Serbs and then all hell broke loose. I really think that's a fable. I think Rugova had already gone beyond his sell-by date by the time these events took place. Rightly or wrongly, few were listening to him. And what is barely addressed in the report is the rebirth of Adam Demaci and radical elements within the political establishment of the Kosovar Albanian world.

Such diasporic pressures are familiar. You see them in other situations. Jewish communities and Israel are the clearest example I know of this phenomenon. This mistake goes with the report's credulous account of what is possible in post-war Kosovo. My suspicion is that where these questions were concerned the authors of the report rather listened too much to Bernard Kouchner. Certainly, the report is culpably easy on him. I think those of us who were there when Kouchner assumed power had the distinct impression that for the first six months, Kouchner thought he was in Sarajevo and wouldn't listen to the bad news that he was not in a place where historical commitments to multicultural comity, at least in the cities, were real, but rather in a place where people hated each other. Period, end of story.

I wish this report had talked to more of us who did not have such credulous and romantic (not to say, in Kouchner's case, self-serving) views. Looking at the list of people who were credited with the Commission having interviewed, I see very few people like me who just sort of hang around the first para and watch this stuff happen and too many grandees of the international liberal conference circuit.

Let me tell you what Kouchner really did. When he first arrived in Kosovo, he lectured us all – including the UN officials he was replacing – that there was going to be ethnic comity. It's only six months later, if you actually follow the sort of direct time line of his declarations that he began to say that, you know, we're doing the best of a bad job, blah-blah-blah. In fact, he took the job so that he would be a better candidate for the UNHCR high commissioner's job that, thankfully, he went on to lose. His inability to listen is as vast as his ambition. But what is sure is that had he known

355

what he was getting into, he would almost certainly have stayed in France or moved to New York.

So, beyond inaccuracy, credulousness, and hidden agendas, what else is there to say about the report? Well, there are the report's cognitive confusions. The incessant conflation of humanitarian groups, human rights groups and civil society NGOs as if they all had the same purposes, the same mandates and the same goals, is profoundly misleading. Not just misleading as an account, but misleading to the authors of this report who by being able to lump these actors together could come up with a much neater and, frankly, more palatable moral fable than what really happened in Kosovo.

There is, for example, a statement in the report at one point that Mercy Corps, a U.S. medical NGO, was monitoring human rights violations. Well, Mercy Corps is actually doing a lot more than that. Mercy Corps was letting officials of the Soros Foundation pose as humanitarian actors and do human rights reporting pretending to be aid givers. There was far too much of this. At its most extreme, it took the form of the Care Canada officials who were arrested as spies by the Serbs sometime during the Kosovo crisis. We all thought, 'there go the Serbs again.' But the Care officials were spies, just as the Serbs alleged, in the sense that their job was to report on what was going on to the Canadian government – one of the belligerents. But they had been admitted as humanitarian officials, that is, as people who were purportedly neutral.

The report also minimizes in its account of the humanitarian crisis how damaging the role their funders from the NATO countries demanded they play was for the humanitarian NGOs. Kosovo was a crisis for humanitarians, for the humanitarian international. It may have been a glorious moment for the human rights movement, but contrary to this report, the human rights movement and the humanitarian movement are not the same thing, despite their overlaps. Kosovo was the instance where most main line humanitarian organizations found themselves in a position of siding with, and literally administering, more or less as sub-contractors, the refugee problems of one of the belligerents – that is, NATO. That is what really happened to the humanitarian agencies in Kosovo. There was a notable exception, Doctors Without Borders, which refused to take money from any NATO country for its operations there on the good and sufficient grounds that that would put them, in effect, as subcontractors to the belligerents in the war.

Mohonk International Peace Conference: Lessons from the Conflict in Kosovo

The refugee crisis in Kosovo, which this report deals with in a few very, very unsatisfactory pages, was a thunderbolt in the humanitarian world. It's an event from which the main line humanitarian agencies have not yet dealt with, are still digesting, are still arguing about. It put into question the whole principle of humanitarian action, the ineluctable, bedrock principle of humanitarian action that is impartiality and neutrality. No humanitarian actor, even Doctors Without Borders with its brilliant tradition of testimony of being unwilling to keep quiet about what it sees, has ever suggested, indeed, no reputable humanitarian actor, to my knowledge, has ever suggested that you can put to the side in the interest of a just war or a good cause impartiality and neutrality. And yet, whether wittingly or unwittingly, by providing this humanitarian cover for a war which was again and again described by all the NATO powers as a humanitarian war, by implicating the humanitarian international in this, the whole humanitarian project that begins with the para-formations of Doctors Without Borders in Biafra a third of a century ago was endangered. That is a really serious issue. But from the report, you'd never know it was a problem.

Predictably, the report is as incredibly romantic and hagiographical about civil society and NGOs as it is ignorant about humanitarianism. It makes the usual left liberal confusion about civil society by confusing a descriptive term for a prescriptive one. For the authors of this report, civil society never includes the bad guys in the National Rifle Association, or, to use a Balkan example, Radovan Karadzic's SDS. Civil society is 'us,' the international good guys. That is how the report can once more deploy the tired suggestion that a priority must strengthening civil society. Mix the NGOs, preventive diplomacy, and the democratic forces, and you will get a good result. Rubbish! Civil society is not ipso facto "the good guys", and the whole con of civil society, and frankly in my view of international humanitarian law, is that it wants to avoid the real problems of politics, of having to take sides. But for the authors of the report, civil society is the liberal equivalent of George Bush's missile shield.

What this position permits one to do is pretend one does not have to take political sides, with all the moral hazards that implies. I remember people in Bosnia taking this stance. "I'm just responding to these terrible violations," they would say, "these war crimes, this humanitarian thing." And then they would often say, "It's not that I support the Bosnian government. It's that the heroic victim people of Bosnia are being murdered by those mean Serbs on the hill."

How convenient. How consoling. No moral problem, n'est-ce-pas? And for a side benefit, take such a position and you can also condescend to the Americans and all their crude, vulgar bellicism. You can say how can they take these political things? You can say what's all this grayness? Why can't we have principles? And then you can use your principles like a prophylactic against reality.

I am struck by how the report relied on the Danish government's claim that what is needed after Kosovo is "a framework for principled humanitarian intervention. Criteria: Serious violations of human rights or international humanitarian law. A failure by the UN Security Council to act. Multilateral bases for the action undertaken only necessary in proportion for its use. Disinterestedness of intervening states." Excuse me. On what planet is there the disinterestedness of states? In what universe do states act with such altruism? It's nonsense. And pernicious nonsense, because it's an attempt to make an end run around politics and history by talking about – by enshrining the law as a totem.

When you put a crisis like Kosovo in terms of criminal violations, the challenge becomes a species of police work. As if these wars were crimes. But these wars are not only or even mainly crimes, except in that social-democratic never-never land where war has become inconceivable. These wars are expressions of long political conflict, long historical crises. This does not mean there should never be outside military intervention. Those of you who know my work will know I was a great supporter of military intervention in Bosnia. But I was always, though perhaps never as clearly as I wanted to be, a bitter opponent of humanitarian intervention. I was a supporter of military intervention because the Bosnian side was right, and my government, the U.S. government, should have helped them. Simple as that.

Now, I may have been right or wrong. Those of you who didn't think as well of the Bosnians would have been correct in taking the opposite view. But then, at least, the argument would have been on the correct grounds – political ones. In a democracy like the United States, somebody would have won and somebody would have lost. Perhaps the wrong side. But we wouldn't have one side holding up the supposedly unanswerable claim of international law, which is just going to get us in, in my view, into the worst kind of trouble, the worst kind of intellectual misapprehensions and wishful thinking and sanctimony, and into blind faith in modalities like prevention and conflict resolution that do not have a hope of working in the real world.

Let's talk for a minute about prevention. The report makes great play of the fact that not enough was done before, and that the international community didn't get involved early enough or decisively enough. But the recommendations of the report are for the international community to have taken sides in the dispute. Over and over again the report says we should have supported these elements or those elements; in the case of Kosovo, the LDK.

What is that except imperialism to come back to Benjamin Barber's argument? But then he should say so. If you want to say we're for a new world order, no irony intended, in which the major powers say these forces in the minor powers are the ones we want to support, and you want to go into that, fine. But then say what you're doing. Don't pretend you're a human rights actor, and don't pretend that this is easy or that there are no responsibilities or that the good guys that you support may not turn out to be tomorrow's bad guys – as in Rwanda, incidentally – if you're really going to do it on that basis.

I find something deeply immodest about this report, for all its fine language. There is the astonishing presumption that if the international community, whatever that may be, will only strengthen international institutions, expand international laws, and above all vest more power in the UN, these problems of failed states and intractable ethnic conflicts can be addressed successfully.

The UN? Please! The United Nations has failure inscribed in its DNA. Largely speaking, it is a useful, but a subaltern institution. And in any case, what the report is actually suggesting is that some version of the institutions we have confront the dozens of wars in the world and know what to do about them and know what action to take, and be able to galvanize politicians in powerful countries to send their children to die stamping out these brush fires.

Excuse me, but let me ask a human rights non-believer's question: On what moral basis? The only moral basis I can see is this fetishized edifice called international law which is presented as justifying anything.

I, myself, with all due respect to Judge Goldstone, am not surprised that Kofi Annan welcomed this report in advance of its conclusion, because frankly Kofi Annan is preaching the same idea. In the 54th meeting of the General Assembly, Kofi Annan made a speech in which he said we must do for Sierra Leone and Angola what we did for Kosovo and East Timor.

That is a declaration to the world of attempting to persuade people to engage in what would be decades of humanitarian war.

Of course Kofi Annan wouldn't dream of using the word war. He has actually never even used the word humanitarian intervention. But it is war he has in mind. But that, he knows, would make many of his own constituencies uncomfortable. So instead, he and people like him use the crime analogy. They say, we're not really going to war. We're just arresting human rights violators, and we're going to use the minimum force. Of course, then when the Americans don't use all the force people want, they spit on the Americans, and when they use too much force for the tender stomachs of governments in Stockholm or Ottawa, they spit on them as well.

Secession Without Independence?
Comments on the Report of the Independent Commission on Kosovo
Professor *Robert Keohane*, Duke University

I am not an expert on the Balkans any more than Benjamin Barber is. I'm a student of international relations and international institutions, and I am violating here a principle of one of my colleagues. He says a political scientist should never write or speak about a country he hasn't at least flown over. I don't even pass the fly-over test here. So I'm not going to focus on the Balkans. I'm going to focus on the context of international relations within which the report's recommendations ought to be placed.

And I think we should emphasize, as Richard Falk has, the need for humility here. As President Bowen in his comments about the history of Mohonk indicated, for 20 odd years very intelligent people in the international arbitration movement met here every year and behaved in a way that we would regard now as naïve; and yet there is no evidence that they were any less intelligent or less public spirited than we are. So it may be that when people read these records in 100 years, they will think we were very naive, but that's the risk we take.

I'm not going to also focus on the humanitarian intervention part of the report, largely because I'm too sympathetic to it. I thought it was a very thoughtful discussion. I agreed with almost all of it, and I also think that we can't just look on when large numbers of people, whether it's 10,000 or 800,000, are killed. Since states often act in their own self interest, intervention, of course, can be abused, and that's precisely why one needs criteria for humanitarian intervention. So the notion that one should simply accept it as somehow morally right to intervene but one doesn't need criteria is incoherent. Any kind of moral point of view requires a general moral philosophy basis for making judgements, not simply an emotional concern that one is on one side or the other.

One need not be an optimist to favour humanitarian intervention. Vaclav Havel in the 1980s before his triumph made a very interesting distinction between optimism and hope. He said that optimism is the belief that things will turn out all right. Hope is the commitment to try to make sure that things do come out all right. It's a very different phenomenon. So one has to have some hope to take action, but not necessarily optimism.

I'm going to focus on what the Commission calls its central recommendation, that Kosovo embark on a path towards conditional independence. I'm
focusing on this because it's the recommendation that I'm most critical of
in the report. The Commission reaches this recommendation after rejecting
a set of other possibilities, maintaining Serbian sovereignty or a UN protectorate indefinitely would, it believes, generate resentment. The implication is that terrorism and civil war might result. Yet, partition or full independence, it is argued, could lead to international war, in Kosovo and Serbia or other neighbours. So conditional independence is seen as the only
way to satisfy Kosovo national aspirations without sparking violent conflict with its neighbours.

One could ask why partition is not the best solution. What is so sacred
about the internal boundaries of the former Yugoslavia? Why can Serbs in
Kosovo be expected to accept Albanian rule if Albanians in Kosovo cannot be expected to accept Serb rule? Do atrocities by the military, paramilitaries and police of one side justify such an asymmetrical solution to
be maintained indefinitely in the future? Since I'm not a Balkan expert, I
simply ask these questions rather than pursuing them.

I, in my own remarks, am less concerned with where boundaries should be
drawn than with questioning whether boundary drawing should be seen as
the heart of the issue. The starting point of my analysis is my political belief that the Commission's recommendation for conditional independence,
whatever its merits, does not seem politically feasible in its present form
for three reasons.

First, Kosovo's independence will be more difficult to arrange now that
Milosevic has been forced from power in Serbia, since the legitimacy of
secession was fostered by the presence of an oppressive regime, a prior
regime in Serbia.

Secondly, Serbia is unlikely to offer to engage in a dialog if such a dialog could be interpreted as accepting a pathway towards Kosovo's independence, and especially a new regime, democratic but nationalist, and
accused by Milosevic of being traitors. It would be very, very unwise politically for a democratic Serbian government to appear to be giving away
Kosovo. It reminds one a little too much of the Weimar Republic, later accused by Hitler of a stab in the back.

And thirdly, Russia and China and other countries with discontented minorities will strongly object to any precedent committing the international
community to the legitimacy of secession, which I will come back to.

So, as written, it seems to me that the Commission's recommendation is very thoughtful, very interesting from the point of view of learning about and reflecting on Kosovo, probably a political dead end. And furthermore, the Commission's language of conditional independence is itself ambiguous. Independence will be conditional on a demonstration that Kosovo's people "could live in peace with each other and with the neighbouring states in the region." "Only as it established conditions of internal and external peace would Kosovo earn recognition from other states as a fully independent national state." So at some point, in one, three, five, or ten years, the prospect of such full independence, classic sovereignty, is held out as a prize for good behaviour.

Now, I think the Commission is on the right track in inquiring into the conditions for a solution rather than simply arguing for one set of boundaries rather than another. But I think its language of independence will lead to difficulty, both by raising the short run problems of feasibility that I discussed and if implemented by creating unfortunate precedents in the longer term.

There seem to be two major problems with short run feasibility: first, how to make secession more tolerable to Kosovo's neighbours, and secondly how to make secession more tolerable to other countries including Russia and China. But in the long run, the problems are, in a sense, more interesting. In the long run the problem is to avoid creating a new source of international conflict in the region centred on a sovereign Kosovo. It doesn't take a great imagination to imagine an international politics of the region in which Kosovo played a difficult role. One can think of Serbia's own role before 1914 in its region.

After Kosovo became fully independent, after all, its leaders could become more militant again, making demands or taking actions that would destabilize the region. So suppose that Kosovo receives conditional independence and the conditions are met, and then it becomes a shallow democracy to use the obverse of Ben Barber's deep democracy. In such a situation, a nationalist xenophobe could come into power; and then we have a sovereign Kosovo, nominally but not really democratic, as a thorn in the side of its neighbours.

The answers, I think, to both the short and long run problems lie in the structure of European political institutions, which are considered in the Commission's report but whose significance could be further discussed. To reassure Kosovo's neighbours, Kosovo's sovereignty, in my view, should be not only conditional, but *permanently limited*. There is precedence for such action with respect to a more important country, the Federal Republic of Germany. In 1954, the Paris agreement signed by seven European states, the United States and Canada, prevented Germany from developing nuclear, biological or chemical weapons, and assigned German forces to NATO's integrated command. The German pledges were reinforced by a joint pledge by Britain, France and the United States to act against any resort to force in violation of the UN charter by a German government.

West Germany became, in a phrase of a political scientist, a semi-sovereign state. Its sovereignty was not merely conditional, but limited, and for all intents and purposes in 1954 permanently limited, and remained so throughout the Cold War. Similar arrangements may be needed for Kosovo. The dense institutional context of Europe should make this easier, and the European Stability Pact discussed by the report seems to me to be an essential aspect of this institutional landscape.

The implication of my suggestion is that sovereignty should not be seen anymore as something that a state has or has not. It should be seen as more of a continuum in which entities can be partially sovereign. Note that all of the members of the European Union are only partially sovereign now. They have pooled much of their sovereignty and delegated powers to entities such as the European Court of Justice and for some of them the European Central Bank. The classically sovereign states are diminishing in the world community; the United States and China are the two leaders. After that, it becomes harder and harder to see classically sovereign states.

The second task, then, is to make Kosovo's secession from Serbia more palatable to China, Russia and other states. In this regard, the crucial additional conditions involve regional institutions. In my view the biggest single misstep in the report is the statement that conditional independence for Kosovo "would effectively commit the international community to the proposition that national minorities have a right of secession when they have been subjected to a systematic abuse of their human rights together with a systematic denial of their right to self government." This commits the international community to a right of secession and by implication, I think, independence, even if conditional, to these national minorities.

Now, such a commitment by the United Nations could generate a great deal of conflict. I'm not worried about this report being a license for UN intervention around the world. I agree with Co-Chair Carl Tham that the problem is too little inclination to intervene and not too much. But it certainly could generate incentives for lots of national liberation movements to do exactly what the KLA did: to attack oppressive regimes, goad them into especially oppressive acts against civilian populations from which the guerrillas slip away, and then generate the conditions under which secession and independence are valid. The incentives that this precedent would give to liberation movements, so-called, from the Tamil Tigers to the KLA, to keep fighting, hoping that they can legitimate their activities and become legitimately seceding entities, are large. I don't like them.

So, because of these perverse incentives and also because of the interests of states whose leaders want to repress their national minorities, a right to secession is not on the horizon. By proposing a solution to Kosovo that implies a worldwide right to secession, the Commission, I think, has doomed its report to political irrelevance.

So in my view, the Commission has not taken its own language of conditions seriously enough. It has not thought especially deeply about the conditions that were necessary to create a right of oppressed groups to autonomy. And I use the word autonomy deliberately, because I think that the language of independence and sovereignty get in the way of a reasonable solution. *Full sovereignty and complete independence are part of the problem, not part of the solution.*

The reason that sovereignty is part of the problem is that it raises the stakes for boundary-drawing. The group that constitutes the majority within a given territory benefits from winner-take-all under sovereignty rules. The winners rule, the losers suffer. Of course, then, the battle over how to draw the boundaries is intense and usually involves – draws in states whose majority populations sympathize with the minority in the disputed region. Cyprus, which Turkey invaded and partitioned more than a quarter century ago, is a case in point. With winner-take-all sovereignty rules, the endemic suspicion and rivalry described by so-called realist students of international relations will result, and not surprisingly the history of minority treaties in the Balkans and East Central Europe, both before and after World War I, is a history of failure. Once sovereignty has been handed over, arrangements for minority protection and autonomy are unlikely to be successful in situations with as much animosity as exists in the former Yugoslavia today.

Hence, what should be granted to the seceding entity is not independence, but limited autonomy within the context of constrained sovereignty. Autonomy, in my sense, does not mean a self-governance within the structure of a given state, as a self-governing or an autonomous region in a sovereign state, it means self-governance within a supranational institutional structure. This is the kind of autonomy that members of the European Union have now. The autonomous entity could have membership in the United Nations and European institutions, but it would not have the traditional sovereign rights of external independence from outside authority and internal supremacy, neither of which members of the EU retain today. Its right to secede does not imply the classical prerogatives of sovereignty. In other words, I want to separate the right to secede from the right to sovereignty. These two rights are linked in the report, I think implicitly and without thinking about the connection sufficiently.

As I indicated earlier, the entity's right to autonomous status should be limited. Autonomy should continue only as long as the groups governing authority conforms to regional standards guaranteeing human rights. These standards must be enforceable. Hence, there need to be regional organizations monitoring human rights and backed by the most powerful states in the region. These states must be willing to help enforce human rights standards if necessary. Under these conditions, international organizations may be able to act as human rights entrepreneurs or normative intermediaries as the OSC High Commissioner on National Minorities has done during recent years.

My point is that conditional independence is a recipe for trouble, because it implies sovereignty and a winner-take-all solution. Even limited autonomy would be likely to leave the conflict of autonomy as granted in a void without strong regional institutions. In my view, oppressed ethnic groups should only be given rights to secession if regional structures exist that are sufficient to limit sovereignty. Such limitations are necessary to insure with a reasonable probability that secession will not simply lead to aggravation of violent conflict. Europe is the only region of the world with such institutions today. They include the Council of Europe Framework Convention for the Protection of National Minorities entered into force in 1998, as well as the European Stability Pact, the Organization for Security and Cooperation in Europe, and the European Union itself. These institutions provide standards for state behaviour towards minorities and support by powerful members provides incentives, positive as well as negative, for implementation of the standards.

Limited autonomy for Kosovo, therefore, in my view, would not commit the international community, *per se*, to recognize the right of even secession, much less independence, for oppressed and abused national minorities worldwide. What it would do is commit states and international organizations to the right of secession, but not full sovereignty, to oppressed peoples *in any region in which an affected institutional structure already existed.* That is, regional institutions would have to be sufficiently well developed to insure with a high probability that succession would not lead to further conflict. Only as regions other than Europe develop such institutional structures would the precedent of Kosovo's limited autonomy become relevant to them.

So, to conclude, focusing on conditions as the Commission does is a good idea, but we need to get away from conceptions of independence and sovereignty in the traditional sense. My version of limited autonomy adds two conditions. First, it provides for permanent limitations on sovereignty on the model of the restrictions in 1954 on the Federal Republic of Germany. Second, it requires that regional institutions providing a guarantee of security and minority protection be in place. These limitations would, I think, make secession for Kosovo more acceptable to its neighbours and to China, Russia, and many other members of the United Nations. They could therefore make the Commission's creative focus on conditions more politically feasible as a basis for serious international discussion.

Reflections on the Recommendations of the Independent Commission on Kosovo
Ivo Daalder, Senior Fellow, Brookings Institution

This is, in general, an extraordinarily well-researched and written report. I agree with most, if not all, of the history and many of its conclusions.

What I wanted to do is confine my remarks to two particular aspects, and one more than the other. I wanted to look at the Commission's very pertinent reflections on the problems and prospects of humanitarian intervention. And I also wanted to spend a moment on the question of Kosovo's future status now that Milosevic in fact has been defeated in free the elections that have been held.

Unlike the Commission, I no longer believe, though I did when I did my own study on this issue, that Kosovo ought to be independent whether conditionally or not because the politics in the region has changed fundamentally since October 5th. Unlike, I guess, Professor Falk, I was not displeased with either those changes or, in fact, the consequences for Kosovo thereof. But let me return to that at the end.

First, I want to really talk about and spend the bulk of my presentation and remarks on the Commission's discussions and suggestions with regard to humanitarian intervention. I applaud the Commission for taking on this difficult, legally touchy and problematic issue, and to do so in an open and most non-dogmatic way. Particularly, I am impressed with the Commission's ability to achieve consensus among its members, which is a diverse group of people from various backgrounds, not all of whom would share the perspectives or proclivities that NATO members would bring to this issue, and yet the Commission has come out with a consensus recommendation that, as the discussion this morning proves, hardly is soft in its implication.

The framework that the Commission proposes is interesting, and I think it does move the ball forward, although like the Commission, I recognize that there's a long way to go to turn this framework into a consensus for a declaration by the United Nations members, let alone as a basis for amending the charter, which, perhaps, falls more in the hope than optimism category that Bob Keohane mentioned in his analysis.

The Commission recognizes, and I think rightly so, that there are two approaches that are raised by the issue of the "Kosovo precedent," if that it is. There is a legal approach, which the Commission's report spends a lot of time talking about in regard to the question of international law and the legitimacy of action. But there's also a political approach and a political precedent that was set by Kosovo with regard to the requirements for intervention and the willingness of states to do so.

The Commission devotes most of its report, as I said, to the legal issues. I, in fact, don't have much to add to it, one because I'm not a lawyer, and if I were it might only confuse things. But secondly, because the Commission does not spend much time on the political precedent, that's what I want to do. The only legal issue I want to raise, the only issue of law that I think is important, is that the Commission's report ignores the very extensive discussion on the legality of NATO's intervention that the NATO members had among themselves. This was not just an issue that was only discussed in the UN councils, but it was in fact an issue that dominated deliberations within the NATO council among NATO members, so much so that the actual intervention may well have been delayed because of that very debate.

And within that debate, which was in some senses theological in nature, basically three religious doctrines emerged. There was a Catholic approach represented by France, which basically said that the rules for intervention are very clear, that we cannot intervene in this case because intervention would violate those rules, but of course we all sin once in a while, so in this case we can. There was the Lutheran approach prominent in discussions by the Brits and the Germans which was the rules can be adapted in a way that is consistent with the intent – where the emergence of the notion that there is an immediate humanitarian emergency that intervention is designed to prevent. And then there was the agnostic approach by the United States which basically says the rules are really interesting, but now we need to act.

So this debate, which went on through most of 1998, was very much a debate about the legality of the action, and NATO in what I think is an innovative way decided that there was a legal basis for action, they just never spelled it out, because there was no agreement on what exactly that legal basis was. Therefore, I would not conclude, and I think no NATO government would conclude, that this was an illegal action. It was an action that was legal, although the legal basis thereof was indeed debated, if not debatable. So much for the legal issue.

The political precedent, what I want to focus on, is the issue of the United States and the question of intervention in humanitarian cases. Does the Kosovo War set a precedent for future humanitarian intervention as far as the United States is concerned, and what is the implication of that, if there is such a precedent? Immediately after the end of the Kosovo War, President Clinton in Macedonia famously declared as follows: "We can say to the people of the world whether you live in Africa or Central Europe or any other place, if somebody comes after innocent civilians and tries to kill them en masse because of their race, their ethnic background, or their religion, and it is within our power to stop it, we will stop it." Thus was borne the putative Clinton Doctrine. It proved to be short lived.

Just a month after President Clinton spoke these words, his National Security Advisor added a significant modifier. Sandy Berger speaking at the Council on Foreign Relations in July 1999 said: "The United States and its allies will not fail to act when first, there is a systematic effort by a government to eliminate an entire people through genocide or near genocide. Second, when we have the capacity to act. And third, when we have a clear national interest at stake." The third condition was new.

By the end of the administration, Sandy Berger, summing up the Clinton administration's general perspective on the matter, wrote in the most recent issue of *Foreign Affairs* that: "I believe the United States should not send military forces into conflict where America's national interests are not at stake. And the reality is that we have not. For all the talk of humanitarian intervention," Berger continued, "the only instance when America has used force purely for humanitarian reasons was Somalia in 1992."

The perspective on humanitarian intervention that dominates at the end of the Clinton administration is likely to be amplified further under an administration headed by George W. Bush, given, in fact, that candidate Bush has stated repeatedly first, that the United States should use military forces only in defence not just of national interest, but of vital national interest. As he said yesterday, "we should protect our property and our people." Parenthetically I'm not sure I'd agree with the ordering of that.

Second, he has said that genocide is not in and of itself sufficient reason for using military force. He has repeatedly, when asked whether genocide in Africa, for example, was reason to intervene, said no, it was not.

And third, although I think Sandy Berger is correct that the United States has not used military force in the Clinton administration except when a national interest was at stake. Candidate Bush has repeatedly said that the

Clinton administration has over-committed the U.S. military for humanitarian and other non-vital interest purposes. Given that mind set, one can expect that the likelihood for American participation in humanitarian interventions in a George W. Bush administration are going to be even less than under a Clinton administration.

I've gone over this evolution of American thinking in the last year and a half in some detail because I firmly believe that the future of humanitarian intervention depends not on what the rest of the world does, but depends on what the United States does. In this area, the United States truly is, for better or for worse, the indispensable power. Any intervention involving the use of military force will require American military participation. No other single country or group of countries possesses the military resources required to organize, lead, or conduct these type of operations.

In that regard, the question of how to intervene is as important as the questions of whether, why, and when. On that very important issue, the report is, however, largely silent.

The fact is that military intervention for support of humanitarian ends is far from easy. No matter whether the humanitarian tragedy is caused by deliberate government policy or because it results from the breakdown of state authority.

In either case, it takes decisive force. It took 30,000 U.S. Marines in Somalia to establish a modicum of a secure environment, and it would have taken an estimated 150,000 to 200,000 combat troops to go into Kosovo, three-quarters of which would have had to been American. This is not the place to dwell in detail on the precise military requirements for intervention. It is only to suggest that the scope and extent of these requirements will, in almost all cases, be beyond the means of the vast majority of states. Our European friends, in fact, have recognized that. They have understood that Kosovo showed that their incapacity militarily was unacceptable and have embarked on providing themselves with the military means to intervene for peace keeping and crisis management purposes in the aftermath of Kosovo.

However, there is considerable doubt, not just here in the United States, but even in Europe, whether sufficient financial and material and organizational resources will be provided to mount an effective force in Europe. Even when Europe meets the stated goal of deploying 60,000 troops within two months for a period of up to one year, this will be a geographically restricted capability. This is not the capability that is going to do Sierra Leone, let alone East Timor, if and when it is necessary, at erra Leone, let alone East Timor, if and when it is necessary, at least not without American help.

For these reasons, the U.S. perspective on humanitarian intervention post-Kosovo, I believe, is crucially important, because we won't have a humanitarian intervention of any size, and that's what will be necessary if it is in fact to be justified, without the United States to participate. And the evolving debate in the United States on this issue to me and to those of us who believe that humanitarian intervention may well be necessary in the future, is indeed disturbing.

To conclude, therefore, whatever the legal precedent that Kosovo has set, the political precedent is very uncertain indeed. To a considerable extent, it is disturbing. The American political consensus is such that the likelihood of an American administration deciding to intervene for humanitarian purposes outside of Europe, quite frankly, is close to zero. That's sad, but that is what the Kosovo precedent has underscored. And those who would wait for other countries to be able to mount that kind of force, I think it would be helpful if that were to occur, but we'd have to wait years, if not decades, before other countries would be in a position to mount that kind of force. Unfortunately, while focusing on the legal aspects of humanitarian intervention, the Commission's report neglected to study the military requirements thereof, which inevitably would have to lead to a major debate about the United States role there.

Let me conclude with a few words about the Commission's recommendation regarding Kosovo's future status. First, I agree with the Commission that neither partition nor outright independence offer a way out. I also agree that a UN protectorate is not a long-term solution, and that the implication that it is will likely lead to dangerous instability within the area and dangerous conflict between the international presence and the local population. That leaves autonomy and conditional independence.

I'm on record as favouring conditional independence, the same solution that the Commission has come up with and for much the same reason. A Serbia ruled by the kinds of people that were ruling Serbia for the last ten years hardly is the kind of place to have any control over Kosovo. But, like the Commission, my support for this proposal was predicated on the belief that Mr. Milosevic would remain in power for some time. Like the Commission, I was fortunately proven wrong. Assuming that the opposition wins in two weeks in Serbia, this is not the time to push for an independent Kosovo, whether conditionally or not. They recognize that this is also not the time to insist on Serb sovereignty over Kosovo. In fact, the new powers are likely to be far more accommodating on the question. Better to use that opportunity to refashion the entire federal structure – to address relations among Serbia, Montenegro, and Kosovo within such a new federal republic of Yugoslavia. Of course, if Serbia and Montenegro decide together, or if Montenegro, God willing, decides on its own to part company and become fully independent, that would raise major problems for Kosovo.

The situation in Serbia and Kosovo is still too unsettled today to finalize this issue now. The best we can hope for is what Veton Surroi, the Kosovar Albanian newspaper editor, has called the "three Taiwan solution." Serbia, Montenegro and Kosovo would continue along the path of becoming entities, fully self governing and able to stand on their own feet. The FRY would for now remain the internationally recognized state to which these three entities belong. This kind of solution of a "three Taiwan solution" represents a transition from where we are today to either three new independent states or a new arrangement among them. But that could only work if the issue of Kosovo status is deferred and the international protectorate established under 1244 remains, at least for the time being, in place. In that sense, I think the Commission is wrong to say that 1244 does not offer a viable solution at least in the short term, while I agree it doesn't offer a solution in the long term. It also means that Montenegro will have to defer its decision on independence for now, which in any case it would be wise to do for other reasons.

And finally, and most crucially and most difficult, it would mean that power in Belgrade needs to shift clearly to a Serbia that is preoccupied with recovery and consolidation of democracy, rather than with its relationship either with Montenegro and Kosovo. And it also means that power needs to migrate from the FRY to where it is located now, at least democratic power, in a newly democratic Serbia.

I recognize that the danger of excluding independence for Kosovo, per se, may lead some in Kosovo to take up arms against the international community. That, indeed, is a danger, but it's something that the international community so far has prevented through managing the situation there. And we did have an election in Kosovo which firmly repudiated the views of that very minority. And to suggest that we are to in fact move our policy on the question of independence because there may be a minority that does take up arms because they don't like the political situation in which they are in, that doesn't seem to me to be the right way to pursue this policy.

I'm a little concerned we may be driving a policy because of concerns about a bunch of KLA rebels not wanting to live in the kind of society that is emerging in Kosovo. I mean, we cannot accept the proposition that just because there are a bunch of KLA people running around who want independence that the international community then just has to give it to them. The vast majority of the Albanians living in Kosovo today want to get on with their lives. They don't want to be dominated by Serbs, but they're perfectly happy, for the moment at least, to be protected by a NATO force under a UN mandate and run with a UN administration. They would like to have more say over their affairs, but there isn't a clamour here for a flag and independence.

Far better, in fact, to make very clear to anybody that the force of arms is not the way you achieve your objectives. NATO took upon itself a responsibility when it intervened, not only to make sure that the Kosovar Albanians could come back when they had been kicked out and to protect them, but also to make absolutely sure that the people who were engaged in an armed struggle would not continue that armed struggle in a way that some of them might want to. And I don't think that our policy ought to be driven by those very people. That's why it's so important, for example, to prevent what is happening right now in Presovo.

Kosovo's Future and the Future of the Balkans
Jonathan Levitsky, Former Senior Consul to Ambassador Holbrooke, U.S. Mission to United Nations

I want to thank Justice Goldstone and the members of the Commission for their very detailed and extremely thoughtful report. I think it's a matter of record that's been well established before the group this morning that my government doesn't agree with every recommendation or idea expressed in the report. But I do think it's an extremely exhaustive and interesting document. I appreciated the opportunity to read it, as I know did many other American officials.

As a participant in the events described, I was particularly interested to see the issues from the many different vantage points that you were able to gather. I had my own role in it, but one tends to have a worm's eye view associated with the particular part of it you played. It was an extremely interesting document, I thought.

Let me turn to Kosovo and the Commission's recommendations on its future a bit backwards, if I can, through the lens of the remarkable developments that have taken place in the region over the past months, which for the first time since the break-up of the former Yugoslavia provide an opportunity for this devastated part of the world to get back on its feet.

The leadership change in the region has been dramatic. I was in Dayton, Ohio a week or so ago with Ambassador Holbrooke celebrating the Fifth Anniversary of the Dayton Peace Accords. The remarkable thing about that event is that all three of the major leaders who took centre stage during the peace negotiations had left the scene. Tudjman passed away, and he's been replaced by President Stipe Mesic, an honourable man who ran on a platform of full support for the Dayton Accords. President Izetbegovic of Bosnia has taken a well-deserved retirement after years of distinguished service. And, of course, Milosevic, the arsonist of the Balkans, who bears so much responsibility for the horrible events of the last years, has been toppled in a peaceful revolution, a remarkable exhibition of people-power that I don't think any of us Balkan analysts predicted would come as rapidly or as peacefully as it did.

These are very hopeful developments. The changes are good news for Bosnia, which stands a chance to finally be cut free from neighbours' intent on undermining the Dayton Accords, whatever their public pronouncements to the contrary were.

It's good news for Montenegro, which finally stands a chance – after the December 23rd elections – to negotiate with the democratically elected leadership in Serbia and the Federal Republic of Yugoslavia about its future and their future relationship. They seem poised to do that.

Finally, and I take into account the concerns professed by Professor Falk, I think it's also good news for Kosovo, although the situation there is still very difficult.

Consistent with UN Security Council Resolution 1244, the first democratic elections in Kosovo's history were recently held. The people of Kosovo voted overwhelmingly for democratically minded and basically civilian leaders. The end of Milosevic's rule also means that Kosovo no longer faces the serious near term threat of military attack by Serb military forces, and that is a dramatic positive development and a significant change. Finally, Milosevic's exit presents an opportunity to end a series of policies that he was pursuing *sub rosa* in an effort to destabilize the situation in Kosovo, building upon the high level of ethnic tension that was pre-existing and exacerbating that tension.

These positive developments cannot, of course, obscure the grave challenges that Kosovo continues to face. But I think most of them are internal rather than external. They have a lot less to do with the future status of Kosovo than with the discrete problems that Kosovo faces in and of itself for wholly different reasons. Let me lay them out for you. I class these problems as: combating Kosovo's own political instability and problems of criminality; managing and stopping the mistreatment of non-Albanians remaining in Kosovo; getting Kosovo back on its economic feet; avoiding the greater Albania trap, which goes to the Presovo Valley issue that Professor Falk raised and I'll say a little bit more about in a minute; and finally political status, an issue that everybody likes to talk about over coffee and cigars, but one that in fact probably has very little impact on the lives of the people in Kosovo on a day-to-day basis, for now anyway. So I'll get to the status issue, but let me talk about the other things that I think are more important from the perspective of people actually living in Kosovo.

The first challenge is to get the transition to democratic government right, and to avoid the political instability and corrosive criminality that are so pervasive in post-conflict situations. A critical part of the problem for the Kosovars is insuring that they can develop a democratic process that really works. It's not an easy thing, despite the fact that they have a sizeable number of NATO troops on the ground to help provide basic security.

The recent attacks on political party members in Kosovo are not a very good sign, for example. There is a serious risk that Kosovo could develop a weak democracy rather than a deep democracy. The Kosovars must avoid a situation in which the democratic system, although formally in place, is so wholly subverted by criminal elements and people acting outside the confines of the system that the duly elected government's formal writ of authority doesn't extend much beyond its own capital building. This is a real risk. It is something that the international community is going to have to exercise continuing vigilance over, and it is probably one of the gravest risks that Kosovo faces.

I would add to the list the continuing mistreatment of the Serbs and the other non-Albanians in Kosovo, which is, as everyone acknowledges, wholly unacceptable, even if somewhat understandable given the horrible things that were done to Albanians by Serbs both in the run up to the conflict and during the NATO campaign. As David Rieff has accurately pointed out, there are really deep rooted hatreds in Kosovo. And as anybody who has spent a lot of time in Kosovo and Bosnia both will know, those hatreds are sufficiently deep rooted in Kosovo that I think the differences between the two places are one of kind rather than merely degree.

Kosovo has also got to get its economic house in order, and to some extent that is linked to status issues. There is no doubt that there is a level of investor confidence that is hard to come by when people are not sure what the long term value of the economic assets that they are investing in a place are going to be. There's no question that is true. But if you go to Kosovo and spend a little time there, I think it becomes clear that that's really the least of the problems. The fundamental problems in Kosovo go back to the issues of criminality, of forming stable and functioning governmental institutions. Indeed, investment is already starting to trickle in, including international investment, in the most appealing industrial properties anyway.

Now to the greater Albania trap. This is sort of an old canard in a way that the Kosovo Albanians are seeking to create a pan-Albanian union, which would bring in a part of Macedonia and a part of Serbia. This would be incredibly destabilizing in the region. And it's certainly true that there are a handful of extremists who are acting now in the ground safety zone across the way from the Kosovo border, the internal boundary, who are creating real concern at the moment. My government spends a lot of time telling these people, directly and through people who know them, that they have to cut it out, that they're doing no good for Kosovo or for the cause that they profess to care about. This is a neuralgic problem that we will continue to deal with. It's not very pleasant, but I think the important thing about it is that it really reflects the views of a small and disgruntled minority rather than being a mass movement. Again, that's something that you find out if you go to Kosovo and talk to people, not just from conversations in the Pristina coffee houses, but through talks in the villages across the way from the Presovo Valley.

Now, finally we get to the status issue. This is the headline issue that everybody wants to talk about. The news about this is fairly straightforward, really. The process for dealing with Kosovo's future status is laid out clearly in Resolution 1244, but that does not mean that the answer is laid out. Let me say a few things about 1244, which I had a hand in drafting, though I won't accept responsibility for all the bad things that people say about it, because, as you all know, it was the product of a tough negotiation.

First of all, contrary to what I am afraid is some sloppy language in the Commission's report, Resolution 1244 doesn't require renewal. It is self-renewing. That was a point that was much negotiated in Bonn. Resolution 1244 will continue in force indefinitely until the status issue is resolved. That's the first point.

The second thing is that Resolution 1244 leaves open the issue of Kosovo's future status, at least in my government's view. There is disagreement in the international community about this, a matter of interpretation. But in our view, all the options are on the table, and nothing is either required or precluded. Resolution 1244 says clearly that there's going to be an international process to resolve status at some future date. In our view, the references to sovereignty and territorial integrity in the preambular language are carefully bracketed and sufficiently counterpoised by other language in the text that they're not the defining elements of the document. All of those bits and pieces were heavily negotiated. I know I've gone through this with Gareth Evans, and I would be happy to go through it with any others who are interested in hearing our legal reasoning as to the interpretation of Resolution 1244. But needless to say, this is the position of the United States government, and we spent a lot of time insuring that Resolution 1244 would leave those issues open.

Now it's clear that before the status issues are addressed Kosovo is going to have to develop democratic self-government. Resolution 1244 is unambiguous about this step in the process. The municipal elections were an important first step, but it's not done. UNMIK is planning on moving toward – UNMIK meaning the UN Mission in Kosovo – is planning on moving forward toward Kosovo-wide elections in the spring. Then over time UNMIK is going to transfer authority to these new Kosovo institutions, although it will retain some crucial powers. The analogy that I have in mind here is really sort of like the High Rep's office in Bosnia. In the end, the people of Kosovo are going to run their own lives. There will be a residual role for the United Nations to preserve the rights and interests of minorities and to insure that Resolution 1244 is protected, but the UN and its associated pillars will get out of the business of trying to run Kosovo on a day-to-day basis. This is all to the good, frankly, because the UN is not particularly well-suited to the job, and the institutional arrangements that we bequeath to the United Nations in order to carry out this goal have hampered rather than aided that task. And then we'll see.

The fact is that the parties are very far apart. While Milosevic's departure permits a serious conversation for the first time, it doesn't change the Serbs' basic position that Kosovo can't be split with Yugoslavia, and that the Serb refugees have to have a chance to come home. Nor does it in any way affect the almost universal Kosovo Albanian desire for independence. Resolving this impasse is going to be a major challenge for the next administration. But I'll say one thing that is clear. Both sides are going to have to accept the deal, whatever the final deal is, because otherwise the war is going to restart, and the international community's efforts will all have been in vain.

The critical thing to note for now is that neither party is pressing us to resolve this issue. In fact, to the contrary, I think they would all be delighted if we would not put this issue on the table right now. Kosovo needs democratically elected leaders who can represent it at the highest levels. Forcing the Kosovars to have a conversation about their status before the issue of who leads them is settled is extremely dangerous, frankly, for the leadership class in Kosovo and for the development of democracy there. Similarly, Serbia needs to consolidate its democracy. A rapid movement forward on status issues and putting the new Yugoslav government and the Serb government under pressure to resolve those issues would do grave damage to the democratic forces in Yugoslavia.

Above all, the situation needs some time to calm down. We all have to remember that we are just a year and a half away from a brutal war. We need to resist the desire to push the parties to rapidly resolve a dispute that they themselves are not particularly eager to resolve right now.

Let me wrap up by making a general point that I think holds true for the region as a whole, and it follows up on something that Bob Keohane said. We are not going to be able to make progress anywhere in the Balkans until the traditional notions of sovereignty begin to give way to something greater, until the people of the region start thinking of themselves as much as Europeans as Albanians, Serbs, Croats and Muslims. The zero-sum nature of the current game makes it extremely difficult to move forward. That means giving real meaning and content to this vague notion of a European future for the Balkans, in which national boundaries matter a lot less than a common European identity.

I am very aware as an American official that it is not for me to dictate to my European colleagues how this ought to be done. And I am well aware of the tensions generated within the EU on sovereignty issues, particularly in the context of further widening of the Union. But this must be done. For in the end, in my view, the international community's exit strategy from the Balkans must be an entrance strategy for the Balkans into Europe.

Intervention, Protection and Humanitarian Assistance in Kosovo
Joelle Tanguy, US Executive Director, MSF/Doctors without Borders

The discussion on the Commission's Report is quite illustrative of a new trend: with all the talk about humanitarian intervention, there was no mention of humanitarianism at all and none of the experts on the panels ever framed it in a humanitarian perspective!

Should we, humanitarians, rejoice in this re-appropriation of the humanitarian concept and ideals by the political community at large? I am not so sure.

My purpose here will be to highlight humanitarian issues, paradoxes and challenges in Kosovo, and especially those brought about by the concept and practice of military intervention.

You will hear me make the following key points that, I believe, were too little addressed by the commission:

-   That the principles, roles and responsibilities of humanitarian actors were challenged at a fundamental level during the 1999 Kosovo crisis.
-   That the lack of humanitarian protection inside Kosovo was a dramatic flaw of the intervention, a fundamental challenge to its alleged humanitarian nature
-   That NATO's direct involvement in humanitarian action and refugee assistance should be questioned
-   That a key UN agency, UNHCR, should be seriously strengthened rather than undermined as it was in the Kosovo crisis
-   That the relationship between NGOs and the State agencies financing them is too often an incestuous and pernicious one, blurring the lines and ultimately challenging the consolidation of a community of impartial and independent humanitarian actors.

But first, we need to have a hard look at the expression that filled the commission's report: that of "humanitarian intervention".

Military or humanitarian intervention?
As Rony Brauman developed last year in an editorial in *Le Monde*, humanitarian intervention, grounded in the Geneva conventions, was defined over the years by the practice of independent, impartial humanitarian actors. It conveys the *civilian* action to provide assistance in the face of the

consequences of crises, and it does not include the *political and military* actions deployed in response to the *causes* of crises.

Humanitarianism seeks not to stop or influence the outcome of a war but to provide a modicum of humanity at the heart of the war, to assist the most vulnerable, to limit the impact of conflicts on the life and dignity of men, women and children caught in the war-zones.

The words "Humanitarian intervention" do not describe the political and military intervention whose aims, while potentially complementary, are clearly distinct since, unlike humanitarian action, the military and political may seek to prevent conflict, enforce peace or ensure accountability of governments towards minorities rights.

New-age "military interventions" – defined as deployments of military might undertaken in situations involving mass crime or terror – may be at times not only appropriate, but necessary, required, just, desirable, maybe even effective; they could also become legitimate and accountable with a little help. But that does not make them humanitarian.

The expression itself "humanitarian military intervention" and its associated legalistic rationale the "right to intervene", or "authority to intervene", mix two approaches which, though not mutually exclusive, weaken each other when they are combined. Both approaches may be necessary, but in order to serve their purposes, we believe that humanitarian and military work must carried-out independently.

You may wonder why I insist, at this important moment, on a matter of simple semantics. Let me be clear: this is not about semantics, nor is it the last effort of a humanitarian "arrière-garde" to stick to an old and obsolete model! More than an oxymoron, more than a confusing slogan, "humanitarian (military) intervention," it is a dangerous one.

The danger we see is the legitimate suspicion that would then be cast on humanitarians on the ground, that they and the intervening military forces and their political coaches are no different, that aid workers are the infantry of NATO or other intervention forces. This suspicion, were it to rise, would lock forever access to the needy civilians in the war zones and make relief workers undesirables, even hostages or targets.

It would have a disastrous impact on the perception of and therefore the capacity of humanitarian agencies to respond to humanitarian challenges. As has been acknowledged, military intervention would favour only a few situations where humanitarian needs line up with a modicum of national interest. For the vast majority of the 39 million refugees and displaced, of millions caught in war or social conflict, the confusion of roles would instead hinder relief operations.

The Commission states that in its intent to codify the conditions for such interventions it does not seek to "let the genie of human rights imperialism out of the bottle but to prevent a doctrine of intervention from becoming a license for the unprincipled exercise of great power politics". It sounds great, but I wonder, given the inter-changeability in the commission's report between the words "humanitarian intervention" and the meaning of "states' military intervention", if we might not be inadvertently letting another genie out of the bottle: a toxic one for humanitarian action. I don't think any of us here are ready to move forward on the recommendation of the Commission at the cost of sacrificing the identity and challenging the capacity of the independent civilian humanitarian movement to be credibly and responsibly responding to the 99% other humanitarian crises.

So, let's agree to talk about humanitarian intervention when referring to civilian action, military intervention when referring to military action, and to forget the fallacious slogans of military humanitarianism, and military-humanitarian interventions.

On the rationale for intervention
The role of humanitarians in calling for intervention
Some critics point out to an inconsistency in the thinking of humanitarians. They highlight the fact that "it is humanitarian agencies and human rights groups, not governments that have tended to demand militarised humanitarian responses" They highlight that "national militaries tend to be opposed to such actions [...And that in the case of Kosovo,] it was humanitarian groups themselves that, through media campaigns and private lobbying with governments, helped build the consensus for military intervention."

MSF did not formally call for the interventions in Somalia, Bosnia, or Kosovo. We actually consciously abstained. In the case of Kosovo, we also attempted to resist – not always successfully I reckon – the pressure to join or feed the NATO propaganda machine. Nevertheless, it is true that our vision of humanitarian action, with its central notion of "témoignage", implies that each volunteer is not only providing medical care but also bearing witness, seeking, locally and internationally, to build outrage and stimulate action. If this vision of solidarity captures the mind of Americans and Europeans and stimulate political action, it's all for the better.

But we must again make a distinction between humanitarian and political actions. Humanitarian crises are the symptoms and consequences of severe political crises, for which political initiatives are required locally and sometimes internationally. Military intervention is then a tool of political intervention seeking to address the root causes of the problem.

I think it is worth repeating that "International humanitarian law spells out the role of humanitarian actors – as distinct from political actors – in the protection of civilians in times of war. Protection is defined by two components. One aspect of protection is the provision of *material assistance* to civilian victims, which is coordinated by U.N. agencies and nongovernmental agencies, such as MSF. The second aspect is the responsibility of humanitarian actors to monitor vigilantly the conditions of war that impinge on civilian safety. Such conditions may include the deliberate targeting of civilians, diversion of food aid, manipulation of humanitarian assistance to achieve strategic advantage, or forced regroupment of populations. Humanitarian actors on the ground must identify these wrong doings and demand that they be stopped."

In our recent field experience, we have seen numerous failings on the political front, accompanied by a blurring of roles, as those who are entrusted with implementing the diplomatic response have become more involved in the provision of humanitarian aid – masking their inability to resolve the underlying conflict.

Even the ICRC is outspoken on this point and states that "there is no substitute for the political will to find a political solution. Such political commitment is essential if military and humanitarian action are to remain effective". Well, we saw the results in Srebrenica...

I believe however that a modicum of political will was engaged in the case of the Kosovo intervention, I just deplore that we had to dress a political initiative in humanitarian clothes.

On the rationale for intervention
The manipulation and blurring of roles
I'd like to come back on the rationale for intervention and focus on the manipulation and the blurring of roles. Let me explain:

In the presence of a modicum of political will but the absence of true political (public) consensus and leadership, belligerent states and forces had to appear acting in direct humanitarian action in order to make the intervention palatable to the public. That is exactly what happened. But it was achieved through a major reshuffling and blurring of roles. And that was done at the cost of the identity of independent humanitarian actors in the region and potentially at the cost of their future positioning in humanitarian crises in general.

These points are illustrative of the tremendous blurring of roles occurred in the theatre of the Kosovo operation:

- Most relief organizations supported belligerent propaganda and accepted a role of contracted service providers for belligerent states. Through bilateral initiatives belligerent countries sidelined the agency legally entrusted with the negotiation of the protection of refugees,
- NATO forces supposed to be addressing human rights violations in Kosovo actually chose to not take risk there and postured as relief operators in Albania and Macedonia.
- Several North-American humanitarian organizations allowed themselves to be infiltrated by staff from political, human rights and other institutions and helped them pose as humanitarian actors.
- Several international humanitarian organizations were plagued by inner dissent brought about by divergent national sensitivities to the conflict.
- When UNMIK was set up, the UN humanitarian agency UNHCR was brought into the infrastructure of a UNMIK government progressively drawn into the political conflict, thereby finally undermining UNHCR stance of impartiality.

In our 1999 annual report, we attempted to look back at the series of events that progressively transformed the Kosovo theatre into a rather confused circus, and noted that: "Within days of bombing Kosovo and Serbia, NATO and its member states gave logistical support toward the humanitarian effort. Given the size and speed of the humanitarian need, this was necessary – as in many other circumstances this decade – but risked extending to a de facto control of independent and impartial humanitarian efforts."

Seeing the public relations advantage toward their home-publics, NATO and its member states began building refugee camps in the region. Either directly or in collaboration with NGOs, they also wanted to manage those camps. Yet despite the disproportionate financial cost to NATO, in Albania for example, only a small proportion of refugees were actually housed in NATO-built camps. The vast majority were accommodated privately in the homes of Albanians, or scattered throughout the country in make-shift camps and collection centres.

By assuming a so-called humanitarian role, NATO was trying to improve its public image. However, many of its actions were incorrect, so that in some cases sites were poorly selected, and camp-layout and water and sanitation services had to be re-done according to correct UNHCR standards.

MSF refused to collaborate with NATO or its member states on refugee camp management, and unequivocally refused funding from NATO member states. Why? Because as actual parties at war in the conflict, they could not be seen as impartial supporters of humanitarian action, and collaboration of this kind could put the security of refugees at risk. This was born out when Serbian forces began shelling into Albania in regions where camps had been set up.

Meanwhile governments' propaganda was seeking to further blur the lines. In a good public-relations gesture – actually supported by several US humanitarian agencies! – President Clinton announced the establishment of an 800 number: 1-800-US AID KOSOVO. While the number was featured to and by the media as channelling citizen's private funds to independent private agencies, it was actually managed by FEMA and USAID who soon found a way to suggest that this government agency should take over and channel through a re-granting process some of the funds received!

These moments also highlighted the difficulty among humanitarian agencies to focus on principles and affirm the distance from national propaganda. This was true here, in the USA. It was also well illustrated in the difficulties of Greek sections of international humanitarian agencies (MSF and MDM) to resist the temptation of state sponsored humanitarian intervention in Serbian territory.

In such situations when the government turns belligerent, few agencies are able to affirm their independence, and protect the special place of civilian humanitarianism.

MSF sought to preserve this independence and resolved to fund its operations during the war exclusively on private donors' funding, refusing NATO funding and rebelling against the Clinton-FEMA-USAID artifice. As I mentioned, we also attempted to enforce the separation of mandates and duties in the field. Nevertheless, within the "humanitarian community", these moves remained a minority gesture and ultimately led possibly to a more symbolic than effective impact.

Meanwhile, funding dependency, other incestuous ties and a confusion on principles, led several agencies to misinterpret their own mandate. In one the two worse cases developed yesterday by David Rieff, accusations of spying led to the arrest of 2 representatives of Care Canada in FRYI.

I enjoyed Benjamin Barber's comment that we have globalised markets, economies, labour, disease, crime, terrorism without enabling the globalisation of governance and civil society, factors which still remain confined within the box of nationality – in other words that we enabled a "globalisation of our vices without globalisation of our virtues". It is essential that the humanitarian movement, grounded in civil society take on that challenge, and that relief organizations, now generically labelled "NGOs", choose their path between being grounded in civil society or being instruments of foreign policy.

If I insist on this it is also because what keeps us, humanitarians, alive in the middle of war zones is not the military forces we bring along, it is more ultimately the clarity of our humanitarian purpose and principles, and the transparency of our intent, our value for the community and the perception of impartiality and neutrality. That perception not a given but is acquired though each day, each relief-worker, each action. "Our weapons are our transparency, the clarity of our intentions, as much as our medicines and our surgical instruments". Forgetting this may mark the end of effective humanitarian assistance and close the path to the victims of war and civil conflict.

On Protection and Security
I'd like now to say a few words on the respective cornerstones of humanitarian and military interventions: protection and security.

As the bombing campaign intensified, NATO's public relations increasingly focused on the work NATO was doing outside Kosovo for the refugees. In contradiction to this, MSF systematically surveyed and publicly released the stories of people leaving Kosovo; their experiences of rape, massacre and torture, and the beaten, killed, abandoned or lost family members remaining behind.

In one survey conducted in Montenegro at the end of April, 28% of refugees had left at least one member behind in Kosovo, and 10% had wounded, killed or missing family members. At the height of the bombing and NATO's public relations campaign, MSF publicly called attention to the 'forgotten' people still inside Kosovo in the hands of the Milosevic government- those without humanitarian protection or assistance.

But our message seemed to be only partially heard: the plight of the Kosovar described by our teams seemed to strengthen the public resolve to support NATO but never achieved to challenge publicly NATO in its approach to protection issues within Kosovo. Therefore I appreciate the Commission effort to finally highlight this point and state that "once hostilities began, the exclusive reliance on air power proved incapable of stopping civilian expulsions, ethnic cleansing and murder" and that in the future we "must take measures to protect all civilians".

There is again a contradiction though.

The report states that the military operation was illegal but legitimate. Legitimate because of its stated humanitarian intent, or in the words of Richard Goldstone: " *The NATO operation was clearly illegal, in contravention of the UN charter; but it was somehow legitimate in the sense that it was morally and politically justifiable, as massive breach of human rights cannot be ignored because of sovereignty.*"

Yet, when it cam to strategizing, the plight of civilians within Kosovo proper was ignored. While the 800,000 refugees certainly had needs, those people who remained trapped and brutalized inside Kosovo were completely without humanitarian protection and security.

Even on the refugee side, the protection aspects seemed to have been handled questionably. And that was best illustrated by the side-lining of the UN High Commissioner for Refugees. Effective registration of refugees – a fundamental first step to protecting their political rights as refugees – became all but impossible. As the lead UN Agency in this setting, UNHCR had the legitimate responsibility of setting humanitarian priorities around assistance and protection, and ensuring that these are implemented. It failed.

Ethics and International Law
Among issues raised by the Commission are issues of ethics and international law. The first such question that comes to mind is:

> If we are really committed to the safeguarding of human rights even militarily, is it really compatible with a war doctrine in which we're willing to kill but not to die?

The Kosovo intervention actually brought about a lot of questions in this area. When the military must be immortal, and only civilians, journalists and aid-workers are allowed to die in a conflict, the military strategies are limited. So-called "surgical strikes" in Serbia did not provide the protection needed on the ground in Kosovo and actually precipitated the sudden and massive deportation of Kosovars, accelerating the spread of civilian violence in the region while actually provoking the humanitarian crisis that the intervention sought to prevent.

On the issue of legal framework, I do not feel qualified to comment on the specific Commission's recommendation of principles to qualify and codify military intervention in response to grave violations of human rights. But somehow all of us, confronted since the Gulf War to various forms or intervention reportedly started on humanitarian impulse, can only ask the following:

> If we are really committed to the safeguarding of human rights even militarily, shouldn't we have the instruments to make intervention legitimate and accountable? The NATO intervention was illegal, not having sought the blessing of the Security Council. Worse, is the Security Council a credible arbitrator for peace?

Then, even Security Council initiated operations have limited accountability and transparency mechanisms. Peacekeepers have repeatedly breached human rights and humanitarian laws themselves!

A key obstacle to decisive action by the U.N. Security Council is the ability of any of its five permanent members to veto a public security resolution dealing with the protection of civilians. In the case of Chechnya, it is notable that the Council has not even been able to discuss the issue of protection of the civilian population, presumably because Russia would veto any Security Council action in the conflict. When considering protection of civilians, the Security Council should adopt new rules related to the use of the veto, and to the rationale behind each state's vote.

The Security Council must also affirm the independence of U.N. agencies such as UNICEF and the U.N. High Commissioner for Refugees (UNHCR) to implement humanitarian assistance that is independent from its own political priorities. The humanitarian independence of these agencies is compromised when the U.N. is also engaged in political measures such as sanctions or peacekeeping operations. This has been the case in numerous situations, such as Sierra Leone and Angola, where U.N. humanitarian agencies have not set up programs in areas controlled by a faction upon which the U.N. system was applying political pressure.

Beyond Kosovo

Let me conclude this discussion on Kosovo by leaving Kosovo for a while.

Forty million people are displaced by conflicts, most of them resource-less and traumatized. Eighty percent of them are women and children. Displacement easily leads to 30 fold increases in mortality. The children under 5 are the first to die. Their elders, if they stay alive, are often stripped of their dignity and rights. Surviving on humanitarian assistance is no great solution and definitely not a long term one. In public health terms, being a refugee in a camp, being dependent of food aid, is a most precarious condition that often leads to excess mortality and morbidity. In human terms it's unbearable.

I need not say more about the plight of civilians caught in the violent collapse of their countries, of their communities, witness and victims to mass crime or terror. It is those very situations that the new age "military interventions" or "protective interventions" would seek to address. Military deployment would seek to root out the causes of the massive mortality and suffering whereas humanitarian assistance only acts out as a palliative. What is at stake is great.

With that in mind, let me leave one plea and two questions with you. First the plea: let us abandon the label of "humanitarian intervention" for military ones. Then the questions:

If we are really committed to the safeguarding of human rights even militarily, shouldn't we have the instruments to make intervention le-gitimate and accountable?

If we are really committed to the safeguarding of human rights even militarily, is it really compatible with a war doctrine in which we're willing to kill but not to die?

A Commission Response
Professor *Richard Falk*, Princeton University

It is a privilege to be part of this process of reflection and reconsideration, I was very stimulated and challenged by the earlier remarks, but I will resist the temptation to respond directly, because it would, I'm afraid, consume the whole time available for my presentation.

Let me say that the basic perspective, I think, that underlay the approach of the Commission and my own thinking was to seek to do our best to learn from the Kosovo experience and to translate that learning into a perspective that might enable a somewhat more successful response to subsequent challenges which we regarded as part of the texture of international society as it is evolving in this post-Cold War world. In that context of learning from the successes and failures of responses to humanitarian catastrophe, I think it's very important to have humility in our relationship to these confusing, and often ambiguous, realities. They are extraordinarily complex to begin with, and because of the complexity and the effort to mobilize political consciousness in one or another direction, there is a strong temptation to manipulate the mind of the public and of the media in a preferred policy direction. This tendency to "spin" the news about human suffering overseas makes it that much more difficult to penetrate the opaqueness of the factual reality. This opaqueness of the reality is one of the reasons, I think, why ethically motivated and intelligent individuals can take very opposite views as to the viability and desirability of a particular interventionary response. It has been commonly observed that there is no ideological coherence with respect to the debate over instances of humanitarian intervention such as Kosovo, with critics and advocates interspersed across the entire left/right political spectrum.

And I must say, just speaking personally for a moment, that I have been generally over the years critical of interventionary diplomacy, even when it has a humanitarian cover. I suppose this scepticism partly exhibits the lasting effects of my opposition to the Vietnam intervention. And what altered my view in relation to the NATO War to a significant extent was the experience of being in Kosovo itself, and with it the opportunity to observe the realities on the ground. I think it was very important to the work of the Commission to have had this direct contact with the existential experience of the sort of suffering that Serb domination had brought to the majority Albanian population Kosovo for so long. From an emancipatory perspective, military intervention played an indispensable role in freeing 90% of the Kosovo population from a regime of oppression. It is important to realize that even if the search for a diplomatic solution at Rambouillet had succeeded, it would not have had a comparable emancipatory impact to that achieved by NATO, and then a strong UN presence. At the same time it is necessary to acknowledge that this emancipatory effect became tainted due to failure to prevent the reverse ethnic cleansing at the expense of the suddenly beleaguered Serb minority (and their ethnic allies) in Kosovo. There were definite failures by the UN and KFOR to be more robust in their early efforts early to protect these newly vulnerable minorities. It had been the case that it was the majority that was the vulnerable and threatened constituency in Kosovo. One of the effects of the NATO War that should have been anticipated and acted upon, was to make the relatively small minority suddenly extremely vulnerable to retaliatory acts of vengeance. This failure contributed to an overall sceptical view as to the claimed humanitarian motivations for the intervention.

I think Benjamin Barber's remarks this morning were very useful in contextualising Kosovo in a wider global setting. I would like to add only a footnote to what he said. When this transition from the Cold War world to the post-Cold War world occurred at the start 1990s, one of the shifts in world order concerns was from a preoccupation with what strong states might do to one another if there interaction crossed the war threshold to a preoccupation with the global instabilities generated by weak states. If you leave aside the anomalous Gulf War, I think it has become characteristic of this period that the real dangers to world order have emerged out of weak state structures. The adverse effects of these weak or deformed state structures have posed an enormous challenge to those that have been making global policy in leading states and international institutions. It has also been necessary to interpret this altered global setting in such a way as to develop a coherent approach to the challenge of weak state instability. How can these issues be addressed in an international framework that continues to give legal and moral deference to sovereignty and the territorial supremacy of states. What kind of balance should be struck between sovereign rights and the protection of fundamental human rights? Who should interpret this balance, especially if leading states cannot agree on a common course of action? These issues were underscored by the controversy that has surrounded all phases of the Kosovo intervention, and remains unresolved.

There is a further element that needs to be taken into account when one adopts a broad historical view of intervention and is appropriately scepti-cal of any ethical claims made on its behalf. It is relevant to note that the rise of an international human rights culture and awareness is something that has emerged gradually, and only in this very recent period has it given rise to credible advocacy of interventionist diplomacy. Of course, there is a long history of interventions undertaken by the strong states of the North, usually accompanied by normative justifications, but these uses of force seemed invariably self-serving and a dimension of colonialist diplo-macy. With the advent of international human rights as a significant di-mension of world order there is generated for leaders and citizens an an-guishing dilemma – either watching while a humanitarian catastrophe un-folds, or doing something about it in a hurry. The challenge to act is too complex and contextual to indict a society that chooses the option of non-intervention. The effects of intervention are so uncertain that it is never clear beyond a reasonable doubt that the benefits of action will outweigh the harm done. Each case requires a subtle assessment of the factors at work, including the willingness of the prospective interveners to bear the burdens and accept the risks of their own possible losses.

It is important to seek a high degree of convergence between the political engagement undertaken, and the moral imperative that prompts interven-tion. I completely agree with David Rieff's realist insistence that we not expect to recruit interveners from among the ranks of disinterested states. The absence of strategic incentives should not operate as a prerequisite for a valid instance of humanitarian intervention. Rather such an absence should be treated as an alarm bell that warns us that any undertaking will likely be inconsequential, and may easily backfire. Paradoxically, it is rarely, if ever, advisable to support a humanitarian intervention that is dis-interested. The experience with Somalia in the early 1990s suggested the logistical precariousness of a humanitarian intervention that seemed genu-inely motivated by a mainly American concern for the human suffering of Somali civilian society. Such an intervention lacks a realist quality of commitment that will withstand resistance in the traumatized society, and therefore the engagement made can quickly evaporates under pressure, as occurred when American casualties resulted. The political culture of inter-vening states is moralistic at the level of rhetoric, but realist at the level of human costs to itself, and will not bear these costs unless they turn out to be nominal or can be justified in more traditional terms of vital national interests. This observation is applies generally, but is particularly applicable to the United States due to its interventionist capabilities, its moralistic pretensions, and its realist and self-regarding political culture.

And just one further point about the comparative results of various interventions is the relevance of political will. Part of the difference between the failure in Bosnia and the relative success in Kosovo was that the main political actors could not afford to allow NATO to fail, whereas they didn't mind the UN failing. It is fundamental to understand that the success of NATO or the failure of NATO was a matter of strategic significance. It was because there existed this strategic interest converging with a humanitarian imperative that established in the Kosovo setting the political grounds for a credible commitment to address the humanitarian catastrophe in an effective way. The absence of such a strategic interest in Bosnia, Rwanda, and many other places, explains either non-action or a trivial response. It is of great importance to identify those strategic interests of intervening states that make it far more likely that a humanitarian intervention will achieve its essential goals. Two further points are relevant. First of all, it is conceptually possible for humanitarian challenges to be regarded as "strategic," but it is not currently the case for most ruling elites and the citizenry of most countries. Secondly, that because there exists a strategic concern, it does not ensure the success of an intervention. Such a conclusion emerges from the long highly dedicated intervention by the United States in Vietnam.

I want now to address briefly the central distinction that the Commission draws between understanding the Kosovo campaign or war as illegal, yet nevertheless regarding it as legitimate. Such a distinction amounts to an attempt to identify the deficiencies of a purely law-oriented approach to behaviour in international relations. This is a risky venture as the word legitimate can be used to evade desirable legal inhibition on the behaviour of states, especially with respect to the use of force. The Commission attempts to walk a tightrope, suggesting that one needs to take seriously Charter inhibitions both on the use of force and on intervening in matters that are normally within the domain of territorial sovereignty, while at the same time recognizing that in exceptional circumstances these constraints need to be loosened for the sake of humanitarian values.

And that one can't just wish away this tension between legality and legitimacy by relying on the sort fancy, high-priced lawyers that became so prominent in the legal battles to resolve disputes about the outcome in Florida that would decide the outcome of the 2000 presidential elections. That fiasco confirmed the sense that skilled lawyers can tell you anything you want to hear, which is one of the more dubious gifts of the legal profession to the daily workings of democracy. But to confuse this sort of fession to the daily workings of democracy. But to confuse this sort of lawyering with effort to bring law to bear in international life is a disservice to this fundamental undertaking to use law as an instrument to promote a more humane world. We need to respect and protect the autonomy of international law, especially with respect to the use of force. Yet in this instance one was confronted here in the aftermath of Srebrenica and in light of the UN failures in Bosnia, with an additional unfolding catastrophe that could not be allowed to happen. It presented an unacceptable outcome that threatened to tarnish European hopes after the Cold War. So the political and moral preconditions for humanitarian intervention existed even though the legal preconditions were not present. The Commission was sensitive to these realities, and to the tensions produced. It acknowledged the legal difficulties with efforts to validate the NATO War and at the same time affirmed the legitimacy of the undertaking, but exhibiting appropriate discomfort about offering such a disjunction. This discomfort is reflected in the Commission efforts to propose a new way of thinking about how the UN should function in these sorts of situations in the future, and what should be done by "coalitions of the willing" that embark on intervention outside the UN framework.

It was against this background that the Commission attempted to formulate a framework for principled humanitarian intervention that set forth a series of eleven considerations that should be taken into account before, during, and after. The essence of these eleven factors is to make prospective interveners satisfy conditions that increase the prospect that a humanitarian intervention is genuinely, and to the extent possible, "humanitarian." I think the separate elements of the approach are worthy of detailed substantive discussion. Unfortunately, in the settings of our discussions such an inquiry would be far too time consuming. What the framework does try to underscore is that recourse to interventionist force should always be a last resort. Beyond this, that the UN should be given every opportunity to address the reality under its authority. But if the UN cannot act, then the international responsibility does not automatically terminate. This is particularly true if available information makes clear that a humanitarian catastrophe is in the making and that there exists the political will and logistical capability to respond effectively to the challenge. In these circumstances, the failure to achieve a UN mandate should not be treated as a conclusive inhibition on the legitimacy of the intervention, but that its degree of legitimacy should be determined by its degree of adherence to the framework of principles.

Given this kind of understanding, the eleven factors or principles also are trying to suggest that a great deal of emphasis should be given in the course of intervention to the means used to carry out a humanitarian mission of this sort. The primacy of the well being of the population that is being protected should operate as a decisive consideration during all stages of the undertaking, including the post-conflict relationship of the interveners (or their successors) to the country in question. In that post-conflict engagement, there should be a maximum commitment of resources and efforts to establish some kind of civic normalcy as rapidly as possible, a necessary condition for humane state-building and democratic governance.

So that what this framework for humanitarian intervention tries to achieve is to set forth some very demanding constraints that will restrict claims to instances of necessity. The Commission is not endorsing a new form of global crusade that casts aside sovereign rights. But it is saying that under exceptional circumstances where the political will, the moral imperative, and some kind of collective commitment is present, then is a beneficial role can be played by intervening to alleviated human suffering in these extreme situations. And it needs to be clearly understood that these are extreme situations, and that only in extreme situations are interventionist claims being vindicated. To meet the combination of conditions will be possible only in most unusual circumstances. These qualifying situations do not fit easily into a world order that is at once predominantly realist in outlook, and must guard against all forms of imprudent risk-taking, whatever the humanitarian motivations. For many suffering peoples the narrowness of this aperture is tragic. From an ethical perspective, something should be done to help the peoples of the Sudan and several other entrapped countries in sub-Saharan Africa. Even in Kosovo the work is not finished by any means, and it could be done better in the future. It is too soon to evaluate the overall results for the peoples involved. The wider effects, including the democratising impacts on Serbia need to be taken into account, but the main basis of evaluation is related to Kosovo, and whether it finds a way for its people to exercise their right of self-determination and to establish within their borders some form of humane governance that protects the dignity of individuals and groups regardless of their ethnic identity.

Let me in concluding just say a word or two about the displacement of Milosevic as the leader of former Yugoslavia. As soon as I heard this welcome news, I worried about its implications for the future of Kosovo. I applauded the removal of Milosevic, and especially his removal through a constitutional process that involved his repudiation by Serbians. At the same time, it seemed to me that it was very likely that this would have the unintended side effect of once again removing Kosovo from the visible political agenda of Europe and the United States. In effect, there would be such a strong impulse to see that Kostunica succeeded that a maximum effort would be made by Washington and NATO not to undermine his nationalist credentials by pushing him hard on Kosovo. And this in turn, one had to assume, would cause great anxiety to the Kosovars who are most mindful of being forgotten by the international community, and of the dire consequences that can follow. The Kosovars were worried that such a process would likely push them back across the threshold of violence. Much of the population in Kosovo "learned" in the 1990s that the only way they can be heard internationally is by generating some kind of violence that will then produce a reaction, an overreaction by the Serbs, which will act to awaken the international community. This seems to be precisely what has been in recent months in Kosovo. Because of the electoral drama in Florida and the second intifada in the Middle East diverted world attention, events in the Balkans slipped again into the background of media and political consciousness in this period. We did not read much about Kosovo developments, but there were operations by Kosovar militants in the Presovo Valley Albanian villages where the KLA has penetrated, killed Serbian police, and then to a greater extent in Macedonia where the KLA joined with indigenous Albanians to challenge the established order.

It becomes clear that unless the humanitarian goals of the NATO campaign are sustained in this altered setting, the credibility of the initial diplomacy could be eroded, if not altogether undermined. A second phase of humanitarian catastrophe for Kosovo cannot be ruled out, and it would likely spread beyond Kosovo. Events in Macedonia already prefigure such a process. So we are confronting, I think, a very serious new challenge as to whether the moral and political resolve that led to the earlier NATO/UN commitment in the first place can be sustained in this new situation. I think it is very important that people in civil society here and in Europe concerned about the Balkans do let the policy makers and leaders forget Kosovo once more.

Conclusion
Honorable *Carl Tham,* Commission Co-Chair

When we look at the Kosovo intervention, it becomes clear that it did not so much create a precedent for intervention elsewhere, as it raised vital questions about the legitimacy and practicability of the use of military force to defend human rights and humanitarian values in the 21st Century. We've added a little more by pointing out the problems of how this may be accomplished – and the difficulties implicit in the idea of protecting human rights by military means. We conclude that there is a lesson here calling for scepticism and caution.

Of course, that was also the starting point of the seminar, when we discussed the future of humanitarian intervention. We suggested that it should be brought into the framework of the United Nations. This is not really a very new idea or even a bold one, because it has been suggested repeatedly by other institutions and also, as you know, by the Secretary General and, in fact, by his predecessor as well. We recognize that there is certainly a natural, and in some cases a well-founded, suspicion among what we can call the Third World countries against the idea of intervention. They have in their history, both distant and recent, the memory of numerous colonial interventions, and in many cases long wars of liberation. So for them intervention could be seen as Western interference in what they perceive to be legitimate domestic affairs.

So for these reasons, we feel it is very important to put this discussion of humanitarian intervention into the context of the United Nations, and hopefully, into the charter. At the very least as we've talked about the possibility of a General Assembly resolution. This is what we mean when we discuss the somewhat idealistic idea of a "code of citizenship" for nations, which both protects states against interference and at the same time guarantees their inhabitants protection when human rights are systematically abused. We, of course, understand that it is not easy to create such a "code of citizenship" but we hope that we can start a discussion.

We also think here it is very important to have a free discussion not only among the UN's member governments and official institutions, but also among the institutions of civil society around the world, about how to redefine the rights of citizens and states in that context.

To comment on the need for preventative diplomacy, I think you can say that hopefully diplomacy is a means of preventive action. There are also efforts to take action in cases where crises have not yet fully emerged. But this is difficult to accomplish, given the suspicion that naturally still complicates relations between the North and the South. For example, the European Union has recently tried to put pressure on the government of Burma in regards to human rights, but that resulted in a reaction not only from Burma, but unfortunately also from many other Asian states or governments. They believe human rights in Burma are not the concern of the European Union, that it is purely the concern of the Burmese government and its people. So the pressure to improve the human rights situation in Burma was not fully successful. This just illustrates that we have an uphill struggle to get these kinds of ideas and policies accepted.

The key problem of preventive diplomacy is, of course, that if there is a lot of pressure on a specific government and then nothing happens, what to do next? There is, of course, the threat of force as a last resort. But then the threat of force in itself, which I think we illustrate clearly in the case of Kosovo, may undercut the diplomatic effort to reach a solution. So the threat of force is always a dangerous thing to put into the context of a diplomatic effort. On the other hand, it may be the only way for the preventive diplomacy to have any impact. This was the dilemma in the case of Kosovo. On the one hand, given the experience of Milosevic and what happened in the Balkans during the 1990's, it was rather unreasonable to believe that only the threat of force would move Milosevic to any kind of negotiations. On the other hand, the threat of force, that is, forced negotiations with the threat of force, is against the UN charter, making it more difficult to reach an agreement, not only because of Milosevic's position, but also because of the KLA position. Another problem about the threat of force in this case was that it threatened exactly what the KLA wanted, NATO intervention.

We also spoke about the problem that the legitimacy of intervention, specifically a military intervention, would be strongly influenced by the outcome of the action. This is why we think there's a strong link between saying the action was illegal but legitimate, and the proposal of conditional independence for Kosovo. The moral issue was, after all, to liberate the Kosovo Albanians from repression and to give them a chance to create their own future, as well as to create a framework for peaceful governance in the Balkans region and between the different countries in the region. That was the moral basis for the intervention, and if that fails, it fails because of the lack of involvement from not only the NATO countries, but also the European Union and ultimately the United Nations. If it fails because of that lack of interest and involvement, then the legitimacy of the operation will be severely undermined and eroded, and the critics will be right.

So that is the reason why we specify, rather in detail, how this process of conditional independence should be developed. It was said that we should have done this in more detail. But I think all the members of the Commission were surprised that we could produce a report at all in this very short period of time. We couldn't do everything, but I still think we were quite extensive as it was, and we specified the principles on minority rights which have been used here, and which have already been developed by the OSCE as a basis for the future. We discussed how this constitutional regime should be adopted, the role of the United Nations Security Council, and of course the future of the process and the necessity of an international security presence. This is not a proposal for today or tomorrow, we are talking about a long process.

The role of the European Union in this process was briefly discussed as well. First of all, there are those in the European Union who hope that everything is all right and that now that we have done this, we don't need to talk too much about it. It is a question of the past, and hopefully, with the change of government in Serbia, everything will be sorted out given the proper support. But that is certainly wishful thinking. There is much that still has to be done.

The complication is that there is a process for the enlargement of the European Union involving many of the Central European countries, and there are extensive conditions linked to EU membership. There are at least 96,000 rules, which must be accepted and adopted by the countries wishing to join the Union. This means an enormous adjustment, and the countries in the Balkans cannot do this in the foreseeable future.

On the other hand, one can foresee an emerging division in the Balkans between Croatia and Slovenia on the one hand, and the other countries that cannot possibly hope to adopt these conditions in the foreseeable future on the other. The future of the European Union in this regard may be crucial, as well as very complicated. What is needed is another kind of arrangement, and perhaps as we discuss in the report, the Stability Pact could be a model. But that is still one of the many uncertainties you have today in the policies of the European Union. There is much to be learned, and an important task for the future.

May I then address what we have not yet discussed as much, the work of humanitarian organizations. There is a long discussion of this in our report. Certainly, it was and still is a problem that many of the humanitarian agencies have had to work in the context of a military situation, and were constrained by NATO operations.

Peacekeeping includes a humanitarian dimension, and there's a need for greater NATO and EU training in humanitarian activities. What we can say about the humanitarian organization in this context, is that it is impossible to have a clear-cut line between humanitarian activities and security activities. There is also a need for security protection for those people working for humanitarian organizations. Even the Red Cross, which is very strict about maintaining its independence, has now adopted a kind of cooperation with NATO in Bosnia, just for the protection of its personnel. So it's really not possible in such an environment to be totally independent of security considerations.

We have no clear conclusion, we just say that this is a debate, which must continue. There must be more training in cooperation. Again what we stress very strongly is the role of the UNHCR, and here again, this is indeed a lesson for the future, but unfortunately also something which is too often repeated over and over again, primarily because the UNHCR is and has been severely under-funded for a very long time. It has not had enough funding to maintain a proper organization. As soon as there is a new crisis, there is a demand for more money to get through the specific emergency, and the High Commissioner has to shop around in the major capitals for support for the immediate problem. In Kosovo the UNHCR had no information, as there was no information shared between NATO and the UNHCR before the war started. Perhaps NATO had no idea what would happen, and as we say in the report, there seems to have been an underestimation of what the Serbian forces would do during the bombing war.

The UNHCR had no information and consequently it took a lot of time to recruit personnel. They had to take people from other corners of the world to bring to Kosovo, which took time. They also made some errors, of course, and there has been an extensive study of the UNHCR, which we also discussed in the Commission. Our conclusion was that there were mistakes, but the basic problem is still that the UNHCR did not have the necessary resources to cope with a new crisis. Of course, there is always a need for additional personnel. I suppose you can never have a large enough an organization to cope with a crisis of that size, but there must be a stronger core at the UNHCR, and this is very much a lesson for the future. But unfortunately, it is a lesson that has been repeated over and over again, with the same result. The Nordic countries, the Netherlands, Canada, and a few other countries are, in practice, responsible for most of the core funding of the UNHCR, at least in relation to their size. It has been an extraordinarily excessive burden on these countries, while the major powers, the big countries, are paying a rather small share.

I would like to add just one point more about which we haven't yet talked, and that is the role of the media. We haven't made a very large study of this in our report, but we do reflect a little on media issues. I think it was said in a BBC television documentary that the war was won by spin, and we take up this question. Certainly, there was a propaganda war in Serbia and, of course, there were many examples of exaggerated or misleading news from NATO. It is difficult to say if NATO was being deliberately misleading, since it is never clear what happens in a war. But certainly there were mistakes made by NATO in the public relations department, and there was pressure in the NATO countries to give a picture of what was going on which would favour the NATO intervention.

However, even if there was such an effort, which can be disputed, it was not successful. All during the war there was a heavy debate in all NATO countries, more or less, about whether the NATO intervention was correct and if it was efficient or effective. There was a lot of criticism, in fact. So if there was an effort to manipulate the media, it was not successful. Still our main point as a lesson for the future, is that if there is an intervention for humanitarian reasons, it is more important than in so-called normal military operations to disclose all the facts relevant to the public's right to know, and that only very strict military necessity can justify distortion or withholding any information.

Of course, the reason for this is rather evident. Humanitarian intervention depends on the legitimacy of the democratic consent of the countries concerned, and that cannot be based on manipulation. This is always important, but it is more important in humanitarian interventions than in strictly military operations, which are based on other considerations. So we draw a parallel to what we say about warfare. Warfare in humanitarian intervention must be subject to more stringent rules. That is also the reason why we are very critical of the use of cluster bombs and some other forms of conflict. You can see the same theme in our discussion of the media.

At the end, of course, you cannot say that Kosovo was a watershed event and there is a post-Kosovo world order. We do not really believe that. As you may recall, after the Kuwait intervention, the previous President Bush proclaimed a new world order. This was discussed for a few months and then the concept disappeared. Of course, all international events of that size have an impact on international security and the world order. But what happened in Kuwait hasn't changed our entire security perspective. What we say is that Kosovo could be used as an example, and a lesson, about how to protect human rights more efficiently in the future, and that is the hope expressed in our report.

Conference on *Nation Building in East Timor*,
Lisbon, 21-23 June 2001
organized by the Portuguese Centre for the Study of Southeast Asia
and the School of Oriental and African Studies of London University

Nation Building in East Timor

Graça Almeida Rodrigues*

A meeting on *Nation Building in East Timor* was held at the Geographical Society of Lisbon, from June 21 to June 23, 2001. It was organized under the auspices of the Portuguese Centre for the Study of Southeast Asia and the School of Oriental and African Studies of London University.

The main purpose of the meeting was to bring together academics and practitioners in the hope of creating a synergy of complementary experiences. There was a strong presence of Timorese, both academics and practitioners. Most of the Western participants were academics, some of whom had first hand experience of East Timor. A representative of the Embassy of Indonesia in Lisbon took an active part in the debate. The presence of the President of the Pearson Peacekeeping Centre, Alex Morrison, reinforced the notion sometimes absent from academic meetings, that in *Nation Building* action and thought – practice and theory – have to go together to achieve the desired goals. An idea that can only be reinforced by the New Peacekeeping Partnership which brings together military and civil roles and personnel.

East Timor's new nation presents a unique, and to a large extent overwhelming, experience in that its people have never had the opportunity to establish their own autonomous/independent institutions. From 1515 to 1975 East Timor was a Portuguese Colony, with a short interruption by the Japanese invasion and occupation from 1941 to 1945. In 1975 while decolonisation was taking place in the former Portuguese empire, Indonesia unlawfully annexed East Timor as its 27th province.

During the meeting, six working sessions were held namely on Human Rights, Institution Building, Post Colonial Identities and Nationalism, Legacy of Colonialism, Gender Issues and Peacekeeping/Peace Building.

---

* Coordinator of the Seminar, Professor at the Universidade Nova de Lisboa.

M. Bothe and B. Kondoch (eds.),
International Peacekeeping. The Yearbook of International Peace Operations, Volume 7, 2001, 403–408.
© 2002 *Kluwer Law International. Printed in the Netherlands.*

Although some papers focused on theoretical aspects proper [Ivo Carneiro de Sousa, José Manuel Sobral] or on the colonial past of East Timor and the legacies that were passed on [Howard Wiarda, Teotónio R. de Souza], the main focus of the meeting was decisively on the present situation and the future.

The first important conceptual issue was naturally on what constitutes a nation [Armando Marques Guedes]. How are the Timorese going to conceive their own nation? What unites them? Not language. Not ethnicity. No clear-cut feelings of nationalism or national identity. The looting of East Timorese patrimony [Justino Guterres, Virgilio Simith] during the Indonesian occupation presents added difficulties in the consolidation of an East Timor national identity.

Quoting Benedict Anderson, [Armando Marques Guedes] Indonesia's ultimate failure to successfully annex and integrate East Timor was an incapacity to conceive of East Timor as part of their country. How are the East Timorese going to imagine their own national community? Further, quoting Garibaldi, "We have made Italy. We must now make Italians."

East Timor's road to independence was only possible after the end of the Cold War and when the Timorese people received momentous regional and international support. International support to East Timor took years to come. The attention drawn by the press to the Santa Cruz massacre in 1991, the Nobel Peace Prize award to Bishop Ximenes Belo and José Ramos Horta in 1996, were decisive in finally having a United Nations sponsored referendum in 1999.

However, the continued support of the international community is essential [Arnold Kohen]. The repatriation of those East Timorese who want to return from West Timor and other places is a difficult and vital task. The border between East and West Timor remains highly militarised and peacekeeping forces will be necessary for the foreseeable future.

A major danger is the rampant discontent of unemployed youth who see their future threatened by a lack of employment and, in some ways, more difficult access to education than before the withdrawal from Indonesia. The generation gap is also a language gap. Those over 35 usually speak Portuguese, the younger generation was educated in Bahasa Indonesian and spoke Tetum at home. This is a major challenge.

On the positive side there is the role of the new civil society engaged in good governance and organizations devoted to human rights, women's issues, reconciliation, the environment, relief and reconstruction. Most of these groups are led by people under 35 years of age.

There is a clear need for capacity building. As one Timorese put it "East Timorese must be free to make their own mistakes".

These concerns lead to the unprecedented mandate of the United Nations in East Timor [Boris Kondoch], a role that also calls for the need for special training of its staff, particularly in the background and culture of the people they came to assist. This role, with its new responsibilities and demands, is now called the 4th generation of a peacekeeping mission.

The new mandate, besides providing security and maintaining law and order, calls for new responsibilities. This includes the establishment of an administration, assistance in the development of civil and social services, the coordination and delivery of humanitarian assistance, rehabilitation and development, the support of capacity-building for self-government, assistance in the establishment of conditions necessary for sustainable development (S/RES/1338 2001). The new UN terminology is "transitional administration". In a nutshell, to promote good governance. And as quoted from Secretary-General Kofi Annan, "In post conflict settings, good governance can promote reconciliation and offer a path for consolidating peace."

The search for good governance was also emphasized in other ways. Economic justice [Jacqueline Woodman] is essential in post conflict situations for peace and reconstruction, given that the inequity and inefficiency of economic exploitation are invariably destabilizing. Furthermore, the control of resources is critical to ensure that the new nation has the possibility to establish sustainable peace and development. To further this argument, it was regrettable that Minister Mari Alkatiri found it necessary to cancel his participation in the meeting at the very last moment, fortunately, precisely because of engagements in the East Timor Gap's negotiations.

It was also argued [Peter Slinn] that in the search for good governance East Timor may benefit from an international framework support, such as that which the Commonwealth has provided to some 54 countries. This organization could also secure technical and development co-operation between the member states in the perceived needs of East Timor. Could the Community of Portuguese-speaking Countries (CPLP) provide such a framework?

A set of guidelines to outline a strategy for development in East Timor [A. Almeida Serra] was presented, stressing a priority for rural and agriculture development and the need to build a "development-friendly" institutional framework. The role of foreign investments was given close attention.

The meeting welcomed a strong representation of vocal Timorese women. Gender issues were debated [Ivette Oliveira, Milena Pires, Ana Vicente] based on data provided by amongst others, FOKUPERS (Communication Forum of East Timorese Women), the United Nations Civil Police in East Timor, East Timor's Women's Congress reports, UN Human Rights Commission and interviews carried out with Timorese refugees living in the outskirts of Lisbon in 1999. The results were unanimous in showing an unacceptably high proportion of violence against women, in the crimes that were reported. Although it was clearly emphasized that in a society that is pre-eminently patriarchal, women may not report sexual abuse for fear of being judged and treated as outcasts by their families and community. The real numbers are therefore higher than the very high ones already recorded.

Given the cultural and social climate in East Timor, the Catholic Church was often the only institution to receive reports of rape, sexual slavery and general sexual abuse.

In March 1985, Bishop X. Belo reported from Dili a list of people killed in the Craras massacre in 1983. 400 males, adult and children, were killed by the Indonesian military, as a result some 200 women became widows. The only organization to help the victims was the Catholic Church. Recently, in a pastoral letter, dated March 2001, the same Bishop wrote that one of the most serious problems facing East Timor was the violence against women.

The results of the *Survivors Interview Project* [Peter Carey] point to the fact that the reintegration of sexually abused women into Timorese society will be an indicator of the degree of tolerance in the new independent nation. It will show how much traditional East Timorese society has been capable of change. Here again the role of the Church will be challenged, from helping victims to accept different sexual mores, such as contraception and abortion.

Now that the road to independence seems to be open, "the hardest part has yet to be achieved". These are the words of the historic leader, Xanana Gusmão.

A crucial aspect of nation building will be the way in which past conflicts – the atrocities committed – are resolved [Catherine Jenkins]. Inspired by the South African *Truth and Reconciliation Commission*, the National Council of East Timor, approved in June 2001, the UNTAET draft regulation establishing a *Commission for Reception, Truth & Reconciliation in East Timor*. The Timorese Commission will have, in a way, more work than its predecessor, as it will have to deal with the serious issue of the return of refugees. It will also have fewer responsibilities, as it will not be empowered to accord amnesty for "gross" violations of human rights, though it will deal with lesser offences.

It was pointed out that institutions such as Truth Commissions cannot be transplanted from one society to another as some sort of universal panacea. The South African Commission had unquestionable benefits and gave sustaining hope to a new nation. East Timor has a blueprint to follow but also to improve upon. The recommendations presented at the meeting fall well inside the concepts of good governance: promotion of human rights, accountability, redress, tolerance, realistic expectations, social justice, economic development and the celebration of difference. Bishop Tutu's famous statement can well be applied to East Timor, "the rainbow people of God".

A concern for Human Rights – the lifeblood of good governance – permeated the meeting, with one session being dedicated to it exclusively [Isabel Ferreira, William Schabas, Stephen Hopgood, Paula Escarameia].

From a conceptual point of view, a new actor has entered the scene in world affairs, "the international community." This community, with an influence that is being built all over our present world, is prevalent in the UN administration in East Timor. Its agenda includes three aspects, namely the setting-up of a market society, the creation of a political system based on the liberal model instituted in the Constitution, and the respect of human rights (UNTAET has been accused of too high a standard of accountability in this respect). It was considered that the same model was being applied by the international community everywhere, irrespective of the particular circumstances of the case and that its implications were highly negative.

An analysis was made of the state of affairs of the present situation of crimes committed in East Timor. A Special Human Rights Court was created by Indonesia on November 3, 2000. Its material jurisdiction is based on the definitions of the Statute of the International Criminal Court of crimes against humanity and war crimes, with some omissions and excluding pre-referendum acts in East Timor. These courts are not actually functioning. Indonesia has claimed that it has problems in appointing judges. UNTAET regulation 2000/15, gave jurisdiction to East Timorese courts to judge crimes against humanity and war crimes, amongst others, committed in East Timor, without any temporal restrictions, but separating the judgements of regular crimes from those of these special crimes. However, there has been to date but one complete judgment for the perpetration of these serious crimes.

In the broader issue of amnesty vs. prosecution of crimes, the previous position of NGOs and the international community favouring amnesty, has completely changed in the last years, backing now prosecution. This is noticeable with the creation of the Ad Hoc Tribunals for former Yugoslavia and Rwanda by the Security Council, and the International Criminal Court by States at the international level, as well as by the domestic regulations on universal jurisdiction of national courts. Security Council resolutions concerning Timor stressed the importance that justice be proportional to the crimes committed. Although prosecution seemed preferable to amnesty, due to the importance of not erasing history, the impossibility of judging, in practical terms, all those involved in crimes, seemed to indicate the need for institutions such as truth and reconciliation commissions.

The President of the East Timorese Commission on Human Rights focused on the human rights situation in East Timor under Indonesian occupation and at present. She made a report of the major atrocities that took place since the invasion of 1975 and, more recently, in the period before and after the popular consultation. She then analysed the present situation under UNTAET administration and stated that, in some aspects, violations of human rights worsened, mainly because there is no operational judicial system at present and there are abuses by the international police, with arbitrary detentions and few guarantees of defence for those who are arrested.

A selected number of papers will be published in July 2002 by the Pearson Peacekeeping Centre, Canada, edited by Graca Almeida Rodrigues and Heather Wharton.

Civil and Military Administrations
in International Peacekeeping Operations
– Focus on Kosovo –

*Dieter Fleck**

With the Conference on 'Civil and Military Administrations in International Peacekeeping Operations', held at the U.S.-German George C. Marshall European Centre for Security Studies in Garmisch-Partenkirchen from 12-16 March 2001, the Legal Advisor of the United States European Command and the Director, International Agreements & Policy, at the German Ministry of Defence continued a series of meetings for military and civilian lawyers from NATO Member and Partner States on issues of common interest and practical relevance. Previous conferences had been devoted to questions such as the law of visiting forces[1], the application of operational law in military missions and legal issues of European regional peace operations[2]. The focus this year was on different aspects of the peace process in Kosovo. The process has involved the United Nations, OSCE, UNMIK, KFOR, numerous non-governmental organizations and the media, and has required the support and cooperation of military and civilian officials. Traditional patterns of military operations in post-conflict situations have quickly changed and so has the need for and reliance by civilian authorities on military support in such situations.

Ambassador Vladimir Shustov Ministry of Foreign Affairs, Russia, assessed the recent development of 'Transitional Civil Administration within the Framework of UN Peacekeeping Operations' in his contribution to the Conference, which is published in this Volume. He compared past operations such as the UN Council for Namibia (1967-90) and the UN Transi-

---

*   Dr. iur., Director, International Agreements & Policy, Federal Ministry of Defence, Bonn. All opinions expressed herein are personal.

[1]   As a result of this cooperation, the new *Handbook of the Law of Visiting Forces* (edited by D. Fleck in collaboration with S. Addy, W.T. Anderson, R. Batstone, M. Bothe, J.A. Burger, F. Burkhardt, P.J. Conderman, T. Dörschel, E. Heth, H. Honma, M.S. Johnson, J.P. Lavoyer, J.M. Prescott, A.P.V. Rogers, P. Rowe, D. Sonnenberg, D.A. Timm, B. Tuzmukhamedov, B. de Vidts and M.D. Welton), xxxv, 625 pp., was published by Oxford University Press in July 2001.

[2]   See the Articles by B. Tuzmukhamedov, G. Zolotukhin, V. Lozinskiy, and D. Fleck (1/2000) 6 *International Peacekeeping* (Kluwer Law International/The Hague) 1-19.

M. Bothe and B. Kondoch (eds.),
International Peacekeeping. The Yearbook of International Peace Operations, Volume 7, 2001, 409–415.
© 2002 *Kluwer Law International. Printed in the Netherlands.*

tional Authority in Cambodia in the early '90s with the present United Nations Interim Administration Mission in Kosovo (UNMIK). Drawing on his experience as a co-author of the "Brahimi Report" to the UN Secretary-General on the future of peacekeeping[3], Shustov questioned whether UNMIK's current administrative structure, which combines legislative and executive powers, will contribute to the creation of a "substantial autonomy" within the framework of the Federal Republic of Yugoslavia, as provided for in Security Council Resolution 1244 (1999). He considered the current displacement from Kosovo of the majority of Serbs and other ethnic groups, the non-participation of Kosovo Serbs in the November 2000 municipal elections, the inadequate security conditions hindering the return of refugees and the abiding shortcomings in the functioning of judicial procedure. Shustov submitted that problems of democratic self-government in Kosovo should be tackled in conjunction with Yugoslavian authorities and that a basic task of UNMIK was to prevent the spreading and deepening of separatist roots.

Tom Koenigs, Deputy Special Representative of the UN Secretary-General for the Interim Administration of the United Nations in Kosovo, offered insight into the role of UNMIK and its efforts to establish and support a political network comprising relevant international organizations and all ethnic groups in the region. He explained the unique mandate of UNMIK, whereby the UN for the first time ventured a "government" provided with wide-ranging responsibilities and considerable powers in a region. The UN had under the circumstances performed quite well, but the following lessons could be drawn: local problems need to be addressed locally, taking local perspectives into account; there is a constant need for security in order to protect against extremists as well as to build institutions and shape a civil society. Along with other speakers Koenigs stressed the importance of enhanced security in the region, elections with widespread participation and the continued long-term engagement of the international community.

The OSCE's role in the region was addressed in terms of its distinct activities in Kosovo. Dr. Rolf Welberts, Director, Human Rights and Rule of Law, OSCE Mission in Kosovo, outlined the organisation's work in establishing a functioning police force. The force consists mainly of native but internationally trained officers, that is to say people who are conscious of

---

[3]   Report of the Panel on United Nations Peace Operations, A/55/305-S/2000/809 (21 August 2000).

the working environment but also of the applicable law as enriched by human rights standards. Welberts stressed the need to train lawyers and support judicial structures in the region. This work involves a fundamental review of the penal code and criminal procedure that are to be applied in Kosovo and will be accomplished by supporting the still-underdeveloped sector of private practitioners with the services of the Kosovo Judicial Institute, a Criminal Defence Resource Centre and Kosovo's Ombudsperson. Dr. Sebastian von Münchow, Acting Director of the Kosovo Law Centre in Pristina, described the establishment, mandate and program of his institution and its first achievements in compiling existing law in Kosovo and supporting law curricula at Pristina University. Practical aspects of the cooperation between OSCE, UNMIK and KFOR were illustrated by Polizeidirektor Alexius Schubert. Schubert explained his tasks as Regional Commander of the Kosovo Police Force between September 1999 and June 2000. The Force was put together by UNMIK and has experienced severe difficulties due to its late establishment, small size and diverse international composition.

Similarities and differences regarding the situation in neighbouring countries were discussed. Julian Harston, Deputy Special Representative of the UN Secretary-General in Bosnia and Herzegovina, described developments in this region where three and a half years of war have resulted in the deaths of some 220,000 people, the flight or internal displacement of 2.2 million more and the brutal transformation of a multiethnic society into mono-ethnically dominated regions. The United Nations Mission in Bosnia and Herzegovina (UNMBH), established under Security Council Resolution 1035 (1995), operates under a clear and – in comparison with Kosovo much more limited – mandate, namely to "provide a safe and secure environment for all persons by ensuring that civilian law enforcement agencies operate in accordance with internationally recognized standards and with respect for internationally recognized human rights and fundamental freedoms". The UNMBH mission has provided training for police and improved law enforcement agency structures. In 2002, the Security Council will have to determine an appropriate follow-on presence to consolidate its achievements.

Military lawyers in the field made substantial contributions to the Conference, assessing the current position of judges and prosecutors in Kosovo, the difficulties in defining and compiling existing laws and the problems of applying rules of evidence. The status of civilian judiciary and civilian law enforcement was discussed in the context of KFOR's potential role in detentions. While the overall assessment was confirmed by UNMIK and OSCE representatives, various improvements were discussed, including the education of law students.

Addressing the role of the media, Edward Girardet, President of Media Action International, and Rod Curtis, its correspondent in Kosovo, considered on the importance of needs-based information in alleviating crises. They described the benefits of having a locally-oriented international media service and concluded that such a service is as important in this context as food and shelter. They argued that peacekeeping or humanitarian operations cannot succeed without an effective media component serving the needs of the local population, refugees, aid agencies and peacekeepers for relevant information and exchange about basic social and security issues.

The goals and accomplishments of the Stability Pact for South Eastern Europe were assessed by its Deputy Special Coordinator Donald B. Kurch. The Pact does not act in an executive but in a mobilizing capacity among other actors in the Balkans. Accordingly, the main concern is to gain the support of international donors and countries in the region for common activities. A funding conference, which took place in Brussels, helped to raise € 1.2 Billion for regional investments. That conference has had to be followed by another drive. A second regional funding conference with a significant private sector component was envisaged for fall 2001 to raise funds for the Federal Republic of Yugoslavia as well as for other countries in the region. Long-term benefits from the Stability Pact are thus expected also for Kosovo.

Dr. Isabelle François of NATO's Defence Planning and Operation Division explained how Partnership became a fundamental security task of the Alliance. Reviewing institutional as well as operational developments, she highlighted the contribution made by Partners to NATO activities (including key initiatives such as the Defence Capabilities Initiative (DCI), the South East European Initiative (SEEI) and the Membership Action Plan (MAP)) and specifically commented on Partnership prospects towards defence reform, a current Alliance priority.

Baldwin de Vidts, NATO Legal Advisor, while considering the insertion of Partners into the NATO legal framework, stressed the importance of appropriate Security Arrangements and Agreements on the Legal Status of Liaison Officers, in particular the Brussels Agreement of 1994[4]. He also

---

[4]   Agreement on the Status of Missions and Representatives of Third States to the North Atlantic Treaty Organisation of 14 September 1994.

stressed the importance of Partners reviewing, and where necessary revising, their national legislation to enable them to send their forces abroad and to receive foreign troops. He called for the ratification of the PfP SOFA with its Additional Protocols, and he discussed different requirements for and ways of supplementing SOFA provisions.

Brigadier General Dorel Siminiuc, Head of the Legal Department at the Romanian Defence Ministry, briefed participants on his country's activities within the MAP process: new national legislation provides for sending forces abroad and receiving foreign forces; considerable experience had been gained by Romania since 1991 in various peacekeeping operations and its contribution to stabilizing the Balkans is widely welcomed as preparation for full NATO and EU membership.

Anton Thalmann, Swiss Ambassador to NATO, offered insight into the growing tendency of his country to support various forms of cooperation with UN, OSCE, PfP/EAP and EU (including its observer status in the WEU) without joining an alliance[5]. He underlined Switzerland's readiness for interoperability without accepting irreversible dependence and its willingness to support Chapter VII operations short of participating in combat actions to impose peace. Countries in the Balkans and the Caucasus were advised to consider Switzerland's multiethnic tradition and experience as a possible model.

James A. Burger, Associate Deputy General Counsel (International Affairs) of the Secretary of Defence, described legal issues in peacekeeping and humanitarian assistance as comprising both general peacekeeping policies and specific legal issues that arise during missions. From longstanding U.S. experience, he characterized the relevant Presidential Decision Directives as a basis for the interagency decision making process and the Dayton Accord as a model for solving complex operational issues in a multilateral context. (Burger's contribution is also published in this Volume.)

Hans B. Weisserth from the Office of the Secretary-General of the European Union (Policy Unit) traced the development of the European Security and Defence Policy (ESDP) from its origins in the 1948 Brussels Treaty (WEU) and the 1950 Treaty on the European Defence Community (which failed in 1954). Under the revised EU Treaty improvements in European capabilities will be effected in phases with a view to becoming fully operational by 2003. The complementarity, transparency and inclu-

---

[5]   See http://www.NATO.INT/Org./Partner Countries.

siveness of this process were stressed. The EU is not an exclusive community, and a EU/NATO strategic partnership remains essential.

The role of non-governmental organizations was discussed in terms of public attention, role specialization and mutual support during peacekeeping operations. Carsten Stahn, Research Fellow at the Max-Planck-Institute for Comparative Public Law and International Law in Heidelberg, moderated major parts of this discussion. He published his views on the issues, prospects and lessons learned separately.[6]

As at previous conferences, experience from practical legal work in implementing operational law was introduced. Special insight was offered into target selection and the role of US judge advocates in this elaborate process. The final report to the Prosecutor of the International Criminal Tribunal for the Former Yugoslavia (ICTY) on alleged violations of international humanitarian law during Operation "Allied Force"[7] was presented and discussed. The debate about the fundamental legality of NATO's use of force against the Federal Republic of Yugoslavia, which was the focus of last year's conference[8], was renewed by Professor James T. Johnson of Rutgers University. Particular consideration was given to the moral meaning of sovereignty and the contemporary use of armed force, the protection of human rights as a just cause for action, the erosion of the idea of non-combatant immunity as well as the aim of peace in contemporary armed conflicts. Although important questions remained open (such as what justifies humanitarian intervention; who should decide to end intervention and when it should be done), participants agreed on the relevance that moral categories have for this discussion.

Conference participants, expressing their gratitude to the George C. Marshall Centre for its hospitality, have encouraged the two sponsors to continue this series on contemporary legal issues, focussing on well-selected issues concerning standards of military conduct in different areas, such as international humanitarian law, anti-corruption measures, peace

---

[6]   C. Stahn, 'NGOs and International Peacekeeping – Issues, Prospects and Lessons Learned' (2-3/2001) 61 *ZaöRV* 379-401; see also C. Stahn, 'International Territorial Administration in the Former Yugoslavia: Origins, Developments and Challenges ahead' (1/2001) 61 *ZaöRV* 107-176.

[7]   Final Report to the Prosecutor by the Committee Established to Review the NATO Bombing Campaign Against the Federal Republic of Yugoslavia, July 2000.

[8]   See D. Fleck, 'Contemporary Legal Issues: Legal Issues of European Regional Peace Operations' (1/2000) 6 *International Peacekeeping* (Kluwer Law International/The Hague) 16-19.

operations (including preventive diplomacy and lessons learnt), arms control and the role of legal advisors to the military.

Transitional Civil Administration within the Framework of UN Peacekeeping Operations

V. Shustov*

The report of the panel established last year by UN Secretary-General Kofi Annan on UN Peace Operations underscores the complex character of transitional civil administration. The report also notes that it is very likely that the United Nations will be required within the framework of peacekeeping operations to perform administrative functions in the territories covered by Security Council resolutions. At present, such a task is conferred by Security Council mandate and is being fulfilled by UN missions in Kosovo, the Federal Republic of Yugoslavia (FRY) and East Timor.

The Panel, headed by former Algerian Foreign Minister Lakhdar Brahimi, recommended that the UN Secretary-General invite international legal experts, including persons with experience in UN operations, "to evaluate the feasibility and usefulness of developing an interim criminal code, including any regional versions as required, for use by such operations, pending the re-establishment of local rule of law and local law-enforcement capacity."

Based on the wording of this recommendation, the following conclusions may be drawn. First, the code in question should be interim in nature. Second, "regional versions" of the code should be considered, corresponding to the specific character of the territories in which transitional administration is carried out. (The situation in East Timor, where local administration is newly established with the UN's help, differs from that in Kosovo, which is recognized by UN Security Council resolution as an integral part of Yugoslavia.) Third, the code should facilitate the re-establishment of local law and order.

The United Nations has accumulated some experience of field operations with elements of transitional civil administration. In particular, at the 5th Special Session of the General Assembly in 1967, a transitional administrative body was established to administer Namibia. The UN Council for Namibia dealt with important matters of administration in the country. One decision, for example, that has played an important role in Namibia's development was the Decree on Protection of Natural Resources, which

---

* Ambassador, Ministry of Foreign Affairs, Russia, Co-author of the Brahimi-Report.

M. Bothe and B. Kondoch (eds.),
International Peacekeeping. The Yearbook of International Peace Operations, Volume 7, 2001, 417–423.
© 2002 *Kluwer Law International. Printed in the Netherlands.*

declared that all natural resources belong to the country's people. With the election of the Constituent Assembly in 1990, the Council for Namibia completed its task and was dissolved. Throughout its existence, that transitional administrative body worked in strict compliance with the Security Council resolutions, one of which approved the "Plan for Namibia", setting out action to be taken by the United Nations in that country for its development.

The activities undertaken in the early '90s in Cambodia by the UN Transitional Authority, which included military, police and civil components, constitute another experience of a field operation with elements of transitional civil administration. Despite the difficult conditions wrought by the military confrontation of the parties, the mission, with the collective support of foreign states, was able to complete the task set by the Security Council. It succeeded through patient and persistent effort in conducting general elections, which resulted in the establishment of the national administration in Cambodia. Having completed this task, the land forces (10,200 persons) and other military and civilian personnel (12,000 persons) left the country.

The UN Transitional Authority in Kosovo, led by the Special Representative of the Secretary-General, was established in accordance with Security Council Resolution 1244 of 10 June 1999. As in the two aforementioned operations, which are generally considered to have been successful, the Council's resolutions constitute a political mandate that the UN Mission should follow in its activities. The "Brahimi Report" justifiably states that it would be desirable to define the mandates as clearly and precisely as possible. If a mandate is approved by the Council, it should be strictly adhered to, or the goal set will not be achieved. Hence, when assessing a mission's activities, one should take into account how faithfully it implements its mandate.

I once visited the NATO air base in Ramstein with a group from several OSCE countries. We had been invited by the Alliance's military leaders to acquaint them with the activities of the all-European organization in the field of security and arms control. At the time, NATO was engaged in its first air strikes against facilities and materiel of the Bosnian Serb army in BiH. The NATO Supreme Allied Commander, Europe, General Joulwan, explained to us that the strikes were being carried out by the Alliance following the decisions of the NATO political leadership. UN peacekeeping missions can only be guided by the Security Council mandate, however, and the mandate did not then provide for NATO air strikes. Any action contrary to a UN mandate cannot be considered legal under international law.

There are two closely-related aspects in UNMIK activities, namely the political and the legal. The political aspect is governed by the following provisions of Security Council Resolution 1244:

- confirming, on behalf of all UN member states, commitment to the "sovereignty and territorial integrity of the Federal Republic of Yugoslavia";
- establishing "an interim administration for Kosovo under which the people of Kosovo can enjoy substantial autonomy within the Federal Republic of Yugoslavia";
- assuring "the safe and unimpeded return of all refugees and displaced persons to their homes in Kosovo".

The legal aspect of the interim administration activities consists mainly in fulfilling "basic civil administrative functions" and gradually transferring "its administrative responsibility to interim local authorities". These authorities comprise the interim legislative, executive and judicial bodies whose structure and powers have been discussed in various international fora. I do not intend to dwell on the details of these discussions; my assessment is based on the UN Secretary-General's reports, some publicly-available documents of UNMIK, the text of the Rambouillet Accords and press reports. I would like to outline here the structure of the interim administration in Kosovo, so as to express my personal opinion about its present and future functioning.

Under the UN Secretary-General Special Representative's instructions of 14 January 2000, a Joint Interim Administrative Structure (JIAS) was established, which remains in place despite several changes. JIAS's main goal is to enable local political forces in conjunction with UNMIK to provide an interim administration of the territory. The Special Representative's instructions state that "a fair representation of all communities" in Kosovo (evidently national communities) should be included in this structure.

The Transitional Council serves as a consultative body of JIAS while the Interim Administrative Council functions as its executive. The latter consists of eight members appointed by the Special Representative (four from among UNMIK staff and four from the local population, three of whom are Albanian and one Serbian). In the absence of consensus, decisions in the Administrative Council are taken by a two-thirds majority.

Which national community's position will prevail in such decision making can be easily guessed.

Specific management functions have been delegated to administrative departments. The local government system is comprised of municipalities headed by UNMIK-appointed administrators. The UN Secretary-General's Special Representative, who is entrusted with all legislative and executive power, sits atop this hierarchy. It would be difficult to call such an administration democratic in the true sense of the word; the administration resembles rather a kind of protectorate. Being purely transitional, however, it may have the right to exist given the prevailing local conditions. An adequate basis for the future democratic sustainability of transitional administrative institutions must be developed immediately. During this process, decisions contradicting the grounding or subsequent resolutions of the Security Council should not, of course, be taken.

A question naturally arises here: how does the present administrative structure really function and to what extent will it contribute to the creation of a "substantial autonomy" within the framework of FRY, i.e. to the achievement of Resolution 1244's goal? To answer this question the political aspects of UNMIK activities must be addressed.

First, the achievement of the said goal is hindered by the current displacement of the majority of the Serbian population and other ethnic groups from Kosovo. Neither international military nor civilian presence have so far been able to ensure a "safe and free return of all refugees and displaced persons to their homes", as provided for in the Security Council resolution. (The Secretary-General's report of 15 December 2000 states that during the year 92,000 Albanians but only 2,000 Serbs returned to Kosovo).

Second, a democratic and stable multinational society and local government cannot be established without adequate security conditions. This reality was clearly demonstrated by the November 2000 municipal elections in Kosovo. The same report of the Secretary-General, while calling these elections "the key achievement of UNMIK", acknowledges that "Kosovo Serbs did not participate in the municipal elections and voter turnout for Romas and Turks was low to negligible". Those were monoethnic elections and as such cannot be characterized as successful.

A properly functioning system of judicial procedure has not been established in Kosovo over the past year and a half. The December report of the UN Secretary-General speaks of a "biased attitude of local judicial bodies towards representatives of minorities". One year after the establishment of UNMIK, the US newspaper *Christian Science Monitor* wrote that even international judges receive death threats from Albanian extremists unless they sentence Serbs as the Albanians demand. "It is very, very difficult to get any justice here as long as some extremists are still operating", observed a Swedish judge.

Finally, the lack of adequate security conditions will make it extremely hard to resolve the future status of Kosovo. This opinion has been expressed by the new authorities in Belgrade. It is also contained in the UN Secretary-General's report: "Continued implementation of substantial autonomy depends upon the existence of security, respect for security and human rights and democratic development".

The UN Secretary-General and his representatives in Kosovo have called upon the Kosovo Serbs to return to their homes and to broaden their cooperation with UNMIK. Their appeals will only find a response if the "international presence", primarily military, police and judicial, resolutely suppresses killings, bus explosions, arson and other terrorist acts against the Serb community. Similar acts by Serbs should also be severely punished. The territory's population should be made to see and understand that practical measures to enforce law and order are being taken in pursuance of the UN Security Council resolutions. Passive "international presence" is tantamount to non-fulfillment of the Security Council mandate and can only exacerbate the problems in Kosovo. The British newspaper *Guardian* reported last February that KFOR, deployed in southern Serbia on the administrative border of Kosovo, observed Albanian extremists rearm in preparation for provocations, but that it did not react at all. The newspaper went on to state that "The concern of the official London is noticeable that the ethnic Albanian extremists in Presevo valley could cause a new war in the Balkans and the British military circles firmly believe that KFOR reacted 'too late'".

While preparing for this seminar, I was asked whether it would be possible to apply the trusteeship system in Chapter XIII of the UN Charter to Kosovo. Under Article 77 of the Charter, a territory can be voluntarily placed under the trusteeship of a world organization by a state responsible for its administration with the goal of preparing the territory for independence. After the Second World War, Chapter XIII was applied to the "territories held under mandate". Since Resolution 1244 recognizes Kosovo as a part of Yugoslavia, however, Chapter XIII is inapplicable.

Until security in Kosovo is assured so as to permit the return of refugees and displaced persons, it is hard to conceive of a temporary status of this region as an extended autonomy within Yugoslavia. Nonetheless, some of its elements seem to be mandatory in light of Resolution 1244 and the Rambouillet Accords.

It is clear that such a temporary status will provide for a democratically and freely elected legislative body. A census to determine the composition of the electorate should precede these elections, as an arbitrary division of the Kosovo population into ethnic communities by the UN Secretary-General's Special Representative would be unacceptable. However, a fair census depends again on assuring security in Kosovo so that refugees and displaced persons return to their homes. The elections should be monitored by the OSCE.

In determining the mandate of the future legislative body – let us call it an Assembly – the Rambouillet Accords should be taken into account. According to the relevant provisions a temporary administrative body responsible for implementing decisions of legislative bodies should be set up. This must be an efficient body whose activities would be carried out by respective ministries or agencies.

The Prosecutor's office and judicial system should function according to legislation adopted by the Assembly. The federal courts and laws and the Kosovo judicial system should be linked so that, for example, Kosovo citizens could seek FRY rulings based on laws applicable in Kosovo. Such a procedure is specifically provided for in Article V, paragraph 3, of the Rambouillet Accords. Incidentally, Yugoslavia's legislation has always been considered in Europe as sufficiently developed, and should be taken into account.

International civilian presence, including the Special Representative, should control the development of transitional institutions of democratic self-government, facilitating the institutions' establishment rather than imposing them. That is the intent of paragraph 11 of Resolution 1244 (sub-paragraphs a, b and c).

Decisions in transitional bodies of the Kosovo autonomy should be made by consensus, thereby taking into account their multinational composition. Consensus decision making will require major efforts, but after such decisions are made, they would become the most binding guidance for enforcement.

Problems of the democratic self-government in Kosovo should be resolved in conjunction with FRY authorities. According to the UN Secretary-General's reports, UNMIK maintains contacts with Belgrade through the Committee on Kosovo and Metohia in Pristina. There are several other channels within the framework of the Military and Technical Agreement (e.g. the exchange of information on the situation in the land and air security zones). Maintaining contacts is, however, only preliminary to the more important task of finding mutually acceptable solutions. The intention of the UN Secretary-General's new Special Representative, Mr. Hekkerup, to open a UNMIK office in Belgrade and to interact more closely with FRY in general is therefore to be welcomed. Representatives of national minorities should more actively participate in municipal structures. As noted in the UN Secretary-General's reports, however, their participation is hindered by the lack of adequate security.

UNMIK is faced with significant challenges in forming the transitional self-government in Kosovo. One of its basic tasks is to prevent separatism from further taking root. The very idea of Kosovo independence, which contradicts the UN's intention, would serve to increase tension and instability in the Balkans, trigger new conflicts and undermine regional and international security. This fear is not groundless, as observation of the political and ethnic situation in the region attests.

Legal Issues in Peacekeeping and Humanitarian Assistance

James A. Burger*

Since the end of the Cold War the armed forces of the United States have been highly involved in peacekeeping missions, and despite any indications of change in the United States policies in regard to peacekeeping, they are likely to continue to be so involved for the foreseeable future. While the present Administration has indicated a desire to reduce the numbers of forces committed to peacekeeping missions, there are major missions where the United States will still be required to commit forces such as in the continuing missions in Bosnia and Kosovo. And it will still be requested to provide support to the United Nations and to forces of other nations where the U.S. will play a supporting rather than a lead role. Also, the basic policies in deciding whether and how to commit U.S. forces will continue in force. There seems to be no immediate need to change these polices. This paper will look at both the policies of the United States, and some of the legal issues that have been raised in recent peacekeeping missions.[1]

The policy lead for peacekeeping and humanitarian assistance issues within the U.S. Department of Defence comes under the Deputy Assistant Secretary of Defence for Peacekeeping and Humanitarian Affairs (DASD PKHA). The DASD PKHA reports to the Assistance Secretary of Defence for Special Operations and Low Intensity Conflict, then to the Under Secretary of Defence for Policy, and then to the Secretary of Defence. The functions of the DASD PKHA, are to provide policy advice and oversee policy administration, to monitor crises and ongoing missions require-

---

* James A. Burger, Associate Deputy General Counsel for International Affairs in the Office of the General Counsel of the Secretary of Defence, Washington D.C. Colonel Burger, U.S. Army Judge Advocate General's Corps, served as IFOR Legal Advisor in Sarajevo from December 1995 to November 1996, and now provides advice on operational legal issues including peacekeeping in the Office of the General Counsel of the Secretary of Defence. Any of the opinions expressed in this article are solely those of the author, and do not represent the views of the Office of the General Counsel or of the United States Department of Defence.

[1] This article is based upon a presentation given at the George C. Marshall Centre in Garmisch, Germany, in the spring of 2001on the subject of peacekeeping and humanitarian assistance. Colonel Burger presented an overview of U.S. policies on peacekeeping, and reviewed legal issues raised during U.S. participation in peacekeeping missions.

M. Bothe and B. Kondoch (eds.),
International Peacekeeping. The Yearbook of International Peace Operations, Volume 7, 2001, 425–435.
© 2002 *Kluwer Law International. Printed in the Netherlands.*

ments, and to oversee U.S. readiness to conduct and support peacekeeping operations and humanitarian activities. He also develops policies for U.S. humanitarian demining programs, and policies for non-combatant evacuation missions (NEOs), and he is tasked to help strengthen UN and third party peacekeeping and humanitarian assistance capacities.

The United States has traditionally played a limited role in UN peacekeeping operations. It presently contributes approximately 42 military personnel and over 800 civilian police to eight UN peacekeeping operations. This compares with over a total of 36,000 military personnel from all nations involved in 15 UN peacekeeping operations worldwide, and almost 8,000 civilian police. On the other hand, the U.S. also contributes almost 11,000 military personnel in 3 non-UN peacekeeping operations. These include SFOR in Bosnia, KFOR in Kosovo, and the Multinational Force (MFO) in the Sinai. And it is frequently called upon to provide logistic, training or other support to UN forces for other UN operations and non UN multinational operations. These requests typically come from the United Nations in New York. The U.S. has a military liaison office at the U.S. Mission to the United Nations in New York which transmits such requests to the State Department and Department of Defence in Washington. Other requests might come from NATO in Brussels where the U.S. as well as other NATO members have military representatives at NATO Headquarters.

The nature of peacekeeping has evolved over the years, and U.S. policies in regard to peacekeeping have developed through actual experience in peacekeeping operations. There are three key Presidential Decision Directives (PDDs) which have served as the basis for U.S. policy. The U.S. began drafting its first PDD on peacekeeping in 1993,[2] and it was signed in 1994 during the UN peacekeeping operation in Somalia. U.S. experience in Somalia was reflected in the second peacekeeping PDD which was drafted during the peacekeeping operation in Haiti and at the beginning of the Bosnia IFOR and the SFOR missions.[3] It was signed in late 1997. The third peacekeeping PDD in turn reflected experience in Haiti and Bosnia. Drafting began in early 1998, and the PDD was signed in January of 2000.

---

[2]   Presidential Review Decision 13, sometimes incorrectly referred to as PDD 13, initiated a review on American participation in international peacekeeping activities. For discussion see the record of the Defence Appropriations Act of 1994 (Senate Record – October 18, 1993, pp. S13567 – S13568).

[3]   For a discussion of the problems experienced in Somalia see the book, *Black Hawk Down,* which has become standard reading in U.S. military schools. M. Bowden, *Black Hawk Down* (Penguin Books, New York, 1999).

Each PDD thus drew from the experience of the peacekeeping operations at the time, and were planned to adapt policies to the need for future peacekeeping operations.

Decisions on whether and how to participate in peacekeeping operations are made through what is referred to as a "policy coordinating committee" chaired by the National Security Council (NSC). The committee responsible for peacekeeping decisions may be comprised of representatives from the State Department, the Office of the Secretary of Defence, the Joint Staff, the Military Staff Committee to US Mission to the United Nations in New York, and appropriate representatives from the U.S. intelligence community. It may consider USG peacekeeping policies and initiatives, react to the need for new peacekeeping operations, and monitor and make decisions in regard to current peacekeeping operations. It may also provide interagency management, and coordinate issues with the Congress.

The basic U.S. policy under the Clinton administration was found in Presidential Decision Directive 25, *Reforming Multilateral Peace Operations.*[4] This directive was signed in May of 1994. Presidential Decision Directives are issued by the President, and set out policies on a particular subject. PDD-25 established an interagency policy making process for peace operations. Issuance of the directive responded to a generally recognized need to have a formalized process to decide when and how the United States should involve its military forces in peacekeeping missions. It therefore set out factors to guide USG decision-making on when to support and participate in peace operations. It established command and control policy for US forces' participation in multilateral peace operations. It outlined initiatives to improve US and international capabilities to conduct peace operations. PDD-25 provides "factors for consideration" to guide US deliberations on whether to support and/or participate in a peace operation.

In order to decide whether to initiate or continue a peacekeeping operation the directive indicates that specific questions should be asked. These questions include whether U.S. interests are involved, whether there is a threat to peace or security, whether there are clear objectives, whether adequate resources are available, if the objectives of the mission are achievable, and if the duration of the mission is acceptable. As to whether

---

[4]   PDD-25, "Reforming Multilateral Peace Operations," signed by President Clinton on 3 May, 1994. The unclassified version of this directive can be found in U.S. Department of State Publication Number 10161 released by the Bureau of Organizational Affairs in May of 1994.

U.S. troops in particular should participate, additional questions must be answered, and these include whether the appropriate U.S. forces are available, whether U.S. participation is necessary, whether there would be Congressional and domestic support, and if the command and control arrangements are acceptable. There are also additional questions to be asked if U.S. troops are likely to be involved in combat operations. In this regard, it must be asked whether sufficient forces are involved, if there is a plan to achieve the objectives in a decisive manner, and it is pointed out that there is the need to continually assess the situation and make adjustments.

PDD-56, *Managing Complex Contingency Operations,* was a follow-on directive to PDD-25.[5] Benefiting from experience in Haiti and Bosnia, it was written with the intention of integrating the political, military, humanitarian, economic, and other dimensions of U.S. government planning for complex contingencies. President Clinton signed the Directive in May of 1997. PDD-56 called for the integrated policy development, planning and execution. It does not guide decisions on when and where to intervene, but does guide the development of an integrated intervention strategy. As indicated above, it places the responsibility for coordinating interagency training and publishing an interagency handbook upon the DASD PKHA. PDD-56 established an interagency process to manage three types of smaller scale contingencies.

The first type of contingency addressed is peace accord implementation such as the NATO mission in Bosnia, the MFO mission in the Sinai, and the UN mission in Haiti. The second contingency addressed is humanitarian intervention such as Provide Comfort in Northern Iraq and UNITAF in Somalia. The third contingency is foreign humanitarian assistance such as Operation Sea Angel in Bangladesh and Operation Support Hope in the Great Lakes region of Africa. The PDD-56 "process" is similar to that used to manage the initial peacekeeping strategy for Haiti, and incorporates lessons learned from that experience. At the centre of the process is a "political-military plan" developed by an interagency working group, and addressing functional elements such as elections, resettlement, human rights monitoring, security, development, enhancing indigenous police and humanitarian assistance. The need for rehearsal is indicated as a key part in the process.

---

[5]   PDD-56, "Managing Complex Contingency Operations," signed by President Clinton in May of 1997. Published in a White Paper, "The Clinton Administration's Policy on Managing Complex Contingency Operations: Presidential Decision Directive May 1997."

The third and most recent PDD is Presidential Decision Directive 71, "Strengthening Criminal Justice Systems in Support of Peace Operations and Other Complex Contingencies."[6] President Clinton signed the directive in February of 2000. PDD-71 is designed to enhance the capabilities of U.S. and international organizations and other countries to conduct effective CIVPOL (Civilian Police) operations and to support complementary police, justice, and penal system development. It established the State Department as the lead agency for coordinating U.S. participation in CIVPOL and international criminal justice development activities. It also established guidance to facilitate an early transition of law enforcement responsibilities from military peacekeeping forces to the effective restoration of civilian police authority.

The three directives together see peacekeeping as a vital tool for conflict management resolution, and peacekeeping operations as one of several instruments in the "toolbox" of conflict containment and mitigation measures. Other instruments include diplomacy, sanctions, and assistance to bolster force posture and/or relieve hardships. Conflict containment instruments may also include measures such as no-fly zones or safe areas. And lastly there is the additional measure of war crimes adjudication. While care is needed in utilizing such measures, the underlying needs for peacekeeping are likely to continue, and the world community in general and the U.S. in particular will have to consider when and if peacekeeping operations are warranted and whether they are likely to be successful. Despite the fact that the previous Administration issued these PDDs, many elements of these PDDs are likely to have continuing validity in analysing whether and if the UN and individual states should become involved in future peacekeeping operations.

In the same way the PDDs are valuable in analysing peacekeeping missions, there are also legal considerations that have to be taken in view when deciding on how and whether to participate in PK operations, and in deciding the nature of support to these operations. These legal considerations are the result of both U.S. and international experience. Lawyers are important members of peacekeeping missions, and any peacekeeping mission in which the U.S. has a large contingent will include a military attor-

---

6   PDD-71, "Strengthening Criminal Justice Systems in Support of Peace Operations and Other Complex Contingencies," signed by the President on February 24, 2000. Published as "The Clinton Administration White Paper on Peace Operations, 24 February 2000; Summary of Presidential Decision Directive 71 State Department, 24 February 2000; and Fact Sheet on PDD 71: Strengthening Criminal Justice Systems, State Department 24, February 2000.

ney. Legal considerations begin with the need for authority to establish the operation – a clear mandate, rules for the conduct and employment of personnel and equipment – standing operations orders and rules of engagement, status of personnel and equipment – SOFA issues, civilian military cooperation, and other issues such as war crimes adjudication.

In regard to the mandate, the mandate must first of all be based upon international authority such as a UN Security Counsel Resolution under Chapter VI, Pacific Settlement of Disputes, or Chapter VII, Threats or Breaches of the Peace. However, the UN Charter also provides for regional arrangements under Chapter VIII. The UN Security Council may call upon regional organizations to implement a peacekeeping mission, or regional organizations may take action on their own authority. In this regard it is important to note that regional organizations exist independently from the United Nations, and may take actions, including self defence, upon their own initiative. Another important Charter provision to note is Article 55 under which the UN may promote economic, social, health and human rights, and Article 56 under which it may call upon members to join in cooperative actions. These other provisions provide the basis for the United Nations to involve itself in the "civil" side of peacekeeping missions.

Preferably there should be a written mandate which sets out the authority for the mission, the expected duration of the mission, the size of the force, the objectives to be achieved, the composition of the force, and special directives and limitations. The Dayton experience is particularly helpful in this regard, because more than in other peacekeeping operations this mandate was set out with great detail. This mandate is found in there General Framework Agreement, Annex 1-A, the Agreement on Military Aspects of the Peace Settlement, and the Appendix to Annex 1-A which contains the status of forces agreements (SOFAs) with Croatia, with Bosnia and with Yugoslavia.[7] Other details are found in Annex 1-B, the Agreement on Regional Stabilization, and additional annexes on boundaries, elections, a constitution, arbitration, human rights, refugees, civilian implementation and an international police task force (the IPTF).

The rules governing a peacekeeping operation first and foremost include customary and codified international law, and in particular the laws

---

[7]   General Framework Agreement for Peace in Bosnia and Herzegovina, negotiated and initialled at Dayton, Ohio, and signed at Paris, in December of 1995. Texts of the Dayton documents can be found in International Legal Materials, Bosnia and Herzegovina-Croatia-Yugoslavia: General Framework Agreement of Peace in Bosnia and Herzegovina with Annexes (1996) 35 *ILM* 75-169.

of armed conflict including the Geneva Conventions of 1949 and the Hague Conventions of 1899 and 1904. There are also the 1971 Protocols to Geneva Conventions of 1949. While the United States is not a party to these Protocols, the U.S. recognizes much of the content of the protocols as customary law, and U.S. forces in Bosnia had no problem working with other nations which were parties to the Protocols. National laws to be considered include both local laws and the laws of the participating states. These laws may differ, and nations must consider their differing laws in cooperating in peacekeeping operations. Finally, there are the rules established by the military commander for the peacekeeping force. Generally, there will be an order to establish rules for good order and discipline. Such orders may be established separately by the international and the national forces. These orders may cover such activities as controlled substances, black market activities, respect for local religion or buildings, and they are important factors in maintaining discipline. While the international command will have a responsibility to assure that discipline is maintained, the actual enforcement will be handled through the individual national military disciplinary systems. International commands do not exercise disciplinary authority. Discipline is the responsibility of the national authorities.

The most important rules for a peacekeeping unit are the rules of engagement, the ROE. These rules are written to provide the authority for the use of force to carry out the mandate and the mission. Countries such as the United States have standing rules of engagement which are then tailored for the particular mission.[8] NATO and the UN also have similar standing rules, although in the Bosnia operation it was the first time that NATO issued rules of engagement for a land operation. In an international mission there may be both ROE for the international command, and national ROE established by individual participating states. Generally the national forces will operate under the international ROE, but the international ROE will allow for national implementation. Differences in implementation may cause problems, but these are worked out in the planning for the mission and for particular operations. When I was in Bosnia as IFOR Legal Adviser, the IFOR commander would assemble his subordinate commanders prior to any new mission to assure that there would not be problems caused by differing national rules.

---

[8]   Standing Rules of Engagement for US Forces, 15 January 2000. Enclosure A is the unclassified version. Rules of Engagement are generally classified, but they also will often have a shortened unclassified version, or a releasable version. The NATO rules also have a short summary appendix which is open to the public.

Under the Dayton agreement, the Military Annex authorizes "...the use of necessary force to assure compliance ... and to protect IFOR ..."[9] Authority to enforce the mission was a key addition to the authority allowed to UNPROFOR, which could only use force in self defence. Lack of enforcement authority was a key factor in UNPROFOR not being able to fulfil its mission. The main task for IFOR was to separate the parties, and to have them withdraw and disarm. Then there were supporting missions to assure conditions for associated tasks, to assist movement of humanitarian organizations, to assist the UNHCR and humanitarian organization, to prevent the interference with the movement of the civilian population, and to monitor the clearing of minefields and obstacles. All of these tasks are especially set out, and they are reflected in the IFOR/SFOR ROE. The ROE provide the authority to use force to accomplish these tasks. As indicated the main difference between the UN ROE in the UNPROFOR operation and IFOR ROE was the authority of enforcement. If the parties refused to separate, put away their arms, or hinder the freedom of movement, the peacekeepers could use force to make them comply. It is noteworthy that IFOR recognized the applicability of the laws of armed conflict if appropriate, and that it was provided in its ROE with the authority to detain war criminals.

ROE is an area requiring special attention, and great care must be taken to design ROE and provide for particular missions. ROE should be written by operational officers, but will also involve attorneys expert in operational law. When I was at AFSOUTH preparing for deployment to Sarajevo, I chaired a committee of operational officers representing all of the services, land, sea and air, who provided input to the ROE before they were submitted to the commander of AFSOUTH for approval. ROE must provide for the use of force for self-defence and to enforce the mission. They will consider proportionality, military necessity and preventing collateral damage. They will set out definitions for threat, minimal force, and hostile intent or action. They will provide for weapons release authority, types of weapons, and special authorities such as to detain war criminals.

An equally important area for consideration is the status of personnel and equipment in the receiving state. The grandfather of all status of forces agreements is the NATO Status of Forces agreement.[10] However,

---

[9]   Para 5, Article VI of the Agreement on the Military Aspects of the Peace Settlement, Annex 1-A of the General Framework Agreement, *supra*, n. 8.

[10]   Agreement between the Parties to the North Atlantic Treaty regarding the status of their forces. Signed at London June 19, 1951, entered into force August 23, 1953. 4 UST 1972: TIAS 2846; 199 UNTS 67.

the United Nations also has a Model Status of Mission (SOMA) or Status of Forces Agreement (SOFA) to be used when UN forces deploy on peacekeeping missions.[11] Status for forces agreements provide for the right of entry and exit, the wearing of uniforms, and bearing of arms. They reserve criminal jurisdiction over military and civilian personnel serving in the peacekeeping mission to the sending state. They provide for the right to bivouac, manoeuvre and billet, and the use of areas or facilities for support, training and operations. They provide for the right to import and export equipment and supplies free of taxes and duties. They provide for the right to contract for supplies and services, and to hire local personnel. In sum, they provide for all of the things that are necessary to bring about a successful operation. It is necessary to have a SOFA to provide for these matters since the consent and the cooperation of the host state is essential. This is a question not only of non interference with the sovereignty of the host state, but also the need to have the active support of the host state.

Rules and procedures must also be established to provide for civilian military cooperation. Under Dayton Agreement, the High Representative coordinates the activities of civilian organizations.[12] He attends and offers advice on civilian matters in the Joint Military Commission which is a group chaired by the military (IFOR/SFOR) commander, and which is comprised by both military and civilian representatives including the non-governmental organizations (NGOs). When I served as IFOR Legal Advisor in Bosnia, the IFOR Commander chaired weekly meetings which reviewed civilian aspects of the mission, and how the military forces would provide security to and otherwise support the civilian organizations. Under Dayton this organization was formalized in the Framework Agreement, but in other peacekeeping missions if it was not formally created there would have to be an equivalent organization or process created. The end goal of any peacekeeping mission is to re-establish civilian control and functions, and the military cannot fulfil its own mission without the support and cooperation of civilian agencies.

---

[11] United Nation Status of Mission Agreement or Status of Forces Agreement, a copy of the UN SOMA/SOFA may be found at p. 3-17 of the Operational Handbook, the Judge Advocate General's School, Charlottesville, Va. 1997.

[12] The function of the High Representative is set up under the Agreement on Civilian Implementation of the Peace Settlement, Annex 10 to the General Framework Agreement, *supra* note 8. However, it is the military commander who chairs the Joint Military Commission. The High Representative attends Commission meetings, and offers advice on matters of a political-military nature. Article VIII of Annex A-1.

One of the most important of these civilian issues is the police function. Under Dayton the International Police Task Force monitors, advises, trains and facilitates law enforcement activities.[13] SFOR protects and assists as directed. The military peacekeeping unit will provide the essential security necessary for the police to operate. It may be called upon to extricate the civilian police from difficult situations if security breaks down. Military civilian police cooperation involves significant legal issues. Military personnel are not trained, nor for the most part are they authorized to serve as police. In the early days of a peacekeeping mission it may be necessary for military personnel to fulfil a need to police because civilian police are inadequate or do not exist. But this responsibility must be handed off to civilian police as soon as possible. The military then transfers its support to providing the security necessary for the civilian police to perform their appropriate mission. Even the IPTF was not created to act as a police force, but to monitor and provide training as the local police took back their responsibilities.

War crimes is an issue which was not originally expected by the IFOR commanders and staff in Bosnia, but the authority to detain war criminals was provided in the IFOR rules of engagement. After some initial difficulty, an understanding was worked out as to the circumstances when the IFOR military authorities would detain persons accused of war crimes. Basically they would detain PIFWC (persons indicted for war crimes) when they came across such persons in the course of their other duties, but they would not seek PIFWC out or carry out an arrest on behalf of the ICTY (International Criminal Tribunal for Former Yugoslavia). This understanding is still in effect today, and numerous PIFWIC have been detained and turned over to the authorities in the Hague. When the IFOR commanders and staff met at The US Army War College after finishing their mission there was general agreement that the war crimes issue had to be addressed. However, it was categorically agreed that this should not be the responsibility of the military. The military should provide support, but war crimes matters should not be one of their primary missions.

The UN peacekeeping mission in Kosovo provided new challenges, but all of the same problems were present. A mandate was needed, and UN Security Council resolution 1244 provided for both KFOR (Kosovo Force) on the military side, and for UNMIK (United Nations Mission in Kosovo),

---

[13]   Agreement on International Police Task Force, Annex 11, of the General Framework Agreement, *supra* note 8.

on the civilian side.[14] ROE were needed, and were quickly provided based upon the IFOR/SFOR model. These also were NATO ROE since NATO was entrusted with the military implementation. A SOFA has never been signed, but KFOR and UNMIK jointly agreed on regulations which would fulfil the need for SOFA type provisions. The fact that UNMIK provided for civilian government was a special aspect of the Kosovo mission. Recall that in Kosovo it is UNMIK which is providing government functions in absence of a viable local government. War crimes issues have been addressed also as ICTY's jurisdiction equally applied to Kosovo as to the rest of the Former Yugoslavia. Lastly, UNMIK had to establish civilian courts which would try regular criminal offences as well as offences which might be considered lesser war crimes.

In summary, issues to be analysed for the success of peacekeeping missions must be viewed as comprising both the general peacekeeping policies on when and how to organize peacekeeping missions, and the many specific legal issues which come up during peacekeeping missions. This article has described both the general peacekeeping policies of the United States, and illustrated specific legal issues which we have had to deal with in recent peacekeeping missions. These policies and the legal issues are closely interconnected. In all of the areas it is the policy which commits to a particular mission, and the legal issues are the problems which must be resolved in order to properly support the mission. The bottom line is that peacekeeping is ripe with legal issues, and lawyers play a vital part in making peacekeeping work.

---

[14] UNSCR 1244, dated 10 June 1999, provides both for KFOR to provide the security function (para 9), and for UNMIK to provide the civilian function (para 11).

Book Reviews

Nassrine Azimi & Chang Li Lin (eds.), The Nexus between Peacekeeping and Peace-Building: Debriefing and Lessons, Report of the 1999 Singapore Conference. London: Kluwer Law International, 2000, 288 pp.
*Cedric de Coning**

The first thought that came to my mind when I picked up this book, was how can the report of a conference that took place in 1999 possibly still be of interest two, three or more years later. In our fast paced world journals and quasi-academic magazines, not to even mention electronic journals, have almost replaced books as the medium through which to publish material still relevant to the ever changing current context. A report of a conference, published as a book a year later, thus seemed, at first, to defy common sense. As I paged through and then started reading, however, I realized that this collection of papers, presentations, debriefings and recommendations is an incredibly rich collection of knowledge and information on the nexus between peacekeeping and peace building, that is, and will remain for some years to come, essential reading for anybody who wants to stay on top of the developing knowledge base in this field.

We all become so conference fatigued that it has become rare to come across a meeting that seem to have really achieved what so many set out to do, but fail. I have not attended the November 1999 Singapore Conference, but when reading the Report, almost two years later, it becomes clear that the co-organizers: the United Nations Institute for Training and Research (UNITAR), the Institute of Policy Studies in Singapore (IPS) and the Japan Institute of International Affairs (JIIA), managed to bring together an extraordinary group of participants from the United Nations, development agencies and humanitarian organizations, governments, the military and then created an environment within which these two groups could exchange information, knowledge and analysis that resulted in a very meaningful set of recommendations and conference papers.

The Conference took place at a time when the United Nations and other multilateral and bilateral agencies were struggling to conceptualise and implement peace-building strategies in the wake of military operations in Kosovo and East Timor. The Conference reviewed four peacekeeping op-

---

* Civil Affairs Officer with the UN Transitional Administration in East Timor (UNTAET).

M. Bothe and B. Kondoch (eds.),
International Peacekeeping. The Yearbook of International Peace Operations, Volume 7, 2001, 437–453.
© 2002 *Kluwer Law International. Printed in the Netherlands.*

erations: Angola, Cambodia, Haiti and Mozambique. Lessons of the nexus between peacekeeping and peace building were drawn from these missions and the Conference then tried to apply them to two (then) new operations: the United Nations Interim Administration in Kosovo (UNMIK) and the United Nations Transitional Administration in East Timor (UNTAET). I am sure the events unfolding in these two regions at the time of the Conference must have served as a constant reminder of the significance of the work being undertaken by the participants. The *Summary of Discussions* and the *Conference Co-chair's Recommendations* captures the inspiration and motivation the participants must have felt, and one comes away with a feeling that a sense of measured optimism prevailed at the Conference.

The papers collected in this volume provide a comprehensive review of all six cases, both from the perspective of those who were involved, as well as from those that could observe compare and analyse these missions against existing theories, policies and trends.

Part One captures the introductory remarks and keynote speeches, including a message from Kofi Annan, the Secretary General of the United Nations, and presentations by Prof. S. Jayakumar, the Minister of Foreign Affairs and Minister of Law of Singapore; Hedi Annabi, an Assistant Secretary General for the United Nations Department of Peacekeeping Operations (DPKO); Jacques Forster, Vice-President of the International Committee of the Red Cross (ICRC) and the principals of the co-organisers, IPS, JIIA and UNITAR.

Part Two is a debriefing by the research and policy community on the existing knowledge base on the nexus between peacekeeping and peace building. Part Three contains the lessons learned from Angola, Mozambique, Haiti and Cambodia. This section contains the various background papers on these past operations. In most cases these are by practitioners, e.g. on Angola by Dame Margaret Anstee, a former Special Representative of the UN Secretary General (SRSG) for Angola, and on Mozambique by Denis Jett, a former US Ambassador to Mozambique and now with the Carter Centre. The organizers have chosen their presenters well and almost all of these background papers are full of insights and useful facts. Denis Jett, argues, for instance, that there is not only a nexus between peacekeeping and peace-building, but a tension as well. Peacekeeping involves specific steps to be accomplished on a fixed timetable whilst peacebuilding requires the strengthening of local institutions and local capacity that can take years if not decades. He argues that given the cost of large, multi-dimensional peacekeeping operations, the emphasis will be on conducting peacekeeping quickly without adequate attention, time or resources for peace-building.

Part Four focus on the lessons that can be learned from the four case studies for the new missions in Kosovo and East Timor and is prefaced by insightful introductory remarks by Lakhdar Brahimi, the UN Secretary General's Special Envoy. The section on Kosovo includes a presentations by Philip Wilkinson of the Joint Doctrine Concepts Centre of the UK Ministry of Defence; Paolo Lembo the Special Advisor on Kosovo for UNDP and Francis Amar, Head of the International Organizations Division of the ICRC. East Timor, barely one month after UNTAET was established, was covered by Hedi Annabi, ASG of DPKO; Omar Bakhet the Director of the Emergency Response Division of UNDP and Toni Pfanner, the Head of the Southeast Asia region of ICRC.

Part Five is the Summary of Discussions and Co-Chairs' Recommendations. Although the different peacekeeping missions considered shared similar goals, the responses in each case differed depending on the context and conflict environment. Based on the discussions, however, the Co-chairs' identified a number of traits common to all of the case studies, namely: the importance of the internal and the international political context and the question of timing; the design and architecture of the mission; financial resources; selection of the SRSG and the independence of his/her authority; mandate and quality of the military component; exit strategies, and communications.

The Co-chairs also provide a summary of the discussions on each of the case studies. These can probably best be summarized by using the anonymous quote the editors used to preface each discussion: on Angola – "No peace can prosper without genuinely sustained political will on the part of all the parties to a conflict, and this was plainly lacking in Angola"; on Mozambique – "Two single' parties do not make for multi-partism"; on Haiti – "Elections do not a democracy make" and on Cambodia – "Mission must be allowed the necessary flexibility to adapt the implementation of the mandate to the changing realities on the ground".

Part Six contain various annexes, including additional remarks on the nexus between peacekeeping and peace-building by Ahmad Khamal, the Chairman of the Board of UNITAR and a very useful summary of the history and development of peacekeeping missions, entitled: Cascading Generations of Peacekeeping: Across the Mogadishu Line to Kosovo and Timor by Ramesh Thakur of the United Nations University in Tokyo.

The Conference struggled with many issues that are as relevant – and half-answered – today as they were in November 1999. The Co-chairs summarize the fundamental questions as follows: "Where does peacekeeping stop and peace-building begin? When does peace-building end and development activities begin? What is the nature of the overlap, and what mutual re-enforcement can be achieved?". They go on to explain that "in struggling with these fundamental questions and reflecting on the case studies, participants felt that many of these concepts need not be sequential but could exist concurrently, rather tan chronologically, depending on the context. In all the cases reviewed, however the peacekeeping forces could have played a key role in supporting peace-building initiatives. In its simplest form it was agreed that, where adequate security was not established, peace-building efforts invariably suffered."

The Co-chairs found that the nature of today's peacekeeping and the necessity for broader missions has led to at least two new sets of problems. The first is the careful articulation of the scope of the mission so as to avoid leaving to large a gap between the peacekeeping and peace-building aspects of the mission. The second is the challenge of coordination among the various segments of the UN system and the many intergovernmental and non-governmental organizations operating in the same field and working for similar purposes. The Conference Co-Chair's suggest how these problems can best be addressed and they come up with a concise but powerful set of recommendations that address the wide spectrum of issues, but very neatly cover them all in 16 points. I have made a note of them so that I can easily refer to them in future, and I am sure you will find them equally useful.

The Co-chairs conclude that the participants recognized that though each peacekeeping case was unique, they shared many similarities and therefore it was reassuring that the conceptual plans for the missions in Kosovo and East Timor seemed to have benefited from lessons learned in past cases.

Despite my initial doubts as to the continued relevance of a conference report that took place in November 1999, I have found this collection of papers, summaries and recommendations most useful in broadening my understanding of the nexus between peacekeeping and peace-building, and would recommend this volume as essential reading for all of us who are either involved in studying peacekeeping or who are responsible for the operational aspects.

Abiodun Alao, John Mackinlay and Funmi Olonisakin, Peacekeepers, Politicians, and Warlords: The Liberian Peace Process. Tokyo, New York, Paris: United Nations University Press Series on the Foundations of Peace, 1999, 216 pp.
*Jens Bernhardt**

The book is the product of field research carried out in Liberia, Sierra Leone and Nigeria. With painstaking effort the authors have analysed local newspapers, operational planning documents and staff lists and have interviewed participants. Highlighted is the Liberian peace process, which constituted the first post-cold-war regional peacekeeping operation and the first co-operation between UN military observers and a regional peacekeeping operation. The book does not claim to offer a definitive assessment of the conflict in Liberia. The peace process is discussed through snapshots of the most important peace agreements of Cotonou and Abuja. Chapter One describes the traditional principles of UN-peacekeeping, the changing nature of conflicts and the shifting interests of the Security Council's permanent members after the Cold War. African countries in particular were no longer a main concern of the great powers. Their loss of interest required regional organisations to address conflicts in Africa.

Chapter Two outlines the historical development of Liberia. It has been characterised by the unequal treatment of the country's various ethnic groups. The internal political tension was aggravated by the coup of Samual K. Doe in 1976. He oppressed the opposition and other ethnic groups, which led to emergence of the NPFL, a violent opposition headed by Charles Taylor, in 1989. This caused the civil war by creating new warring factions.

The next chapter deals with the regional intervention of ECOMOG in Liberia. The Monitoring Group was put into action by the Economic Community of West African States (ECOWAS) with the agreement of President Doe. ECOMOG was initially intended to serve as a peacekeeping force, but enforcement operations arose that required more than self-defence. This changed role and the dominance of Nigerian troops within the Monitoring Group brought allegations of partiality on the part of ECOMOG.

Many peace agreements were concluded through ECOWAS's mediation, but they signally failed to achieve their objectives. Their implementation was under the discretion of ECOMOG. ECOMOG itself had to strug-

* Cand. jur , Johann Wolfgang Goethe-University, Frankfurt/Main.

gle with flaws in its command. ECOWAS and ECOMOG were suffering financial and structural problems in proceeding with this operation. The third chapter concludes that the mission brought a measure of order and stability to Liberia, but that to further the peace process, a stronger intervening organisation like the UN was needed.

The Cotonou Agreement of July 1993 is the subject of Chapter Four. The Agreement concerns primarily a cease-fire and secondarily disarmament, demobilisation, elections, repatriation of refugees and a general amnesty. Besides ECOMOG, the UN observer mission in Liberia (UNOMIL) was intended to supervise and monitor the Agreement's implementation. Although the violence stopped, it is argued that the Cotonou Agreement was flawed in its conception and was doomed to failure.

Cotonou did not succeed. A main reason was the lack of a powerful authority that could provide shelter and control the processes of disarmament, resettlement and election. The spheres of authority of the different groups were not clearly defined. The plans for disarmament did not take into consideration the fact that the security required for weapons to become superfluous for the combatants did not exist in the country. Here the authors point out that the inner structure of the warring factions should have been strengthened so as to enable them to create a secure environment. The time for implementation was too short. Moreover, there was an inattention to detail and no long-term strategy for success. At the end of the chapter, the authors suggest that Cotonou should be considered as a first step on a much longer journey to recovery.

Chapter Six makes a comparison to the first Abuja Accord, in which the peace process was planned with greater attention to detail and expertise. The co-ordination between the participating groups was improved, and the Accord was signed by all concerned. In the event, a gap between planning and implementation was revealed. There was mistrust between the warring factions and no movement towards peace. Financial resources were not available to carry out the intended tasks. The stagnation of the peace process led to a rising number of cease-fire violations, climaxing in the heaviest fighting of the civil war in Monrovia.

The second Abuja Accord achieved a lasting end to the violence. It retained the first Accord without amendment, but it should remain in force for an additional nine months. The implementation schedule was revised, and a sanction scheme for violations was put into effect. Despite the very unpropitious overall circumstances (resources were still not available; an encampment of the combatants was not possible; and reintegration programs were turned down), the Accord led to the disarmament of 23,000 combatants. The way towards elections was paved.

Chapter Eight shows how all hopes of ensuring peace were pinned on the influence of Charles Taylor and his NPFL. This faction had not been opposed by ECOMOG since 1997. Taylor trusted the peace process and his electoral chances, as he was prepared best. On July 19th Taylor took 75% of the votes in elections declared free and fair by international observers. It is now up to the new government to rebuild the country. The book highlights the problems it will face in rebuilding the armed forces, the economy and the social infrastructure, especially as regards the child soldiers.

The last chapter draws some lessons from the experience in Liberia. The fiction of an existing state was maintained and the centres of real power ignored, just as fatefully as the power within the warring factions was misjudged. Massive changes in a country's social structure must be factored into such assessments. Exhaustion and unbearable outside pressure were the reasons why the warlords gave up their relatively secure and lucrative lifestyle. ECOMOG was a key factor in that regard. The authors conclude that though ECOMOG as a traditional peacekeeper may be impugned for its alleged partiality and looting, ECOMOG has nonetheless been a strong, powerful force promoting the peace process. *"A lesson of this experience has been that the principles of traditional peacekeeping are no longer relevant to complex emergencies. It may be that, rather than a powerful and highly organised intervention dominated by northern defence forces, an African solution is the best form of intervention in an African emergency."*

The most important peace agreements dealt with in the book are reprinted in an appendix.

The book offers a good perspective of the Liberian civil war and peace process. The process is examined, and mistakes are pointed out. In addition, it draws parallels to conflicts of the same kind. The book helps to explain such conflicts and may help to prevent the recurrence of the same mistakes elsewhere. Lastly, the authors propose novel solutions as to how best to handle some of the various problems that typically arise in peace processes.

Aleksandar Fatić, Reconciliation via the War Crimes Tribunal? Aldershot: Ashgate Publishing, 2000, 117 pp.
*Florence Feyerbacher**

With the growing popularity in recent years of war crimes tribunals as a peacekeeping and/or peacemaking tool (e.g. in Rwanda or the Former Yugoslavia), it has become vitally important to understand the efficacy of such bodies' work in war-torn countries. Of particular interest is not only the degree to which justice is achieved in a given area, but also the way in which tribunals can contribute to the peace settlement, the defusion of accumulated aggressions and lasting stability by overcoming ethnic hatred and strife. Aleksandar Fatić's book addresses precisely these issues. However, contrary to what the book's title might suggest, Fatić does not analyse the reconciliatory function of war crimes tribunals generally; instead he focuses specifically on The International Criminal Tribunal for the Former Yugoslavia (ICTY).

In his introduction, Fatić names three goals of the ICTY: to create moral and legal justice, to stabilize peace and to foster reconciliation among the countries of the Former Yugoslavia. According to the author, the third goal is the most important, because it facilitates the political, economic and social progress that can in turn lead to stability in the region. Fatić claims that, judged on this basis, the ICTY has not fulfilled its mission but has contributed to the lasting instability in the Balkans. His most serious allegation is that the ICTY has served as a political tool to impose victors' justice on the Former Yugoslavia and has therefore failed to find credibility with the region's population.

The author, who is a Senior Fellow at the Institute of International Politics and Economics in Belgrade and the President of the Management Centre in Belgrade, begins with an analysis of "The Background and Diplomatic Significance of the ICTY". The first chapter develops the doubts about the ICTY's reconciliatory function hinted at by the question mark in the book's title. The author criticizes the actions taken by the ICTY so far, describing the Tribunal as lacking the impartiality, consistency and courage to prosecute all war criminals regardless of their military, social and political rank or ethnic background. Fatić also criticizes the exclusion of the countries of the Former Yugoslavia from decision-making in The Hague. This exclusion, he claims, has lessened the credibility, effectiveness and tendency to co-operation between the countries and international

* Cand. jur , Johann Wolfgang Goethe-University, Frankfurt/Main.

organizations generally and the ICTY specifically. The keywords for Fatić are credibility and effectiveness. The ICTY allegedly lacks this credibility by serving not only as a judicial but also as a diplomatic tool, leaving the political leaders – the true warmongers – unindicted. The possibility of achieving catharsis through the ICTY goes unrealised. (Fatić's criticism that only Serbian suspects had been indicted as to the date of publication cannot be refuted. Since Fatić finished writing in early 1999, however, recent developments have undermined it: e.g. Slobodan Milošović has been extradited, and Croatian leaders have been indicted and their extradition requested.)

Fatić discusses next "The Nature of Peace in the Former Yugoslavia" and how to distinguish war criminals from war heroes. According to Fatić, the ICTY's main task should be to define clearly the criminal responsibility of individuals, be they the "ordinary man" or political and military leaders. This definition is necessary in order to publicly convey an unambiguous message about the legitimacy and illegitimacy of wartime acts. The author recommends the establishment of a "hierarchy of guilt", according to which the political and military leaders implicated in ethnic cleansing and other war crimes should first be prosecuted. Only by also prosecuting those atop the chain of command who instigated war crimes can the ICTY achieve popular credibility and thereby serve as a forum for reconciliation. (Accordingly, Fatić calls for NATO's political leaders as well as its troops to be held responsible for violations of international humanitarian law.) Fatić stresses that "the most notorious proof of failure" of the ICTY has been its non-indictment of Franjo Tudman and his associates. Additionally, Fatić argues that the Tribunal's lack of decisive and consistent action has given rise to the accusations of opportunism on the part of the ICTY and the international community as a whole. Delays in prosecution have also enabled many war criminals to assume the status of war heroes within their communities, a status that becomes ever more difficult to overthrow as more time passes. In order to avoid further deterioration in the ICTY's credibility, Fatić proposes the introduction of a "deontic type of justice", which would be applied regardless of the practical consequences (due to its basis in substantive moral principles) and which would not permit a distinction between morally justified and unjustified actions.

Fatić's third chapter concerns itself with "The Political Landscape of Peace in the Balkans". He begins by describing the special character of the ICTY. In contrast to earlier war crimes tribunals, it was established to resolve tensions and achieve justice in the aftermath of civil war. The ICTY could thus have served as a model for a new type of war crimes tribunal. Fatić then explains why the ICTY has not lived up to its expectations. The author recapitulates the events of the Yugoslav civil war between 1991 and the end of 1995, when the Dayton Peace Accords were signed. It is demonstrated that already at this stage, the partiality of the "international community" – a term Fatić dislikes due to its alleged lack of differentiation – and thus that of the NATO troops led to the failure of the ICTY. The author goes on to argue that Dayton's "civil provisions" could have brought about the re-establishment of civil society in Bosnia – assuming prior reconciliation and regeneration of mutual trust – only if the IFOR presence had been based on the utmost impartiality. This very impartiality was allegedly lacking, however, and political stability was consequently not achieved.

One of the most urgent civil problems in the Balkans, particularly in Bosnia, was the return of refugees. Fatić strongly accuses the countries hosting refugees of violating fundamental civil rights. According to him, the host countries used the planned "return of refugees" as an excuse to expel them mainly for economic reasons, which inflicted additional harm on already once displaced persons.

Fatić continues by summarizing the history of war crimes tribunals and the rationale behind the establishment of the ICTY. The ICTY was above all intended to deter new atrocities. Since some of the most serious war crimes were committed after its establishment in Dayton, however, the Tribunal failed to fulfil this objective, thereby damaging its credibility severely. The ICTY was also intended to restore confidence in the international community. The author closely analyses the Tribunal's initial indictments, in which only Serbs were charged with war crimes. This fact is cited in support of his claim of a lack of impartiality.

The author demands that individual responsibility be determined in order to enable true reconciliation in the region. Fatić does not tire of arguing that those who encouraged or initiated the commission of war crimes should in particular be held individually responsible. (He does, however, concede the difficulties of doing so.) The author rejects thereby the concept of the collective guilt of an entire country.

Fatić analyses NATO's strategic interest in the Balkans, concluding that ignorance about its social, military and political circumstances has exacerbated tensions in the region. Nonetheless, he acknowledges the benign nature of the European policy of moderation, contrasting it to the dangerous radicalism governing the relations among Balkan groups. The author urges the reader, however, to distinguish clearly between the region's ruling elites and the "simple" population on which the elites imposed their nationalist ideology. Fatić traces the origins of the conflict back to insecurities that the rulers sought to overcome through political radicalisation.

The accusations repeatedly thrown at NATO and the "international community" as a whole become somewhat tiresome, particularly since Fatić, when referring to the Serbian population, does not tire of emphasizing the importance of impartiality and the determination of individual rather than collective guilt. Similarly remarkable is that the Serbian army's atrocities are considered worthy of mention merely in passing. In contrast, the intervening powers' mistakes are pointed out over and over again, but no real alternatives to their actions are suggested. Indeed, many of Fatić's criticisms take the form of keywords, lacking elaboration.

Fatić's book does provide insight into an important aspect of the conflict that international organizations might have so far overlooked: the perception of the ICTY by the population of the Former Yugoslavia, particularly war crimes victims. The author delivers their point of view very clearly, highlighting the shortcomings of the international community, NATO, IFOR and the ICTY. The delivery is uncensored and the criticism harsh and unsparing. Unfortunately, the reader is often left to wonder how matters might be improved, as Fatić largely fails to propose practicable alternatives to the current policies. Some measures to increase or even reestablish the ICTY's credibility with the region's population are at suggested. Many of the highlighted problems go, however, unanswered, though they pose obvious and important questions.

Fatić accuses the ICTY of serving as a political tool and yet he at times comes dangerously close to becoming one himself. (It is true that many of the recent developments, such as Milošović's extradition, were still unimaginable when the author finished writing and could therefore not be taken into consideration in the analysis. Nonetheless, this means that some of the author's observations and criticisms may soon be out of date.) Fatić repeatedly alleges that NATO troops also committed war crimes, though he never offers detailed proof. He calls for the prosecution of political leaders from the intervening powers, equating them with the warmongering Milošović and his troops. None of the early efforts by international organizations to find a peaceful solution are mentioned, except once, when the attempts at reconciliation by the Clinton administration are favourably referred to.

Despite such shortcomings, Fatić's book makes a useful contribution to a highly necessary debate. It is of vital importance to understand the desires and feelings of participants in a civil war. Only with such under-

standing can international war crimes tribunals like the ICTY play a leading role in the re-integration of the population, the re-establishment of mutual trust and the rejection of old aggressions - in a word, in reconciliation.
The directness of Fatić's language and analysis enables the reader to see
some of the structural and organizational mistakes more clearly, albeit often only from one perspective. His observations provide us with the opportunity to learn from these mistakes in carrying out the ICTY's work at present and in establishing similar tribunals in future.

The author never mentions the technical difficulties that the ICTY has
had to face: neither the usual difficulties in searching for testimonies and
collecting evidence nor the unusual difficulties due to the exceptional fact
that the ICTY was established in the aftermath of a civil and not an interstate war. Fatić is unfortunately inclined to present only one side of the
story. Nonetheless, his emphasis on the importance of impartiality in the
reconciliatory function of the ICTY is convincing. The determination with
which the author demands a reform of the ICTY has the potential to serve
as a wake-up call. The ICTY's reform is essential, if its reconciliatory
function in the Balkans is to be realized and more if its statute is soon to
serve as a blueprint for war crimes justice. Fatić represents a group that
has recently voiced its concerns about the ICTY more loudly and that has
received increasing attention from the media and the general public. Fatić
would like to see the abandonment of black-and-white thinking about the
events in the Balkans and a move away from the idea of the collective
guilt of an entire nation towards a system of individual responsibility.
Fatić does not reject the ICTY as such. He merely claims the right to an
impartial ICTY, serving as a tool of justice and not diplomacy. If asked
whether war crimes tribunals can contribute to reconciliation, Fatić would
likely answer, "yes, but."

Otto Triffterer (ed.), Commentary on the Rome Statute of the International Criminal Court. Baden-Baden: Nomos Verlagsgesellschaft, 1999, 1295 pp.
Rita Silek*

The Statute of the International Criminal Court is one of the biggest achievements of the United Nations. The idea of a permanent international criminal court to serve as a deterrent for the most serious international crimes was raised as early as the end of World War II. The drafting process began shortly thereafter at the UN but was interrupted for several decades by the Cold War, to be resumed in 1989. The matter was referred to the International Law Commission, then to an Ad Hoc Committee on the Establishment of an International Criminal Court, and then to the Preparatory Committee on the Establishment of an International Criminal Court. In June-July 1998 a diplomatic conference was convened in Rome which finally adopted the Statute of the International Criminal Court on 17th July. The conference also decided on the establishment of the Preparatory Commission for the International Criminal Court which is charged with drafting further documents necessary for the functioning of the Court, such as the Elements of Crimes and the Rules of Procedure and Evidence.

The aim of the International Criminal Court is to, as UN Secretary-General Kofi Annan stated, to end the culture of impunity, that is not to leave unpunished the perpetrators of the most serious international crimes. Upon entry into force, the International Criminal Court will have jurisdiction over those international crimes which are regarded by the international community as the gravest crimes, namely genocide, crimes against humanity, war crimes and aggression, provided that the latter is ever defined by the Preparatory Commission. Since there is currently profound disagreement over the issue, conferral of jurisdiction over aggression is not to be expected in the near future.

The jurisdiction of the Court is complementary, that is the perpetrators of the international crimes will be tried by the Court only if the states which would normally have jurisdiction are either unwilling or unable to prosecute. Accordingly, prosecution of these crimes remains primarily a state responsibility.

*   Legal officer of the International Law Department, Ministry of Foreign Affairs, Hungary.

The Statute of the International Criminal Court has been ratified to date by 56 states and is expected to enter into force in July 2002.

The Commentary on the Rome Statute of the International Criminal Court was edited by Professor Otto Triffterer of the University of Salzburg and includes contributions by 51 authors from 25 countries, representing all continents and major legal systems. The aim of the Commentary is to present information from those who participated at the Preparatory Committee and the Rome Conference about the process of codification, as well as to provide the readers with an interpretation of the Statute which takes into account its history. The intent thereby is to assist with the Commentary those persons who are responsible for the implementation of the Statute, on national and international level, states which are still considering signing it, as well as academics and NGOs. The other declared goal of the book is to preserve the information about the work of the Preparatory Committee and that of the Rome Conference.

The Commentary is introduced by Cherif Bassiouni and Philippe Kirsch who present the drafting history of the International Criminal Court and evaluate the future role of the Court. Kirsch describes, in particular, the positions of various groups of states participating in the process and gives an overview of those provisions that were included at the initiative of the so-called Like-Minded Group in order to create a strong and effective Court. The author also points out those provisions which were the results of compromises among the groups.

Triffterer's preliminary remarks serve to put the ICC in a broader perspective. After the historical overview the editor of the Commentary discusses the theoretical foundation and the function of an international criminal jurisdiction. He also briefly describes the main features of the Statute and the compromises made during drafting. The author ends his introduction with the assessment of the results of the Rome Conference and the future perspectives of International Criminal Court.

The articles of the Statute are presented one by one in a unified system. Each analysis is headed by the article's text and the relevant literature. The authors continue with the drafting history of the articles which are followed by analysis and interpretation. Special remarks are added to some chapters.

The Commentary offers a comprehensive and thorough analysis of the Statute which Philippe Kirsch called an international instrument on a very sensitive subject, with the aim of promoting a culture of accountability at the end of 20th century. It will be of great use to all those who work on the implementation of the Statute, participate at the sessions of the Preparatory Commission, as well as for scientific purposes.

Bibliography

Aboagye, F., *Towards New Peacekeeping Partnerships in Africa?*, African Security Review, Vol. 10, No. 2, 2001, p. 19.

Adebajo, A./Sriram, C., *Managing Armed Conflicts in the 21st Century*, 2001, 288 pp.

Akhavan, P., *Beyond Impunity: Can International Criminal Justice Prevent Future Atrocities,* American Journal of International Law, Vol. 95, No. 1, 2001, p. 7.

Alao, A./Olonisakin, F., *Economic Fragility and Political Fluidity: Explaining Natural Resources and Conflicts*, International Peacekeeping (Frank Cass), Vol. 7, No. 4, 2000, p. 23.

Alexander, B.C., *East Timor: Will There be Justice?*, Human Rights Brief, Vol. 8, No. 1, 2000, p. 5.

Ankenbrand, B., *Humanitäre Interventionen: Anwendungsvoraussetzungen für ein politisches Konzept*, Vierteljahresschrift für Sicherheit und Frieden (S+F), Vol. 19, No. 3, 2001, p. 132.

Antonopoulos, C., *Whatever Happened to Crimes against Peace?*, Journal of Conflict and Security Law, Vol. 6, No. 1, 2001, p. 33.

Assenburg, M., *Der Nahost-Friedensprozess und der Beitrag der EU - Bilanz und Perspektiven,* Die Friedens-Warte, Vol. 76, No. 2-3, 2001, p. 257.

Badsey, S./Latawski, P. (eds.), *Britain, NATO and the Lessons of the Balkan Conflict*, 2001, 288 pp.

Barnes, S.H., *The Contribution of Democracy to Rebuilding Postconflict Societies*, American Journal of International Law, Vol. 95, No. 1, 2001, p. 86.

M. Bothe and B. Kondoch (eds.),
International Peacekeeping. The Yearbook of International Peace Operations, Volume 7, 2001, 455–475.
© 2002 *Kluwer Law International. Printed in the Netherlands.*

Beck, M., *Defekte Architektur und gesellschaftliche Widerstände - Zur Problematik des israelisch-palästinensischen Friedensprozesses*, Die Friedens-Warte, Vol. 76, No. 2-3, 2001, p. 179.

Bell, C., *Peace Agreements and Human Rights*, Oxford University Press, 2000, 380 pp.

Benvenuti, P., *The ICTY's Prosecutor and the Review of the NATO Bombing Campaign against the Federal Republic of Yugoslavia*, European Journal of International Law, Vol. 12, No. 3, 2001, p. 503.

Berdal, M., *Lessons Not Learned: The Use of Force in 'Peace Operations' in the 1990s*, International Peacekeeping (Frank Cass), Vol. 7, No. 4, 2000, p. 55.

Betram, C., *Starting Over Again*, NATO Review, Vol. 49, Spring, 2001, p. 12.

Booth, K., *The Kosovo Tragedy*, Frank Cass, 2001, 280 pp.

Bothe, M./Dörschel, T., *The UN Peacekeeping Experience*, in The Handbook of Law of the Visiting Forces (Fleck (ed.), Oxford University Press, 2001), p. 487.

Bothe, M./Marauhn, T., *UN Administration of Kosovo and East Timor: Concept, Legality and Limitations of Security Council Mandated Trusteeship Administration*, in Kosovo and the International Community (Tomuschat, C. (ed.), 2001), p. 217.

Bothe, M., *The Protection of Civilian Population and NATO Bombing on Yugoslavia: Comments on a Report to the Prosecutor of the ICTY*, European Journal of International Law, Vol. 12, No. 3, 2001, p. 531.

Boulden, J., *Peace Enforcement: The United Nations Experience in Congo, Somalia and Bosnia*, Praeger Publisher, 2001, 176 pp.

Boyer, Y., *France and European Security and Defence Policy: A Leadership Role Among Equals*, Vierteljahresschrift für Sicherheit und Frieden (S+F), Vol. 19, No. 2, 2001, p. 69.

Brody, R./Ratner, M. (eds.), *The Pinochet Papers*, Kluwer Law International, 2000, 520 pp.

Brooks, D., *Messiahs or Mercenaries? The Future of International Private Military Services*, International Peacekeeping (Frank Cass), Vol. 7, No. 4, 2000, p. 129.

Bruha, T./Bortfeld, M., *Terrorismus und Selbstverteidigung – Voraussetzungen und Umfang erlaubter Selbstverteidigungsmaßnahmen nach den Anschlägen vom 11. September 2001*, Vereinte Nationen, Vol. 49, No. 5, 2001, p. 161.

Brzoska, M., *Der Schatten Saddams - Die Vereinten Nationen auf der Suche nach zielgerichteten Sanktionen*, Vereinte Nationen, Vol. 49, No. 2, 2001, p. 56.

Buo, S., *Reflections on United Nations Peace Operations in Africa*, International Law FORUM du droit international, Vol. 3, No. 2, 2001, p. 87.

Burger, K., *Alliance Agrees SFOR Cuts*, Jane's Defence Weekly, Vol. 35, No. 23, 2001, p. 3.

Büllesbach, R., *Aufgaben öffentlicher Sicherheit für KFOR-Soldaten im Kosovo*, Humanitäres Völkerrecht-Informationsschriften, Vol. 14, No. 2, 2001, p. 83.

Byron. C., *Armed Conflicts: International or Non-International?*, Journal of Conflict and Security Law, Vol. 6, No. 1, 2001, p. 63.

Campbell, K./Mitchell, D., *Crisis in the Taiwan Strait?*, Foreign Affairs, Vol. 80, No. 4, 2001, p. 14.

Carey, H.F., *'Women and Peace and Security': The Politics of Implementing Gender Sensitivity Norms in Peacekeeping*, International Peacekeeping (Frank Cass), Vol. 8, No. 2, 2001, p. 39.

Carment, D./Schnabel, A. (eds.), *Conflict Prevention - Path to Peace or Grand Illusion*, Brookings Institute, 2001, 460 pp.

Carpenter, T.G. (ed.), *NATO Enters the 21st Century*, Frank Cass, 2000, 200 pp.

Cerone, J., *Minding the Gap: Outlining KFOR Accountability in Post-Conflict Kosovo*, European Journal of International Law, Vol. 12, No. 3, 2001, p. 469.

Chesterman, S., *Just War or Just Peace?*, *Humanitarian Intervention and International Law*, Oxford University Press, 2001, 300 pp.

Chopra, J., *The UN's Kingdom of East Timor*, Survival, Vol. 42, No. 3, 2000, p. 27.

Clapham, C., *Rethinking African States*, African Security Review, Vol. 10, No. 3, 2001, p. 7.

Clements, P., *Coups and the Fiji Military*, Peacekeeping and International Relations, Vol. 30, No. 1-3, 2001, p. 1.

Conlon, P., *United Nations Sanctions Management: A Case Study of the Iraqi Sanctions Committee, 1990 – 1994*, Transnational Publisher, 2000, 220 pp.

Cooper, N., *Conflict Goods: The Challenges for Peacekeeping and Conflict Prevention*, International Peacekeeping (Frank Cass), Vol. 8, No. 3, 2001, p. 21.

Cortright, D./Lopez, G., *The Sanctions Decade. Assessing UN Strategies in the 1990s*, Lynne Rienner Publishers, 2000, 275 pp.

Cortright, D./Millar, A./Lopez, A., *Smart Sanctions: Restructuring UN Policy in Iraq*, Lynne Rienner Publishers, 2001, 41 pp.

Croft, S./Terriff, T. (eds.), *Critical Reflections on Security and Change*, Frank Cass, 2000, 272 pp.

Cryer, R., *The Boundaries of Liability in International Criminal Law, or "Selectivity by Stealth"*, Journal of Conflict and Security Law, Vol. 6, No. 1, 2001, p. 3.

Daase, C., *Terrorismus - Begriffe, Theorien und Gegenstrategien. Ergebnisse und Probleme sozialwissenschaftlicher Forschung*, Die Friedens-Warte, Vol. 76, No. 1, 2001, p. 55.

Daglish, K., *The Crime of Genocide?: Nulyarimma v. Thompson*, International and Comparative Law Quarterly, Vol. 50, No. 2, 2001, p. 404.

Davis, A., *Taliban Plans Offensive*, Jane's Defence Weekly, Vol. 35, No. 22, 2001, p. 14.

Debiel, T., *Strengthening the UN as an Effective World Authority: Cooperative Security versus Hegemonic Crisis Management*, Global Governance, Vol. 6, No. 1, 2000, p. 25.

Dee, M., *Coalition of the Willing and Humanitarian Intervention: Australia's Involvement with INTERFET*, International Peacekeeping (Frank Cass), Vol. 8, No. 3, 2001, p. 1.

Degroot, G.J., *A Few Good Women: Gender Stereotypes, the Military and Peacekeeping*, International Peacekeeping (Frank Cass), Vol. 8, No. 2, 2001, p. 23.

Dekker, I., *Illegality and Legitimacy of Humanitarian Interventions: Synopsis of and Comments on a Dutch Report*, Journal of Conflict and Security Law, Vol. 6, No. 1, 2001, p. 115.

Deluce, D., *Media Wars*, NATO Review, Vol. 48, Winter 2000-2001, p. 16.

Detter, I., *The Law of War*, Cambridge University Press, 2000, 546 pp.

Dicke, K., *Standpunkt: Weltgesetzgeber Sicherheitsrat*, Vereinte Nationen, Vol. 49, No. 5, 2001, p. 163.

Dobbins, J., *Steady as She Goes*, NATO Review, Vol. 49, Spring, 2001, p. 9.

Donelly, C., *Rethinking Security*, NATO Review, Vol. 48, Winter 2000-2001, p. 32.

Dreist, P., *Rechtliche Aspekte des KFOR-Einsatzes*, Neue Zeitschrift für Wehrrecht, Vol. 43, No. 1, 2001, p. 1.

Drew, C., *The East Timor Story: International Law on Trial*, European Journal of International Law, Vol. 12, No. 4, 2001, p. 651.

Egan, P.T., *The Kosovo Intervention and Collective Self-Defence*, International Peacekeeping (Frank Cass), Vol. 8, No. 3, 2001, p. 39.

Eisele, M., *Die Vereinten Nationen und das internationale Krisenmanagement. Ein Insider-Bericht*, Verlag Josef Knecht, 252 pp.

Erhardt, H.-G., *Leitbild Friedensmacht? Die Europäische Sicherheits- und Verteidigungspolitik und die Herausforderungen der Konfliktbearbeitung*, Vierteljahresschrift für Sicherheit und Frieden (S+F), Vol. 19, No. 2, 2001, p. 50.

Fenrick, W.J., *Targeting and Proportionality during the NATO Bombing Campaign against Yugoslavia*, European Journal of International Law, Vol. 12., No. 3, 2001, p. 489.

Ferencz, B.B., *A Nuremberg Prosecutor's Response to Henry Kissinger*, Vierteljahresschrift für Sicherheit und Frieden (S+F), Vol. 19, No. 2, 2002, p. 86.

Finke, J./Wandscher, C., *Terrorismusbekämpfung jenseits militärischer Gewalt – Ansätze der Vereinten Nationen zur Verhütung und Beseitigung des internationalen Terrorismus*, Vereinte Nationen, Vol. 49, No. 5, 2001, p. 168.

Findlay, T., *The Blue Helmets' First War? Use of Force by the UN in the Kongo*, 1960-64, The Canadian Peacekeeping Press, 2000, 192 pp.

Finlay, B./O'Hanlon, M., *NATO's Underachieving Middle Powers: From Burdenshedding to Burdensharing,* International Peacekeeping (Frank Cass), Vol. 7, No. 4, 2000, p. 145.

Fischer, H./Kress, K./Lüder, S.R. (eds.), *International and National Prosecution of Crimes under International Law,* Berlin Verlag, 2001, 873 pp.

Fleck, D. (ed.), *The Handbook of the Law of Visiting Forces,* 2001, 600 pp.

Fox, G.H./Roth, B.R. (eds.), *Democratic Governance and International Law,* 2000, 600 pp.

Fox, M.-J., *The Idea of Women in Peacekeeping: Lysistra and Antigone,* International Peacekeeping (Frank Cass), Vol. 8, No. 2, 2001, p. 9.

Franckx, E./Pauwels A./Smis, S., *An International Trusteeship for Kosovo: Attempt to Find a Solution to the Conflict,* Studia Diplomatica, Vol. 52, No. 5-6, 1999, p. 155.

Freeman, M., *The United Nations and the Promotion and Protection of Human Rights: Identifying Strenghts, Weaknesses and Limitations in a Complex System,* Vierteljahresschrift für Sicherheit und Frieden (S+F), Vol.19, No. 3, 2001, p.110.

Friman, H., *Justice in the Aftermath of Peace?,* African Security Review, Vol. 10, No. 3, 2001, p. 63.

Frulli, M., *Are Crimes against Humanity More Serious Than War Crimes?,* European Journal of International Law, Vol. 12, No. 2, 2001, p. 329.

Gardam, J.G./Jarvis, M.J., *Women, Armed Conflict and International Law,* Kluwer Law International, 2001, 308 pp.

Gazzini, T., *NATO Coercive Military Activities in the Yugoslav Crisis (1992-1999),* European Journal of International Law, Vol. 12, No. 3, 2001, p. 391.

Gerson, A., *Peace Building: The Private Sector's Role*, American Journal of International Law, Vol. 95, 2001, No. 1, p. 102.

Gordon, D.S./Toase, F.H. (eds.), *Aspects of Peacekeeping (The Sandhurst Conference Series)*, 2001, 312 pp.

Goredema, C., *Transnational Crime Initiatives and Legislative Reform in Zimbabwe*, African Security Review, Vol. 10, No. 3, 2001, p. 78.

Gowlland-Debbas, V., *The Limits of Unilateral Enforcement of Community Objectives in the Framework of Peace Maintenance*, European Journal of International Law, Vol. 11, No. 2, 2000, p. 361.

Gowlland-Debbas, V. (ed.), *United Nations Sanctions and International Law*, Kluwer Law International, 2001, 408 pp.

Göbel, D.H., *Riot Control Agents im Kosovo - Zur völkerrechtlichen Zulässigkeit des Einsatzes von Reizstoffen durch KFOR*, Humanitäres Völkerrecht-Informationsschriften, Vol. 14, No. 1, 2001, p. 34.

Göbel, R./Guilliard, J./Schiffmann, M., *Der Irak – Ein belagertes Land*, 2001, 243 pp.

Graham-Brown, S., *Sanctioning Saddam: The Politics of Intervention in Iraq*, I. B. Tauris, 1999, 380 pp.

Gray, C., *International Law and the Use of Force*, Oxford University Press, 2000, 250 pp.

Gries, T., *Der aktuelle Fall: der lange Arm des nationalen Richters: Demokratische Republik Kongo v. Königreich Belgien*, Humanitäres Völkerrecht-Informationsschriften, Vol. 14, No. 1, 2001, p. 19.

Gryst, R., *More than Eunuchs at the Orgy: Observation and Monitoring Reconsidered*, International Peacekeeping (Frank Cass), Vol. 8, No. 3, 2001, p. 59.

Gustenau, G. (ed.), *Humanitäre militärische Intervention zwischen Legalität und Legitimität,* 2000, 207 pp.

Harhoff, F., *Unauthorised Interventions - Armed Violence in the Name of Humanity?*, Nordic Journal of International Law, Vol. 70, Nos. 1-2, 2001, p. 65.

Harmon, C.C., *Terrorism Today*, Frank Cass, 2000, 320 pp.

Haslam, E., *Information Warfare: Technological Changes and International Law*, Journal of Conflict and Security Law, Vol. 5, No. 2, 2000, p. 157.

Hasse, J./Müller, E./Schneider, P. (eds.), *Humanitäres Völkerrecht*, Nomos, 2001, pp. 597.

Hebel, H.A.M. v./Lammers, J.G./Schukking, J. (eds.), *Reflections on the International Criminal Court*, Kluwer Law International, 1999, 230 pp.

Heiligsetzer, E., *Religiös-fundamentalistischer Terrorismus im Vergleich: Extremischer Protestantismus in den USA und fundamentalistische Gewalt im islamischen Orient*, Die Friedens-Warte, Vol. 76, No. 1, 2001, p. 81.

Heintze, H.J., *Zur Durchsetzung der UN-Völkermordkonvention,* Humanitäres Völkerrecht-Informationsschriften, Vol. 13, No. 4, 2000, p. 225.

Heinz, W.S., *Internationaler Menschenrechtsschutz durch die VN – Menschenrechtskommission (MRK): Chancen und Grenzen*, Vierteljahresschrift für Sicherheit und Frieden (S+F), Vol. 19, No. 3, 2001, p. 120.

Heisbourg, F./Wijk, R. de, *Is the Fundamental Nature of the Transatlantic Security Relationship Changing?*, NATO Review, Vol. 49, 2001, p. 15.

Henderson, C., *RCMP and Navy Join Forces at the DILI Police Academy*, Gazette, Vol. 62, No. 2, 2000, p. 18.

Henkin, A.H. (ed.), *Honoring Human Rights*, Brookings Institute, 2001, 40 pp.

Hill, L., *Turkey Slows Build-up of EU Defence*, Jane's Defence Weekly, Vol. 35, No. 22, 2001, p. 21.

Hill, L., *EU Military Staff Goes Operational*, Jane's Defence Weekly, Vol. 35, No. 25, 2001, p. 2.

Hills, A., *The Inherent Limits of Military Forces in Policing Peace Operations*, International Peacekeeping (Frank Cass), Vol. 8, No. 3, 2001, p. 79.

Hilpold, P., *Humanitarian Intervention: Is There a Need for a Legal Reappraisal?*, European Journal of International Law, Vol. 12, No. 3, 2001, p. 437.

Hoffman, M.H., *Peace-enforcement Actions and Humanitarian Law: Emerging Rules for "Interventional Armed Conflict"*, International Review of the Red Cross, No. 837, 2000, p. 193.

Holdanowicz, G., *Czech-Polish-Slovak Link Aims to Set up Special Brigade for NATO-EU Operations*, Jane's Defence Weekly, Vol. 35, No. 25, 2001, p. 20.

Hughes, L., *Can International Law Protect Child Soldiers?*, Peace Review, Vol. 12, No. 3, 2000, p. 399.

Jones, C./Kennedy-Pipe, C. (eds.), *International Security in a Global Age*, Frank Cass, 2001, 256 pp.

Jorgensen, N.H.B., *The Responsibility of States for International Crimes*, Kluwer Law International, 2000, 360 pp.

Kalkku, E., *The United Nations Authorisation to Peace Enforcement with the Use of Force in the Light of Practice of the UN Security Council*, Finnish Yearbook of International Law, Vol. 9, 1998, p. 349.

Kamto, M., *Le cadre juridique des opérations de maintien de la paix des Nations Unies*, International Law FORUM du droit international, Vol. 3, No. 2, 2001, p. 95.

Karamé, K.H., *Women in Military Positions in Peace Operations: Experiences of the Norwegian Battalion in UNIFIL 1978–1998*, International Peacekeeping (Frank Cass), Vol. 8, No. 2, 2001, p.85.

Kassin, A.F., *Der Friedensprozess von Oslo: Nur eine Lösung*, Die Friedens-Warte, Vol. 76, Nos. 2-3, 2001, p. 241.

Keen, D., *War and Peace: What's the Difference?*, International Peacekeeping (Frank Cass), Vol. 7, No. 4, 2000, p. 1.

Khan, R., *United Nations Peacekeeping in International Conflicts: Problems and Perspectives*, Max Planck Yearbook of United Nations Law, Vol. 4, 2000, p. 543.

Kissinger, H., *The Perils of Universal Jurisdiction*, Foreign Affairs, Vol. 80, No. 4, 2001, p. 86.

Knaus, G./Cox, M., *Whither Bosnia?*, NATO Review, Vol. 48, Winter 2000-2001, p. 6.

Kobe, R., *Entwicklung und Perspektiven der deutschen Zivil-Militärischen Zusammenarbeit*, Humanitäres Völkerrecht-Informationsschriften, Vol. 14, No. 1, 2001, p. 4.

Kondoch, B./Silek, R., *Special Court for Sierra Leone*, Conflict Trends, No. 1, 2001, p. 28.

Kondoch, B., *Neueste Entwicklungen im Völkerstrafrecht aufgezeigt am Beispiel Sierra Leone, Kambodscha und Ost-Timor*, Vierteljahresschrift für Sicherheit und Frieden (S+F), Vol. 19, No. 3, 2001, p. 126.

Kondoch, B., *The United Nations Administration of East Timor*, Journal of Conflict and Security Law, Vol. 6, No. 2, 2001, p. 245.

Kouchner, B., *The Challenge of Rebuilding Kosovo*, NATO Review, No. 3, 1999, p. 12.

Kühne, W., *Zukunft der UN – Friedenseinsätze Lehren aus dem Brahimi Report*, Blätter für deutsche und internationale Politik, Vol. 2, 2000, p. 1355.

Kühne, W., *Friedenseinsätze verbessern - der Brahimi-Report*, SWP - aktuell, No. 63, 2000, 8 pp.

Lapidoth, R., *Israel und die Palästinenser: Einige rechtliche Aspekte*, Die Friedens-Warte, Vol. 76, Nos. 2-3, 2001, p. 211.

Lewis, F., *Problems of UN Peacekeepings*, International Law FORUM du droit international, Vol. 3, No. 2, 2001, p. 80.

Lightburn, D., *Seeking Security Solutions*, NATO Review, Vol. 48, Winter 2000-2001, p. 12.

Linde, H., *Massenvernichtungswaffen, eine Herausforderung für die Verbreitung der Genfer Konventionen und ihrer Zusatzprotokolle*, Humanitäres Völkerrecht-Informationsschriften, Vol. 14, No. 1, 2001, p. 37.

Lobel, J., *The Use of Force to Respond to Terrorist Attacks: The Bombing of Sudan and Afghanistan*, Yale Journal of International Law, Vol. 24, No. 2, 1999, p. 537.

Lorenz, F.M., *A Series of Reports from Kosovo*, Peacekeeping and International Relations, Vol. 30, No. 1-3, 2001, p. 13.

Lüder, S.R., *Die völkerrechtliche Verantwortlichkeit der Nordatlantikvertrages-Organisation bei der militärischen Absicherung der Friedensvereinbarung von Dayton*, Neue Zeitschrift für Wehrrecht, Vol. 43, No. 3, 2001, p. 107.

Lüder, S.R., *Zur Rechtsnatur des Internationalen Strafgerichtshofes*, Humanitäres Völkerrecht-Informationsschriften, Vol. 14, No. 3, p. 136.

Lynch, D., *Russian Peacekeeping Strategies in the Cis: The Cases of Moldova, Georgia and Tajikistan*, Palgrave, 2000, 226 pp.

Madsen, W., *Genocide and Covert Operations in Africa 1993-1999*, African Security Review, Vol. 10, No. 3, 2001, p. 142.

Magaš, B./Žanić, I. (eds.), *The War in Croatia and Bosnia-Herzegovina, 1991-1995,* Frank Cass, 2001, 416 pp.

Malan, M., *'Layered response' to an African Conflict*, African Security Review, Vol. 10, No. 2, 2001, p. 75.

Malik, O., *Enough Definition of Terrorism*, Royal Institute of International Affairs, 2000, 88 pp.

Malone, D.M./Wermester, K., *Boom and Bust? The Changing Nature of UN Peacekeeping*, International Peacekeeping (Frank Cass), Vol. 7, No. 4, 2000, p. 37.

Maresca, L./Maslen, S., *The Banning of Anti-Personnel Landmines*, Cambridge University Press, 2000, 698 pp.

Matheson, M.J., *United Nations Governance of Postconflict Societies*, American Journal of International Law, Vol. 95, No. 1, 2001, p. 76.

Matlose, K./Pule, N.W., *The Military in Lesotho*, African Security Review, Vol. 10, No. 2, 2001, p. 63.

McCormack, T.L.H./Tilbury, M./Triggs, G.D. (eds.), *A Century of War and Peace*, Kluwer Law International, 2001, 305 pp.

McCoubrey, H., *The Protection of Creed and Opinion in the Laws of Armed Conflict*, Journal of Conflict and Security Law, Vol. 5, No. 2, 2000, p. 135.

McCoubrey, H., *From Nuremberg to Rome: Restoring the Defence of Superior Orders*, International and Comparative Law Quarterly, Vol. 50, No. 2, 2001, p. 386.

McGregor, L., *Individual Accountability in South Africa: Cultural or Political Facade?*, American Journal of International Law, Vol. 95, No. 1, 2001, p. 32.

MacKinnon, C., *The Day the World Changed: A Reflection on Democracy in a Time of "Globalized" War, Peacekeeping and International Relations*, Vol. 30, No. 4, 2001, p. 2.

Mejcher, H., *Die Anfäng des Nahostkonflikts, 1897-1920*, Die Friedens-Warte, Vol. 76, Nos. 2-3, 2001, p. 147.

Melven, L., *A People Betrayed - The Role of West in Rwanda's Genocide*, African Security Review, Vol. 10, No. 3, 2001, p. 139.

Millard, A., *Children in Armed Conflict*, Security Dialogue, Vol. 32, No. 2, 2001, p. 187.

Muguruza, C.C., *Strengthening the European Union's Common Foreign Policy: The European Council's Decision to Develop an Autonomous Military Crisis Management Capability in the Context of Petersberg Tasks*, Humanitäres Völkerrecht-Informationsschriften, Vol. 13, No. 4, 2000, p. 206.

Müller, E./Schneider P., *Funktionsbedingungen Internationaler Gerichtsbarkeit*, Vierteljahresschrift für Sicherheit und Frieden (S+F), Vol.19, No. 3, 2001, p. 158.

Nieuwkerk, A.v., *Regionalism into Globalism? War into Peace?*, African Security Review, Vol. 10, No. 2, 2001, p. 7.

Oeter, S., *Terrorismus - ein völkerrechtliches Verbrechen? Zur Frage der Unterstellung terroristischer Akte unter die Internationale Strafgerichtsbarkeit*, Die Friedens-Warte, Vol. 76, No. 1, 2001, p. 11.

Olsson, L., *Gender Mainstreaming in Practice: The United Nations Transitional Assistance Group in Namibia*, International Peacekeeping (Frank Cass), Vol. 8, No. 2, 2001, p. 97.

O'Shea, B., *Macedonia on the Brink?*, Peacekeeping and International Relations, Vol. 30, No. 4, 2001, p. 1.

O'Shea, B., *The Future of United Nations Peacekeeping*, Peacekeeping and International Relations, Vol. 30, No. 4, 2001, p. 17.

Othman, M., *Peacekeeping Operations in Asia*, International Law FORUM du droit international, Vol. 3, No. 2, 2001, p. 114.

Politi, M./Nesi, G. (eds.), *The Rome Statute of the International Criminal Court*, Ashgate, 2001, 340 pp.

Potier, T., *Conflict in Nagorno-Karabakh, Abbkhazia and South Osetia*, Kluwer Law International, 2001, 336 pp.

Rapoport, D.C. (ed.), *Inside Terrorist Organisations*, Frank Cass, 2001, 288 pp.

Ratner, S.R./Abrams, J.S., *Accountability for Human Rights Atrocities in International Law*, Oxford University Press, 2001, 398 pp.

Rauchhaus, R.W. (ed.), *Explaining NATO Enlargement*, Frank Cass, 2001, 232 pp.

Reschke, B., *Der Bericht des UN-Generalsekretärs über den Schutz von Zivilpersonen in bewaffneten Konflikten: Ein Beitrag zur Effektivierung des humanitären Völkerrechts?*, Humanitäres Völkerrecht-Informationsschriften, Vol. 14, No. 1, 2001, p. 10.

Richards, L., *Building Multi-Ethnic Peace in Bosnia*, Gazette, Vol. 62, No. 2, 2000, p. 19.

Richards, L., *International Training - RCMP partnerships: Building Skills to Serve the World's Communities*, Gazette, Vol. 62, No. 2, 2000, p. 34.

Richards, L., *MICAH Continues Canada's Civilian Support in Haiti*, Gazette, Vol. 62, No. 2, 2000, p. 11.

Richards, L., *MINUGUA: Canadian Police Monitoring Human Rights in Guatemala*, Gazette, Vol. 62, No. 2, 2000, p. 26.

Richards, L., *RCMP Forensic Teams in Kosovo*, Gazette, Vol. 62, No. 2, 2000, p.36.

Richards, L., *RCMP International Training and Peacekeeping Branch: Supporting the Peace Builders*, Gazette, Vol. 62, No. 2, 2000, p. 10.

Richards, L., *UNMIK: Building a Fragile Peace in Southeastern Europe*, Gazette, Vol. 62, No. 2, 2000, p. 23.

Richards, L., *UNTAET: Cooperation and Community Policing in East Timor*, Gazette, Vol. 62, No. 2, 2000, p. 14.

Richards, P., *War Crimes and the RCMP - Changing Investigations and Future Challenges for the Force*, Gazette, Vol. 62, No. 2, 2000, p. 30.

Rikhye, I., *The Politics and Practice of United Nations Peacekeeping: Past, Present and Future*, The Canadian Peacekeeping Press, 2000, 182 pp.

Roberts, A./Guelff, R. (eds.), *Documents on the Laws of War,* Oxford University Press, 2000, 765 pp.

Rozès, A., *Angolan Deadlock - Chronicle of a War With No Solution,* African Security Review, Vol. 10, No. 3, 2001, p. 17.

Rotberg, R. et al., *Peacekeeping and Peace Enforcement in Africa: Methods of Conflict Prevention*, Brookings Institute, 2001, 214 pp.

Ruffert, M., *The Administration of Kosovo and East-Timor by the International Community,* International and Comparative Law Quarterly, Vol. 50, No. 3, 2001, p. 613.

Rytter, J.E., *Humanitarian Intervention without the Security Council: From San Francisco to Kosovo - and Beyond*, Nordic Journal of International Law, Vol. 70, Nos. 1-2, 2001, p. 161.

Sarooshi, D., *The United Nations and the Development of Collective Security,* Oxford University Press, 2000, 334 pp.

Sauerwein, B., *Swiss Vote to Arm Peacekeepers*, Jane's Defence Weekly, Vol. 35, No. 25, 2001, p. 16.

Schabas, W.A., *An Introduction to the International Criminal Court*, Cambridge University Press, 2001, 336 pp.

Schabas, W.A., *Genocide International Law*, Cambridge University Press, 2000, 640 pp.

Schnabel, A./Thakur, R. (eds.), *Kosovo and the Challenge of Humanitarian Intervention*, United Nations University Press, 2000, 500 pp.

Schneider, M., *Der aktuelle Fall: Geiselnahme von humanitären Helfern in Somalia – der völkerrechtliche Schutz von Hilfspersonal*, Humanitäres Völkerrecht-Informationsschriften, Vol. 14, No. 3, p. 153.

Schreuer, C., *Is There a Legal Basis for Air Strikes against Iraq?*, International Law FORUM du droit international, Vol. 3, No. 2, 2001, p. 72.

Schürings. H., *Versagen im Angesicht des Völkermords - Die unabhängige Untersuchung zur Verantwortlichkeit der internationalen Gemeinschaft in Rwanda 1994*, Vereinte Nationen, Vol. 48, No. 2, 2000, p. 53.

Schüßler, R., *Humanitäre Interventionen und gerechter Krieg*, Vierteljahresschrift für Sicherheit und Frieden, No. 3, 2001, p. 138.

Serfaty, S., *Lasting Liaison*, NATO Review, Vol. 49, Spring 2001, p. 6.

Sharp, W.G., *Jus Paciarii: Emergent Legal Paradigms for UN Peace Operations, in the 21st Century*, Paciarii International, 1999, 392 pp.

Sharp, W.G., *The Use of Armed Force against Terrorism: American Hegemony or Impotence?*, Chicago Journal of International Law, Vol. 1, No. 1, 2000, p. 37.

Skjelsbæk, I., *Sexual Violence in Times of War: A New Challenge for Peace Operations?*, International Peacekeeping (Frank Cass), Vol. 8, No. 2, 2001, p. 69.

Sloan, E., *Speeding Deployment*, NATO Review, Vol. 49, Spring 2001, p. 30.

Socín, C./Dugone, A.C., *The Challenge of Avoiding Darkness in a Soldier's Mind*, Peacekeeping and International Relations, Vol. 30, No. 1-3, 2001, p. 2.

Sorel, J.M., *La responsabilité des Nations Unies dans les opérations de maintien de la paix*, International Law FORUM du droit international, Vol. 3, No. 2, 2001, p. 127.

Spillmann, K.R./Krause, J., (eds.), *Kosovo: Lessons Learned for International Cooperative Security*, Peter Lang Publishing, 2000, 245 pp.

Spoerri, P., *Die Fortgeltung völkerrechtlichen Besetzungsrechts während der Interimsphase palästinensischer Selbstverwaltung in der West Bank und Gaza*, Peter Lang Publishing, 2001, 323 pp.

Sriram, C.L., *Truth Commissions and the Quest for Justice: Stability and Accountability after Internal Strife*, International Peacekeeping (Frank Cass), Vol. 7, No. 4, 2000, p. 91.

Stahn, C., *Die Umsetzung des Rom-Statuts in nationales Recht - Ein erster rechtsvergleichender Überblick*, Humanitäres Völkerrecht-Informationsschriften, Vol. 13, No. 4, 2000, p. 200.

Stahn, C., *International Territorial Administration in the Former Yugoslavia: Origins, Development and Challenges Ahead*, Zeitschrift für ausländisches öffentliches Recht und Völkerrecht, Vol. 61, No. 1, 2001, p. 107.

Stein, T./Meiser, C., *Die Europäische Union und der Terrorismus*, Die Friedens-Warte, Vol. 76, No. 1, 2001, p. 33.

Stemmet, A., *Regulating Small Arms and Light Weapons - The African Exprience*, African Security Review, Vol. 10, No. 3, 2001, p. 90.

Strohmeyer, H., *Collapse and Reconstruction of A Judicial System: The United Nations Missions in Kosovo and East Timor*, American Journal of International Law, Vol. 95, No. 1, 2001, p. 46.

Talmon, S., *The Cyprus Question before the European Court of Justice*, European Journal of International Law, Vol. 12, No. 4, 2001, p. 727.

Taylor, M./Horgan, J. (eds.), *The Future of Terrorism*, Frank Cass, 2000, 320 pp.

Thakur, R./Schnabel, A. (eds.), *United Nations Peacekeeping Operations - Ad Hoc Missions, Permanent Engagement*, United Nations Publications, 2001, 280 pp.

Thakur, R./Newman, E. (eds), *New Millennium, New Perspectives,* United Nations Publications, 2001, 366 pp.

Thouvenin, J.M., *Le statut juridique des forces de maintien de la paix de Nations Unies,* International Law FORUM du droit international, Vol. 3, No. 2, 2001, p. 105.

Toggia, P./Lauderdale, P./Zegeye, A. (eds.), *Crisis and Terror in the Horn of Africa,* 2000, 296 pp.

Tomuschat, C., *"Uniting for Peace" - ein Rückblick nach 50 Jahren*, Die Friedens-Warte, Vol. 76, Nos. 2-3, 2001, p. 289.

Thränert, O., *Zwischen Hoffnungen und Befürchtungen: Die USA und die Europäische Sicherheits- und Verteidigungspolitik*, Vierteljahresschrift für Sicherheit und Frieden (S+F), Vol. 19, No. 2, 2001, p. 81.

Tripodi, P., *Peacekeeping: Let the Conscripts Do the Job*, Security Dialogue, Vol. 32, No. 2, 2001, p. 155.

Turns, D., *Some Reflections on the Conflict in Southern Lebanon: The 'Qana Incident' and International Humanitarian Law,* Journal of Conflict and Security Law, Vol. 5, No. 2, 2000, p. 177.

Waters, C., *Legal Education in Kosovo*, Peacekeeping and International Relations, Vol. 30, No. 4, 2001, p. 7.

Watson, G.R., *The Oslo Accords, International Law and the Israeli-Palestinian Peace Agreements,* 2000, 320 pp.

Weber, S., *Rules of Engagement: Ein Paradigmenwechsel für Einsatz und Ausbildung?,* Humanitäres Völkerrecht-Informationsschriften, Vol. 14, No. 2, p. 76.

Wedgewood, R., *Responding to Terrorism: The Strikes against Bin Laden,* Yale Journal of International Law, Vol. 24, No. 2, 1999, p. 559.

Wheatley, S., *The Foreign Affairs Select Committee Report on Kosovo: NATO Action and Humanitarian Intervention,* Journal of Conflict and Security Law, Vol. 5, No. 2, 2000, p. 261.

Wheeler, N.J., *Saving Strangers, Humanitarian Intervention in International Society,* 2000, 352 pp.

White, N., *Commentary on the Report of the Panel on United Nations Peace Operations (the Brahimi Report),* Journal of Conflict and Security Law, Vol. 6, No. 1, 2001, p. 127.

Wilde, R., *From Danzig to East Timor and Beyond: The Role of International Territorial Administration,* American Journal of International Law, Vol. 95, No. 3, 2001, p. 583.

Wilkinson, P., *Terrorism versus Democracy,* Frank Cass, 2001, 448 pp.

Wilkinson, P./Jenkins, B.M. (eds.), *Aviation Terrorism and Security,* Frank Cass, 1998, 184 pp.

Williams, P./Vlassis, D. (eds.), *Combating Transnational Crime,* Frank Cass, 2001, 272 pp.

Wouters, J./Naert, F., *How Effective is the European Security Architecture? Lesson from Bosnia and Kosovo,* International and Comparative Law Quarterly, Vol. 50, No. 3, 2001, p. 540.

Wulf, H., *Kleinwaffen – die Massenvernichtungsmittel unserer Zeit – Die Bemühungen der Vereinten Nationen um Mikroabrüstung,* Vereinte Nationen, Vol. 49, No. 5, 2001, p. 174.

Zagorski, A., *Great Expectations,* NATO Review, Vol. 49, Spring 2001, p. 24.

Zahar, M.J., *Protégés, Clients, Cannon Fodders: Civilians in the Calculus of Militias,* International Peacekeeping (Frank Cass), Vol. 7, No. 4, 2000, p. 107.

Peacekeeping Chronicle of Events
July 2000 – June 2001

A. General

6 July
Hans Corell, Under-Secretary-General for Legal Affairs and the United Nations Legal Council, completed formal discussions with the Royal Government of Cambodia on the establishment of a tribunal to try Khmer Rouge leaders in Phnom Penh. The tribunal envisaged would be a Cambodian Court with the participation of international judges and prosecutors. Because the outstanding substantive issues were resolved by the Secretary-General and Cambodian Prime Minister Samdech Hun Sen, the discussions focused on technical issues involved in forming the tribunal. Mr. Corell provided his Cambodian counterpart, Mr. Sok An, Senior Minister and Chairman of the Council of Ministers, with a draft Memorandum of Understanding that would govern the relationship between Cambodia and the United Nations. The Memorandum of Understanding would be signed by the United Nations and Cambodia after the Cambodian Parliament passes legislation that is in keeping with the understanding between the parties. As Mr. Corell and Mr. Sok An agreed in a post meeting press conference, the responsibility for moving the process towards completion now lies squarely with the Government of Cambodia. (UN Press Release SG/SM/7481)

7 July
The United States introduces a resolution in the UN Security Council calling on all countries that contribute UN peacekeepers to counsel their troops on sexually transmitted diseases and to track the incidence of HIV/AIDS among their soldiers. The resolution reflects a growing conviction among American policymakers that the AIDS epidemic represents a threat to international peace and security, particularly in Africa. (WP, 7 July, p. A18)

9 July
UN Secretary Kofi Annan said Foday Sankoh, the rebel leader being held by Sierra Leonean authorities, should face trial for war crimes despite an amnesty enshrined in a 1999 peace accord. (WP, 9 July, p. A22)

12 July
A group of United Nations liaison officers will arrive in Ethiopia and Eritrea by the end of next week, in the first stage of a peacekeeping operation to enforce the cease-fire that the two nations signed last month, a senior United Nations military official said in Asmara, the Eritrean capital. But the official, Maj. Gen. Timothy Ford, said it would be several months before the full force was deployed. (NYT, 12 July, p. 8)

13 July
The Unites States paid some of its back dues to peacekeeping operations, including $40 million for Kosovo and $53 million for East Timor. By international agreement, Washington is billed 31 percent for every peacekeeping mission, but Congress has ruled that 25 percent is the limit, and arrears continue to build. United Nations accounts show the United States debt totals $1.65 billion. (WP, 13 July, p. A2)

20 July
Richard C. Holbrooke, taking aim at both Congress and the Clinton administration, said today that American reluctance to sufficiently pay for United Nations peacekeeping could cost the United States much more down the line in emergency relief and the direct involvement of American troops. "The tragedy is that by lagging behind in funding peacekeeping operations, we often inadvertently, unintentionally contribute to conditions in which peacekeeping fails and refugee and relief assistance is then required," he said. (NYT, 21 July, p. 10)

22 July
The Secretary General of the United Nations Annan has presented a catalogue containing 55 proposals for a better child protection in war- and after-wartime. (NZZ, 25 July, p. 2)

24 July
UN Secretary-General Kofi Annan said Monday all violations have been cleared along the line of demarcation between Lebanon and Israel and hopes to see Lebanese and UN troops patrolling the border "in the next few days".
He said that after the Israelis withdrew the UN troops had been patrolling, but "They haven't been deployed actually to the border. I hope to see that done in the next few days."
"What had held us up is we were hoping to clean up all the violations on the 'blue line' before we did that," he said referring to the demarcation line. Israelis were verified June 16 to have withdrawn behind the line. "The violations have all now been cleared," and he would report that to the panel later in the day "with the latest developments on the ground." Annan also said he planned to speak by telephone with Lebanese President Emile Lahoud about troop deployment.
"UN troops would deploy to the border and the Lebanese will also deploy their own troops alongside the UN troops," Annan said. He said the two commanders were working on the details. "So, I hope that in the next few days you will see our troops on the border," said the secretary-general.
Last Friday Annan warned in his latest report to the council on Lebanon that "the potential for serious incidents still exists" along the Israel-Lebanon line and recommended beefing up and extending the 5,075-strong UN Interim Force in Lebanon peacekeeping mission another six months. He would like to see two battalions added to the force, but so far has not received any offers.

"While an enormous improvement compared to the past, the situation in the Israel-Lebanon sector falls well short of peace and the potential for serious incidents still exists," the secretary-general said. He said the situation in UNIFIL's areas of operation has been "generally calm" since the end of May. (United Press International, 24 July)

25 July
Syria has asked the United Nations to take control of a partitioned town near the Golan Heights rather than giving part to Lebanon and leaving the rest under Israeli occupation, the Foreign Ministry Farouq al-Shara said on Tuesday.
Mr Shara told Annan the UN represented by its UNIFIL and UNDOF forces, should shoulder its full responsibilities to ensure the unity of the town and its people far from the Israeli forces. A ministry spokesman added that the UN chief expressed support for this humanitarian request and promised to exert his goodwill efforts to keep the town undi-

vided and under the control of the UN peacekeeping forces until the implementation of UN resolutions 242 and 338 calling for Israeli withdrawal from the Golan Heights to the (pre-war) June 4, 1967 line. (Reuters, 25 July)

27 July
Late Tuesday, the United Nations had delayed the redeployment of the UN Interim Forces in southern Lebanon (UNIFIL) down to the Israeli borders-which had been scheduled for Wednesday-because of the four new Israeli violations of Lebanese territory.
In the wake of the Israeli withdrawal from southern Lebanon on May 24, the Lebanese government has opposed the deployment of UN peacekeepers right up to the border until Israeli troops cease to encroach on its territory. UN Secretary General Kofi Annan has hoped that the UNIFIL Redeployment would be "immediately followed by the deployment of the composite Lebanese unit," consisting of soldiers and members of the internal security forces. (Agence France Presse, 27 July)

30 July
The United Nations overcame a last minute block by Hizbollah guerrillas Sunday to finish deploying its peacekeepers at four positions along the Israeli-Lebanese frontier. Successful negotiations between the UN Interim Force in Lebanon (UNIFIL) and the guerrillas, finally allowed UN peacekeeping forces to move into the last of four positions in south Lebanon, vacated by Israel two months ago. (Reuters, 30 July)

3 August
France has blocked a US proposal to create a senior position for an American official in the United Nations' peacekeeping department, dealing a setback to Washington's efforts to enhance its oversight of UN military operations. The Clinton administration says the new post of deputy under-secretary would enhance the effectiveness of UN peacekeeping operations, and that it should be filled by a respected American who can improve the organisation's relations with Congress and the Pentagon. The United States also advocates beefing up the UN peacekeeping department in New York, which employs 410 people, about half as many as those working at the world body's department of public information. But France, which controls the top peacekeeping post, viewed the initiative as a challenge to its influence at the United Nations, according to diplomats. (WP, 4 August, p. A14)

4 August
The small but brutal wars of Sierra Leone and Congo have brought the United Nations to a moment of truth. The choice that looms is captured in a few candid, thought-provoking phrases by Kofi Annan. "We have in the past prepared for peacekeeping operations with a best case scenario: The parties sign an agreement, we assume they will honour it, so we send in lightly armed forces to help them," Annan said. But recent events, led by the capture of some 500 UN peacekeepers (now released) by Sierra Leone's rebels and the collapse of peace efforts in Congo, have convinced Annan that "time has come for us to base our planning on worst-case scenarios; to be surprised by cooperation, if we get it. And to go in prepared for all eventualities, including full combat, if we don't." This would be a major philosophical turn for a political body built on good intentions, not on coercive power. But Annan says that the UN peacekeeper will become an endangered species if the transformation does not come. The most important member nations have shown

themselves unwilling to provide troops, money or timely logistic help for more assertive UN peacekeeping, even as many of them step up their criticisms of the world body's effectiveness. But the destructive power of modern weapons available to any rogue force is turning the priorities upside down. (WP, 4 August, p. A29)

7 August

The UN agency responsible for preventing the proliferation of nuclear weapons is facing a financial crisis and may soon have to cease key operations because the United States and other countries refuse to pay their bill on time, according to senior diplomats here. "If this perilous situation continues, it could undermine critical safeguard operations that verify the safe uses of nuclear energy," said the Director General of the International Atomic Energy Agency. (WP, 8 August, p. A1)

23 August

In Geneva and New York, a group of experts presented Secretary General Kofi Annan a plan of reform for the peacekeeping missions of the United Nations. The plan contains both an upgrading of the UN peacekeeping missions as well as several measures to accelerate the deployment of UN units and to strengthen the positions of troops. These measures are to prevent failures like Rwanda in 1994 and Srebrenica in 1996. Until now the means didn't meet the expectations of UN missions. The plan proposes that in a situation of international conflict, UN troops should be stationed within 30 days to reach a truce. In case of internal conflicts the term is set on 90 days. On top of that, UN troops should be better equipped, to maintain themselves in an emergency situation. To be able to guarantee a quick deployment of UN soldiers, an education is proposed for troops on standby, consisting of 100 military members and 100 policemen of different nations. (NZZ, 24 August, p. 2)

26 August

The first American soldiers have arrived in Nigeria this week to train about 4,000 Nigerian troops as UN peacekeepers for Sierra Leone, though there are concerns about instructing troops from an army known for recent serious human rights violations. US troops have also arrived in Ghana on a similar mission. (IHT, 26 August, p. 4)

2 September

With President Clinton preparing to visit New York this week for a meeting of world leaders at the United Nations, the American ambassador, Richard C. Holbrooke, said that the United States must focus more on its ties with the organisation, which he called "indispensable" to American foreign policy. "American dollars spent on the UN are worthwhile," Mr. Holbrooke said in an interview. "We need to fix it and save it, rather than walk away from it or weaken it." Mr. Holbrooke, who is completing a year as ambassador to the UN, has found much of his time consumed in lobbying his administration colleagues on international issues and in carrying out demands made on the UN by Congress. A group of congressmen who have often been hostile to the United Nations have established multiple hurdles to full American participation, blocking payment of past dues and some new assessments. Mr. Holbrooke's potential foreign policy role in a new Democratic administration – if Vice President Al Gore wins the presidency in November – is the focus of unending speculation among other diplomats. But he said he intended to "work straight through until January 20" no matter what the outcome of the election. His arrival here was delayed a year by congressional blocks and federal ethics investigations, largely into his contacts with American embassies after he left a federal post. (NYT, 4 September, p. 6)

3 September

A paramilitary police force is being established by the European Union to intervene in conflict areas across the world to protect the community's political and economic interests. Brussels has drawn up plans for a 5,000-strong armed police capability able to carry out "preventative and repressive" actions in support of global peacekeeping missions. Critics say it is a deliberate challenge to the United Nations. The new body, which may be given the name European Security and Intelligence Force (Esif), would work alongside a 60,000-strong EU defence force that is also being set up. The security force would be intended primarily for use in trouble spots such as Kosovo. It is expected to be fully operational by 2003. Critics fear, however, that its units, armed with light machineguns and trained to operate alongside EU ground troops, may eventually be used to suppress disorder within member states. No restrictions on its sphere of operations have been placed in the regulations so far agreed by EU governments, and detailed "rules of engagement" have not yet been drawn up. "There is no attempt at all to reduce the role of the UN," a spokesman said. There was also "no question" of the force being used within the EU. The new police units, like the EU's defence arm, will be under the control of a political and security committee, composed of ambassadors from each EU country. Effective operational command, however, will be in the hands of Javier Solana, the Spanish former secretary-general of NATO who is now secretary-general of the council of ministers. The impetus for the creation of the force has been the perception of Britain, France and Germany that the UN failed to act effectively in preventing bloodshed in the Balkans. (ST, 3 September, Home news)

4 September

The United Nations came under fire from a joint Cabinet committee as Tony Blair prepared to fly to America for the organisation's millennium summit. A report, by Robin Cook and his Liberal Democrat counterpart Menzies Campbell, said that the UN's recent operations in Rwanda, Sierra Leone and the former Yugoslavia had been marred by "brutally evident" shortcomings. The report from the Government's Joint Consultative Committee with the Liberal Democrats indicated Britain intended to take a tough line on UN reform at the meeting. UN soldiers had been prevented by their mandate from taking action while atrocities were being committed, it said. "No longer must UN 'blue helmets' stand by while the most serious crimes against humanity are being committed," it said. "The doctrine of peacekeeping which evolved in the 1950s ... is no longer valid for the intrastate conflicts of the 21st century." The report called for UN-trained soldiers to be on standby at all times to provide a rapid response as conflicts break out, and said that all contributing countries had to meet a "baseline of military competence." Concerns extended to civilian staff as well as soldiers, it added: "We have been starkly reminded in Kosovo and East Timor how difficult it is to recruit qualified personnel for missions. Where do we find police officers quickly, or judges, or people to run correctional institutions?" The paper called for more rigorous mandates for troops, better co-ordination of policy once peace had been established and the establishment of a UN staff college – possibly in the UK – to train officers. It also urged the expansion of the UN's main decision-making body, the Security Council, and said Germany and Japan should become permanent members along with one representative each from Latin America, Africa and Asia. (TI, 5 September, p. 2)

4 September
President Clinton's foreign policy aides say he plans a diplomatic whirlwind in New York over the next three days, including what one senior official called "the last real chance" to jump-start the failed talks between Israel and the Palestinians and what may be prove to be a tense session with China's president over Beijing's continued missile exports to Pakistan. Those meetings are part of a jammed schedule for Mr. Clinton. Tomorrow, he is to open a three-day series of speeches and discussions by more than 150 world leaders at the United Nations. Clearly intent on not sitting on the sidelines while the presidential campaign speeds into its last two months, Mr. Clinton plans to announce American support for a plan to strengthen the UN peacekeeping department. But Mr. Clinton also plans to use the UN meeting to insert himself in an array of simmering world conflicts – from the Middle East to Cyprus to the Korean Peninsula. Mr. Clinton's United Nations speech tomorrow will also endorse a report, issued by a special advisory group to Secretary General Kofi Annan, that the peacekeeping department be augmented by an interdepartmental panel that could do more continuous planning and make peacekeeping less of an ad hoc operation. "In principle we are supportive of what is in the report for a peacekeeping operation," Mr. Berger said. "It parallels what we have been recommending for several years." (NYT, 5 September, p. 1)

4 September
Robin Cook "ethical" foreign policy may be dead but the Foreign Secretary said that he was still committed to putting human rights at the heart of British policy abroad. Unveiling the latest in a series of ambitious and potentially controversial initiatives, he showed that, despite criticism, he planned to put Britain at the forefront of peacemaking in world trouble spots. Yesterday Mr. Cook, with the support of Menzies Campbell, the Liberal Democrats' foreign affairs spokesman, proposed reform of the United Nations Security Council and an overhaul of the UN's peacekeeping operations. In a move likely to upset the other permanent Security Council members Mr. Cook proposed that the body be enlarged to take in Germany and Japan and one representative each from Latin America, Africa and Asia as well as four non-permanent members. By far the most ambitious suggestion, which will be circulated this week among the 150 leaders gathered in New York for the millennium summit, is the call for a permanent UN rapid reaction force and the establishment of a UN military academy based in Britain. (TT, 5 September)

5 September
More than 150 Presidents, Prime Ministers and potentates, the largest gathering of world leaders in history, descended on New York for the UN millennium summit. The three-day meeting will conclude with a formal declaration calling for the eradication of poverty, the promotion of education, and the spread of democracy and renewed combat against the Aids virus. The world leaders are expected to agree unanimously to the summit declaration, which also calls for increased respect for human rights and the sparing of "no effort to free our peoples from the scourge of war". Those attending will also address less elevated topics, however, such as the thorny issue of how to divide the costs of UN peacekeeping efforts. (TT, 6 September)

7 September
President Clinton opened the summit meeting of world leaders at the United Nations to-day, urging the huge gathering to prepare the institution for a new age in which international forces will have to reach regularly and rapidly inside national boundaries to protect threatened people. Mr. Clinton also used the moment to try to settle some of the disputes that have dogged his presidency, from the Middle East to Russia to Southeast Asia. The president met separately into the evening with Prime Minister Ehud Barak of Israel and then with the Palestinian leader, Yasir Arafat, in hopes of picking up the broken pieces of the peace agreement to which they came tantalisingly close at Camp David in July. Mr. Clinton was deliberately vague on the question of when the UN should step into civil wars or ethnic and religious disputes. "These conflicts present us with a stark challenge," he said. "Are they part of the scourge the UN was established to prevent? If so, we must respect sovereignty and territorial integrity, but still find a way to protect people as well as borders." During his speech, he also made an oblique reference to Washington's $1.7 billion in arrears to the UN, saying that as the organisation expands its missions, "all these things come with a price tag, and all nations, including the United States, must pay it." He also took a clear shot at conservative Republicans who have attacked the UN, saying, "Those in my country or elsewhere who believe we can do without the UN, or impose our will upon it, misread history and misunderstand the future." Shortly after Mr. Clinton spoke, he met with the president of Vietnam, Tan Duc Luong. The two men discussed Mr. Clinton's desire to visit Vietnam before the end of his presidency, which would make him the first American president to set foot on Vietnamese soil since the end of the war nearly 30 years ago. But the stated purpose of this vast meeting of leaders is much broader: to set new priorities and directions for the United Nations, which at age 55 seems creaky and unprepared for a host of new challenges. On Friday the leaders are scheduled to sign a millennium declaration, calling for a new peacekeeping structure; a report to Mr. Annan calls for a strengthened corps of commanders in New York, ready to organise peacekeeping operations in a week or two. The declaration also sets goals for reducing poverty and illiteracy during the next 15 years, and contains carefully formulated language about guiding economic globalisation so that it benefits the poor as much as the rich, and small, uncompetitive nations as much as the developed world. But as with any document that is signed by so many, the language is so watered down that discerning its specific meaning is difficult at best. And it is particularly difficult to pin down the United Nations' role in managing economic globalisation and development. More and more, that role has fallen to the institutions that were created at the end of World War II to manage the world economy – the World Bank, which focuses on poverty, and the International Monetary Fund, which seeks to prevent and manage economic crises. (NYT, 7 September, p. 1)

7 September
Under U.S. pressure at the millennium summit this week, the 15 members of the UN Security Council agreed to renegotiate the assessments for peacekeeping, a 27-year-old formula that Washington believes places an unfair financial burden on the United States. U.S. officials said the agreement was reached after months of negotiations with China, which resisted a change that could require it to pay substantially more for UN peacekeeping operations, which it often opposes as interference in the internal affairs of sovereign states. The scale of assessment was established in 1973 as a temporary measure to fund the first UN peacekeeping mission, in the Sinai Desert between Egypt and Israel. Like

many other developing countries at the time, China was given a steep discount on its share of the cost. But as the economies of China and other emerging economic powers have grown, their financial obligations have not been adjusted. "The Chinese are virtually certain to have to pay more because of a strengthened economy," said a senior U.S. official. "The Russians are facing the opposite situation. The amount they are paying would decline." The breakthrough will give Richard C. Holbrooke, the U.S. ambassador to the United Nations, some leverage as he seeks to persuade the organisation's 189 member states to also reduce the U.S. share of the regular operating budget. (WP, 8 September, p. A24)

8 September
World leaders at the UN Millennium Summit wrapped up what may have been the largest diplomatic talk-fest in history today with a wildly ambitious declaration to end poverty, halt the spread of deadly infectious diseases and bolster the ability of UN peacekeepers to do their jobs. But the three-day extravaganza may best be remembered for President's Clinton failure to jump-start the Middle East peace process, the brutal murder – just hours before the summit's opening – of three UN relief workers in western Timor and an unplanned handshake between Clinton and Cuban leader Fidel Castro. At a reception Wednesday, Clinton inadvertently made history when Castro slipped into line behind other world leaders and, after patiently waiting his turn, grabbed the president's hand. The handshake was apparently the first between the communist leader and a sitting American president and has angered some Cuban Americans. Participants concluded the summit with a declaration that pledged to slash in half the percentage of people living in extreme poverty, halt the spread of AIDS and provide primary school education for all children by 2015. "The central challenge we face today is to ensure that globalisation becomes a positive force for all the world's people," the declaration stated. "As leaders we have a duty to all the world's people, especially the most vulnerable and, in particular, the children of the world, to whom the future belongs."(WP, 9 September, p. A16)

15 September
The 2000 Olympic Games in Sydney opened with the politics of healing on parade. Australia's indigenous Aborigines were honoured in an emotional pageant. Newly independent states debuted in the alphabetical order of nations. And athletes from North and South Korea – countries long joined in mutual hostility – marched hand-in-hand behind a single "unification" flag. The picture of athletes from North and South Korea parading together into the stadium was the most dramatic sign yet of the two nations' new desire to rejoin their riven peninsula. The 150 athletes and sporting officials from the two countries, nearly indistinguishable in their matching blue blazers, khaki pants and bright orange ties, received a thunderous standing ovation as they put aside a half-century of bitter conflict and walked into Olympic Stadium here following a placard that simply stated "Korea." Also joining the procession of athletes were a group from Palestine, a first team from Eritrea and a contingent from war-ravaged Bosnia-Herzegovina that consists of, for the first time, Muslims, Croats and Serbs. Four competitors from the newly independent nation of East Timor joined the procession. Because East Timor still is administered by the United Nations and does not yet have an active sports federation, the four athletes were forced to wear white uniforms and carry the Olympic flag. But Australians, who led an international peacekeeping force to secure the territory last fall, gave the four a spirited standing ovation similar to that for the Koreans. (WP, 16 September, p. A1)

2 October
The UN Security Council was deadlocked late on Monday in formulating a reaction to clashes between Palestinians and Israeli security forces that have claimed at least 48 lives in the past five days, mainly among Palestinian demonstrators.
Members at the session, requested by Palestinian UN observer Nasser al-Kidwa, met for more than five hours without reaching an agreement on a statement and will try again before a formal meeting convenes on Tuesday with more than 30 speakers.
Earlier al-Kidwa accused Israel of "massacring and injuring numerous Palestinian civilians" and called for an immediate Security Council intervention to put an end to the fighting and salvage the Middle East peace talks. He said the 15-member body should call for immediate withdrawal of Israeli forces from Muslim holy sites in Jerusalem and the vicinity of Palestinian cities as well as investigate the violence. "The intervention of the Security Council is needed so that it might salvage the Middle East peace process and if possible resuscitate the efforts to reach a peaceful settlement between the parties," al-Kidwa said in identical letters to the council and UN Secretary-General Kofi Annan. "What is urgently needed at this time is ensuring the withdrawal of Israeli security forces from al-Haram al-Sharif and from the vicinity of Palestinian cities and towns, in addition to investigating the events of the last few days." (Reuters, 2 October)

3 October
The European Union today rebuffed an American request to have Washington's dues to the United Nations lowered, as a crucial review of how much each country should contribute to the organisation's budget began. The European message echoes voices of opposition from Japan, other Asian countries and a number of developing nations that reject a reduction in dues for the United States, the country with the world's largest and arguably strongest economy. The United States, still the United Nations' largest debtor, has been arguing that a restructuring of assessments is overdue, and Ambassador Richard C. Holbrooke, the American envoy who is under an ultimatum from Congress to cut American contributions, has been casting a revision of the payment scale as a broader reform measure here. Many other nations agree that the scale needs reworking, but only to reflect real changes in the world economy. Budget assessments are based on a nation's share of the world gross national product and on currency movements. By that standard, some countries in financial trouble should pay less and a number of newly affluent countries should pay more, but the United States – with about 27 percent to 29 percent of the total world gross national product and an assessment rate of 25 percent – would not qualify for a reduction. Europe's collective share of the world GNP is also about 29 percent. In addition to the bill for 25 percent of the United Nations regular annual $1 billion budget, the United States is charged for 30 percent of the separate, fluctuating peacekeeping budget, which in the coming year is likely to total more than $2.5 billion. Congress has already lowered peacekeeping payments to 25 percent – a move seen here as a violation of treaty obligations – and is now demanding that the regular budget share be reduced to 22 percent. (NYT, 3 October, p. A12)

7 October
Following intensive negotiations over recent days that often lasted until the early morning hours, the Security Council has passed resolution 1322 deploring the recent provocation in Jerusalem and the resulting violence which left over 80 Palestinians dead. The Council condemned "acts of violence, especially the excessive use of force against Palestinians"

and called upon Israel, the occupying Power, to abide scrupulously by its legal obligations under the 1949 Fourth Geneva Convention on the protection of civilians in times of war.

The resolution also called for "the immediate cessation of violence, and for all necessary steps to be taken to ensure that violence ceases, that new provocative actions are avoided, and that the situation returns to normality in a way which promotes the prospects for the Middle East peace process."

In addition, the Council stressed the importance of establishing a mechanism for a "speedy and objective inquiry into the tragic events" with the aim of preventing a repetition. The resolution welcomed "any effort in this regard."

The text, which was adopted just before 8 p.m. on Saturday, also called for the immediate resumption of negotiations within the Middle East peace process on its agreed basis with the aim of achieving an early final settlement between the two sides. (UN News, 7 October)

9 October

Faced with the worst assault on Middle East peace since he entered the White House, President Clinton asked the Egyptian president, Hosni Mubarak, to convene an urgent summit meeting where Mr. Clinton could meet the leaders of Israel, the Palestinians and Jordan, a senior administration official said today.

The rapid deterioration in the Middle East, which threatened to undo the peace accords of Mr. Clinton's two terms, was encapsulated in a United Nations resolution passed on Saturday night, with the United States abstaining. It criticized Israel for what if called excessive use of force against the Palestinians.

The United Nations secretary general, Kofi Annan, left for the region tonight in an effort to get all sides to retreat from belligerent threats. (New York Times, 9 October)

10 October

Thanks to the budget surplus, the Republican majority in Congress is said to be moderating its indifference to America's international responsibilities. Earlier this year, the Republicans allocated just over $13 billion to the foreign operations budget, about $2 billion short of what the administration had requested; that meant short-changing everything from AIDS relief to embassy security. In the past few days, however, there have been signs that Congress is ready to give the administration most of what it wants. The most important concerns United Nations peacekeeping. The administration wants $846 million to pay America's share of the UN's peacekeeping costs. The House earlier this year set aside only $498 million, while the Senate offered a mere $287 million. Since the United States has voted in favour of the UN missions that give rise to these bills, there is no justification for the United States to refuse to pay its part of them. (IHT, 11 October, p.8)

12 October

The United Nations often has been viewed in Israel as favouring the Arabs, but Israel's acceptance of Secretary-General Kofi Annan as a Mideast mediator is evidence of a recent change in Israel's attitude to the world body.

Only Saturday, the Security Council adopted a resolution condemning Israel for provoking two weeks of violence that have left more than 90 dead, most Palestinians.

Israeli officials nevertheless see the secretary-general as a well-placed negotiator who may be able to stop the fighting, reduce tensions, and bring Israel and the Palestinians back to the negotiating table.

Many observers attribute Israel's willingness to accept UN Mideast mediation to the role Annan and his envoys played in certifying Israel's withdrawal from southern Lebanon earlier this year. In addition, Israel in May ended 50 years of UN isolation by finally being welcomed into a regional group that allows it to participate fully in the work of the organization. (Associated Press/Nando Times, 12 October)

16 October

US media have been ignoring or downplaying an important dimension of the ongoing turmoil in the Middle East. On October 7, the United Nations Security Council voted 14 to 0 for a resolution condemning Israel's "excessive use of force against Palestinians" and deploring the "provocation" of Israeli opposition leader Ariel Sharon's September 28 visit to the Temple Mount. (Fairness & Accuracy in Reporting, 16 October)

17 October

Human Rights Watch stressed that the current crisis in the Middle East highlighted the need for the UN to establish a standing body of independent international criminal justice investigators to be available for deployment by the UN at short notice whenever the need arises for independent, impartial investigations of a criminal justice nature. (Human Rights Watch, 17 October)

20 October

Just hours ahead of Friday's agreed ceasefire deadline, the deaths of a Palestinian and an Israeli in the West Bank have dampened international hopes for a swift and peaceful resolution to the Middle East crisis.

The remaining hours before the Friday afternoon deadline would be a crucial test of the commitment of Israelis and Palestinians to the Sharm el-Sheikh truce, UN Secretary General Kofi Annan said Thursday.

Meanwhile in Geneva, the UN Human Rights Commission meeting agreed in an emergency session to set up a commission of inquiry into human rights violations by Israel in the Palestinian Territories. (Agence France Presse, 20 Octobre)

21 October

The UN General Assembly late Friday adopted a resolution that condemned the "excessive use of force by Israel against Palestinian civilians". The resolution gave support to the agreement reached on Monday at the Egyptian resort Sharm el-Sheik, calling for a ceasefire and for Israel and the Palestinian Authority to implement steps aimed at defusing tensions and restoring calm. It called for the "immediate cessation of violence and use of force and upon the parties to act immediately to reverse all measures taken in this regard since 28 September 2000 and acknowledges that necessary steps have been taken by the parties in this direction since the summit at Sharm el-Sheik". It branded the Israeli settlements in the "occupied Palestinian territory, including Jerusalem, as illegal and an obstacle to peace, and called for the prevention of illegal acts of violence by Israeli settlers".

The resolution supported an inquiry into the events leading to the violence. The Sharm el-Sheik agreement called for an inquiry commission composed of the United States, Israel and the Palestinian Authority to work in consultation with the UN to carry out the investigation. (Deutsche Presse-Agentur, 21 October)

23 October
Arab leaders demanded yesterday that a United Nations war crimes tribunal should prosecute Israel for the deaths of more than 120 Palestinian demonstrators after Ehud Barak pulled out of the peace process and five more Palestinian demonstrators after Ehud Barak pulled out of the peace process and five more Palestinians were killed in Gaza and the West Bank.
In a display of angry unity, kings, presidents and political leaders from more than 20 Arab states meeting at a summit in Cairo called on the UN Security Council to set up a tribunal like those dealing with Rwanda and the former Yugoslavia. They asked the UN to investigate Israeli massacres and said the Arab state would use international law to prosecute those who had caused "these barbaric practices". (Times, 23 October)

25 October
A senior Palestinian official said on Wednesday Palestinians want Europe, China, Russia and the United Nations, along with the United States, to take part in any future talks with Israel. Palestinians have long demanded the participation of the UN and EU, believed to be more supportive of the Arabs, in the talks because they consider Washington, which has monopolised sponsorship of the peace process, biased towards Israel. The summit ended with a statement read by U.S. President Bill Clinton calling for an end to the current wave of violence and an examination within two weeks of the possibility of renewing peace talks. (Reuters, 25 October)

25 October
A promise by George W. Bush that, if elected president, he would negotiate the removal of American troops from peacekeeping duties in the Balkans and leave such work to the Europeans has provoked a collective sigh of anxiety and even weariness among European diplomats, officials and analysts. These officials said the proposal enunciated by Mr. Bush during a presidential debate and elaborated upon by Mr. Bush's foreign-policy adviser, Condoleezza Rice, could divide the NATO alliance, undermine the current European effort to increase its military capacity and question the post-war rationale for NATO's existence, which has revolved around the Balkans. Ms. Rice dug new ground with the idea that the American military should be reserved for war-fighting, in the Persian Gulf or the Pacific, while the weaker European forces should concentrate on peacekeeping at home. Any wariness by the allied governments was enhanced by the strong suspicion – expressed for example by Lord Roper, the British defence analyst and Liberal Democratic peer – that Ms. Rice intended her comments politically, to underline the usual Republican charge that, as he put it, "the Democrats get Americans involved in long wars." Still, the Bush-Rice proposal is not new, but an extension of a doctrine put forth by Gen. Colin L. Powell under the last Republican president, Mr. Bush's father. General Powell's belief was that American troops would essentially be reserved for a real crisis where overwhelming force could be brought to bear, to ensure victory and limit casualties. (NYT, 25 October, p. A12)

28 October

For the first time in more than half a century of dealing with issues of war and peace, the United Nations Security devoted a special session to women, who are demanding to be included at the negotiating table in many regions, most prominently in Africa. Angela King, an assistant secretary general and special adviser to the secretary general on the advancement of women, said women could readily expand debates to include social issues at a time when global conflict is harming more civilians than soldiers. Women should also play a bigger role in peacekeeping missions, she added. "Gender equality issues are absolutely essential to the success of any peace operation," Ms. King said. (NYT, 29 October, p. 2)

31 October

If elected president, Al Gore says he will use U.S. military power to halt Bosnia-style massacres, America's economic influence to press failing states to embrace democracy and the carrot of trade accords to encourage the adoption of Western-style labour and environmental standards. George W. Bush, in contrast, argues that an overextended U.S. military should gradually pull out of the Balkans – a step that the Europeans view as abandonment by the world's most powerful nation. The Texas governor insists on charging ahead with a national missile defence system – which Russia and China have vowed to defeat by building up new nuclear forces to overwhelm defensive interceptors. Beneath their words lie very different priorities, and probably very different styles, in managing America's relations with both allies and enemies. The vice president has repeatedly portrayed himself as a man who has come to believe in vigorous U.S. intervention abroad, a reversal of Democratic philosophy for most of the time since the end of the war in Vietnam. He describes how the experience of seeing the Clinton administration move too slowly to end the killing in Bosnia drove him to conclude that America must be prepared to prevent disaster, and how two successive global financial crises reshaped his understanding of the central role economic stability must play in the foreign policy agenda. Mr. Bush has woven a middle ground between two battling factions of his party – internationalists who support engagement with great powers like China, and isolationists who are deeply suspicious of the UN, the International Monetary Fund and the World Trade Organisation. "There may be some moments when we use our troops as peacekeepers, but not often," Mr. Bush said in the final presidential debate. (IHT, 31 October, p. 1)

1 November

Secretary-General Kofi Annan has stressed the need for the Lebanese Government to take effective control of the whole area and assume full responsibilities there, including putting an end to continuing provocations on the Line of Withdrawal, know as the "Blue Line". In a report on the United Nations Interim Force in Lebanon (UNIFIL) released today covering events over the past three months, Mr. Annan says that the deployment of both UNIFIL and the Lebanese Joint Security Force proceeded smoothly, and the return of the Lebanese administration was ongoing. (UN News, 1 November)

8 November

The Security Council will meet Friday with Palestinian leader Yasser Arafat, who wants a UN force sent to protect Palestinian civilians, the Council president said Wednesday. The Dutch ambassador to the United Nations, Peter van Walsum, said Council members held consultations on Wednesday and discussed a Palestinian proposal for an international protection force for Palestinian civilians. (Agence France Presse, 8 Novembre)

10 November
Palestinian President Yassir Arafat on Friday before the United Nations Security Council again called for a UN peacekeeping force to be established in Israeli-occupied areas as a means of stopping violence that has over six weeks killed more than 190 people, most of them Palestinians and Arabs. (Deutsche Presse-Agentur, 10 November)

10 November
With a steady increase in peacekeeping operations and relief missions around the world, Dileep Nair, the United Nations inspector general, recommended today that the organisation needs to review how to police itself better. Corruption and mismanagement have been persistent problems in the isolated, quickly organised missions thousands of miles from New York that now characterise much more of the organisation's work. Complicating efforts to account for money and materials is the growing use of non-governmental organisations – private relief agencies – to deliver services on behalf of the United Nations, especially in refugee work, the report found. (NYT, 10 November, p. A5)

14 November
The UN Security Council has told Lebanon that it must abide by international law and take control of the area in the south of the country which was vacated by Israel in May. The Security Council has reminded Lebanon that the UN resolution calling for the Israeli withdrawal also required Lebanon to take full control of the area. The Council also called for an end to what it called the dangerous violations on the border with Israel. Israel objects to the daily bouts of stone throwing by Lebanese and Palestinian tourists at the Fatima Gate- a former border crossing into Israel.
Lebanon is demanding from Israel the return of the farms in the foothills of the Golan Heights – but the UN disputes Lebanon's claim to the land. Beirut's position is that while Israel is illegally occupying Lebanese land, Hezbollah is justified in continuing its campaign. Hezbollah controls the former occupation zone, despite the presence of UN peacekeepers in southern Lebanon. (BBC, 14 November)

15 November
The size of the UN peacekeeping force in Lebanon could be sharply reduced next year and its role downgraded to a purely observational one, a Western diplomat said Wednesday. Though the peacekeepers have been in Lebanon since 1978, with their mandate renewed by the United Nations Security Council every six months, they only came into their own last May with the end of Israel's occupation. (Agence France Presse, 15 Novembre)

15 November
As recently as the early 1990s, American and European soldiers formed the backbone of UN forces trying to keep the peace in Cambodia, Somalia and the Balkans. But today, UN peacekeeping largely is subcontracted to Third World soldiers who endure the physical risk while rich countries bear the financial cost. This situation, which has developed gradually as the United States and other developed countries have scaled back their involvement in UN missions, increasingly is under attack as unfair. "You can't have a

situation where some people contribute blood and some contribute money," said Lakhdar Brahimi, a former Algerian foreign minister who headed up a UN panel that studied peacekeeping and presented proposals for reform in August. "That's not the UN we want." Bangladesh, a major troop contributor, proposed this week that the UN Security Council's five permanent members – the United States, Russia, Britain, France and China – each be required to provide at least 5 percent of the troops for any UN peacekeeping operation that they authorise. None of the permanent members supported the proposal, and it was dropped. Developing nations now contribute more than 75 percent of the nearly 30,000 UN troops taking part in 15 missions around the world. The five largest troop contributors – India, Nigeria, Jordan, Bangladesh and Ghana – supply about 13,700 soldiers, well over a third of all UN "blue helmets." The United States, Japan and European countries, on the other hand, provide relatively scant numbers of troops but will be billed for more than 85 percent of the $3 billion cost of UN peacekeeping this year. (WP, 15 November, p. A36)

17 November
President Clinton arrived in Hanoi, becoming the first president to visit Vietnam since Richard Nixon visited American troops in 1969. Mr. Clinton said earlier that he wanted to focus on Vietnam's economic and political potential and that he did not believe that America owed an apology to Vietnam for its wartime role. He is to be greeted today by President Tran Duc Luong and will give a speech at Hanoi National University that Vietnamese officials said would be broadcast nation-wide. Senator-elect Hillary Rodham Clinton arrived in Hanoi separately, earlier in the day. (NYT, 17 November, p. A2)

20 November
The European Union has come up with the 60,000 combat troops for a rapid-reaction force that could eventually handle small, international emergencies for Europe. The plan will be announced Monday in Brussels, according to EU officials. The plan amounts to the first tangible step by the European Union to create a multinational force by 2003 that will give Europe military clout of its own. The drive to create a European-only force has taken on new urgency in the light of the U.S. presidential campaign, in which Republicans, who control Congress, have signalled reluctance to see the U.S. military take on extensive peacekeeping duties in Europe. EU governments feel that they would weigh more heavily in trans-Atlantic bargaining if they had a force of their own that promised to be a useful complement to U.S. power. Getting a force, even just on paper, represents a milestone in relations between the EU and NATO, Western officials said. NATO, led by the United States, protects Europe against a major war, but the EU reaction force could act autonomously – meaning without NATO authorisation – in smaller crises. "What we got here is not a European army or even the beginning of one - what we've got is an agreement to try to work together," a defence official said in Paris in a briefing on the EU's progress. EU military activity is decided among heads of state and does not involve the European Commission. The policy is managed by Javier Solana, the EU security and foreign policy chief, who was NATO secretary-general during the Kosovo conflict. The EU force could operate far from Europe, especially in missions under the auspices of the United Nations. In developing over the last two years what they call "an autonomous force,". European leaders caused some heartburn in Washington, which initially wanted the Europeans to subordinate the force to NATO. U.S. concerns have eased recently, a

Clinton administration official said, because the EU seemed closer to fulfilling its pledges of complete "transparency" with NATO. (IHT, 20 November, p. 1)

26 November
Proposals for a new unit for gathering information and improving planning for United Nations peacekeepers, which officials see as crucial to faster and more effective responses to crises, could be blocked by developing nations in the General Assembly in the next few weeks. Some diplomats from the developing world, opening another fissure between rich and poor nations in the organisation, say they are wary of giving the United Nations what amounts to intelligence-gathering functions. Others say that the proposed unit is redundant, since the existing Department of Political Affairs is supposed to be watching world trouble spots. The proposed policy planning staff, which would draw on expertise from several departments, was one of many recommendations in a report produced in the summer by a panel of outside experts led by Lakhdar Brahimi, a former Algerian foreign minister and frequent trouble shooter for the United Nations. His proposal was widely welcomed at first as a way to give peacekeepers, who can take months to reach a crisis, a sharper operation. The Security Council passed a unanimous resolution on Nov. 13 commending the report and promising to do its part by giving clearer mandates to peacekeeping operations. The Council suggested that deadlines for fielding missions should be set at 30 days for traditional operations and 90 days for more complex deployments. It underlined the need for better analysis and planning. (NYT, 26 November, p. 30)

28 November
A week after President Laurent Kabila shuffled his government to give it an international image, Congolese officials have agreed to allow a United Nations observer mission, precursor to a 5,000-member peacekeeping force, to function effectively. Plans for a force have been stalled since February because the government refused to give it the freedom of action it needs. President Thabo Mbeki of South Africa, meeting African leaders in Mozambique to discuss the Congo war, said progress may now be possible. Nelson Mandela failed to persuade Burundi's president to accept African peacekeepers during a transition period meant to end seven years of civil war. Mr. Mandela, who has worked for more than a year to broker a peace deal, met over the weekend with representatives of Burundi's government, the army and Hutu and Tutsi parties to discuss a cease-fire and a transitional government. The groups agreed in August to an ethnically balanced army and legislature but the issues of transitional leadership and a cease-fire remain unresolved. Two Hutu rebel groups boycotted the talks, being held in Arusha, Tanzania. (AP) (NYT, 28 November, p. A12)

7 December
President Bill Clinton has made a spirited pitch for continued engagement around the world. In what amounted to a foreign policy farewell address at the University of Nebraska, Mr. Clinton spoke today of the importance of building relationships with Russia and China. Both nations are former adversaries that present new challenges to American policymakers as they wrestle with restructuring their economies and opening to the West. Mr. Clinton offered this message to them: "If you will accept the rules and the responsibilities of membership in the world community, we want to make sure you get the full benefits, and be a full partner, not a junior partner. We also have to say, we have to feel

free to speak firmly and honestly when we think what you do is wrong." Mr. Clinton also counselled against the isolationist sentiment held by many Americans who remain deeply suspicious of institutions like the United Nations and the World Trade Organisation. (IHT, 11 December, p. 3)

7 December
With less than two days to go at a meeting to put finishing touches on the International Criminal Court, a group of nations friendly to the United States is scrambling, with diminishing confidence, to strike a deal that would let the Clinton administration sign on to the tribunal. The new court will be the first permanent international tribunal for trying individuals charged with war crimes, genocide and crimes against humanity. Since the Nuremberg trials of Nazis, criminal tribunals have been ad hoc creations like the courts for war crimes in Rwanda and the Balkans. This week, several countries – among them Australia, Britain and Switzerland – have suggested that a limited exemption given to France in 1998 when the treaty establishing the court was approved in Rome should be extended to the United States and other countries who sign. That exemption gave France seven years of immunity for war crimes in return for a promise to sign and ratify the treaty, which France subsequently did. The French said they needed time to align their military training and laws. The United States poses a different problem, however. It is arguing for a permanent exemption for itself and for countries that do not sign. The Pentagon has demanded guarantees that no American soldier or official on duty abroad could ever be tried by the court, a stipulation that President Clinton, while professing to support the court, has shrunk from overruling. If the administration signs before Dec. 31, it does not have to ratify the treaty immediately. After that date, any country has to both sign and ratify the treaty to take part. (NYT, 7 December, p. A6)

7 December
Britain said Wednesday it would put a draft resolution to the Security Council designed to break the deadlock over a Palestinian request for 2,000 unarmed UN observers. Britain's ambassador to the United Nations, Jeremy Greenstock did not go into details, but British diplomats said the draft resolution would likely endorse the general principle of an international presence in the territories without giving it a size or mandate. The council was due to resume its consultations on Thursday afternoon. British diplomats said the draft would probably ask UN Secretary General Kofi Annan to make recommendations about the size and structure of the presence. Annan is already holding consultations with the Israelis and the Palestinians at the request of the council. (Agence France Presse, 7 December)

7 December
United Nations Secretary General Kofi Annan Thursday appointed Stefan de Mistura as his new personal representative for southern Lebanon, replacing Rolf Knutsson who has been in the post since August 9, according to a UN statement released in Beirut. De Mistura's new job comes as the United Nations reiterates calls for restraint and respect of the so-called "Blue Line" set by the international organization to verify Israel's withdrawal from the area. (United Press International, 7 December)

9 December
The European Union made its position final: Europe will not pay higher UN dues to off-set any reduced payments by the United States. "What is our bottom line is that we will not pay more," said Ambassador Jean-David Levitte of France, which holds the rotating presidency of the EU until the end of the year. The General Assembly finance committee, which Mr. Levitte addressed Thursday, has until Dec. 22 to reach agreement on how, or if, the U.S. demand can be accommodated. Europe's negative response throws the burden on the rest of the world to find a way to pay more if Washington is to be accommodated. Ideas are being discussed, but no firm plan has yet taken shape. At issue are U.S. demands to lower the percentage of the UN operating budget that Washington pays to 22 percent from 25 percent, and the peacekeeping assessment to 25 percent from 30 percent. Congress cut peacekeeping contributions in defiance of international agreements in 1995. (IHT, 9 December, p. 5)

13 December
Sen. Joseph R. Biden Jr. (D-Del.) offered a possible compromise today for U.S. funding of the United Nations, saying he would urge his Senate colleagues to lower their sights on a reduction in the U.S. share of the UN peacekeeping budget if the world body agrees to cut Washington's portion of its regular administrative budget. "I'm of the view that if there is movement in the direction of the U.S. position, there would be an opportunity to be flexible on peacekeeping," Biden told reporters after an address to the Security Council. The announcement provided the first hint that Congress might be willing to compromise over the terms for payment of U.S. debts to the United Nations, which total more than $1.6 billion by the organisation's count and about $1 billion by Congress's count. Biden's message also appeared to reflect the mounting concern in Washington that the United Nations' 189 member states were on the verge of flatly rejecting the U.S. request for a reduction in its share of the $3 billion annual peacekeeping budget. The United States now pays 30.4 percent of all UN peacekeeping costs. Congress wants to cut that share to 25 percent. (WP, 13 December, p. A6)

15 December
After five weeks a winner in the U.S. presidential contest has been determined at last; George W. Bush will be the next president of the United States. He has already begun working with Colin Powell and Condoleezza Rice, respectively his likely secretary of state and national security adviser. (IHT, 16 December, p. 6)

18 December
The Security Council failed by one vote Monday to approve a resolution calling for "a UN force of military and police observers" in Israeli-occupied Palestinian territories. The proposed resolution, introduced in the council by Namibia, supported the October 7 resolution calling for an immediate cessation of hostilities that began September 28 between Palestinians and Israel and an end to "excessive use of force" by Israel against Palestinian protest. (United Press International, 18 December)

22 December
CNN founder Ted Turner has offered to make up the $35 million difference between the dues that the United States owes to the United Nations for 2001 and the amount Congress is willing to pay. Turner's offer is intended to help U.S. Ambassador Richard C. Hol-

brooke clinch a deal for a permanent reduction in the U.S. share of the UN budget and to bring an end to Washington's chronic debts to the world body, U.S. officials and a Turner representative said. Turner has stepped into the middle of this picture, showing an apparent taste for the limelight through high-profile philanthropy as well as a passionate conviction that the United States should be more deeply involved in the United Nations. He previously pledged to donate $1 billion to the organisation's work, but had said he would not help pay America's dues. (WP, 22 December, p. A1)

22 December
New proposals from the United States and the European Union failed today to end a deadlock over how to revise the dues for member nations in order to give Washington reductions it is demanding. As midnight approached, diplomats said they expected to be in session until dawn, with no promise of an agreement. Diplomats said tonight that many other problems remained as nations bickered over their assessments. Mr. Holbrooke said just before midnight that a division had widened between the Europeans, who have said that they will not pay more, and developing countries who say they cannot afford to accept increases. The Russians, however, agreed to double their contributions, but their dues are only a very small fraction of the American assessment. Earlier today, with the General Assembly bargaining strenuously over how to revise dues, the Europeans introduced an idea that could complicate negotiations further for the United States. Ambassador Jean-David Levitte of France said the Europeans were proposing that if Washington wins the cut in dues that it is seeking, Congress would have to release the money to pay all American debts by 2003. If that deadline is not met, he said, "then we will have to see whether we will have to push up the United States again." (NYT, 22 December, p. A12)

24 December
The UN General Assembly formally voted today to reduce America's dues, eliminating a major source of friction between the United States and the United Nations. The accord will reallocate the cost of running the United Nations among its 189 members and place the world body on a more solid financial footing, easing years of antipathy toward the United States for withholding more than $1 billion in dues. "This agreement should remove a major source of tension among member states," Secretary General Kofi Annan said today. "We can now look forward to a normal and constructive relationship with the United States." The budget pact will slash the U.S. share of the $1.1 billion UN administrative budget to 22 percent from 25 percent--saving American taxpayers about $35 million a year. It also will bring down Washington's share of the separate, $3 billion UN peacekeeping budget in stages, from 30.4 percent to about 28 percent in 2001 and then to 26 percent by 2003. While the new UN financing arrangements fall slightly short of what American Congress demanded, Sen. Joseph R. Biden Jr. (D-Del.), the ranking minority member of the Foreign Affairs Committee, said today he is confident Congress will approve the deal if the Bush administration embraces it. U.S. Ambassador Richard C. Holbrooke brokered the agreement after 16 months of emotionally charged negotiations and a pledge by CNN founder and UN advocate Ted Turner to donate up to $35 million to help close the deal. The agreement, however, failed to resolve a dispute between the United States and the United Nations over the amount of the U.S. debt to the world body, which the UN Secretariat calculates at $1.3 billion and the United States at about $800 million. (WP, 24 December, p. A16)

27 December

A UN expert panel last week completed a report to the Security Council laying out in impressive detail what the Council's members should have known for some time: That the rebel force that has been raping and dismembering the people of Sierra Leone while making a mockery of UN peacekeeping is empowered by the illegal arms and diamond trafficking of President Charles Taylor of Liberia. Mr. Taylor, the panel said, "is actively involved in fuelling the violence in Sierra Leone"; he oversees the smuggling of diamonds mined by the Revolutionary United Front and dedicates part of the money to paying off rogue arms dealers who, in turn, use Liberian-registered planes to deliver large quantities of weapons back to the revolutionary front. Mr. Taylor is not the only helpmate. The UN report also fingers Burkina Faso, which it says has facilitated weapons shipments to Liberia; Gambia, which has also allowed diamond smuggling; and Ukraine, the source of illegal weapons shipments. Strong measures were recommended by the report. These include a boycott of diamonds from Liberia and Gambia, an international travel ban on Mr. Taylor and other senior Liberian officials, the grounding of Liberian-registered aircraft outside the country, and an embargo on Liberian timber exports. (IHT, 27 December, p. 6)

31 December

In a move certain to upset his European allies, George W. Bush plans to begin withdrawing American peacekeepers from the Balkans shortly after he moves into the White House next month. Senior advisers to the Republican president-elect have told The Sunday Times that America will have removed all 10,000 of its ground troops from Bosnia and Kosovo within four years, leaving only logistical and intelligence teams behind. John Hulsman, a conservative analyst tapped as a Balkans adviser for the new administration, said Bush was concerned about "imperial overstretch" – a buzzword within the new national security team for America's involvement in "nation building" abroad during the presidency of Bill Clinton. (ST, 31 December)

1 January

The United States signed a treaty today to establish a permanent international criminal tribunal, after President Clinton overrode objections from the Pentagon and defied Republicans in the Senate. Mr. Clinton's decision is not legally binding without Senate approval, which appears unlikely any time soon. Still, it represents a powerful American endorsement of the treaty's goals, and poses a political and diplomatically challenge for the incoming administration of George W. Bush. The treaty, if ratified by 60 nations, will create the International Criminal Court, the world's first standing court with jurisdiction to try individuals on charges of genocide, war crimes and other crimes against humanity. In a statement released by the White House, Mr. Clinton said he remained concerned about "significant flaws" in the treaty that he hoped would be corrected in negotiations before the court becomes a reality. He said that, nevertheless, it was important to sign the treaty to "reaffirm our strong support for international accountability" and to place the United States in a better position to negotiate changes in the court's structure and rules. When the treaty was negotiated in 1998, President Clinton refused to endorse it. While administration officials have strongly supported the creation of an international court. Mr. Clinton had until today heeded warnings from the Pentagon that such a court would subject American troops, diplomats and other officials to frivolous or politically motivated prosecutions. Under the treaty's provisions, nations had until the end of today to sign a step that amounts to a statement of intent to support the court, which will ultimately be created in the Netherlands. After today, nations could only become party to the treaty by taking the formal step of ratification. (NYT, 1 January, p. A1)

3 January

In signing the treaty establishing an international criminal court, President Clinton served American interests and the cause of justice world-wide. The court will enter into force when 60 countries ratify the treaty, which should happen in a few years. The court will then be empowered to try people accused of genocide, crimes against humanity and war crimes. The Senate must still ratify the treaty, which is not likely to happen soon. But by signing it, Mr. Clinton has insured that Washington can have a voice in affecting the shape of the court. Washington's co-operation is under attack from conservatives in Congress and members of the incoming Bush administration. The most common objection is that American troops abroad might be subject to politically motivated prosecution. But the court is designed to deal with the most serious international crimes, and will try people only if they are not prosecuted at home. There are safeguards to prevent frivolous prosecutions. This mischievous bill is no favour to the Bush government, though some top Bush appointees have opposed establishment of the court. The bill would severely constrain the administration's ability to form a balanced foreign policy in the critical opening months of the new administration and could also constrain its operations abroad. The new administration might be unable to take part in peacekeeping missions it finds important. It could also be forced to cut off aid to nations like South Korea or Colombia that are likely to ratify the treaty. (NYT, 3 January, p. A16)

10 January

Jesse Helms, the Senate's fiercest critic of the United Nations and its budget structure, said today that he would allow the release of $582 million in American back dues to the world body, even though his goals for reform have not been fully met. Mr. Helms, who has used his leadership position on the Foreign Relations Committee to demand reductions in American contributions to the United Nations budget and its peacekeeping operations, declared himself satisfied with a deal brokered last month by Richard C. Holbrooke, the American ambassador. Mr. Helms, Republican of North Carolina, led the committee's Senators in a standing ovation for Mr. Holbrooke, who has toiled for years to win the changes sought by Mr. Helms and the ranking Democrat, Senator Joseph R. Biden Jr. of Delaware. It was an oddly giddy scene – witnessed by several foreign ambassadors – that belied the long struggle by Clinton administration officials to conduct diplomacy under the stigma of being a deadbeat nation. Under the deal, the American share of the United Nations administrative budget of $1.1. billion would drop to 22 percent, which Congress required, from 25 percent. The American contribution to the $3 billion annual peacekeeping budget would be reduced from 31 percent to 26 percent by 2004. The rollback in peacekeeping dues was not quite the 25 percent cap demanded under Helms-Biden, but Mr. Helms indicated that it was close enough, noting that it would save Americans $170 million over two years. Mr. Holbrooke said the American share of the budget was reduced by increasing allocations from other countries. The United States will save $100 million next year and an additional $70 million the year after, he said. Several ambassadors to the United Nations attended the committee meeting, including envoys from Australia, South Korea, Argentina, Colombia, South Africa and Japan. With the exception of Japan, the other countries have agreed to increase their United Nations dues under the new allocation. Russia and China will take on the biggest increases in terms of their share of the budget, Mr. Holbrooke said. Penny Wensley, the Australian ambassador, stiffened the mood slightly by voicing impatience with what many governments saw as strong-arm tactics by American lawmakers. She called on Congress to formally lift its 25 percent ceiling on United Nations payments, a restriction introduced by Senator Nancy Kassebaum in 1994. (NYT, 10 January, p. A8)

10 January

Senator Helms, chairman of the Senate Foreign Relations Committee, agreed today to a compromise that will allow the United States to repay a large portion of its debt to the United Nations. Helms said he would allow the release of about $585 million of back dues in return for the 189-member UN General Assembly's decision last month to slash the U.S. share of the UN budget. Helms lavished praise on Holbrooke, the U.S. ambassador to the UN, for accepting changes in the formula for allocating its operating expenses and peacekeeping costs. Under a bipartisan agreement fashioned more than two years ago by Helms and Senator Biden Jr., Congress agreed to repay $926 million of debts to the UN in three annual payments. But the deal was contingent on the organisation's agreement to cut the U.S. share of its administrative budget from 25 percent to 22 percent and the U.S. share of peacekeeping costs from 30 percent to 25 percent. In the end, Holbrooke persuaded other countries to make the full cut demanded by Congress in the U.S. contribution to the administrative budget. But he agreed to compromise on the peacekeeping budget, winning a reduction in the U.S. share to about 27 percent, 2 percentage points more than Congress wanted. In an interview after the hearing, however, Holbrooke said the incoming Bush administration still must tackle some thorny financial matters, including more than $500 million in disputed dues. (WP, 10 January, p. A20)

14 January

As his last days as United States ambassador here dwindle down through the single digits, Richard C. Holbrooke has yet to run out of ideas for fixing the United Nations. In a scant 17 months, Mr. Holbrooke has made himself an unapologetically assertive proponent of American interests at the United Nations, pulling off some feats that many diplomats believed were doomed to fail. The impossible mission this time was the high-wire act Mr. Holbrooke deftly maintained before the General Assembly three weeks ago when, employing the sort of arm-twisting a professional wrestler might envy, he persuaded other member countries to restructure the assessment of United Nations dues. The agreement cut the American share of administrative costs to 22 percent, down from 25 percent and its peacekeeping costs to 26 percent by 2004, down from 31 percent. But more than that, it cut through the long American stand-off with the organisation, and allowed Senator Jesse Helms, chairman of the Foreign Relations Committee and Congress's most powerful critic of the United Nations, to release $582 million the United States owed in dues. When Mr. Holbrooke briefed the Senate committee on his achievement, he received a standing ovation. Mr. Holbrooke has also steered the United States back onto the General Assembly's budget committee, which had taken away the American seat after Washington consistently fell behind in its payments. To break down the animosity that had developed over the years between Congress and the United Nations, Mr. Holbrooke brought members of Congress – Senator Helms among them – to the United Nations headquarters as well as escorting ambassadors from the world organisation to Capitol Hill. Mr. Holbrooke said the resolutions denouncing Israel put forward by countries in the non-aligned movement "are both deleterious to the peace process in the Middle East and damaging to the efforts to build a strong United Nations." Mr. Holbrooke, a Clinton administration appointee, is leaving the United Nations to join the Council on Foreign Relations, and he plans to write a book about the history of American diplomacy. His successor at the United Nations has yet to be named. But Mr. Holbrooke is not done yet. Next Friday, on his final day as United States ambassador, he has asked the Security Council to hold an open session on the problem of AIDS and the United Nations' failure to prevent peace-keeping troops from spreading the disease. (NYT, 14 January, p. 1-10)

14 January
A recent editorial cartoon by Matt Davies of the Journal News showed Bill Clinton trying to make a diving catch of a huge ball. The ball, labelled "Greatness," lands just out of his reach. The drawing provided a haunting visual metaphor for the near-miss quality of a presidency that never quite measured up to the potential that every supporter and most critics knew resided within Mr. Clinton. Yet simply stating the fact that Mr. Clinton is not destined to enter the pantheon of great, universally respected presidents does not capture the richness, complexity and drama of these eight years. No citizen is likely to forget them or, for that matter, to quit debating the man's remarkable gifts and the narcissistic indiscipline that diminished them. His White House years have been marked by prosperity, rancour, achievements, disappointments and something approaching a national psychodrama involving Mr. Clinton himself. Trying to separate Mr. Clinton from the times he presided over is like trying, in Yeats's phrase, to tell the dancer from the dance. Mr. Clinton presented himself as an agent for change. But with or without him, the 90's were bound to be a decade when change rolled across the economy, international relations and the political culture with a grinding inexorability. Historians will surely record Mr. Clinton as the first president to be impeached since 1868 and as having presided over America's longest economic expansion. That's the easy sentence to write. But they may also come to see him as the shaper of some main themes of governance for the 21st century. President-elect George W. Bush, who gained a lot of votes from Clinton fatigue, will not be able to ignore the policies Mr. Clinton installed or the expectations he created.
Setting a Course
For Mr. Clinton, a string of decisions on the economy belies his reputation as a poll-driven politician. In many cases, Mr. Clinton relied instead on gut instincts and was proved right. Another bold move came when he stood up to his party's orthodoxy and embraced opening trade barriers with the North American Free Trade Agreement with Mexico and Canada, the accord to create a new World Trade Organisation and the upgrading of trade relations with China. It is too soon to be positive that these will bring the benefits Mr. Clinton promised, but there is no doubting that he planted himself on the right side of history. Mr. Clinton has been at his best and most memorable in advocating engagement in the world in order to lift everyone's hopes for freedom and economic growth.
Days of Battle
Two of Mr. Clinton's biggest achievements flowed from that stand-off. First, on the environment, the president was persuaded by Vice President Al Gore and others to fight Republican efforts to eviscerate the Clean Water Act. Thereafter he vetoed repeated congressional attempts to weaken environmental standards and compiled the best conservation record of any president since Theodore Roosevelt. Among his achievements were tighter air pollution controls, new protections for wilderness areas, national forests and national parks, and the negotiation of a still non ratified global warming treaty. The second outgrowth of the confrontation with Congress was Mr. Clinton's determination to build a progressive record step by step. Among the accomplishments are an expanded

earned-income tax credit for millions of poor families; a health initiative covering 3.3 million poor children; welfare-to-work aid enacted in the years subsequent to his signing of welfare reform; a doubling of Head Start and school aid for the disadvantaged; and an expansion in college tuition aid for low- and moderate-income students. The administration estimates that in all an extraordinary $64 billion is now newly channelled annually to working-class and poor families, far more than might have been enacted in one big program. None of this can outweigh the failure to install the universal health care he promised in 1992. But for the first time in at least two decades, the lowest-income families have gained from good times, and indeed have gained the most.

A Dangerous World

Mr. Clinton has had difficulty finding a theme to sum up his approach to the world. His inattention led to missteps in the Balkans and Africa. But nowhere, this page not excepted, could one find flawless guidance and predictions on Serbia and Rwanda. Mr. Clinton's personal involvement with Prime Ministers Yitzhak Rabin and Ehud Barak of Israel, and with Yasir Arafat and King Hussein of Jordan, surely speeded the possibility of a settlement in the Middle East, even though a final deal has eluded him. In general, Mr. Clinton has rightly broadened the definition of national security to encompass the spread of disease, poverty and ethnic strife, ending his term with honourable involvement in the world and revitalisation of the United Nations and regional peacekeeping alliances. (NYT, 14 January, p. 4-16)

14 January

After almost a decade of much fuss about Africa by the Clinton administration but little to show for it, Gen. Colin L. Powell seems to believe there is room for improvement. He chose the Africa bureau as his first stop during his get-acquainted tour of the State Department, an interesting signal by the first African-American secretary of state-designate and a man best known for his hard-nosed military doctrine and sense of Realpolitik. In sub-Saharan Africa itself, where most countries have seen things go from bad to worse in the last decade, and where leaders and intellectuals look at the West with increased mistrust, the signal was noted with a mix of cynicism and expectation. Under General Powell, the tone of the American relationship with Africa – as with much of the world – will almost certainly be overhauled. The specifics are not yet clear, but there are some tantalising clues. At one point, the general asked crisply: What about Nigeria and South Africa? These are the two powerhouses of the continent, large in size, rich in resources and situated like two anchors astride wars, poverty and disease. Both are democracies under stress: Nigeria, which has swung between military dictatorships and civilian leadership, is in a democratic phase but is deeply troubled by corruption and growing income disparity; South Africa is in economic doldrums. One approach that might suit General Powell would be to send more American military assistance to these two governments to improve their peacekeeping abilities. The Clinton administration has just finished training two Nigerian battalions whose soldiers are supposed to go to Sierra Leone. But congressional aides, who are enthusiastic about using Nigerian forces there, complain that the American training has been too meagre. In pointing to Nigeria, General Powell was also recognising a vital American interest: oil. Little is said about it, but Nigeria and Angola have become important suppliers of oil. Nigeria now is the United States' fifth biggest supplier, Angola the eighth. Their oil is highly desirable light sweet crude, and it is in offshore fields, making it relatively easy to drill for the major companies like Chevron. (NYT, 14 January, p. 4-6)

14 January

Foreign policy has not played a decisive role in electing a president since 1968, the height of the Vietnam War. Since 1992, at the end of the cold war, foreign policy has become an electoral afterthought. Perhaps we should feel grateful that foreign policy has lost its political prominence. The sense of menace that once made the world matter urgently to us has lost its political prominence. But if today's world is less dangerous, it is also more complex. Think about the new phenomenon of disintegrating states or economic globalisation. Forces both smaller and larger than the state now play a crucial role in foreign affairs. And as the terrain has changed, so have the terms of the debate. The words "interest" and "values" points to one way in which the foreign-policy debate has realigned itself since the end of the cold war. The words correspond roughly to the realism of traditional European diplomacy and to the idealism associated. Ms. Rice said in the journal Foreign Affairs when foreign policy is centred on values the 'national interest' is replaced with 'humanitarian interests' or the interest of 'the international community'. She does not believe in humanitarianism as a goal of foreign policy. For George W. Bush and his team is helping humanity a second-order effect. The central theme of the new administration's military policy will be national missile defence. The core issue is Bush cares enough about the nuances of a complex world. Colin Powell will probably become Secretary of State and Condoleezza Rice will be national security adviser. A Bush administration is likely to have the kind of foreign policy the corporate community likes – less focus on human rights, more on free trade. The great difference between Bush and Clinton will have to do with military and defence policy. Bush and his team believe that only by constructing a national missile defence the United States can offer security in a world with access to weapons of mass destruction. The Bush team also wants that American soldiers won't continue with peacekeeping around the globe, but prepare for global engagements. A lot is said about the supposedly harmful effects of "low intensity" interventions on the U.S. military, less is said about the human beings on the other end. (NYT, 14 January, p. 6-28)

14 January

If George W. Bush's campaign rhetoric and Cabinet choices are any indication, the president-elect is not inclined toward the kind of muddled interventionism or ill-fated peacekeeping that has characterised American foreign policy in recent years. The secretary of state-designate, Powell, is a leading opponent of using the military to solve diplomatic and humanitarian problems. But the real test for Bush will come when the first inevitable international crisis bursts forth on CNN. Wherever it occurs, persuasive and emotional cries for U.S. intervention will reverberate around the world. The United States should not risk further erosion of its war-fighting capabilities; it should not allow its military forces to be drawn into small war and peacekeeping missions that can last years or decades. It the UN and its member nations believe that peacekeeping is important, it is time for the world's lesser powers – "middle" developed countries – to participate in greater numbers. During the previous decade, the United States was coerced into taking a leadership role in several UN missions primarily because middle powers were no able to provide the military resources necessary to cope with the challenges of a Somalia or Bosnia. The United States needs a UN that is capable of operating complex peacekeeping operations. Otherwise, it will be forced to take on the role of rescuer by default. The United States can partially pays its UN dues by providing support for these peacekeeping missions: logistics from existing U.S. bases, intelligence data, communications assistance. (WP, 14 January, p. B3)

15 January

In 1993 the American military force was ambushed in Somalia. One of President Clinton's senior foreign-policy advisers recently recalled with agony a delegation of congressional leaders descending on the White House to lay down terms to Clinton for bringing forces home from Somalia. Foreign leaders watched the administration's piteous performance and may well have concluded that this naïve young president was hardly a force to be reckoned with. Bruce Jentleson, who served in Clinton's first term, said the new team that autumn learned a brutal lesson: "If you don't do foreign policy, it does you." The way the president reconciled himself to this truth was one of the most striking evolutions of the Clinton years. How did this change happen? Holbrooke, Clinton's ambassador to the United Nations, said Clinton realised that the skill at which he excelled – politics – had as much currency overseas as it did at home. This revelation came haltingly. But as it came, Holbrooke said, Clinton learned he had the ability "to look at a problem in political terms and to find its political essence. This allowed him to look at something from the perspective if how another leader looked at it." So evolved a highly personal brand of diplomacy. Yet, if this administration foreign policy over time reflected its leader's strengths, so, too, did his infirmities show. At times, critics called him gushingly naïve. At times, Clinton's view that foreign problems could be understood in American terms caused his own advisers to cringe. Inattention could carry large costs. Failed diplomacy led to military confrontation. Among foreign-policy experts, there remains a debate over whether Clinton's record should be called a policy at all. As many see it, he leaves office as he came to it: with a loosely twined bundle of good intentions, some in conflict with each other, and most pursued in fits and starts. A secondary question is whether this improvisational style was a liability – or perfectly suited for the times. Clinton is the first American president to serve his entire tenure without the Cold War. He laboured to bring focus to America's mission abroad. The Clinton administration was unable to rally Congress around this so-called new agenda. Meanwhile, problems from the old agenda persisted. National security adviser Berger said, "He understood that the old paradigm of win-lose that dominated the Cold War was no longer sufficient". There is one place where Clinton's "body of practice" has won wide acclaim: international economics, which under Clinton reached pre-eminence it seldom if ever had among his predecessors. "At first he felt uncomfortable only because he had not done that much," said Panetta, who served as chief of staff in the first term. "He relied on his national security team and his vice president to provide guidance." In addition, Clinton's early latitude on foreign policy was limited by then-Chairman of the Joint Chiefs of Staff Powell. Powell had made plain his scepticism about military intervention except under strictly limited circumstances, which had "an enormous intimidating effect" on Clinton during discussions of Bosnia, an aide recalled. Powell retired and Clinton's confidence that he really was the commander in chief gradually rose. Some members of the first-term team say the turning point came in 1994, when Clinton ordered intervention in Haiti. Holbrooke describes in his memoir, "To End a War", an astonishing scene from the summer of 1995. Clinton was not aware that his administration had agreed to send troops to rescue stranded UN personnel. Given this reality, he reasoned, why not make an all-out for peace? Clinton ordered air strikes against the Bosnian Serbs to make clear the price of not reaching a settlement. Advisers feared that this could prove disastrous to his 1996 re-election. But a paradox soon unfolded. Once Clinton defied public opinion to do what he thought was right, public confidence in his foreign-policy judgements began to rise. After

Dayton, Ohio and a Bosnia deal in November 1995 Clinton's foreign-policy ratings went up and stay high for the rest of his presidency. Clinton over time refashioned his relationship with his foreign-policy team. During the first term, he often deferred to Lake, Secretary of State Christopher and Defence Secretary Perry. In the second term, Secretary of State Albright and Defence Secretary Cohen and Berger surrounded him; there was never a doubt that he was the dominant force. One place where Clinton's personal diplomacy and powers of persuasion brought him far, was the Middle East. With the end of his presidency nearing, Clinton brought the two sides' closer than almost anyone thought possible. Former secretary of State Kissinger argues that the Mideast gambit reflects a shortcoming of Clinton's personal diplomacy. "I don't think he ever learned to differentiate between foreign and domestic policy," Kissinger said. "In domestic policy, if you come to an agreement, the problem is over. In foreign policy, everything depends on accumulating nuances over and extended period of time." Perhaps the not-quite completed negotiations over a battle-scarred Promised Land are a fitting legacy for Clinton. He won the confidence of leaders on both sides, brought them further anyone expected. Yet the force of his personality was still insufficient for the task, triggering a backlash from extremists on both sides and leaving the unanswered question of whether the world is better of because Bill Clinton strove for the ultimate prize abroad as well as at home. (WP, 15 January, p. A1)

18 January
As a 63-year-old four star general acquainted with the old world of the Soviet Union and its weapons, Gen. Colin L. Powell set out today to convince his polite Senate inquisitors that he was suited to be secretary of state because he knew the new world of the Internet and the information revolution. But just as the Internet was essential to the new world, so was national missile defence, said General Powell, who stressed repeatedly in his confirmation hearings before the Senate Foreign Relations Committee that the Bush administration was determined to move forward with the plan, even in the face of allied opposition. "I have also been through several things like this over the years where people see something new come along and they are terrified," General Powell said comparing the fears in Europe about national missile defence with fears in the 1980's when there was public opposition in Britain and Germany to the installation of American Pershing nuclear missiles to deter the Soviets. But, the general declared, "If it's the right thing to do, you do it anyway." General Powell broke no new ground in his testimony or in answers to questions, saying that the Bush team would "careful" review the commitments made by the Clinton administration to the NATO peacekeeping force in the Balkans. European leaders have expressed alarm that even the threat of withdrawing American troops from the Balkans missions would weaken NATO and destabilise Kosovo and Bosnia just at a critical moment of their repair. As if to respond to that concern but not willing to concede the apparent contradiction that withdrawing troops would affect NATO, General Powell said in his testimony that NATO was the "bedrock of our relationship with Europe." On Iraq, General Powell made the case that sanctions, as he has said before, needed to be reinvigorated and that this could be done by pointing out more vigorously to nations in the region that Saddam Hussein was threatening them with weapons of mass destruction. Elsewhere in the Middle East, the general distanced himself from the all-out Clinton effort to reach an accord between the Palestinians and Israelis, saying that Syria was needed for a comprehensive settlement. On the crisis in Congo, General Powell described the situation as "very confuse" and warned that Congo was the most difficult peacekeeping task for the United Nations. On the International Criminal Court General Powell told the panel not to be "standing on your tippy-toes waiting for the Bush

the panel not to be "standing on your tippy-toes waiting for the Bush administration to ask for any – any – movement toward ratification of the treaty." General Powell gave the impression that that the Bush administration would not seek passage of the Comprehensive Test Ban Treaty at all, though in his oral delivery he modified that to say they would not seek passage in the current congressional session. (NYT, 18 January, p. A-17)

20 January

Every president takes office believing he can set the foreign policy agenda for his administration, only to discover that a major portion of that agenda has already been set by the world. The crises of the world do not take a time-out for a new American leader. President Clinton arrived hoping to focus on domestic issues, but was immediately faced by crises in places like Somalia, Haiti and Taiwan, along with hardy perennials like Russia and the Middle East. President-elect George W. Bush was confronted by the killing of the president of Congo this week, and might see the election of a hawkish prime minister in Israel and the crumbling of the peace accord in Northern Ireland in his first month in office. Further down the line, Mr. Bush's enthusiasm for a missile-defence system is certain to generate fierce opposition in Europe and in Russia. Even with Slobodan Milosevic deposed, the Balkans are not going away. Mr. Bush has said he would "very much like to get our troops out" of the Balkans, where more than 9,000 American soldiers are stationed in Bosnia and Kosovo. But the Europeans and the Kosovar Albanians will oppose that. The 1995 Dayton agreement was an American-imposed peace and Bosnia and Herzegovina is an American-designed country. Five years later, the peace is holding, but the country is badly riven by ethnic nationalism. Will a Bush administration redesign Bosnia and the Dayton accord if it intends to withdraw troops? Kosovo is becoming more explosive, with new attacks on Serbs by the supposedly disbanded Kosovo Liberation Army outside of Kosovo but under the eyes of American peacekeeping troops. Mr. Bush will have to consider how much pressure to place on the government when popular unhappiness with a bad economy, power shortages and a restive Montenegro is reaching its peak. (NYT, 20 January, p. A-19)

20 January

The Security Council confronted the issue of United Nations peacekeepers who carry the virus that causes AIDS and who may spread it in the countries where they are assigned. The heads of the United Nations' peacekeeping department and AIDS agency promised to work together to make peacekeeping troops more aware of the peril of AIDS and more sensitive to the rights of local people left vulnerable by armed conflict. (NYT, 20 January, p. A7)

20 January

The Security Council today confronted the problem of United Nations peacekeepers that carry the virus that causes AIDS and could spread it in the countries where they are assigned. In a session held at the insistence of the departing United States ambassador, Richard C. Holbrooke, the heads of the United Nations peacekeeping department and the AIDS agency acknowledged the situation. They promised to work together to make peacekeeping troops more aware of the peril of AIDS and more sensitive to the rights of local people left vulnerable by armed conflict. The General Assembly has left it up to the countries, some of which cannot afford to test and treat soldiers for AIDS and want to avoid any stigma attached to the disease. This keeps the United Nations from ensuring that soldiers are HIV-free before sending them on peacekeeping missions. Peter Piot, the executive director of the Joint United Nations Program on HIV/AIDS, said, "The role of HIV testing in peacekeeping missions is a complex issue, and nothing raises the emotional temperature of these debates more quickly." This brings its total contributions to the United Nations for combating AIDS to $15 million this year. Mr. Holbrooke, in his last day on the job, said he was encouraged by what he heard, but not satisfied. He asserted that confronting AIDS must become part of peacekeeping and be built into every mission's budget. (NYT, 20 January, p. A-7)

30 January

Calling for an end to violence in southern Lebanon, the Security Council on Tuesday unanimously agreed to cut the UN force which is helping to restore peace following Israel's troop withdrawal in May. The Council urged Lebanon to deploy its troops throughout the territory "to ensure the return of its effective authority and presence in the south." Lebanon has so far refused to send its army to the border, saying it does not want its troops to serve as Israel's border guards.

Secretary-General Kofi Annan said the simplest way to ensure calm in the area was for all sides to respect the blue line, which marked the withdrawal positions, and for Lebanon to assert its authority up to the line. Endorsing Annan's recommendations, the Security Council resolution called on the two sides to respect the blue line and exercise "utmost restraint." It condemned "all acts of violence, expresses concern about the serious breaches and violations of the withdrawal line and urges the parties to put an end to them." The council also welcomed Lebanon's establishment of checkpoints in the area vacated by Israel and encouraged the Lebanese government "to ensure a calm environment throughout the south, including through the control of all checkpoints." (Associated Press, 30 January)

8 February

Ending a bitter dispute with the United Nations, the Senate voted today to immediately release $582 million the United States owes in back dues, recognition that the world organisation has made significant strides toward revamping its operations. The Senate vote – 99 to 0 – came less than two months after Richard C. Holbrooke, who served as the Clinton administration's United Nations ambassador, brokered a deal to reduce American dues for the first time in more than 28 years. In a game of brinkmanship, Congress withheld a portion of the United States' dues to the United Nations for more than a decade, arguing that the American people were paying too much for peacekeeping missions and that the United Nations was mismanaging its money. The stand-off complicated diplomatic relationships and drew criticism from other nations, which labelled the United States an arrogant, deadbeat superpower. In 1999, Senator Helms and Senator Joseph R. Biden Jr., the ranking Democrat on the committee, drew up a three-year plan to release the money if the United Nations agreed to a series of goals. Chief among them was the question of reducing the United States' dues. Under the deal that was reached by Mr. Holbrooke, the American share of the United Nations' $1.1 billion administrative budget would drop to 22 percent, which Congress stipulated, from 25 percent. The American contribution to the $2.5 billion annual peacekeeping budget would be reduced, in increments, from 31 percent to 26.5 percent by the end of 2002, and eventually to 25 percent. Other United Nations members did not agree to scale back in the short term to the 25 percent that Mr. Helms originally wanted, but came close enough. The Senate released the first $100 million under the plan's initial phase. The third chunk of money – $244 million – will be released next year, on the condition of changes in some auditing procedures at the World Health Organisation and other independent agencies. In his speech today, Mr. Helms said the reduction in dues would save $170 million a year in dues that the United Nations had billed taxpayers. Mr. Holbrooke spent almost all of his 17 months as ambassador trying to broker an agreement on American payments. What unfolded over that time was a defiant speech to the United Nations Security Council, the first ever to by a member of Congress. Mr. Holbrooke argued that the dues charged for peacekeeping had not changed since 1973 and had failed to keep pace with a quickly changing world. But opposition was fierce. Some newly prospering countries did not want to see their dues rise, while others did not want to bow to an ultimatum from Congress. The United Nations and the United States still disagree over the amount that is actually owed. United Nations officials say the United States owes another $500 million in dues. (NYT, 8 February, p. A9)

8 February

The Senate voted without dissent yesterday to repay $582 million of the United States' debt to the United Nations as part of a deal that also reduces the U.S. share of UN operating and peacekeeping costs. The way was cleared for passage of a bill releasing the funds after Foreign Relations Committee Chairman Helms gave his blessings to an agreement. The agreement was worked out two months ago by the United States and the United Nations aimed at ending a six-year funding dispute and repairing relations that had suffered as a result of it. The legislation releasing the funds was the second step in a three-phase process Congress approved two years ago. It calls for payment of $926 million in U.S. debts in exchange for improvements in UN operations and a reduction in the U.S. share of the international organisation's costs. Congress approved a $100 million down payment in 1999. Another $244 million is due next year if the UN follows through on further budget improvements involving the World Health Organisation and other agencies affiliated with the UN. The U.S.-UN deal, which was brokered last year by the former U.S. ambassador of the UN Holbrooke, calls for cutting the U.S. share of the UN operating budget from 25 percent to 22 percent. American contributions to peacekeeping costs would drop from 31 percent to 28 percent this year and 26 percent in future years. A law passed in 1994 put caps in U.S. contributions, including 25 percent for peacekeeping but eventually agreed to higher amounts, sealing the deal. But the change required new legislation to free up the money. (WP, 8 February, p. A17)

10 February

Paula J. Dobriansky and David B. Rivkin wrote "Out of the Balkans". They made a pitch for President Bush's proposed strategic division of labour between the United States and its allies, "including redeployment if more than 11,000 American troops from the Balkans." They argued that "the withdrawal of U.S. 'peacekeepers', if handled with even a modicum of diplomatic finesse, would neither destroy NATO, destabilise Europe nor undermine U.S. global leadership." It is this kind of simplistic thinking that kept the United Nations out of the Balkans – and out of the UN protection force – during the three-year period of genocidal warfare. Some members of the alliance have argued that if the United States were to withdraw troops from Bosnia or Kosovo, the French, British, Germans and others would be sure to follow. This sounds like a recipe for a resumption of warfare in the Balkans. (WP, 10 February, p. A22)

11 February

The Senate passed a bill reducing the U.S. share of the $1.1 billion United Nations administrative budget from 25 percent to 22 percent and cutting U.S. support of the world body's $2.5 billion peacekeeping budget from 31 percent to 25 percent. The bill signal U.S. approval of steps the United Nations has taken, under American prodding, to prune its bureaucracy and require more affluent nations to pay a greater share of UN expenses. It authorises payment of $582 million in tardy U.S. dues that Congress has been holding back while awaiting UN reforms. (WP, 11 February, p. T6)

18 February
In his presidential campaigns George W. Bush said he would protect America's "national interests" and that America would conduct a "more humble foreign policy". No one was quite certain what it all meant. The past few weeks Mr. Bush has begun defining his terms, setting his priorities, but he doesn't plan to show it. Last week, Mr. Bush set a broad new direction for America's military, told reservists that he would bring a halt to the "over deployments" of troops around the world and talked about gas exploration and new immigration policy with President Fox of Mexico. A few examples, in the past few days Defence Secretary Rumsfeld has declared that Moscow's role as an "active proliferator" of missile technology helped propel the White House toward developing a national missile defence. Treasury Secretary O'Neill told Russia to pay off the old Soviet Union's debts and forget about new aid until it cleans up rampant corruption. It sends a message: don't expect us to leave home as often, and don't expect us to whip out our American Express card when we do. Mr. Zelikow, the director of the Miller Center of Public Affairs at the University of Virginia said, "the two words they use the most are discipline and strategy". He argued that Mr. Bush's team is "trying hard to recover choice". This fits all nicely intro Mr. Bush's preferences for pragmatism over ideology. He tends to attack problems through personal relationships. The flip side of Mr. Bush predilection for the personal is a lack of much real enthusiasm for the multilateral institutions that Mr. Clinton saw as the vital wiring of a globalise world. The fear in Europe and Asia, of course, is that the talk of consultation is just for show – that Mr. Bush wants to put a multinational patina on views he's already arrived at. The real test of America's new management won't come until grand pronouncements confront some global reality. (NYT, 18 February, p. 1)

23 February
F. T. Liu, a Chinese-born United Nations official who worked closely with the American Nobel laureate Ralph J. Bunche during the Congo crisis of the 1960's and in many other trouble spots, died on Feb. 16 in his home in Bronxville, N.Y. He was 82. Mr. Liu joined the United Nations in 1949 and went to work for Dr. Bunche in the Trusteeship Division, charged with helping colonial territories gain their independence. In 1960 he moved to the Office of Special Political Affairs. Mr. Liu played an important role in planning and organising United Nations peacekeeping operations around the world. He was senior political adviser to the United Nations' huge peacekeeping operation in Congo from 1963 to 1964, then worked with the peacekeeping force in Cyprus and with the United Nations Truce Supervision Organisation in the Middle East. In 1970 he became secretary to the United Nations Good Offices Mission to Bahrain, helping that country's transition to independence. He retired from the United Nations in 1982 and became an associate professor at the University of Nice in France. But later that year he returned to the United Nations as a consultant on peacekeeping. (NYT, 23 February, p. 17)

2 March
The Pentagon today unveiled a weapon that uses electromagnetic waves to disperse crowds without killing, maiming or, military officials say, even injuring anyone slightly. The weapon is the fruit of 10 years of research and is intended to help American soldiers in the quasi-military roles they have increasingly been asked to play as peacekeepers or police in places like Kosovo and Ethiopia. The weapon would fire bursts of electromagnetic energy capable of causing burning sensations on the skin of people standing as far as 700 yards away – without actually burning them, officials said. Colonel Fenton said about the weapon that the new system fires waves that are shorter and at higher frequencies than microwaves. That means, he said, that while the waves could penetrate clothing, they would barely enter the skin, reaching a depth of only one sixty-fourth of an inch. The weapon, which to date has cost taxpayers $40 million, already has its sceptics. Senior military adviser to Human Rights Watch Arkin described it as a "high-powered microwave antipersonnel weapon" that should be more carefully studied before it is used on crowds containing elderly people, children or pregnant women. The weapon, which to date has cost taxpayers $40 million, already has its sceptics. William M. Arkin, the senior military adviser to Human Rights Watch, described it as a "high-powered microwave antipersonnel weapon" that should be more carefully studied before it is used on crowds containing elderly people, children or pregnant women. The weapon is still in development and probably will not be ready for deployment by troops for at least five years, Colonel Fenton said. American troops now typically use tear gas, rubber bullets or beanbags fired from shotguns to disperse crowds. The electromagnetic weapon would be superior to those techniques, Colonel Fenton said, because it would have much longer range. (NYT, 2 March, p. 14)

16 March
The United States will probably veto any United Nations Security Council resolution calling for the dispatch of international observers to the West Bank and Gaza Strip, Israel's UN ambassador said Friday. The Palestinian Authority under President Yassir Arafat has called for international observers to protect Palestinians from Israeli forces as the Palestinian-led intifada (uprising) continues with daily violence and deaths.
Israel however rejects UN intervention, saying the presence of international observers would exacerbate the tense situation there. (Deutsche Presse-Agentur, 16 March)

19 March
The long-running fight between the United States and the United Nations ended supposedly back in December. Other countries agreed to pay more so that the U.S. dues could be reduced. In return, the U.S. was supposed to pay its UN debt and resume its leadership position within the institution. Unfortunately, Congress has yet to deliver its end of the bargain. The most obvious delay is in the House, which had failed to match the Senate in passing a bill to pay off $582 million of UN debt. There are two other problems need to be fixed. A 1995 measure known as the Dole amendment forbids the U.S. from paying more than 25 percent if UN peacekeeping costs. In December the UN accepted that share as reasonable and agreed to abandon the old requirement that the U.S. pay 31 percent. But the December deal reduces the American obligation in phases. Unless Congress acts to repeal the Dole amendment soon, the U.S. will accumulate new arrears and so renege on the spirit if the December agreement. Congress also needs to address the timing of its payment. Since the 1980s the U.S. has paid January bills only at year-end. Because the U.S. is it biggest contributor, this makes life difficult for the UN. (WP, 19 March, p. A16)

23 March
Part of the expansiveness of U.S. foreign policy during the past decade was to some degree tied to the soaring U.S. Dow and Nasdaq and the sense they produces of boundless American power. There were plenty of good reasons to intervene to halt mass killings in the Balkans, but the soaring markets made these and other interventions much easier. There wasn't great public support for many of these operations, but there also wasn't much opposition because the costs were not big enough to notice. The soaring Nasdaq was not the only reason for American expansiveness abroad in the past decade. It had also to do with the fact there is no military draft, none had to give up their stock options to serve in Bosnia or Haiti. Those who did go went with the assumption that these would be "zero-casualty wars". Public moods alone don't determine foreign policy and would never stand in the way of wars of no choice. But the point about the post-cold-war era is that we feel if gives us more choices to intervene or not. And the markets will affect public 's choices, especially if they turn costly. (NYT, 23 March, p.19)

23 March
Kofi Annan, the first leader of the United Nations, said today he would accept a second five-year term as secretary general. He is likely to be re-elected at the end of his first term, Dec. 31 2001. Washington welcomed Mr. Annan's decision. Mr. Annan is popular within the organisation and has become a celebrity figure outside the United States, where the United Nations is generally held in higher regard and as a higher visibility. (NYT, 23 March, p. 7)

26 March
Kofi Annan's candidacy for a second five-year term as UN secretary general is welcome and deserves the strong endorsement President Bush gave it on Friday. Mr. Annan's has strengthened the UN's management and moral credibility and repaired its once frayed ties with Washington. He commissioned tough reviews of past UN peacekeeping failures in Rwanda and Bosnia, even though he led the peacekeeping department during those operations. For the past year he has pressed member nations to make peacekeeping more effective. He has also emerged as a voice of conscience on a variety of international issues. Further reforms are needed to enable the organisation to live up to its founding ideals. A second term would allow Mr. Annan to make additional changes and cement a constructive relationship with the new Bush administration and Congress. Mr. Annan must strengthen the under-staffed peacekeeping department. To serve again he needs the support of the Security Council, including the five permanent members. A successful secretary general must court Washington and the Security Council's other permanent members. Those countries generally decide when to impose or lift international sanctions on misbehaving countries and where to send peacekeeping operations. The secretary general must also be a voice for the needs of smaller countries. Mr. Annan has managed both roles with competence and grace and should be kept on the job. (NYT, 26 March, p. 18)

27 March
There are two competing foreign policy camps emerging in the Bush administration: an ideologically conservative Pentagon and a more moderate State Department. At the Pentagon side, secretary of Defense Rumsfeld is collecting a hard-line group of advisers. At the State Department Secretary of State Powell is on board. General Powell is likely to place more emphasis on working with his allies than is Mr. Rumsfeld, who has a history of supporting a

unilateral approach. Mr. Bush has acknowledged that he will rely on his most senior policy advisers. Vice President Cheney collected his own foreign policy specialists and is likely to become an important arbiter. Mr. Cheney is seen as leaning more toward the Pentagon, where he served as secretary of defence. Ms. Rice, the national security adviser, didn't make clear her predilections. Tests of how the competing spheres are reconciled will come in several areas: Iraq, Taiwan, Russia, the Balkans, North Korea. (NYT, 27 March, p. 1)

28 March

Voting against efforts to establish a United Nations observer force to protect Palestinian civilians, the United States last night vetoed a draft resolution expressing the Council's readiness to set up such a mechanism.

The Council would have expressed its full support for the work of the Fact-Finding Committee established at Sharm el-Sheikh and would have called upon all parties to cooperate fully with it, and to resume contacts on implementation of reciprocal security commitments. The Council would also have called for an end to the closures of the occupied Palestinian territories; full cessation of settlement activities; the transfer by Israel to the Palestinian Authorities of all due revenues; and the institutional of additional confidence-building measures, including unequivocal public statements supporting all commitments made at Sharm el-Sheikh.

The Observer for Palestine said that tonight's negative result meant that the Council had been prevented from following through with its duties in maintaining international peace and security. Palestine had made every possible effort to arrive at a positive conclusion, even at the expense of its own position. Ultimately, it could not give up the legitimate needs of the Palestinian people, including the need for international protection, especially since no alternative text had been tabled. Palestine would be present at a later date to see what could be done in cooperation with the Council members who were ready to work for peace, justice and legitimacy. (UN News, 28 March)

28 March

The Bush administration has made clear its desire for an early withdrawal of American peacekeeping troops from the Balkans. This cannot be achieved until sufficient stability has been brought to the region to allow the removal of outside military forces without risking a rapid return to armed conflict. Recent raids into Macedonia and southern Serbia by armed bands of ethnic Albanians show just how volatile the military situation remains. The specific remedies needed in Macedonia, southern Serbia and Kosovo are different. But in all three areas, Western governments should work closely with moderate Albanian leaders who reject violence and promote the interests of their community by political means. Albanians in Macedonia want equal constitutional status for Slavs and Albanians, a more decentralized government, official status for the Albanian language and international monitoring of the next census. In Kosovo, the most urgent need is building new structures of self-government to replace the ousted Serbian administration. Last year successful local elections were held, now the United Nation's administrator needs to move on to a province wide vote. In southern Serbia, the new democratic government must regain their confidence by working co-operatively with elected Albanian local officials and by bringing more Albanians into the police and military forces. Improving political and economic conditions in the Balkans will take time, as the slow progress in Bosnia has shown. More inclusive political arrangements in all three areas will reduce the potential for violence and speed the completion of NATO's mission. (NYT, 28 March, p. 20)

29 March
The Bush administration is prepared to certify that Yugoslavia is co-operating with the war crimes tribunal at The Hague, thus meeting the requirements of an American law and allowing American economic assistance to resume, officials said. (NYT, 29 March, p.2)

6 April
An article last Friday about peacekeepers in Eritrea and Ethiopia referred incorrectly to the involvement of Canada in United Nations missions to Africa in recent years. Canadians have indeed served more recently than 1993 – in Rwanda, the Western Sahara and the Central Africa Republic, and currently in Sierra Leone and Congo, in addition to Ethiopia and Eritrea. (NYT, 6 April, p. 3)

3 May
After monitoring the Lebanese border for 23 long years and overseeing the withdrawal of Israeli forces last June, the UN Interim Force in Lebanon (UNIFIL) is beginning a phased withdrawal of its troops from one of the most volatile hotspots in the Middle East. In a report to the Security Council this week, Annan said that the reconfiguration of the UNI-FIL will be achieved through the non-replacement or reduction of military units during their normal rotations. (IPS, 3 May)

10 May
The House is scheduled to vote today to pay $582 million in back dues to the UN this year but to freeze a final instalment of $244 million scheduled to be paid next year, unless the U.S. regains its seat on the UN Human Rights Commission. Members of both parties predicted yesterday that the measure would pass easily on a wave of exasperation with the UN. Though the Bush administration shared Capitol Hill's frustration over the loss of the traditional U.S. seat, the State Department dispatched officials to oppose the amendment freezing the next instalment. Although American officials said they were surprised by the outcome in the secret balloting last week, a State Department official wrote a memo before the vote warning that the U.S. was in jeopardy of being ousted, according to sources familiar with the document. But the memo became mired there because of disagreements over the seriousness of the danger and the proper tactical response. The warning did not reach Secretary of State Powell of Deputy Secretary of State Armitage "until the eleventh hour," a senior State Department official said. Powell and other top administration officials learned on the eve of the vote that defeat was possible and discussed the prospect, but is was already too late to sway outcome, sources said. Holbrooke, the American ambassador to the UN under Clinton, said the setback last week reflected a lack of diligence on the part of the U.S. and its European Union allies. The U.S. agreed to pay $244 million next year. The sum is the third and final instalment to clear its debts under an arduously negotiated deal that also sharply reduces the American share of the UN's operating budget and peacekeeping expenses. Holbrooke brokered the deal in the final weeks of the Clinton administration. He said yesterday that he regrets that the arrangement may now be rewritten but can support the House measure because he is confident that the U.S. will be voted onto the human rights commission next year. UN Secretary General Annan urged the U.S. not to overreact to its defeat. Annan said, "We are all surprised by the vote. I am confident that next year they will be able to get onto the commission and this situation will be corrected." (WP, 10 May, p. A14)

11 May

The House voted yesterday to withhold $244 million in UN arrears next year, striking back at the world body for its decision to oust the U.S. from a seat on a UN human rights panel. The move came despite warnings from the Bush administration that the action could shuttle a deal aimed at settling a long-running dispute over U.S. debts to the UN. The vote was for a proposal that would allow Congress to pay $582 million in UN back dues this year but suspend the next instalment unless the U.S. regains its seat on the UN Human Rights Commission. The proposal underscored the depth of anger on Capitol Hill in the wake of last week's vote to remove the U.S. from its traditional seat on the human rights panel as well as the degree to which lawmakers remain uneasy with America's close ties to international organisations. It remains unclear whether the Senate will also approve the proposal. (WP, 11 May, p. A1)

12 May

President Bush pledged an initial $200 million to a new global trust fund to combat AIDS yesterday, saying it was "almost beyond comprehension" that 36 million people around the world are believed infected with the virus that causes the disease. Standing with UN Secretary General Annan and President Olesegun Obasanjo of Nigeria, Bush said there would be "more money to follow as we learn where our support can be most effective." Bush said he thought a world-wide consensus was forming on the basic elements of the fund. He also emphasized that the fund "must respect intellectual property rights as an incentive for vital research and development." Anna, who has said $7 billion a year is needed for the developing world to stem the spread of AIDS and HIV that causes it, called Bush's pledge "a visionary decision that reflects your nation's natural leadership in the UN." Bush made no mention of where the $200 million would come from. (WP, 12 May, p. A19)

24 May

A guy named Makinawe said "My brother Colin Powell is in Africa." Another one, called Maepa, said that Powell is a black man. It represents Africans' profound ambivalence about Colin Powell, who arrived in Mali today to begin a four-nation tour of the continent. Powell told reporters that this visit to Africa gave him an "emotional twinge". He also said he was "moved by the fact that I'm the first African American secretary of state to visit Africa." When he leaves Mali, Powell is scheduled to come to South Africa, then travel to Kenya and Uganda. A political analyst in South Africa, Seepe, said, "Colin Powell is a difficult call for a lot of Africans. This is the highest position a black person has ever held in the U.S. There is the sense that you have a black person in the position and so he understands poverty and discrimination." "On the hand he made his name in a political party that has historically been hostile to Africa, that was an avowed ally of apartheid South Africa. Add all that up and what Africans really want to know is: Who is Colin Powell loyal to?" Many Africans say they see Powell's tour as a sign that Africa will indeed be a priority in the Bush administration's foreign policy, despite Bush's assertion during the campaign that the continent was not strategic for the U.S. (WP, 24 May, p. A1)

24 May

The past year in West Africa demonstrates that even a minimal commitment to armed peace making can yield positive results. It demonstrates that the international community remains mostly unwilling to muster that limited effort, with the result that hundreds of thousands of people have lost their homes and livelihoods. The bush administration should pause to consider this African lesson. The first lesson comes from Sierra Leone. Before the British showed up last year it seemed to demonstrate the hopelessness of peace making after a 10-year civil war: A UN force in the country had been humiliated by the country's limb-chopping rebels, who took several hundred of their soldiers hostage. The British arrived and secured the capital. They don't see why they should shoulder all the risks in the absence of U.S. or European back up. Having eschewed the type of response that is sure to be effective – NATO-intervention – the international community has reverted to the second-best formula of UN troops plus West African forces. The hope is that this combination will prove more effective than previously. In Guinea, spill over fighting has driven more than 300,000 people from their homes and provoked the Guinean government to respond with incursions into Sierra Leone and Liberia, which shares a border with both countries. You might think the international community would follow with an intervention in Guinea. But instead the refugees have been left to the mercy of assorted militias. The Bush administration has sympathetic words for Africa, and Powell is currently visiting the continent. Yet the U.S. response to West Africa's crisis is inadequate. (WP, 24 May, p. A38)

27 May
The change in party control will affect the major committees: Democratic control of the committee will mean the departure as chairman of Helms, a strong conservative who has used the committee to block nominations, arms control treaties and funding for the United Nations. It also means tougher questioning of the Bush administration's policies on national missile defence, negotiations with North Korea and peacekeeping in the Balkans. While Biden is in line to be chairman, the committee would adopt a more sceptical posture toward the administration's handling of these issues regardless of who assumes the top post. Though many Democratic members have supported research and development of some missile defence technology, the administration's determination to build a national shield costing more than $ 50 billion has drawn criticism from the Democrats. They question whether the system can be developed and whether it would serve U.S. interests. The change of control will also put more congressional pressure on the administration to explain its reluctance to continue missile talks with North Korea. When Bush abruptly suspended those negotiations in March, saying the United States had concerns about the verification of agreements with the Pyongyang government, Democrats on the committee vigorously objected that this would undermine efforts to stabilise the Korean peninsula. If Biden becomes chairman, the committee will likely pay far more attention to the administration's policies in the Balkans. He has been particularly critical of remarks by officials indicating the U.S. plans to withdraw its peacekeeping troops from the region. (WP, 27 May, p. A10)

29 May
The US got voted off the island at the UN Human Rights Commission three weeks ago. The vote that got the US booted off the Human Rights Commission was a wake-up call, a signal that the world will push back against radical Bush policies. When President Bush trashed the Kyoto treaty on climate change, the message the world got was that the Bushies will do whatever they please, on a range of issues, and if the world doesn't like it – though. When the members of this UN commission got a change to vote anonymously on whether the US

should be a member, they stuck it to us. The fact is, the world is full of problems that touch America, that the UN handles – problems of poverty; problems of refugees; problems related to AIDS. There are now 16 UN peacekeeping missions. All these problems would exist whether the UN was there or not. So what the UN provides 95 percent of the time is a body for co-ordinating our response to problems we care about. And it does it in a way that the burden of costs is shared, so that the US doesn't have to pay alone, and that the burden of responsibility is shared. So wars the US wants fought, or the peace accords the US wants kept, have a global stamp of approval, not made-in-USA. The dirty little secret of the Human Rights Commission vote is that it is precisely because 95 percent of the time the UN is simply a tool of the US that a few countries, when they got a chance to stick us, did so. But if we can't understand that on just about every other day the real vote at the UN, the vote that matters, is 95 to 5 – 95 percent of the time it acts in our interests and 5 percent not – then shame on us. (NYT, 29 May, p. 15)

3 June
One of the bitterest voting campaigns is going on Switzerland. The debate is about whether Swiss soldiers can be armed while serving on peacekeeping missions abroad. The vote also goes to the core of Switzerland – its neutrality, independence and outreach to help people. The latest opinion polls indicate that the vote is close. The government is mindful that in 1994, voters rejected a proposal to let troops take part in peacekeeping missions of the United Nations, to which Switzerland does not belong, though the UN European headquarters are in Geneva. Another vote on membership, however, is coming up next year and next week's vote is in some ways a test run. The government makes no secret of wanting to edge Switzerland away from its isolationist, island-in-Europe status, over time, integrate it with its neighbours in the European Union. A turn away from engagements abroad would assault traditions that have kept the country prosperous and at peace. And no action is more disturbing to them than changing the Swiss military, which is a militia-style army similar to the National Guard system in the United States. A change in the law is necessary, government officials say, because individual soldiers abroad are barred from carrying guns, and can't adequately defend themselves. (NYT, 3 June p. 8)

4 June
In the late 19880's Mozambique was no-go territory: the rebel Renamo movement terrorized the countryside, and aid workers cowered in the capital. But Lonrho, a British company, chose that moment to buy a large swath of the country and farm cotton on it. Lohrno had hired a force of mercenaries. The dilemma posed by mercenaries is growing sharper. These days it's governments that hire them. In Sierra Leone and Angola mercenaries have performed effectively, raising the question of whether they should be used more often in peacemaking operations. The case for Lonrho's behaviour in the 1980s was not all that different from the case for government-hired mercenaries today. In an ideal world, the state would provide for public safety. In poor countries, the state is all but helpless. The choice is often mercenary-protected investment or no investment at all. In an ideal world strong countries would help war-torn ones by sending in their soldiers. Rich countries are, however, sick with the Somalia syndrome: no troops for Africa, even not to prevent genocide. So the choice often comes down to mercenary peacekeeping or no peacekeeping. Rich governments refuse to acknowledge the bottom line, like Lonrho did. They find the idea of mercenaries embarrassing. The result of this squeamishness is that a lot of people die. Unwilling to commit troops yet unwilling to pronounce the "m" word, governments have devised a peacekeeping system that is mercenary in all but name. This arrangement might be fine if it

keeping system that is mercenary in all but name. This arrangement might be fine if it worked properly. Sadly, it does not. In 1995-97 a South African firm was paid $1.2 million a month for its Sierra Leone operation; it hammered the rebels so thoroughly that they ran to the negotiating table, clearing the way for an election. A UN peace force was necessary, with the cost of $47 million a month. The critics of mercenaries say that paid war makers cannot promote peace in the long run. The critics charge that mercenaries won't be held accountable for battlefield atrocities. Burkhalter, a Washington human-rights activist, has words for the common squeamishness about mercenaries. "Watching a Rwanda genocide or a Srebrenica unfold without anyone's lifting a finger is what I find obscene – not using paid professionals to put a stop to it." She's right. (WP, 4 June, p. A19)

10 June
Carlos Saul Menem made history as Argentina's president between 1989 and 1999, selling off much of the bloated state bureaucracy, pegging the value of the peso to the dollar to control hyperinflation, and reorganizing the army to become a major player in United Nations peacekeeping operations. Now he has made history again, as the first democratically elected president arrested under another democratic government, on suspicion that he led a conspiracy to smuggle arms to Croatia and Ecuador between 1991 and 1995. If formally charged and convicted, he could be sentenced to 10 years in jail. (NYT, 10 June, p. 2)

11 June
When Bush departs for Europe tonight to make his case for building missile defences, he will be carrying in his luggage a familiar playbook: the one used to get his tax cut through Congress. The issues and audiences are entirely different. But Bush's strategy will be the same, his advisers say. He will listen to opponents, but ultimately he will not swerve from his original agenda. The Europeans are worried that Bush's willingness to forgo the 1972 Anti-ballistic Missile Treaty to build a missile defence system will set off a new costly new arms race. Democrats in Congress were worried that his tax cut would cause cutbacks in government programs. The Europeans and Russia complain that they haven't been consulted adequately and accuse the U.S. of an arrogant unilateralism. Outwardly, the Bush administration has told European allies that it is eager to discuss differences and celebrate common interests and administration officials say the president has no intention of abandoning his missile defence plan. Bush's domestic critics say the allies may be forced to swallow his missile defence plan, though at the cost of international goodwill Bush may need in the future. "Unilaterism has been strong in Congress for a number of years, a go-it-alone approach to solving the world's problems, and I think it's had quite an impact on his early positions," said former representative Hamilton. When necessary or desirable, Bush has been willing to compromise. Analysts say there are costs to unilateral action overseas. Blinken of the Centre for Strategic and International studies, warned that allies may start to balk at co-operating on issues such as weapons proliferation, crime, terrorism, disease and international military actions. Overseas, the protests about U.S. assertiveness have been more symbolic than damaging. Analysts agree that Bush faces obstacles to unilateral action overseas than he does at home. "The problem in the American Congress is the votes aren't there," said Donnelly of the Project for the New American Century, which favours an aggressive foreign policy. "In foreign policy we've got all the votes. The funny trick of leadership is the more people are convinced you're going to do it come hell or high water, the more likely they are to join in." Missile

defence is just one of the issues on which Bush will consult with foreign leaders. In Belgium, he will likely warn NATO members about his eagerness to reduce U.S. participation in peacekeeping missions in the Balkans. In Sweden, he will face EU-leaders furious over his dismissal of the Kyoto treaty on global warming. In Slovenia, he will meet Putin, who is irked not just by missile defence but also by planned NATO expansion. (WP, 11 June, p. A1)

13 June
The Security Organizations of the Government of Israel (GOI) and of the Palestinian Authority (PA) reaffirm their commitment to the security agreements forged at Sharm el-Sheikh in October 2000, embedded in the Mitchell Report of April 2001.
The operational premise of the work plan is that the two sides are committed to a mutual, comprehensive cease-fire, applying to all violent activities, in accordance with the public declaration of both leaders. In addition, the joint security committee referenced in this work plan will resolve issues that may arise during the implementation of this work plan. The security organizations of the GOI and PA agree to initiate the following specific, concrete, and realistic security steps immediately to re-establish security cooperation and the situation on the ground that existed prior to 28 September. (Al-bab, 13 June)

14 June
Syrian President Bashar al-Assad called on UN Secretary General Kofi Annan Thursday to work toward the application of UN Security Council resolutions on peace in the Middle East. In a meeting with Annan Thursday morning, Assad reaffirmed "Syria's stable position concerning the peace process, based on the resolutions of the United Nations and on international principle." (Agence France Presse, 14 June)

18 June
UN Secretary General Kofi Annan is continuing to work for a meeting between Palestinian Authority Chairman Yasser Arafat and Foreign Minister Shimon Peres. There is concern in the Prime Minister's Office that Annan's presence in the region at this time signals the start of a new initiative based on UN and European efforts to help Arafat. In his discussion with Prime Minister Ariel Sharon, Peres, and former justice minister Yossi Beilin, Annan raised the idea of a multi-faceted program that he thinks could improve the climate of confidence between Israel and the Palestinian Authority.
The first element would be the establishment of a team that would supervise the implementation of the cease-fire. A second element would be to establish a time framework so that both sides would know when talks on a final status agreement would begin. A third element would be creating a permanent third party presence in the area; and the fourth element raised by Annan was a Peres-Arafat meeting. (Ha'aretz, 18 June)

24 June
When it comes to military matters, New Zealanders are more likely to hear from the minister of disarmament than the minister of defence these days. Having angered the United States and other allies in the 1980s by banning visits by nuclear-powered or – armed warships, New Zealand now has opted to be the first advanced country to virtually scrap its air defences. The left-of-centre government announced last month that is was junking the

air force's combat jets, turning the air force into a transport service. The small army is being remade into a peacekeeping force and the navy cut to just two ocean-going warships. The army also has been instructed to study setting up a peace school at which soldiers would sit in seminars with aid workers and peace campaigners to discuss methods and share experiences. New Zealand may be small and far away from just about everywhere, but the Labour Party government believes it can set an example to the world on defence. Opponents of the cuts contend the government is pursuing total disarmament by stealth, cloaking its true aim with talk about peacekeeping because most New Zealanders want a strong defence. Prime Minister Clark insists the changes be justified because there is virtually no chance of New Zealand being attacked. New Zealand is investing in the army to carry out peacekeeping missions with the UN and other world bodies, she said. "This defence strategy is very opposite of being isolationist." Many legislators in the governing party were deeply influenced by the opposition to New Zealand's military involvement in the Vietnam War in the 1960s and the movement in the 1980s against nuclear weapons and power. Robson, the government's disarmament minister, said disarmament and arms control are "just as important" as what the country does with the armed forces. Outsiders, who say the country is isolationist "are misleading their people and misleading the world," he said. New Zealand has a long and proud military tradition, having sent troops to aid Britain during the two world wars and taking part in the Korean and Vietnam wars. Military analysts and former defence chiefs argue the government's policy will leave New Zealand defenceless and alienate allies. "We're really becoming a passive onlooker, and they will conclude we have no plans to work on collective security in a time of trouble," said Hensley, a retired senior defence official. (WP, 24 June, p. A16)

25 June
Three Arab countries are pushing for what they see as a more balanced western role in resolving the Palestinian Israeli conflict. Saudi Arabia's Crown Prince Abdullah has criticised what he calls America's one sided support for Israel. Egypt's pro government press says Washington should be pushing for a political solution and Syria's president Bashar al Assad is expected to begin his visit to France on Monday with a call for a bigger European role in the crises. Prince Abdullah bin Abdulaziz, who effectively runs the country, was quoted on Monday as saying that Europe should play a more prominent role. (BBC, 25 June)

28 June
A New York City law restricts smoking in all public spaces and office buildings, but the air in many areas of the United Nations building is thick with the smell of Pall Malls. Past efforts to enforce smoking laws here have been met with open hostility. The former Secretary General Boutros-Ghali once suggested that attempts to do so would require the services of the peacekeeping department. (NYT, 28 June, p.14)

28 June
Secretary General Kofi Annan and other officials have praised the role of AIDS activists here, but they still expect them to mind protocol. About 25 protesters who stood outside a conference room carrying signs and shouting security officers ejected slogans on Tuesday and their credentials confiscated. After some negotiations, seven got back in today. The protesters were from Oxfam, Act Up and other groups. Such groups were briefed before the session on "the procedures and rules of the United Nations," said a spokeswoman,

Susan Markham. "We don't allow people to carry signs of any fashion," she added. (NYT, 28 June, p.14)

28 June
The Secretary Council nominated Secretary General Kofi Annan to a second term today, months ahead of a deadline at the end of the year. The General Assembly is expected to elect him officially on Friday, for a five-year term beginning Jan.1. Although some Asian countries had argued that is was their region's turn to provide a leader, Mr. Annan's wide popularity within the organisation and its 189 member countries has made his re-election all but certain months ago. Now working with the Bush administration, Mr. Annan draws on a long relationship with Secretary of State Powell. Before becoming secretary general, he was under secretary general for peacekeeping. As secretary general, Mr. Annan has made significant management changes within the United Nations, while promoting a more aggressive defence of rights, even at the expense of national sovereignty. (NYT, 28 June, p. 14)

28 June
The UN Security Council voted unanimously today to nominate Secretary General Anna to serve a second five-year term at the helm of the United Nations. The action by the 15-member council is all but certain to be endorsed Friday by the 189-nation General Assembly. Annan ran unopposed in an election six months before his term formally ends Dec. 31. The nomination was applauded by diplomats, human rights activists and UN staffers who credited Annan with slimming the organisation's bureaucracy, raising the profile of human rights and increasing the UN's role in peacekeeping. In a news conference, Annan said he was "deeply honoured" and thanked the council for its "trust and support." But he declined to speak at length about the election until the General Assembly has voted. Instead, Annan promoted the UN's current conference on AIDS and appealed for financial support for an international find to battle the disease. (WP, 28 June, p. A21)

29 June
Kofi Annan became the seventh United Nations secretary general at the worst of times. The organisation was bankrupt, at war with the United States Congress and ridiculed for peacekeeping fiascos on several continents. On Friday, Mr. Annnan, will be given a second term by acclamation in the 189-member General Assembly. No nation thought twice about other candidates; he was considered unbeatable. In the last few years, the United Nations has achieved a better budget balance. Relations with Washington have improved dramatically, and searing reports on peacekeeping operations gone wrong have cleared the air and allowed for new thinking on how to tighten up existing missions or create more realistic new ones. Mr. Annan has also weathered a rising tide of anger against international organisations and protests over globalisation, while at the same time opening the doors of the UN to co-operation with some of the same corporations reviled on the streets. Mr. Cunningham, the acting American ambassador, said today that the Security Council hastened the selection process, which would normally taken place near the end of the year, because everyone agreed that Mr. Annan should have as much time as possible to get started on his next term. Mr. Annan has worked hard to persuade African leaders to take charge of solving the continent's problems wherever they can, while pressing for more outside aid in helping them battle diseases and economic imbalances. More generally in the developing world, Mr. Annan has been criticized for his strong advocacy of the need for outside intervention when their governments are abusing the human rights of people. President of the UN Association of the

United States, Luers said that Mr. Annan's ability to "keep cool" had made a difference as he tried to rebuild good relations with Washington. Mr. Luers said the message Mr. Annan had often taken to Capitol Hill or relayed to members of Congress was: "This isn't a world government. This is an organisation trying to co-ordinate the work of everybody who has to work together." (NYT, 29 June, p. 8)

B. Operations

NATO

6 January
The United Nations said it had found evidence of radioactivity at 8 of 11 sites tested in Kosovo that were struck by NATO ammunition containing depleted uranium. NATO has come under pressure from several European governments over claims that depleted uranium in NATO weapons had caused death or illness among peacekeeping troops. (NYT, 6 January, A6)

6 January
The United Nations announced today that it had found evidence of radioactivity at 8 of 11 sites tested in Kosovo that were struck by NATO ammunition with depleted uranium. The discovery from the sampling of sites was a preliminary finding that the United Nations' Environmental Program reached at laboratories in Sweden, Switzerland, Italy, Britain and Austria. NATO has come under pressure from several European governments over claims that depleted uranium in NATO weapons caused death or illness among peacekeeping troops in Kosovo. Depleted uranium is used in the tips of missiles, shells and bullets to increase their ability to penetrate armour and can be pulverized on impact into a toxic radioactive dust, military experts say. A United Nations report in May had warned that much of Kosovo's water could be so contaminated as to be unfit to drink, and that a cleanup of the province could cost billions of dollars. It warned staff members not to approach any target that might have been hit by a depleted uranium weapon. (NYT, 6 January, p. A6)

12 March
NATO now finds out what the consequences are of a refusal to deal seriously with the problems and aspirations of the Albanians it went to war to protect. There's still instability in the Balkans. Once the West could blame Milosevic, yet his ouster has created new difficulties and uncertainties. A senior Western diplomat said, "NATO has become the single guarantor of stability and security in the Balkans, but it is not clear that NATO wants to do the job. Mr. Samardzic, a senior adviser to President Kostunica of Yugoslavia, has worked with NATO on the idea of allowing the Yugoslav Army back, gradually, into the three-mile zone of separation in Serbian territory around Kosovo. And the method of the militant groups led by the Kosovo Liberation Army is not to solve minority problems in a democratic way, but to make this zone of insecurity even more insecure, to step-by-step consolidate more land and make new frontiers". The United Nations resolution that ended the Kosovo war promises Kosovo substantial autonomy but leaves its final status unresolved, subject to some future negotiation, while confirming that the territory is a sovereign part of Yugoslavia. (NYT, 12 March, p. 1)

Afghanistan

16 January
Muhammad Khaled Mihraban, a polite, soft-spoken 26-year-old Pakistani, thinks he has already killed at least 100 people. Maybe more; he isn't really sure. A gifted student, he was soon asked to train others in-group camps near Khost. "But I wanted to act, not teach," he explained. So after a stint waging war in Kashmir, he returned to Kabul to fight alongside the Taliban forces that control most of the country. If the international terrorism that has haunted Americans for the last decade has a home, it is Afghanistan, the place that comes closest to the extremists' ideal of a state ruled by the strict code of Islamic law. Afghanistan is an inspiration, an essential base of operations, a reservoir of potential suicide bombers and a battlefront where crucial ties are forged. It is also, American officials say, where Osama bin Laden is experimenting with chemical weapons. Participants in nearly every plot against the United States and its allies during the last decade have learned the arts of war and explosives in Afghan camps, authorities say, including the defendants in the 1998 bombings of two American Embassies in East Africa. The Central Intelligence Agency estimates that as many as 50,000 to 70,000 militants from 55 countries have trained here in recent years. The agency says the Taliban permit a wide range of groups to operate in Afghan territory, from the Pakistani militants who trained Mr. Mihraban to Mr. bin Laden's organisation Al Qaida (Arabic for The Base). Middle East officials said that as many as 5,000 recruits have passed through Mr. bin Laden's camps. American and Middle Eastern intelligence officials believe that Mr. bin Laden maintains a network of a dozen camps in Afghanistan that offer training in small arms and in explosives and logistics for terrorist attacks. The officials said the embassy bombings, which killed more than 200 people, were rehearsed on a model built to scale at one of Mr. bin Laden's Afghan camps.
The Training
Middle Eastern officials estimate that in the last six months, more than 100 men recruited by Mr. bin Laden's and affiliated groups have been trained at the camp. The camp is part of a large complex of such training sites known as Darunta, about eight miles from Jalalabad, an Afghan eastern provincial capital, down a dusty road that runs atop an old stone dam of the same name. According to Western and Middle Eastern officials, a cache of chemicals is stored in the reinforced caves of nearby mountains and naturally protected underground tunnels.
The Inspiration
The Afghan cause has inspired several generations of young men determined to wage holy war. Thousands came here in the 1980's to fight the Soviet forces in response to a fatwa, or religious order, from leading Islamic scholars. Thousands more have come since then to help the Taliban expand their power, or to be trained for jihads elsewhere. Taliban officials boast that they have imposed true Islamic rule, cleansing Afghan society of Western influence. Since their capture of Kabul in 1996, they have among other things banned education for girls and most work for women, and instituted harsh punishments for blasphemy, playing cards, watching television, listening to music and trimming one's beard. Mr. bin Laden arrived in Afghanistan in 1996 after he was expelled from Sudan. American officials and Afghan opponents of the Taliban say their loyalty to him has been well earned. The officials say Mr. bin Laden provided the Taliban with some of the cash they used to buy off local warlords in their march to power. His financial support of the Taliban is said to continue. Several diplomats and aid workers in Afghanistan estimated that he had put up millions of

dollars – one diplomat's estimate was $40 million – to rebuild roads destroyed in the war against the Soviets and the ensuing civil war. Mr. bin Laden is also said to be providing the Taliban with military help.

The Enablers

American officials acknowledge that they have limited influence over the Taliban, who they say have a powerful regional ally in Pakistan. (NYT, 16 January, p. A1)

16 February

UN drug control officers said the Taliban Islamic militia had virtually wiped out opium production in Afghanistan since banning poppy cultivation in July. A team from the UN Office for Drug Control searched most of the country's largest opium-producing areas for two weeks and found so few poppies that it said it did not expect any opium to come out of Afghanistan this year. (WP, 16 February, p. A21)

30 March

India's new ambassador to Washington, Mansingh, said in an interview that his country was "the most affected victim" of the arrival of the Taliban in neighbouring Afghanistan. The end of the cold war did not bring a "peace dividend" to South Asia, he said. He described the Taliban as an "evil force combining religious fanaticism and the drug trade." The ambassador said his priority is to "continue the momentum" in U.S.-Indian relations and to work on removing some of the "irritants," such as sanctions on military and economic assistance. (WP, 30 March, p. A24)

Bosnia

11 July

The fifth anniversary of the "ethnic cleansing" in Srebrenica where 7,000 to 8,000 Muslim men were killed is marked by 1,000 to 2,000 Muslims. Thousands of peacekeeping troops and police were mobilised to prevent trouble at the ceremony, which was purely religious, despite the presence of Bosnia's President, Alija Izetbegovic, international officials and diplomats. (Ind./NZZ, 12 July, p. 16, p. 5)

5 August

Police and soldiers of the United Nations secured non-approved weapons and documents, in a police-watch in Bosnia. United Nations declared that the razz in Vares served the surveillance of the local authorities. The material wasn't used for ordinary police-duties, a UN police officer said. (NZZ, 7 August, p. 2)

6 August

According to current local lore, Radovan Karadzic has been hiding in the forested mountains of south eastern Bosnia. His influence over the Bosnian Serb republic, which he founded, is said to be waning. Yet Dr. Karadzic is still at large and his unrepentant presence glowers over every issue in this ruined society. The American ambassador insists that arresting Karadzic is still a priority, because he symbolizes resistance. Without him, that will collapse. It is expected that Karadzic will flee to Bosnia, eventually. (NYT, 7 August, p. 3)

18 November
Richard Holbrooke, the U.S. ambassador to the United Nations and architect of the 1995 Dayton agreement, predicted today that a trend toward hard-line nationalism in Bosnia would soon be reversed. At a commemoration of the fifth anniversary of the peace deal, Holbrooke also called for a stronger central government in Sarajevo, with a united army and an end to corruption. Holbrooke, then assistant secretary of state, worked out the Dayton Accord with Balkan leaders in 1995 at Wright-Patterson Air Force Base here. The deal redrew the map of Bosnia, where 250,000 people were killed in three years of fighting. Half of the country went to the Bosnian Serbs, the other half to a Muslim-Croat federation. The three ethnicities share power through a federal presidency. The United States and its allies want to make Bosnia stable and multi-ethnic so they can withdraw peacekeeping forces. But in elections last weekend, the nationalist Serbian Democratic Party (SDS) and Croatian Democratic Union (HDZ) did well. "These people will not lead the Bosnian people where they want to go. They will not help them achieve the economic prosperity that everyone in Bosnia wants. They will not help Bosnia heal its deep wounds," Holbrooke said. "As these facts become clearer, I believe we will continue to see the power and influence of such racist and separatist and criminal elements whittle away."
(WP, 18 November, p. A5)

24 November
The European Union, which has taken prime responsibility for reconstruction and stability in the Balkans, will hold its first summit meeting with regional leaders, their task made easier by the election of the new Yugoslav president, Vojislav Kostunica. The idea for the summit meeting in Zagreb, Croatia, came from President Jacques Chirac of France before the fall of Slobodan Milosevic last month, and was designed to further isolate him. But Yugoslavia's re-entry into the world of international meetings, with all its high-blown rhetoric about peace and regional cooperation, has brought new substance to the idea of a more integrated European Balkans. And Mr. Kostunica's presence, alongside other leaders of what was once Tito's Yugoslavia, will have impact. In Zagreb, Mr. Kostunica is also expected to meet the United Nations administrator of the Serbian province of Kosovo, Bernard Kouchner, for the first time. To help develop market activity and promote democracy and regional trade, the EU is offering the main countries of the western Balkans - Macedonia, Croatia, Bosnia, Yugoslavia and Albania - 4.65 billion ($3.92 billion) from 2000 to 2006. In return, the Europeans are requiring democratic and legal behaviour. They are negotiating agreements with these countries, called Stabilization and Association Agreements, which lay out reforms that could put these countries on the path toward joining the European Union. In Zagreb, Macedonia will sign such an agreement with the European Union, while the host, Croatia, will formally begin its negotiations toward one. Even five years after the Dayton peace agreement that ended the Bosnian war, Bosnia-Herzegovina is not considered ready even to begin such talks. (IHT, 24 November, p. 5)

11 January
A UN prosecutor today publicly accused former Bosnian Serb president Plavsic of planning, ordering and overseeing the killings of thousands of ethnic Croat and Muslim civilians in Bosnia at the outset of the former Yugoslav republic's brutal civil war in 1992. A
lawyer, Simic, who accompanied Plavsic, told reporters that Plavsic would deny the
charges and had surrendered so that she could have a forum to defend herself. In an indictment prosecutor Blewitt charged Plavsic with genocide, crimes against humanity,
"extermination, murder, and wilful killing." In this indictment, Plavsic and two other
Bosnian Serb leaders, Karadzic and Krajisnik are accused of organizing the mass executions of more than 900 civilians in at least 18 incidents between April and November of
1992. She is also blamed for forcing thousands of ethnic Croats and Muslims into 20
detention camps where some were summarily executed and others were raped or tortured
to death. Plavsic was a key figure in the Bosnian Serb leadership from 1990 to 1998, in
1995 she became president of the Serb Republic. She won Western support for her re-
election to that post after breaking with Karadzic and Krajisnik in 1997 and promising to
allow ethnic Croats and Muslims who were allegedly expelled on her orders to return to
their homes. She never kept the promise. The current Bosnian Serb government hopes
that Plavsic will be free on bail pending any trial. Western officials say that she surrendered to the tribunal after being threatened with arrest by NATO peacekeeping troops.
(WP, 11 January, p. A24)

4 March
Judge Mumba of the war crimes tribunal convicted three Bosnian Serbs of rape and sexual
enslavement. For the first time, a war crimes tribunal ruled that rape was a crime against humanity. The United Nations made the crucial decision to expand the list of crimes to include
abuses of women. (NYT, 4 March, p. 5)

8 March
The head of the international peace mission in Bosnia dismissed the Croat member of the
Balkan's state's three-man presidency after he threatened to declare self-rule in Croat-
controlled areas. Petritsch, who is charged with overseeing the peace in Bosnia, removed Jelavic from the country's inter-ethnic presidency and barred him from public office. He said
the move was punishment for attempting to undermine the constitutional order of Bosnia and
one of its autonomous regions, the Muslim-Croat federation. The firing of Jelavic, head of
the main Bosnian Croat nationalist party, was one of the toughest moves taken by Petritsch
who has authority to remove anyone he considers an obstacle to the peace process. (WP, 8
March, p. A18)

29 May
In the five years since international police officers were sent to Bosnia to help restore law
and order, the UN police mission there has faced numerous charges of misconduct, corruption and sexual impropriety. But in virtually every case the officers have been sending
home, often without a full investigation. The troubles of the UN police mission in Bosnia
have important consequences for the Bush administration. Eager to scale back military
commitments, Secretary of Defence Rumsfeld is pushing to reduce the 3,350 American
soldiers on peacekeeping duty in Bosnia and replace them with civilian police. But some
UN and European officials question the wisdom of shifting responsibility onto the international police force without first addressing its flaws, including low recruitment stan-

dards, a hazy command structure and the ability of individual officers to act with near impunity. Among the 1,832 UN police in Bosnia are 161 officers from the U.S. Although the record of the U.S. contingent is no worse than others, senior American officials acknowledge serious problems in selecting and training U.S. police officers to serve in Bosnia. That job is given to a private corporation, DynCorp. In the past year alone, at least three American policemen were removed from the Bosnian mission for sexual misconduct and exceeding their authority, according to UN officials. International police have diplomatic immunity from prosecution in Bosnia, and unless their governments waive that immunity, the most severe punishment the UN can impose on renegade officers is to send their home. Miller, the U.S. ambassador in Bosnia, conceded that in a race to find American police willing to serve abroad, the U.S. contingent accepted some officers who were unfit to serve on the International Police Task Force, IPTF. American officials say the failings are due to inexperience in international policing and the absence of a national police force. American participation in civilian police missions, CivPol, had increased since 1993. President Clinton issued a directive in February 2000 acknowledging that "the current process used by our government to recruit, prepare, train and deploy civilian police officers to CivPol operations is not adequate." Last summer, the White House asked the FBI and police commissioners from major U.S. cities to provide a reserve of police officers who could be sent abroad to serve in UN missions. But the FBI and big city police departments demurred. When the UN mission in Bosnia began in 1996, DynCorp scoured U.S. police departments in search of bored or underpaid officers looking for a change of pace. According to UN and DynCorp officials, many of the U.S. officers have performed nobly, even donating money and labour to local charities. The main trouble with American officers was that they were difficult to command. Although UN officials said they were disappointed in the Americans, they conceded that the U.S. contingent was far from the weakest in the mission. Others could not speak English or drive a vehicle. The IPTF was created by the Dayton peace accord, which ended Bosnia's civil war in 1995. It task was to integrate the country's warring Muslim, Croat and Serb officers into a national police force and monitor their activities. However, the UN officers are prohibited from carrying arms and do not have authority to make arrests; their role is mainly to monitor and advise local police. Holbrooke described the police mission as the "weakest" component. Among the problems is a fuzzy command structure that gives the UN brass limited authority over police officers recruited from more than 45 countries that widely varying law enforcement systems. Kroeker, former police officer in Bosnia, said, "There were so many overlapping policies and rules and laws that it made it very diffuse." The final say in disciplinary matters, according to UN officials, rests with the home government, which seldom are interested in prosecuting or even thoroughly investigating the muddy allegations that arise in the Balkans. Under questioning by UN police investigators some of the officers admitted having had sexual relations with women they had rescued, according to UN sources and an internal UN document. (WP, 29 May, p. A1)

31 May
Despite the Bush administration avowed eagerness to pull U.S. troops out of the Balkans Secretary of State Powell once again assured NATO governments this week that the U.S. would not act unilaterally. The administration accepted a NATO decision to make only a minor reduction of forces during the next six months. By doing so, President Bush avoided yet another blow-up with the European allies, who are already deeply unsettled

by his initiatives in the environment and missile defence. At the same time, his administration confirmed a minimalist approach to U.S. engagement in the region that has repeatedly, proved a failure over the past decade. Mr. Powell encountered a group of NATO ministers in Budapest once again disturbed and confused by the administration's public statements. Mr. Powell has repeatedly pledged that U.S. and European forces will "come out together" from the Balkans. But Secretary of Defence Rumsfeld The Post earlier that he intended to "keep pushing" to get U.S. troops out. Mr. Powell said he had tried to assure the European allies that there is unanimity within the U.S. government. In recent weeks a new war brook out in the Balkans between the government of Macedonia and ethnic Albanian insurgents. Efforts by European diplomats to head off the conflict in Macedonia. The Bush administration has been literally and figuratively absent from the region; the clear message it sends is that it is hoping to confine its Balkan policy to arranging U.S. troop withdrawals. And yet, as a host of Balkan politicians and European ministers have been quietly trying to tell the administration, the U.S. is needed in the region more than ever. The 11,000 U.S. troops now serving in Bosnia and Kosovo represent a small fraction of the international peacekeeping forces. The U.S. is the only Western country that enjoys real credibility and leverage with the Albanians and their leaders. The steadily escalating warfare now underway in Macedonia cannot be ended unless the legitimate political aspirations of Albanians in both Macedonia and Kosovo are fully addressed; it is unlikely what will happen without deep U.S. involvement. The Bush administration's reluctance to commit diplomatic energy and capital to the Balkans is hardly novel. Both the Clinton and first Bush administrations also tried to avoid involvement in Balkan conflicts and hand off their mediation to the Europeans. The result was bloody wars in Bosnia and Kosovo that ended only after U.S.-led military campaigns. Perhaps this time the Bush administration's bet on disengagement will pay off. More likely it is repeating the mistakes of the past decade. (WP, 31 May, p. A24)

24 June
The team of auditors had just begun studying the records inside a Bosnian bank suspected of criminal connections when an angry, shouting mob of ethnic Croats appeared on the street outside. Within minutes, the protesters had pressed against the doors and closed off escape. This confrontation on April 6 underscored the new reality of peacekeeping in the Balkans: increasingly powerful alliances between ethnic nationalist politicians and organized criminal groups now from the greatest impediment to long-term reconciliation. U.S. and European troops that came to Bosnia in 1995 to keep warring armies apart find themselves unprepared to tackle this threat. Western officials say politician-gangsters who want to set up a Croat-only state in Bosnia organized the riots here. It was "the most serious crisis of the Dayton accords," the cease-fire agreement that ended in the Bosnian war said Austrian diplomat Petritsch. Many Western officials now say the rule of law will never take hold in the Balkans unless peacekeeping forces aggressively and expertly target the link between criminals and top politicians. (WP, 24 June, p. A1)

24 June
Headquartered in Mostar, the Herzegovachka Bank is controlled by a group of ethnic Croats known as the "young generals", men who became rich during the 1992-95 Bosnian war selling arms and food and were rewarded by appointments to military rank, mostly without formal training. Some are also senior officials of the Bosnian branch of the hard-line nationalist Croatian Democratic Union, the leading wartime party and the dominant political power in

Bosnia's Croat-populated southwest region. The party's main theme is that Croat interests are under siege from the governmental structure set up by the Dayton accords: Croats and Muslims in a federation that controls about half of Bosnia's territory, Serbs in a republic that controls the rest. Miller, the U.S. ambassador, says is mostly a ruse. Some top officials in the party "are engaged in a lot of criminal activity and have used government as a veneer," he said. Two recent Western decisions, taken under the broad authority granted here by UN Security Council resolution, set in motion events that disrupted the system. Election rules were changed to allow Muslims to vote for Croat politicians, which resulted in Croat hard-liners' losing seats in the Bosnian parliament. And the 55-nation Organisation for Security and Co-operation in Europe (OSCE) began poking around the party's finances. With Western pressure growing, Croat political leaders declared in March that Croat areas of Bosnia were withdrawing from the federation. They established a rump government and began paying Croat members of the Bosnian army to detect. (WP, 24 June, p. A1)

24 June

Alarmed by the possibility that the Dayton accords might unravel, the U.S. government secretly gave the Western governments' Office of the High Representative in Bosnia $1 million in March to pay for Operation Athena: the forcible seizure of the Herzegovacka Bank and auditing of its account by the private U.S. corporate security firm, Kroll-O'Gara. Throughout the 1990's, Western governments doled out $5 billion in aid but paid little attention to corruption. Now the Western powers planned to force the officers of an allegedly corrupt bank to hand over records at gunpoint. For Petritsch, the West's top representative, it was not an easy decision. Upon arriving in Bosnia in 1999, he had concluded, "we don't need crises." But this spring, he said he recalled the private advice in 1999 of General Clark, then NATO's commander in chief: "You need to create crises, And we are going to help you." The audit teams burst into the bank's branches between 7 and 9 a.m., ordering all employees to leave. Shortly afterward, men appeared outside many of the branches, carrying trays of eggs and rocks to give to people in gathering crowds. Schoolchildren were placed at the front of the crowd while men with pistols and rifles stood at the rear. A week and a half later, NATO troops conducted a second raid at the bank headquarters in Mostar. This time a group with experience in civil disorder in Northern Ireland accompanied them. This time, things went smoothly. But investigators said that vital information had been wiped from the hard drive of the bank's main frame computer. Munro, the West's representative in Mostar, said he believes that "this is the hard-liners' last stand." But he added that Western success "will require a decision by capitals to exert a much greater degree of control" all over Bosnia. (WP, 24 June, p. A1)

Burma

31 March

Burma's military government has given permission for the new UN human rights envoy for the country to visit in early April, a senior Foreign Ministry official said yesterday. Diplomatic sources in the capital of Rangoon said Brazil's Pinheiro would meet representatives of both the military government and the opposition National League for Democracy. The national league won Burma's most recent elections, in 1990, by a landslide but has never been allowed to govern. (WP, 31 March, p. A17)

Cambodia

10 August

UN Secretary-General Kofi Annan has urged Cambodia to have at least started the debate before the UN General Assembly meeting in mid-September. The UN has threatened to pull out of the deal if Cambodia delays too long, but has not set a firm deadline. (South China Morning Post, 10 August)

29 December

Cambodia National Assembly has approved Article One of a draft bill that will set up to try former Khmer Rouge leaders for their roles in the deaths of at least 1.7 million people during their 1975-1979 rule. National Assembly President Prince Norodom Ranariddh told legislators that he hopes the draft bill, which has 48 articles, will be adopted by next week. Cheam Yeap, a parliamentarian from the ruling Cambodian People's Party, explained that the bill targets only senior leaders of the Khmer Rouge and the people most responsible for the genocide. Opposition leader Sam Rainsy expressed strong support for the draft bill, saying it reflects the will of the UN

The new legislation would establish three special tribunals to try the war criminals, with five judges at a trial court, seven at the appeals stage and nine at a supreme court. There will be three Cambodian and two foreign judges at the trial court, four Cambodians and three foreigners at the appeals level, and the supreme court would be presided over by five Cambodians and four foreigners. Rulings will require super-majorities at the respective levels of four out of five, five of seven and six of nine. According to the bill, the tribunal will be located in Phnom Penh and the proceedings conducted in Cambodia's official language Khmer, with English, French and Russian translations.

The UN and Cambodian agreed on the nature, composition and procedures for the tribunal in July this year, and also decided to have co-prosecutors and co-investigating judges. Once the bill is adopted by the lower house, the Senate will review it and pass it to the Constitutional Council for constitutional examination. Finally, it will be signed by the king who will promulgate the new law. Cambodia and the UN will also sign a Memorandum of Understanding on the issue before moving forward with the trial. (Japan Economic Newswire, 29 December)

2 January

The Cambodian National Assembly unanimously approved the draft law to establish an extraordinary chamber to the try Khmer Rouge leaders. (Crimes of War, Magazine: The Tribunals)

15 January

The draft law was passed by the Cambodian Senate. (Crimes of War, Magazine: The Tribunals)

3 February

The United Nations has accused Cambodian authorities of backtracking on key elements of an agreement to create an independent war crimes tribunal to prosecute former leaders of the Khmer Rouge, the communist movement responsible for the deaths of more than 1.7 million people in the 1970s.

The United Nations' senior lawyer, Hans Corell, wrote in a January 9 letter to the Cambodian government that a new law to establish the tribunal lacked provisions designed to ensure UN oversight and to guarantee that prosecutors have authority to pursue suspect currently shielded by amnesty. The Law was passed last month by Cambodia's National Assembly and Senate.

Following more than two years of negotiations with the United Nations, Cambodia agreed last May to create a court to try those who had the greatest responsibility for mass killing in Cambodia. Only four senior leaders of the Khmer Rouge, including two who are in prison in Cambodia, are expected to face trial before the court.

Under the agreement, Cambodia pledged to introduce legislation that mirrored an agreed-to document that serves as a blueprint for a UN-sponsored court headed by foreign and Cambodian prosecutors, investigators and judges.

The United Nations discovered, however, that several key provisions from the initial agreement had been omitted from the law passed by the Cambodian National Assembly on January 2, potentially diluting the court's independence. In the most glaring reversal, Cambodian lawmakers removed a provision ensuring that "an amnesty granted to any person falling within the jurisdiction of the [court] shall not be a bar to prosecution." (Crimes of War, Magazine: The Tribunals)

12 February

The Constitutional Council was passed the draft law, which flagged a technical discrepancy for correction. Since Article Three of the draft law proposes the death penalty as the maximum punishment when there is currently no death penalty under the Cambodian Constitution, the Council sent the draft law back to Parliament to be amended before it is sent to King Norodom Sihanouk for his signature, which represents the final stage in the legislative process. (Crimes of War, Magazine: The Tribunals)

5 June

Cambodia and the United Nations agreed in April last year on how to try former leaders of the radical communist group, blamed for an estimated 1.7 million deaths during their 1975-1979 "killing fields" regime. Although legislation to create a tribunal was approved by Cambodia's parliament earlier this year, Prime Minister Hun Sen kick it back to the government in mid-February to have all references to the death penalty removed. Cambodia does not have a death penalty. The process has been stalled since then. (Reuters, 5 June)

27 June

The United Nations issued a press release stating that the current draft tribunal law has to be in conformity with a Memorandum of Understanding to be signed between the United Nations and the Government of Cambodia. To the extent that Cambodia has not yet signed this Memorandum of Understanding, there are still several steps remaining before a trial can be convened. (CNN Worldnews, 27 June)

28 June

A United Nations official has announced that Cambodian Prime Minister Hun Sen Prime had assured him that long-delayed plans to form a Khmer Rouge tribunal would be accelerated. At the end of a six-day visit, Peter Leuprecht, told reporters that Hun Sen had informed him that bureaucratic hurdles blocking the passage of a law allowing the formation of a tribunal had been resolved.

"The Khmer Rouge draft law has gone to parliament...... [after which] it should be ready to signed [into law] by the King," Leuprecht said. "I was encouraged to hear from Prime Minister Hun Sen that the tribunal will be able to operate free of interference and independently."

Leuprecht is the Canada-based Special Representative of the Cambodian office of the UN High Commissioner for Human Rights. Hun Sen has told reporters in Tokyo on June 13 that a tribunal could be functional by as early as December. Efforts to create a controversial "mixed tribunal" of Cambodian and international jurists to prosecute the former top leaders of the Khmer Rouge stalled in February because of objections to the law's references to the death penalty, which is prohibited in Cambodia.

Leuprecht specifically outlined the UN's concerns about the potential for political for political influence on Cambodian judges and prosecutors chosen to participate in the tribunal. "When the tribunal gets into operation it will be up to the prosecutors to see who will be tried," Leuprecht said. The doubts about the capabilities of the Cambodian judiciary, which is universally described as incompetent, corrupt and subject to political influence, were also raised by Leuprecht. The "mixed tribunal" formula is designed to prosecute the top Khmer Rouge leaders and "those most responsible" for the deaths of approximately 1.7 million Cambodians between 1975-1979 by execution, starvation and overwork. (CNN worldnews, 28 June)

Congo

21 August

A Nigerian general who presided over his country's return to democracy last year is being sent to the Democratic Republic of the Congo by the UN secretary general, Kofi Annan, in an effort to try to salvage what is beginning to look like a doomed peacekeeping operation. The appointment follows a warning from Mr. Annan to the Security Council this week, that the Congo operation may have to be reconsidered in light of the failure of President Laurent Kabila's government to cooperate with an advance UN mission and to provide the necessary conditions for the deployment of peacekeeping troops. Meanwhile, in Kisangani, a contested diamond-mining centre in eastern Congo, a British UN official sent as a part of an advance party was found hanged in his hotel room. UN officials have said they do not know whether his death was a murder or suicide. (IHT, 21 August, p. 2)

25 August

A week of conflicting signals from President Kabila of Congo ha left the Security Council no closer to knowing when, if ever, a peacekeeping mission can be sent to the country. The council this week decided that United Nations officials who have been in Congo preparing for the peacekeepers could stay until Oct. 15, giving the Secretary General and the council time to reconsider the operation. After announcing on Thursday that the peacekeepers and support forces, totalling about 5,500 people under current plans, could have free access in Congo, Mr. Kabila's government appeared today to be backtracking, officials said here. Complicating the picture for a peacekeeping mission, Mr. Kabila said this week that he was freezing a peace accord signed last year in Lusake, Zambia. In one positive move, Mr. Kabila, who refuses to meet with political opponents, has established a human rights panel in Congo and allowed United Nations monitor to visit the country in recent weeks. The monitor had been barred from Congo for several years. (NYT, 26 August, p. 3)

4 September
Fifteen months after restoring democracy to Africa's most populous nation for the second time in 20 years, President Olusegun Obasanjo of Nigeria said today that he was ready to step into a larger role in mediating an end to his continent's debilitating wars, beginning with Congo. Mr. Obasanjo, whose troops the United States is now training for peacekeeping duties in Sierra Leone, said he recently volunteered to go to Congo and talk to President Laurent Kabila. Mr. Kabila has been the primary roadblock to efforts to end the war, which involves a half dozen African nations, and has been uncooperative with both the United Nations and the Organisation of African Unity. Mr. Obasanjo's offer was turned down by Secretary General Kofi Annan, he said. "I wanted to go, and I told the secretary general, and I was told that it was not opportune yet for me to go," Mr. Obasanjo said. He said he was also appealing to President Charles Taylor of Liberia, who has been complicit in Mr. Sankoh's, the rebel leader of the Revolutionary United Front who resumed the war this year and captured 500 United Nations peacekeepers, rebellion and is accused of funnelling diamonds from Sierra Leone through his country to raise money for arms. Speaking of "doing what needs to be done as quickly as possible" in Sierra Leone, he said, "What needs to be done is disarmament, demobilization of everybody." (NYT, 5 September, p. A12)

14 December
A faltering advance mission preparing the way for a peacekeeping force in Congo got help Thursday when the Security Council lengthened its life and doubled the number of monitors there. Leonard She Okitundu, who was named Congo's foreign minister in a government reshuffle last month, was in New York to speak to the council. He pledged that his government would not impede the work of UN troops. There have been many confrontations over the last year between UN officials and Mr. Kabila's government. Until very recently, there had been scant hopes in the council that a full-fledged peacekeeping force could ever be sent to Congo, although the force of 5,537 was authorized nearly a year ago. But a series of meetings among African leaders, rebel commanders and countries with combatants in the region, the scene of Africa's widest war, have produced some new optimism. "There is certainly a political will in the region to move forward," said Jean-David Levitte, the French delegate and sponsor of the council resolution, which was adopted unanimously. "But there is in the region a real difficulty to identify the way forward."
(IHT, 16 December, p. 5)

20 January
Heads of the three rebel movements battling for control of Congo remained at a loss as to how to react to the killing of President Laurent Kabila, unsure of whether his son and successor, Maj. Gen. Joseph Kabila, would be another foe. (NYT, 20 January, p. A-6)

23 January
Joseph Kabila became the new President of Congo, after his father Laurent Kabila was killed. He has inherited the dysfunctional government of a nation mired in poverty and war, while being introduced to a world eager to take his measure. One close associate said, "Joseph doesn't want to fight anymore." By all accounts, his father stood as the major impediment to a peaceful settlement of war launched in August 1998 to unseat him. A peace accord he signed in the summer if 1999 remained unfulfilled largely because he kept staging new offensives while blocking deployment of UN peacekeepers in government-held territory. Diplomats who met Joseph last week emerged clutching a hope those things have changed. The diplomats were summoned on Thursday. Rounding out the list was Marjane, he represents UN Secretary General Annan and the Congo peacekeeping mission, called MONUC. One of Kinshasa residents said, "I haven't heard a good word about Joseph. I think, on general principle, the idea of Kabila's son slipping in bothers them." But there is big difference. Laurent was a self-designated rebel leader and had a second career as a bar owner and gadabout in Tanzania. He came of age as a Marxist. Joseph was educated in schools on the British model. Friends describe him as "Western thinking" and "very correct". The war settled into the stalemate that continues today, Joseph Kabila is described as ready to accede to the will of Congo's allies and embrace diplomacy. (WP, 23 January, p. A12)

25 January
Laurent Kabila did not lift a finger to raise his country as president of Congo. The shared goal of communist and ultraconservative ideologues that government should wither away was realized by the ex-Marxist turned robber baron, who took his opportunities where he found them and squeezed them dry. Congo has in fact been without a functioning government since the extended sunset years of its previous tyrant, Mobutu Sese Soku. But Kabila's assassination brought other reactions, including fevered finger pointing and a search for meaning if it fit preconceived ideological needs. This illuminates much of what is wrong with current thinking on Africa. Spokesmen for the left and right eagerly paused the historical videotape of a century of rack and ruin in Africa's wounded heart to show only those frames that suited their case. Leftist mobs turned out in Kinshasa on Sunday to assign responsibility for Kabila's death and Congo's plight to Western imperialism. Kabila came to power by accident and guile, not through the force of neo-colonialism, Marxism or the CIA. Rwanda needed a local front man for its advance into eastern Congo (then called Zaire) in 1997 to put down cross-border raids. Kabila used the unexpected and instant evaporation of Mobutu's army to stroll into Kinshasa. Briefly he seemed to offer the chance for a fresh start. It was; after all, hard to believe Kabila could be as feckless or corrupt as Mobutu had been. The Clinton administration built aid programs and diplomatic strategies around Kabila and then watched in disbelief as he too made government a criminal enterprise. Knowing few Africans and little about the harsh facts of life that prevail on their continent, Westerners projects onto Africa their own political hopes, fears and prejudices more readily than they do in Europe, Asia and Latin America. For some, Kabila's career trajectory and demise are reasoning enough to give up on a continent that dared flirt with socialism in the independence era. Others will see the iron being hot, or the clay being wet, or whatever metaphor is needed to convey the sense that Kabila's death is a new movement of opportunity to rescue Congo. Perhaps it can be done. The Bush administration will want to explore with its main European partners a joint effort to help end the civil war through sustained diplomatic and economic pressures

and incentives. But rescue will have to be as long and systematic a process as has been destruction. No single explanation or piece of the past will suffice to illuminate the enormous task facing Africa and those who would help. (WP, 25 January, p. A19)

3 February

Joseph Kabila, Congo's new president, came before the Security Council today and pledged to open an unreserved dialogue with his opponents at home in hope of ending the nation's long civil war. Mr. Kabila, who was thrust into leadership by the assassination of his father, Laurent Kabila, on Jan. 16, used the prestige of the Security Council to invite his "Congolese brothers" of all origins and opinions, "including those who have taken up arms," to discuss peace, without interference from abroad. Secretary General Kofi Annan, who joined the Security Council session, stressed that peace would not return until all parties held a meaningful dialogue on how Congo would be governed. Mr. Annan urged Mr. Kabila to show his commitment to negotiations by allowing a more liberal political climate. In the last two weeks, the secretary general said, United Nations observers in Congo had reported almost no cease-fire violations. The Council authorized a peacekeeping mission with as many as 5,537 troops for Congo. So far, only a little more than 200 have been sent because the government cannot guarantee their protection. On Dec. 14, when the Council renewed the mission's mandate for six more months, it asked Mr. Annan to come up with a new concept for the operation by mid-February. Today, the acting United States ambassador, James B. Cunningham, said that while Mr. Kabila's government had a right to demand that uninvited foreign forces depart, "the governments of Rwanda and Uganda have a right under the UN charter to demand that Congolese territory not be used as a launching pad for attacks against their countries." At a news conference, Mr. Kabila dismissed the contentions of both countries that their troops entered Congo to stop cross-border raids by insurgents. He said Uganda had no such claim, and Rwanda's ethnic problems should be addressed by the international community because Rwanda failed to prevent the mass killing of Tutsis by Hutus in 1994. Before coming to New York, Mr. Kabila visited Washington, where he met with the Rwandan leader, Paul Kagame. Mr. Kabila said he had met Mr. Kagame to establish a basis for discussing problems between the two countries, and had told him that "the forces of Rwanda are not welcome" in Congo. Asked about the killing of his father, Mr. Kabila said he expected to know more about whom was responsible in a few weeks. As to whether another country was behind the killing, Mr. Kabila said, "It's a possibility that we cannot rule out." (NYT, 3 February, p. A-7)

13 February

The United Nations is working on plans to send fewer peacekeeping troops to Congo than planned, but to send them sooner, to take advantage of the change in leadership, an official said. The plan reduces the number of troops and observers to 3,000 from the 5,537 authorized last year. (NYT, 13 February, p. A-9)

13 February

The United Nations is hoping to seize the opportunity provided by the change in leadership in Congo. The department peacekeeping is working out a plan to send fewer troops there than originally planned, but send them sooner, the head of the department said today. The plan goes this week to the Security Council. Jean-Marie Guehenno, who became under secretary general for peacekeeping in October, said there was an unexpected opening, with a burst of diplomatic activity since the killing of President Laurent Kabila and the choice for his son Joseph as successor. The new Congo peacekeeping plan would reduce the total number of troops and military observers to about 3,000 from the 5,537 authorizes last year by Security Council. The cuts would be mainly in troops, whose role would be limited to protecting 550 military observers based in Kisangani, Kalemie, Kananga and Mbandaka. The observers would monitor the pullback that various factions and foreign armies agreed in December. Mr. Guehenno said monitors already in Congo had faced few problems so far. Also, because much of their logistical support could be provided by about 400 troops using rivers (in a country largely without roads and railways), the number of soldiers assigned to protect them could be reduced to about 2,000. When they could be sent, however, remains an open question, because the warring sides have not yet pulled back to agreed positions. "It's too early to tell you that the lights are all green," Mr. Guehenno said. On Feb. 21 the Security Council is to open a two-day summit meeting on Congo with government leaders from the region. (NYT, 13 February, p. 9)

16 February
The leaders of rebel groups and governments fighting in Congo made substantial movement in peace talks, but the absence of Rwanda led many observers to worry about the future of the peace process. Congolese President Joseph Kabila announced that he would invite to Congo former Botswana president Masire to come to relaunch talks between the government, opposition and civil groups in Congo. Masire had been appointed as a mediator by regional leaders but was rejected by Laurent Kabila, causing a major roadblock in the peace process. Summit participants asked the United Nations to send a peacekeeping force called for in the 1999 cease-fire agreement reached in Lusaka and signed by most of the countries and rebel factions involved in the Congolese was. The United Nations had said Monday that peacekeepers could be ready to go to Congo within the next few weeks. (WP, 16 February, p. A21)

22 February
The Security Council agreed today on a step by step plan for the withdrawal of all foreign troops in Congo. The agreement is expected to be adopted on Thursday. The plan follows the outline of an agreement reached by all the warring sides in Harare, Zimbabwe, in December, a pact that has not been acted on. The resolution is intended to put more pressure on all sides to do so. Under the force of the resolution the parties will jeopardize any further United Nations involvement in settling the war, including the possibility of a peacekeeping mission, if they don't meet the Council's requirements. The resolution calls for a 14-day period beginning in the middle of March for all foreign troops to complete plans to pull back from battle lines, and a deadline around the middle of May for setting up a timetable for leaving the country, a process diplomats hope can be completed by the fall. The plan calls for a Security Council visit to Congo, to check on progress. Rwanda and Uganda, who invaded Congo in 1998, have already promised to begin pulling back as early as next week. Under the new resolution, the Security Council pledges to station military monitors with the withdrawing troops as a verification and confidence-building measure. (NYT, 22 February, p. 5)

23 February
The main warring parties in the Democratic Republic of Congo agreed today to begin withdrawing more than 40,000 troops within the next month, bolstering the chance that a UN observer force will be sent to help bring an end to the country's civil war. The

agreement reflects revived peace efforts since the assassination of Congo's President Kabila last month. Senior UN officials said they would immediately speed up plans to deploy 3,000 UN peacekeepers and observers to verify the troop withdrawal. The accord was contained in a resolution passed unanimously today by the 15-member UN Security Council. The resolution also set a May 15 deadline for the warring parties to provide the council with a detailed plan for the full withdrawal of foreign forces and for the disarmament of other factions, that are not parties to the agreement. The war in Congo began in August 1998, after Rwandan and Ugandan-backed rebels sought to drive Kabila from power. Angola, Zimbabwe and Namibia subsequently intervened on behalf of the Congolese leader, setting the stage for one of the largest and most complex African wars in a generation. UN Secretary General Annan has sought to play down expectations that UN forces will be able to impose peace in Congo. Their primary job, he has said, will be to observe and document any violations of the agreement. The six main warring parties signed a pact in Lusaka, Zambia, in July 1999 to observe a cease-fire and withdraw all foreign forces from Congo. And they asked the UN to send a peacekeeping force to help enforce that agreement. But is has been repeatedly violated. (WP, 23 February, p. A15)

5 March
The United Nations Security Council agreed last month to a plan for withdrawal of all foreign troops from Congo that could set the stage for a long-delayed UN-peacekeeping mission. Last week Rwanda and Uganda began pulling their troops back from front-line positions in eastern Congo. This pullback puts pressure on Congo's allies – Angola, Zimbabwe, and Namibia – to begin leaving. Congo's new president Joseph Kabila has wisely decided to participate in talks with rival factions on the country's political future. (NYT, 5 March, p. 16)

5 March
Hundreds of Ugandan soldiers left Congo today, a small step toward peace. The Congolese government said it had begun the pullback today, as required in an agreement that was pave the way for a 3,000-strong United Nations peacekeeping force. All sides in the conflict agree the new leadership in Congo has played a role in jump-starting the stalled peace process. Joseph Kabila became President after his father died. Last month, both Rwanda and Uganda agreed to what they called goodwill gestures beyond the agreement toward ending their involvement in the civil war. (NYT, 5 March, p. 7)

8 March
The United Nations will start deploying a peacekeeping force in Congo this month, a UN spokesman in the Central African country said. Toure, spokesman for the UN military mission in Congo, said the bulk of the estimated 1,562 troops would come from Morocco and Senegal, which were sending 614 and 540 troops, respectively. Uruguay and Tunisia will contribute the rest. Toure said this was the first batch of about 2,500 UN troops being sent to back an eventual force of 500 military observers. He said further deployments could be expected "in due course." The forces will be deployed exclusively to guard UN facilities and will not extract other UN personnel from hostile situations or protect civilians harmed by fighting. (Reuters)

9 March
The UN Undersecretary General for Peacekeeping Operations, Guehenno, said there is a distinct possibility for peace in Congo and a window of opportunity for the UN to support the

parties involved if they opt for a long-lasting truce. "If the commitment of the parties is there, what the UN can provide is the ability to monitor disengagement," he said in Washington Wednesday. The 2 ½-year Congo war, which began as a Rwandan-backed rebellion against Kabila's rule, has drawn six African nations into the fray. The vast nation is now divided roughly in half, with Congo, Angola and Namibia controlling the west and Rwandan, Uganda, Burundi and several Congolese rebel factions holding the east. Guehenno said this would be the major first step, which must be followed by an inter-Congolese dialogue. (WP, 9 March, p. A21)

17 April
With a new government in Congo that has expressed openness to United Nations peacekeeping efforts, there is growing pressure on Uganda and Rwanda to rein in their activities in support of Congo rebels, United Nations and Congolese officials and Western diplomats say. The refusal of Rwandan-backed rebels in the major eastern city of Kisangani to allow peacekeepers to land over the weekend represented the main problem for the United Nations. The government of the late Laurent Kabila had been considered the major stumbling block to peace. Mr. Morjane, the United Nations' special envoy to Congo, said that the United Nations' relationship with government of Joseph Kabila was "perfect." The new president has already visited the new administration in Washington, and that has accompanied a major shift in relations between Congo's warring parties and the rest of the world. The government in Kinshasa has seized on this shift. Over the weekend, Mr. Kabila announced a new cabinet, which included only one hard-liner from his father's government. (NYT, 17 April, p. 8)

21 April
"Pressure Rises on Outsiders in Congo War" (news article, April 17) describes the growing impatience of the United States with Rwanda and Uganda because they are dragging their heels about withdrawing their military occupation forces from Congo. (NYT, 21 April, p. 14)

30 April
As foreign armies pull back from Congo's farthest reaches and aid agencies move forward, the human toll of the country's 32-month war is being sketched in apocalyptic terms beyond any previously documented in an African conflict. According to a new "death census" conducted by a private American aid agency, the number of lives claimed by the Congo war now approaches 3 million. The survey by the New York-based International Rescue Committee (IRC) was conducted only in the rebel-held eastern half of the century, where most of the fighting and even more of the accompanying hardship has taken place. The survey attributes a relatively small proportion of the deaths to the battles waged by the Congolese army, its rebel foes and troops from the half-dozen other African countries that have fought on both sides of the conflict. The vast majority of deaths have resulted from starvation, disease and deprivation. Until the IRC sent survey teams into eastern Congo, little was known about the human toll of a war fought largely out of the world's sight. The conflict began in August 1998, when rebels backed by Rwandan and Uganda rose up against Laurent Kabila, then the president of Congo. After Angola, Zimbabwe and Namibia sent troops, warplanes and armour to aid Kabila's army, the war settled into a stalemate that has left the vast country divided roughly in half. An agreement to bring in UN peacekeeping troops has moved forward since Kabila's assassination in January put his son, Joseph, in power. Epidemiologists offer two explanations for the extreme numbers: strife in Africa goes usually unmeasured and the strife in Congo has gone

on for almost three years. Although a National Academy of Sciences committee approved the methodology of the original study, IRC concedes that there were structural imperfections in both tallies. Yet some of IRC's key findings were replicated by a second aid agency in a January survey of one relatively peaceful district of eastern Congo. The British medical aid group Merlin documented 2 ½ tomes more deaths than births in a population that before the war had been growing by 3 percent a year. The estimates for Congo may be higher than those for other African conflicts partly because of the country's size. What make the Congo surveys exceptional are not only their relative ambition, but also how long the conditions they document have been allowed to persist. In Congo, the hugely elevated mortality rates have continued for 32 months, steadily racking up deaths by the hundreds of thousands across a vast region rendered inaccessible to aid because of fighting and the lack of roads. For it latest estimate, IRC ventured into eight health districts scattered in the five provinces that historically define eastern Congo, an area of 20 million inhabitants. There are representative zones selected that could be reached by plane or secure roads. Once a district is chosen, bias should be thwarted by technology. The results were tallied and compared with the number of deaths that the Centres for Disease Control and Prevention say should be expected in a country as Congo: 1.5 deaths per 1,00 people per month. Total deaths in Congo's five eastern provinces from January 1999 to May 2000 were calculated at 2.3 million – 1.7 million more than what would have been expected in the absence of war. IRC estimates that 40 percent of Congo's wartime deaths could have been avoided by access to the kind of basic health care that was becoming scarce even before the rebellions that have defined Congo over the last five years. Further aggravating the situation is Congo's economy; the world's fastest-shrinking since the war began. Even so, IRC estimated that 200,000 of the first 1.7 million deaths were by violence, almost all of them civilians. Untold thousands who no longer feel safe in their homes but are ill equipped for living in the bush now populates Congo's vast jungles. As assessments of Congo's devastation accumulate, help has been very slow in coming. A January plea from the World Food Program to more than double its Congo food aid to $110 million has been barely one-third funded by rich countries. (WP, 30 April, p. A1)

2 May

They may control much of Africa's third-largest country, but the foreign powers involved in Congo's war are fighting more over public opinion than over turf – and Rwanda and Uganda appear to be losing. Joseph Kabila, who succeeded his father Laurent as Congo's president this year, is being received in Europe as a peacemaker and embraced by the UN. Morjane, the chief UN official in Kinshasa said, "The situation has changed fundamentally. We have excellent relations with the government." Three years ago, before Rwanda and Uganda fomented the rebellion that started the Congolese war, President Clinton hailed the presidents of the two countries as "Africa's new generation of leaders." Last month, in a UN report detailing about Congo, Museveni of Uganda and Kagame of Rwanda are described as "on the verge of becoming godfathers." The controversial report of a UN panel of experts on the illegal exploitation of natural resources so infuriated Museveni that he announced Sunday that Uganda would no longer participate in the official peace plan for Congo. In Washington Monday, the State Department urged Uganda to reconsider its withdrawal from the accord. Because Museveni also announced that Uganda would continue to withdraw its troops from Congo the practical effect of abandoning the accord remains to be seen. But analysts said the announcement reflected the frustration of a government that had enjoyed one of the shiniest images on the continent before it became involved in Congo. In the 80-page UN report, Uganda stands accused of "wide-scale looting" and "systemic exploitation." The document lists diamond exports totalling $3 million over the last two years from Uganda, a country that has no diamonds of its own; Congo is among the world's leading diamond producers. Rwanda, meanwhile, is calculated to have taken in at least $250 million in 18 months by exporting Congolese cool-tan, a once-obscure mineral essential to the production of some computer chips. Independent observers also criticized the report for its frequent reliance on vague attribution and, in some cases, raising allegations without any support. UN officials indicate the panel's tenure will be extended, in part to investigate Congo's allies. But whatever the final outcome, analysts say, even the flawed current report reinforces the widely held impression that Congo's government is no longer the primary obstacle to peace. During Laurent Kabila's rule, Congo constantly frustrated implementation of the Lusaka accord. His son has opened government territory to UN peacekeeping troops who are to monitor the cease-fire and pulled back Congolese troops from frontlines. While both Rwanda and Uganda pulled back front-line troops weeks before deadlines, the Congolese rebel groups that they sponsor have begun causing problems. Bemba, whose Congolese Liberation Movement was created by Uganda, refused to move his forces from central Congo until the UN sent troops to take their place. The request went beyond the UN mandate, which is merely to observe. The population of Congo welcomes UN troops. "This is a political message the population is giving to all the parties," Morjane said. "I hope they will all get the right message." (WP, 2 May, p. A18)

16 May
Twelve of 15 Security Council members left New York today for an intense round of talks intended to hasten the end of the war in Congo. Ambassador Levitte of France, who is leading the mission, said in an interview that this is the moment for a concerted push on Congo. In recent months, Mr. Levitte said, a cease-fire has held; troops from Rwanda and Uganda, which invaded Congo in 1998, have been pulling back as promised. Diplomats say it is the right time to talk about the departure of Zimbabwean, Angolan and Namibian forces fighting on the government's side. The Security Council hopes not only to encourage momentum for the pullbacks but also to win the approval of African governments for an international conference on the economic and political development of Congo's neighbourhood, the lakes region of east central Africa. The Council trip is a gamble. The United Nations does not have large numbers of troops to send to Africa now for peacekeeping duties. (NYT, 16 May, p. 5)

16 June
The Security Council extended the peacekeeping mission in Congo for another year, buoyed by a cease-fire that has lasted four months and small but steady steps toward settling the issues that brought half a dozen nations into the war. There are 2,400 United Nations monitors and peacekeeping troops in Congo, and more may be sent if the situation continues to improve. A force of up to 5,537 has been authorized. (NYT, 16 June, p. 4)

Croatia

22 February

The war crimes suspect Gen. Mirko Norac turned himself in to the police, ending a two-week search that set off anti-government protests. The announcement of his detention came after Prime Minister Ivica Racan said a Croatian court would try the general and not be extradited to the United Nations war crimes tribunal in The Hague. (NYT, 22 February, p. 8)

Cyprus

19 October

Turkish jets buzzed Greek warplanes that were taking part in Greek Cypriot military manoeuvres on the divided Mediterranean Island of Cyprus, officials said. The incident occurred just days after Turkish fighters blocked Greek warplanes from taking part in NATO war games in the eastern Aegean Sea. "There was an attempt by Turkish aircraft to harass the planes coming for the exercise, but they were intercepted by other Greek fighters," a defence ministry spokesman here said. Two A-7 Corsair II bombers were buzzed on their flight to Cyprus and on their way back to their Greek base, the spokesman said. Greece and Turkey, both NATO members, have long been at loggerheads over the division of Cyprus as well as territorial rights in the Aegean Sea. Military over flights of Cyprus by either country always raise hackles and in the past have spurred tit-for-tat flyovers or landings in a show of brinkmanship. Cyprus has been divided since Turkish forces invaded the north in 1974 after a brief coup engineered by the military authorities then ruling Greece. Turkey maintains some 30,000 troops in northern Cyprus, a breakaway state it alone recognises. (WP, 20 October, p. A28)

8 November

A new round of talks on the future of the divided island has opened in Geneva, with a special envoy of Secretary General Kofi Annan meeting separately with the Greek Cypriot leader Glafcos Clerides and the Turkish Cypriot leader Rauf Denktash. Mr. Annan will join the envoy, Alvaro de Soto, this week on his way to the Middle East. The United Nations has one of the longest-running peacekeeping operations in Cyprus, which has been divided along ethnic lines for more than a quarter of a century. (NYT, 8 November, p. A6)

East Timor

20 June

The National Council of East Timor today unanimously passed an amended regulation on the establishment of a truth and reconciliation commission and in a related move asked the United Nations Transnational Administrator to set up a tribunal to prosecute perpetrators of serious human rights violations in the territory.

The Commission on Reception, Truth and Reconciliation will investigate the human rights violations that occurred in the territory between 1974 and 1979 and also create a community reconciliation body to facilitate agreements between local communities and the perpetrators of non-serious crimes and non-criminal acts committed over the same period. According to the UN Transnational Administration in East Timor (UNTAET), the regulation stipulates that there can be no further civil or criminal liability for those who comply with the conditions of the Commission.

After acting unanimously on the truth commission, National Council Member Aniceto Guterres proposed a regulation calling on the head of UNTAET, Sergio Vieira de Mello, to take steps to establish an International Tribunal to prosecute those responsible for committing serious human rights violations in the territory. That resolution was also passed unanimously.

The National Council then passed a series of amendments to the regulation that established East Timor's defence Force in January. These include amendments inserting a preamble that recognizes the important role played by Falantil and prohibiting the defence force from political affiliation.

A proposal to include in the regulation the observation of principles of international human rights law that apply during armed conflict was also passed unanimously. (BBC, 20 June)

25 July

A soldier from New Zealand was fatally shot in the head today in East Timor during a clash with armed opponents of independence, becoming the first UN peacekeeper to be killed in the former Indonesian territory, the top UN official there said. The soldier was part of a team tracking men who had reportedly crossed the border from Indonesian-ruled western Timor. Captain Hurren, an Australian officer, said airborne infantry and reconnaissance helicopters had been mobilized to find the militia group. The incident was the third serious attack on UN peacekeeping troops in East Timor, de Mello said. The United Nations, with 8,500 troops stationed in the former Portuguese colony, is administering the territory until it is ready to hold its first elections as an independent country. But since UN troops arrived, pro-Indonesian militiamen have regularly crossed the border from western Timor to stage attacks. Much of Timor remains a terrorized wasteland with tens of thousand of refugees. (WP/Ind., 25 July, p. A18)

11 August

Militia groups with ties to the Indonesian military have sneaked into East-Timor and are carrying out bold attacks on UN peacekeepers in the newly independent nation, UN officials and Western diplomats said. The assaults have resulted in the deaths of two peacekeepers in the past three weeks and have escalated tensions along the rugged, 100-mile border separating UN-controlled east Timor from western Timor, the part of the island that remains under Indonesian control. The violence also has complicated efforts to send home more than 100,000 refugees from squalid camps in western Timor end raises the prospect that an international security force will have to remain in East Timor longer than planned to control the militias, which oppose the territory's independence from Indonesia. "It's very clear that the relationships that existed for decades between the Indonesian military and the militias are still there," said a senior Western diplomat. UN Secretary General Annan and the Security Council both called on Indonesia today to halt the infiltration and disarm the militias. The Indonesian government insisted that it cannot control pro-Jakarta militiamen in East Timor. (WP, 12 August, p. A14)

6 September

Thousands of armed militiamen and their supporters rampaged through a UN office in western Timor today, killing at least three workers and burning their bodies. Four UN helicopters, dispatched from newly independent East Timor, swooped down to the site of the violence, the border town of Atambua, and evacuated 54 other UN employees, some of them injured. They were taken to the East Timor border town of Balibo. Witnesses said Indonesian security forces stood by as the mobs burned the UN office and beat the workers. As a result, Indonesian President Abdurrahman Wahid came under new pressure during a UN summit meeting with other world leaders, some of whom charged his government has not done enough to control militia groups in the western part of the island, which is still under Jakarta's control. The three victims were the first civilian aid workers to be killed in Timor. Two peacekeeping soldiers have died in border skirmishes with armed militia infiltrators in East Timor in recent weeks. In addition to the three dead, several foreign staff members of the UN refugee agency escaped, and three were injured, one of them seriously, police in Atambua said. (WP, 7 September, p. A16)

7 September
A further 69 international and local aid workers were evacuated from Atambua in West Timor by the Indonesian military. Nearly 240 UN staff and their dependants have now left for East Timor or the resort island of Bali after three foreign employees of the UN High Commission for Refugees (UNHCR) were beaten to death and burnt. (TI, 8 September, p. 14)

13 December
A United Nations prosecutor in East Timor indicted 11 men for crimes against humanity in what promises to be a first step on a long and contentious road to justice. Among the accused is Lt. Sayful Anwar, a deputy commander of Indonesia's feared Special Forces Command (Kopassus)-the first Indonesian soldier ever to face international prosecution for war crimes. The UN said it would seek Lieutenant Anwar's extradition from Indonesia to face trial in East Timor. The 10 others were members of Team Alpha, a Kopassus-trained militia group based in the northern town of Los Palos. Nine of them are already in custody.

Mohamed Chande Othman, the UN's chief prosecutor in East Timor, said the indictments would send a message to Indonesia's military that there would be no impunity for the rampage that followed East Timor's independence vote in August 1999.

Human rights experts say it's now unlikely that the Indonesian government will be either willing or able to force the military to cooperate. The military has effectively stonewalled the efforts of UN prosecutors to question five military and police officers in Jakarta this week, despite the full cooperation of Indonesian Attorney General Marzuki Darusman. "No officer it is to be investigated or questioned by UNTAET," Armed Forces Chief Admiral Widodo Adisucipto told journalists yesterday after meeting with President Abdurrahman Wahid. The government rejects any intervention or meddling by foreign parties.

Against that backdrop, it's unlikely that an extradition will be allowed. While there was some sentiment for an international tribunal last year, UN support for one-particularly among the Security Council members who would control the process-has evaporated. With the threat of an international tribunal removed, the chance for credible Indonesian prosecutions now appears "slim and none" says an official familiar with the UN's prosecution in East Timor. Mr. Darusman has promised to begin trials of 22 suspects accused of human rights abuses by the end of January.

The team Alpha members were charged with massacring nine people on September 25, 1999, near Los Palos. They have also been charged with forcing the entire population of

Leuro village into Battalion 745's base in Los Palos. Anwar, deputy commander of Kopassus in Los Palos, was charged with the mutilation, torture, and murder of Averisto Lopes on April 21, 1999, at the team Alpha base.

UN investigators in East Timor say that 745's commanders are responsible for the murder of former Monitor contributor Sander Thoenes last September, and an extensive investigation by the Monitor early this year found that Team Alpha worked hand in glove with Battalion 745. (Christian Science Monitor, 13 December)

13 December

Indonesian Military (TNI) Chief Admiral Widodo AS's objection to foreign intervention in the alleged human rights violation in East Timor by a number of military and police officers is a correct attitude, because an intervention by UNTAET (United Nations Transnational Administration in East Timor) in handling this case would make things worse.

Regardless of the Memorandum of Understanding reached between the Attorney General's Office and UNTAET last April in the settlement of the alleged human rights violations, Indonesian citizens are supposed to be tried in their own country, a political affairs observer at the state Padang University Amir Benson said here on Wednesday.

In the meantime on Monday this week UNTAET was reported to have filed the first dossiers of the alleged crimes against humanity by Indonesian troops and pro-Jakarta militias during violence in East Timor last year. (Antara, 13 December, 2000)

14 December

Indonesian Attorney-General Marzuki Darusman said here Thusday 14 December that all human right abusers in the breakaway province of East Timor in 1999 would be tried in Indonesia instead of being extradited to the country's former province. Darusman said that the government will carry out the trial in Indonesia, and those who are allegedly involved in human right abuse cases in East Timor will not be extradited to East Timor, adding that the government and the UNTAET have reached agreement on cooperation on the settlement of human right abuse cases there.

Meanwhile, Speaker of the House Akbar Tandjung said that the DPR agreed with the government in term of Memorandum of Understanding (MoU) signed by Darusman and the Chief of the UNTAET Sergio Vieira de Mello in April 2000 under which the two sides agreed to be cooperative based on the reciprocity principles in connection with the settlement of human right abuse cases in the former province.

Under the MoU, both sides also agreed to, among other things, afford to each other the widest possible measure of mutual assistance in investigations or court proceedings. The MoU also said the UNTAET and the government agreed to take evidences or statement from persons, assisting in the availability of detained persons, ensuring service of judicial documents, executing arrests, searches and seizures, facilitating transfer of persons, and ensuring participation of representatives of authorities in legal proceedings.

Darusman denied any suggestion that personnel of the UNTAET would questioned the wrongdoers and being involved in legal process in Indonesia. "It should be clarified that the UNTAET will not be involved in the legal process against those who are believed to have been implicated in human right abuse in East Timor. They only collected information by visiting Jakarta and attorney-general to get information about the case," Darusman said.

Meanwhile, Darusman indicating that the human rights trial would began some time in January 2001. "The bill on human right trial has been signed by President Abdurrahman

Wahid on 26 November. And it has been taking effect since then," he said. (Xinhua, 14 December)

4 April

In the worst recent violence along the border between East Timor and the Indonesian territory of West Timor, unidentified attackers threw grenades and fired guns at United Nations peacekeeping troops in five separate clashes, United Nations officials said. They said that no peacekeepers had been hurt, but that an East Timorese woman had been wounded. (NYT, 4 April, p. 8)

12 April

The United Nations will face renewed pressure to set up an East Timor war crime tribunal after receiving a report alleging a conspiracy among Indonesian generals was behind 1999's wave of killings and destruction.

The report, by a special UN-appointed investigator, Mr. James Dunn, came as human rights activists and diplomats in Jakarta said yesterday that they believed 22 people named as orchestrating the violence might escape prosecution in Indonesia because of a legal loophole. Mr. Dunn's report contradicts claims by Indonesia's top military officers, including the former armed forces chief General Wiranto, that the violence was a spontaneous reaction by pro-Jakarta Timorese to the UN-administered ballot in which voters rejected Indonesian rule.

The UN Secretary-General, Mr. Kofi Annan, warned last year that the UN would consider setting up an international tribunal if Jakarta failed to prosecute key East Timor culprits. The Indonesian Government is certain to refuse to co-operate with any prosecutions outside the jurisdiction of its own courts.

Before any charges are filled over the Timor violence, a special ad-hoc human rights court must be formed. Parliament approved such a court only last month, and the legislation still has not been signed by President Abdurahman Wahid. However, the Attorney-General, Mr. Marzuki Darusman, argued that the 70-day clock did not begin until the special court had been formed and charges filed. "We are wholly on track here," he was quoted as saying. (Sydney Morning Herald, 12 April)

24 April

Indonesia is setting up a special court to try cases of human rights abuses by Indonesian troops in East Timor in 1999. Officials said President Abdurrahman Wahid has signed a degree to establish the court. The decree also provides for a separate tribunal to prosecute officers accused in the murder of dozens of anti-government demonstrators in Jakarta's Tanjung Priok port district in 1984, presidential spokesman Yahya Staquf said.

Indonesia has been under growing international pressure to prosecute war crime suspects or face the possibility of an international war crimes tribunal being set up. United Nations investigators are expected to indict as many as 400 suspects, including some top Indonesian military generals. An Indonesian government probe has prepared a list of 23 potential suspects. However, no formal charges have been filed

Wahid's move came as East Timor's spiritual leader, Bishop Carlos Belo, urged the UN to set up a tribunal akin to those for the former Yugoslavia and Rwanda. "What is good for Bosnia and Rwanda is also good for East Timor," Belo said in Sydney, Australia.

UN officials believe Indonesian soldiers and paramilitary thugs murdered up to 1,000 East Timorese civilians, when they rampaged through the province in the aftermath of an independence referendum in August 1999. About 80 percent of the housing and infrastructure was destroyed in the rampage that ended with the arrival of international peacekeepers a month later.

A report prepared for the UN penned by the former Australian consul to East Timor, James Dunn, implicated the Indonesian army of tolerating violence against proindependence civilians in East Timor. The report was prepared for UN prosecutors conducting their own investigation in East Timor. (CNN, 24 April)

25 April

News that the Indonesian President has approved the establishment of a human rights court for East Timor which will only try cases of violations committed after the August 1999 popular consultation was greeted with dismay by Amnesty International.

The President Decree issued on 23 April 2001 followed a recommendation from Indonesia's parliament to establish ad hoc Human Rights Courts on East Timor and on the 1984 Tanjung Priok case in which dozens of Muslims protestors were unlawfully killed, "disappeared" or imprisoned.

Amnesty International urged the Indonesian government to demonstrate its commitment to ending impunity by reconsidering its decision to limit the jurisdiction of the ad hoc court, so that the full truth of the 1999 events including on issues of policy and command responsibility are revealed.

Restricting the court's remit to events after the 30 August 1999 vote looks like an attempt to rewrite history – suppressing the truth denies the connection between the post-ballot violence and the pattern of events throughout the year in which militia were established, armed and trained by the Indonesian military before being let loose on the East Timorese population. In particular it means that suspects in two of the major cases investigated by the Attorney General's office will now not be brought to trial.

The Presidential Decree comes only days after the UN Commission on Human Rights adopted a statement recommending, among other things, that those responsible for human rights violations in East Timor be brought to justice without further delay – a statement in which the Indonesian authorities agreed to.

"This compromised decision should force the international community to seriously consider the establishment of an international criminal tribunal on East Timor so that the 1999 events can be looked at in their entirety," Amnesty International said.

The organization also emphasised the need to ensure that any Human Rights Court which is set up conforms to international standards. The required steps include further amendments of the legislation on Human Rights Courts to guarantee their competence and independence as well as the rights of suspects; the training of judges and other court officials; and an effective program of victim and witness protection must be established. (Amnesty International, 25 April)

May

The proposed Commission on Reception, Truth and Reconciliation (CRTR) is one of the most commonly misunderstood projects in East Timor. Serious crimes, including murder, rape and torture, would be excluded from the commission, on the assumption that they should go to trial. Less serious crimes, such as destruction of private property-including, perhaps, arson-would be resolved through a community reconciliation procedure. The idea of such a commission has been driven largely by East Timorese, and is now being developed with the support of UNTAET's Human Rights Unit, working closely with women's groups and human rights organizations, the Catholic Church and CNRT. In addition to national reconciliation, the commission would aim to facilitate reintegration from West Timor and to establish a historical record of human rights abuses from 1974-1999.

The likely procedure would be for perpetrators to meet with the affected community, offer a public apology, and undertake some form of community service by way of atonement. This agreement would be registered by a court; following completion to the satisfaction of the CRTR, the perpetrator's debt to society would be deemed to have been paid. It is likely that a perpetrator would be required to make some sort of a declaration accepting that the result of the August 1999 popular consultation reflects the will of the majority of the Timorese population.

A separate function would enable victims to enter testimony about violations suffered in the period 1974-1999. There were some initial concerns that this public airing of grievances might interfere with East Timor's first elections. In any case, the CRTR now seems unlikely to be adopted until after elections have been completed, and perhaps not until after independence. (The International Peace Academy, May 2001)

1 May

The United Nations Serious Crimes Unit, in charge of gathering evidence to prosecute those responsible for the violence which swept East Timor in 1999, is on the point of collapse.

The reports – one the Indonesian Government's own investigation and the other by special UN reporter Mr James Dunn – confirmed the involvement of senior Indonesian military figures in the planning and arming of the militias responsible for the violence and revealed details of several mass killings. No-one has yet been tried for crimes related to these events.

By June he said at least six cases would be ready to go to trial involving army-backed militia killings committed in Liquica church, Cailaco, Maliana police station, Oecussi, the murder of priests and church workers in Los Palos, and a rape case committed in Lolotoi. "In these cases, which are all crimes against humanity, we would have a minimum of 60 accused ranging from militia executioners to army commanders. These cases will give a good indication of criminality of all the actors at a district level, then we move on to cases of command responsibility," he said. (Sydney Morning Herald, 1 May)

Ethiopia-Eritrea

10 October

The United Nations began clearing mines from the Ethiopia-Eritrea border to ensure the safe deployment of its peacekeeping force, the United Nations Mission for Eritrea and Ethiopia. The Halo Trust, a charity registered in Britain and the United States, began surveying Ethiopia's Tigray region this month in co-operation with the Ethiopian authorities. They found cluster ammunition, aerial bombs as well as unexploded ordnance and minefields, the mission said.

(NYT, 11 October, p. A6)

4 December
Ethiopia and Eritrea have agreed to a final peace pact, bringing a formal close to a border war in the Horn of Africa that ended militarily in June after claiming tens of thousands of lives. Details of the pact, which include formal demarcation of the disputed border, were confirmed in a letter that President Bill Clinton sent to the leaders of both countries late last week, an official familiar with the talks said. The agreement, brokered by a U.S. envoy, Anthony Lake, and the Organisation of African Unity, is to be signed in Algiers on Dec. 12 by Prime Minister Meles Zenawi of Ethiopia and President Issaias Afewerki of Eritrea. What began in May 1998 as a skirmish over a remote stretch of border exposed a deep reservoir of bitterness. The neighbours, which are among the world's poorest countries, dug in and rearmed, spending hundreds of millions of dollars on weapons. A negotiated cease-fire was reached in June that included a UN peacekeeping force whose commanders have made a symbolic drive across the front lines. When the main force of 4,000 peacekeepers arrives next year, Ethiopian troops will fall back to their 1998 positions. The new agreement is meant to be the "lasting settlement" that will ensure that hostilities do not resume when the UN troops leave. (IHT, 4 December, p. 2)

24 December
More than 700 sick and wounded prisoners of war from the two years of a border conflict between Ethiopia and Eritrea returned home over the weekend with the help of the International Committee of the Red Cross. A chartered Boeing 727 took off from Addis Ababa for Asmara, Eritrea, early Saturday in the first official direct flight since the guns fell silent, carrying Eritrean troops, many of them on crutches, who been brought to the airport on buses. A comprehensive peace treaty between the two countries was signed two weeks ago. With medical assistants on board, the plane returned with Ethiopian soldiers, police and customs officers, who were given a hero's welcome with a brass band and full military honours. In all, 359 Eritreans and 360 Ethiopians were flown across the border. As the ailing prisoners went home for Christmas, clutching the few possessions they had brought from the camps, the Red Cross also brought home more than 1,400 Ethiopian civilians who had been interned in Eritrea. The return of civilians began before President Meles Zenawi of Ethiopia and President Isaias Afewerki of Eritrea signed the peace pact on December 12, formally ending the war. Tens of thousands of soldiers are believed to have been killed in the fighting before both sides agreed to a cease-fire in June.
(NYT, 25 December, p. A20)

8 January
Misgivings are mounting, even among some American officials here, over United States efforts to lift an arms embargo against Ethiopia and Eritrea while the two African countries are still putting in place a fresh peace accord ending a border war that killed tens of thousands of combatants. Secretary General Kofi Annan and some officials at the United States Mission to the United Nations, have expressed doubts about a draft resolution introduced in the 15-member Security Council shortly before the new year that aims to end the arms embargo, Western diplomats said. Canada and the Netherlands have raised in particular, strong objections, which have peacekeepers in Eritrea and Ethiopia as part of some 4,200 United Nations forces who are supposed to oversee the peace accord signed by the two Horn of Africa countries on Dec. 12. The arms embargo is scheduled to expire in May, a year after it was imposed, and several countries want the ban to stay in place at

least until then. It will stay in place unless the Council votes to extend it or until Mr. Annan reports that "a peaceful definitive settlement of the conflict" between Eritrea and Ethiopia has been reached. Most Council members argue that Mr. Annan has not yet issued such a report. Ethiopia and Eritrea continue to trade accusations daily over details of the accord. Under the agreement, Ethiopia is to pull back to positions it held before the war broke out, and Eritrea is to withdraw to 15 miles from Ethiopian positions. But the two nations are still arguing over which areas were under whose administration before the war broke out. The accord also calls for an independent commission to demarcate the 600-mile border, while other commissions are to address compensation for war damages, an exchange of prisoners and the return of people displaced from their homes. The work of the border commission is expected to last three years. (NYT, 8 January, p. A7)

13 February
Ethiopia has begun withdrawing its troops from Eritrea in a redeployment that will formally allow the United Nations to take charge of a buffer zone on the disputed border separating the two countries, officials said today. About 600 Ethiopian soldiers had withdrawn from the Eritrean town of Senafe to Ethiopia's border town of Zalambessa on Sunday, a day ahead of schedule, with mainly military equipment being moved today, United Nations officials said. Some 4,200 United Nations peacekeepers are being deployed to monitor the 15-mile deep buffer zone. The war in the Horn of Africa broke out in May 1998, when Eritrean troops took control of territory claimed by Ethiopia. Eritrea gained independence from Ethiopia in 1993 after a 30-year guerrilla war, but the border was never properly demarcated. The war, in which tens of thousands of soldiers are believed to have been killed, ended with a peace deal last June after Ethiopian forces scored a string of decisive battlefield victories. But arguments over which areas were under whose administration before the war began has delayed the withdrawal of troops and the deployment of the United Nations' peacekeeping mission. The deployment is seen as a success story in the making for the United Nations after a string of troubled peacekeeping missions in Africa. (NYT, 13 February, p. A3)

6 April
Two years of fighting between Ethiopia and Eritrea were fierce by any measure: perhaps 100,000 soldiers died. But the two nations now seem equally committed to the silence between them. For six months, starting last June, they respected a cease-fire, even without the peacekeepers to keep them apart. That is a welcome relief for the 4,100 peacekeepers who have since arrived along a broiling strip of borderland in Eritrea. So much is this considered a model mission that there are more offers for peacekeepers than there is space. This is in stark contrast to the wariness surrounding the United Nations' newest African task, in Congo, which is a muddle of six armies and dozen rebel groups. In a world where conflicts have grown more and more complex the situation here is almost reassuringly direct. This is an old-fashioned war along a definable front. The more common, newer face of war is a struggle for power and resources within a single country, where civilians become targets of rebels or militias with little accountability. Soldiers and United Nations officials say they see no immediate lessons for other, more complicated deployments in Africa's internal wars, particularly in Congo, where the first of some 3,000 peacekeepers took up their posts in late March. In some ways, the relative simplicity of this mission has increased the pressure to get it right after problems in Sierra Leone, Rwanda and Angola. Success hinges, as ever, Ethiopia and Eritrea keep their commitment to not fight. But that doesn't mean the problems between Ethiopia and Eri-

trea is anywhere near a solution. In may 1998, several years of tension between Ethiopia and Eritrea erupted over a relatively unimportant town along their 625-mile border. Formed only in 1993, Eritrea is Africa's newest nation, and because their leaders had been friends and ties were otherwise tight, the border never was formally marked. Three major waves of war cost the lives of thousands of soldiers and severed the once strong economic and cultural ties between two nations on the road to development. By last June Ethiopia had pushed Eritrean soldiers deep into their own territory. A cease-fire took hold, the war was over, and the United Nations then took on the task of deploying peace-keepers and settling the borderlines for good. The overall task is still complex: with trust between them destroyed, Eritrea and Ethiopia have wrangled particularly over the establishment of a demilitarised zone, some 15 ½ miles wide and entirely inside the rugged borderlands of Eritrea. Only in late March did Eritrea finally agree to complete the withdrawal of its troops. That appears to pave the way for a formal creation of the demilitarised zone. (NYT, 6 April, p. 3)

Former Republic of Yugoslavia

3 July
The director of the UN administration in Kosovo has some advice for the next great international mission to rebuild a country; be prepared to invest as much money and effort in winning the peace as in fighting the war. He's caustic about the continuing and worsening violence against non-Albanian minorities in Kosovo, especially the remaining Serbs and Roma, or Gypsies. He says the UN, Western governments and NATO have been too slow and timid in their response. He and others suggested, there is simply a tendency to put an optimistic gloss on events here and to avoid confrontation with former guerrillas who fought for independence for Kosovo or with increasingly active gangs of organised criminals. In the year since NATO took over complete control of Kosovo and Serbian troops and policemen left the province, there have been some 500 killings, a disproportionate number of them committed against Serbs and other minorities. But there has not been a single conviction, the judicial system is still not functioning, international prosecutors and judges are hard to find, to little police-officers are present or not capable of their tasks. Another significant problem has been the lack of "unified command". (NYT, 3 July, p. 3)

7 July
In a case that could have serious repercussions throughout Kosovo, UN police are investigating a shootout in which a former Kosovo Liberation Army commander-turned-politician was wounded. Wildly conflicting versions of what happened to Haradinaj circulated through Pristina, the capital of Kosovo. Police and NATO-led peacekeeping command refused to provide details. Friday's incident is potentially explosive for both the international mission and Kososvo's ethnic Albanian leadership. Haradinaj's party plans to contest local elections in October. (WP, 9 July, p. A22)

10 July
The first agreement between the Serbs and the United Nations administration here may provide better protection for the Serbian minority, but it threatens to unravel key Albanian participation in international efforts to build a democratic, tolerant Kosovo. Ma-

noeuvring by the province's majority Albanians and the Serbs is intensifying ahead of municipal elections scheduled for October. The international administration here hopes that this ballot will be the first step toward cutting Kosovo loose from its foreign lifeline, but so far almost no Serbs have registered to vote. And Albanian leaders jostling for power seem to be increasingly willing to fight out their differences on the streets. Some formal participation by Serbs is considered vital to the success of the western effort to turn Kosovo into a democratic, self-governing entity where all ethnic groups can live peacefully -even if separated into enclaves behind barbed wire and guarded by foreign peacekeepers. Both Serbs and Albanians to are accusing United Nations workers of giving the other party a preferential treatment. (NYT, 10 July, p. 9)

18 July
A night of violence in the divided Kosovo city Mitrovica was followed by another protest against the detention of a Serb suspected of beating an ethnic Albanian. (TL, 19 July)

18 July
The secretary-general of NATO, Mr. Robertson had an optimistic judgement about the situation in Kosovo, on Tuesday when he met with journalists in Prizren. The security-situation had obviously improved under the surveillance of international troops. NATO is planning to erect a multi-ethnic and democratic order. The situation is stabilizing and peace is recognised. The situation around the different minorities has stabilized as well. Reality often seems less positive. Violence is not a rare thing and Prizren for instance has become a centre for criminal gangs. There are indications that they consist partly of former members of the UCK ore are connected to Albanian Mafia. During Robertson's visit there were also incidents in Mitrovica. (NZZ, 20 July)

19 July
A new special unity is appointed to persevere the discipline in the Kosovo-Protection Corps, the civil successor of the UCK. In the last few weeks critics sharpened, because its members were tangled in criminal offences while they displayed themselves as keepers of the law. (NZZ, 20 July, p. 20)

30 July
Roughly half the work force in Yugoslavia is unemployed and high inflation is eating away at citizens' already barren lifestyle. Economic sanctions continue to pinch recovery from war. Hundreds of political activists are in jail, sometimes enduring beatings, assassinations are common. Yet the man who presides over all of this, President Slobodan Milosevic, regarded by the United States and its allies as the greatest single threat to peace in Eastern Europe, is almost certain to secure another four-year-term in elections he has called for Sept. 24, senior U.S. and European officials predict. Opposition is divided and polls also indicate that each of his potential political opponents is even less popular than he is. Besides that Milosevic is bending rules and laws to his own benefit. (WP, 30 July, p. A1)

29 August
After new killings of Serbs in Kosovo, British marines began today to spearhead a new campaign against ethnic violence. As his commandos searched the streets, the new commander of peacekeeping troops in the central region of Kosovo, Brig. Robert Fry, said

that fixed checkpoints would be replaced by patrols to hunt out troublemakers. The deaths provoked protests in the victims' towns. 1,000 protesters gathered in the Serbian enclave of Gracanica to demonstrate against what they said was the inability of the peacekeepers and the United Nations mission to ensure their safety. (NYT, 29 August, p. 8)

3 April

President Kostunica said today that Yugoslavia should not extradite former President Milosevic to The Hague to face war-crimes charges. In the negotiations before Mr. Milosevic surrender to the police early Sunday morning, he sought and received written assurances that his arrest on domestic charges of corruption and abuse of power was not a precursor to a transfer to The Hague. Mr. Kostunica said that the arrest of Mr. Milosevic ends "a very painful period in our lives and in the lives of all these states, a period of lost years." Mr. Kostunica criticizes the tribunal at The Hague that prosecutes war crimes in the countries that made up the larger Communist-era Yugoslavia. He contends that it is political and accuses it of practicing selective justice and following shaky rules of law." Still he said, "one should make certain compromises" and co-operates with the tribunal. Yugoslavia will investigate war crimes and help The Hague to do so, he said, and Mr. Milosevic should be brought to trial on war crimes charges before domestic courts. Officials of The Hague tribunal say Yugoslavia, as a member of the United Nations, is obligated to turn over any indicted people on its territory, including Mr. Milosevic. Ms. Del Ponte, the chief prosecutor, said, "any domestic trial on war crimes charges must still end with his extradition." The tribunal's current indictment against Mr. Milosevic covers the actions by Serbian troops against Kosovo Albanians in 1999. Ms. Del Ponte said today that she was getting ready to sign a new indictment for the war in Bosnia from 1992 to 1995, though she could use a few more months to prepare the case. Mr. Kostunica said he also supported a draft law on cooperation with the tribunal that would allow the extradition of those indicted after a rapid judicial procedure. But the case of a former president is different. "It was not international pressure that brought down Mr. Milosevic," Mr. Kostunica said, "but the Serbian people themselves, by their votes and demonstrations." Mr. Kostunica described a bad economy and infrastructure and a ruined system of judicial and political institutions, all of which must be reconstructed, and an unstable regional environment. He wants to work with NATO and the NATO-led peacekeepers in Kosovo, he said. He understands the fear Washington and the peacekeepers have of becoming targets of Albanians in Kosovo. (NYT, 3 April, p. 3)

22 April

The central issue in Montenegro's parliamentary elections on Sunday is depicted by campaign posters plastered everywhere in the capital with the names of the two rival coalitions, "Victory is Montenegro's" and "Together for Yugoslavia." If the former grouping wins impoverished Montenegro will have taken a crucial step toward becoming the fifth and final republic to wrench itself away from the Yugoslav federation. That's the confident prediction of Djukanovic, president and architect of his party's strategy to pursue independence this year over the objections of the U.S., the EU, the Serbia government and Yugoslav leaders. Djukanovic, whose separatist policies were supported by the West while Milosevic governed Yugoslavia, expressed frustration that U.S. and European officials have switched positions and claimed that its independence could provoke fresh instability in the Balkans. Washington and allied capitals have urged Montenegro to reach a compromise with Serbian and Yugoslav leaders to gain more political prominence within the existing federation. Otherwise, they have said, Montenegro's departure will unsettle Serbia and hasten an independence drive in the neighbouring Serbian province of Kosovo. Djukanovic had said he firmly rejects the West's stated position that with Milosevic gone, Yugoslav officials can respond adequately to Montenegro's desire for elevated status. He asserts that with independence, Montenegro would adopt Western economic reforms more rapidly than Serbia would. Italian and other officials have expressed concern about alleged links between Djukanovic's government and organized crime. These problems have been raised repeatedly by leaders of the opposition "Together for Yugoslavia" coalition. But the coalition has had difficulty presenting an alternate path to prosperity, because many of its supporters are fans of Milosevic and hostile to economic or political integration with the West. (WP, 22 April, p. A20)

India

22 February

The government decided to extend for the third time a unilateral cease-fire in Kashmir where it has been battling anti-India militants since 1989. The cease-fire began in November, but it has not stopped the violence. Pakistan-based militants, who rejected the extension, have made a series of attacks on security forces. And army members fired into protesting crowds recently, killing seven. (NYT, 22 February, p. 8)

Indonesia

23 July

Faced with international pressure for peacekeepers, President Abdurrahman Wahid told 20,000 party supporters that Indonesia can end the fighting on the Molucca Islands by itself. Speaking to backers of his National Awakening Party here, Wahid said UN Secretary General Kofi Annan recently told him of pressure on the Security Council to send international peacekeepers to the remote archipelago. (Ind., 24 July, p. 13)

Iraq
The continued military strikes in the no-flight zones

28 August

Iraq's official daily has chided the US and Britain for imposing no-fly zones on Iraq, saying the two countries has been exploiting the restricted areas "for pure aggressive and espionage purposes."

The unilateral decision by the US and Britain to establish the air exclusion zones has got no authorization from the United Nations Security Council. Iraqi held the US-British alliance "fully responsible" for any consequences of their "illegitimate hostile acts," as Iraq has "full right of self defence" according to the International Law.

Iraq has been challenging the US and British warplanes over flying the two zones since the US-British air strikes in December 1998. Yassin Jasim, major general of the Iraqi Air Defence Command, claimed that the Iraqi anti-aircraft artillery had shot down more than 10 US and British planes. (People's Daily, 28 August)

23 December
President Saddam Hussein told a visiting Chinese delegation Saturday that Iraq suffers almost daily bombings by U.S. and British jets while the UN Security Council does nothing to stop it.
Speaking to a delegation led by Chinese Cabinet official Ismail Amat, Saddam criticized the United States and Britain for what Iraq considers to be violations of Security Council resolutions. The Iraqi people are facing real difficulties and continuous conspiracy from America and Britain when they bomb northern and southern Iraq on a daily basis.
US and British jets have been patrolling no-fly zones over northern and southern Iraq in a program designed to protect Kurdish and Shiite groups against government forces. Baghdad has been challenging the planes since late 1998, saying the zones violate its sovereignty and international law. Iraqi civilians have been killed and injured in the attacks. (Associated Press, 23 December)

18 January
Iraq sent a letter to UN Secretary-General Kofi Annan calling for United Nations condemnation of Friday's attack on the outskirts of Baghdad, which it said killed at least two civilians.
"The UN Secretary-General and the Security Council Chairman should condemn the military aggression and should take appropriate steps to prevent such attacks from happening again," said a letter to Annan from Iraq's Foreign Minister Mohammed Saeed al Sahaf.
Washington said U.S. and British Planes hit Iraqi radar systems five to twenty miles from Baghdad. The attack was designed to remove a threat to planes patrolling no-fly zones set up after the 1991 Gulf War.
Iraq said Western warplanes returned Sunday to patrol the southern zone after having made a similar sortie Saturday, within hours of Friday's air strike.
"Iraq will continue defying American and British aircraft flying in its airspace.and will confront them by all possible means," Iraq's Trade Minister Mohammed Mehdi Saleh told reporters in Baghdad. (Reuters, 18 February)

18 February
The American and British air strikes carried out Friday against radar installations and anti-defence sites near Baghdad will reduce the growing risk to pilots who patrol the southern no-flight zone.
"Operations such as the one last night would not be needed if Saddam stopped attacking us," Prime Minister Tony Blair of Britain said today. "But as long as he does, I will continue to take the steps necessary to protect our forces and to prevent Saddam from once again wreaking havoc, suffering and death. (New York Times, 18 February)

20 February
The latest clashes in the no-fly zones, culminating in the February 16 US-UK attack on Iraqi command and control sites north of the 33rd parallel, are no exception. The February 16 attack was an escalation, in that it targeted installations outside the no-fly zones, but the scale of action in the no-fly zones has increased dramatically since the beginning of 1999. The Iraqi government claims that between December 1998 and the beginning of

2001, 323 civilians have been killed and 960 injured by US and UK attacks in the no-fly zones.

The use of air power in recent conflict has often signalled ambivalence and uncertain policies. The present low-level warfare being conducted by the US and UK in Iraq seems a good example of this absence of strategic thinking. Meanwhile, the February 16 bombing will only reinforce Iraqi civilians' well-rooted view that despite their rhetoric, the US and UK have little or no interest in their welfare. (MERIP, 20 February)

22 February

Pentagon officials have admitted that most of the bombs dropped by US and British warplanes on Iraq last Friday missed their targets. Last Friday's attacks sparked protests around the world, and inflamed UN-Iraqi relations, souring the atmosphere ahead of key talks aimed paving the way for a lifting of the decade-old embargo on Iraq. (BBC, 22 February)

26 February

News Media reports last week that 50 percent of the weapons fired at Iraqi military installations missed their so-called aim points obscures a more disturbing facet of the February 16 attack: The U.S. jets used cluster bombs that have no real aim point and that kill and wound innocent civilians for years to come.

Twenty eight Joint Stand-off Weapons (JSOWs, pronounced jay-sow) were fired by Navy aircraft in the February 16 attack, along with guided missiles and laser-guided bombs. Pentagon sources say that 26 of the 28 JSOWs missed their aim points. (Washington Post, 26 February)

9 May

The danger to the U.S. and British pilots who fly in the two zones has skyrocketed as Iraq's military has made an unusually determined effort to shoot down a pilot. Almost every flight has been fired on by Iraqi antiaircraft guns, and well over 100 surface-to-air missiles have been launched since the last large-scale U.S. and British air raids in mid-February.

In addition, the Iraqis are rarely turning on their air-defence radars, making them harder to target and so lessening the military benefit of flying in the zones. Without radar to guide their missiles, the Iraqis are firing almost blindly, but in such great numbers that U.S. commanders fear that eventually they will get a lucky hit.

Administration officials, including Secretary of State Colin L. Powell in congressional testimony last week, have repeatedly said they intend to maintain the no-fly zones. (Washington Post, 9 May)

The debate on economic sanctions against Iraq

11 July

Russia will gain if the UN lifts sanctions imposed on Iraq, an expert for the Moscow-based Institute for Oriental Studies said on Tuesday. "Iraq is a vast market for Russian goods. Besides, it will be able to return its debt to Russia once the international blockade is over," the head of the Arab department's economic sector, Alexander Filonik, told Itar-Tass. "When sanctions are finally lifted – and they will be abolished some day because they cannot last for ever – Baghdad will be again a partner of Moscow's, the way it was during the days of the former Soviet Union," Filonik said.

However, the head of the Moscow-based Arabists' Association, Vadim Sementsov, said the sanctions must remain in place until Iraqi President Saddam Hussein caved in and gave signs of willingness to co-operate with the international community.

Nevertheless, experts have not come to a unanimous conclusion about whether the lifting of sanctions will help or damage Russia. From the one hand, Baghdad is expected to re-pay its several-billion-dollar debt to Moscow. On the other hand, oil prices may drop once Iraq is allowed to produce fuel on a large scale, which will be an absolutely unwel-come prospect for Russia's export-oriented economy. (ITAR-TASS News Agency, 11 July)

26 July
President Vladimir Putin was to host Iraq's Deputy Prime Minister Tareq Aziz on Wednesday, for talks focusing closely on the easing of UN sanction against Iraq. Setting the tone for the talks, Ivanov said Russia would continue to press the United Nations to lift sanction against Moscow's close Middle East ally. Russia continues to apply maxi-mum pressure for the quickest end, and then permanent lifting of international sanctions against Iraq. Russia, as one of the five major powers in the UN Security Council, strongly supports lifting sanctions enforced against on Baghdad since Iraq's 1990 invasion of Ku-wait. (Agence France Presse, 26 July)

1 August
French Foreign Minister Hubert Vedrine said on Tuesday that the economic sanctions against Iraq imposed 10 years ago should be lifted and the U.S.-British should stop bombing the country. Vedrine said that the sanctions against Iraq have become "cruel, in-efficient and dangerous." It is cruel because they punish exclusively the Iraqi population and the weakest of them. Inefficient because they don't touch the regime which is not pushed to cooperate. Dangerous because they nourish the resentment of "the embargo generation," this generation of the young people who only know war and hardship.

These sanctions also risk destroying the social cohesion of Iraq and in the mid-term threatening the stability of the region. (Xinhua News Agency, 1 August)

2 August
The end of the war could have been the beginning of Iraq's recovery and reintegration into the family of nations. All that was required for Saddam Hussein to meet the require-ments insisted upon by the Security Council. These were designed not to punish Iraq, but rather o prevent renewed aggression, and to gain an accounting of the more than 600 Kuwaitis missing after being abducted by Iraqi forces during the war.

If Baghdad had simply met these obligations, the UN economic sanctions would long ago have been lifted. Instead, Saddam lied repeatedly to UN weapons inspectors and sought to conceal and preserve his capacity to build weapons of mass destruction. Instead, he has chosen to defy the UN, rebuild his military to the extent he can, and exploit the suf-fering of Iraqi civilians in order to gain sympathy for lifting sanctions. This is why Sad-dam so long opposed efforts, led by the United States, to establish an "oil for food" pro-gram to ease the impact of sanctions upon the Iraqi people. The UN sanctions have never prohibited or limited the amount of food or medicine Iraq could import.

As a result, the availability of food to Iraqi civilians has risen significantly. And in northern Iraq, which is subject to sanctions but not to Saddam's misguided administrative control, child mortality rates are lower now than they were a decade ago. In addition, the Clinton administration is devoting additional personnel to the job of processing sanctions-related export requests at the United Nations, so that legitimate goods may be shipped without undue bureaucratic delay. (Korea Herald, 2 August)

4 August
When comprehensive economic sanctions on Iraq were extended under Resolution 687 (1991), the expectation of the Security Council and other parties was that sanctions would be in place for a relatively short time. Whatever the extent of Iraqi non-compliance with the provisions of that resolution, the Council must recognise that the sanctions have contributed in a major way to persistent life-threatening conditions in the country, and that short-term emergency assistance is no longer appropriate to the scale of this humanitarian crisis.
A number of United Nations bodies, including the Security Council and General Assembly, have acknowledged the critical need to device sanctions that are targeted, effective, and credible. Most recently, the 19 July report of the Secretary-General to the Security Council and the General Assembly on children and armed conflict (A/55/163-S/2000/712, section F) stressed the need to protect children from the impact of sanctions. It is essential to apply these insights, conclusions, and recommendations without further delay to the case of Iraq, where the continued imposition of comprehensive economic sanctions is undermining the basic rights of children and the civilian population generally. (Open Letter to the Security Council Concerning the Humanitarian Situation in Iraq, 4 August)

15 September
Egypt reflects the growing discontent among some Arab states in criticism of the sanctions against Iraq. Foreign Minister Amr Moussa, calls for modifying the sanctions regime and discussion on how to suspend the sanctions against Iraq. (Reuters, 15 September)

21 September
Human Rights Watch strongly criticized the government of Iraq for refusing to cooperate with United Nations efforts to asses the country's humanitarian situation. Human Rights Watch wrote to President Saddam Hussein calling for Iraq to reconsider its stance of non-cooperation, and to the Security Council, criticizing the negative humanitarian impact of sanctions. (Human Rights Watch Press Release, 21 September)

7 November
UK Foreign Office Minister Peter Hain has criticised French policy on Iraq and its impact on the UN Security Council's efforts to maintain sanctions against Baghdad. In a speech in London, Mr Hain described French policy as contemptible and destructive.
Mr Hain said Britain wanted to see the sanctions suspended. "There is a new way forward. What we should do is join together and encourage Saddam to take it," he said. "That is why we spent eight months negotiating with the United Nations on Security Council resolution 1284, which would provide for sanctions to be suspended within six months." (BBC, 7 November)

17 January

After a decade of suffering by innocent people, and the deaths of children on a scale far exceeding that caused by any military weapon in history, the sanctions continue to bring misery and degradation to all sectors of Iraqi society except their target, the Iraqi Government.

Surveys by agencies such as the UN Children's Fund and an enormous amount of anecdotal information indicate that the impact of sanctions has seen a dramatic increase in infant mortality and morbidity in the general population in Iraq. As early as 1993 the Food and Agriculture Organisation and the World Food Program reported that the sanctions had virtually paralysed the whole economy and generated persistent deprivation, chronic hunger, endemic under nutrition, massive unemployment and widespread human suffering.

It is time for a change of direction. In particular, it is time to allow the people of Iraq to rebuild their society, to create a future for their children, and to engage with the international community. Economic sanctions should be lifted, but strict sanctions on military materials must remain. (The Australian, 17 January)

18 February

Iraq wants the UN to lift crippling economic sanctions imposed after it invaded Kuwait in 1990. The United Nations says Iraq must first let inspectors back in to make sure President Saddam Hussein is not developing weapons of mass destruction. Under Security Council resolutions, the sanctions cannot be lifted until UN inspectors certify that Iraq's nuclear, chemical and biological weapons have been destroyed. (Associated Press, 18 February)

29 March

The meeting of Arab leaders billed as a step toward regional harmony pledged new financial support for the Palestinian government today, but the arguments on lifting United Nations sanctions against Iraq collapsed in bitterness.

The two-day meeting, an attempt to resume regularly scheduled annual gatherings for the first time since Iraq invaded Kuwait in 1990, ended with the two countries trading accusations of who was responsible for the failure. The Kuwaiti delegation sought to prevent the summit from coming up with a resolution that would open the door to lifting the embargo, against Iraq.

The Kuwaitis, while agreeing with other nations that sanctions imposed against Iraq after the invasion should end, refused to accept any Arab League resolution that lacked an explicit Iraqi promise not to threaten Kuwait again. (New York Times, 29 March)

11 April

Sanctions against Iraq should follow a "Milosevic model" that targets the country's leadership and not its people, Kuwaiti Foreign Minister Sheikh Sabah al-Ahmad al-Sabah was quoted as saying on Wednesday.

Sheikh Sabah spoke to Le Monde after talks in Paris on Tuesday with Foreign Minister Hubert Vedrine of France, which has been highly critical of united sanctions in place against Iraq since Saddam's forces invaded Kuwait in 1990.

The U.S administration has been working on ideas for a new package of "smart sanctions" since taking office in January, in the hope of restoring international solidarity against Iraq acquiring military equipment or materials for weapons of mass destruction. (Reuters, 11 April)

3 May

Nezavisimaya Gazeta reports that Russian-American consultations on lifting sanctions against Iraq have begun in Geneva. Both Moscow and Washington are developing their plans for lifting the sanctions against Iraq. The US promises to submit a "smart sanctions" plan by July that would soften the embargo. Moscow believes the American plan aims not at removing sanctions, but at keeping them in place.

Moscow believes that the easing of the sanctions regime by expanding the list of goods forbidden to be imported in Iraq and by creating a sanitary zone around Iraq, proposed by the Americans, is useless. The only way out of the situation, in the opinion of Russian diplomats that is shared in Arab countries, is the so-called package approach envisaging continued negotiating between the UN and Iraq to establish international monitoring of arms on its territory. (Nezavisimaya Gazeta, 3 May)

27 May

The smarter sanctions are the first part of a broader US effort to toughen policy towards Iraq. The sanctions amendments proposed by the US have the merit of allowing quick access into Iraq of virtually all civilian goods. But the impact of smart sanctions should not be exaggerated. The US plan will not revive Iraq's devastated economy while control over Iraq's oil revenues remains in the hands of the UN, and foreign investment and credits are still prohibited. Sanctions would only be fully suspended when Iraq allows UN weapons inspectors back in and wins a certification that it is free of weapons of mass destruction. (Financial Times, 27 May)

31 May

The US Government has decided to postpone efforts to change the system of UN sanctions against Iraq. The United States and Britain want to answer criticism that sanctions mainly hurt ordinary Iraqis by changing them to focus more on preventing Iraq from obtaining arms and weapons-making equipment. But a US official said it would probably take about a month to deal with concerns raised by Russia, France and China about the new "smart" sanctions. (BBC, 31 May)

1 June

Baghdad pre-empted with flat rejection the British draft resolution for revising the economic sanctions regime. This was formally submitted to the Security Council on May 22. It is unlikely that the council will approve the "smart sanctions" proposal, as London and Washington would like, before June 3, when the oil-for food program comes up for renewal. Under "smart sanctions", most restrictions on trade with Iraq would, theoretically, be lifted. The only items banned would be military-related items, which would be placed on a 30-page list prepared by Washington.

Humanitarian agencies working in Iraq argue that only the total lifting of sanctions can put Iraq, devastated by ten years of blockade, back on the road to economic recovery. (Middle East Times, 1 June)

2 June

The "smart" sanctions under discussion in the UN Security Council this month aim to target the Iraqi regime rather than its people by lifting restrictions on civilian goods tightening controls on arms-related products clamping down on oil smuggling.

If the US-backed British proposals are approved, they might succeed in re-imposing restrictions on Iraqi trade that are collapsing after 11 years. But they may also be impossible to implement effectively; they are not likely to benefit the Iraqi people much; and they will not finish the job of destroying weapons of mass destruction, the original goal of the embargo.

For the Iraqi people, the main improvement would appear to be a faster flow of civilian goods. Instead of having to get UN approval for all imports, everything would be automatically allowed except items that might be used to build weapons. The change in emphasis is meant to improve the efficiency of the UN's oil-for-food scheme, which allows Baghdad to exchange oil for humanitarian goods, but keeps money out of its hands. (BBC, 2 June)

8 June

Britain intends to submit an amended text of its UN Security Council draft resolution to revamp sanctions against Iraq, but Russia questioned the underlying premise of the measure.

Russian Ambassador Sergei Lavrov told reporters on Thursday the draft, backed by the United States and revised somewhat by France, did not tackle fundamental problems of how the UN Security Council should suspend decade-old Iraqi sanctions.

At issue are U.S.-British proposals that would ease controls on civilian goods imported by Iraq but tighten restrictions on military-related supplies and smuggling. The plan is a revision of the oil-for-food program, an exception to the sanctions imposed in August 1990 when Iraq invaded Kuwait. That program allows Iraq to sell oil and order food, medicine and other goods under UN supervision. It was renewed for one month last week in hopes that the new measures could be adopted by July 3.

Iraq, in protest against the entire revision of the sanctions, halted oil exports on Monday. Baghdad wants the embargoes lifted or at least made ineffective and objects to any system that would perpetuate them. (Reuters, 8 June)

11 June

It is common knowledge and no surprise that Turkish and U.S. policies towards Iraq do not converge on the nature of sanctions, intelligent or otherwise. Before the intelligent sanctions, the United Nations, inspired by the United States, introduced and implemented sanctions which may now be thought of as unintelligent in hindsight, as they did not produce the desired results.

Sanctions rarely do succeed in the textbooks, if at all. Heavy-handed policies are generally counterproductive. "Intelligent Sanctions" were not favoured by China, Russia or France, the 3 permanent members of the Security Council, for their own reasons to begin with. Such a start does not give much hope that they will serve a useful purpose. Turkey is not happy with the "Intelligent Sanctions" either.

Turkey's policy towards Iraq is motivated by common interests intending to reinvigorate once-lucrative business and trade relations and not to hamper them with new sanctions, however intelligent. (Turkish Daily News, 11 June)

13 June

Iraq said yesterday that nearly 9,000 of its people, mainly children, had died in April from diseases it blamed on a decade of UN sanctions.

Britain and the United States are trying to promote a new system of "smart sanctions" that would ease restrictions on imports of civilian goods while tightening controls on weapons-related imports and oil smuggling to Iraq's neighbours.

Iraq last week halted oil exports in protest against a Security Council resolution extending the oil-for-food programme for only one month instead of the usual six. The 30 day-period is intended to give council members time to continue negotiations on the U.S.-British plan to overhaul sanctions against Baghdad. (Reuters, 13 June)

18 June

Two former United Nations officials yesterday condemned a U.S.-British proposal to revamp 11-year-old UN sanctions on Baghdad as a move which amounted to increased punishment for the Iraqi people.

Denis Halliday and Hans von Sponeck, who have both headed the UN humanitarian programme or oil-for-food deal, told reporters the proposed "smart" sanctions were designed to extend an embargo imposed on Iraq for its 1990 invasion of Kuwait. "They (smart sanctions) are intended to create an open-ended opportunity to sustain an embargo," said Halliday, who quit as head of the oil-for-food programme in 1998 and has since been a vocal critic of the sanctions.

"We have very carefully studied the draft resolution. We find it a provocation and an intensified punishment of a people for a crime they have never committed," said von Sponeck, a German career UN official. He resigned from the same post last year, criticising the sanctions' effect on ordinary Iraqis.

The UN Security Council is debating an Anglo-American draft resolution that would ease sanctions on civilian imports to Iraq and tighten the ban on military goods. The council is working towards a self-imposed deadline of July 3 to adopt the new resolution. Russia, Iraq's closest ally in the Security Council, has signalled its objections.

In a letter to UN Secretary-General Kofi Annan on June 14, Jordan appealed to the Security Council to drop plans to overhaul sanctions, saying its economy would be devastated if trade was halted. Iraqi media said Syria had also voiced its concern over the new resolution in a letter to Annan. Turkey last week sent its foreign ministry under-secretary to Baghdad, where he was told by Iraq's Deputy Prime Minister Tareq Aziz that Ankara would suffer severe consequences if it implemented the new resolution. (Reuters, 18 June)

20 June

Frustrated by the reluctance of Russia and other members of the UN Security Council to go along with a plan to modify sanctions on Iraq, the Bush administration has accepted delaying UN action on the issue for one month.

Even a successful restructuring of UN sanctions that will improve the lot of Iraq's people and limit Iraq's weapons will be read as a failure in the United States before long. (Washington Post, 20 June)

26 June

Russia has told its key counterparts on the UN Security Council it would reject a U.S.-British resolution to revamp sanctions on Iraq if the measure were put to a vote, diplomats said.

Russia, Iraq's closest ally on the council, has long opposed the embargoes. Foreign Minister Igor Ivanov last week criticized the U.S.-British plan and said he would probably offer an alternative, which diplomats expected at a public meeting on Iraq.

Russia has raised objections to the plan for months, saying the United Nations should instead seek ways to move toward a suspension of the sanctions, imposed when Iraq invaded Kuwait in August 1990.

Before the sanctions were imposed in 1990, Russia supplied Baghdad with military goods worth up to $8 billion to be repaid with oil. Its only chance to recoup some of the outstanding debts is if sanctions are lifted and Russian firms are allowed to invest in Iraqi oilfields.

The new resolution would be part of the oil-for-food plan, an exception to the sanctions, which allows Iraq to sell oil to meet basic demands of ordinary Iraqis. Iraq stopped oil flows on June 4 and threatened to stop trade with its neighbours if the resolution were adopted. If the council does not reach an agreement on changing the sanctions, it would probably continue the current oil-for-food plan.

In order to get sanctions suspended, Iraq has to allow UN arms inspectors back into the country to check on its weapons of mass destruction programs. (Reuters, 26 June)

26 June

As the first casualty of "smart" sanctions against Iraq, Jordan could lose its entire oil supply, as well as its main export market. Under the proposed sanctions regime, to be debated by the UN Security Council next week, civilian trade with Iraq will be relaxed but border checks for military or dual-use goods will be tightened. This will place extra responsibility on Iraq's neighbours, and President Saddam Hussein has threatened to cut trade with any country that helps to implement the sanctions.

The Iraqi threat, says one western diplomat, is both credible and-in the case of Jordan-devastating. "Jordan would have to abide by an international resolution, but Iraq would retaliate. It would be political and economic suicide," the diplomat said.

Jordan gets a combination of free and cheap oil from Iraq, saving up to Dollars 300m a year on market prices. In return, Jordan supplies Iraq with a variety of goods. No money changes hands, but the barter accounts for about one-third of Jordan's exports and thousands of livelihoods depend on it.

Last week the Foreign Office confirmed that Security Council members were holding talks with Jordan about compensating it for any losses caused by "smart" sanctions. (Guardian, 26 June)

27 June

The United Nations Security Council appears to have reached an impasse over sanctions on Iraq, less than a week before the current policy is due to expire. Russia has introduced a draft resolution to suspend the sanctions altogether, but the United States and United Kingdom have dismissed this unacceptable.

That proposal-for targeted measures known as "smart sanctions"-would ease restrictions on civilian goods while retaining the military embargo on Iraq. Russia, Iraq's closest ally on the council, has argued instead that the UN should move towards ending the sanctions, imposed after Iraq's 1990 invasion of Kuwait. Russian Deputy Foreign Minister Sergei

Ordzhonikidze said that Russia was "seriously worried that the so-called smart sanctions may negatively affect the legitimate economic interests of many countries, including Russia."

Before 1990, Russia supplied Baghdad with weaponry worth billions of dollars which was to be paid for in oil. Correspondents say its only hope of seeing at least some of that debt repaid is if sanctions are lifted and Russian firms are allowed to invest in Iraqi oil-fields. (BBC, 27 June)

28 June

Russia yesterday threatened to wield its veto in the United Nations to torpedo US and British plans to introduce a new "smart sanctions" regime against Iraq. The Russian Foreign Ministry Igor Ivanov writing a letter to the US secretary of state, Colin Powell, detailing its objection. He told Mr Powell that Russia would be damaging its own commercial links with Baghdad if it gave the green light to the smart sanctions. (Guardian, 28 June)

29 June

Russia, one of five permanent council members with veto power, has rejected the plan and wants to speed up steps towards suspending the sanctions, arguing the new resolution only tightens the embargoes. Council members must renew the oil-for-food programme by Tuesday. If Russia maintains its objections, the council is expected to extend current program but it is not known for how long. Iraq suspended oil sales on June 4 to protest a British-drafted resolution on the overhaul of sanctions. (Reuters, 29 June)

Ivory Coast

23 July

Authorities said that voting on a new constitution that would begin to return the Western African country to civilian rule would be extended into a second day, citing a lack of ballots and other organisational problems. All major political parties have called for the constitution to be approved, but clauses that set the eligibility criteria for presidential candidates have stirred controversy. Ivory Coast faces increasing military unrest, a battered economy and fears that things could get worse. (WP, 24 July, p. A18)

Kosovo

3 September

Thirteen Serbs, most of them charged with war crimes, escaped from prison on Saturday night, and NATO peacekeepers and United Nations police spent most of today looking for them. The escape was the fifth this year by prisoners in the city of Mitrovica, near the border with the rest of Serbia. Officials in Kosovo's UN-administration conceded that the escapes are an embarrassment that could further erode their credibility among the people in Kosovo. The fugitives escaped by overpowering a United Nations police guard who had accompanied a prisoner back to his cell after a phone call, the UN said. Several prisoners attacked the guard, hitting him over the head with a pistol they had smuggled in. Fifteen prisoners escaped, but peacekeepers recaptured two in prison grounds soon after the breakout. Three of the escapees were being held on genocide charges and four for other crimes linked to the war between Serbs and members of Kosovo's ethnic Albanian majority. Four more were accused of mass murder, one of murder and one of arson and theft. (NYT, 4 September, p. A7)

15 September
NATO peacekeeping troops in Kosovo fought street battles with supporters of Slobodan Milosevic, the Yugoslav President, after they attacked his main election challenger during campaigning in northern Kosovo yesterday. In extraordinary scenes Vojislav Kostunica, who leads a coalition of 18 Serbian opposition parties currently leading the polls for elections on 24 September, was pelted with rotten tomatoes and bottles and was struck on the head by a stone. He had been campaigning in the ethnically divided northern Kosovan town of Mitrovica when a hail of stones and rotten vegetables disrupted his campaign speech. French NATO troops clashed briefly with Milosevic supporters. Eight people were treated for injuries after the violence. (TI, 15 September, p. 13)

19 September
British troops reported that they had foiled a plot by Serb special forces to launch bomb attacks in Kosovo during the forthcoming elections. Six Serbs were arrested at a house in Gracanica in the first evidence of a conspiracy to provoke unrest in Kosovo in the run-up to the Yugoslav presidential elections on Sunday. The counter-terrorist operation involved NATO troops from The Prince of Wales's Royal Regiment, elements of a Swedish battalion, a Royal Engineers "bomb search" unit, Royal Military Police and United Nations police. In all, 300 military and police personnel took part. The six Serbs had been under surveillance for days. The British and Swedish troops found plastic explosives, detonators, timers, a machine pistol and an automatic rifle hidden in the house and at two other addresses, including a bar. British sources said the leader of the Serb plotters, said to be connected to the VJ, the Yugoslav Army, admitted that they had been sent to Kosovo to target members of the UN, which administers the province, and representatives of the Organisation for Security and Co-operation in Europe (OSCE). The OSCE will be monitoring the municipal elections. (TT, 20 September)

23 September
The people of Yugoslavia, battered by a decade of ethnic war and international sanctions, will attempt tomorrow to choose a president for a four-year term in a vote the United States and its allies are watching in nervous suspense. The country has never had a directly elected president, and by all accounts, this first such vote will be an extraordinary political cliff-hanger. Voting will not be independently monitored, and both the government and the opposition have warned of cheating. As a result, neither President Slobodan Milosevic nor his chief challenger, Vojislav Kostunica, may be able to convincingly claim victory. (WP, 24 September, p. A30)

28 September
Once again the American Congress is trying to legislate an end to American military involvement in Kosovo. A conference committee is considering a House bill that would force the withdrawal of all 6,000 U.S. troops now in Kosovo starting next April unless the president certifies that the European allies are providing the bulk of the troops and paying almost all of the cost. Gov. George W. Bush opposes this Republican-sponsored

bill – but only on the narrow grounds that it interferes with a president's prerogatives. At the same time, his own repeated statements – and those of his running mate, Dick Cheney – leave little doubt that the Republican presidential ticket shares the views of the bill's sponsors: Not only should Europe do more but U.S. troops should leave the Balkans – albeit in an "orderly" fashion – since their presence serves no American interests. (WP, 28 September, p. A31)

3 October

Once again the U.S. Congress is trying to legislate an end to American military involvement in Kosovo. A conference committee is considering a House bill that would force the withdrawal of all 6,000 U.S. troops now in Kosovo starting next April unless the president certifies that European allies are providing the bulk of the troops and paying almost all the cost. George W. Bush opposes this Republican-sponsored bill, but only on the narrow grounds that it interferes with a president's prerogatives. At the same time, his own repeated statements leave little doubt that the Republican presidential ticket shares the views of the bill's sponsors: Not only should Europe do more, but U.S. troops should leave the Balkans (albeit in an "orderly" fashion) since their presence serves no American interests. (WP, 4 October, p.8)

12 October

A Bosnian Serb war-crimes suspect detonated a hand grenade and killed himself today as peacekeepers tried to arrest him. Four German soldiers were wounded in the explosion, two of them seriously. A spokesman for the German Defence Ministry said their condition was not considered life threatening. NATO-led peacekeeping troops swept into Foca late Thursday to arrest the suspect, Janko Janjic, 43, who had been indicted on charges of crimes against humanity, including torture and rape, by the United Nations war crimes tribunal in The Hague. "During the course of the arrest, Janjic detonated a hand grenade, which killed him," a NATO statement said. (NYT, 14 October, p. A4)

17 October

For the first time in history an international tribunal issued a subpoena to NATO, ordering the military alliance to disclose how it detained a Bosnian Serb war crimes suspect, who says he was abducted illegally by mercenaries. The UN International Criminal Tribunal for the Former Yugoslavia also summoned an U.S. commander, Army Chief of Staff Gen. Eric Shinseki, to provide evidence on the Sept. 27, 1998, detention of Stevan Todorovic. Shinseki is former commander of U.S. peacekeepers in Bosnia. NATO and the 33 countries it leads in a peacekeeping force were ordered to disclose all documents, reports and audio and videotapes on the detention by Nov. 17. Todorovic claims his arrest took place on Serbian soil outside the mandate of the NATO-led Stabilisation Force for Bosnia. Todorovic, a former police chief in Bosanski Samac in northern Bosnia during the 1992-95 ethnic war, was in charge of detention camps where Muslims and Croats were beaten, tortured, raped and killed on a daily basis, according to his indictment. He is charged with torture, murder and deportation as war crimes and crimes against humanity. The NATO subpoena marked the first time the tribunal, established in 1993 by the UN Security Council, issued a binding order to the U.S.-led military alliance to hand over information. (WP, 21 October, p. A18)

19 October
Bosnian Serb students blocked U.S. peacekeepers from patrolling through the ethnically tense town of Brcko and pelted their vehicles with eggs in a third day of protests demanding that Muslims leave. More than 1,000 young Bosnian Serbs gathered in the centre of town, chanting the name of indicted war crimes suspect Radovan Karadzic and cursing Bosnian Muslims. Protests began Tuesday after a group of Bosnian Serb students beat up a Bosnian Muslim student last week. Serbian and Muslim students share high school buildings but attend classes in separate shifts. After the beating, Muslims demanded better security and the Bosnian Serbs began agitating for separate schools. A multinational unit of riot police, commanded by the NATO peacekeeping force, was sent into town after local police appeared to have lost control. (WP, 20 October, p. A28)

24 October
Unidentified attackers fired a rocket-propelled grenade tonight at the last Serbian community remaining in Pristina, the capital of the Serbian province, the NATO-led peacekeeping force said. There were no reports of injuries. Kosovo's Serbian minority has been a frequent target of ethnic attacks since the arrival in the province of the NATO-led peacekeeping force in June last year. Hundreds have been killed or injured and about 170,000 have fled the province, according to the United Nations high commissioner for refugees. About 40,000 Serbs fled Pristina, leaving a few hundred living mainly in the apartment block that was attacked tonight. (NYT, 24 October, p. A7)

25 October
Some or all of the more than 900 ethnic Albanians from Kosovo imprisoned in Serbia for more than a year may be released in coming weeks, according to Yugoslav officials. The sources said that President Vojislav Kostunica planned to propose a general amnesty for ethnic Albanians accused of illegal involvement in the Kosovo war in 1999. He would then seek Parliament's approval of the measure, possibly as early as late next week. Most of the ethnic Albanian prisoners are young men who were arrested as the Belgrade government of President Slobodan Milosevic tried to purge Kosovo of its ethnic Albanian majority – a campaign that triggered the 11-week NATO air campaign against Serbian targets. (IHT, 26 October)

28 October
Kosovo's ethnic Albanians vote today in the war-torn province's first democratic elections. The party led by Ibrahim Rugova, a moderate separatist intellectual, is expected to win, setting the stage for potential violence by his hard-line opponents. British Royal Marine peacekeeping troops stepped up patrols in the bomb-scarred streets of Pristina, the provincial capital, to provide security for electors as an emotional 45-day campaign for the polls to elect councillors in 30 municipalities ended yesterday. The run-up to the contest, in which 5,441 candidates are competing for 920 assembly seats, has been peaceful, but tension in the province is expected to escalate if Mr Rugova's Democratic League of Kosovo (LDK) defeats the Democratic Party of Kosovo (PDK) led by Hashim Thaci, the 31-year-old former Kosovo Liberation Army strongman. Mr Thaci's supporters dominate the local governments appointed by the UN interim administration that have run the province since the NATO bombing of Yugoslavia. Both main parties contesting the election call for Kosovo to become an independent state, but Mr Rugova's party will probably draw the majority of votes from many of the 901,000 registered voters because of his aristocratic background – from a family that ruled much of central Kosovo for genera-

tions – diplomatic sources say. Britain's 3,000 troops in Kosovo have been reinforced by an extra battalion, to be held in reserve in case trouble breaks out. "We appreciate that there is the possibility that the situation could become enflamed," Lieutenant Nick Mansfield, of KFOR, said.
(TT, 28 October)

30 October
The moderate Kosovo Albanian leader, Ibrahim Rugova, claimed victory for his party today in Kosovo's first post-war elections, saying that unofficial results from the election on Saturday showed that the party had won more than 60 percent of the vote in municipalities across the province. The more militant parties, formed by members of the armed rebel force, the Kosovo Liberation Army, appeared to have fared poorly except in a few areas. If the results hold, it is a sign that Kosovo Albanians have opted for peace and stability and largely rejected the thuggery of some of the people who assumed power after the war last year. Votes were still being counted through the day, and official results were not expected until Monday. But political parties and independent monitoring groups disclosed their calculations. The results from an independent monitoring group, as well as from Mr. Rugova's party, the Democratic League of Kosovo, indicated that the party had won broadly, in particular in all the major towns. The small remaining population of Serbs in Kosovo overwhelmingly boycotted the elections. Today they said the vote was illegal because only the Albanians voted. President Kostunica of Yugoslavia said that he could not recognise the elections and called for the full application of UN Security Resolution 1244, which says Kosovo is an integral part of Yugoslavia. (NYT, 30 October, p. 6)

31 October
Ibrahim Rugova, the Kosovo Albanian who led his people on a 10-year campaign of peaceful protest for independence from Serbia, was confirmed today as the winner of the elections held on Saturday. His party won 21 of 27 contested municipalities. With close to 90 percent of votes counted, international election organisers released preliminary results showing Mr. Rugova's party, the Democratic League of Kosovo, with 58 percent of the votes and the former guerrilla leader Hashim Thaci with 27 percent. Mr. Thaci, who was political leader of the Kosovo Liberation Army before he turned to politics last year after the NATO bombing campaign to drive Serbian forces from the province, won six municipalities. Another rebel commander, Ramush Haradinaj, took about 7 percent. Turnout was close to 80 percent; three municipalities in northern Kosovo populated only by Serbs did not take part in the elections. (NYT, 31 October, p. 5)

2 November
Flora Brovina, a prominent doctor, poet and activist for Kosovo Albanians, was freed from a Serbian prison today by a special pardon from the new Yugoslav president. She was sentenced to 12 years in a Serbian court last year on charges of conspiring to commit terrorism and aiding the rebel force, the Kosovo Liberation Army. She was one of 2,000 Albanian detainees transferred from Kosovo when Serbian forces withdrew and NATO-led peacekeeping troops took control of Kosovo after the war ended in June 1999. Over half have been gradually released, and the return of the remaining 818 has become an urgent concern for the United Nations officials running Kosovo, who say the prisoners are an obstacle to the reconciliation of Serbs and Albanians. Bernard Kouchner, head of the United Nations administration in Kosovo, welcomed Dr. Brovina's release and praised

Mr. Kostunica for making a "crucial step toward healing the wounds that exist between Serb and Albanian communities." (NYT, 2 November, p. A13)

22 November

Belgrade gave warning today that it could be on the verge of a "large scale war" with Kosovo, after suspected ethnic Albanian rebels carried out a two-pronged attack on Serb targets, leaving half a dozen people dead. In the most serious outbreak of fighting since moderates replaced the Milosevic regime in September, hundreds of ethnic Albanian separatist guerrillas reportedly crossed the administrative border from Kosovo and raided police units. Hours later in Pristina, capital of the province, a building used by the Yugoslav representative was ripped apart by a huge bomb explosion. NATO's KFOR peacekeeping force said that one man had been killed in the early morning attack and two injured. Lieutenant-General Carlo Cabigiosu, the KFOR commander, said that more NATO troops would be put on street patrol to deter further actions. Zoran Djindjic, a moderate in the newly elected Government of President Kostunica, said that the guerrillas had surrounded scores of policemen. He said the situation was so serious that the special police – earlier accused of war crimes in Kosovo – should be brought back to help restore security. "Those are big clashes," Mr Djindjic said, claiming that the Albanians were armed with mortars and other heavy weapons. "This could lead to a large-scale war ... We are warning the international community that if it tolerates this, there could be another flashpoint in the Balkans." He said that the rebels were operating in the three-mile demilitarised zone along the administrative border, from which Serb troops are barred. (TT, 23 November)

24 November

Following the escalation of violence, including attacks on Serbian targets in Kosovo and southern Serbia, Bernard Kouchner, the head of Kosovo's UN administration expressed concern in a statement, reading in part: "As I have repeatedly said, Kosovo remains in crisis. The conflict between the two communities is not over." The warnings of war risks came after a bomb exploded in Pristina on Tuesday night, half demolishing the home of the Serbian representative in Kosovo, killing one man and injuring several others. (IHT, 24 November, p. 5)

27 November

NATO and the Yugoslav Army (VJ), which were at war 17 months ago, may begin joint patrols in the buffer zone between Kosovo and Serbia to stop anti-Serb attacks by heavily armed ethnic Albanian "guerrillas". The idea of joint KFOR/VJ patrols inside the five-kilometre (three-mile) demilitarised zone around Kosovo is expected to be among a number of drastic measures to be studied by NATO ambassadors. They hope to prevent a breakdown in the June 1999 agreement with Belgrade, which ended the alliance's bombing campaign and led to KFOR's entry into the province as a peacekeeping force. Any move towards a joint patrolling arrangement would underline NATO's growing anxiety about the attacks launched from within the security zone across the border into southern Serbia. In addition, they would reflect the alliance's determination to meet the concerns expressed by Yugoslavia's President Kostunica. On a visit to Vienna, which he cut short to return home, Mr. Kostunica gave warning of the risk of the whole region being "set ablaze". Addressing foreign ministers of the 55-member Organisation for Security and Co-operation in Europe (OSCE), Mr. Kostunica said that Kosovo was Europe's most critical issue. Later he said it was "crystal clear" that NATO and the UN, which is administering Kosovo, had "failed to do their job properly". (TT, 28 November)

27 November
The flow of ethnic Albanian refugees from south-eastern Serbia to Kosovo threatened to turn into another Balkan exodus today as thousands fled the battlefront between Kosovan guerrillas and Serb police in the Presevo Valley. "Only today 180 cars full of people crossed from Serbia into Kosovo at the Mucbabe checkpoint alone and they are still coming," an official of the UNHCR, the United Nations refugee agency, said. More than 2,000 villagers have crossed into Kosovo from Presevo since the start of the week. The announcement yesterday that American peace-keeping troops from KFOR had persuaded the guerrillas to extend until Friday an uneasy truce has done little to reassure refugees, who say they have been suffering increasing harassment and intimidation from Serb police in recent weeks. The UNHCR said that it can cope with the scale of the exodus so far. "We were prepared for it," one official said. (TT, 28 November)

6 December
A UN envoy has urged the Serbian government and the NATO-led peacekeeping force in Kosovo to act fast to prevent tensions from worsening on the Kosovo boundary. Eric Morris, who represents the United Nations High Commissioner for Refugees in Serbia, Montenegro and Kosovo, spoke on his return from the Presevo Valley in southern Serbia. Albanian militants attacked the Serbian police there last month and seized control of a five-kilometre-wide (three-mile-wide) zone along Kosovo's eastern boundary. "It is urgent that all the concerned parties, including the Yugoslav government, act as quickly as possible so that the Presevo region does not get out of hand," Mr. Morris said in Belgrade, "because the consequences are potentially very, very great." (IHT, 6 December, p. 6)

12 December
A Serbian regional court found nine men guilty today of kidnapping a war crimes suspect in Serbia who was later handed over to NATO peacekeepers in Bosnia, the Beta news agency of Serbia said. The court in the central town of Uzice convicted the men for kidnapping for money Stevan Todorovic, who was taken from Bosnia to the United Nations war crimes tribunal at The Hague in September 1998. The reputed leader of the group, Ignjatije Popovic, was tried in absentia and sentenced to seven years in prison. Others present at the trial received from one and a half to eight and a half years. The war crimes tribunal has asked the NATO-led peacekeeping force in Bosnia for details of the arrest after Mr. Todorovic said mercenaries in Serbia had captured him. In 1995, the tribunal indicted Mr. Todorovic, former police chief in the Bosnian town of Bosanski Samac, and five other men accused of orchestrating a campaign to "ethnically cleanse" the town during the 1992-1995 Bosnian war. A United Nations spokeswoman said at the time of the arrest that Mr. Todorovic was in Bosnia when he was detained. (NYT, 12 December, p. A15)

17 December
Angry Serbs demonstrated in Leposavic, Kosovo, yesterday after Belgian peacekeeping troops shot and killed a Serb in an incident that could strengthen support for Slobodan Milosevic in this week's Serbian elections (John Phillips writes). The protest passed off

peacefully but tension is high. Belgrade claimed that thousands of ethnic Albanian guerrillas are about to mount an offensive inside Serbia. (TT, 18 December)

19 December
The Yugoslav government is urging NATO to let Belgrade's military and police forces move more freely in a security zone that borders Kosovo, to beat back Albanian militants, President Vojislav Kostunica said today. Belgrade has proposed renegotiating the military agreement that ended the 1999 Kosovo war to narrow the three-mile-wide security zone, where the Albanian militants operate with near impunity. The Yugoslav Army and NATO forces are not allowed in the zone, which is in Serbia. With crucial elections for a new Serbian government less than a week away, Mr. Kostunica and his allies are under domestic pressure to react with force against Albanian militants, connected to the former Kosovo Liberation Army, who are conducting attacks in southern Serbia. Mr. Kostunica has heeded Western calls to respond with patience and not violate the zone that separates the Yugoslav Army from the NATO-led peacekeeping force in Kosovo. Just the Serbian police, with light weapons, may enter the zone, and they have been attacked by an Albanian militia called the Liberation Army of Presevo, Medvedja and Bujanovac, three heavily Albanian towns in Serbia that the militants want to annex to Kosovo. (NYT, 19 December, p. A13)

21 December
A Yugoslav military court today ordered three soldiers jailed for more than four years each for the murder of an elderly ethnic Albanian couple in their home in Kosovo. The verdict marked the first official confirmation by the Yugoslav army of its soldiers' involvement in an atrocity during the 1999 war in Kosovo. The panel rendered its verdict after hearing evidence that two of the accused had carried out an order by the third to execute the couple after they refused to evacuate a Kosovo farming village. The verdict comes as a growing number of Yugoslav courts are demonstrating their independence from the policies of the government of former president Slobodan Milosevic, who waged the Kosovo war, lost an election in September and was ousted from power by Serbian demonstrators in October. (WP, 21 December, p. A40)

21 December
In a meeting signalling increased co-operation between NATO and Belgrade against ethnic Albanian insurgents operating along the Kosovo border, the commander of the NATO-led peacekeeping force in Kosovo crossed into Yugoslavia today to meet a senior political leader. Lt. Gen. Carlo Cabigiosu travelled to the town of Bujanovac to talk to Nebojsa Covic, the deputy Prime Minister of Serbia, Yugoslavia's dominant republic, about the security situation in a three-mile neutral zone that separates the two sides. Since January, a growing guerrilla group supplied from Kosovo – now under UN administration – has pressed attacks on Serbian forces in the zone, exploiting a truce Belgrade signed with NATO last year that permits only lightly armed Serbian police to enter the area. "The meeting was constructive, and I am encouraged by the discussion," Cabigiosu said in a statement released by the peacekeeping force after the first public meeting at this level on the issue. "I believe it is possible to find a peaceful solution to this problem, and this meeting was a step in the right direction." The meeting came as the new Yugoslav government of Vojislav Kostunica called for renegotiation of the agreement that ended last year's Kosovo war – which included a 78-day NATO air assault on Yugoslavia and

was followed by NATO-led occupation of the province. Kostunica said Tuesday that the Kosovo buffer zone should be narrowed to about one mile to allow his country's forces to "cleanse" the area of insurgents. NATO and Western governments remain opposed to that option because they believe it would inflame opinion among Kosovo Albanians. Meanwhile, the peacekeepers have been attempting to curtail guerrilla activity by sealing the border area. (WP, 21 December, p. A40)

8 January

NATO warned countries with armies and aid workers in the Balkans months ago about the possible dangers of depleted uranium ammunition, which recently sparked concern as a possible cause of serious illnesses in soldiers who served there. Defence Ministry documents obtained by the Berliner Morgenpost newspaper said NATO warned soldiers and aid workers in July 1999 of a "possible toxic threat" and advised them to take "preventative measures." The ministry said it began health checks on soldiers who had come into possible contact with the ammunition that same month. Despite that, the document said NATO planned no further steps, according to the newspaper. The Defence Ministry said it immediately responded with orders on how soldiers should behave in areas that were targeted with depleted uranium. The renewed concerns over depleted uranium arose in December, after Italy announced an investigation into illnesses suffered by 30 soldiers who served in the region. Twelve had cancer, and five had died of leukaemia. Other countries with troops in the Balkans have since launched testing programs. The head of the UN Environment Program criticized NATO for not being more forthcoming about where it used the ammunition. (WP, 8 January, p. A15)

11 January

Facing a public outcry in Europe about the use of depleted-uranium munitions in Kosovo in 1999, NATO offered full co-operation today with all investigations into the weapons' health consequences for Western peacekeepers in the province. NATO Secretary General Robertson said the alliance had "nothing to hide and everything to share" in seeking to reassure troops and civilians that there were no serious health hazards from the uranium-tipped shells that U.S. planes fired at Yugoslav tanks and other targets during the 78-day air war. NATO's decision for an information offensive was reached at a meeting today by ambassador of NATO's 19 member states. Depleted uranium is used to tip anti-tank shells because its high density and hardness give the weapons a special ability to punch through heavy armour. NATO contends they are crucial to its military readiness. But the discovery of several cancer cases and other ailments among returning European veterans of NATO peacekeeping forces in the Balkans has stirred a political uproar that has defied arguments of medical scientist, who say health risks posed by the weapons are minimal. Robertson conceded that NATO had been slow to provide the information because of what he described as "bureaucratic delays." But he insisted the alliance was determined to be more forthcoming in dealing with the controversy. (WP, 11 January, p. A21)

18 January

As the commander of a United States Army tank company, Capt. Joseph Cantello has trained hard for armoured warfare. These days he is trying to coax wary Serbs and Albanians to agree that they would go to a school where their children will study under one roof, though in separate classrooms. George W. Bush and his aides complained in his presidential campaign that Balkan peacekeeping diverted the military from its primer task of preparing to fight the nation's wars and degraded necessary skills. But a trip across Kosovo provides a different impression of America's role. Most of the scores of American officers and senior commanders interviewed for this article said they believed their mission was important. Many insist that their work in Kosovo is making them better soldiers. Kosovo is a good test case of the effects that peacekeeping is having on American military. With a doctrine that requires that requires the military to prepare for two nearly simultaneous regional wars, the armed forces have plenty to do even without peacekeeping. Critics have portrayed peacekeeping as a poor substitute for intensive combat training at the vast ranges that the Army has established in Europe and the United States. Some troops in Kosovo agree, saying they are soldiers, and not police officers. But others stress that the mission is far more varied than many critics recognise, taking a view that is widely shared by their European NATO counterparts. Peacekeeping in Kosovo not only means staffing checkpoints and escorting Serbian civilians to markets and so on in Albanian areas. It also involves armed patrols along the rugged boundary with Serbia, actions that are intended to stop the flow of arms, food and supplies to Albanian insurgents, who operate in a three-mile strip of Serbian territory that adjoins Kosovo and where Serbian armed forces are banned by the agreement that ended the Kosovo conflict in 1999. Most of the effort, of course, is directed at more traditional peacekeeping, for which the troops received months of training. Even so, soldiers say, their duties provide good experience for intelligence officers, medical and logistical personnel, communications specialists and civil affairs units, all helping restore basic services. With the ambitious training regimen and a steady series of overseas deployments, there has also been concern that extended time away from families will prompt many young soldiers to conclude that the Army life is not for them. So far, that problem seems to be under control here, at least in terms of re-enlistment rates. Maintaining the peace in Pones might seem more like police work than a military mission. But the United Nations police force, made up of personnel from more than 50 nations, is too weak to control Kosovo, and the nascent Kosovo police are inexperienced and untested. The platoon of heavily equipped American soldiers, based in the town, seems to enjoy the most trust. The theory is that Americans will provide the security and space to enable the Kosovars to do more for themselves – and, ultimately, allow the Americans and other international forces to leave Kosovo. But those days are clearly not yet at hand. To build ties between the Serbian and Albanian communities, the Army is promoting plans for the new school that Serbian and Albanian children would attend. The project would be paid by non-military budgets. The Serbs in Pones have balked, saying the Albanians may squeeze them out after the school has been constructed. But the soldiers have not given up. Sgt. Kevin Gleason, 33, has invited the Serbian and Albanian leaders to a new meeting to break the logjam. The place: the American Army platoon's base in Pones. (NYT, 18 January, p. A-8)

21 January
A year ago, just across the boundary line from Kosovo into the rest of Serbia, a ragtag group of about 40 ethnic Albanian guerrillas was just beginning its fight to defend and annex parts of Serbia it would like to attach to an independent Kosovo. The new insurgent force, named the Liberation Army of Presevo, Medvedja and Bujanovac, has the respect of the majority Albanian population in their area of Serbia. It has close ties to the former Kosovo Liberation Army, the rebel group, and increasingly widespread if still shallow support inside Kosovo itself. Commanders of the peacekeeping force insist that interception of their supplies and capture of close to 10 percent of their members have hurt the guerrillas by the peacekeepers. But some senior United Nations officials are not

so sure that the insurgent force – known by its Albanian initials U.C.P.M.B. – is doing anything more than lying low for now. The insurgents have taken advantage of the military agreement negotiated at the end of the 1999 NATO bombing war against Yugoslavia. To separate NATO forces from the Yugoslav Army, Belgrade agreed to a three-mile-wide "ground safety zone," bordering Kosovo but inside Serbia, from which all Serbian forces are banned, except police officers with light weapons. The new insurgency, feeding off the majority Albanian population in the area, used the freedom of the zone to organize, bring in or dig up weapons and stage attacks against the Serbian police. While Slobodan Milosevic was in power in Belgrade, the West did not much care about another irritant to him and his forces in southern Serbia, senior diplomats and military officials concede. But with Mr. Milosevic's ouster and the election of Vojislav Kostunica as Yugoslav president and of his democratic coalition as the new government of Serbia, the insurgent force has become a source of grave concern to both the peacekeepers and to the new Belgrade leadership. The Yugoslav leaders are being criticized for not defending Serbian territory. The ascent of Mr. Kostunica was a painful surprise to Kosovo Albanians, who saw Mr. Milosevic as their best chance to get Western support for Kosovo's independence. A surge in violence in November by the insurgents, in which four Serbian policemen died, is widely interpreted as an effort to get Mr. Kostunica to overreact militarily and to harm his new relations with the West. In fact, the insurgency has helped bring Mr. Kostunica's government and the West closer, leading to formal and informal talks between the peacekeepers, the United Nations and Belgrade that would have been unthinkable before Mr. Milosevic fell. That relationship has further upset people in Kosovo and made the insurgent force all the more symbolic as an instrument of Albanian aspirations. Mr. Kostunica has sharply criticized the peacekeepers for not doing more to stop the insurgency and has called for the zone between Kosovo and Serbia proper to be reduced to just over a mile, or less, to allow Serbian forces more leeway. But that decision is up to NATO, and could turn angry Kosovo Albanians against the peacekeepers. If the fall of Mr. Milosevic has given the West more incentive to consider Serbian grievances and to help Belgrade, to consolidate and preserve democracy there, it has also given Belgrade more incentive to co-operate with the United Nations and the West over interim arrangements in Kosovo. (NYT, 21 January, p.1-10)

1 February
Eighteen months after NATO kicked out Serbian authority in Pristina, the issue of when to hold the first province-wide elections is highlighting some of the most fundamental difficulties in running Kosovo, from ethnic violence to organized crime. The largest problems for the new United Nations administrator, Hans Haekkerup, are the timing of the elections and how to entice Kosovar Serbs to take part. With democratic changes in Belgrade, pressure from the Albanian majority in Kosovo has been growing, to move more quickly toward self-rule, via province-wide elections for a new legislative assembly. First Mr, Haekkerup wants to establish what kind of assembly (with what powers), the vote will be for. That decision could take months and must at least be discussed with Serbs and Albanians, and agreed upon by key members of the United Nations Security Council. Serbs boycotted the October municipal ballot, but participation is essential for the elections to be considered legitimate. Some political encouragement may come from the new authorities in Belgrade, where Mr. Haekkerup will open an office. To secure that help, however, he and the NATO-led peacekeepers need to devise a fairly specific plan for the return home of some of the more than 100,000 Kosovar Serbs who fled the province. The new Yugoslav president, Vojislav Kostunica, says

Serbs should return in large numbers, for their safety, but the United Nations refugee agency and NATO's generals have concluded that the numbers should be smaller and less obtrusive, to avoid protests and attacks by Albanians. Everyone agrees that Serbs should return to Serb enclaves, a move that belies the goal of a multiethnic Kosovo but should provide better protection. Mr. Haekkerup has also said that he intends to confront organized crime and the failures of a judicial system in which witnesses and judges are easily intimidated, and in which only the few international judges and prosecutors have been willing to charge or convict ethnic Albanians. An internal United Nations document given to The New York Times by international officials argues for the pressing need to restore order and stability, even if Western standards of human rights are diluted in a post-war situation where the courts work badly. The issue is a live one for the peacekeeping force as well, which has jailed members and suspected members of an armed Albanian group based in Serbia on fuzzy legal grounds stemming from the authority of the military commander of the force. A struggle also exists between those who want quick elections and those who want perfect ones. The Europeans tend to favour a later vote, for fear of what one European official called "the domino effect" of a legislature. A new assembly would push for legislative powers and might call for Kosovo's independence, or start drafting a constitution – a symbolic but potentially embarrassing gesture. But the democratically elected politicians in power in Belgrade also need an interlocutor to discuss Kosovo's future, and until the province holds elections, no Albanian will have enough political legitimacy. (NYT, 1 February, p. A-7)

1 February
The commander of the peacekeeping forces in Kosovo ordered extra troops and two special police units into the divided town of Mitrovica in northern Kosovo as violence continued for a third day. Grenades wounded eleven French soldiers and several ethnic Albanian demonstrators as Albanians protested the death of a 15-year-old on Monday. (NYT, 1 February, p. A-6)

3 February
A new dilemma for the United States as it tries to keep peace in the Balkans; there's a new dangerous insurgency in a nearby region of Serbia. 60 people of being rebels are jailed at the Bondsteel Detention Facility. The Army says the detentions are necessary to contain the rebellion at Kosovo's doorstep. But after 18 months of preaching respect for the rule of law if Kosovo is to become a democracy, the American military now finds itself in the uncomfortable position of detaining Albanian prisoners who have virtually no legal rights. When the Army was sent to Kosovo as part of an international force, nobody expected that it would end up running a jail for rebels. But the equation was changed by the Albanian insurgency that emerged last year in a strip of Serbian territory outside Kosovo, the province of Serbia inhabited mostly by Albanians. Fearful that the rebellion might destabilize the Balkan region, peacekeepers began seizing shipments of arms intended for the rebels. Trying to contain the insurgency, the peacekeepers have detained suspected members of a rebel group who have ventured back and forth across Kosovo's boundary. The group, the Liberation Army of Presevo, Medvedja and Bujanovac, is known by its initials in Albanian as the U.C.P.M.B. The crowd of prisoners at the Bondsteel Detention Facility is one result. As many as 16 inmates live together in small, windowless wooden bungalows, each of which is surrounded by a wire mesh fence. There is little room for exercise, and the prisoners amuse themselves by smoking, talking and playing chess. American and British officers say they are acting under the authority of United Nations Security Council Resolution 1244, which authorizes the

peacekeeping force to provide a safe and secure environment. Given the peacekeepers' energetic effort to patrol the border, the 530th Military Police Company has contingency plans to expand the detention center. "We are reluctant to be releasing anyone right now knowing that they may go right back across the border and pick up where the left off," Colonel Gross said. "The quandary is that we are holding them based on some intelligence and perhaps not based on judicial evidence that would go forward in a court of law. That flat-out is the truth." (NYT, 3 February, p. A-4)

11 February
The West has been hard to ignore in Kosovo since NATO bombing halted Slobodan Milosevic's Serbian campaign to subjugate Kosovar Albanians 18 months ago. Between the NATO peacekeeping troops, the United Nations-run government and police force and the numerous non-governmental agencies at work in this Yugoslav province, about 60,000 foreigners live here now. But beyond providing a chance to meet people from countries Kosovo's youth could once only experience by tuning in the BBC, the Voice of America or German satellite television, the Western presence has given young people an unprecedented amount of freedom. Before the war, during a 10-year crackdown on the culture of this overwhelmingly Albanian province, teenagers would generally stay in at night because there wasn't much to do, and the Serbian police would harass them if they did venture out. Now, however, young people are asserting their independence. Teenagers and 20-somethings are also producing plays, publishing magazines and mounting art shows. But music seems to be their main passion. Western rap and rock music – readily available on counterfeit CD's for about $2.30 a pop – has inspired a home grown music scene drenched in a kind of American street sensibility. Many young people flock to Pristina's discos and bars, where there are no age restrictions. Alcohol and drug use has increased, according to those who work with Kosovar youth. Greater availability accounts for part of the upsurge, as does the sheer number of young people in Kosovo: 50 percent of Kosovo's population of 2.3 million is under the age of 25. Impending changes in education, work and politics – all reflecting Western approaches – have young people keenly aware that their homeland is in transition. Among the measures taken to help Kosovo's youth recover from the war are the creation of nearly 300 youth centres and youth associations since the war. Much of the funding – an estimated $6 million – has come from the United Nations and such organisations as the International Rescue Committee and the International Medical Corps. Kosovo's education system still reflects the rigid curriculum favoured in the rest of Yugoslavia, a system that, according to the Ministry of Education, rewards memorization, recitation and ideology, not creativity or imagination. But the World Bank estimates that nearly 29,000 teachers need to be retrained and nearly half of the 800 school buildings need reconstruction and repairs. Kosovo's economy remains at a near standstill. With an unemployment rate estimated by the Ministry of Labour and Employment to fluctuate between 60 percent and 80 percent, young people are wondering what to do with their lives while such industries as textiles, agriculture and mining recover from the war or long-term neglect, even as they are bracing themselves for the introduction of a market economy. The fear is that before jobs appear, many youths will be recruited by organized crime, or leave for work in the West and not return. As for how Kosovo's youth will face the future, perhaps a concert poster pasted up all over Pristina a few months ago provided a clue – or at least a wish. Alongside the show's date and location were the words: "Love Your Present, Create Your Future." (NYT, 11 February, p. 4-3)

17 February
A roadside bomb blew apart a bus in north-eastern Kosovo, which killed seven Serbs and more than 40 were injured. The attack was interpreted by Serbian leaders as a sign that extremists among Kosovo's Albanian majority would resist any move to disband armed Albanian insurgents who have taken control of a zone of southern Serbia. The assault today also hinted at more trouble for Kosovo' peacekeepers. Almost immediately, Serbs in Gracanica, a village just south of Kosovo' capital, Pristina, retaliated by blocking a main road and burning at least one car belonging to the United Nations mission, which has administered the province since the NATO war against Yugoslavia ended in June 1999. Bracing the NATO for further violence, Lord Robertson, the secretary general of NATO, extended sympathy to the families of the victims and expressed "hock and outrage at this disgraceful and cowardly incident." Serbian leaders linked the attack to opponents of the government's proposals, presented this week, to bring peace to the tense Presevo region of southern Serbia, where Albanian rebels have taken advantage of the agreement ending the Kosovo war to assert control of an area from which NATO had barred Serbian troops. At the news of the violence, legislators in the Yugoslav Parliament interrupted a debate on an amnesty law that had promised to free hundreds of Albanian prisoners still being held in Serbia. The 18-party alliance that secured victory for Mr. Kostunica over Slobodan Milosevic in the elections last September went on to mount a revolt that toppled Mr. Milosevic in October and then to win Serbian parliamentary elections in December. But those politicians are only now taking control of the levers of power and appointing new police chiefs, prosecutors and judges. While the government wants to turn its attention too much needed economic measures, it has been preoccupied by the violence in and around Kosovo, and arguments with Serbia's smaller sister republic Montenegro, which is threatening to secede. Organized crime also represents a dangerous problem, ministers warned this week. The new Interior Minister, Dusan Mihajlovic, had a run-in with armed gunmen in downtown Belgrade during the night, and warned today that organized crime gangs connected to the old leadership of Mr. Milosevic were aiming for members of the new government. A gunman fired on the minister's security escort as it slowed at an intersection at about 1 a.m., although it is not clear if the attack was intended for the minister himself. But Mr. Mihajlovic said he had already received a number of threats and said he was sure there would be more. "All of us in the government are targets and they are trying to eliminate us," he said. Mr. Kostunica appealed to all in Kosovo to reject violence and opt for peace. It was high time for the Albanians in Kosovo to realize that the violence against Serbs and other minorities in the province "has done them immense harm and that they find the strength and courage to confront it," the statement said. But Mr. Kostunica added a strong plea to Serbs not to retaliate either and to trust international peacekeepers and the United Nations police to guarantee that all ethnic groups could live in Kosovo. United Nations officials have repeatedly warned of the dangers of renewed violence in Kosovo since last fall, when the political shifts in Belgrade and the West's embrace of Mr. Kostunica and the other new Serbian leaders began to alarm the Albanians and made them feel vulnerable. The Yugoslav government has drafted an amnesty law that – when passed – would free at least half of the Albanians, as well as absolve thousands of draft-dodgers in Yugoslavia. Nearly 200 of the Albanian prisoners are charged with terrorism and may not be included in the amnesty; they are expected to have their charges commuted by the Supreme Court and then be released. (NYT, 17 February, p. A-1)

18 February
British peacekeepers and the United Nations police said today that 11 people including a baby had died in the bomb blast that destroyed a bus full of Serbs escorted into Kosovo by Swedish peacekeepers on Friday. The bombing was one of the bloodiest and most brazen attacks on Serbian civilians since NATO-led peacekeepers and United Nations administrators took control of the province 20 months ago. The attack has raised tensions across Kosovo and set back the return of any Serbian refugees incalculably, United Nations officials here said. With some exceptions, Albanians expressed weariness at the violence, and shame that Kosovo is still in the grip of advocates of terrorism. Some accused the Serbs of orchestrating the attack; others cast it as continuing revenge for the 1999 war. About 2,500 people demonstrated in the northern town of Mitrovica – home to the biggest Serbian enclave remaining in Kosovo – and commemorated those who died on Friday by laying flowers on the bridge that divides the town's Albanian and Serbian communities. (NYT, 18 February, p. 4)

22 February
The chief of the NATO-led peacekeeping force in Kosovo, Lt. Gen. Carlo Cabigiosu, left, ordered increased patrols along the border with Macedonia after reports of movements of ethnic Albanian fighters in border villages. The Macedonian military has already clashed with one armed group in an ethnic Albanian village and has linked the appearance of armed men in Macedonia to the growing conflict over the border in southern Serbia. (NYT, 22 February, p. 8)

23 February
There is a climate of fear in Kosovo: few will speak out, let alone act against the perpetrators of violence. The Geci family took a courageous step of a different kind, gathering the people of their village to denounce the bomb attack last Friday. The Geci brothers decided with the bomb blast that enough was enough. The violence in Kosovo has acquired new dimensions in the last few months. There are now daily clashes between Albanian rebels and Serbian forces across the border east of Kosovo. Extra troops have been sent to join the American soldiers patrolling the eastern border. In Kosovo, peacekeepers and United Nations police officers are more cautious in their assessment, but they say that it takes only a handful of men to start something, and if they are determined, terrorists can get through the most stringent security measures. The international peacekeeping mission is looking increasingly troubled, and contributing nations are divided as how to proceed. Although the police have a good lead with two men arrested at the scene, the general climate of fear and threats will make it difficult to find the ringleaders behind the bombing. Mr. Geci also wants the United Nations administration to give the people of Kosovo a stronger voice with parliamentary elections this year. (NYT, 23 February, p. 9)

1 March
Heavy shooting erupted in two separate ethnic Albanian areas just outside Kosovo today, as NATO dispatched a team to one of the front lines in hopes of capping new violence in the Balkans. Though separated by borders, the two conflicts appeared to be similar; both sparked by insurgents in heavily ethnic Albanian areas in apparent hopes of joining them to Kosovo as part of the rebels' ultimate goal of achieving independence for the Serbian province. Serbian forces and Albanian militants clashed only hours ahead of scheduled talks with NATO officials on possibly narrowing a tense southern Serbian buffer zone with Kosovo, where the rebels have taken up positions. In Macedonia, state television re-

ported that ethnic Albanian rebels in the border village of Tanusevci opened fire on soldiers and police. Across the border, in Debelde (Kosovo), reporters heard shooting and saw about a dozen ethnic Albanian rebels running across the mountainside, apparently away from government fire. In Brussels on Tuesday, the NATO allies urged ethnic Albanians and Serbs to begin direct talks and said the Atlantic alliance would consider a "phased and conditioned" reduction of the demilitarised buffer zone between Kosovo and central Serbia. The "ground safety zone" in southern Serbia was originally designed to separate NATO-led peacekeeping forces in Kosovo from heavily armed Serbian and Yugoslav forces. NATO officials stressed that the Yugoslav army would be allowed to return to the zone only after the Serbian government implemented confidence-building measures toward the local ethnic Albanian majority. A NATO team arrived in Bujanovac on the edge of the zone today for talks with Serbian Deputy Prime Minister Covic on details of the proposed buffer zone reduction. (WP, 1 March, p. A16)

8 March
NATO soldiers in Kosovo opened fire and wounded two ethnic Albanian gunmen, raising the prospect that the peacekeeping force could become tangled in a violent Albanian insurgency that has flared in neighbouring Macedonia. (NYT, 8 March, p. 2)

8 March
The UN war crimes tribunal proposed a compromise to overcome a stand-off with Belgrade over the trial of former Yugoslav president Milosevic. Deputy prosecutor Blewitt said the International Criminal Tribunal for the Former Yugoslavia would be willing to hold part of Milosevic's trial in Belgrade. He also said new indictments charging Milosevic for the first time with responsibility for war crimes in Croatia and Bosnia would be issued soon, adding to a 1999 indictment over the war in Kosovo. (Reuters)

14 March
A temporary cease-fire between Albanian and Serbian forces had been signed. Nearly two years after NATO forces entered Kosovo to protect its Albanian population from Serb violence, NATO finds itself facing some dangerous unfinished business. In recent weeks, ethnic Albanians have repeatedly attacked Serbs just beyond Kosovo's border, an area of Serbia populated mostly by ethnic Albanians. Similar violence has broken out in Albanian-dominated areas of neighbouring Macedonia. As the fighting escalates, Western officials are increasingly worried that Western troops patrolling the area might get drawn into fire fights. The level of violence is low compared with the recent past, but political analysts here see all the incendiary ingredients for another Balkan war. Albanian nationalism and rebels seeking an independent state in Kosovo sparked a campaign of repression in 1998 by Milosevic, then president of Yugoslavia. NATO intervened the following year and has inherited the issue now that Serb-led Yugoslav forces have left. Western governments hope to bring calm through a political settlement worked out with the new Belgrade government to address civil liberty concerns of Albanians in the buffer zone along the Kosovo border. Last week NATO persuaded the guerrillas to sign the cease-fire and has allowed Serb forces re-enter the buffer zone. NATO contends that under its watchful eye, the new Belgrade government will not resort to the brutal tactics employed by Milosevic. Since taking control of Kosovo, a province of Serbia, NATO and the United Nations have tried to foster a multi-ethnic society in which Serbs live alongside Albanians. But the Serbs who remain are stuck in isolated enclaves, unable to ven-

ture out their neighbourhood for fear of being attacked. Other worries that if the NATO takes the hard line necessary to stop the attacks and disarm the rebels, it could lead to bloody clashes. Many analysts here say Western governments deserve some of the blame. NATO has made the safety of its troops a top priority leading to caution in the field. This has allowed rebels to smuggle arms and recruit and train soldiers in and around the buffer zone. U.S. Sgt. Shackelford said, "We treat them all the same. We're just trying to keep one from bashing the other." (WP, 14 March, p. A18)

17 March

A group of ethnic Albanian guerrillas battling for control of a hillside overlooking this frightened provincial city Tetovo said today their sole aim is to win more economic and political rights alongside Macedonia's Slavic majority. The Albanian rebels specifically said they wanted the Macedonian government to provide adequate schools staffed with Albanian-speaking instructors. The guerrillas said in interviews their armed violence was sparked by a decade of discrimination at the hands of the Macedonian Slavs who make up nearly two-thirds of the country's 2 million inhabitants. Their statement seemed designed to counter charges from Macedonian and Yugoslav officials that the uprising here had been helped along by ethnic Albanians in the neighbouring Serbian province of Kosovo, southern Serbia and Albania itself, united behind the goal of a greater Albanian super-state. Ethnic Albanians in several villages near Tetovo said they had begun forming armed self-defence groups to keep Macedonian police from passing through their towns to encircle the rebels and cut off their supplies. The fighting has thrown Macedonia's ethnically mixed government into crisis. The parliament held an all-day closed session today to debate ratification of a state of emergency plan that would give the police new powers. Ethnic Albanian politicians threatened to boycott the government if the proposal was accepted, and no decision was reached. A group calling itself the General Headquarters of the National Liberation Army issued a communiqué urging all ethnic Albanians to enlist the battle. Depicting themselves as acting solely in self-defence, the guerrillas said they had no direct casualties and blamed government forces. NATO Secretary General Robertson said in Athens that "we are determined that ... stability is not going to be threatened by a small number of extremists" in Macedonia. But the alliance announced no concrete actions to deal with the guerrillas. There is little agreement in Macedonia about one of the guerrillas' key demands, new schools staffed by Albanian-speaking teachers. At present, only elementary schools offer instruction in that language. While ethnic Albanians see the school issue as a matter of human rights and economic opportunity, many Macedonian Slavs consider the creation of more Albanian-language schools a recipe for enhanced Albanian nationalist and separatist sentiments. (WP, 17 March, p. A1)

18 March

Army en police troops took up positions today in the centre of Kosovo, to fire on ethnic Albanian rebels in the surrounding hills for a fourth consecutive day. The fighting was part of a government counteroffensive. The German troops, in Macedonia as a backup for the peacekeeping mission in neighbouring Kosovo, moved 500 troops farther north after coming under fire on Friday. It is not clear who fired on them. The heavy fighting on the fringes of Tetovo was much more serious than the insurgency in remote mountain villages of the previous week, the United Nations Balkans envoy Bildt said. (NYT, 18 March, p. 4)

22 March

Two years ago NATO went to war to rescue Kosovo's ethnic Albanians from predatory Serbs. Today the U.S. and its European allies are taking measured steps to help Serbia and Macedonia resist predatory Albanians. Such is the progress in the Balkans. Washington and its European partners need to focus again on the West's responsibilities and capabilities in the Balkans. That development actually represents progress compared with the drift and uncertainty of recent months, when it appeared that the new Bush administration might significantly and prematurely diminish U.S. involvement in the peacekeeping operations in Bosnia and Kosovo. By demonstrating patience and perspective during this spasm of violence, NATO governments can forge a new sense of unity and purpose for the vital tasks that remain ahead. It is a clearly progress when the West can co-operate with democratically elected administrations in Macedonia and Serbia on a common program to contain factional violence. Western co-operation with Belgrade and Skopje is a wholly unintended consequence for the ethnic Albanian guerrillas. Revenge is likely to be the most direct measure of progress for them. The shadowy guerrillas want to expand and internationalise their conflict in hopes of mobilizing Western sympathy and ultimately support against their Slav "oppressors," as the guerrillas' Kosovo brethren did in 1999. This is likely a miscalculation by the guerrillas, which have unclear ties to the Kosovo liberation movement that NATO did eventually rescue. Determined civilian and military efforts by the UN, NATO and the European Union have kept the peace in Bosnia and Kosovo. A functioning local government is slowly emerging in Kosovo, which has settled into an uncomfortable but manageable limbo in which eventual independence is neither guaranteed nor denied by its protectors. The future is still to be gained, or lost. (WP, 22 March, p. A29)

25 March

Of the roughly 5,600 U.S. troops on the peacekeeping mission in Kosovo, the happiest appear to be the 500 military police. They are at the centre of the international effort, patrolling constantly and interacting with the population. The infantry and other combat units, by contrast, tend to hate it. The central role played by the MPs represents a sharp reversal of the traditional military hierarchy of prestige, where infantry, armour and aviation usually rank the top. And of all the support forces, the MPs tend to be resented by other troops because part of their job is to hand out speeding tickets and generally police the force. But all that's changed in the peacekeeping missions that have dominated the U.S. military's attention for the last decade. At the main U.S. base Camp Bondsteel here, MPs head out to patrol the exotic towns and snow-capped mountains of this Balkan province. MPs are old hands at using the least amount necessary to get the job done, a key skill here. Commanders of the multinational force here increasingly agree that police skills are what Kosovo needs. One reason is that MPs tend to be more comfortable with a mission in which the goal isn't victory but stability. (WP, 25 March, p. A21)

26 March

All too often the American government has, in its handling of Balkan affairs, pursued a policy of "Do as I say and not as I do." Last week Serbian Prime Minister Djindjic was on the receiving end of this treatment during his visit to Washington. The Bush administration is threatening to cut off $100 million aid package and block World Bank and International Monetary Fund support for Belgrade if the authorities there do not arrest Milosevic before March 31. The idea is that Belgrade's new leaders must abide by the international community's norms of behaviour if they hope to reap the benefits of being in the international community. This means arresting Milosevic. The U.S. government, in the past decade, has a spotty record of honouring its commitments and obligations in the Balkans, and this has contributed to the region's continuing instability. In 1992 the first Bush administration went through the motions of condemning the Serb-led attack on Bosnia but did nothing to counteract it. The problem was handed of to the Clinton administration, which dishonoured itself, as the war raged on, by making eloquent protestations and promising vigorous action and then doing little except blaming its European allies for dithering. An U.S.-led bombing campaign ended the war in 1995, but the peacekeeping force, spearheaded by U.S. troops, shied away from arresting indicted war criminals. The same reluctance to do the hard work on the ground has hobbled the U.S.-led peacekeeping force in Kosovo. There is a new administration in Washington and, with it, the possibility that these obligations will be met. Whether President Bush likes it or not, the U.S. government is a key player in the Balkans. Just as the Serbs need to do the right thing, the Bush administration must do its job, too. (WP, 26 March, p. A25)

28 March
Around Tetovo in Macedonia there were shootings between Albanian guerrillas and Macedonian security forces. On Sunday night the guerrilla commanders gave an order to the fighters: hide your weapons and join civilians in fleeing across the border into NATO-occupied Kosovo province. It was a surprising decision by the guerrilla army said several fighters who arrived in Kosovo. It helps explain the past two days of relative quiet in Macedonia. NATO officials and international diplomats are trying to use the lull to broker a lasting peace and encourage the government to pursue political concessions aimed at satisfying the minority ethnic Albanian population. NATO troops monitoring the violence from here on the Kosovo side of the border say they doubt that the guerrillas have disbanded but they cannot explain why the fighting abated to quickly or predict what might happen next. To get answers, German military police and intelligence officers have been combing the woods south-east of here to find members of the guerrilla army and glean some information about their plans. (WP, 28 March, p. A16)

29 March
Government forces mounted an operation against ethnic Albanian rebels in the north, near the Kosovo border, in a last effort to rout the guerrillas before political talks begin. A spokesman said the government wanted a "political and economic dialogue" with ethnic Albanian political parties. (NYT, 29 March, p.2)

30 March
Heavy mortar fire from the direction of Macedonia rained in an ethnic Albanian village in NATO-occupied Kosovo province today, killing two residents and a British journalist. The attack occurred as Macedonian government forces across the border pressed an offensive against Albanian guerrillas. The Macedonian army has been under pressure from Western governments to avoid civilian casualties. The Macedonian government last night denied that its troops were responsible for the attack, but promised to investigate further. A senior NATO official said there was little doubt the Macedonian government was responsible. American soldiers and UN police in Kosovo, showing signs of embarrassment that the violence had occurred in Kosovo, attempted unsuccessfully to seal off the scene of an attack that could inflame Albanian anger. Mortar fire from Macedonia had been

drawing steadily closer for two days, residents said. Their village is nestled in a gully about 2 ½ miles from the border. The Macedonian government has vowed to drive the guerrillas out of Macedonia and into the arms of NATO peacekeepers in Kosovo, who have said they will attempt to detain any rebels entering the province. UN officials in Kosovo's capital Pristina said the Macedonians thought they were pursuing a band of about 60 guerrillas at the time of the attack. (WP, 30 March, p. A21)

8 June

International officials in Kosovo, who are under pressure to show results, are reconsidering a plan to return Serbian refugees to the province despite shelving the idea last year because of security concerns. The UN refugee agency refused to support previous plans to return Serbs to Kosovo because of the dangers involved. But the agency is going along with the plan this time: Lubbers, the UN high commissioner for refugees, discussed the issue with President Kostunica of Yugoslavia this week. Afterward he said he would support the return of a limited number of refugees to villages near the border with Serbia. The dangers of the scheme are stark: in February, a bomb attack on a bus full of Serbs killed 10 and injured dozens more, despite the presence of peacekeeping troops. Mr. Haekkerup, the UN administrator in Kosovo, has already presented the plan to return Serbs to Kosovo to a joint council of Serb and Albanian leaders in the province. The constitutional framework that Mr. Haekkerup has devised for Kosovo reflects the new firmness, and it gives nothing to Albanian aspirations for independence. The framework lays out the legal basis for a system of self-government, including elections to a ruling assembly and the nomination of a president, which will be in effect until a final settlement on Kosovo's status is reached. It does not say when or how that final status will be decided. In an interview, Mr. Haekkerup said he thought a final settlement would be closer to 5 years away, rather than 20 years, but added that he was going to make the Albanians, and the Serbs, work for it. (NYT, 8 June, p. 11)

18 June

Russia and Yugoslavia said today that Kosovo was the main cause of instability in the Balkans and urged world leaders to ensure that Albanian "terrorists" in Kosovo and the region were completely disarmed. President Putin of Russia visited Yugoslavia and warned later that Macedonia could be a repeat of Kosovo, if Western pressure pushed the Macedonian leadership to give in to the demands of the rebels. Mr. Putin was making a short working visit to Belgrade to show support for the eight-month-old government of President Kostunica. He visited Russian peacekeeping troops at their base at Pristina in Kosovo and met United Nations officials. Mr. Putin said he agreed with Mr. Kostunica that the international community should do more to fulfil the UN resolution that regulates Kosovo and has made it a UN protectorate since NATO's war with Yugoslavia in 1999. Some 3,000 Russian troops are serving in Kosovo as part of the 38,000-member peacekeeping force led by NATO in Kosovo. Mr. Kostunica repeated his now familiar criticism of the UN mission in Kosovo. "The crisis in Kosovo, and many wrong moves by the international community in Kosovo have caused instability in the entire region," he said. Russia is seen as an ally of Serbia by most by most Albanians, and Russian troops have come under attack in Kosovo. Macedonian leaders have failed to forge an agreement on political reforms to answer the grievances of the Albanian minority after three days of closed negotiations. Mr. Putin also criticized the UN's new framework for self-rule in Kosovo, drawn up by Haekkerup, the head of the UN mission in Kosovo. The framework was too like a constitution and did not emphasize strongly enough that Kosovo remained a sovereign and territorial part of Yugoslavia, he said. (NYT, 18 June, p.8)

Lebanon

22 September
An American federal judge yesterday ordered the government of Iran to pay $355 million in damages to the family of Marine Lt. Col. William R. Higgins, who was taken captive and killed in 1989 while on a United Nations peacekeeping mission in Lebanon. The ruling came in a lawsuit filed by Robin L. Higgins, who contended that terrorists backed by Iran were behind her husband's kidnapping, torture and eventual death. U.S. District Judge Colleen Kollar-Kotelly said expert witnesses convinced her that Iran controlled Hezbollah, the group that she found responsible for the acts. Iran has not responded to any of the lawsuits, losing all by default, and has shown no sign of paying the awards. Robin L. Higgins was kidnapped in February 1988, one of 18 Americans taken hostage during the war in Lebanon. He was killed 18 months later at the age of 44. (WP, 22 September, p. A10)

21 October
Within the next several months, former hostage Anderson and his family are scheduled to receive $41.2 million in compensatory damages, and former Lebanon hostages David P. Jacobsen, Joseph J. Cicippio and Frank H. Reed will receive $9 million, $30 million and $26 million respectively. The family of slain Marine Col. William R. Higgins will get $55.4 million. More than $213 million – plus significant interest payments – will be distributed to eight families that have won judgements against Iran in a series of U.S. court cases. In a precedent-setting turn of events, the money is coming from the U.S. Treasury, with the U.S. government assuming responsibility for collecting on the claims from Iran, either through the international claims tribunal or negotiations with Iran. The action marks the first time that foreign countries will pay damages under a 1996 anti-terrorism law. Anderson and others said they believe the payments will make it easier for future plaintiffs to collect awards and may deter terrorists. (WP, 22 October, p. A01)

31 January
The Security Council extended the mandate for the United Nations peacekeeping presence in southern Lebanon for another six months, but scaled back the contingent from 5,800 troops to 4,500. The mission has been in Lebanon for nearly 13 years. The Council again urged Lebanon to reassert authority in the south and speed up troop deployments following Israel's withdrawal. (NYT, 31 January, p. A-6)

31 January
The UN Security Council voted unanimously today to reduce the size of the UN peacekeeping force in southern Lebanon from 5,800 to 4,500 troops, and it urged the Lebanese government to send in its army to take charge of Lebanon's southern border with Israel. The decision comes two weeks after UN Secretary General Annan recommended a reduc-

tion, citing the restoration of relative calm in the region after the withdrawal of the Israeli army from southern Lebanon in June. The United Nations Interim Force in Lebanon, UNIFIL, was created in 1978 to implement a Security Council demand that Israel ends its occupation of southern Lebanon. The UN certified that Israel had completed its withdrawal in June and demarcated a line of separation between the two countries, known as the blue line. The United States has backed a UN request last summer to enlarge the UN force in Lebanon, fearing such cross-border attacks against Israel. But the United States supported the Security Council's decision today. "We remain concerned about the ongoing tensions along the borders and urge all parties to exercise restraint and respect the blue line," US ambassador Soderberg said. "We have been urging [the Lebanese] to exercise ... their full authority in the south." (WP, 31 January, p. A22)

1 February
As part of a United Nations decision to reduce its peacekeeping role in Lebanon, Irish Army troops will leave the country after 23 years. An Irish Defence Forces spokesman said 600 soldiers will start their last six-month tour of duty in May. (NYT, 1 February, p. A-6)

9 March
The Christian Maronite Patriarch of Lebanon, Cardinal Nasrallah Boutros Sfeir, lunched with 15-congressman Wednesday and met with House Speaker Hastert yesterday to plead for implementation of the U.S. and Saudi-sponsored Taif accords of 1989. Those accords provided the framework for ending civil strife in Lebanon and called for the pullout of some 40,000 Syrian troops from the country. Sfeir was rebuffed on the recommendation of the U.S. embassy in Beirut and other advisers in Washington, who are nervous about alienating Syria and its Lebanese allies. Sfeir expressed fears that cross-border attacks by guerrillas from Lebanon's Hezbollah movement based in South Lebanon could trigger a major Israeli retaliation. He also lamented the exodus of young Lebanese professionals to seek a more stable future elsewhere. (WP, 9 March, p. A21)

Macedonia

17 March
Fierce fighting has broken out in this Balkan nation. The insurgents are trying to claim parts of Macedonia that are overwhelmingly Albanian, and the population is quickly dividing between Slavs and Albanians, just as in Kosovo. There is little practical help offered to the Macedonian government. The main opposition parties were in negotiations to form a government together with the ruling coalition, uniting Slavs and moderate Macedonians. The aim is to unite all political parties in Macedonia, a fragile nation that broke from Yugoslavia a decade ago and since has made progress toward democracy. (NYT, 17 March, p. 1)

18 March
The ethnic Albanian guerrilla army that launched a surprise offensive in Macedonia this month was organized over a long period and intends to take over the entire region in western Macedonia, where Albanians make up the majority of the population, a senior guerrilla official said today. Ameti, a guerrilla, said his side was interested in opening a dialogue soon with the Macedonian government, which is dominated by Macedonian Slavs. The guerrillas' bottom-line demand will be that they get control over the city Te-

tovo and all other cities where Albanians have "historically ... owned territory," Ameti said. He also said that the guerrillas plan to establish a separate army and police force in this region, a goal that goes well beyond the rebels' previous statements of wanting only to protect Albanians' rights. While Macedonia's government says it is keen to avoid incidents that would provoke further ethnic hostility, ethnic Albanians have made unconfirmed charges of police brutality in the past two weeks. Macedonian Slav civilians are now furious over the guerrillas' attacks. Many ethnic Albanians here have said they sympathize with the guerrillas' demand for enhanced political en economic rights; they say that the majority Macedonian Slavs have discriminated against them since the country was forged during the break-up of Yugoslavia a decade ago. Unemployment is high in villages now controlled by the guerrillas. But Macedonia is in the midst of a difficult transition from communism, and Slavs are also experiencing growing unemployment. (WP, 18 March, p. A21)

18 March
U.S. peacekeepers in Kosovo, watching warily as ethnic Albanian guerrillas launch new attacks just across the border in Macedonia and southern Yugoslavia, are bracing for possible confrontations in Kosovo with the guerrillas or their supporters. Stepping up patrols on the border to block the flow of men and weapons from Kosovo to the insurgents, the peacekeepers risk becoming targets them if the guerrillas feel threatened. NATO waged a 78-day bombing campaign against Yugoslavia in 1999 to end a brutal crackdown by that country's Serb-dominated army against an Albanian insurrection in Kosovo. But U.S. Army peacekeeping troops here see the recent attacks as confirmation that the Albanians are now the problem. NATO has been co-operating more and more closely with its former adversary in the war. Earlier in the week, the alliance allowed Yugoslav troops to re-occupy a 10-square-mile sector of a buffer zone just outside Kosovo, where Albanian guerrillas have been attacking Yugoslav police. Serb civilians who remained in their homes when the Yugoslav army pulled out in 1999 are in constant danger from Albanians, who either want revenge or a Kosovo without Serbs. U.S. troops are guarding isolated Serb enclaves, religious sites and homes. Despite the efforts, Albanians manage regularly to terrorize Serbs. Many Serbs say the peacekeepers are too concerned about taking casualties and should apply their full military muscle to establish order and confiscate weapons used by Albanians during the war against Yugoslavia. (WP, 18 March, p. A22)

24 March
The Macedonian government voiced frustration today at the limited U.S. role in the conflict here, saying more vigorous U.S. diplomacy could reduce support for ethnic Albanian guerrillas who have launched a rebellion in the hills along the border with Kosovo. Under pressure from the European Union, which hosted president Trajkovski of Macedonia at an EU summit in Stockholm today, Macedonia has launched only sporadic shelling of rebel positions in the mountainous region north of Tetovo, 25 miles west of Skopje, the capital. Intelligence from U.S. drone aircraft has been provided to the Macedonian military, but civilian officials have begun to bridle at what they perceive as U.S. diplomatic passivity in the face of a conflict that could yet spiral out of control. In their view, the U.S. role in driving Yugoslav troops out of Kosovo in 1999 has given Washington enough influence with ethnic Albanians to persuade the rebels here to abandon violence. The government's principal goal in soliciting U.S. diplomatic support is to turn around

growing support for the guerrillas among the wider ethnic Albanian population of Macedonia. (WP, 24 March, p. A14)

25 March
The war of the United States and NATO against Milosevic's Yugoslavia also justified their alliance with Albanian extremists. Those extremists are now trying to do in Macedonia what the U.S. and NATO did to Serbian authority in Kosovo. It is called a "blowback"; the bad consequences of actions taken earlier for other reasons, or in other settings. The militants' goal is to consolidate ethnic Albanians (in Kosovo or Macedonia) under Albanian rule. Mr. Milosevic tried to destabilize multiethnic, democratic Macedonia by forcing thousands of Kosovo Albanians to leave their homes and cross the border. In a matter of weeks extremist Albanians have succeeded where Mr. Milosevic could not, bringing bloodshed to the one country of the former Yugoslavia that had avoided it. How did they do this? NATO became to liberate after the war. Washington and NATO closed their eyes to organized efforts to drive out non-Albanians from Kosovo, to murder moderate Albanian politicians. Officials acknowledge that former leaders of the Kosovo Liberation Army have been involved in all these activities and that the UN administration and the peacekeepers have been slow or reluctant to crack down. The peacekeeping force has been lax about sealing Kosovo's borders. A senior Western diplomat concedes NATO is rushing to try to finally seal the border. (NYT, 25 March, p. 16)

27 March
In the hills above Tetovo is a rebel group active, who are an offshoot of the Kosovo Liberation Army, known as the National Liberation Army. They came under renewed pressure from the West to make good on their promise to move more quickly to address the political concerns of the ethnic Albanians. The NATO secretary general Robertson and Solana, the current European Union security chief, visited the President and other politicians in Macedonia. The visitors offered support for the Macedonian State, praise for what they consider a proportionate military response and encouragement to act quickly to show Albanians living in Macedonia that progress is possible without gun. Macedonian officials privately worried that the rebels would turn to urban terrorism or emerge in more widely spread towns, stretching the small Macedonian security forces. There were a few incidents reported today. Two policemen were wounded today when their vehicle was machine-gunned on a road between Skopje and the border with Kosovo. There was also shooting at army positions near the town of Gracani, near the village of Germo and in the mountains closer to Kosovo. (NYT, 27 March, p.6)

9 June
In a new bid to halt a five-month guerrilla rebellion, Macedonian President Trajkovski in a speech to parliament proposed a partial amnesty today for fighters who lay down their arms. At the same time, the government launched its fiercest artillery bombardment so far against the guerrilla strongholds. The proposal signified growing frustration at the spreading violence in Macedonia, provoked in February by experienced and well-equipped ethnic Albanian guerrillas that say they are defending the country's largest minority. In recent days, the fighting has begun to draw closer to the capital of Skopje and the airport, which NATO uses to ferry food and supplies to Western peacekeeping troops in neighbouring Kosovo. The violence also has grown more chaotic, with organized groups of civilians attacking ethnic Albanian businesses and homes in reprisal for battlefield

losses by Macedonian forces. In scenes reminiscent of the start of total breakdown in other Balkan countries in the 1990s, the predominantly ethnic Albanian population of Aracinovo has begun to flee. Western officials estimate that the conflict has already displaced at least 18,000 people inside the country and forced another 18,000 into neighbouring nations. Solana, the top security official of the EU, returned to the capital here tonight to prod the government to make political reforms that might defuse the violence, according to a diplomatic aide. Under Solana's prodding, major Macedonian Slav and ethnic Albanian parties agreed last month to create a unified consensus government. But so far, it has not yielded any concrete moves to address what ethnic Albanians describe as their long-standing grievances about discrimination. Several thousand civilians remain holed up in the basements of homes in six villages of north-eastern Macedonia, where most of the fighting has occurred in the past two months. The rebel group, the National Liberation Army, has refused to organize mass evacuations, saying it fears police retaliation against civilians, according to Western observers. Today's shelling of homes in the villages of Slupcane and Matejce raised clouds of dust and smoke that could be seen several miles away. Trajkovski told the parliament that the operation would yield great success within a few days and that by next week "your lives" will return to normal. At the same time, he said that emotions should not rule policymaking and that some "terrorists" should be given a chance to be reintegrated into society. He also urged a major build-up of the army's capabilities and more efforts to promote political reform. (WP, 9 June, p. A13)

12 June
Ethnic Albanian rebels and the Macedonian government announced cease-fires today, a day after the rebels threatened to train their artillery on airports, police stations and other targets in the capital, Skopje, and other cities. The government said it hoped the lull would enable aid groups to deliver food to thousands of civilians in villages battered by fighting and alleviate water shortages in Kumanovo. Rebels took control of the reservoir there more than a week ago, leaving the 100,000 residents without water. On Sunday they threatened to bombard the cities unless government forces stopped their assaults. The militants, who began their insurgency in February, say they are fighting for more rights for ethnic Albanians. The government contends that the rebels are separatist and has waged an offensive to drive them from their bases in the north. More than 37,000 refugees have fled to Kosovo in the past three days, according to a UN official. The EU cautiously welcomed the cease-fires but warned that the situation remained worrisome. (WP, 12 June, p. A18)

21 June
The NATO alliance announced today that it was prepared to send up to 3,000 European troops to Macedonia to help disarm ethnic Albanian rebels if a peace agreement is reached that ensures a cessation of hostilities. Ambassadors from the 19 NATO countries ordered military planners to begin drawing up operational plans for the force. The NATO troops would not be a formal peacekeeping mission, but would seek to fulfil a short-term task of disarming the guerrillas and then leave the country, perhaps within six weeks. In a joint statement, the 19 allies emphasized the "urgent need for a successful outcome of the political dialogue between the different parties in the former Yugoslav Republic of Macedonia and the cessation of hostilities as an essential precondition for any NATO assistance." Macedonia's government and ethnic Albanian leaders have been negotiating for

the past six days on the terms of a peace deal that would ostensibly enhance the political rights and cultural status of the Albanian minority. President Trajkovski, a member of Macedonian Slav majority, said that the talks appeared to have reached an impasse because of what he described as unreasonable demands by the Albanians. He said the Albanian negotiators appear to be holding out "in the expectation that the international community will intervene and support their unreal political demands, which would include cementing terrorist positions in temporary, occupied territories." The EU's foreign chief Solana, is scheduled to travel to Skopje on Thursday in a bid to break the deadlock and disabuse the Albanians of the notion that armed struggle finds sympathy in the West. He will also press the government to deal with what Western countries see as legitimate Albanian grievances. Solana has taken the lead in trying to broker a peace deal, with the U.S. playing a lower-key role. He said the negotiations have now reached a critical point and that Western allies "must now do our outmost to avoid war in Macedonia." Under the plan NATO has approved, the disarmament force would be a "coalition of willing nations" answering a call for assistance by the Macedonian government. It would not require a UN Security Council mandate. The new force would require fresh troops to be sent into the Balkans region, where the alliance now heads up peacekeeping missions in Bosnia and Kosovo. NATO already has based 3,000 troops in Macedonia, but they are logistical units, unsuited for combat, who help supply the Kosovo force. (WP, 21 June, p. A19)

Middle-East

1 July
Amid rising concern over the conduct of the trials, a military court sentences 30 Lebanese convicted of collaborating with Israel to prison terms ranging up to 120 years. The court has sentenced 605 people since it began work June 5 and intends to try about 2,200 Lebanese. Amnesty International has called the trials "a parody o justice" that "can in no way help national reconciliation." (NYT, 2 July, p. 4)

1 July
The quick deployment of United Nations peacekeepers and Lebanese forces into the stretch of southern Lebanon, that Israel abandoned in May after 22 years of occupation has been thrown into doubt with the controversy over a series of apparent Israeli incursions across a border line drawn in 1923. The Secretary General of the United Nations, Kofi Annan, certified two weeks ago that Israel had indeed pulled out its troops, but Lebanon protested the findings. Mr. Annan brushed these objections aside, saying there where only a couple of border violations by Israel and they would be cleared up swiftly. But then there were more transgressions, and United Nations relations with both Lebanon an Israel became strained. The United nations has sent officers from the peacekeeping force that has patrolled the south for more than 20 years to survey and map the border, with orders to report back to New York headquarters daily. This week, they found nine violations by Israel. Most of them were said to be minor. But the violations have become a political issue, and have drawn a threat from the leader of the Hezbollah militia to take unspecified action if the United Nations does not resolve the dispute. (NYT, 2 July, p. 4)

5 July

Israel accused Lebanon Wednesday of petty-mindedness in the row over continued Israeli border violations following the end of the occupation of southern Lebanon.

Deputy defence Minister Ephraim Sneh said Israel had complied with UN Security Council Resolution 425 calling for it to withdraw from Lebanon and it was now up to Beirut to do the same.

A United Nations report to the Security Council Monday outlined 12 violations by Israel of Lebanese territory, including technical fences or equipment that lie on the Lebanese side of the line of withdrawal. The United Nations Interim Force in Lebanon (UNIFIL) report dated Sunday said five violations involve fences encroaching a few meters (yards) into Lebanese territory, and the remaining seven consist of patrol tracks or the position of Israel next to the border line.

The United Nations drew the "blue line" to verify that Israeli forces had completely withdrawn from Lebanese territory on May 24. The Security Council certified the Israeli retreat on June 23, but UNIFIL has accused Israel of a number of violations on Lebanese territory. The Lebanese government asked the United Nations to put an end to these violations and opposes the deployment of UN troops in the territory from which Israel withdrew until the situation is rectified. UN chief cartographer Miklos Pinther and UN special envoy Terje Roed-Larsen are due in Beirut Friday in a bid to resolve the dispute. (Agence France Presse, 5 July)

11 July

A federal judge order the government of Iran to pay $327 million to the families of two Americans killed in a suicide bus bombing in Israel, saying the evidence showed former Iranian officials aided the terrorists who carried out the attack. The ruling marked the fourth time a federal judge has ordered Iran to pay damages under a 1996 U.S. law intended to provide U.S. victims of terrorist acts recourse in the courts. Iran has not responded to any of the lawsuits and has given no indication that it will pay the judgements, which total nearly $ 1 billion. Legislation is pending in Congress that would help families with claims against Iran gain access to Iranian assets frozen by the United States government. (WP, 12 July, p. A5)

14 July

The top Hezbollah commander in Southern Lebanon, Sheik Nabil Qaouk, discussed in a rare interview with a Western journalist, in unusual detail how Hezbollah learned to improve its effectiveness, strategy and weaponry, and how to videotape its successes for distribution to the media. He said "the use of media as a weapon had an effect parallel to a battle." (NYT, 19 July, p. 12)

20 July

With President Clinton's departure for Japan, the energy drained from the Israeli-Palestinian peace talks as the delegations, trying to recover from the roller-coaster drama of late Wednesday night, slept late and then worked with the American peace team to determine how to move beyond the impasse and the mutual accusations of bad faith. Israel's apparent willingness to give up some control of East Jerusalem has roused fears among the Arab residents there of a compromise that would fall short of Palestinian aspirations for full sovereignty, while putting at risk jobs, social services and unimpeded travel access. (NYT, 21 July, p. 2)

24 July

Over a month ago the UN Security Council confirmed that Israel had indeed fulfilled Resolution 425 calling for a complete withdrawal from Lebanon. Israel went to considerable lengths to obtain this international imprimatur, in a number of cases blowing up military posts located just meters from the international border.

In recent weeks, Israel has been busy trying to correct minor violations of the UN-drafted "blue line" that will be the border until a permanent frontier can be negotiated between Lebanon and Israel directly.

At the same time, the United Nations has not moved as quickly as expected to expand UNIFIL and move that force to the border with Israel. Even if the long-awaited deployment of an enhanced UNIFIL contingent is completed as expected, such action is insufficient if it is not accompanied by a similar deployment by Lebanese government forces, both army and police.

Lebanon's and the UN's fastidiousness with respect to confirming the obvious-that Israel has withdrawn from Lebanon-is in sharp contrast with their fervour for implementing the other, now urgent, portions of Resolution 425. That resolution, as Israel continuous to point out, provided for the restoration of international peace and security and the return of Lebanese authority to the area.

Since Israel's complete withdrawal from Lebanon, the United Nations has taken little interest in Lebanese violations of the border or Lebanon's failure to deploy its army in the South. In any case, such a deployment alone should not be considered sufficient; its purpose should be to disarm Hezbollah and prevent disturbances on the border.

The international interest in restoring peace to southern Lebanon is not just a matter of Israeli security and UN credibility, but a humanitarian necessity. The residents of the area, naturally, crave such stability, but it is also the key to allowing the Lebanese who fled to Israel to return to their homes.

Israel, both officially and as a society, has responded with a large degree of sympathy and generosity toward its Lebanese allies who became refugees following Israel's withdrawal. But decent treatment now cannot erase the bitter feelings of abandonment, the undignified rush to the border, or tensions that grow over time from living in a foreign land.

A general amnesty for South Lebanese Army veterans would, as is reportedly being considered, encourage such a process further.

The current quiet in southern Lebanon should not be read as providing unlimited time to establish a new, stable, and peaceful order in the area. Israel's swift withdrawal, though promised, was somewhat unexpected.

The hesitancy of the French and others, for example, to contribute to the expansion of UNIFIL-on the grounds that the border is quiet-risks being a self-negating prophecy. Israel and the international community should not regard UNIFIL as the major guarantor of a peaceful border-which responsibility lies with the Lebanese government. But UNIFIL can be an important vehicle of international attentiveness to the problem, and therefore should be utilized to the fullest extent. (Jerusalem Post, 24 July)

27 July

Late Wednesday, a UN spokesman told AFP on condition of anonymity that Israel had "firmly pledged to rectify the violations during the night and we hope that the redeployment of United Nations troops will start as of tomorrow." (Agence France Presse, 27 July)

27 July
Lebanese and United Nations experts will head to southern Lebanon later Thursday to check if Israel had rectified four fresh border encroachments, Lebanese Prime Minister Salim Hoss said.
Late Tuesday, the United Nations had delayed the redeployment of the UN Interim Forces in southern Lebanon (UNIFIL) down to the Israeli borders-which had been scheduled for Wednesday-because of the four new Israeli violations of Lebanese territory.
In the wake of the Israeli withdrawal from southern Lebanon on May 24, the Lebanese government has opposed the deployment of UN peacekeepers right up to the border until Israeli troops cease to encroach on its territory. UN Secretary General Kofi Annan has hoped that the UNIFIL redeployment would be "immediately followed by the deployment of the composite Lebanese unit," consisting of soldiers and members of the internal security forces. (Agence France Presse, 27 July)

28 July
Lebanon is preparing to pursue a claim for compensation against Israel for its 22-year occupation of south Lebanon at the International Court of Justice, the government said Friday.
An official statement said Prime Minister Selim al-Hoss headed a meeting of legal and diplomatic specialists to finalize plans to press a case that included compensation for "direct and indirect losses resulting from Israeli aggressions." It gave no figure for the damages to be sought, but officials have previously talked about billions of dollars in losses that Israel inflicted on Lebanon. (Reuters, 28 July)

30 July
Israel withdrew its forces from a 15 km (nine mile) occupation zone on May 24, ending 22 years of occupation and honouring a decades old UN Security Council resolution. Hizbollah had led the fight to oust Israel from the zone.
Thirty Indian UNIFIL troops with two armoured personnel carriers and three trucks took up a position near the village of Abbasiyah on the edge of the eastern sector Sunday, a Reuters correspondent said. Five Hizbollah guerrillas with machineguns watched the deployment, while Israeli soldiers observed it from the other side of the border. Thirty soldiers of UNIFIL's Swedish and Finnish units with six armoured personnel carriers, two jeeps and a bulldozer moved into another border position facing the Israel village of Mutella. (Reuters, 30 July)

6 August
United Nations peacekeeping troops finally began spreading out in force along Lebanon's border with Israel today, after weeks of haggling over just where the border is and 22 years after presence was first authorized. Hezbollah guerrillas, the effective force on the ground, quietly turned over the fortified strongholds and observation posts they had taken when the Israelis abruptly departed two months ago, leaving the Christian-led militia called the South Lebanon Army to flee in their wake. "But the guerrillas are not giving up their weapons, which they will stash away in their hoes and other hiding places," a Hezbollah official said. The United Nations Interim force in Lebanon, or UNIFIL, is being expanded from about 4,600 troops to about 6,000. A Lebanese force of 500 soldiers and

500 security police is supposed to follow the UN troops into the south. (NYT, 6 August, p. 4)

8 August
Lebanese Interior Minister Michel Murr had given the go-ahead for a joint Lebanese force of army troops and police to deploy in the former occupied zone early Wednesday. Murr said that the 1,000-member force will start deploying at 3 a.m. after the Lebanese government was informed by UN peacekeepers that they had completed their first phase of deployment inside the liberated border zone.
Meanwhile, a UN statement distributed in Beirut said that UN peacekeepers are preparing to expand their presence in southern. The statement quoted UN Secretary- General Kofi Annan's deputy spokesman Manoel de Al Meida e Silva as saying that the UNIFIL has deployed in 17 new positions along the UN drawn withdrawal Blue Line and will deploy in 11 more positions in the next few days. (Deutsche Presse-Agentur, 8 August)

12 August
In the Middle East, Lebanon's refusal to have its forces go all the way to the border is widely seen as a move by Syria, which has virtually controlled Lebanon for a decade, to maintain pressure on Israel to return the Golan Heights. By leaving control of the border uncertain, the line of reasoning goes, Syria reserved the threat of possible future action by Hezbollah, or other proxies, such as Syrian-based Palestinian groups. The Lebanese government says it will deploy its troops on the border only in the context of a complete regional peace agreement, including the turnover of the Golan Heights and the return of Palestinian refugees. "What the Lebanese seem to be unaware of is that UNIFIL's end is near," a UN official said. "Lebanon can't go on indefinitely ignoring its responsibility for the border and the border region alike." (NYT, 13 August, p. 13)

23 September
Most recently, Israel has been deliberating on an American proposal that would grant the United Nations Security Council control over the Temple Mount as a way to break the Israeli-Palestinian deadlock over the sacred file. That deadlock emerged at the Camp David talks in July as the major obstacle to a comprehensive settlement.
According to today's issue of the Israeli newspaper Haaretz, in fact, Israeli diplomats are working assiduously to promote the idea that only international control of the 35-acre holy zone would resolve competing Israeli and Palestinians claims on the site – by rising above them.
Under the latest proposal, the Security Council would assume sovereignty, granting control over the Islamic sites to the Palestinians while the Israelis kept the western Wall. The seeming Israeli willingness to seek Security Council guarantees for such an arrangement is seen here as a sign of how Israel's relations with the United Nations have improved since it withdrew from southern Lebanon and advertised a new willingness to surrender much of East Jerusalem in a peace pact with the Palestinians. For more than three decades, Israel has been the target of regular condemnation by the United Nations for its occupation of lands seized in war. (New York Times, 23 September)

22 October

Arab leaders condemned Israel's "gruesome atrocities" in recent clashes with Palestinians and suggested that a war crimes tribunal similar to those established after ethnic massacres in Rwanda and Bosnia be set up to prosecute the Israeli opposition leader Ariel Sharon and others. But despite rhetoric that reflected Arab anger over three weeks of street battles between the Israeli Army and Palestinian protesters and the Palestinian police, the final communiqué of an emergency Arab summit meeting stopped short of ordering any immediate, across the board, economic or diplomatic punishment of the Jewish state, as hard-line Arab countries had desired. Instead the conference recommended that any new steps toward normal relations with Israel be postponed and that participation in regional economic meetings or other conferences involving Israel be suspended. A billion-dollar fund to support the current Palestinian uprising, through direct aid to the families of those wounded and through a broader push to keep Arab control over Islamic holy sites in East Jerusalem, was also established at the behest of Saudi Arabia. The United Nations was also called on to investigate alleged war crimes and even to interject peacekeeping forces directly into Israel to stop what the Arab leaders deemed "barbaric" acts that have claimed well over 100 Palestinian lives in three weeks of violence. (IHT, 23 October, p. 1)

6 November

In a vote of no-confidence in the United States before this week's Washington summit, Yassir Arafat demanded that America involved Russia, the European Union and the United Nations in the Middle East peace process. The Palestinian leader laid down his new terms, which would effectively end the Oslo peace process and start a new round of negotiations, after having accepted an invitation to the White House. The demands were another signal that Mr Arafat, and above all his own people, have lost faith in the US as an impartial mediator. Thousands of Palestinian demonstrators jeered Mr Arafat yesterday for having agreed to attend the summit in Washington on Thursday. Mr Arafat also called for an international army of peacekeepers to be deployed on the West Bank and in Gaza. In the past five weeks 160 Arabs, almost a third of them children, have been killed by Israeli security forces. "I am asking for international forces ... to protect us," he said. Ehud Barak, the Israeli Prime Minister, who accepts that Mr Arafat is trying to restrain the violence, rejected his proposal for a peacekeeping force yesterday. He said: "An international army may even make it (the conflict) worse." (TT, 7 November)

8 November

Secretary General Kofi Annan said today that he does not see how a United Nations force could be inserted between Palestinians and Israelis unless both sides agreed to it. The Palestinians are asking for an international "protection force" for the West Bank and Gaza. Israel's Prime Minister, Ehud Barak, has ruled out such a mission. Diplomats say the Security Council, which is planning to discuss the Mideast crisis in general terms on Wednesday, is unlikely to act anytime soon on the Palestinians' request. The Palestinian observer mission here has circulated a proposal calling for a United Nations force of 2,000 uniformed monitors in territories occupied by Israel since 1967. The troops would provide "safety and security for Palestinian civilians," according to the plan. Five Security Council resolutions since 1987 have called for protection of the civilian Palestinian population. Diplomats here are divided on the prospect of any peacekeeping force being stationed in Israeli-occupied territory. The United States has warned that any resolution that condemns the Israelis will be vetoed. Russia, with the war in Chechnya to consider, and China, with calls for action in Tibet, are generally opposed to intervention on principle. (NYT, 8 November, p. A10)

12 November

Ehud Barak arrived in Washington last night to seek a treaty that would upgrade Israel's status in relations with the United States to that of "strategic ally". The Israeli Prime Minister was asking President Clinton to take the step, which would cement the already strong links between the two countries. Israel already gets about $3billion (Pounds 2.1billion) a year in US military aid. When Yassir Arafat, President of the Palestinian Authority, met President Clinton last week, he pressed the Palestinian case for an international observer force to be sent to Palestinian-controlled areas of the West Bank and to those still under Israeli military occupation. The welding together of the United States and Israel in this way would end any real chance of any future US President negotiating a permanent peace between Israel and the Palestinians. Arab leaders, attending the opening of the three-day summit of the 56-member Organisation of the Islamic Conference, supported Mr Arafat's called for a UN peacekeeping force. There was also a demand for "deeds not words" from the Arab world by Crown Prince Abdullah of Saudi Arabia, in what he said was their holy struggle against Israel. (TT, 13 November)

20 November

United Nations Secretary General Kofi Annan is set to begin negotiations with Israel and the Palestinian Authority on the establishment of an international observer mission in the Palestinian territories. The move represents a significant expansion of the UN chief's role in the Middle East, and could increase pressure on Prime Minister Ehud Barak of Israel to accept an international presence in East Jerusalem, Gaza and the West Bank. Mr. Barak has rejected the idea of UN observers, except perhaps to monitor a peace settlement. President Bill Clinton has stressed that no UN force can be sent without Israeli consent. But the United States has joined other members of the 15-nation Security Council in backing Mr. Annan's mediation effort. "The Security Council has asked me to explore with the parties how we can move forward," Mr. Annan told reporters after the Security Council's closed- door meeting Friday. "And obviously that means thinking through what sort of observer group will be acceptable." Mr. Annan told the council he is exploring two options. The first is to broaden the mandate of a fact-finding committee, led by the former Senate majority leader George Mitchell of Maine, to include monitoring the violence. A second option, Mr. Annan said, is to create a team of UN observers or to expand the mandate of an existing UN observer mission, possibly the Jerusalem-based UN Truce Supervision Organisation. Any mission, Mr. Annan said, would require the agreement of Israel and the Palestinians, and he asked the council to grant him "flexibility" in brokering an accord.
(IHT, 20 November, p. 8)

24 November

Ehud Barak, the Israeli Prime Minister, telephoned Yassir Arafat, the Palestinian leader, today during his talks in the Kremlin with President Putin and, in a three-way conversation, discussed ways of jump-starting Middle East peace talks. Mr Barak's unusual interruption – almost unprecedented in Kremlin talks with foreign leaders – came as Mr Putin was insisting that all talks and meetings would be useless if there was no drop in the level of violence. Regretting the "sad, tragic events in the Middle East", he said that Russia was in close and permanent contact with Israel and expressed confidence that things would soon change for the better. Mr Arafat's fleeting visit here is part of his campaign to persuade Russia and Western Europe to play a bigger role in the region and to support his call for an international force to protect the Palestinians from Israeli attacks. Mr Putin made clear that such a force could be deployed only if it had the agreement of both Israel and the Palestinians. He added that Russia saw the idea of a United Nations peacekeeping force in the region as unrealistic. (TT, 25 November)

7 December
Israel has used "excessive and often indiscriminate" force against Palestinian civilians and has discriminated "in law and practice against ethnic and religious minorities" and women, a leading U.S. human rights organisation charged today. In its 11th annual report reviewing human rights practices around the globe, Human Rights Watch said Israel's actions since a Palestinian uprising began last September had "greatly overshadowed and put into question" the country's earlier human rights improvements, including a decrease in the use of torture and a reduction in the number of people detained without charge. The report also said that Palestinian security services, in dealing with their own citizens, "continued to operate with impunity, despite recurring cases of torture, arbitrary arrests and prolonged detention without charge or trial." (WP, 8 December, p. A48)

Philippines

20 January
President Joseph Estrada resigned amid a corruption scandal as tens of thousands of protesters marched on his residence. The country's vice president immediately took the oath of office in an effort to end the Philippines' worst crisis in years. (NYT, 20 January, p. A-1)

Rwanda

7 July
An independent panel assembled by the Organisation of Africa Unity said that nations and institutions that failed to prevent or stop the 1994 genocide that killed up to 800,000 people should pay a "significant level of reparations" to Rwanda. The panel singled out France, the United States, Belgium, The United Nations and the Roman Catholic and Anglican churches as those most guilty-in addition to Rwanda's Hutu-led government- of complicity or negligence as Hutu militias rampaged through the country, massacring ethnic Tutsi and moderate or anti-government Hutu who defended them. In a report full of stinging rebukes, the panel asked Secretary-General Kofi Annan to establish a commission to name the countries that owe Rwanda the money to rebuild a devastated country and to formulate an appropriate scale of compensation. It also demanded cancellation of Rwanda's international debts.

9 July
Secretary of State Madeleine K. Albright says that an international panel was wrong to blame the United States for failing to prevent the slaughter of more than 500,000 people in Rwanda. "In my entire tie at the UN," she said, "I followed instructions because I was an ambassador, but I screamed about the instructions that I got on this. I felt they were very wrong, and I made that point. But I was an ambassador under instructions." She added: "The truth, though, that has to be kept in mind is that the whole thing exploded rapidly. There wasn't a UN force capable of taking this on." (WP, 10 July, p. A4)

6 September
Less than two weeks after experts told the United Nations that it needed an in-house policy centre to work on areas of tension before they turn into international crises, President Paul Kagame of Rwanda came along this week with a case in point. More than six years after a frenzy of ethnic killing tore his small African country apart, armed militia and former soldiers thought to be guilty of some of the killings are still roaming free in neighbouring Congo. A plan to deal with them should have been worked out long ago by UN officials drawing on their collective skills, Mr. Kagame said in an interview. To him, they are the reason there is a war in Congo. In New York for the summit meeting of world leaders, Mr. Kagame said that until the Hutu responsible for killing Tutsi and their moderate Hutu allies are disarmed and resettled somewhere in peace, Rwandan troops will stay in Congo. The presence of foreign troops – from Rwanda, Uganda, Zimbabwe, Angola and Namibia – is also a major impediment to dispatching a United Nations peacekeeping operation. Mr. Kagame, who has tempered the fury he first expressed at the failure of the United Nations and its leading members, including the United States and France, to prevent or end the massacres, now focuses his criticism on what he sees as an international failure to recognise that a country so profoundly wounded cannot be treated like just any place. (NYT, 7 September, p. 14)

5 February
The president of Rwanda, a central player in the long war in Congo, is warning American and United Nations officials that they must seize the opportunity to search for a peace settlement with a new Congolese leader while the political situation there remains fluid. President Paul Kagame, who has known the new Congolese president, Joseph Kabila, for years, said in an interview last week that Mr. Kabila, thrust into power after his father, Laurent Kabila, was killed on Jan. 16, appeared to be more open to peace and more co-operative with the outside world. "The opportunity is available and is not going to be there forever," Mr. Kagame said. Mr. Kagame urged timely international action in Congo after a year of fruitless debate in the United Nations Security Council, which has been unwilling or unable to send even a small peacekeeping force because of the continued warfare and the elder Kabila's refusal to allow political dialogue. The Congo conflict is Africa's widest war and involves the armies of five outside nations: Rwanda, Uganda, Angola, Zimbabwe and to some extent Namibia. "I think one can give him the benefit of the doubt that maybe he can do better than his father," Mr. Kagame said of Joseph Kabila, who met with the Security Council on Friday. "From what I've learned, he might be interested in going forward with peace. What I've not understood fully yet is what formula he wants to use to achieve that. Whether it is a formula that satisfies all the parties concerned is something we have yet to understand." Hundreds of thousands of Rwandans died before the attackers fled into Congo ahead of a Tutsi-led guerrilla force commanded by Mr. Kagame, who took power in Rwanda later that year.

Members of the Security Council have grown increasingly concerned that the outside powers in Congo, including Rwanda, are taking advantage of the chaos there to exploit its vast mining and mineral resources, which have in turn been used to fuel still more fighting. "On one hand, the international community is there claiming to be looking for a solution to the problem," he said. "On the other hand, it is allowing this problem to be recycled," he added, meaning that the militias are being allowed to fight, regroup and cross borders as governments in the region help them or look the other way. Mr. Kagame suggested a solution that he said had helped nearby Angola in its long civil war against rebels of the National Union for the Total Independence of Angola, or Unita. The Security Council has put the group under an embargo. Mr. Kagame, who was widely regarded as a favourite of the Clinton administration, said he hoped the Bush administration would continue American support. He said he was pleased with his meeting last week with Secretary of State Colin L. Powell. "There seems to be a good understanding and a readiness to be useful," he said. "That was the sense I got." (NYT, 5 February, p. A-4)

11 February
A People Betrayed – The Role of the West in Rwanda's Genocide – By Linda Melvern
On April 9, 1994, three days into the genocide in Rwanda, Gen. Dallaire watched as the European troops arrived and began evacuating their citizens. The new arrivals were clean-shaven, well fed and heavily armed, a marked contrast with the ragged, ill-equipped force that General Dallaire had battled his own headquarters to arm, shelter and feed. Estimates of the number of dead in the capital were already approaching 10,000. He knew that without outside help his troops could not deter the machete-wielding, largely Hutu militiamen who appeared bent on exterminating moderate Hutu and ethnic Tutsi citizens. His forces were even running out of ammunition, fuel, water and food. General Dallaire had pleaded with the Security Council for troop reinforcements, supplies and the authority to protect civilians. None of these were forthcoming. Finally, on April 21, with reports of some 100,000 Rwandans dead, the Security Council, in perhaps its most shameful hour, slashed the flimsy peacekeeping force further, leaving 450 troops to tackle tens of thousands of killers. A vast array of international decisions, non-decisions and decisions not to decide ensured that the Rwandan people and the peacekeepers would be abandoned to their fates. Two international investigations of the disaster have already been completed. The current United Nations secretary general, Kofi Annan, who at the time of the genocide was the head of the United Nations' peacekeeping department, commissioned an independent inquiry in May 1999 that proved harshly critical. Drawing on these reports, interviews with peacekeepers and previously unpublished records of private Security Council deliberations, Melvern offers a vivid picture of the role of Western nations in abetting, ignoring and allowing Rwanda's genocide. She singles out "accomplices" like France, which, with an eye to preserving its dominance in the region, provided the murderous Hutu regime with arms, money and even protection (allegations France has denied). And she documents the fatal lapses of the more remote bystanders, who, from their offices in New York, Washington, London, Brussels and Paris, failed Rwanda at every juncture. By capturing the cold, calculating debates at the United Nations, she has contributed a valuable behind-the-scenes version of the events that Gourevitch described so movingly on the ground. In the months before the mass killings began, official Western "Rwanda watchers" ignored warnings that Hutu militias were mobilizing for extermination of the Tutsi minority. Annan's peacekeeping office flatly rejected General Dallaire's requests to seize weapons. And once the killing had begun, American and European policy makers insisted on withdrawing peacekeepers, refused to jam radio broadcasts inciting

murder and issued only tepid and belated condemnations of the massacres. To defuse pressure to act, they also notoriously refrained from labelling the slaughter "genocide." Stung by the loss in 1993 of 18 American soldiers in Somalia, and vocal Congressional pressure to steer clear of United Nations operations, the Clinton administration was the most adamant opponent of sending reinforcements. American policy makers insisted that the United Nations pinpoint its exit strategy precisely before it would vote to allow even other countries to deploy a rescue mission, and also complained about the cost of any expanded peacekeeping presence. While Melvern offers an important account of the international response to the crisis, "A People Betrayed" only begins to tell the story of how and why the United Nations and its member states failed Rwanda. France, Belgium and the United Nations have at least been pressured into investigating their roles. But in the United States, President Bill Clinton's administration rejected Congressional calls for an investigation into the American response and refused requests for high-level co-operation with the United Nations investigation. "Accountability" was a concept that the last administration rightly pursued for the perpetrators of genocide but wrongly evaded itself. Many count the Rwandan genocide as one of the defining events of the post-cold-war world. It has become commonplace to hear international statesmen trumpet the importance of "reforming peacekeeping." But if that effort stands any chance of success, Western leaders will have to do more than open their eyes after genocide. They will have to commit troops and resources to risky missions, and open their classified files on past disasters. (NYT, 11 February, p. 7-33)

30 April
The bulky neo-Classical Palace of Justice in Brussels suggests a yearning for order and rules, but anarchy and bloodletting are the focus in one of its courts. There are four charges of complicity in multiple murders during the frenzy in Rwanda in 1994 in which an estimated half million civilians were shot, hacked or beaten to death. For the first time a jury of 12 citizens is judging people accused of war crimes in another country. Until now, military or civilian magistrates have decided such cases. The trial has stirred wide interest among lawyers and human rights advocates, who see this as a new chapter of human rights law. Supporters of a trial maintain that Belgium bears a special responsibility for the killings in Rwanda. When the Hutu majority began its bloody rampage against the Tutsi minority, Belgium pulled out of the United Nations peacekeeping force there. It took a Belgian parliamentary inquiry six years to bring the case to trial. But the political mood changed last year, when the new Prime Minister Verhofstadt visited Rwanda and apologized for Belgium's failure to do more to prevent the slaughter. The trial is now seen as a way to repay a moral debt to Rwanda's victims and to revive credibility in Belgium after scandals over corruption and an inept judicial system. The proceedings in Brussels are running parallel to other trials dealing with the Rwanda genocide. The International Criminal Tribunal for Rwanda, set up by the UN in Arusha, Tanzania, has so far convicted eight people. In Rwanda 4,500 people have been tried, with close to 100 executed. More than 100,000 people await trial there. The defendants are charged under Belgian laws that allow trials here for people accused of war crimes elsewhere. In the first days of trial, the 12 jurors and their 12 alternates have been given a crash course in Rwanda's ethnic divisions and turbulent history by a number of expert witnesses. (NYT, 30 April, p. 3)

1 May
Seven years after a state-orchestrated genocide claimed the lives of more than half a million ethnic Tutsi in Rwanda, the world is still struggling to establish a measure of accountability

for the mass killings. In Brussels four Rwandan Hutu are being tried on charges of slaughter. The trial marks the first time that a jury of civilians from one country is being asked to judge people accused of war crimes committed in another. The case opens a promising new frontier in the evolution of international criminal law. The four defendants have been charged under Belgian laws adopted to comply with international human rights convention. They are accused of collaborating with ethnic Hutu militias in several instances of killing. Ideally, trials should be conducted in the country where the crimes occurred, but Rwanda lacks the resources and judicial expertise to provide adequate trials. Belgium bears a measure of responsibility for the massacres in Rwanda. As Rwanda's former colonial master, Belgium helped lay the historical groundwork for the genocide. When Hutu militias began killing Tutsi in the spring of 1994, Belgium pulled out of the United Nations peacekeeping force after 10 Belgian soldiers were killed. That abrupt departure prompted the withdrawal of most of the rest of the UN force. The United States also blocked effective UN action in Rwanda, leaving Rwanda's Tutsi to their fate. The principle of universal jurisdiction is based on recognition that certain crimes are so serious that all of humanity has reason to bring the perpetrators to justice. (NYT, 1 May, p. 22)

Sierra Leone

1 July

Gunmen ambushed a UN convoy in Sierra Leone today, killing a Jordanian peacekeeper and wounding four others in the most lethal challenge to the UN mission since the withdrawal of several hundred British troops two weeks ago. UN officials said the attack occurred in a rebel-controlled area about 80 miles from Freetown. A UN spokesman could not confirm that the rebel Revolutionary United Front (RUF) had carried out the attack but said the group has repeatedly attacked civilians and UN posts in the region during the last week. The ambush rekindled fears among UN diplomats about the fate of more than 230 UN peacekeeping troops and military observers, who remain surrounded by rebels. Charles Taylor, the Liberian President, is the main UN hope for freeing the UN troops and observers. That's why the UN top diplomat in Sierra Leone warned the Council that a British resolution singling out Liberia as a potential target for sanctions over its role in smuggling arms and diamonds for the RUF, could complicate efforts to obtain the peacekeepers' release. The United Nations last night delayed banning the sale of "blood diamonds" from Sierra Leone, which for years have been used to finance and arm the country's rebel movement. The trade is estimated to be worth 50 million Pounds a year. Experts gave warning that the embargo would be meaningless, as it was in Angola, unless it was enforced properly. The United States, meanwhile, began circulating a proposal for an UN-sanctioned criminal court to prosecute RUF officials, including the group's leader, Foday Sankoh, for war crimes. The proposed resolution would have the United Nations help Sierra Leone establish a "mixed court" of Sierra Leonean and UN-appointed judges. (WP/TL, 1 July, p. A19)

5 July

The Security Council has voted to impose a worldwide ban on the purchase of rough diamonds from Sierra Leone until the country's government can establish a system to certify the origin of stones and begins to assert its authority over the diamond fields. The resolution Wednesday, sponsored by Britain, is experimental and intended to get at the roots of war. The Sierra Leonean ambassador said:" The root of the conflict is and remains diamonds, diamonds and diamonds". The time limit on the embargo will be, after French proposal, 18 months. The United States, while backing the resolution, opposed having a time limit, especially one so short. The Security Council is also working on a resolution to increase the size of the peacekeeping force in Sierra Leone to 16,500 from about 13,000. But the Clinton Administration, facing a refusal by Congress of money to pay the US share of such a peacekeeping operation, is reluctant to approve the increase, council members say. (IHT, 7 July, p. 4)

5 July
President Bill Clinton visited the UN to sign an international protocol forbidding the forced recruitment of children to fight in wars. The Revolutionary United Front has long been accused of using child soldiers and giving them lethal weapons. (Ind., 6 July, p. 14)

13 July
Britain has been warned by a leading human rights group about humanitarian abuses in the Sierra Leonean war- this time perpetrated by government forces, who are being advised by British military experts- against suspected rebels. The attacks killed at least 27 civilians and wounded 50 more in the three towns, to the north and north east of the capital, Freetown, the human rights group said. (Ind., 13 July, p. 15)

16 July
In a rare display of force, hundreds of United Nations troops, who picked up a distress signal today, rescued all 222 peacekeepers and 11 military observers trapped by rebels inside peacekeepers' base in eastern Sierra Leone since May 1, United Nations officials said. No one in the UN aircraft was hurt, but the rebels suffered "serious casualties". The decision to mount a rescue was made after the United Nations force in Sierra Leone received a distress call from the detainees about dwindling food and medical supplies, according to a United Nations statement. It was the first time that the UN peacekeepers in Sierra Leone had taken direct action to rescue detained international troops. (NYT, 16 July, p. 8/ TL, 17 July)

17 July
The United States, in person of Thomas Pickering, under-secretary of state for political affairs, has warned Liberian President Charles Taylor in a meeting. If he does not quickly halt his support of rebels in neighbouring Sierra Leone, his government will be treated as an international pariah and subjected to unilateral and international sanctions, according to U.S. and Liberian officials. While Taylor acknowledges his historic ties to the RUF, he strongly denies aiding them now and has said he will accept UN monitors on the porous Liberia-Sierra Leone border to verify no weapons pass through it. Taylor was furious over the tone of the meeting and blasted back in a nationally broadcast radio and television address July 19. Taylor said that while the United States may be satisfied with the evidence against him, "I have said, 'What you have is a diabolical lie ... Even a condemned man deserves his day in court. Bring the evidence. You cannot be the judge and jury at the same time.' Sources close to the rebels said a meeting from Taylor with senior rebel commanders and political representatives in Monrovia was scheduled for this weekend or later this week. (WP, 30 July, p. A27)

22 July

Today Britain has produced the first 1,000 Sierra Leonean soldiers for the government's long running war against the rebels of the Revolutionary United Front (RUF). A different kind of battle must now be fought to make sure the soldiers are properly paid, fed, kept together as a unit and supported in the field. British forces are expected to be in the country for another five years-rather than the three officially announced- training up to 4,000 men. But most British officers believe it will be the Sierra Leoneans who ultimately win or lose this war. (TL, 23 July).

22 July

An offensive by UN peacekeepers has pushed a breakaway military faction from a strategic road leading into Sierra Leone's capital. The operation involved heavily armed UN ground troops and helicopter gun ships. At least one peacekeeper was wounded and an unknown number of renegades were killed, a United Nations military officer said. (NYT, 24 July, p. 3)

31 July

The United States and Britain threatened today to impose sanctions on Liberia and Burkina Faso unless those West African countries cut off military assistance to rebels in neighbouring Sierra Leone. Representatives of Liberia and Burkina Faso denied the allegations. But outside experts testified at the hearing that Liberia exports at least 40 times more diamonds than it is capable of producing domestically. "A year ago, the RUF were machete wielding thugs," Holbrooke said. "They are now acquiring machine guns, shoulder fired surface-to-air missiles and the means to shoot down aircraft. This is extraordinarily dangerous, not only for the region but for the United Nations." (1 August, WP, p. A19)

2 August

The United States has repeated its warning that it will impose sanctions on Liberia unless it determines that the West African country has halted support for rebel forces in neighbouring Sierra Leone. Two weeks after Under-secretary of State Pickering visited President Charles Taylor to warn of sanctions, Liberian Foreign Minister Monie Captan met with Pickering today and promised new co-operation on ending the war in Sierra Leone. Captain said in an interview Monday that his government would encourage the rebels to give up the diamond fields and would invite UN observers to Liberia to monitor its border with Sierra Leone for any illicit trade in arms and diamonds. Captain told US officials this week that Liberia is working with rebel commanders to select a new spokesman to replace the movement's jailed leader, Foday Sankoh, and restart a peace process that stalled in May after rebel forces attacked UN peacekeeping forces in Sierra Leone and took 500 of them hostage. But Captain argued against a US proposal to establish a UN-sponsored war crimes court to try Sankoh and other rebels suspected of atrocities, saying that could torpedo any efforts to resume the peace process. (WP, 3 August, p. A23)

4 August

After weeks of resisting appeals by Secretary General Kofi Annan for more UN troops for Sierra Leone, the Clinton administration said today that it would ask Congress for funding to send thousands of additional peacekeepers to the troubled West African country. The additional peacekeepers would help Sierra Leone's elected government take control of rebel-held territory, including the country's lucrative diamond mines. Republican leaders however have rebuffed very new request for additional peacekeeping funds, even for operations in Kosovo. (WP, 5 August, p. A16)

14 August
The Security Council voted unanimously today to create a special court to prosecute rebel leaders responsible for killing and maiming tens of thousands of people during Sierra Leone's civil war. The resolution authorizes secretary General Kofi Annan to negotiate with Sierra Leone's government to set up an independent court, with a mixture of local and international judges, to prosecute crimes against humanity, war crimes and other serious violations of international and Sierra Leonean laws. (WP, 15 August, p. A6)

25 August
Secretary General Kofi Annan called for increasing the United Nations peacekeeping force in Sierra Leone to 20,500 troops to help the government regain control of the country from rebels. United troops are now authorized to concentrate on helping the government extend its authority by deploying at strategic locations and 'by responding robustly to any hostile actions or threats of force.' (NYT, 26 August, p. 3)

25 August
A group of British troops in Sierra Leone has been taken hostage by a ruthless band of renegade soldiers loyal to the country's former ruling military junta. Masiaka highway in what had hitherto been regarded as a safe area. They were captured in a small village called Forodugu on their way back from a routine liaison visit to a unit of the Sierra Leone army at Benguema, southeast of Freetown and taken to the West side Boys' base in nearby hills. Military sources believed that the abduction may have been motivated by a desire to acquire the vehicles, which bristle with weaponry. (TL, 27 August)

27 August
A specialist team of British negotiators and SAS hostage-rescue experts arrived in Sierra Leone to join efforts to free 11 Royal Ireland Regiment soldiers who were kidnapped three days ago. The militia group issued its demands. It said that it wanted food, medicine, and the release of a leader from prison. He was named as General Papa, alias "Bomb Blast", who has been at the central prison in Freetown for nearly two months. The group also demanded a meeting with the Sierra Leone Government, raising hopes that the soldiers might be freed soon. (TL, 28 August)

28 August
Hopes are growing of an early resolution to the hostage crisis in Sierra Leone as the kidnapped British soldiers' commander officer twice met the leader of their abductors. In London, Ian Duncan Smith, Shadow Defence Secretary, said the Government had to think seriously about whether to keep the training team of 250 British soldiers in Sierra Leone. (29 August, TL)

1 September
The rebel group holding six British soldiers hostage in Sierra Leone said yesterday they would not be released until its demands to be included in the West African country's government was met. Five of the soldiers, who were captured seven days ago, were released

on Wednesday and negotiations were continuing yesterday to free the others and their Sierra Leonean guide. A spokesman for the West Side Boys said the soldiers were taken to force Britain to put pressure on Sierra Leone's government to recognise the militia, release their leaders from prison and include them in a new administration. Earlier the Armed Forces minister, John Spellar, confirmed that the 11 soldiers were captured after they left the main road back to their base near the capital, Freetown. The admission that the three-vehicle UK convoy did enter rebel territory followed complaints from Brigadier General Mohammed Garba, the Nigerian deputy commander of the UN peace- keeping force. He accused the British troops of "Rambo-like" behaviour deep inside jungle controlled by the rebels and said they laid themselves open to capture by failing to tell peacekeepers of their movements. British negotiators refused to say if a deal had been made to secure the soldiers' release. (TI, 1 September, p. 2)

9 September
The UN peacekeeping mission in Sierra Leone has become paralysed by infighting among its top officials and has failed to halt new waves of human rights violations – including abductions and rapes – by the country's armed factions. The deep divisions in the UN mission were described in interviews with diplomats and UN officials in Freetown, the capital, and dramatised in an unusually blunt and angry memo written by Maj. Gen. Vijay K. Jetley, the Indian commander of the 13,000 UN troops dispatched to bring peace to this badly bruised West African country. In bitter terms, Jetley accused his deputy commander, Gen. Mohammed Garba, and the UN secretary general's special representative, Oluyemi Adeniji, both of whom are Nigerian, of undermining the UN mission and of insubordination. He also alleged that Nigerian officers had secret contacts with the main Sierra Leone rebel group, the Revolutionary United Front (RUF), which, he implied, led them to profit from the illegal diamond trade. In his memorandum Jetley wrote that Adeniji and Garba believe "keeping the Nigerian interests was paramount even if it meant scuttling the peace process." Jetley also wrote that the "Nigerian army was interested in staying in Sierra Leone due to the massive benefits they were getting from the illegal diamond mining" and that Adeniji and Garba "have worked hard to sabotage the peace process and show Indians in general and me in particular in a poor light." The two officers denied the charges. But the memo has so divided the UN leaders here that they barely speak to each other and give conflicting commands, leaving the mission adrift in recent months, UN officials and diplomats said. (WP, 10 September, p. A1)

19 September
The United Nations Security Council delayed a vote to increase the peacekeeping force in Sierra Leone yesterday because the UN has not managed to secure enough troops from its members, diplomats and UN officials said. The council had planned to vote today on a resolution increase the force from 13,000 to 20,500-strong. (TI, 20 September, p. 15)

20 September
India will gradually withdraw its contingent from the UN peacekeeping force in Sierra Leone, raising new problems for the troubled UN operation there, according to Indian and UN diplomats. India's 3,000 troops form nearly a quarter of the 13,000-member UN Mission in Sierra Leone (UNAMSIL) and provide it with essential helicopter gun ships. It remains unclear whether the United Nations can find adequate replacements. For months, the UN force has been effectively paralysed by a power struggle between its In-

dian commander, Maj. Gen. Vijay Jetley, and Nigerian political and military officials in the operation. India's decision to quit the force comes after UN Secretary General Kofi Annan asked New Delhi to replace Jetley. "We have told the United Nations secretariat that we are withdrawing from Sierra Leone," said a spokesman at the Indian mission to the United Nations. "We are going to be withdrawing everything." U.S. Army Special Forces teams are training Nigerian and Ghanaian units to join UNAMSIL, and U.S. officials have voiced hope that those units will be available in the coming few months. Annan has asked several countries--including Britain, Turkey, Malaysia, Morocco and Tunisia--to take the Indians' place. "We were already in touch with troop contributing countries," said Shashi Tharoor, the UN communications director. "There was a process for reviewing the composition of the force in the context of a possible expansion." (WP, 21 September, p. A30)

9 October
Several hundred more British troops are expected to be sent to Sierra Leone to prop up the crumbling United Nations peacekeeping force there, under measures due to be announced by the Government in the Lords as early as today. The move is expected to provoke controversy and accusations that the Government has embarked on a deeper commitment without properly calculating the dangers to British Armed Forces deployed in the former colony. The British reinforcements will be sent to help to save UNAMSIL, the 13,000-strong UN peacekeeping force, which has had a disastrous record since its deployment. Last month, just when the UN had begun to gain some credibility in the country, India announced that it was pulling out its 3,000 troops, the largest and most capable of all UNAMSIL contingents. Since India's announcement, Jordan has also threatened to pull out its contingent unless the UN force receives help from a NATO country, preferably Britain. Despite growing reservations at the Ministry of Defence about the dangers of further commitments, the Government has said that it regards Sierra Leone as a test case for all future conflict resolution in Africa. The British are hoping that by announcing more troops for Sierra Leone, they will be able to share the burden and attract other contributors from NATO countries, possibly Canada and The Netherlands. (TT, 9 October)

18 October
President Charles Taylor of Liberia has suggested that UN peacekeeping troops be allowed to move into rebel-held diamond-producing areas of Sierra Leone while the rebels return to the negotiations that were shattered in May by their breach of a peace accord. Mr. Taylor, who has been close to the Revolutionary United Front, as the insurgents in Sierra Leone call themselves, floated the proposal Saturday to a Security Council mission that was visiting Liberia as part of a West African tour. The proposal, which could be a significant step toward a peace pact in Sierra Leone, was conveyed to the Security Council in a closed session Monday by Britain's chief representative, Sir Jeremy Greenstock. Some council members treated the proposal as possibly a tactical ploy by Mr. Taylor, who denies widespread allegations that he is prospering from diamond and arms trade with the rebels. The proposal has coincided with some hints from the rebels themselves that they may be looking for a way out of the war they started. Meanwhile, the United Nations has embarked on a program of expanding its presence, now about 12,500 troops, helping to stabilise the Sierra Leone government and strengthening the military force assembled by a coalition of West African countries. It also helped set up a system to certify

diamonds legally exported from Sierra Leone, in an effort to stifle international demand for illicit stones mined by the rebels. (IHT, 18 October, p. 6)

25 October

Jordan has decided to withdraw all of its 1,800 troops from the UN peacekeeping mission in Sierra Leone, dealing another blow to the beleaguered operation, UN officials said. The decision comes a month after India announced the phased withdrawal of its 3,000 troops from the 13,000-member mission. The withdrawals will deprive the force of its best-trained-and-equipped troops, and they have prompted Secretary General Kofi Annan to search for replacements. Bangladesh, Kenya and Ghana have offered to provide about 3,000 additional troops to fill the gap. Ukraine and Slovakia are considering supplying armoured vehicles and trucks. Britain, meanwhile, pledged this month to double the number of military instructors training the Sierra Leonean army to about 400 and to provide 10 military officers to the UN mission. Marie Okabe, a UN spokeswoman, said that Annan would appeal to the Jordanian government to delay the departure of its soldiers until he had a chance to bring in replacement forces. (WP, 25 October, p. A25)

1 November

Britain's military commitment to Sierra Leone has taken a further significant leap forward today when a senior British Army officer was assigned to a top post with the United Nations peacekeeping force in the West African state. Brigadier Alastair Duncan, 47, a highly experienced officer who served in Bosnia, will take over as Chief of Staff at the United Nations Mission in Sierra Leone (Unamsil) headquarters in Freetown. The UN asked for a British officer to fill the post of chief of staff. Britain's military reputation in the West African state is unrivalled since the rapid deployment of 700 paratroops to Freetown in May, when it was feared that rebel forces were about to seize the capital. The disarray in Unamsil and the end of the rainy season – bringing fears of new military action by the rebel Revolutionary United Front – put pressure on Britain to step in once again to steady what was seen as an increasingly wobbly mission. In a few weeks Britain's commitment has grown steadily. A team of 250 soldiers training the Sierra Leonean Army has risen to 400; the short-term instruction programme has lengthened by 18 weeks; a special operational brigade headquarters of 100 staff officers has been set up and a Royal Navy Amphibious Ready Group, with 600 Royal Marines, has been dispatched. (TT, 2 November)

6 November

United Nations peacekeepers and Sierra Leone police officers opened fire today to disperse hundreds of youths that were burning tires and demanding that a curfew be lifted, witnesses said. At least 13 civilians, including two children, were wounded. The government had imposed the curfew to prevent rebel attacks, but people were angry over a spate of armed robberies during curfew hours. The youths said the curfew, from 11 p.m. to 6 a.m., prevents them from mobilizing to protect their neighbourhoods from robberies. The acting defence chief of staff, Tom Carew, appealed to protesters to go home while authorities looked into their grievances. The curfew was put in place earlier this year in an effort to prevent incursions by Sierra Leone's rebel Revolutionary United Front, which controls much of the country's jungle interior. UN officials in Freetown could not be reached for comment, although a duty officer at the United Nations headquarters in New York, Edoardo Bellando, said he had been informed "third hand" that United Nations troops had been present when "police fired in the air to disperse a mob of thieves who were throwing rocks." (NYT, 6 November, p. A10)

10 November
Less than an hour after it was signed, a cease-fire reached on Friday between the government and rebels of Sierra Leone was thrown into doubt after a rebel leader said the deal was no guarantee of an end to Sierra Leone's nine-year civil war. After the first high-level talks between the two sides since the rebels re-ignited the civil war in May, Sierra Leone's government and rebel leaders agreed to a 30-day cease-fire. It would allow United Nations peacekeepers to deploy in rebel territory, including areas around the lucrative diamond mines that the rebels have used to finance the war. But Col. Jonathan Kposowa, the leader of the rebel Revolutionary United Front, immediately called the deal a "stepping stone," and said he could give "no guarantees it means the end of the war." (NYT, 12 November, p. 12)

4 December
The United Nations Secretary General, Kofi Annan, appealed to Sierra Leone's rebels today to show their commitment to peace efforts by opening up areas under their control to the government and peacekeepers. Mr. Annan, wrapping up a two-day visit to Sierra Leone in the capital, Freetown, also urged the rebels to guarantee the security of all who came from abroad to help put the shattered West African country back on its feet. Mr. Annan later left for Benin, where he will attend a democracy conference. He will also visit Ethiopia and Eritrea, which have been at war and where peacekeeping will again be on the agenda. He will also attend an AIDS forum in Ethiopia. (NYT, 4 December, p. A4)

20 January
President Taylor said today that he has ended support of a brutal insurgency in Sierra Leone and is willing to international scrutiny of his finances. Taylor said Liberia would adopt several measures demanded in a recent UN report, including supervision of the sale of Liberian diamonds. A UN panel and others have accused Taylor of receiving diamonds from Sierra Leone's Revolutionary United Front (RUF) in exchange for shipments of weapons to the rebels. In an interview Taylor said "it is the intention of Liberia to sever all links to the RUF, both formal and informal." Taylor's pledge of "complete disengagement" from the RUF came as Liberia faced a new round of international sanctions. The Security Council is to take up measures that would impose a worldwide ban on sales of Liberian diamonds and timber and prohibit international travel by its officials. The sanctions would "kill Liberia," Taylor said. Taylor acknowledged long-standing ties between his government and the RUF, but denied that they included swapping guns for diamonds. He said the relationship was aimed at bringing peace to Sierra Leone. He said Liberia's moderating influence on the RUF could contribute to peace prospects in the region. Last month, a report compiled by a UN panel accused Taylor and his government of profiting from their support of the RUF. Taylor called the report "a political document" but said his government accepted the paper with "deep reservations." In July 1999, RUF leader Sankoh signed a peace agreement to end Sierra Leone's war and agreed to accept a UN peacekeeping force in the country to monitor the accord. But the agreement fell apart last May when the RUF took several hundred peacekeepers hostage. Officials stressed there can be no peace in the region until the RUF loses the ability to trade diamonds

mined in areas under their control for weapons and food. Taylor said he had ordered the grounding of all Liberian-registered aircraft until they could be inspected and registered to prevent their use in diamond or arms trafficking. He said he would also ask a UN group to oversee the legal sale of Liberia's diamonds. He said the United States was engaged in a campaign to "demonise" him and "bring this government down, or maybe even assassinate the president." Taylor asked, "What has Liberia done that is so bad to deserve this? We have been allies for 150 years, but they shut every door on us. So what else can we conclude but that this is what happens when they want to take a guy out? It is terrible." (WP, 20 January, p. A21)

31 January

A presidential election due in February has been called off because of insecurity over the country's civil war, its justice minister said. Solomon Berewa said a parliamentary vote set for March would also not take place. (Reuters)

19 February

All sides in the conflict about Sierra Leone agree that unless the troubled UN peacekeeping mission quickly begins to fan out across Sierra Leone, one of the most brutal wars in Africa in recent years will likely resume. UN officials say that even with almost 10,000 troops, there are not enough to deploy beyond a few positions. The mission, UNAMSIL, costs $1.5 million a day and is heavily concentrated in Freetown and a few other urban centres. The inability of peacekeepers to deploy, according to UN officials and diplomats, could seriously hinder efforts to repatriate tens of thousands of Sierra Leonean refugees who fled to neighbouring Guinea to escape escalating fighting. The international peacekeeping mission began after the government and the Revolutionary United Front (RUF) signed an agreement in July 1999. They designed to end war in which rebels kidnapped thousands of children and turned them into combatants, razed hundreds of villages, raped woman and hacked the arms and legs of thousands of civilians. The agreement collapsed last May when the rebels refused to disarm and briefly took 500 UN peacekeepers hostage, plunging the country back into war. UN officials said the number of troops, authorized at 20,000 following the hostage taking last year, should stabilize at about 12,000 by the end of March. UN officials said a more rapid deployment would open UN forces to new hostage-takings or attacks. Besides breaking the initial peace agreement, the RUF has repeatedly promised to turn over hundreds of weapon taken from the UN forces and allow the free movement of people and relief agencies in the areas they control. None of the commitments has been met. Within the RUF a growing number of rebels want to disarm but are being prevented from doing so by their senior officers. An officer of RUF said, "They are waiting for UNAMSIL, If UNAMSIL is there to guarantee their safety, many, many will surrender." On the other side is the government. The government is threatening an all-out offensive against the RUF to retake taken areas. The UN officials strongly oppose such a move, arguing they are not here to fight or take sides in the conflict – a position that is stirring anger and frustration among people outside rebel territory. Many Sierra Leoneans say that, given the brutal history of RUF and its breaking of the peace process, the UN troops should force their way into rebel territory if necessary. (WP, 19 February, p. A29)

24 February
Parrot's Beak has become the focus of a widening war in West Africa and home to what United Nations officials describe as the world's worst refugee crisis. Parrot's Beak begins where the borders of Guinea, Sierra Leone and Liberia intersect, as do conflicts in the three countries. It has become the haven for as many as 140,000 refugees who have been pushed there by fighting in Sierra Leone and Liberia. Recently, as fighting has spilled over the border into Guinea, the atmosphere has grown less than welcoming for foreigners in a small country that already holds hundreds of thousands of people displaced by war and is wary of its region's contagious conflicts. Many of the refugees have already gone to government-controlled areas in Sierra Leone, travelling by boat after making their way to this country's capital, Conakry. In the camp at Massakoundou the population has tripled to 30,000. A recent United Nations report charges that Liberia has used its place as the centre for arms and diamond trafficking in the region to stir up the war in Sierra Leone. The United Nations Security Council is considering sanctions against Liberia for its support of the rebels and for its flouting of an embargo on arms imports. The crisis here began a few months ago with an attack on Macenta, a town near the Liberian border and the hub of the regions diamonds mining activities. For Guinean people the basis of the fresh conflict was clear. For years Guinea harboured up to half a million refugees from Sierra Leone and Liberia, two countries ravaged by interlocking conflicts. Today about 300,000 of the refugees here is from Sierra Leone and about 120,000 from Liberia. Tensions have long simmered between Guinea and Liberia, each of which has provided rear bases for rebels committed to overthrowing the other's government. But the tensions erupted in recent months into aerial bombings and guerrilla attacks, involving the armies of the three countries as well as several militias. Relief officials and Western diplomats say the shifting alliances appear to pit the Guinean and Sierra Leonean militaries, Liberian rebels and the Sierra Leonean tribal hunters of Kamajors on one side, against the Liberian military, Guinean rebels and the rebels from Sierra Leone. (NYT, 24 February, p. 1)

4 March
At every street corner in the centre of Freetown you see the small boys and girls missing a hand or a foot. They are the casualties of Sierra Leone's brutal civil war. They are the ones who were left behind when the corpses had been counted and the rebels of the Revolutionary United Front (RUF) had returned to their camps in the bush. Sierra Leone, no longer in the headlines, remains a country locked in violence. The democratically elected government controls only about half of the nation's territory, with the aid of 13,000 UN peacekeeping troops. RUF rebels continue to hold the diamond-producing regions. Profits from the diamonds are routed through Liberian President Taylor, who buys weapons for the RUF and enriches him and his RUF allies. If Taylor remains in power in Liberia and the UN troops leave, the entire country will in all likelihood soon be awash with blood. And it will not stop at Sierra Leone's border. The Bush administration should do all within its power to prevent this. It should use its leadership in the Security Council to ensure the continued presence of UN troops in Sierra Leone, with a mandate sufficiently robust to protect both themselves and the civilians under their care. And, ultimately, to help Sierra Leone's government recaptures the diamond regions and put the RUF out of business. The administration should also support the Special Court for Sierra Leone. The UN at the urging of the United States created this body, and it will be sleeker than the similar tribunals for Rwanda and Yugoslavia. Without the support and funding of the U.S., the court will languish. The international community did little while rebels took

away the future from countless Sierra Leonean children and threatened the stability of all West Africa. Belatedly, the Clinton administration took a leadership role in bringing the atrocities to an end and laying the groundwork for a better tomorrow in Sierra Leone. The Bush administration should now take up that leadership mantle. (WP, 4 March, p. b7)

8 March

The United Nations Security Council voted unanimously to bar all diamond exports from the West African nation in two months if Liberia did not stop supporting a rebel army that has devastated Sierra Leone. (NYT, 8 March, p. 2)

31 March

The UN Security Council demanded that Sierra Leone's rebels allow UN peacekeepers into diamond mine areas they control and authorized an increase of UN troops to 17,500 from 10,350. In a resolution adopted by a 15 to 0 vote, the council extended the mandate of the UN Mission in Sierra Leone, known as UNAMSIL, for another six months. (Associated Press)

14 April

The breadth and brutality of Sierra Leone's 10-year civil war was evident everywhere in a visit to this town, headquarters of the rebel Revolutionary United Front. The rebels, who reneged on previous peace agreements, gained international notoriety by forcing thousands of children into combat, raping woman and hacking off the arms and legs of civilians. But two days of conversations with a visitor painted a picture of a rebel force reassessing its future. Senior leaders of the RUF said they realized the possibility of military victory was gone, and offered unconditional talks with the government. For the first time, they apologized for taking more than 500 UN peacekeepers hostage last year. They pledged to allow the UN troops to deploy freely across the 60 percent of the national territory that the rebels' control. To push the peace process forward, the RUF leaders said they have named a peace commission headed by Golley, a British-educated lawyer who has represented the rebels in the past. Diplomats and analysts reacted to the RUF statements with scepticism, because the rebels have reneged on past peace agreement. Still, some aid there were signs that the war may be winding down. The big question, they said, was whether rank-and-file troops would go along with a peace agreement. Whether the government should take up the offer to talk is a point of debate. In a report issued earlier this week, the International Crisis Group, a Brussels-based research and advocacy group, said that the Sierra Leone government should make no further deals with the RUF, demand its surrender and prepare to move militarily if the answer is no. Several factors have combined to spur the RUF leadership to reassess its situation. These include the increased presence of UN peacekeepers, the reduction of support from neighbouring Liberia and the imprisonment if its leader and founder, Sankoh. To show that the RUF has a political and social side as well as a military one, the RUF allowed journalist unusual access to the rebels. The RUF commanders and combatants said their peace overtures carried none of the demands that the RUF had made in the past. Because the RUF assigned a person from its propaganda wing to accompany a visiting journalist on a tour of the town, it was hard to gauge the level of popular support for the rebels. When asked what the RUF had done for the town was the highest praise any of the locals offered that the RUF let them live. Massaquoi, a senior RUF commander and official spokesman acknowledged that the RUF has committed widespread atrocities during the war and said it supported an international inquiry. That, he said, would show that all parties to the conflict had used the same brutal tactics of rape, amputation and scorched earth destruction of villages. Human rights groups have long agreed that all sides are guilty of such atrocities and that the most vicious tactics began in 1997, when, for nine months, a military junta and the RUF, leading to the bloodiest phase of the war jointly governed Sierra Leone. The war drew to a temporary halt after the 1999 Lome accord, which granted RUF a share of political power in exchange for disarming and called for deployment of UN peacekeepers to monitor the process. The agreement fell apart last May, when the RUF, refusing to disarm, took 500 peacekeepers hostage and marched toward Freetown. Britain, the former colonial power here, dispatched several thousands troops to defend the capital and work with the government army, halting the RUF advance. Although a tenuous cease-fire signed in November has generally held, there have been no talks between the RUF and the government. The most formidable factor enforcing the peace is the threat of intervention by the British. At the same time, Liberian President Taylor, a long time patron of the RUF, is no longer able to support the rebels. He is under increasing international pressure to cut his ties to the RUF or face stiff international sanctions. Sankoh no longer leads the RUF. The new RUF leaders are more flexible and realistic, according to sources who deal with the RUF regularly. The most formidable factor enforcing the peace is the threat of intervention by the British, who have several hundred trainers working with the army, a warship off the coast and an "over the horizon" force of several thousand poised for rapid intervention. At the same time, Liberian President Charles Taylor, a long time patron of the RUF, is no longer able to support the rebels. In the past, Taylor has supplied them with weapons, logistical help and an avenue to sell diamonds to finance the war. But Taylor is under increasing international pressure to cut his ties to the RUF or face stiff international sanctions, and his economy is crumbling. He is also facing a growing war in his own country as Liberian insurgents based in Guinea inflict heavy losses. Sankoh's replacement, Sessay, and Massaquoi have become the leading proponents of seeking a political end to the conflict. At the same time, the UN contingent is slowly beginning to carry out its mandate to deploy across the country, including into RUF territory. UN spokeswoman Novicki said the peacekeeping mission would be up to its fully authorized strength of 17,500 troops by the summer. Massaquoi and other RUF commanders said they were allowing the UN deployment to go ahead in part because the presence of UN troops ensured that their positions would not be attacked by the army or the British. (WP, 14 April, p. A1)

26 May
Children are being released as soldiers by the Revolutionary United Front (R.U.F.), the rebel group that has terrorized this country for the last decade by kidnapping children and chopping off the arms of ordinary citizens. A year after the rebels took more than 500 United Nations peacekeepers hostage and raised doubts about the West's commitment to peacekeeping in Africa; the situation has clearly begun improving in recent weeks. About 2,600 rebels and pro-government militia members have surrendered their weapons in the last week and almost 600 child soldiers have been freed. But the government says the rebels still hold 1,400 children. Peacekeepers have begun deploying again in rebel-held territory. British troops continue to train Sierra Leone soldiers and rebuild its army. Military officials from the United States have been training West African peacekeepers, and about 1,500 American-trained Nigerian soldiers are now in Sierra Leone. At the same time, while the situation is stable in Sierra Leone, it has deteriorated in Liberia and neighbouring Guinea. In recent months, the Li-

berian-supported revolutionary front has fought against Guinean troops on the border between Sierra Leone and Guinea, because the government of Guinea is believed to be supporting Liberian rebels. The fighting has caused a refugee crisis in Guinea. The rebels have begun talking peace, United Nations officials and Western diplomats say. The UN Security Council imposed charges on Liberia this month. UN officials received a reminder of the dangers of the widening war last week when they began disarming combatants in the western region of Gambia, where clashes between the revolutionary front and Guinean soldiers have occurred. The biggest difficulty may be bringing peace to the diamond-mining region in eastern Sierra Leone. Most of that area has been under the control of the revolutionary front. (NYT, 26 May, p. 3)

26 May
The children poured by the hundreds out of trucks and buses and swarmed toward the concrete seats of the rundown soccer stadium, afraid to believe that that they were finally being freed by the rebels who had abducted them. While UN officials and leaders of the rebel Revolutionary United Front (RUF) and Sierra Leone's government gave speeches, the children asked visitors if it was true they were leaving today. The release of nearly 600 child combatants today was the first in Sierra Leone's 10-year civil war and was perhaps the surest sign yet that the conflict may be winding down. The peace process that has been underway in earnest since the government and the rebels signed an agreement in March is not the first attempt at ending Sierra Leone's agony. But observers on all sides say it is the most serious and has the best chance of succeeding. A peace agreement signed in July 1999 fell apart last year when the RUF took 500 UN peacekeepers hostage and resumed fighting. Soon afterward, RUF founder Sankoh was captured and remains in prison. The rebels' leaders who replaced Sankoh found themselves facing a host of reasons the war could not be won militarily. Their supply lines through neighbouring Liberia dried up as international pressure mounted on their most staunch ally, Liberian President Taylor. Britain established a military presence in Sierra Leone and a reinforced UN peacekeeping contingent of about 12,500 troops fanned out across the country. Now peace talks ensued. The advances toward peace have been threatened by an outbreak of fighting in the eastern part of the country. Where Sierra Leone's lucrative diamonds fields lie. Peacekeepers and other observers described today's release of child soldiers as a major sign of hope. Relief workers say they now face a huge challenge in trying to return the children to a normal life. (WP, 26 May, p. A20)

30 May
President Taylor of Liberia today accused Britain of helping to keep alive a regional conflict in West Africa. His forces are battling an insurgency in the north of Liberia by dissidents based in Guinea. He contends that Sierra Leonean militia members trained by Britain are taking part in attacks. "We believe that Britain is on a secret war in West Africa", Mr. Passawe said, when he quoted Mr. Taylor. Britain has denied any involvement in Liberia's was, which is part of a widening regional conflict at the junction of the borders between Liberia, Guinea and Sierra Leone. But Britain and the United States have been the strongest advocates of the sanctions the UN Security Council imposed against Liberia. Britain sent troops to Sierra Leone last year to strengthen the UN peacekeeping effort there after a 1999 peace deal collapsed and rebels took hundreds of peacekeepers hostage. Today, Mr. Passawe quoted Mr. Taylor as having said: "The British troops should be under the command of the UN and not outside its operations". The Economic Community of West African States,

whose force intervened in the 1990's in the Liberian and Sierra Leonean civil wars, has approved a 1,700-member force to patrol the borders between Guinea and its two southern neighbours. (NYT, 30 May, p. 6)

4 June

After more than a decade in the thick of West Africa's most brutal civil wars, "Commander Poison" wants to go home. And he asks to be called Richie. He is among the first of the commanders of the rebel Revolutionary United Front (RUF) to lay down his weapons as part of a process that appears to be nudging this tiny country toward peace. His story offers a window onto the conflicts that have bled the region for years and robbed tens of thousands of people of their childhood. Richie said, "My life is much better now. I am very happy to put down my gun. Now I just want to go home. I have not seen my family for these many years." Home for Richie is neighbouring Liberia. He said he was attending a boarding school there in 1990 when he and most of his classmates were abducted by the forces of Taylor, the rebel leader who is now Liberia's president. After three months of training, he was assigned to Taylor's infamous Small Boys Unit, the group of child soldiers that acted as Taylor's bodyguards and most ruthless combat force. In 1991, while still fighting in Liberia, Taylor helped launch the civil war in Sierra Leone by providing troops, training and supplies to Sankoh, leader of the RUF. Richie was assigned to Sankoh's forces to their first incursion into Sierra Leone and has been fighting here ever since. In 10 years of war that turned broad swaths of Sierra Leone into wasteland, Sankoh's forces amputated the hands and legs of civilians, razed villages and abducted children. Then they were taught to kill. Since Sankoh's capture and imprisonment last year, the new RUF leadership has agreed to a cease-fire, disarmament and the presence of UN peacekeeping forces across the country in exchange for status ad a legal political party allowed to participate in December's presidential and legislative elections. On May 25 the RUF released about 600 child combatants to the UN. A signal they are serious about the peace process. But despite the progress in Sierra Leone, the country still runs the risk of being dragged back into bloodshed by low-level fighting going on in Liberia and Guinea. Regional intelligence reports say that at least one senior RUF commander, Mingo, has gone to Liberia with several hundred men to help Taylor's government battle dissident Liberians who are launching cross-border raids from Guinea. At the same time, Guinea has been providing arms and food for the Liberians fighting Taylor as well as supplying militia groups in Sierra Leone who refuse to accept the current cease-fire and continue to attack the RUF. Richie said he wants no part of it. Though he knows he has lost his childhood, he said he wants to get away from war while he's still young enough to turn his life around. (WP, 4 June, p. A15)

20 June

The former finance minister of Sierra Leone said in an interview this week that while the country has begun to make some progress in restoring peace and rebuilding itself after years of intermittent civil war, corruption threatened to undercut both economic and democratic development. The country is awaiting the establishment of a special war crimes tribunal to deal with Foday Sankoh and other leaders of the Revolutionary United Front. But plans for the court are stalled while Secretary General Koffi Annan struggles to get enough money from United Nations members to set it up. Mr. Jonah gets little expert assistance from Western press organisations. The rest of the world only notices, he said, when the government tries to rein in publications for unsubstantiated negative reports about officials that influence outside investors and international lending organisations. Mr. Jonah described Sierra Leone's president as the country's first political leader in 35 years who was not corrupt. The problem, he said, is the traditional political class. He described them as inured to corruption and devoid of ethical standards. The Africa program co-ordinator Mr. Sorokobi, said that Sierra Leone essentially has no middle class. Many professionals have fled. (NYT, 20 June, p. 9)

Somalia

2 August

In Somalia 2,000 people are at a conference in search of a central government for a nation that lacks one. There is a good reason to be sceptical. Twelve attempts have failed, and the warlords, who have kept Somalia in tatters, are not on board. But the Somalis at this conference say they are determined to reverse the hatred and clan fighting that have made Somalia the no. 1 symbol of chaos in Africa. So far, they have agreed on a national charter- something like transitional Constitution- and within the next week expect to elect a three-year, 225-member National Assembly. They have tentatively picked a temporary capital, in the southern city Baidoa. Already the campaign for the next president of Somalia, to be elected here by the assembly members, is in high gear. The talks have revolved around the country's clans. The clan system has been one of the major forces dividing Somalia, but Somalis here argue, it is the only remaining institution of any strength. Perhaps more important, the new government will have to deal with two regions of the old Somalia that have gone their separate ways since 1991 and established a good measure of order on their own. (NYT, 6 August, p. 3)

25 August

Somalis deserted the dusty streets of Mogadishu and gathered around television sets to watch a 12-day-old parliament choose the country's first president in nearly 10 years. The legislators chose veteran politician Abdiqassim Salad Hassan as president from among 16 candidates. Hassan, 58, held several ministerial posts in the government of former dictator Mohamed Siad Barre. The president is a member of he Hawiye clan, which dominates in the Somali capital of Mogadishu. The leader of the most powerful-armed faction, Hussein Mohamed Aideed, has claimed the presidency. He says he will not recognise the elected government, although he has promised not to use force to obstruct it from taking power. (WP, 26 August, p. A11)

10 September

In a dramatic dawn raid today, elite British troops swooped down on a rebel base in western Sierra Leone and, in a bloody gun battle, rescued six fellow British soldiers and a Sierra Leonean officer, who had been held hostage by the renegades called West Side Boys since August 25th 2000. The British Defence Ministry reported that one British paratrooper was killed and 12 were wounded, one seriously, in what was described as a "fierce" fight that broke out after the hostages had been put aboard rescue helicopters. In running clashes alongside a creek in difficult terrain and swamplands, ministry officials said, 25 militia members also were killed, including three women, and 18 were captured, including the leader, identified as Brig. Foday Kallay. (WP, 11 September, p. A16)

12 September

The United Nations is to replace the head of its peacekeeping force in Sierra Leone as part of a shake-up of the troubled operation. The move comes after Major-General Vijay Jetley, the force's Indian commander, said in a leaked memo that Nigeria was a "major player in the diamond racket". Complaining that Nigeria had placed "stooges" in the right places, he singled out three high-ranking Nigerian officials. The leak triggered an immediate reaction at the UN. (TT, 12 September)

15 October
Somalian President Abdiqassim Salad Hassan arrived in his capital today in a massive show of force to begin his effort to establish a functioning national government in a country destroyed by a decade of anarchy. Hassan, who was chosen president of Somalia in an election in neighbouring Djibouti in August, landed at an airstrip 60 miles from Mogadishu and was escorted into the city by more than 1,000 heavily armed militiamen riding on about 100 pickup trucks, many of them mounted with anti-aircraft guns. The massive security operation, put together by Mogadishu businessmen and Islamic religious leaders, deterred any potential attacks by clan warlords, who have vowed to stop the new president from consolidating a government. Hassan will face a challenge from these warlords, who include the powerful, Mogadishu-based clan leader Hussein Mohammed Aideed. The warlords say they object to Hassan as president because he served as interior minister under former dictator Mohammed Siad Barre. Salad said the first priority of his government would be restoring peace and order. "Without security you can not rebuild infrastructure or the economy," he said, adding that he wanted to negotiate with any opponent interested in peace. (WP, 15 October, p. A32)

31 March
A top faction leader released two of four UN staff members he had been holding hostage as a challenge to the legitimacy of Somalia's new government. The four were on a convoy of 11 international aid workers that came under attack as it left the compound of the humanitarian agency Doctors Without Borders on Tuesday. Faction leader Yalahow, whose group controls the area, said gunmen loyal to him attacked the convoy because he had not been informed that the aid workers would be there. (Reuters)